THE NATIONAL TRUST GUIDE
GUIDE

The pyramidal outline of Roseberry Topping forms a distinctive landmark in the view south over the valley of the Tees. (*NT*/*Joe Cornish*)

THE
NATIONAL
TRUST
GUIDE

Lydia Greeves and
Michael Trinick

THE NATIONAL TRUST

Distributed by
Harry N. Abrams, Inc.,
Publishers

First edition, by Robin Fedden and Rosemary
Joekes, published by Jonathan Cape, 1973
Revised editions published 1977 and 1984

Second edition, by Lydia Greeves and
Michael Trinick, published by The National
Trust, 1989

Revised edition published in Great Britain in
1996 by National Trust Enterprises Limited,
36 Queen Anne's Gate, London SW1H 9AS

Distributed in North America in 1997 by
Harry N. Abrams, Incorporated, New York
A Times Mirror Company

British Library Cataloguing in Publication Data
A catalogue record for this book is available
from the British Library

ISBN 0 7078 0261 X National Trust
ISBN 0 8109 6335 3 Abrams

Designed by James Shurmer

Maps by John Gilkes

Production by Bob Towell

Phototypeset in Monotype Garamond Series 156
by Southern Positives and Negatives (SPAN),
Lingfield, Surrey

Printed and bound in Italy by
Amilcare Pizzi s.p.a.

Contents

Introduction

Almost everywhere in England, Wales and Northern Ireland is within easy reach of a dozen or more National Trust properties open to the public. Some will be great houses, but in any one area there may also be a medieval castle, a dovecote or a barn, a cottage garden or a landscape park, monastic ruins or Roman remains, not to mention coast and countryside of outstanding beauty. This encyclopaedic book is a complete source of reference to what is on offer, with detailed descriptions of all major properties.

No place is quite like any other. Every house has a character of its own, a subtle mix of architecture, decoration, furnishing, setting and associations. Some, such as Uppark in West Sussex or Wallington in Northumberland, crown rising ground; others, such as the enchanting half-timbered Lower Brockhampton near Worcester or Cotehele on the Tamar, lie hidden in valleys. Oxburgh's great gatehouse is a landmark visible for miles across the Fens, and Mow Cop on the western edge of the Pennines and Grange Arch high up on the Purbeck Hills are just two of a number of follies seen silhouetted dramatically against the skyline. Not everywhere or everything is very old. The Trust owns a number of great houses rich in history, Knole, Hardwick and Petworth among them, but Edwin Lutyens's inspired Castle Drogo, superbly sited like a medieval fortress on a steep-sided bluff, was not finished until 1930, while the opulent interiors of Polesden Lacey date from the Edwardian era and Mount Stewart's flamboyant decor from the 1920s. The more recent past enriches the contents of houses too: in the collection of modern art at Dudmaston, in Rex Whistler's unforgettable murals at Plas Newydd and Mottisfont Abbey and in Graham Sutherland's menacing bee pictures at Buscot Park. Several of the gardens, including Sissinghurst, Hidcote and Nymans, were also created this century, and a few, such as Mottistone Manor Garden on the Isle of Wight, are still very young.

Associations are legion. The memory of Winston Churchill draws thousands to Chartwell, where his boldly coloured paintings fill every inch of his garden studio, Ellen Terry lives on at Smallhythe Place, Kipling at Bateman's and Virginia and Leonard Woolf at Monk's House near Rodmell in East Sussex. Personal possessions, from walking sticks to rotund pottery pigs, give these places a very individual appeal. Other connections are similarly evocative. Visitors to Moseley Old Hall can follow the route across the garden and up the stairs which Charles II took when he hid there after the Battle of Worcester, and at Uppark they can see the long whitewashed tunnels down which H. G. Wells chased the maids when his mother was housekeeper there, or the table on which the young Emma Hart, later Lady Hamilton, is said to have danced to entertain Sir Harry Fetherstonhaugh and his guests.

(*Opposite page*) Rex Whistler portrayed himself as a gardener sweeping up leaves in his mural at Plas Newydd, Anglesey. (*NT/Erik Pelham*)

Another pleasure in visiting Trust properties is discovering the many curious and unexpected objects they contain, ranging from enchanting doll's houses at Nostell Priory, Wallington and Calke, to a shoal of silver fish at Ickworth, the instruments of a Javanese percussion band at Claydon House, spinning wheels, early bicycles and Samurai armour at Snowshill and, at Coughton Court, the shift in which Mary Queen of Scots was beheaded, gruesomely topped with a representation of the queen's head. Manuscripts and documents include letters from Oscar Wilde and Florence Nightingale and accounts covering preparations to meet the Armada.

This individuality is particularly precious in an age when regional and local differences are being ironed out with the adoption of standard building styles and ever more commercial farming practices and with the insidious spread of the chain store, converting country towns that were once a charming collection of local businesses into pale reflections of each other. In the countryside, too, the Trust aims to preserve the varied landscapes which until recently characterised most of rural Britain. Significantly, the Trust's very first purchase, in 1895, was four and a half acres of clifftop overlooking Cardigan Bay, and it is now the biggest private landowner in the country. Much of this is enclosed farmland, impossible to open to visitors but glimpsed unknowingly by many who motor through hedged landscapes with well-maintained farm buildings partly shielded by a copse or belt of trees. But vast acreages are available for the enjoyment of those with a pair of walking shoes and an hour or two to spare, including some 550 miles of coast and huge holdings in Cumbria and the Peak District, but also a multitude of lesser-known properties making a patchwork over the country. Some are beauty-spots, others a field or a wood whose acquisition protects the setting of a church or a local viewpoint, or will help preserve the character of an estuary or valley.

Incredible as it may now seem, before the days of planning control substantial areas were threatened by building development, including such prominent and glorious sites as the Devil's Punch Bowl at Hindhead in Surrey, Pentire Head on the north coast of Cornwall, Haresfield Beacon on the Cotswold escarpment in Gloucestershire, and the woods at Glencoyne in the Ullswater valley. Similarly, acquisition by the Trust has prevented open land being covered with the serried ranks of commercial conifer plantations, a fate once mooted for large areas of the central Lake District.

Most places are not as they were when the Trust acquired them. Some houses, such as Erddig, have been substantially rebuilt and many more have required vast sums in restoration and repair. Calke Abbey and Kedleston Hall needed extensive renewal and renovation, and some £3 million was spent in the programme to reclad Castle Coole, James Wyatt's masterpiece in Co. Fermanagh. Textiles and other fabrics are meticulously maintained, and colour schemes changed where those the Trust has inherited seem out of sympathy with the period and character of the house. The re-creation of Erddig's early eighteenth-century formal garden is just one example of the Trust's appreciation of the importance of setting, a sensitivity unfortunately not shared by those who routed the M54 within yards of Moseley Old Hall.

In the countryside there have almost always been telephone or electric cables to bury or resite, an expensive business towards which the 'statutory undertakers', British Telecom and the Electricity Boards, have been able to devote only trifling sums. Involvement in the two world wars of this century left a liberal scattering of army camps, anti-aircraft batteries, gun positions, dragon's teeth and pillboxes, particularly on the coast. With the notable exception of the Needles Old Battery on the Isle of Wight, and the strange, futuristic constructions left by the Atomic Weapons Research Establishment on Orford Ness, nearly all have gone, to the regret of military historians but to the considerable visual improvement of the areas concerned. Less controversially, prominent caravan sites and carparks have been resited where they can be hidden from view or are not obvious.

Positive enhancement takes many forms. Amalgamation of farms has led to replanning of buildings, the removal of ugly corrugated-iron or concrete barns and their replacement by wide-span structures in tanalised timber which settle so well into the landscape. Neglected drystone walls have been rebuilt, hedges nurtured and clipped rather than grubbed out and replaced by fencing, and trees planted or natural regeneration encouraged, partly to perpetuate existing woodlands or to screen or enhance the appearance of buildings, but also to re-establish the characteristic pattern of belt, copse and clump which is fast disappearing in those parts of the country dominated by mechanised agribusiness. Special care is taken of the hundreds of ancient woodlands on Trust land, relics of past vegetation which can never be re-created and which need careful management to ensure their indefinite existence.

Another principal objective in the countryside is management for wildlife conservation. Downs, cliffs and heaths have been cleared of invading scrub and trees, eroded sand dunes restored, grazing regimes carefully controlled and flowery meadows and peat bogs conserved. This approach is clearly in tune with the growing awareness of the environment and the increasing strength of the Green Movement. Some of the Trust's properties, such as Wicken Fen, Blakeney Point and the Farne Islands, are specifically concerned with nature conservation, the wetland character of Wicken Fen now having to be artificially maintained as drainage has lowered the level of the surrounding agricultural land. One of the Trust's recent acquisitions, the Crom Castle estate in Co. Fermanagh, a patchwork of amoeba-like islands and peninsulas separated by fingers of upper Lough Erne, shelters woodland and water species, such as the purple-hairstreak butterfly or the silver-washed fritillary, rarely seen elsewhere in the British Isles. But even the humblest copse can nurture a rich flora and fauna.

Domesticated animals, too, come within the Trust's sphere of interest. Rare breeds farms, such as those established at Wimpole Hall and Shugborough, are designed to foster forms of livestock which have no part to play in current agricultural regimes and which are threatened with extinction. At Wimpole, for example, there are a dozen rare breeds of sheep, including the Manx Loghtan, the Golden Guernsey and the primitive Soay, with its heavy double horns and dark brown fleece. Similarly, the Trust perpetuates now outdated farming systems where this is necessary to preserve historic and much-loved landscapes. The characteristic Lake District scene, with tiny fields edged by stone walls in the valley bottoms and rugged open fell above, reflects the traditional pattern of sheep farming. A way of life that once provided a livelihood for the farmer is now barely viable, and the Trust's decision to encourage the continuance of old forms of land use for the sake of the landscape has involved accepting little or no financial return from estates here.

This policy is linked to the growing appreciation of the historical importance of the countryside. A wealth of prehistoric remains is now preserved on Trust land, from the spectacular stone circles at Avebury in Wiltshire or Castlerigg in the Lake District to a significant number of hill forts, the remains of Bronze Age settlements on Dartmoor and an Iron Age and Romano-British field system at Ringmoor in Dorset. As the Lake District example demonstrates, the countryside also holds many less obvious clues to past settlement and land use, in the pattern of field boundaries and lanes, in ancient coppice and old pollard trees, in patches of rough common and in the farmsteads and other vernacular buildings themselves. Visitors to Wimpole Hall in Cambridgeshire can follow a 'hollow way' or sunken track which appears on a map of 1638, and see the banks and ditches outlining the site of the medieval settlement of Bennall End and the pattern of ridge and furrow in an area of old pasture marking part of the open-field system which once

The National Trust actively preserves the traditional Lake District landscape, with small fields edged by drystone walls in the valley bottoms and rugged open fell above. (*NT/Nick Meers*)

surrounded the village. These precious remains show how much has been lost, ploughed out or buried under ever-expanding towns and cities and their satellite villages.

In all these ways the Trust aims to preserve irreplaceable clues to past landscapes and ways of life. But its properties are in no sense dry museum pieces of interest only to historians. They are there to be enjoyed, to be wandered round at the visitor's own pace. Some people relish viewing a collection of paintings or porcelain. Many will prefer to spend an afternoon strolling through a garden and having tea in one of the Trust's restaurants. And, as Michael Trinick shows so clearly in his pieces on the coast and countryside, there are any number of open spaces for picnickers and walkers to sample.

In the seven years since this book was written, the Trust has continued to grow and develop. To a certain extent, this is reflected in the acquisition of the kind of properties – historic houses and gardens – seen to fall squarely in the Trust's ambit, among them the great eighteenth-century landscape developed at Stowe, the much smaller, but equally important, Prior Park, a landscaped valley on the Bath skyline, and a virtually unaltered Jacobean manor at Chastleton, in the Oxfordshire Cotswolds. In line with recent policy, though, a greater emphasis has been placed on the protection of coast and countryside and on a concern with heritage as a whole. Partly due to the relaunching of the South Downs appeal in 1991, for example, the Trust now protects a substantial acreage of fragile downland landscape, and has also acquired an important foothold in the arcadian green and grey limestone scenery of Upper Wharfedale and a five-mile expanse of Orford Ness, the long shingle spit which is such a distinctive feature of the Suffolk coastline. Equally significant has been the Trust's first venture into modern architecture, with the acquisition of the Hampstead house designed by the Anglo-Hungarian architect Ernö Goldfinger for his own family, and the extension of their range of industrial and vernacular properties, among them, for example, the last remaining water-powered edge tool works in the country, set in a valley on the edge of Dartmoor.

Other changes have resulted from events beyond the Trust's control. Since this book was first written, Uppark, perched on the crest of the South Downs like a giant doll's-house, has been both gutted by fire and brilliantly restored to its former faded elegance; the M40 extension has been taken through the Warmington valley below Farnborough Hall, although its effect is not as deleterious as was feared; and the storms of 1987 and 1990, which left a trail of felled trees and battered gardens across southern England, have also given opportunities for new thinking, as in the replanting at Wakehurst Place.

All major acquisitions are fully described in this new edition but, as before, it has been impossible to include entries on every minor holding. Those of lesser importance and also buildings which are not open are listed in the appendix at the back. Covenanted properties are not included. The location of all properties mentioned in the main text is shown on the maps on pp.396–411, which are designed to help visitors pinpoint the places they are particularly interested in or to plan a tour of an unfamiliar region. It may also be helpful to use the *Guide* in conjunction with the sheet map of Trust properties and the guidebooks to individual properties. A complete register of the Trust's holdings is given in the current *Properties of the National Trust*, while opening arrangements and other practical information, such as admission fees and the availability of tearooms and facilities for the disabled, are enshrined in the *National Trust Handbook*; both these publications are given free to Trust members. Imperial measurements have been used in the text; those who find metres and centimetres more familiar than feet and inches, in particular the younger generation, may find the metric equivalents given below useful. The *Guide* also continues to refer to the pattern of counties established by the local government reorganisation of 1974–5. Some modification of county divisions is expected in 1996, with the re-emergence of some traditional names and areas, such as the old Welsh counties, but the situation is fluid and it seemed more helpful, for this edition, to keep to the geography with which readers are familiar.

All the Trust's accessible countryside properties are denoted by the oakleaf symbol and anyone armed with a good map can enjoy them as they please. In addition, each of the Trust's sixteen regions publishes material about the countryside in its care, much of which enormously enhances a visit to a strange place, so it is well worth writing to the Regional Office (*see* Useful Addresses, p.395) beforehand to see what is available.

Any enquiries about properties, publications or membership should be addressed to the National Trust, 36 Queen Anne's Gate, London SW1H 9AS.

LYDIA GREEVES
London 1996

Metric Conversions

This table gives metric conversions for imperial measurements used in the text.

LENGTH

1 inch (in)		= 2·54 cm
1 foot (ft)	= 12 in	= 0·3048 m
1 yard (yd)	= 3 ft	= 0·9144 m
1 mile	= 1760 yd	= 1·6093 km
1 acre	= 4840 sq yd	= 4046·9 sq m

VOLUME/CAPACITY

1 pint (pt)		= 0·5683 litre
1 gallon (gal)	= 8 pt	= 4·5461 litre

MASS (WEIGHT)

1 ounce (oz)	= 437·5 grains	= 28·35 g
1 pound (lb)	= 16 oz	= 0·4536 kg
1 hundredweight (cwt)	= 112 lb	= 50·802 kg
1 ton	= 20 cwt	= 1·016 tonne

The National Trust Guide

This Gothic Grotto, with a looking-glass window outlined in shells, is on the stairs leading up to the Shell Gallery at A la Ronde. The doll's house façade below is done in quillwork. (*NT/Geoffrey Frosh*)

A la Ronde Devon

2 miles north of Exmouth on A376

On the northern fringes of Exmouth, with views across the Exe estuary, is a delightfully uninhibited late eighteenth-century *cottage ornée*. Looking rather like a human dovecote, A la Ronde is a small sixteen-sided, three-storey house, with rough limestone walls and a steeply pitched conical roof – now tiled but originally thatched – topped off with tall brick chimneys. Dating from a time when Exmouth was a fashionable resort, it was built, almost certainly to designs by the Bath architect John Lowder, for two resourceful spinsters: Jane Parminter, daughter of a Barnstaple wine merchant, and her younger cousin Mary, who had both just returned from a nine-year Grand Tour. The design of the house, with wedge-shaped main rooms divided by triangular lobbies, and curious diamond-shaped windows on the exterior angles, is unusual enough; even more so are the Parminters' decorative schemes, a rare survival of the kind of time-consuming, intricate techniques involving paint and paper, shell and feathers, sand and seaweed, much indulged in by Regency ladies but which, due to their fragility, have mostly been lost. The interior stands out, too, for the skilful use of awkward angles and corners, and for the survival of its original contents.

The main rooms are arranged around a central octagon, with marbled yellow and green architraves to the eight doors off, ingenious seats folding down over the openings, and unique painted chairs with octagon-shaped seats. The west-facing drawing-room has its eighteenth-century tub chairs and sofa, the original marbled skirting and painted pelmet and the Parminters' feather frieze, with a delicate pattern of downy concentric circles. Pictures here include a large silhouette group of the Parminter family in 1783 and landscapes of paper, sand and seaweed, with feathery trees stretching out microscopic branches. A chimney board with shellwork surrounding a watercolour of St Michael's Mount (*see* p.278) is a prelude to the gallery at the top of the house. Alas, so fragile that it can only be viewed on video, this is the Parminters' *tour de force*, with shell-encrusted recesses and a zig-zag frieze setting off feathery bird portraits resting on moss and twigs.

Jane died in 1811, Mary in 1849. Partly due to Mary's will, which aimed to keep the house as it was and to allow only unmarried kinswomen to inherit,

A la Ronde survived remarkably unaltered, despite the attentions of its only male owner, the Rev. Oswald Reichel, who added the third-storey dormer windows and roofline catwalk and introduced a dark Victorian note to some of the rooms. The family struggled to keep the property intact until increasing difficulties brought it to the Trust in 1991.

Aberconwy House Gwynedd

At junction of Castle Street and High Street in Conwy

When Edward I built his great castle at Conwy in 1283, he invited English settlers to colonise the little walled town established at its feet. This medieval house dating from the fourteenth century occupies what would have been a prime site in Edward's new settlement, at the junction of High Street and Castle Street, the two principal thoroughfares, and close to the gate through which most of the town's trade passed down to the quay on the river. Now the oldest building in Conwy after the castle and the church, it is probably typical of the prosperous burgess houses which formed the body of the town, two lower floors of stone supporting a half-timbered upper storey jettied out over the streets. This historic survival now houses a Trust shop and there are furnished rooms illustrating daily life from different periods of the house's history.

Aberdulais Falls West Glamorgan

On the A465, 3 miles north-east of Neath

Only a few miles upstream of the Port Talbot oil refineries and the sprawl of Neath and its satellite villages, the River Dulais flows through a deep wooded gorge, with the spectacular Aberdulais Falls cascading over sheer sandstone cliffs at the north end.

For three hundred years this peaceful leafy valley was also an important industrial site, with the falls harnessed to power a succession of enterprises. The earliest, the first copper smelter in Wales, was built here by the Mines Royal in *c.*1590, and fed with ore shipped across the Bristol Channel from the rich mines of Cornwall. Copper smelting was replaced by iron working, fulling and dyeing, and in the eighteenth century the falls were being used to run a large corn mill which supplied flour to the grow-

The spectacular Aberdulais Falls and the romantic ivy-clad ruins in the woods below have inspired a number of landscape painters, including Turner, Penry Williams and de Loutherbourg. (*NT/Colin Chalmers*)

ing industrial towns of the Welsh valleys. This was the period during which the valley was recorded in the romantic vision of a number of landscape painters, J. M. W. Turner, Henry Gastineau, Penry Williams and de Loutherbourg among them. The present ivy-clad ruins, including a tall chimney, are the remains of a nineteenth-century tinplate works, which ceased working in the 1880s.

Now the falls are harnessed once again, in a unique hydro-electric scheme introduced by the Trust. A 27-foot overshot water-wheel installed in the original wheel-pit for the tinplate works now produces all the power needed for the property, while a very twentieth-century water-powered turbine feeds up to 200kw of electricity into the national grid. Also built into the system is a new fish pass, enabling salmon and sewin to reach the upper Dulais for the first time. Visitors can see all these features, with a memorable view down on to the falls and water-wheel from the roof of the turbine house.

Aberglaslyn Pass Gwynedd

Extending south for 1½ miles from Beddgelert, along both sides of the pass (the A487 and the A498)

High above Beddgelert is the Aberglaslyn Pass, where the River Glaslyn forces its way through the hills to reach the valley running down to Porthmadog, a tidal estuary until 1814 when the Cob embankment was built across its mouth.

With mountains crowding the three valleys which meet at Beddgelert, and the great shoulder of Snowdon four miles away to the north, the setting is dramatic: the gorge planted with pine and larch, the river all that a mountain stream should be, and above it, to the east, Moel Dyniewyd, whose 1,254-foot summit offers a magnificent panorama of mountain scenery.

The Trust owns over a thousand acres south of Beddgelert. Paths from the village lead through the pass and along the route of the old Welsh Highland Railway, with its spectacular tunnels.

Abergwesyn Common Powys

West of Llandrindod Wells

To the west of the River Wye, covering 40,000 acres between Llangurig and Rhayader, lie the great gathering grounds of the Elan valley reservoirs, the building of which to serve the thirsty industrial towns of the West Midlands was one of the great Victorian sagas. Ten miles to the west is now the enormous Tywi Forest, straddling the valley of the River Tywi, while to the south the Irfon Forest does likewise for the River Irfon.

Between the Elan gathering grounds and these great conifer forests is Abergwesyn Common, which has survived as open unfenced country among the spruce plantations because its commoners graze it extensively and had registered their legal rights to do so. Its 16,500 acres run for twelve miles west from Newbridge-on-Wye.

Walking is difficult, as the ground is boggy, tussocky and largely trackless, so much of the common's peaceful wilderness is only seen by grazing sheep. Its undisturbed quietness means that ravens, kites and buzzards can be found, as well as bog plants and insects.

An eight-mile walk from Llanwrthwl in the Wye valley takes one up to the 1,968-foot summit of Y Gamriw, south-east to Drum-ddu, and back to one's starting point; the views north to Plynlimon and south to the Brecon Beacons are unforgettable. Streams tumble off the common into the gorge of the River Irfon, to the west, and the walk from there up Drygarn Fawr, on the common's northern boundary, opens an immense prospect over the vast grassy wastes above the reservoirs.

Acorn Bank Garden Cumbria

Just north of Temple Sowerby, 6 miles east of Penrith on the A66

This little garden on the north side of the Eden valley is set below the bleak moors of the Pennines, the peaty heights of Cross Fell rising to almost 3,000 feet only a few miles to the north. On a little bluff above the fast-flowing Crowdundle Beck sits the old manor house round which it is laid out, a welcoming building of warm red sandstone that is now a Sue Ryder home.

The heart of Acorn Bank is the seventeenth-century walled garden to the south-east of the house, now planted as an orchard with apples, pears, medlars and quinces. In spring the long grass beneath the trees is alive with wild flowers, including the double wood anemone, the yellow wild tulip and the pheasant's eye narcissus, while in May heavy

One of the colourful borders at Acorn Bank, where the cool Cumbrian climate is tempered by high enclosing walls. (*NT/Stephen Robson*)

blossom weighs down the cherry avenue which bisects the orchard. Espaliered fruit trees interspersed with clematis and climbing roses line the walls. A gateway leads south-west into the walled herb garden, where 250 species of medicinal and culinary herbs have been established in the last twenty years, ranging from balm and the gentle evening primrose to the more sinister hemlock and opium poppy, and to such oddities as gipsywort, used by gipsies to darken their skin.

One of the most tranquil parts of the garden is the beautiful wooded bank falling steeply to the little beck, covered with the ancient oaks which gave the house its name and which now provide shelter for a wildflower and bird reserve. Over sixty varieties of daffodil are planted here.

Although the old walled garden was first laid out in the seventeenth century, it was much restored in the 1930s by Dorothy Una Ratcliffe, the Yorkshire travel writer and folk historian, and her second husband, Captain Noel McGrigor Phillips. Dorothy Ratcliffe created the reserve on the bank above the stream and introduced the ornamental iron gates which add so much to the charm of the garden. The Trust established the now famous herb collection, thought to be the largest in the north of England.

Alderley Edge Cheshire

On south-east of Alderley Edge, 4½ miles north-west of Macclesfield, astride the B5087

In a countryside which is a dormitory for Manchester and Stockport, the red sandstone ridge of Alderley Edge rises up sharply to form an escarpment at 600 feet, giving views north to Wilmslow and the South Lancashire plain. To the south the hill, wooded with beech and pine, drops gently back to the rich pastures of Cheshire.

Building would have encompassed the Edge had it not belonged to the Stanleys of Alderley. Although it was originally common land, Lord Stanley planted the area from 1745, and enclosed it with hedges in 1779, but always allowed access to the people of Manchester who thronged here on high days and holidays. In 1938 the Stanley estates were sold, and with great public spirit the 220 acres of the Edge were bought by the Misses Pilkington, with help from Cheshire County Council, and later vested in the Trust.

Alderley Edge was once a prehistoric settlement;

there is evidence of copper, lead and cobalt workings on the slopes, and mining tools as well as weapons and Bronze Age pottery have been unearthed.

Alfriston Clergy House East Sussex

4 miles north-east of Seaford, just east of the B2108, in Alfriston village

Despite its name, this low, timber-framed thatched building, delightfully situated on the green of a leafy South Downs village, was probably built for a well-to-do farmer, becoming known as the Clergy House because it was subsequently owned by the Church; however, it may have been the vicarage at some time in its history. Constructed in about 1350, it is typical of its date, with a central hall rising to the rafters flanked by two-storey blocks on either side, one containing the family's private apartments, the other service quarters. The hall has a rammed chalk floor of a kind local to Sussex, the lumps of chalk being laid and sealed with sour milk.

Bought in 1896 for only £10, Alfriston Clergy House was the first building to come to the Trust, and is one of very few fourteenth-century houses surviving in such a little-altered state. It is surrounded by a small cottage garden.

Alfriston Clergy House, a little-altered survival from the fourteenth century. The oak timber-framing is typical of the vernacular architecture of this part of England. (*NT/ Rob Matheson*)

The magical woodland clothing the steep valley of the River Allen was planted in the eighteenth and nineteenth centuries as part of the pleasure grounds of Ridley Hall. (*NT/Linda Covington*)

Allen Banks Northumberland

3 miles west of Haydon Bridge, ½ mile south of the A69

The Allen Banks are perfect for a half day's saunter with a picnic. These mature deciduous woods cling to the steep banks of the River Allen whose peaty waters, draining from the high moorlands, have cut a deep ravine above the point where the Allen joins the River Tyne. Most of the woods were laid out in the eighteenth and nineteenth centuries as the pleasure grounds of Ridley Hall and they cover 500 acres with many miles of paths. Morralee Wood, on the east side, has a delightful tarn and the landscape varies at each turn of the path.

Anglesey Gwynedd

Off the North Wales coast, approached by either the Britannia or Telford suspension bridges, Bangor

At the north-west tip of Anglesey, Mynydd-y-Garn overlooks the Trust's six miles of coast from Clegir Mawr in Holyhead Bay, north round Carmel Head and east to Cemlyn. The view south-eastward is right across the island to the mountains of Snowdon.

The coast is wonderfully varied, with little beaches, rocky inlets and islands, a salt-blasted pine wood, remains of copper mines, the Skerries reef and lighthouse offshore, and the pool behind the pebble beach in Cemlyn Bay, where the five species of tern which breed in Britain have all been spotted.

Anglesey Abbey Cambridgeshire

In the village of Lode, 6 miles north-east of Cambridge on the B1102

An interest in horse racing led Huttleston Broughton, later 1st Lord Fairhaven, to purchase Anglesey Abbey in 1926. A typical stone Jacobean manor house with mullioned windows and tall chimneys, it was conveniently placed for Newmarket and the stud he owned with his brother at Bury St Edmunds. Apart from the vaulted canon's parlour, now the dining-room, few traces remained of the Augustinian priory founded here in 1135 from which the house takes its name.

Over the next forty years this comfortable gentleman's residence was transformed. Although his sporting pursuits were never neglected, Lord Fairhaven devoted most of the huge fortune his father had made from mining and railway interests in the United States to the acquisition of an outstanding and wide-ranging collection of works of art, for which he adapted and extended the house. More remarkably, ninety acres of unpromising fen were used to create an imaginative and individual garden.

The interior of the house is an Aladdin's cave of priceless furniture, silver, paintings, porcelain, tapestries and statuary, seeming to include examples of every style and period from all the countries of the world. An inlaid Louis XV commode supporting a pair of oriental bronze candlesticks in the shape of deer stands below a Suffolk coastal scene, a rare seascape by Gainsborough. Close by, a Spanish seventeenth-century walnut table is used to display an Egyptian bronze cat dating from about 500BC, two eighteenth-century mortars and a pair of silver Dutch tobacco boxes, as well as a medieval wooden carving of Jerome and the lion, the beast looking up at the saint affectionately. With so many interesting and beautiful pieces set close together, each one can only be fully appreciated by mentally isolating it from its companions.

Lord Fairhaven had a particular liking for nudes by the fashionable Victorian painter William Etty, about twenty of which now hang in the house. He also acquired a unique collection of views of Windsor, where he lived for a time in the Great Park. Displayed in the two-storey gallery he built on to the house in 1955, these paintings faithfully record changes in landscape and architecture over 350 years, ranging in style from the toy castle

A collection of pictures of Windsor Castle at Anglesey Abbey includes this delightful early view, painted during the reign of James I. (*NT/Edward Leigh*)

depicted in an early seventeenth-century canvas to William Daniell's mistily romantic view down the Long Walk. Many consider the jewels of the collection to be two superb paintings by Claude Lorraine, examples of the sublime landscapes which inspired the naturalistic gardens of the eighteenth century. In *The Landing of Aeneas*, each slave rowing the boat carrying the Trojan leader is an individual, two looking over their shoulders to see how far they are from the shore.

Whereas the sumptuousness and muted lighting of the house suggest exotic influences, the garden is quintessentially English. Like the great gardens of two centuries ago, it is conceived on a generous scale, a striking contrast to the inward-looking intimacy of the contemporary layouts at Sissinghurst and Hidcote (*see* pp.291 and 149). Majestic avenues and walks, such as the wide grassy ride lined by double rows of horse chestnuts which runs for half a mile to the west of the house, provide a geometric framework for areas of very different character. Some are sweeping compositions in trees and grass or grand set pieces, like the curved border planted for summer display in the herbaceous garden, a giant orange, red and yellow semicircle at the right time of year. Others are more intimate and

enclosed, such as the small sheltered lawn where William Theed's Narcissus contemplates his image in the still waters of a pond, or the leafy seclusion of the terrace circling the pool in the old quarry, with views to the picturesque corn mill on the River Lode (*see* p.185) just a stone's throw away.

A wide variety of trees, such as the planes, alders, elms, sycamores and willows lining the river, act as shelter belts and backdrops, while many rare and unusual species are displayed on the arboretum lawns, including the Hungarian oak, the Indian chestnut, the Judas tree and the Japanese hop hornbeam. Changes in perspective and scale are enhanced by carefully planned contrasts between the formal and the naturalistic, as if Lord Fairhaven deliberately set out to create his garden from the best of the past. 'Capability' Brown would have approved of the Temple Lawn, where 'islands' of trees are subtly sited to enhance rather than destroy the sweep of the grass and planted to give a range of tone and texture, from the grey and gold of willows, elder and privet to the red and purple of violet willow and purple cotinus. In the centre of the lawn two recumbent lions guard the entrance to a circular yew enclosure surrounding ten Corinthian columns of Portland stone.

Statues, urns and other classical features are used throughout the garden to close vistas and punctuate lawns and avenues. Father Time presides over the Hyacinth Garden, his lichen-stained figure bending over the sundial as if to urge the hours on; haughty stone griffins greet visitors to the Dahlia Garden. Along the grassy Emperor's Walk, over 440 yards long, twelve busts of Roman emperors on marble plinths are incongruously set against a backdrop of Norway spruce.

The setting of the garden contributes enormously to the overall effect. Often it is seen against a powerful East Anglian sky, with towering cloudscapes forming and dissolving over the expanses of the Fens.

Antony House Cornwall

5 miles west of Plymouth via Torpoint car ferry, 2 miles north-west of Torpoint, north of the A384, 16 miles south-east of Liskeard, 15 miles east of Looe

Antony House stands at the end of the long neck of land forming the far south-east corner of Cornwall, an isolated peninsula bounded by the estuaries of the Rivers Tamar and Lynher to the east and north and by the sea to the south. The best way of approaching Antony is by boat, as it has been for

The hall at Antony House is dominated by this moving portrait of Charles I, painted at his trial by Edward Bower, a Westcountryman who is thought to have been a pupil of Van Dyck. (*NT*/*John Bethell*)

7

centuries, crossing to Cornwall by the Torpoint ferry from Plymouth.

The setting of the house is superb. The entrance front faces up a slight rise crowned by a wrought-iron screen, but at the back the ground falls away from a flight of terraces across a sweep of grass. In the distance attractively grouped clumps of trees frame glimpses of the Lynher and of the prodigious arches of Brunel's Saltash railway bridge crossing the Tamar estuary.

The Antony estate has been the property of the Carews, and their descendants the Pole-Carews and Carew Poles, since the early fifteenth century. The main block of the present house, a deceptively simple two-storey rectangle faced with silver-grey stone, was built by Sir William Carew between 1718 and 1729. Red-brick colonnaded wings enclosing a courtyard on the south front were possibly added by the architect James Gibbs. Antony is a charming and entirely satisfying house, one of the best of its date in the West Country. It is not large: modest, oak-panelled rooms lead off the hall and upstairs there are only five principal bedrooms, the space for a sixth being taken up by the magnificent staircase.

Antony is also exceptional for the quality of its furnishings, many of which are contemporary with the house, and for the collection of family and other portraits, including works by Reynolds. Most memorable is the portrait of Charles I painted at his trial which hangs in the hall. The king is shown dressed in black wearing a large beaver hat, his sad eyes pouched with weariness. This is the last of a number of portraits which record Charles's final days and only here has the famous pointed beard turned grey. John Carew, who had sat in judgement on Charles, was himself executed at the Restoration. His tragic elder brother Alexander, whose portrait hangs in the library, suffered the same fate at the hands of the leaders of the Commonwealth, dying with a troubled and divided mind, uncertain which cause was right.

No such doubts assailed the historian Richard Carew, author of the great *Survey of Cornwall*, who inherited the estate in 1564. His striking portrait, painted in 1586 when he was thirty-two, faces Charles across the hall. Two years later he must have seen the Armada sail up the Channel along the coast for which, as deputy lieutenant of the county, he was responsible.

Antony's landscaped setting is partly due to Humphry Repton, who produced one of his earliest

Red Books here and swept away formal parterres to the north of the house. Clipped yew features prominently in the present garden to the west of the lawns sweeping down to the Tamar, hedging a long walk punctuated by a Burmese bell, one of a number of eastern ornaments acquired by General Sir Reginald Pole-Carew, and forming the tall wigwam-like topiary shape which rises conspicuously to one side. Another axial walk following the wall of the old kitchen garden is bordered by espaliered fruit trees and a row of magnolias. An arch in the yew hedge leads to the sheltered flower garden, where four beds set round a crab apple provide a colourful summer display at the same time as the roses on the terraces are in bloom, and there is also a knot garden with interweaving lines of box and germander. Specimen trees include a large ginkgo and an immense cork oak, an eighteenth-century dovecote squats by the house, and beside the Lynher is the Bath Pond House of 1784, with a plunge bath.

Ardress House Co. Armagh

7 miles from Portadown on the B28 Moy road, 5 miles from Moy, 3 miles from Loughgall, intersection 13 on the M1

Ardress House is not quite what it seems. The long two-storey entrance front with an impressive array of Georgian sash windows is partly a sham, one end of the façade being nothing more than a wall with false openings added in the interests of symmetry, while the pedimented portico giving dignity and importance to the front door is not placed centrally between the windows on either side. Both features betray the rather piecemeal approach to the gentrification of what was originally a simple seventeenth-century Irish farmhouse, one room deep.

Ardress's finest feature is the elegant late eighteenth-century drawing-room on the garden front, which seems to have strayed from a Dublin town house. Adam-style decoration in muted greens, pinks and yellows dominates the room, the central plaster medallion on the ceiling being the focus of an intricate pattern of intersecting circles and arcs. Whirls of foliage here are echoed in more extravagant loops and chains framing the oval plaques on the walls. Plaster cherubs along the frieze stand with the right leg crossed behind the left, except in one corner of the room where the stance is reversed. The work of the Dublin stuccadore Michael Stapleton, known for his magnificent interiors in the Irish capital, this decoration was carried out for the architect George Ensor some ten years after his marriage to the heiress of Ardress in 1760. Having executed several commissions in Dublin himself, Ensor probably knew Stapleton well.

George Ensor II's additions to the house, including the extended entrance façade and the curving screen walls flanking the garden front, are less happy. The cavernous dining-room below the library in which he may have written his many provocative works on politics and religion is reached only by a door in the yard at the back of the house. It is now hung with paintings from the collection of the Earl of Castle Stewart, including a rare signed picture by the seventeenth-century Flemish artist J. Myts. The diminutive haloed figure of Our Lord on the road to Emmaus is portrayed in a Northern European setting, with gentlemen in frock coats

Ardress House: a detail of the plasterwork by the Dublin stuccadore Michael Stapleton, whose use of geometrical patterns and neo-classical figures, as here, has led him to be called the Irish Adam. (*NT/Alan North*)

and a cluster of steep-roofed half-timbered houses in the little town in the distance.

French windows lead out to the lawn which slopes down to a sunken rose garden. Behind the house outbuildings set round a cobbled yard are filled with reminders of the working farm Ardress once was, including a dairy, a smithy, a cow byre and a threshing barn complete with horse-powered thresher. Goats, pigs, ducks and other fowl contribute to the farmyard atmosphere.

The Argory Co. Armagh

4 miles from Moy, 3 miles from the M1, exit 14

The barrister Walter McGeough Bond's decision in the 1820s to build on his newly inherited land at Derrycaw was influenced by the terms of a very curious will. He and his three sisters had been left the bulk of their father's fortune, their unfortunate elder brother inheriting only £400, but Walter was not allowed to live at Drumsill, the family house, while two of his sisters remained unmarried. He was wise to provide himself with an alternative establishment, as two of his sisters died in Drumsill, rich and eccentric old spinsters.

Walter McGeough Bond's house is a modest two-storey stone building set on a rise overlooking the Blackwater river, its plain neo-classical façades given added interest by the lengthened centre windows added on the west and south in the late nineteenth century. The Argory was designed by the relatively obscure Arthur and John Williamson, who may have been employed on the recommendation of the much more famous Dublin architect Francis Johnston and whose work betrays traces of Johnston's influence.

The largely original interiors powerfully evoke the lifestyle of the Irish gentry during the early nineteenth century, with mahogany furniture, sumptuous curtains and upholstery, potted plants, an abundance of cushions and *objets* and fur-draped chairs in the drawing-room. The family traditionally entertained at tea-time and the white cloth on the dining-room table is set with china and silver as if awaiting guests. Tea was also occasionally taken at the round walnut table in the organ lobby on the first floor, dominated by the magnificent instrument Walter commissioned from James Bishop of London in 1822. Three surviving six-foot barrels hold a selection of music chosen on the advice of

Samuel Sebastian Wesley, nephew of the founder of Methodism, a mixture of suitably uplifting hymn tunes such as 'See, the conquering hero comes' and excerpts from *The Magic Flute*. The instrument is also playable manually.

Personal possessions in the bedrooms suggest the family has only just left. A wardrobe is filled with Lady Bond's early twentieth-century outfits, including fashionable narrow-waisted jackets and tiny Italian shoes. Another holds her hats. Ugly gas lamps disguised as candles on the dressing-tables are examples of the Argory's unaltered early nineteenth-century lighting arrangements, the most impressive being the six fittings with pale green conical shades which hang low over the billiard table. Originally oil, the fittings were subsequently converted to gas, run from the plant still to be seen in the stable yard, installed by the Sunbeam Acetylene Gas Company of Belfast in 1906 at a cost of £250. Although the gas lighting has not been restored, there is still no electricity in the house.

A little Victorian rose garden, with small-flowered polyantha and China roses in box-edged beds, leads into the pleasure ground sloping down to meadows fringing the Blackwater river. There is a pair of garden pavilions, of the same date as the house, linked by a long curving walk, and a wide lawn is studded with two yew arbours and a hand-kerchief tree and framed by borders planted with a collection of shrubs and other plants raised or introduced by Leslie Slinger of the Slieve Donard Nursery.

Miss Rosalie Chichester (*right*), here with her companion Miss Peters in New Zealand in 1928. Rosalie filled Arlington Court with mementoes she brought back from her travels. (*NT*)

Arlington Court Devon

7 miles north-east of Barnstaple on the A39

The plain, grey stone façades of this neo-classical house are no preparation for the cluttered Victorian interior, with boldly patterned and coloured wallpaper, mahogany furniture and display cabinets overflowing with shells, snuffboxes, model ships, pewter and precious objects. The setting of this Aladdin's cave was created in 1820 for Colonel John Chichester by the Barnstaple architect Thomas Lee, who had just completed the Wellington Monument in Somerset (*see* p.357). But the collections themselves are all the work of Rosalie Chichester, the last of the Chichesters of Arlington, who lived here for eighty-four years until her death in 1949.

Only child of the flamboyant and extravagant

Bruce Chichester, who created the opulent staircase hall hung with yachting pictures more suited to a gentleman's club than a private house, Rosalie had been taken on two world cruises in her father's schooner *Erminia* before she reached her teens. Perhaps fired by these early experiences, she was always an enthusiastic traveller, one of the many delightful photographs on display showing her with her diminutive companion in New Zealand, both of them in sensible shoes and heavy suits with skirts down to their ankles. She was also a collector, acquiring tea caddies, candle snuffers and paperweights to add to the Pacific shells and other mementoes she brought back from her travels. Although her stuffed birds, Maori skirts and

African clubs are no longer in the house, Arlington is still full of her treasures, with her favourite piece, a slightly malevolent red amber elephant from China, prominently displayed in the White Drawing Room, one of three sunny rooms on the south front which form a long gallery. In the anteroom next door hangs the mystical watercolour by William Blake which was found on top of a cupboard at Arlington in 1949.

On the first-floor landing another watercolour, of Miss Chichester's parrot Polly, reflects her passionate love of all living plants and creatures. This undoubtedly eccentric lady kept budgerigars and canaries in brass cages in the house and allowed her parrots to fly free, causing incalculable damage to the curtains. The Jacob sheep and Shetland ponies still in the park are the descendants of those she established as part of a wildlife refuge.

Shady lawns surrounding the house are planted with specimen trees, including an ash collection. Some distance away is a small formal garden laid out in 1865, where a delightful conservatory against a high brick wall at one end looks down over three grass terraces and a fountain pool guarded by metal herons, the birds of the Chichester crest. A more informal note is struck by the wilderness pond hidden in a huge clump of rhododendrons further down the hill and by the walk which threads its way to the lake on the River Yeo half a mile below the house, where two great piers are all that was built of the suspension bridge Rosalie's father had planned to carry his grand new drive. He also constructed the imposing colonnaded stable block west of the house, beyond the little parish church filled with Chichester memorials. With the images of the family photographs still strongly in mind, it is easy to imagine Miss Rosalie seated in one of the well-preserved carriages now displayed here, although the collection was brought together after the Trust took over the house.

Arlington is the centre of a thriving agricultural estate, as it has been ever since the Chichester family came here in the sixteenth century. Hidden within the farmland is a $2\frac{1}{2}$-mile stretch of the thickly wooded valley of the River Yeo, a haven for wildlife as Miss Rosalie intended. Early or late in the day there may be glimpses of wild red deer among the trees from the rides and paths along the Yeo and up the two re-entrant valleys leading to North Woolley and Coombshead; a hide has been erected on the lake below the house so the wild duck and other birds which congregate here can be observed without disturbance. Neglected by Miss Rosalie because she hated felling trees, the woods have now been rejuvenated by the Trust.

Ascott Buckinghamshire

$\frac{1}{2}$ mile east of Wing, 2 miles south-west of Leighton Buzzard, on south side of the A418

Entrepreneurial talent rarely passes from generation to generation, but Mayer Amschel Rothschild (1744–1812), who founded the family banking business in Frankfurt during the Napoleonic Wars, was blessed with five sons whose drive and ambition matched his own. While one inherited his father's mantle, the others dispersed to Paris, Naples, Vienna and London to set up branches of the firm. The wealth generated by the activities of this extraordinary clan financed the collection in

The important collection of paintings at Ascott includes this Renaissance masterpiece, Andrea del Sarto's *Madonna and Child with St John*. It typifies the dream-like quality of the artist's work (*NT/John Hammond*)

this rambling neo-Jacobean house overlooking the Vale of Aylesbury as well as the more flamboyant magnificence of Waddesdon a few miles away (*see* p.350).

Ascott is the creation of Leopold de Rothschild, great-grandson of the founder of the family fortunes and son of Baron Lionel, the first Jewish MP. The little Jacobean half-timbered farmhouse he took over in 1876 is now buried in the gabled ranges added by the architect George Devey in the years that followed, transforming the house into a massively overgrown cottage. But, despite Ascott's size, the rooms are pleasingly domestic in scale, with the intimate atmosphere of a beautifully furnished private house.

Predominantly Dutch and English paintings include Aelbert Cuyp's panoramic *Dordrecht on the Maas*, its wide shallow canvas filling one wall of the low-ceilinged dining-room. The town lies on the left, a low sun lighting up a row of gabled houses on the glassy river and giving a warm glow to the clouds heaped overhead. A faint mark in the centre of the painting shows where the canvas was once divided to be sold in two halves. Gainsborough's Duchess of Richmond, her flaming red curls set off by the silky sheen of her blue satin dress, is one of a number of fine English portraits at Ascott. There are three of Stubbs's distinctive horse studies, including the only known canvas in which he shows mares without any foals, and a major work from the Italian Renaissance, Andrea del Sarto's arresting *Madonna and Child with St John*. Elegant eighteenth-century English furniture, such as the two oval pie-crust tables and the walnut and mahogany chairs covered with tapestry and needlework in the library, contrast with the contemporary French pieces elsewhere.

Leopold's son Anthony, besides acquiring paintings and English furniture, also introduced the oriental porcelain which is now such a prominent feature of the house. This starts with ceramics from the Han (206 BC–AD 220), Tang (618–906) and Sung (906–1280) dynasties, with the cream of the collection, in deep rich colours, from the Ming (1368–1644) and K'ang Hsi (1662–1722) periods. These were the centuries which produced sophisticated, three-colour ware in vibrant shades of blue, purple and burnt yellow, such as the elegant vases decorated with flowing chrysanthemums.

The extensive Victorian gardens were laid out by the leading Chelsea nursery of James Veitch & Sons, the wealth of evergreen trees and shrubs probably reflecting the fact that Leopold originally intended to use Ascott mainly in the winter, as a hunting lodge. Terraced lawns with panoramic views to the Chilterns fall away from the house, planted with widely spaced specimen and ornamental trees, predominantly chosen for their coloured and variegated foliage. Clipped yew hedges and a high retaining wall like a ha-ha beyond the lawns conceal an unexpected formal garden. A long herbaceous walk ending in a colonnaded pavilion looks over the circular lawn framing Waldo Story's Venus fountain, with winged seahorses pulling the goddess's shell-chariot. Another Story fountain crowns the long, narrow Dutch garden, where circular beds are planted for summer show and a tufa grotto adds a romantic note at one end. The highlight of a wealth of topiary and clipped hedges is the giant sundial set out at the east end of one of the terraces. Roman figures in box encase the central egg-shaped gnomon of golden yew grafted on to Irish stock, while an outer circle of yew spells out the legend 'Light and shade by turn but love always', an echo of the Victorian proverbs carved on a cornice in the house. An alternative route back to the carpark leads down a wide grass alley to the sheltered lily pool, where white and coloured blossoms carpet the water in summer.

Ashdown House Oxfordshire

2½ miles south of Ashbury, 3½ miles north of Lambourn, on west side of the B4000

Set high up on the rolling, windswept Berkshire Downs, some two miles from the nearest village, this bizarre seventeenth-century building most closely resembles a gigantic doll's house. Diminished by distance, it looks as if the front might come off to reveal a series of beautifully furnished miniature rooms. This air of unreality derives from the square plan with four almost identical honey and cream façades and from the fact that the house is extraordinarily tall and narrow, its height increased by the crowning cupola. It is as if one of the contemporary town houses that fight for ground space along the canals of Amsterdam had been suddenly uprooted and put down in this isolated spot. Ashdown would look even more strange were it not for the fact that its starkness is softened and broadened by detached pavilions on either side,

Ashdown House, like a lifesize doll's house, stands high up on the Berkshire Downs. A corner of the formal box and gravel parterre fronting the south façade is just visible to the right of the roof. (*NT/B.K.S. Surveys Ltd*)

possibly added some twenty years after the main block was built.

Ashdown was created for William, 1st Lord Craven, in about 1663. One of the richest figures of the seventeenth century, Lord Craven is remembered particularly for his devotion to Charles I's unlucky sister, Elizabeth of Bohemia, who reigned for only one winter before being forced into exile by the defeat of her husband's forces by the Habsburg Emperor. There is a family tradition that Lord Craven chose the site of his house so Elizabeth would have a refuge from plague-ridden London, but sadly she contracted a fatal disease without ever seeing the completed building.

Today Lord Craven's devotion to the Winter Queen is reflected in the portraits of her and her family which the Treasury presented to the Trust from the Craven Collection in 1968 to hang in the hall and on the staircase rising the height of the building. With three exceptions, all the works are by, or after, two Dutch artists, Michel Miereveldt and Gerard van Honthorst, echoing the strong associations of the exterior.

Ashleworth Tithe Barn, showing the two projecting wagon porches. (*NT/Nick Meers*)

The architect of the house is not known, but it was probably built by William Winde, who spent his early years with exiled Royalists in Holland and would have seen similar buildings in Leiden, Amsterdam and The Hague. A formal parterre based on a seventeenth-century engraving, such as he might have designed, now fronts the house, the twists and curves of box and gravel seen to particular advantage from the roof. There are also spectacular views over the wooded Berkshire Downs from here, long breaks cutting through the trees on either side of the house marking the north-south ride which shows clearly on Kip's engraving of 1724.

Ashleworth Tithe Barn

Gloucestershire

6 miles north of Gloucester, 1¼ miles east of Hartpury on the A417, on west bank of River Severn, south-east of Ashleworth

Ashleworth barn stands in a group of picturesque buildings on the banks of the River Severn, only yards from a riverside inn and a fine medieval house and just west of the largely fifteenth-century parish church. Although smaller than Great Coxwell or Middle Littleton (*see* pp.133 and 199), this 126-foot limestone building with two projecting wagon porches is still impressive, an immense stone-tiled roof supported on timber trusses stretching the width of the barn. It was built in about 1500, probably by the canons of St Augustine's, Bristol, who were lords of the manor here.

Attingham Park Shropshire

4 miles south-east of Shrewsbury, on Telford road

Few family mottoes can be more apposite than that of Noel Hill, 1st Lord Berwick: 'Let wealth be his who knows its use.' This wily politician, who obtained his peerage through expedient loyalty to William Pitt the Younger, poured the fortune he inherited into this grandiose classical house, set, like Wallington (*see* p.353), in full view of a public road, from which it was devised to look as magnificent as possible.

Designed in 1782 by the individual Scottish architect George Steuart, and a rare survival of his work, Attingham consists of a main three-storey block linked by colonnaded corridors to pavilions on either side, with a classical portico running the full height of the house on the entrance front. Seen from the bridge taking the road over the River Tern, the façade stretches 400 feet from pavilion to pavilion, while inside there are eighty rooms, an unusually large number for a house of this period. The layout of the interior is equally singular, with the rooms on the west side, including the library and dining-room, making up a set of masculine apartments, and those on the east, including the drawing-room, a set of feminine rooms.

On the 1st Lord's untimely death at the early age of forty-four, Attingham passed successively to his two elder sons, who were responsible for the splendid Regency interiors which are now such a feature of the house. Acquisitions during a lengthy Grand Tour in Italy formed the basis of an extensive collection built up by the 2nd Lord, who also commissioned John Nash to add the grand picture gallery in 1805–7. One of the first to be built in a country house, this room is notable for the revolutionary use of curved cast-iron ribs supporting the windows in the roof, a forerunner of the design of the Crystal Palace. Although the paintings for which the gallery was designed were largely dispersed in the sale following the 2nd Lord's bankruptcy in 1827, the mixture of Italianate landscapes and copies of Old Masters now hanging two and three deep conjures up the splendour of the original collection. A pair of Neapolitan landscapes by Philipp Hackert (1737–1807) includes a view of Pompeii showing the small extent of the excavated area at the end of the eighteenth century and the garlanded vines still seen in this part of Italy. The Regency flavour is similarly strong in the dining-room, bold red walls with moulded panels picked out in gold being overshadowed by the display on the ceiling, where a lacy plaster wreath of vine leaves stands out dramatically white against the background red. Frail tendrils of foliage and medallions depicting cherubs set against rose-tinted clouds on the domed ceiling of the tiny boudoir are from an earlier age, part of one of the most delicate late eighteenth-century schemes to survive in England.

The paintings and furniture now seen in the house were collected by the diplomatist 3rd Lord – described by Byron as the only Excellence who was really excellent – during his twenty-five years in

Nash's revolutionary ceiling for the picture gallery at Attingham was one of the first to use curved cast-iron ribs, although the large oval lights he originally proposed, shown here in a gouache of *c*.1805 by A. C. Pugin, were not adopted. (*NT/Jonathan Gibson*)

Italy. He was responsible for the elegant pale-blue drawing-room filled with white and gold Italian furniture, some of which may have come from Napoleon's sister's Neapolitan palace, and for the glittering silver displayed in the old wine cellars, once stocked with some 900 bottles of sherry, port and madeira.

Parkland dotted with mature oaks, elms, beeches and pines slopes gently down to the Tern. The initial layout, of 1769–72, was by Thomas Leggett, but the planting schemes reflect the hand of Humphry Repton, who produced a Red Book for Attingham in 1797. A grove of Lebanon cedars marks the start of the Mile Walk, bright with wild flowers in spring and with rhododendrons later in the year.

Avebury Wiltshire

6 miles west of Marlborough, 1 mile north of the A4 Bath road, at junction of the A361 and the B4003

The picturesque village of Avebury, set in a shallow valley below the ridge of the Marlborough Downs, lies at the centre of a rich and diverse prehistoric landscape. Over about fifteen hundred years, between *c*.3500 and *c*.2000 BC, neolithic peoples transformed this open downland with an impressive sequence of works. Most obvious is the great stone circle now enmeshed with the village, like some surreal sculpture park, with a massive bank and ditch enclosing the remains of a ring of sarsens. Nearly a mile in circumference, this vast composition can be seen as a whole only from a hill above the village; at close quarters, its extent is obscured by buildings and trees. The bank, originally measuring fifty feet from crest to ditch, screens Avebury from the world. Built only with the aid of antler picks and ox shoulder-blade shovels, such as those now displayed in the little site museum, Avebury must represent tens of thousands of hours of labour. The stones are unworked, unlike those at Stonehenge, but there were originally ninety-eight in the main circle, plus two smaller circles, and the largest boulders are some twenty feet high. Over the centuries, many of the stones were broken up and incorporated in the village, with grassy hollows marking where they once stood, and in the superstitious Middle Ages the circle was deliberately buried. Most of the thirty or so stones seen standing today were re-erected in the 1930s by the innovative amateur archaeologist Alexander Keiller, who bought several of the Avebury sites.

From the top of the bank, the north-east horizon is closed by the bushy crest of Fyfield Down, from where the sarsens – the remains of a sheet of hard sandstone which once capped this landscape – were dragged two miles or so down to Avebury; there are views over the rounded humps of Bronze Age barrows, their outlines transformed into giant hedgehogs by nineteenth-century plantings of beech trees; and, to south-east, the remains of what was once an impressive stone avenue, originally consisting of about a hundred pairs of stones, meanders gently uphill into the distance.

Most of the outlying monuments are more elusive than the circle. The course of the Avenue leads 1½ miles from the village to a field on the ridge of the Downs by the main A4 Marlborough road, where a series of low concrete blocks and stubby posts marks out the tight concentric circles of what is known as the Sanctuary, originally a composition in wood and stone thought to date from c.3250 BC. The long-distance prehistoric route known as the Ridgeway starts here, three-quarters of a mile of which, together with a group of seven Bronze Age barrows, is now in Trust hands. Beside the A4 too, seen from a viewing platform by the road, is the equally enigmatic Silbury Hill. Set strangely low in the landscape, in the valley of the Kennet, this huge man-made mound, the largest in Europe, is a steep-sided grassy pudding, its purpose unknown. Standing 130 feet high, and thought to have taken 18 million man-hours to build, it is as arresting now as it must have been when first constructed, c.2700 BC.

On the crest of the Downs just to the south, reached by a stiff ten-minute climb from the road, is the atmospheric West Kennet long barrow. This tapering grassy mound was a place of burial, in constant use for perhaps a thousand years from c.3700 BC. At the east end, confronting visitors as they reach the top of the hill, is the opening to the interior, where massive sarsens – one, flanking the entrance, showing the grooves of neolithic axe sharpening – frame a central passage and five burial chambers. It seems the dead were buried here mostly in a disarticulated state, after the flesh had gone, and that those honoured in this way represented a select group within prehistoric society, marked out by birth rather than achievement. A wall of sarsens almost blocking the entrance was a later addition, after the barrow was no longer in use. In the gathering dusk of a late winter's afternoon this is a haunting place, stirring the imagination.

Most elusive are the neolithic remains on grassy Windmill Hill, to the north-west of the village. On the northern side of the gently swelling summit low bumps and indentations in the sward and, in one place, a well-defined ditch and bank, the result of excavations by Keiller and others, mark the site of a large causewayed camp, originally consisting of three concentric banks and ditches. These earthworks were never impressive and were frequently

Sarsen slabs mark the processional way known as the Avenue leading south-east from Avebury. (NT)

broken by the causewayed approaches which give the monument its name. Unlike the later Iron Age hill forts, this was not a defended position, but a place where neolithic farmers came to trade, gossip and make contacts. Excavations have found remains of young animals, nuts, berries and ears of grain, suggesting the site was in use almost throughout the year. Windmill Hill is the most insubstantial of the neolithic sites, but the views are well worth the climb: the village is half obscured by trees in the valley below, but beyond it, to the south, is the hard outline of Silbury, while to north and north-west is a panorama over sparsely populated countryside, with the crest of Cherhill Down marked by the assertive finger of the Lansdowne Monument (*see* p.64) closing the western horizon. The Trust now owns or manages all these prehistoric sites, and has devised a series of walks, some taking only an hour or so, others involving half a day or longer, round the village and out into the wider landscape.

With the exception of the Iron Age, Avebury has links with almost every period of settled man. A Roman road, a section of which is now owned by the Trust, ran past Silbury Hill, and an early Saxon and medieval village stood close to the Kennet, with the church between it and the pagan circle. In the centuries following the Reformation, as the mists of superstition gradually cleared, the village crept eastwards into the circle, where the narrow street is now lined with some fine eighteenth-century houses. The Trust owns most of this later development, and also the old manor on an originally monastic site outside the circle bank. A charming classical gateway is approached through what was the manor farmyard, past a thatched and weather-boarded great barn and a moss-encrusted sixteenth-century dovecote. Set back across a stretch of grass is a long, asymmetrical, many-gabled range, with tall chimneys and some stone-mullioned windows. This is the eastern wing of a rambling building set round three sides of a small courtyard, which developed from a medieval hall house. The earliest part, facing south, has a delightful eighteenth-century façade, with a parapet instead of the original gables and a classical porch with fluted pilasters. The eastern range is partly an addition of 1548, with the later incorporation of an old brew-house at the northern end, while the western side of the house is a 1920s library in the same spirit as the medieval and Tudor building, with a pretty flight of stone steps leading down into the garden.

The picturesque assemblage is the backdrop to the extensive compartmental garden developed by Colonel and Mrs Jenner, who lived here from 1900 to 1935 and restored the house, adding on the library. Using an existing framework of medieval, Tudor and eighteenth-century walls in stone and mellow red brick, Mrs Jenner devised a series of formal, strongly architectural layouts, each different but all featuring clipped yew and box. A rose garden with box-edged beds is overlooked by the pinnacled tower of St James's church just beyond the garden wall; topiary yew surrounds the orchard, newly planted with Wiltshire varieties of apples; and there is a yew walk and a serene pond garden, where geometric topiary echoing the designs of the plaster ceilings inside the house encloses a rectangular pool. In season, lilies flower profusely here. Most memorable, perhaps, is a long half moon of yew with box buttressing set against a gently curving, lichen-spotted brick wall.

This is a garden of surprises and unexpected vistas, with echoes of Lytes Cary (*see* p.194), where Mrs Jenner probably had a hand in her brother-in-law's design, and of Sissinghurst (*see* p.291), whose chatelaine, Vita Sackville-West, was a frequent visitor to Avebury.

Badbury Rings Dorset

4 miles north-west of Wimborne Minster, 6 miles south-east of Blandford Forum, immediately east of the B3080

This is one of the larger and more impressive Iron Age hill forts in Britain, with three tiers of concentric ramparts enclosing a wooded interior. From the air, Badbury looks like a coral atoll, with an 'island' of trees surrounded by chalky 'reefs'. Bronze Age burial mounds and field systems surround the hill fort and Badbury was also of significance in Roman times, lying at the junction of routes from Bath, Old Sarum and Dorchester.

The chalk grassland is rich in butterfly-attracting downland plants, among them the greater butterfly, frog and bee orchids, bastard toadflax, adder's tongue fern and knapweed broom rape. The clump of trees which is now such a feature of the fort were first planted in the eighteenth century and have been re-established in recent years.

Badbury Rings is part of the extensive estate which came to the Trust with the seventeenth-century mansion of Kingston Lacy (*see* p.167).

Baddesley Clinton from the north-east, showing the crenellated gatehouse and a glimpse of the interior courtyard. (*NT/Jonathan Gibson*)

Baddesley Clinton Warwickshire

¾ mile west of the A41 Warwick–Birmingham road, at Chadwick End, 7½ miles north-west of Warwick, 13 miles south-east of central Birmingham

This perfect medieval manor house set in an ancient park lies in a remnant of the Forest of Arden. Although only ten miles south of Birmingham, the surrounding countryside still has an essentially medieval character, criss-crossed by a network of sunken lanes and with the waves of ridge and furrow visible in fields now under grass.

Encircled by a thirteenth-century moat – all that remains of the farmstead built here when the forest was first cleared – the present house dates from the fifteenth century. It is built round three sides of a courtyard, the only way in being over the two-arched red-brick Georgian bridge which leads to the crenellated gatehouse. Grey walls punctuated with mullioned windows fall sheer to the water on either side, tall red-brick Elizabethan chimneys forming splashes of colour against the roof. Despite its guarded appearance, this is not a forbidding place. Its small panelled rooms filled with mostly seventeenth- and eighteenth-century oak furniture are intimate and homely, a rare survival from the world of the lesser gentry.

For most of its history Baddesley Clinton has been connected with the Ferrers family, who lived here from the early sixteenth century until 1939. The remarkable Elizabethan antiquary, Henry Ferrers, did much to enlarge and embellish the house he inherited, introducing the rich oak panelling and highly decorated overmantels in many of the rooms. He also emblazoned his descent through several generations in rich armorial glass. He was the first of many of his family to suffer for his Roman Catholicism and this remote house became a haven for recusants in the late sixteenth century, when Catholics were persecuted with particular severity. Looking at the hiding place formed out of an old drain in the kitchen – one of three in the house – it is difficult to believe that nine men evaded capture here in October 1591, standing motionless with their feet in water for four hours. The simple little sacristy above is another testimony to the faith which took men to their deaths. Fined heavily for their religious beliefs, the family was also impoverished by the Civil War, in which they supported the king. The shortage of funds which so plagued the Ferrers ensured that Baddesley survived unchanged.

The medieval atmosphere of the house was particularly appreciated by the extended family group who lived here at the end of the nineteenth century. Marmion Edward Ferrers married the talented Rebecca Dulcibella Orpen, whose romanticised portraits of her friends and life at Baddesley now enhance the house. For financial reasons the couple were joined by Rebecca's literary aunt, Lady Chatterton, well known as a romantic novelist, and her husband Edward Dering. All four revelled in the antiquity of the place and re-created a Catholic chapel, sumptuously fitted out with leather hangings decorated with flowers and birds in gold, pink and blue. Both Lady Chatterton and Rebecca liked to paint in the bay window of the great parlour, where, today, the high barrel ceiling, sparse furnishings and rippling reflections from the moat create a sense of airy spaciousness contrasting with the dark intimacy of the rest of the house.

The Balston Collection

West Midlands

In the Bantock House Museum, Bantock Park, south-west of Wolverhampton town centre on the B4161

Thomas Balston (1883–1967), author, art historian and a partner in the publishing company Duckworth's, built up this interesting collection of over 400 Staffordshire earthenware figures. Almost all depict personalities of the Victorian age, many of them accurately portrayed. The earliest pieces, stylised portraits of Victoria and Albert, date from the year of the young queen's wedding in 1840, later

figures showing Victoria holding a baby in long clothes or accompanied by children in short skirts marking the arrival of the numerous royal progeny. Royal engagements also inspired commemorative pieces, such as the figures of the Prince of Wales and Princess Alexandra.

Here, too, are great statesmen of the age, the Duke of Wellington rubbing shoulders with Lord Shaftesbury and Sir Robert Peel, while the Crimean War produced a flood of pieces, Florence Nightingale and the Turkish commander Omar Pasha among them. The worlds of entertainment, literature and crime are also represented, including figures of Jenny Lind, the Swedish nightingale, of Byron, Burns and Scott and of notorious Victorian murderers.

Apart from its historical interest, the collection marks a new era in the output of the Staffordshire potteries, with richer colouring than seen on earlier figures and larger, simpler designs. Also on view at the Bantock House Museum (not owned by the Trust) are eighteenth-century English enamels, Worcester porcelain and collections of Georgian and Victorian japanned tin and papier mâché.

Barrington Court Somerset

2 miles north of the A303 between Ilchester and Ilminster, at east end of Barrington village, ½ mile east of the B3168

Twisted finials and chimneys reaching skywards from every gable and angle transform Barrington's roofline into a forest of stone fingers. Although not as grand as Montacute only ten miles or so to the east (*see* p.202), which it predates by about forty years, this fine sixteenth-century house has the same indefinable charm, a blend of romance, fantasy and age. Built to a characteristic Elizabethan E plan, with long wings projecting either side of the original entrance court on the south front, the honey-coloured façades with their generous mullioned windows and buttressed gables are typical of the best architecture of the day. Barrington's flamboyant roofline, reminiscent of the extravagant self-advertisement of Francis I's contemporary French châteaux, heralds more fully developed Renaissance features at Montacute. And the connection between the two houses is not only architectural, as Barrington was briefly owned by the Phelips family of Montacute in the early seventeenth century.

But, unlike its grander neighbour, Barrington

A bridge across the moat leads into the walled formal garden at Barrington Court. (*NT/Peter Craig*)

over the house in 1920 when it was a gutted shell and filled it with his collection of interior fittings from contemporary derelict buildings. Barrington is now leased to Stuart Interiors for the display of period and reproduction furniture and is arranged as a series of showrooms.

The enchanting formal garden, laid out as a series of outdoor rooms within the warm brick walls of Elizabethan cattleyards, is another twentieth-century creation. Originally planted to plans by Gertrude Jekyll, the raised beds bordering the fountain pond in the Lily Garden still reflect her colour schemes, with azaleas, wallflowers, marigolds and dahlias flowering orange and red in vivid displays. A brick path leads through an arch to the restful Iris Garden flowering pink, blue and purple round a sundial, and to the cool White Garden planted with a range of silver-foliaged and pale-blossomed herbaceous and annual species. Two arms of the moat enfold the house, one bridged by the path which brings visitors from the carpark, the other forming a long lily-encrusted corridor bordering the grassy entrance court. Espaliered apples, pears and plums are trained along the high brick walls of the large kitchen garden, thriving in the sun which turns the Ham stone of the house to gold.

Basildon Park Berkshire

Between Pangbourne and Streatley, 7 miles north-west of Reading, on west side of the A329

This neo-classical mansion standing high above the River Thames a mile or two upstream from Reading was built between 1776–83 by the Yorkshire architect John Carr. Ranked as one of his masterpieces and his only house in the south of England, it was commissioned by another Yorkshireman, Francis Sykes, who had bought the Basildon property in 1771. Sykes, later 1st Baronet, was one of the successful men who returned from India with vast fortunes accumulated in the service of the East India Company. Although less corrupt than many, he appears to have been particularly wealthy, and was able to spend lavishly on his new house. Several other nabobs lived in the tranquil countryside round about, including his friend Warren Hastings, and Lord Clive himself had tried to purchase Basildon in 1767.

John Carr's Palladian villa, built out of beautiful honey-coloured Bath stone, is both restrained and

was not designed for a high-flying politician. Although the Daubeney family who owned the estate in the early sixteenth century were ambitious members of the Tudor court, Sir Giles serving as Henry VII's Ambassador to France and his son a participant in the Field of Cloth of Gold, it seems they were content with the moated medieval house they inherited and that the new building was commissioned by William Clifton, a prosperous London merchant to whom the property was sold in 1552. William Strode, whose father had acquired Barrington in 1625, was responsible for the fine late seventeenth-century stable block in the style of Wren only a stone's throw away from the house, its tall red-brick chimneys echoing the Elizabethan roofline.

Barrington still preserves a largely sixteenth-century layout, although few original internal features survive. Deceptively authentic oak panelling and other decoration, including a remarkable honeycomb of wooden ribs covering the ceiling of the small dining-room, was brought here between the First and Second World Wars as part of the restoration initiated by Colonel A. Lyle, who took suitably grand. The main three-storey block dominated by a pedimented portico – the massive columns etched white against the shadowy recess behind on sunny days – is separated by courtyards from the two-storey pavilions on either side. Although all three parts of the house were originally linked internally, this is no longer so and the windows and doors on the exterior walls of the courtyards are only dummies.

Carr's neo-classical decoration in the hall, with its delicate plasterwork ceiling subtly coloured like expensive wrapping paper in pink, lilac, green and stone, survives unaltered. His magnificent staircase is little changed, lit by graceful lunettes from above and with an elegant wrought-iron balustrade curving gently upwards. But Francis Sykes did not finish his new house, perhaps because he never recovered from the investigation into his dealings in India, which lost him his parliamentary seat and left

St Paul, from a set of eight pictures by Pompeo Batoni at Basildon Park depicting seven of the apostles and God the Father. These paintings illustrate another side of the artist who is chiefly remembered in Great Britain for his portraits of Englishmen on the Grand Tour, but who valued his historical and religious works – of which the examples at Basildon are the finest collection in the country – more highly. (*NT/Angelo Hornak*)

him £11,000 poorer, or because of his disappointment in his sons, one dying young, the other a spendthrift. In 1838 the decline in the family fortunes forced his grandson to sell to the Liberal MP James Morrison, a self-made man whose upward path in life had been eased by marriage to his employer's daughter. Now a merchant prince, he needed a suitably grand setting to display his considerable collection of pictures. Morrison employed his architect-friend J. B. Papworth to complete the house and he and his ten children lived here in style. This was Basildon's golden age. A fast train link with London brought many distinguished visitors, J. M. W. Turner and Bishop Samuel Wilberforce among them.

Sadly, with the death of Morrison's daughter Ellen in 1910, the contents were dispersed and the house remained empty for over forty years. During this period Basildon survived a scheme to re-erect it in America (no purchaser could be found) and lost some sections of plasterwork, which were sold to the Waldorf Astoria Hotel in New York. It was saved by the 2nd Lord and Lady Iliffe, who bought it in 1952, restored it with great skill and filled it with period furnishings and paintings, including portraits by Lely, Hoppner and Mytens as well as one or two twentieth-century works, such as Frank Salisbury's lovely painting of Lady Iliffe in a simple white dress. One of the glories of the house today is the Octagon Drawing Room, with its three great windows looking out over the Thames and the beech woods beyond. Pompeo Batoni's vivid portrayals of seven of the apostles and God the Father clustered round the doors on either side of the room are typical of the fine Italian paintings that Sir Francis Sykes might have acquired on a Grand Tour, and the deep red of the walls on which they are displayed is in accord with eighteenth-century taste.

Parkland studded with carefully placed chestnuts, beeches and limes still comes right up to the entrance front, as it did in Sir Francis Sykes's day. James Morrison added the balustraded terrace walk which now frames a lawn at the back of the house, and he was also responsible for the pair of carved stone dogs on the north side of the grass, which he bought on a trip to Italy in 1845–6. Lord and Lady Iliffe laid out the small formal rose garden with beds of old-fashioned species edged with lavender and introduced most of the other garden ornaments.

Bateman's East Sussex

½ mile south of Burwash on the A265; approached by road leading south from west end of village or north from Woods Corner

Bateman's is a modest Jacobean house of local sandstone, with six brick columns forming a massive central chimneystack above the gabled façades. The date 1634 over the porch almost certainly records the year in which it was completed. In the early seventeenth century this part of southern England was benefiting from the wealth created by the Wealden iron industry, then at its height, and there is a tradition that the house was built by a local ironmaster.

Rudyard Kipling's love of the East is reflected in the oriental rugs and china in the parlour at Bateman's, which include a long Samarkand prayer rug, made for children to pray on, under the refectory table. A Tiffany lamp, one of two in this room, stands to the right of the Dutch cabinet displaying blue and white Chinese Nanking ware. (*NT/John Bethell*)

The particular interest of this modest building lies in its association with Rudyard Kipling, who bought the property in 1902 and lived here until his death in 1936. The great man broods over the stairs in a painting by John Collier, his dark three-piece suit slightly too big for him, the eyes behind the glasses tinged green and blue. In tune with Edwardian appreciation of seventeenth-century furniture and design, he and his wife created interiors that perfectly complement the building and which are still as the Kiplings left them. The heart of the house is the book-lined study at the top of the stairs, where Kipling wrote at the long early seventeenth-century walnut refectory table under the window, flinging himself down on the day-bed when inspiration deserted him. His tidily arranged 'writing tools' look as if he has just gone out for the afternoon, with the fur seal he used as a paperweight and his boxes of pins and clips flanking the blotter. The large Indian waste-paper basket to the right of the desk has just been emptied, awaiting further discarded drafts of the stories and poems that Kipling wrote and rewrote conscientiously to produce what are now classics of the English language.

Kipling wrote some of his greatest works here, including *Puck of Pook's Hill*, called after the hill visible from the house, *If* and *The Glory of the Garden*. For these he drew his material from the Kent and Sussex countryside, no longer looking east to the India of his childhood for inspiration. But the house also reflects his strong links with the subcontinent, with oriental rugs in many of the rooms and Kipling's large collection of Indian artefacts and works of art displayed in the parlour. His delightful bookplate shows a diminutive figure reading on top of an elephant.

The peaceful garden running down to the River Dudwell owes much to the Kiplings, who laid out paths and hedges and planted the rose garden. Kipling's sundial is engraved with the words 'It is later than you think'. As might be expected from the author of *Kim*, the pond was designed with young people in mind, shallow enough for his children and their friends to use it for boating and bathing. It is immortalised in the visitors' book, where the initials FIP stand for 'fell in pond'. The grounds also contain two oasthouses that were built in the late eighteenth century and the mill on the river which Kipling harnessed for electricity when he first came to Bateman's. Now restored to working order, it is used for grinding flour.

Bath Assembly Rooms Avon

In Alfred Street, north of Milsom Street, east of the Circus

This elegant place is straight from the world of Jane Austen, the setting for a thousand card parties and for the routs and masquerades with ices and claret cup that Emma Woodhouse would have revelled in. Although Bath had been known as a spa since Roman times, it was only under the influence of Beau Nash's forceful personality in the eighteenth century that what had been a provincial watering place was transformed into an international resort. By 1769, when the Assembly Rooms were begun – the third set to appear in the town – John Wood the Elder's showpieces, Queen Square and the Circus, were already completed, the start of the magnificent sequence of terraces and streets that was to culminate in his son's Royal Crescent.

John Wood the Younger's Assembly Rooms echo the fashionable elegant world which created them, a place where the company could amuse themselves with dancing, drinking tea or playing cards, strolling from one pursuit to another as the fancy took them. Those who came here were expected to conform to certain standards of dress and behaviour, as laid down by the Master of Ceremonies. Captain William Wade, the Rooms' convivial and decorative host from their opening in 1771 until 1777, still scrutinises visitors from Gainsborough's full-length portrait. His published rules included instructions on where to sit, as well as exhortations such as 'no Lady dance country-dances in a hoop of any kind'.

Set impressively across a wide pavement, the Rooms dominate their surroundings, with two rather austere classical façades rising either side of the central pedimented entrance. This plain exterior gives no hint of the splendours within. The magnificent hundred-foot ballroom, the largest eighteenth-century room in Bath, would once have been filled with 800–1,200 on ball nights, five great candle-lit chandeliers illuminating the glittering company below and the orchestra housed in the apse on the south wall. Rising the height of the building to a high coved ceiling, this superb classical interior is lit only at second-floor level, where Corinthian columns flanking the windows and lining the interior wall are picked out in white against the blue of the walls.

The lofty tearoom with a double screen of columns at one end is similarly splendid. Completing the original suite was the octagon, or card-room, where an organ was provided to entertain the company when card playing was banned on Sundays, but in 1777 another card-room was added to cope with the numbers who flocked here. Concerts graced by such celebrities as Johann Strauss and Liszt continued to be popular, but the Assembly Rooms lost their attraction in the nineteenth century, closing at the start of the First World War. They were restored by the City of Bath after they had been presented to the Trust in 1931, only to be severely damaged by bombs in 1942. Reconstruction began in 1946, initially under the close supervision of Sir Albert Richardson, whose determination ensured the accurate reproduction of original features. Subsequent redecoration, and major restoration in the late 1980s, has been based on original colour samples found in the City Archives, thus re-creating the complete eighteenth-century scheme. A Museum of Costume (not owned by the Trust) is housed in the basement.

Bath Properties Avon

On Claverton Down, 1 mile south-east of Bath, and north-east of the city respectively

Bath's beauty owes a great deal to the way it sits among a bowl of hills. It is essential to this beauty that the skyline, largely wooded, should be preserved. The Trust plays its part in this preservation, holding over 500 acres of the hills immediately south-east of the city. Rainbow Wood Farm on Claverton Down was the first acquisition in 1959, Smallcoombe Farm at Bathwick and farmland at Bushey Norwood nearby were added later, and in the early 1990s the Trust acquired both the twenty-nine acres of Fairy Wood and Klondyke Wood and the crucial twenty-eight acres of Prior Park (*see* p.268). Bushey Norwood is bounded on the north by the rampart of an Iron Age hill fort on Bathampton Down, where a single bank and ditch enclosing an area of some seventy-eight acres overlie an earlier field system. There is access by public footpath, giving country walks close to the centre of Bath.

Little Solsbury Hill, north-east of the city, rises to 625 feet. The ramparts of its hill fort, probably built in about 300BC, are faced with well-preserved drystone hedging. From the top of the hill there are wide views over Bath and the Avon valley.

Beatrix Potter Gallery Cumbria

In Hawkshead, next to the Red Lion inn

Like Hill Top, the little farm which she purchased in 1905 (*see* p.151), and the village of Sawrey, the nearby market town of Hawkshead was captured in several of Beatrix Potter's delicate illustrations for her children's books. The town still looks very much as she knew it in the late nineteenth and early twentieth centuries, a cluster of small limewashed houses ranged round three squares and two main streets. Next to the Red Lion inn overlooking one of the squares in the centre of town is the low,

Beatrix Potter in the porch of Hill Top, her first purchase in the Lake District. (*NT*)

cream-coloured building where Beatrix Potter went to consult the local solicitor W. H. Heelis & Son on her property purchases in the district, all of which came to the Trust on her death. William Heelis, the junior partner she saw regularly over the years, not only gave her advice on her acquisitions, but also kept an eye on her property when she was away and attended sales on her behalf. In 1912 he asked her to be his wife.

Four small rooms, two created out of the large upstairs office which William shared with his uncle and cousin, are now the setting for a changing exhibition of Beatrix Potter's sketches and water-colours. There are also photographs of the Heelis and Potter families and of some of Beatrix's farms. Downstairs, what was the clerks' room has been refurnished as a nineteenth-century solicitor's office, using some of the original desks and furnishings.

Beesands Cliff Devon

½ mile south of Torcross, 3 miles north of Start Point

Beesands Cliff is miles away from other Trust property, but worth seeking out. The great sweep of Start Bay is best seen from Little Dartmouth (*see* p.98), and the A379 follows the beach for two miles between Slapton and Torcross, where it turns sharply west for Kingsbridge. A mile beyond, hidden by high ground, is the fishing hamlet of Beesands. In the cliff to the north, and south of the Limpet Rocks, a narrow cleft the width of a horse and cart is the entrance to a wildly picturesque quarry, where more than a century ago roofing slates were dug to roof the houses of the South Hams, and carried there direct as they were needed.

Bellister Northumberland

¼ mile south of the A69, astride the Haltwhistle–Alston road

Just outside Haltwhistle, in the South Tyne valley west of Hexham, the 1,100 acres of Bellister are a rare survival of a small manorial estate which has escaped absorption by the large surrounding properties. The castle (not open to the public) originally stood on the north bank of the river, but in 1799, when the river changed its course, it was left well to the south. The former river banks lend character to the valley land, their gravelly hummocks showing all stages of colonisation, from herb-rich grassland to scrub woodland. The steep wooded cliffs above the river provide pleasant walks and run up to open moorland.

Belton House Lincolnshire

3 miles north-east of Grantham on the A607 Grantham–Lincoln road

Belton is at peace with the world. Built in the last years of Charles II's reign to an H-shaped design by the gentleman-architect William Winde, its simple Anglo-Dutch style seems to express the confidence and optimism of Restoration England. Symmetrical honey-coloured façades crowned with a cupola look out over the tranquil, wooded park, the grandeur of the broad flight of steps leading up to the pedimented entrance front offset by domestic dormers in the steeply pitched roof.

The interiors reflect Belton's long association with the Brownlow and Cust families, descendants of the ambitious and wealthy Elizabethan lawyer who bought the estate in 1617. Family portraits hang in almost every room, from Reynolds's imposing study of Sir John Cust, Speaker of the House of Commons from 1761–70, which greets visitors in the coldly impressive marble hall, to Lord Leighton's magical portrait at the top of the stairs of the last Countess Brownlow as a young girl, the colour of the bouquet she holds against her long white dress echoed in the autumnal trees behind.

High-quality decorations and furnishings, including magnificent wall mirrors, a brilliant-blue Italian lapis lazuli cabinet and the remnants of an extensive collection of Old Masters, speak of wealth well spent. Glowing panelling lines the formal seventeenth-century saloon in the middle of the house, setting off delicate limewood carvings with beautifully detailed fruit and flowers that suggest the hand of Grinling Gibbons. Early eighteenth-century gilt wall mirrors between the three long windows looking on to the garden reflect two sets of Charles II walnut chairs arrayed on the pink and green Aubusson carpet, their seats and backs upholstered in faded crimson velvet and a host of cherubs adorning the frames. Two more cherubs, their grumpy expressions perhaps due to their rather precarious position, perch uncomfortably on the monumental reredos in the largely unaltered north-facing chapel, where an exuberant baroque

A continuous garden party adorns the walls of the Chinese Bedroom at Belton, the one habitually used by Edward VIII on his visits to the house when he was Prince of Wales. (*NT/Martin Trelawny*)

plaster ceiling by Edward Goudge contrasts with James Wyatt's classical compositions of the 1770s upstairs.

Apart from the silver awarded to Speaker Cust for his service to the House of Commons, some of the most prized pieces at Belton are the vast garden scenes by Melchior d'Hondecoeter acquired by the last Earl. He and his wife presided over a golden age in the late nineteenth century, when Belton was sympathetically restored and redecorated and the formal gardens introduced in the early nineteenth century to the north of the house were re-created. The sunken Italian garden, with urns and clipped yews around the central fountain pond, complements Jeffry Wyatt's elegant orangery of about 1820. More yews line the path through the Dutch Garden to the eighteenth-century sundial clasped by Father Time, one of several pieces of sculpture and a variety of ornamental urns and vases providing points of interest.

The little Palladian temple facing down a short canal on the east side of the garden, the unrestored wilderness to the west and the avenue stretching away across the park, a tall arch silhouetted against the sky at the far end, are all survivals of the eighteenth-century layout depicted in Thomas Smith's bird's-eye views in the breakfast room. Twentieth-century portraits hanging here include a painting of the 6th Lord Brownlow, Lord in Waiting to Edward VIII during his brief reign and a close friend of the king. Edward stayed several times at Belton, perhaps deriving strength from the serenity of his surroundings.

Bembridge Windmill Isle of Wight

½ mile south of Bembridge on the B3395

Set on a hill about a mile from the easternmost point of the Isle of Wight, this weathered four-storey stone mill with its great thirty-foot sails is a familiar landmark and has inspired generations of artists, J. M.W. Turner among them. A fine example of an eighteenth-century tower mill, Bembridge was built in about 1700 and still contains original wooden machinery. The turning gear which rotated the wooden cap to bring the sweeps into the wind is still visible on the outside of the mill; the miller would originally have operated it by walking round the building hauling on a chain. For some 200 years until the outbreak of the First World War the mill ground flour, meal and cattle feed for the village and surrounding countryside. Derelict by the 1950s, it has now been partly restored, the only windmill on the Isle of Wight to have survived.

Beningbrough Hall North Yorkshire

8 miles north-west of York, 2 miles west of Shipton, 2 miles south-east of Linton-on-Ouse

Finished in 1716, dignified Beningbrough Hall is a product of the cultivated, secure decades of the early eighteenth century. The house is set on a slight rise above the water meadows of the Ouse, little pavilions crowned with cupolas framing the solid red-brick rectangle with stone dressings which stares confidently across the entrance court. A splayed flight of steps rises to the central front door, over which two life-like stone horses struggle to escape the sculptured drapery which envelops them. Tiny attic casements one-third the size of the long sash windows in the two principal storeys are set just beneath the roof, sandwiched between massive console brackets supporting an overhanging cornice.

Built for John Bourchier, whose family had acquired the property by marriage in the previous century, the construction was supervised by the local carpenter-architect William Thornton, possibly with advice from Thomas Archer, although Thornton alone was responsible for the exceptional woodcarvings which are such a feature of the house. Mouldings and friezes usually executed in plaster are here realised in wood, such as the three-dimensional acanthus leaves which curl out of the deep ornamental frieze in the state bedroom. Beningbrough is also remarkable for the central corridor running the length of both floors, with a vista at ground level into the greenery of the conservatory at one end. Although the house has none of its original contents, it is furnished in period style and now also displays some hundred paintings from the National Portrait Gallery, including Kneller's portraits of members of the Kit-Kat club.

The formality of early eighteenth-century life is reflected in the suite of state rooms for honoured guests traditionally sited on the ground floor, and in the long saloon used for balls and large family gatherings. Rising through two storeys, the great hall which would have greeted all visitors is one of the most impressive baroque interiors in England.

Japanned chairs, lacquered cabinet and panels from a coromandel screen setting off a Kneller portrait at Beningbrough reflect the early eighteenth-century taste for the exotic. (*NT/Andreas von Einsiedel*)

A flagged stone floor and soaring stone-coloured pilasters set against grey walls contribute to an overall effect of dignified elegance.

Another insight into the eighteenth century is provided by the intimate closets where important guests could receive their closest friends or relax in private. Always richly decorated, those at Beningbrough are crowded with oriental porcelain displayed on stepped ledges over the fireplaces. The contemporary taste for the exotic also shows in the sections of Chinese screen set into the panelling in one of the dressing-rooms, with a Chinese lacquer cabinet standing below.

A door in the wall of the cobbled yard opposite the fully equipped nineteenth-century laundry leads into the garden spread along the south side of the house, where two formal layouts enclosed by yew hedges have been planted in contrasting colours, the plants in one flowering orange, yellow and red, those in the other cool-coloured and set round a pool with a fountain. Double borders are filled with peonies, irises, bush roses and climbing plants, including the rare *Jasminum beesianum*, and plants of North American extraction are featured in the area beyond the now grassy kitchen garden. The view south over the ha-ha to the water meadows has a feeling of the eighteenth-century landscaped park that once surrounded the house.

Benthall Hall Shropshire

1 mile north-west of Broseley on the B4375, 4 miles north-east of Much Wenlock, 6 miles south of Wellington

Although only a couple of miles from Coalbrookdale, the traumas of the Industrial Revolution passed Benthall by, precipitous wooded slopes successfully isolating the house on its plateau above the gorge of the River Severn. Seat of the ancient Benthall family whose origins stretch back to Anglo-Saxon times, the exterior has changed little since it was built in the late sixteenth century. Mullioned and transomed windows gleam in the south front looking towards the Shropshire Hills, its charming asymmetrical façade punctuated by two-storey bays on either side of the projecting porch. Five gables pierce the roofline and giant sixteenth-century brick chimneystacks rise from each end of the house. Five stone tablets set in a playing-card pattern above the door in the porch, perhaps alluding to the five wounds of Christ, were

probably advertising the family's Catholic sympathies, also indicated by the hiding place in the little room above.

Early seventeenth-century interiors include a carved staircase of c.1618, with grotesque heads adorning the massive newel posts and the leopard of the Benthall crest proudly displayed on the panel at the turn of the stairs. In the sunny, welcoming drawing-room, flooded with light from south- and west-facing windows, an elaborate white plaster ceiling and frieze merge with off-white oak panelling. Lions, horses, stags, griffins and other mythical creatures look down on the room from their plaster roundels. Rococo chimneypieces of c.1760 here and in the dining-room were added by T. F. Pritchard, architect of the Iron Bridge spanning the River Severn just to the north, perhaps the most evocative symbol of the Industrial Revolution.

The intimate garden, sheltered and enclosed by trees, is largely the work of Robert Bateman, son of James Bateman who created the individual nineteenth-century layout at Biddulph Grange (*see* p.28). During his tenancy (1890–1906), he laid out the terraces, rockeries and rose garden, built up the shrub banks and carried on the tradition of peopling the garden with unusual plants that had been established by the distinguished botanist George Maw and his brother in the mid-nineteenth century. George Maw was responsible for the display of autumn and spring crocuses in the patch of woodland bordering the lawn, and with his care the Glory of the Snow (*Chionodoxa luciliae*) flowered at Benthall for the first time in Britain in 1877. The rich green leaves of the little mouse plant (*Arisarum proboscideum*) from the Pyrenees appear here and there, herbaceous geraniums, including *Geranium nodosum* and Mourning Widow (*G. phaeum*), have become naturalised under the trees, and there is much else of interest.

Berrington Hall Hereford & Worcester

3 miles north of Leominster on west side of the A49

Berrington is the creation of Thomas Harley, the 3rd Earl of Oxford's remarkable son, who made a fortune from supplying pay and clothing to the British army in America and became Lord Mayor of London in 1767 at the age of thirty-seven. The architect of his austere three-storey house, with its domestic quarters clustered round a courtyard behind, was the fashionable Henry Holland, who also decorated Claremont for Lord Clive and built Carlton House for the Prince Regent.

The house is beautifully set above the wide valley of a tributary of the River Lugg, with views west and south to the Black Mountains and Brecon Beacons and north-west to the Iron Age hill fort of Croft Ambrey (*see* p.92). This was the site advised by 'Capability' Brown, whom Harley took to see the estate in 1775, shortly after he had acquired it, and who was to landscape the park, creating the lake with its artificial island (Berrington is one of the best examples of his work). Holland, Brown's son-in-law, started on the house three years later.

Approached through an entrance lodge built in the form of a triumphal arch, the rather plain neo-classical exterior with a central portico and a wide flight of steps leading to the entrance gives no clue to the lavishness of the interior. Feminine plaster ceilings now decorated in muted pastel colours adorn the principal rooms. Holland is at his most fanciful in the drawing-room, where a number of roundels thought to be by Biagio Rebecca are set off by white plaster cherubs leading seahorses by blue ribbons over a lavender background. Biagio Rebecca probably also executed the prominent grisaille panels in the library, deep shadows in those showing eminent Englishmen of letters on the ceiling giving them a three-dimensional quality as if they were made of plaster. Bacon and Chaucer are easily recognisable; Pope the only one of the eight to be shown in full profile.

Holland's masterpiece is the staircase hall. Rising to a central dome, it shows an extraordinary ability to use perspective and space to dramatic effect, recalling the contemporary engravings of Piranesi. The rooms are set off with a collection of French furniture, including pieces which belonged to the Comte de Flahault, natural son of Talleyrand, and Napoleon's step-daughter Hortense.

In the dining-room, vast panoramic paintings of battles at sea, three of them by Thomas Luny, are a tribute to the distinguished Admiral Rodney. Father-in-law of Harley's daughter Anne and one of the most eminent naval admirals of the eighteenth century, he played a prominent role in the American War of Independence. The scene to the right of the fireplace shows the destruction of the *Santo Domingo* off Cape St Vincent. Clouds billow from the stricken ship, only a fragment of which has survived the massive explosion. More poignant reminders of members of the Cawley family, to whom the estate was sold in 1901, hang in Lady Cawley's room. One of the photographs shows the 1st Lord Cawley and his four sons on horseback in front of the house, ready for a day's hunting. A few years later three of the young men had lost their lives in the First World War.

Biddulph Grange Staffordshire

Off Grange Road on the A452, north of Biddulph town and 4 miles south of Congleton

The garden created over twenty years from 1842 on this cold, wet site at a height of 500–600 feet just below Biddulph Moor is one of the most exceptional in England. A wide range of trees, shrubs and other plants from all over the world reflects the many new species being brought back to England from the Far East and the Americas by David Douglas, Robert Fortune and others at this period. In this respect, Biddulph is no more than a garden of its time, although the links with collectors are particularly close. But the variety of picturesque settings providing diverse growing conditions suitable for a wide range of plants, the use of banks, rocks and tree-trunks to enclose and separate areas of the garden and planting schemes which aim for aesthetic effect as well as the display of individual species put this garden in a class of its own.

The genius of James Bateman, its creator, emerges most strongly away from the house, beyond the formal terraces falling to the lake below the south front. Huge boulders piled one on top of another, all of them laboriously brought to the garden from a quarry nearby, form the sides of a naturalistic glen with a collection of ferns thriving in the many nooks and crannies and semi-aquatic plants growing along the stream devised to flow down its length. At one end is the rhododendron ground, a brilliant display of colour at the right time of year, and from here a tunnel through more rockwork leads to the pinetum. Many tons of earth were moved to produce gently rising slopes on either side of a winding path and a range of soils and situations was contrived to cater for all requirements. Impressive groups of monkey puzzles, deodars and pines are mixed with golden yew and hollies and a variety of oaks.

A second tunnel at the other end of the glen emerges in the enchanting Chinese Garden, a

A delicate glass dome lights Henry Holland's staircase at Berrington Hall. (*NT*/*Jonathan Gibson*)

willow-pattern plate brought to life. A hump-backed bridge and a gaily painted temple hung with bells and decorated with dragons and grebes are reflected in the still waters of a pool. Completely enclosed with earth banks and walls of vegetation, this secluded heart of the garden once sheltered an impressive range of plants, including the first two golden larches to be cultivated in England, one of which still survives, a variety of tree peony and hostas, variegated bamboo and the Japanese anemone. Japanese maples set off an imitation of the Great Wall of China which partly bounds the garden. Even more remarkable, perhaps, is the Egyptian Court, with two pairs of stone sphinxes guarding a pyramid and obelisks of topiary yew. An ape-like god squats in an inner chamber, luridly lit through coloured glass in the roof above. At the

back the pyramid is miraculously transformed into a half-timbered Cheshire cottage looking down the pinetum. More an architectural fantasy than a re-creation of the local vernacular, the cottage's decorative façade carries the date, 1856, when it was built, and the intertwined initials of James and Maria Bateman.

James Bateman's interest in plants began with a passion for orchids, his work on the species of Mexico and Guatemala – the first part of which was produced in 1837 when he was only twenty-six – earning him an international reputation and secur-ing his election as a Fellow of the Royal Horticul-tural Society shortly afterwards. While absorbed in Biddulph he continued to cultivate orchids in the hot-houses of Knypersley Hall, his father's house only a short distance away. He was a frequent visitor

The individual garden at Biddulph Grange includes a topiary pyramid flanked by yew obelisks and guarded by a pair of stone sphinxes.
(*NT/Ian Shaw*)

to George Loddiges's nursery in Hackney and while there may have first met the man who was to help him with his creation, the marine artist and occasional garden designer Edward Cooke. Although Cooke was probably responsible for all the architectural features in the garden, the overall plan was conceived by Bateman, with the help of his wife Maria. Sadly, it seems this enterprise overstretched the small fortune James had inherited from his grandfather, a wealthy industrialist: although Maria's ill-health was a major reason for the couple's decision to leave Staffordshire in the late 1860s, it is also clear they could not afford to stay on there. The Italianate mansion James designed to complement his garden was largely destroyed in a fire in 1895 and only the wings now remain, unhappily married to a late Victorian block built in Renaissance baronial style by Robert Heath, son of the successful industrialist who bought the property in 1872. For most of the twentieth century the house has been a hospital, and although the garden continued to be well maintained there was no conservation or renewal and from the late 1960s it suffered enormously from vandalism. Since Biddulph came to the Trust in 1988, a major eight-year restoration programme has returned the garden as closely as possible to Bateman's original scheme. The elaborate, yew-enclosed formal garden near the house, which includes a long dahlia walk and a sequence of parterres, has been re-created, as has the extraordinary stumpery, a mass of stumps and roots piled up to a height of ten to twelve feet on either side of the tortuous path up from the Chinese Garden, and in 1996 the restoration work culminated in the replanting of Bateman's great Wellingtonia avenue.

Blackdown Hills Somerset

2 miles south of Wellington on the A38, ½ mile east of the Wellington–Hemyock road

The Blackdown range runs east and west for twelve miles, south of the M4 and west of Taunton. The Trust owns only sixty acres of natural woodland on the ridge above the small town of Wellington. The visitor does not come here for the views over the Taunton Vale to the Quantocks, and on a clear day right across the Bristol Channel to Wales, for one can do this just as well elsewhere, but to see the extraordinary memorial to the Iron Duke (*see* p.357).

Black Down West Sussex

1 mile south-east of Haslemere, between the A286 and the B2131

At 918 feet the summit of Black Down is the highest point in Sussex and the views are splendid. The down stands proud above the Weald (*see* p.356), and in Victorian times all the world knew that it was here, at Aldworth, that Alfred, Lord Tennyson had built his laureate's mansion.

The ridge is of sandstone, the dry acid soil supporting heather with bilberries, gorse, birch and pine. The latter is winning the battle for survival, having encroached steadily, as has *Rhododendron ponticum*. Roe deer live in the fringes for there is much private woodland adjoining. Steep clefts, wet bottoms with sphagnum moss and bog plants, and the occasional small landslip, provide some tough scrambling. This is a place for a proper walk, and on the north side is the contrasting Valewood Park, a mix of meadow and open parkland with a pattern of sunken tracks and field banks, bringing the Trust's holding here to over 700 acres.

Blackwater Estuary Essex

10 miles east of Chelmsford

The Blackwater estuary is a lonely place, each farm with its sea wall, its saltings and mudflats. The area is intimately known to farmers and wildfowlers but it is a remarkable survival of what is still *terra incognita* to the millions of people living within a forty-mile radius.

The Essex Naturalists' Trust has been active in acquiring some of the best of this precious area, but the Trust also now has a substantial presence here. Copt Hall, purchased in 1989, has 300 acres of farmland, sea wall and salt-marsh. At the head of the estuary, Northey Island, 300 acres much cut about with creeks, is connected by a causeway to a further 200 acres at South House Farm on the mainland. The farm is believed to be the site of the Battle of Maldon fought in AD 991 between the Vikings and the Anglo-Saxons. Ray Island – cut off only at high water – lies in the Strood Channel which separates from the mainland the much larger Mersea Island, close to the small resort of West Mersea. A haunt of waders and wildfowl, it is leased to the Essex Naturalists' Trust with whom arrangements should be made for visiting.

Blaise Hamlet   Avon

4 miles north of central Bristol, west of Henbury village, just north of the B4057

John Nash, who designed these nine rustic cottages set round a green outside Bristol, was once heard to say that no palace had ever given him as much pleasure as Blaise Hamlet. His tiny settlement is certainly individual. Built in 1810–11 for the Quaker banker and philanthropist John Harford, who had bought the Blaise Castle estate in 1789, it was one of the first 'picturesque' estate villages, an example of the growing appreciation of the intrinsic attractiveness of traditional vernacular architecture (*see also* Selworthy, p.284). In this vision of an idealised village each building is different. Some are thatched, some tiled, and all have varied rooflines, with gables and dormers at different levels. Porches, verandahs, sheds and lean-tos ensure no profile is the same and contribute to the deliberate asymmetry. Even the pump on the green is placed defiantly off-centre. But everything in the hamlet is to the same scale, and all the cottages have soaring brick Tudoresque chimneys, now seen against a backdrop of mature trees as Nash intended. And the aged retainers whom Harford housed here were all provided with a small garden and an outside seat where they could doze on summer afternoons.

One of the three thatched cottages at Blaise Hamlet, John Nash's bizarre model village. (*NT/M. Allwood Coppin*)

The Blewcoat School   London

At 23 Caxton Street, near the junction of Buckingham Gate and Caxton Street, SW1

A statue of a boy in a long blue tunic and yellow stockings in a niche over the front door symbolises the many children from desperately poor backgrounds who were given a start in life in this modest Georgian building. In the one airy pine-panelled room set over a semi-basement, children from the slums of Westminster were taught to read and write and then found positions suited to their station, the girls going into domestic service or apprenticed to seamstresses and fan-makers, the boys placed with joiners, tailors, watermen and a wide variety of other trades. Part of a nationwide charity school movement financed by subscriptions from local tradesmen, the Blewcoat School was built in 1709 at the expense of William Green, a local brewer. Although small, it is both elegant and dignified, a pleasing mixture of red and yellow brick with stone dressings, decorative pilasters and a parapet concealing the hipped roof. The original oak double doors of the entrance front now lead into a Trust shop.

Blickling Hall   Norfolk

On north side of the B1354, 1½ miles north-west of Aylsham on the A140, 15 miles north of Norwich, 10 miles south of Cromer

Blickling is not a house to be trifled with. Built of warm red brick with stone dressings, Robert Lyminge's Jacobean mansion for Sir Henry Hobart, James I's distinguished Chief Justice of the Common Pleas, looks confidently out at the world, the gilded vanes on the corner turrets and the generous leaded windows glinting in the sun. Ornate Dutch gables are repeated on the service ranges extending like outstretched arms either side of the entrance court, their lines continued by dark walls of yew.

The medieval manor which had fired Sir Henry's imagination – home of Anne Boleyn, Henry VIII's ill-fated second queen, and Sir John Fastolfe,

(*Opposite page*) The 123-foot long gallery at Blickling Hall, turned into a library in the mid eighteenth century, still has its Jacobean plaster ceiling, commissioned at 5s 6d per square yard. The floor is now bare, without the matting seen here. (*NT/Jeremy Whitaker*)

inspiration for Shakespeare's tragic clown — has long disappeared, but its ghost lives on in the dry moat, now festive with roses, hydrangeas and hostas, and in the layout of the courtyard house. Partly remodelled in the eighteenth century by Thomas and William Ivory for John Hobart, 2nd Earl of Buckinghamshire, Blickling is a harmonious combination of Jacobean and Georgian, the Ivorys' ranges on the north and west melding beautifully with Lyminge's work.

The most spectacular room is Sir Henry's long gallery running 123 feet down the east front, adorned with Edward Stanyon's intricate plaster ceiling, on which heraldic motifs, including the Hobart bull, are intermingled with delightful depictions of the senses. In one panel a stag listens entranced to a man playing the mandolin, his lady following the music for him with her finger; in another, a woman lifts a brimming glass to her lips, her lap full of luscious fruit. In about 1745 the gallery was converted into a library to house the remarkable collection inherited from Sir Richard Ellys, a distinguished theologian and antiquary, the 12,000 volumes now housed here including a very rare Eliot Indian bible printed in Massachusetts in 1663 and a unique maritime atlas of the same period. J. H. Pollen's delicately painted frieze above the bookcases, full of timid rabbits and other wildlife of the Norfolk countryside, is part of the Pre-Raphaelite mural decoration commissioned by the 8th Marquess of Lothian shortly after he inherited the house in 1850.

A door from the gallery leads into one of the rooms fitted out in 1778–82 to display the works of art acquired by the 2nd Earl during his congenial three-year posting as Ambassador to the court of Catherine the Great. The Empress's parting present, a magnificent tapestry showing Peter the Great triumphing over the defeated Swedish army at Poltawa in 1709, was perhaps a response to the Earl's good looks and affability.

Rolling wooded parkland landscaped in the eighteenth century stretches away from the house, with beeches and sweet chestnuts and huge mature oaks framing a long artificial lake. The main garden borders the Jacobean east front, a long rectangle focused on a central path running east to the little pedimented and colonnaded temple Matthew Brettingham designed for the 1st Earl, set high up on a massive terrace overlooking the park. Immediately in front of the house, red brick edges a Victorian

sunken garden, remodelled in the 1930s by Norah Lindsay, who filled the four parterre beds set round a seventeenth-century fountain with brightly flowering herbaceous plants, islands of yellow and orange, purple and blue. Clipped yews mark the corners of rose beds and yew grand pianos guard the steps leading up to the Temple Path. In the formal wilderness either side of this axis, two sets of radial walks meeting in circular clearings are lined by avenues of Turkey oak, lime and beech or cut through oak woodland. On the southern perimeter, half hidden in the trees and set with its back to the garden looking out over the park, is the late eighteenth-century orangery, possibly by Samuel Wyatt. A secret garden with a summerhouse and a sundial in the northern wilderness is all that remains of an early eighteenth-century layout when the garden was first designed to an east-west plan, while the earthwork defined by the brick Victorian bastion to the north of the parterre may be an even earlier survival, the only remnant of Sir Henry Hobart's formal Jacobean garden, laid out on a strong north-south axis.

Boarstall Tower and Duck Decoy Buckinghamshire

Midway between Bicester and Thame, 2 miles west of Brill

This enchanting three-storey tower, with hexagonal turrets rising from each corner of the battlemented roofline, is all that remains of the fortified moated house built here in the early fourteenth century by John de Handlo. The only entrance to his carefully guarded property was through this gatehouse, its massive three-foot limestone walls falling sheer to the waters of the moat and surviving arrow slits suggesting the grim prospect it must once have presented.

Today Boarstall seems charmingly domestic, an array of Tudor and Jacobean windows surveying the world, octagonal chimneystacks rising almost to the height of the turrets, and approached over a two-arched brick and cobble bridge. A beautiful room running forty feet across the length of the third floor, now occasionally used for chamber concerts, was probably once a dormitory for the men of the establishment.

At the back of the tower, peacocks strut across romantic informal twentieth-century gardens. Just over the fields a tree-fringed lake marks Boarstall

Informal gardens set off the romantic south façade of Boarstall Tower, dominated by the large seventeenth-century windows lighting the room which runs the length of the third floor. The tower is the only medieval military building left in Buckinghamshire. The only known test of its defences occurred during the Civil War, when a Royalist garrison was besieged here and surrendered on 10 June 1646. (*NT/Fay Godwin*)

Duck Decoy, one of the few surviving working examples of a once-common feature of the English countryside, introduced from Holland by Charles II. A trained dog entices the ducks into netted-over channels leading off the lake, each one ending in a narrow point. Once an important source of winter food, the birds are now ringed for scientific purposes.

Bodiam Castle East Sussex

3 miles south of Hawkhurst, 1 mile east of the A229

By 1372, halfway through the Hundred Years War, England had lost control of the Channel and began to suffer the devastating French raids which resulted in the destruction of both Winchelsea and Rye within a few years. In 1385, anxious for the security of his household, Sir Edward Dalyngrigge, a veteran of the wars in France, asked Richard II for permission to fortify his manor of Bodiam, which lay only some ten miles from the Sussex coast and at the furthest navigable point of the River Rother.

The fine castle which still stares south across the Sussex marshes was started in 1385 and completed some three years later. Built just before siege artillery changed the approach to castle design, its

Bodiam Castle from the north-west, showing the approach over the moat to the massive twin-towered gateway. (*NT/Oliver Benn*)

strength lay in the height and might of its tower-studded circuit walls, which rise sheer from a broad moat. Three bridges connecting two islands lead from the north bank to the massive gateway, bristling with machicolations and gunports. Originally, to repel any attacker, this approach involved a dog leg to the west bank, three drawbridges and an outlying barbican, the remains of which stand on one of the islands. A ground-hugging pillbox by the path up from the car-park shows how much things have changed since.

Although now in ruins, enough of the interior survives to give a vivid picture of the realities of castle life. The deep well and the remains of a pigeon loft suggest the preoccupations of a garrison expecting to be besieged, but the remnants of traceried windows and a number of fireplaces tell a different story. Edward Dalyngrigge was a nobleman and had the means to live as luxuriously as the resources and uncertainties of his times would allow. The great courtyard reached through the forbidding gatehouse is surrounded by the outlines of domestic accommodation, including a traditional great hall with adjoining buttery, pantry and kitchen, such as would have been found in any mansion of the period, and personal chambers for Dalyngrigge and his wife. Separate quarters, each suite with its own fireplaces and garderobe, were provided for his household, with additional provision for a military garrison. A chapel catered for the spiritual needs of the retinue and their lord. Like many contemporary buildings in France and England which Dalyngrigge must surely have seen, Bodiam combines domestic comfort with the trappings of defence.

Bodnant Garden Gwynedd

8 miles south of Llandudno and Colwyn Bay on the A470

This extensive, eighty-acre garden is alive with the sound of running water. It splashes over the worn baroque French fountain on one of the broad terraces which descend like a giant staircase into the valley of the River Hiraethlyn, trickles into the lily pond flanked by two majestic old cedars and feeds the long canal mirroring the classical façade of a stuccoed pedimented mill. In the ravine below, the Hiraethlyn tumbles several feet over a weir, water from the pool behind once being used to power a Tudor blast furnace. Minor streams and rivulets plunge precipitously to join the river on either side, helping to feed the Conwy only a short distance further downstream.

Whereas the gardens near the Victorian house (not owned by the Trust) are formal and open, with views across the Conwy to the mountains of northern Snowdonia, the depths of the valley are wild and enclosed. Conifers over a century old have thrived in the sheltered conditions, several of them, such as a fine *Abies grandis*, wellingtonias, redwoods and western hemlocks, now over a hundred feet tall. Seen from the bridge crossing the weir, trees interlace in a green arch over the water downstream, as if to protect the valley from prying eyes. A second mill stands on the banks of the Hiraethlyn, a long two-storey granite and slate construction once used to grind flour, a functional building that is a world away from the elegant summerhouse in the formal gardens above. Rhododendrons, azaleas and magnolias flourish beneath the trees, while hydrangeas planted along the river form unexpected splashes of blue in summer.

Apart from a number of fine beeches, cedars and oaks planted earlier in the nineteenth century, Bodnant has been created since 1874 by Mr Henry Pochin, his daughter Laura and her son and grandson, the 2nd and 3rd Lords Aberconway, ably assisted by three generations of the Puddle family who have served as their head gardeners. Now with all the beauty of a well-cared-for mature garden, Bodnant is notable for its collections of rhododendrons, magnolias and camellias among a wide range of trees, shrubs and other plants. The rhododendrons, ranging from dwarf alpines to trees sixty to eighty feet high, are particularly magnificent, and include many species from the Far East and Himalayas planted when they were first introduced into England in the early twentieth century by collectors such as George Forrest, Frank Kingdon-Ward and Dr J. F. Rock. Most of the Chinese species grown from seed sent back by Dr E. H. Wilson between 1900 and 1906 are represented here, and there are also examples of the many hybrids raised by the 2nd Lord Aberconway, a pioneer in this field, including *Rhododendron* 'Elizabeth', R. 'Winsome', R. 'Fabia Tangerine' and a hedge of R. 'Bluebird'. Some species particularly suited to the garden, such as *Eucryphia glutinosa* and *Camellia* 'J. C. Williams', are planted extensively, and many specimens of the Chilean fire tree, *Embothrium lanceolatum*, several of them a special form raised from seed brought back from the Andes by Harold Comber of Nymans (*see* p.235), dot the garden with patches of brilliant scarlet in late May.

Two of the five terraces are devoted to roses, with a rose-hung pergola framing the steps leading to the lower of the two. The Italiante theme is continued in the little open-air stage which closes one end of the Canal Terrace, facing down the water to the classical mill. Set several feet above the terrace, the stage is fronted by a curving hemispherical wall and bordered and backed by wings and hedges of clipped yew. Even more memorable is Henry Pochin's laburnum arch at the very top of the garden, transformed into a long feathery yellow

The upper garden at Bodnant looks over the Conwy valley to the mountains of Snowdonia. (*NT*)

tunnel in early summer, with thousands of strongly scented blossoms dangling only inches above visitors' heads. No wonder that Henry Pochin chose to be buried here, the sturdy granite tower which he built as a mausoleum on a bluff above the valley now also the last resting-place of his daughter and her son.

Bookham, Headley Heath, Holmwood and Limpsfield Commons Surrey

Running west to east along the North Downs

There are four sizeable Surrey commons, all different, all immensely valuable, on the fringes of London. The Bookham Commons, two miles west of Leatherhead, lie on clay, and are therefore different in character from the typical Surrey heath. Thickly wooded in the north, with open spaces to the south-west and ponds where all three species of newt breed, they have a good bird life. Four miles to the east lies Headley Heath, which was much churned up by tank training during the Second World War. The heathland, with scattered birch on the flatter, upper parts, has been extended by active habitat management, whilst the steeper slopes carry mixed woodland and areas of chalk downland. At Holmwood Common, a mile south of Dorking, the land is clay again. Grazing ceased in 1960 and birch scrub is becoming established, followed by oak and beech, but the wide, grassy rides provide sunny clearings and glades and valuable remnants of the former open common. Four Wents Pond in the south-east corner is the honeypot. Limpsfield Common, on Surrey's boundary with Kent, lies on a greensand ridge at 500 feet. Steep slopes combine with a well-varied vegetation, and the common has the classic ragged and irregular shape, funnelling out along numerous roads.

Borrowdale and Derwentwater

Cumbria

Running for 3 miles south of Keswick

From Scafell Pike the busy streets of Keswick are only eleven miles away, as the crow flies. Within this short distance is every sort of scenery. Borrowdale runs down 2,000 feet from the stark grandeur of

Scafell, Glaramara and the fells to the wooded shores of the lake. Almost entirely obscured now are the remains of the graphite workings at Seathwaite which brought the pencil industry to Keswick and wealth to the landowners. In the late seventeenth century the Statesmen, or yeoman farmers, of Borrowdale rebuilt their farmhouses which are so good to look at today. By far the greater part of the valley now belongs to the Trust, and virtually all the high ground.

At 3,206 feet, Scafell Pike is for the stout walker, but for the less agile the popular route from Seathwaite up Sty Head Gill, past the three tarns – Sty Head Tarn, Sprinkling Tarn below Great End and Angle Tarn – and down to Great Langdale is wholly satisfying. Rather less frequented is the delightful path from Stonethwaite up the Langstrath Beck and over the Stake Pass to Great Langdale.

Rain Gauge Cottage at Seathwaite has a good claim to be the wettest house in England, with an average annual rainfall of 125 inches. Below the hamlet the valley drops down to Derwentwater, through a mixture of well-tended fields, whitewashed farmhouses, numerous little woods and old mine workings now grown over, and with the famous Bowder Stone looming over the Jaws of Borrowdale. As in so many places, the Trust has provided footpaths to help walkers avoid cars. Some stay close to the road, others climb away from it, and it is perhaps the middle-height walks which are the most exciting.

To the east, tucked away behind Grange Fell, is the Watendlath valley, with the two farms of Stepps End and Fold Head and a café making up the hamlet. Here several old packhorse tracks meet: from Keswick, from Thirlmere, from Langdale across Stake Pass, and from Honister via Rosthwaite. A considerable mess when the Trust acquired the farms in the 1960s, the hamlet has now recovered its calm and simplicity.

Two places are particularly good for middle-ground walking. Ashness Farm, running from High Seat down to the lake shore, with the Ashness Woods beside the road from Barrow Beck to Lodore, forms the backdrop to the south-east end of Derwentwater. At Ashness Bridge, half a mile up the Watendlath road from Ashness Gate, is the superb view north to Skiddaw. Half a mile further up the road, the Surprise View suddenly opens down into Borrowdale, on to Derwentwater 500

Catbells above Derwentwater, familiar to generations of children from Beatrix Potter's illustrations for *The Tale of Mrs Tiggy-Winkle*. (*NT/Robert Thrift*)

feet below. The counterpart height south-west of the lake is beautiful Catbells above Brandelhow, where generations of children searching for Mrs Tiggy-Winkle's home have been tempted, like Lucy, to drop a pebble down the chimney of the farmhouse at Little Town. Far below, out in the lake, is St Herbert's Island, home of Old Mr Brown, the sinister owl in *The Tale of Squirrel Nutkin*. (*See also* Buttermere, Crummock Water and Loweswater; Coniston Valley; Ennerdale; Eskdale and Duddon Valleys; Grasmere Valley, Rydal, Hawkshead and Sawrey; Great and Little Langdale; Ullswater, Hartsop, Brotherswater and Troutbeck; Wasdale; Windermere.)

Bourne Mill Essex

1 mile south of centre of Colchester, in Bourne Road, off the Mersea road

This unusual little building with dormer windows in its steeply pitched roof and fanciful pinnacled Dutch-style gables was built by Sir Thomas Lucas as a fishing lodge in 1591. Constructed of rubble and brick from the ruins of the Abbey of St John in Colchester which had been dissolved some half a century before, the walls incorporate Roman remains and various medieval moulded stones, and the four-acre mill pond may have been the monks' stewpond. A weatherboarded projecting sack hoist and the surviving machinery, including an eighteen-foot overshot waterwheel with sixty-four buckets, date from the mid-nineteenth century, when the mill was first used to grind corn. For the previous 200 years it had played a part in the East Anglian cloth industry, used to spin yarn and for fulling woven cloth. Golden-yellow butterworts and other water-loving plants along the mill stream and borders filled with herbs and medicinal plants contribute to the special appeal of this property.

Bradley Manor Devon

On outskirts of Newton Abbot, on the A381 Totnes road

From the top of Wolborough Hill just outside Newton Abbot, there is a panoramic view over rolling countryside to the barren heights of Dartmoor, a thick blanket of oak and beech in the foreground almost obscuring the gables and tall chimneys of this L-shaped medieval manor house hidden in the steeply incised valley of the River Lemon. A long, low building, home of the Yarde family for over 300 years, it is built of roughcast local limestone limewashed white, with granite doorways and fireplaces and a slate roof. Despite some intrusive nineteenth-century castellations, the striking east façade is almost entirely fifteenth century, from the projecting chapel with a magnificent Perpendicular window at one end to the original cusped Gothic lights in the gables.

The interior is medieval in plan, with the hall to one side of the screens passage running across the house. The rooms are mostly low-ceilinged and rough-walled, with a massive granite fireplace in the old kitchen. Only the hall, rising to the rafters, is spacious. There is a carved oak screen in the arch leading to the chapel and a brightly-painted Tudor coat of arms high on an end wall and, in an upstairs room, three-dimensional seventeenth-century plasterwork, with life-like depictions of roses, tulips, primroses, acorns and beech husks echoing the flowers and trees in the woods around the house.

Bradnor Hill Hereford & Worcester

½ mile north-west of Kington, north of the A44

The Welsh Marches provide some of the least-known but most wildly beautiful open country in Britain. Bradnor Hill, to the north of the hilly little market town of Kington, has a golf course laid out across its steep contours, but for once this use does not impair the hill's beauty, which depends on its

shape, the way it perches above the valley of the River Arrow, and the views from its 1,284-foot summit. From the top one can see for miles: east into the woods and meadows of fruitful Herefordshire, south down the great Wye valley, west to Radnor Forest and the ramparts of Wales.

Braithwaite Hall North Yorkshire

1½ miles south-west of Middleham, 2 miles west of East Witton on the A6108

This remote seventeenth-century stone farmhouse is the centre of a hill farm in Coverdale on the eastern edge of the Pennines. Massive chimney-stacks frame the gabled principal façade with mullioned windows looking north to Wensleydale. Original interior features include seventeenth-century fireplaces and panelling and the exceptional oak staircase with turned balusters which rises from the stone-flagged hall.

Bramber Castle West Sussex

In Bramber, south-east of Steyning, just north of the A283

Like Cilgerran or Dunstanburgh (*see* pp.70 and 106), Bramber occupies a natural defensive position, set high above the River Adur on a steep escarpment of the South Downs. This once-mighty Norman castle, the stronghold of William de Braose, was intended to guard the vulnerable route inland from the coast, and there are panoramic views east over the river estuary and the low-lying land on either side.

Completed by about 1100, some 200 years before Dunstanburgh or Cilgerran, Bramber is one of England's earliest stone castles and is also one of the few mentioned in Domesday Book. Now only fragments remain, a stone finger sixty to seventy feet high marking the site of the massive square keep which once crowned the motte. The walls of flint, chalk and rubble have been continually mined for building materials but surviving portions are still five to six feet thick. There are also traces of the curtain wall and a deep ditch marks the site of the former moat. Occupied into the fourteenth century, it seems Bramber was then abandoned by its owners, the Howards, later Dukes of Norfolk. By the sixteenth century the castle had already become part of history.

Branscombe and Weston Mouth

Devon

On the south coast, stretching for 4 miles from Branscombe Mouth to Dunscombe Cliff, and overlooking Sidmouth

The south-east coast of Devon has a character all of its own. From the shingle beaches the ground rises steeply to 500 feet but the cliffs are not sheer; rather they are broken and tumbled. Only at Branscombe Mouth and Weston Mouth do valleys lead down to the coast. The geology is mixed, and worth sorting out, for it very clearly conditions what the visitor sees. Clay with flints covers the high ground; beneath it is cretaceous greensand and chalk, with red Triassic Keuper marl below.

The steep land, on the chalk and greensand, is scrubby, in some places wooded and excellent for exploring, but at Branscombe by no means all is owned by the Trust. Nearly all the farmed land between the village and the sea, the attractive wooded fringe of the escarpment and the beach itself belong to the Trust, but the cliffs, including Branscombe Humps, are in other hands.

At Weston Mouth to the west, south-east of the village of Salcombe Regis, the Trust owns a mile and a half of the cliffs and much of the wooded Dunscombe valley leading down to the sea. Here are more Humps, as at Branscombe, where chalk was burnt to make lime and piles of discarded flints remain. In recent years a quarry was reopened to provide the particular stone needed for restoration work at Exeter Cathedral.

Rempstone Rocks, above the west side of Weston Mouth, rise to 520 feet, the highest point on Devon's south coast, with views east to Portland and inland to Dartmoor. Because of the chalk and limestone on or under the soil, the flora is considerably varied, including several orchids and an abundance of blue gromwell, and while the more common seabirds nest here, as do jackdaws and kestrels, it is the smaller birds which find the scrubby thickets so attractive: chaffinch, chiff-chaff, dunnock, linnet, grasshopper warbler and wren.

The superb landscape surrounding the town of Sidmouth is protected by the Trust which owns Salcombe Hill to the east and Peak Hill to the west. Both hills offer marvellous panoramas stretching over forty miles in either direction from Portland Bill to Start Point, and at a height of over 500 feet they are some of the finest cliffs on the south coast.

Brean Down Somerset

2 miles south-west of Weston-super-Mare, the south arm of Weston Bay

The motorist driving west on the M5 from Bristol sweeps effortlessly over the spectacular Failand gorge. Running down the hill beyond, there is the glint of water ahead: the Bristol Channel between Clevedon and Weston-super-Mare. Beyond Weston a great hump, like a submerging hippo, projects for three-quarters of a mile into the sea.

The peninsula, of hard carboniferous limestone, is 300 feet high, and was an island until the draining of the marshes of the Bleadon Levels, on the mainland at the mouth of the River Axe. Man has probably lived here since the end of the Ice Age, 10,000 years ago. There are Bronze Age barrows and burial cairns, an Iron Age fort, Celtic field systems and, on the second highest point of Brean Down, the foundations of a Roman temple built between AD340–367. It is possible to reconstruct in some detail the dignified design of this building, a square sanctuary within a tower, an entrance porch flanked by Tuscan pillars, an ambulatory, a vestibule and two annexes.

Much later, in the Middle Ages, the peninsula was used as a rabbit warren, easily enclosed from the mainland and with an artificial mound to house breeding stock. In the nineteenth century a 'Palmerston' fort (not owned by the Trust) was built on the tip of the peninsula, and occupied as recently as the Second World War. The final development, an attempt to build a pier and construct an artificial harbour, failed when the works were swept away in a storm. There is a lot to see within a small compass and the vegetation of the western-facing slope is almost unique in Britain.

Brecon Beacons Powys

5 miles south of Brecon, east of the A470

The Brecon Beacons lie close to the industrial towns of South Wales: Merthyr Tydfil is only ten miles to the south. They are much frequented, much written about and necessarily much organised by the admirable staff of the National Park. The immense views from the summits are superb.

At the west end of the dramatic cliffs above Cwm Sere and Cwm Cynwyn, carved out by the glaciers of the Ice Age and by erosion over thousands of

years since, the Old Red sandstone reaches its highest point in Wales at Penyfan's 2,906 feet. Penyfan and Corn Ddu, half a mile to the west, stand at the centre of the Trust's 9,000-acre holding. From the latter the scramble along the ridges of Gwaun Taf and Fan Ddu is thrilling.

To the south and west, the grassy moors drop rather more easily down to the Merthyr reservoirs beside the A470, and the walker wanting something quite different in character can find it here by taking the track from the Storey Arms down Glyn Tarrell to the Trust's farm of Blaenglyn, and then back across the valley to the A470: a tumbling stream, little woods, shelter, peace.

Bredon Barn   Hereford & Worcester

3 miles north-east of Tewkesbury, just north of the B4080

Once slumbering peacefully on the banks of the River Avon, the rural tranquillity of this cathedral-like building has been destroyed by the ceaseless roar of traffic on the M5. Built in 1350 for the Bishops of Worcester, lords of the manor here for about 600 years, Bredon barn is beautifully constructed of local Cotswold stone, with stone tiles on the steeply pitched roof. It is the only aisled barn in the old county of Worcestershire: eighteen great posts like the columns of a nave march down the interior, some blackened timbers being a salutary reminder of the fire which badly damaged the building in 1980.

External stone steps lead up to a room over one of the two porches on the east side, comfortably equipped with a fireplace and a garderobe. From here the bishop's reeve could look down into the barn to check the corn being brought in and the threshers at work.

Bredon Barn, showing the steep stone steps leading up to the reeve's room over one of the porches. Since this photograph was taken, the building has been fully restored after being badly damaged by fire in 1980. (*NT/ A. F. Kersting*)

Brent Knoll   Somerset

3 miles east of Burnham-on-Sea, 1 mile north of exit 22 on the M5

The 480-foot hill of Brent Knoll rises suddenly from the uninspiring scenery of the Somerset Levels, east of Burnham-on-Sea, and gives its name to a service station on the nearby M5.

The triangular hill fort is particularly well preserved, perhaps because it is composed of a hard deposit of Midford Sand rising above the limestones and clays of the lower slopes. Re-used in late Roman times, it may have become a stronghold in the troubled period after the Romans withdrew.

The views are unimpeded in this flat landscape: north to South Wales, west to the Quantocks and Exmoor, with Glastonbury Tor (*see* p.126) prominent to the south.

Bridestones Moor   North Yorkshire

12 miles south of Whitby, 7 miles north-east of Pickering, east of the A169

Ten miles west of Scarborough, Staindale drains part of the enormous conifer forest of Dalby, eventually flowing into the River Derwent. Between the forest and the A169 lies the Trust's 1,200-acre Bridestones property.

(*Opposite page*) Penyfan, 2,906 feet, the highest point of the Brecon Beacons. On a clear day the view from the top extends north to Cadair Idris, some sixty miles away, and south to the Bristol Channel over the industrialised Welsh valleys. (*NT/David Noton*)

From the Forestry Commission's carpark beside the Staindale Beck, one can walk through an attractive open wood of oak and larch up the curiously named Dovedale Griff, with the hill farms of High and Low Pastures rising to the west. The valley forks and up Bridestones Griff becomes open moorland on either side, with the extraordinary Bridestones rising out of the heather, for all the world like the great rock figures of Easter Island. The stones, of Jurassic sandstone, are wider at the top than at the bottom, the lower strata of softer rock having weathered away more quickly than the harder rock above. The largest are named the Pepper Pot and the Salt Cellar, though it is not easy to see why. Nearby, hidden in the heather, are the remains of a number of prehistoric barrows which were excavated in the nineteenth century.

To the east, across Crosscliff Beck, is Thompson's Rigg, a substantial island of moorland in a sea of conifers. At its north end is Blakey Topping, a delightful pointed heathery knoll 876 feet high.

The sandstone slabs of the Bridestones rise out of the heather of the North Yorkshire Moors like Easter Island statues. (*NT*/*Dick Makin*)

Bridge House Cumbria

On a bridge over the Stock Ghyll, in the middle of Ambleside

This quaint two-storey building precariously poised over the Stock Ghyll in the middle of Ambleside, its rough stone walls and a slate-flagged roof typical of early Lakeland construction, has been immortalised by numerous artists, including Turner and Ruskin. Dating from the seventeenth century and consisting of just two rooms, one above the other, it was originally a summerhouse which also acted as a covered bridge for the Braithwaites of Ambleside Hall up the hill. Said to have housed a family of eight in the mid-nineteenth century, it has also served as a cobbler's shop and a tearoom and is now a Trust information centre and shop.

Brimham Moor North Yorkshire

8 miles south-west of Ripon, 10 miles north-west of Harrogate

At Brimham Moor the Trust's 400 acres of open moorland stand high above Nidderdale, with a profusion of millstone grit 'stacks' eroded by thousands of years of weathering. Many of the stacks are named in a rather pedestrian way:

Bridge House, Ambleside. After a severe storm in June 1953 Stock Beck, only a trickle here, rose almost to the top of the arch carrying the house. (*NT*)

Mushroom, Flower Pot, Pulpit, Baboon's Head, Sphinx, Rhinoceros. The most imaginative is the Druid's Writing Desk.

Brockhampton Hereford & Worcester

1–2 miles east of Bromyard, mostly on the north side of the A44 Worcester road

Due west of Worcester the A44 winds its way through gentle hills to the unassuming little town of Bromyard. At the top of the hill, two miles before the town, a tiny neo-Greek lodge marks the gate into Brockhampton Park. The house, built in the 1760s in pleasant plain red-brick, is not what people come to see and is privately occupied. Colonel John Talbot Lutley, who left his 1,700 acres to the Trust in 1946, wanted Brockhampton preserved as an example of an English agricultural estate, with its park, farm and woods.

Trees grow well on this rich sandstone soil: ash, Douglas fir, larch and, in particular, oak. Paths and rides lead through the extensive woods and in places open over views to the surrounding countryside. As well as groups of farm buildings, there is the fourteenth-century moated house of Lower Brockhampton (*see* p.188). All is seemly, traditional, peaceful; this is a place for picnicking, for Sunday walks, and for reflecting on how fortunate we are for the good intentions of people like Colonel Lutley.

Brownsea Island Dorset

In Poole harbour, about 1½ miles south-east of Poole; boats run from Poole quay and Sandbanks

Since the Trust acquired Brownsea Island in 1962, great changes have taken place in Poole harbour and its surroundings. Poole is very much part of the prosperous south-east, and the boating industry, already well established there, has become a major business, with its full accompaniment of boat yards, chandlers, marinas and holiday flats. More than this, the large oilfield centred at Wych Farm, immediately to the west, has also brought new developments. The Trust's initiative in saving Brownsea Island from exploitation has therefore been tremendously worth the major effort involved, ensuring the preservation of an oasis for wildlife in a highly commercialised natural harbour.

One lands at the quay with a feeling of relief. At once peace envelops the visitor, for the island is remarkably inward-looking and self-contained. It is not the views that one remembers but what one finds within its 500 acres: reedy marshes, quiet beaches, heath and woodland, a place where one needs time to saunter.

The island belonged to the monks of Cerne Abbey and after the Dissolution of the Monasteries it was fortified by Henry VIII during his major revamping of coastal defences. Henry's castle was held for the Parliamentarians during the Civil War but had become a ruin by the Restoration. Thereafter the island passed through many ownerships until it was bought by a rich man, Charles van Raalte, in 1901. He lived here in great splendour and in 1907 invited General Baden-Powell to hold the first camp here from which sprang the Boy Scouts' Association.

The last private owner, Mrs Bonham Christie, lived here in seclusion from 1927 to 1961. She actively discouraged visitors and took no steps to control the rapidly encroaching undergrowth which, in the soft coastal climate, began to turn the island into a jungle, a paradise for wildlife during her time, but a problem for the Trust.

There is a little village at the quay, cottages formerly needed by the staff at the castle (now let as a holiday centre) and by the coastguards, and a little church. The cottages, strung out along the edge of the beach, add much to the island's character. Dating from the early nineteenth century, they are in a delightfully whimsical Gothick style, ornamented with battlements, armorial shields and even arrow slits. Marble steps and octagonal turrets flag the landing-stage for the castle, which was rebuilt in pseudo-medieval style after a fire in 1897. The rest of the island is wholly undeveloped. It is one of the few places where the red squirrel survives in Britain and it is an important breeding site for terns, visiting waders and wildfowl. The Trust has not opened it up in a ham-fisted way; rather, it has very gently cleared rides, modified the undergrowth and freed the rarer plants from being smothered. The process is continual but remarkably unobtrusive. The northern half of the island, including a freshwater lagoon, is let to the Dorset Wildlife Trust and managed as a nature reserve. Tours of the reserve are available, and it is possible to see a wide variety of bird life. There are avocets in season, sandwich and common terns breed on gravel islets in the

The fine carving decorating the Norman south doorway of Buckingham Chantry Chapel. (*John Bethell*)

lagoon, and reed and sedge warblers are attracted to the vegetation along the water's edge.

Bruton Dovecote Somerset

½ mile south of Bruton across railway, ¼ mile west of the B3081

Nothing remains of the Augustinian abbey which once dominated the little town of Bruton except a section of wall and this unusual dovecote standing alone on a hillock in what was the abbey's deer park. Adapted by the monks from a gabled Tudor tower with mullioned windows, it is now roofless.

Buckingham Chantry Chapel

Buckinghamshire

On Market Hill, Buckingham

The fine Norman south doorway, probably brought here from elsewhere and originally intended for somewhere grander, is the most memorable feature of this tiny, 38-foot rubble-built fifteenth-century chapel, the oldest building in Buckingham. It was used as a school from the Reformation until 1907 and was substantially restored by Sir George Gilbert Scott in 1875.

Buckland Abbey Devon

6 miles south of Tavistock, 11 miles north of Plymouth

Francis Drake's tiny *Golden Hind* left Plymouth on a cold winter's day in December 1577 and did not return until nearly three years later, on 26 September 1580. This historic voyage was the first circumnavigation of the globe by an Englishman, involving what must have been a terrifying passage across the unknown expanses of the Pacific Ocean. A national hero on his return, Drake needed a house which reflected his newly acquired status, ironically choosing to purchase the abbey which had been so recently converted by his rival, Sir Richard Grenville. It was from here that he planned his assault on the Spanish Armada a few years later.

Set among sloping green lawns and exotic trees and shrubs on the edge of the sleepy Tavy valley, Buckland Abbey is rich in associations with Drake and in echoes of the great monastery it once was, the last Cistercian foundation in England, established some 140 years after Fountains (*see* p.121) in 1273. Like Lord Sandys at Mottisfont (*see* p.205), Richard Grenville chose to form his house out of the thirteenth-century abbey church rather than using the domestic buildings of the community. The exterior of his mansion is dominated by the abbey's great crossing tower, the arch of the demolished south transept outlined clearly on the wall below, while the tracery of the chancel arch and ancient mouldings are visible inside.

Imaginative displays in the long gallery running the length of the top floor outline the history of the abbey from medieval times to the present day. Carved stones, pieces of tracery and floor tiles help recall the monastic community which lived here for some 300 years, growing gradually richer on an income derived from tin mines in the Tavy valley as well as from the tenants on their estates. Drake's coat of arms over the fireplace, on which a fragile ship is guided by the divine hand of providence, heralds the Drake Gallery on the floor below. Gorgeous flags – one showing the golden leopards of England on a red ground – may have flown on *Golden Hind*. Other cases contain Elizabeth I's commission of 5 March 1587, giving Drake command of the fleet with which he 'singed the King of Spain's beard', Armada medals, the first ever struck to commemorate a historical event, and finds from Spanish ships that foundered off Ireland. A fascinating document details the Armada accounts from December 1587, early entries covering payments ('to drummers, carpenters, cooks, mariners, surgeons') concerned with preparations to meet the Spanish, later months including terse references to engagements. Marginal notes in Treasurer Lord Burghley's thin spidery hand record sums reimbursed, such as the payment in October 1588 to cover the loss of a fireship. Here too is Drake's drum, which was with him on his epic voyage and when he died of dysentery off Panama in 1596. It is said to beat if England is ever in danger.

The only complete interior surviving from these times is the fine sixteenth-century great hall. Dating from Sir Richard Grenville's conversion, it is warmly panelled in oak and decorated with an elaborate ceiling and a holly and box frieze adorned with carved figures. Contemporary plasterwork on the end walls symbolising Grenville's retirement to Buckland shows his shield hanging on a tree and a large pile of discarded arms. A Georgian dining-room and the elegant staircase curling up through four floors were added during late eighteenth-century improvements.

A picturesque group of granite outbuildings with lichen-stained roofs includes an ox-shed introduced by the agricultural improver William Marshall, who spent four years at Buckland in 1791–4. Only yards from the abbey is the huge, heavily buttressed monastic barn, built in about 1300. Almost 160 feet

long, it is one of the largest in Britain, eloquently suggesting the wealth of the community. Sinuous box hedges like window tracery enclose a little herb garden, where it is easy to imagine white-robed figures moving silently from bed to bed collecting lovage, balm or sweet cicely.

Burrow Mump Somerset

2½ miles south-west of Othery, just south of the A361

At only nine and a half acres, Burrow Mump is tiny, but, pimple that it is, it rises boldly above the flat wastes of the Athelney marshes south of Sedgemoor. At Burrow Bridge the River Tone joins the River Parrett which flows on to Bridgwater and the sea. The Mump, Triassic limestone with a cap of Keuper marl, stands at the rivers' confluence. It was an island before the levels were drained in the Middle Ages, and in a wet season when the levels flood it still gives the impression of being completely surrounded by water.

The most notable feature is the shell of a late eighteenth-century church on its summit. In fact the building, on the site of an earlier church, was never completed but the ruin gives great character to the little hill. From it there are views in all directions.

Buscot Park Oxfordshire

Between Lechlade and Faringdon, astride the A417

This extensive estate straddling the River Thames in the fertile valley above Oxford was the scene of an extraordinary agricultural experiment in the nineteenth century, when a rich Australian, Robert Tertius Campbell, turned Buscot into the most progressive farm of his time. Largely given over to sugar beet, the grandiose schemes which eventually overwhelmed his resources included a distillery for converting the sugar into spirit and over six miles of narrow-gauge railway for bringing in the crop.

Two years after Campbell died in 1887, Buscot was sold to Alexander Henderson, later 1st Lord Faringdon, politician, financier of exceptional ability and connoisseur. The art collection acquired by this remarkable man was enriched by the 2nd Baron, a prominent socialist, who seems to have inherited many of his grandfather's talents.

The house itself is a rather severe late eighteenth-century neo-classical building, probably designed

by the then owner, Edward Loveden Townsend. Two pavilions set either side, and the imposing flight of steps flanked by bronze centaurs leading up to the pedimented entrance front, were added by Geddes Hyslop in the 1930s for the 2nd Baron, who also did much to reinstate the original character of the house. The interiors are both sensuous and cultivated, with extravagant chandeliers, inlaid and painted Regency and Empire furniture, richly coloured carpets and gleaming mahogany doors.

An original filigree ceiling looks down on the Italian paintings in the drawing-room, including Pier Francesco Mola's powerful *St Jerome*, and Palma Vecchio's strangely asymmetrical *Marriage of St Catherine*. Here, too, is the delightful *Rest on the Flight into Egypt*, attributed to Andrea Previtali, showing the Holy Family enjoying a substantial picnic of bread and cheese, the food carefully set out on a white cloth on the ground. The Faringdons' catholic collection also embraces paintings by Gainsborough, Rembrandt and Reynolds, as well as some twentieth-century works, including two menacing bee pictures by Graham Sutherland. A number of canvases reflect the 1st Lord's interest in the Pre-Raphaelites, perhaps inspired by his neighbour, William Morris, whose house at Kelmscott lies close by over the fields. Works by Rossetti, Watts and Millais are overshadowed by Burne-Jones's cycle based on the Sleeping Beauty story, *Legend of the Briar Rose*, his richly coloured panels set in a gilt framework running round the walls of the saloon like a mural. The knight who has come to wake the beautiful princess faces her across the room, as if he has to fight his way through the rose forest on the walls to reach her, past the sleeping knights of the court entangled in thorny branches and the old king himself, slumbering on his throne, his grey beard reaching to his waist.

Such dense thickets still feature in the woodland sloping down to the large lake created when the park was landscaped in the eighteenth century. A chain of cascades, basins and canals, fed by a dolphin fountain and crossed by a little hump-backed balustraded bridge, stretches in a long vista through the wood, box hedges framing the view on either

A dolphin fountain feeds Harold Peto's cool water garden at Buscot Park, a long green vista punctuated by the temple on the far shore of the lake. (*NT/Vera Collingwood*)

side. Created by Harold Peto in the early twentieth century, there can be few more restful places than this cool Italianate water garden, constantly lulled by the background murmur of falling water.

Buttermere, Crummock Water and Loweswater   Cumbria

9 miles from Keswick via Newlands Pass

The Trust owns or protects some 12,000 acres of this beautiful and vulnerable Lakeland valley, including the three lakes strung along its length, the whole of Buttermere Commons, four farms, one of which has been brought back to life by the Trust, and pockets of woodland. From the bare rugged heights of the Honister Pass, where the Trust owns only the roadside strips (and can thus prevent road-widening), with protective covenants over Buttermere Fell and Fleetwith Pike on either side, the visitor pauses at Gatesgarth for the superb view over Lake Buttermere, with the great ridge of High Stile and Red Pike to the south providing a dramatic backdrop. Crummock Water lies a mile further down the valley, the great bulk of Brackenthwaite Fell and the 2,791-foot summit of Grasmoor rising

(*Opposite page*) The shell of a late eighteenth-century chapel silhouetted dramatically against the sky on the summit of Burrow Mump, an island in the Athelney marshes. (*NT/Fay Godwin*)

above it. Completing the picture is little Loweswater, in gentle farming country, with Holme Wood on its far side. In only eight miles harsh wilderness has become pastoral beauty.

Cadbury Camp Avon

2½ miles east of Clevedon

Although not easy to find, Cadbury Camp stands high above the dramatic section of the M5 where the motorway carves its route through the high Failand ridge east of Clevedon. It has the inevitable Iron Age hill fort and should not be confused with the very fine Cadbury Camp overlooking the Exe valley north of Exeter, nor, nearer at hand, with the Cadbury Camps at South Cadbury or Congresbury.

Calke Abbey Derbyshire

9 miles south of Derby, on the A514 at Ticknall between Swadlincote and Melbourne

However you approach it, this imposing three-storey classical house is hidden in a fold of the landscape. Set some distance from any public road, Calke Abbey lies buried in its beautiful eighteenth-century park, the thousands of trees grouped in picturesque clumps and windbreaks and framing a chain of ornamental lakes seeming to provide insulation from the world outside.

Calke was built in 1701–4, but the symmetrical grey sandstone façades decorated with fluted pilasters and a balustraded roofline conceal the substantial remains of earlier buildings, some of the stonework perhaps recycled from the priory of Austin canons established here in the early twelfth century. Embellishments by William Wilkins the Elder in 1793–1811 include the pedimented entrance portico and the sophisticated suite of Georgian reception rooms on the first floor.

Like Kedleston only a few miles to the north (*see* p.164), Calke has been in the hands of the same family for hundreds of years, each generation of the Harpurs and Harpur Crewes contributing to the extraordinary individuality of the house. More remarkably, little has been changed since the mid-nineteenth century, providing a unique insight into mid-Victorian England.

William Wilkins's drawing-room, with its yellow silk curtains and gilded wall mirrors by the fashion-able Georgian cabinet-makers Tatham and Bailey, is still as cluttered as it appears in a photograph of 1886, a *mélange* of embroidered chairs and stools, numerous occasional tables and ornaments under glass domes. Display cases full of glistening polished stones are no preparation for the contents of the saloon next door, remodelled by Henry Isaac Stevens in 1841. Stevens's coffered ceiling decorated with the Harpur boar and his elegant panels hung with family portraits fade into insignificance beside the cases of stuffed birds and geological specimens and the stag trophies mounted on the walls. A noble head even looks down on Tilly Kettle's charming portrait of Lady Frances Harpur and her son.

These unusual exhibits reflect the interests of Sir Vauncey Harpur Crewe, the idiosyncratic recluse who inherited Calke in 1886 and filled the house with his collections. Increasingly unpredictable, Sir Vauncey took to communicating with his servants by letter, would make off into the woods when his wife entertained, and forbade his tenants to cut hedges so as to provide maximum cover for the birds. Carriages now displayed in the stable yard reflect his insistence that motor vehicles should not be allowed on the estate.

Sir Vauncey seems to have had nothing in common with the three Georgian baronets, two Sir Henrys and Sir Harry, whose keen interest in the turf is commemorated by paintings of racehorses by Sartorius and Sawrey Gilpin in the library and by three florid eighteenth-century racing cups. Sir Harry's wife Lady Caroline was given the sumptuous state bed, its beautiful Chinese silk hangings embroidered with dragons, birds, deer and other traditional motifs in rich blues, reds, greens and oranges still as fresh as when it arrived in the eighteenth century. This treasure was found in a packing case, and many more gems also lay forgotten behind closed doors or languished in outhouses – Victorian dolls in mint condition, books full of dried flowers, a Georgian chamber organ and a harpsichord by Burckhardt Shudi. Household objects which would have been thrown away long ago in other establishments, such as the row of leather fire buckets and the antiquated kitchen equipment, have also survived here: a reflection of instincts that would drive the houseproud mad.

Several members of the family lie buried in the graveyard and vaults of the undistinguished early nineteenth-century church, a remodelling of an Elizabethan building which crowns a rise to the

The drawing-room at Calke Abbey has remained virtually unchanged since 1886, crowded with furniture and display cases full of polished stones. (*NT/Mike Williams*)

south of the house. Nearby, hidden by a screen of trees, is the large late eighteenth-century walled garden, a combination of the ornamental and the practical. Mixed borders against the walls and geometrical beds in the lawn of the flower garden echo Victorian planting schemes, and historical varieties of fruit and vegetables, many of them known in the 1770s when the garden was created, mark the site of the original physic garden. Of the four-acre kitchen garden, only some old fruit trees trained against the walls, a summerhouse and three ornamental ponds survive.

Specimen trees, including a wide variety of exotics, delicate shrubs and carpets of bulbs in spring adorn Sir Harry's pleasure ground round the house, separated from the park by a sunken wall. Red and fallow deer which were latterly allowed to

wander here, causing considerable damage, are now restricted to the north-east corner of the park and varieties of trees and shrubs popular in the mid-nineteenth century are being planted. The park beyond is rich and varied, including patches of bracken woodland and stretches of closely cropped grassland grazed by a flock of rare Portland sheep. Gnarled old oaks, descended from the medieval woods out of which the park was created, harbour an unusually rich insect population, suggesting unbroken continuity with the primeval forest cover.

Canons Ashby Northamptonshire

On the B525 Northampton–Banbury road

Set in the rolling, thinly populated country of south Northamptonshire, this ancient courtyard house seems lost in a time warp, summed up in the motto 'Ancient as the Druids' set over the drawing-room fireplace. A lime avenue from the garden leads to an unexpectedly grand church, all that remains of the Augustinian priory which gave Canons Ashby its name and which once dominated a thriving medieval village, now only bumps and furrows in the grass. Although reduced to a quarter of its former length, the church is extraordinarily impressive, with a striking red and white arcade on the west front and a massive pinnacled tower visible for miles.

John Dryden's modest H-shaped Tudor manor, built with material from the demolished east end of the church, now forms the great-hall range of the house, with its unusual squat tower like an echo of a Cumbrian pele rising over the south front. The wings to the east enclosing the cobbled internal courtyard were added by his son Sir Erasmus, the 1st Baronet. Unlike the finished stone and brickwork of the exterior, the courtyard walls are rough and irregular, patterned with lichen and moss and set with leaded windows.

Some recently uncovered murals painted in greyblue monochrome date from Sir Erasmus's time, the most complete showing a great sailing ship at anchor in front of a walled city. Sir Erasmus was also responsible for the striking domed ceiling arching over the drawing-room, every inch crowd-

The west front of Canons Ashby seen across the Green Court. This was the main entrance to the house before Sir Henry Dryden's alterations in the mid-nineteenth century. (*NT/Mike Williams*)

ed with elaborate plasterwork, with thistles and pomegranates set on curving branches and the heads of strange disembodied Indian princesses staring down. Three long sash windows lighting this room, added when Edward Dryden remodelled the south front in 1708–10, look out over a rare formal garden of the same date. A flight of terraces falls away from the house, stained stone steps linking one level to another. The character of the garden changes down the slope, the smoothly mown grass and topiary yew of the two upper terraces giving way on the third to an orchard planted with varieties of apples and pears known in sixteenth-century England, while the lowest level is a wild garden with meadow flowers in long grass. Florid baroque gateposts pierce the enclosing walls. Edward was also responsible for Canons Ashby's dignified west front, now looking out over a grassy court but for centuries, from 1550 to *c.*1840, used as the main entrance to the house. Edward's imposing baroque doorway dominates the façade, and he probably commissioned the sculptor Jan Van Nost to supply the leadwork coat of arms above the entrance and figures for the garden, of which only a statue of a shepherd boy survives. The classical *trompe-l'oeil* decoration in the painted parlour also dates from Edward's time, executed by his cousin Mrs Creed, and it was he who purchased the exquisite needlework-covered furniture in the Tapestry Room, embroidered with flowers and pastoral scenes.

The present entrance to the house, across the cobbled courtyard and into the great hall, was arranged by Sir Henry Dryden, the much-loved Victorian squire of Canons Ashby known as the Antiquary. Fired by a lifelong interest in medieval architecture, Sir Henry largely preserved the house as it was, his only major addition being the oak bookcases in the little library where he wrote his learned articles. Leather-bound volumes now filling the shelves include the works of the three important literary figures associated with the house: the poet Edmund Spenser (1552–99), author of *The Faerie Queene*, who was a cousin of Sir Erasmus Dryden's wife; the poet laureate John Dryden, who visited the house as a very young man in the 1650s to pay court to his cousin, daughter of the 3rd Baronet; and the playwright and novelist Samuel Richardson (1689–1761), who is said to have written much of *Sir Charles Grandison*, his improbable moral tale about a virtuous paragon, at Canons Ashby.

A corner of the drawing-room where Thomas Carlyle wrote *The French Revolution* and where his wife received many eminent figures, including Tennyson, Thackeray and Darwin. This was also the room in which Carlyle died, at 8.30am on 5 February 1881. (*NT/Michael Boys*)

Carlyle's House London

24 Cheyne Row, London SW3 – off Cheyne Walk, between Battersea and Albert Bridges on Chelsea Embankment

When the historian and philosopher Thomas Carlyle and his wife Jane moved to London from Scotland in 1834, they decided to rent this unpretentious Queen Anne house in the then unfashionable area of Chelsea. Here they lived until their deaths, hers in 1866 and his fifteen years later, furnishing the house with good but unremarkable Victorian pieces and a wealth of books and pictures. Still filled with the Carlyles' possessions, the walls crowded with photographs, watercolours and drawings of themselves, their families and places they loved, this otherwise unexceptional house conveys a remarkable impression of the great man and his lively and intelligent wife.

The kitchen with its cast-iron range where Carlyle would smoke so as not to offend Jane is very little changed, and so too is the sitting-room, with its *chaise-longue* covered in black horsehair and the cloth over the table brought from Mrs Carlyle's Scottish home. The book-lined drawing-room upstairs is where Carlyle wrote *The French Revolution*, the work that was to establish his reputation, painstakingly recasting the first volume after it had been accidentally burned while on loan to John

Stuart Mill. In the attic room, which the great man built on in 1853 in a vain attempt to provide himself with a sound-proofed study, a scorched fragment of manuscript is all that remains of the original draft.

While Carlyle wrote with vision about the condition of mankind, his wife is remembered for her witty and caustic correspondence with family and friends and for the wide circle of eminent figures she received in Cheyne Row, including Dickens, Tennyson, Browning, Thackeray, Ruskin and Darwin. While Carlyle's reputation has dimmed in the twentieth century, her stature has grown, and her observant letters are now regarded as among the best in the English language.

Carneddau Gwynedd

8 miles south-east of Bangor, astride the A5, near Capel Curig

The Carneddau is divided from the Snowdon massif by the Llanberis Pass, and here the Trust owns 17,430 acres of superb hill country, most of which was acquired with Penrhyn Castle (*see* p.254).

The area is divided by the A5, which crawls up the Nant Ffrancon Pass to Llyn Ogwen, and then gently descends to Capel Curig. To the south of the lake is a great semicircle of mountains, long beloved of climbers and geologists, but also of botanists, for here, miraculously preserved, is a prime example of the effect of the Ice Age on a volcanic landscape.

Beautiful Tryfan rises 2,000 feet, from the shore of Llyn Ogwen to its peak of 3,010 feet, in little more than half a mile. Glyder Fach, to the south, is slightly higher, while Glyder Fawr, to the west, is tallest of all at 3,278 feet. The range turns north to Y Garn and the semicircle is complete, enclosing the lake of Llyn Idwal, on the former site of a glacier. Here, and on the slopes of Cwm Idwal in which it lies, are alpine plants of the utmost rarity, such as the Snowdon lily. Travellers in the eighteenth century, on their last stage from London to Holyhead, thought the mountains were 'horrid'. Our twentieth-century eyes can only find their screes and precipices magnificent.

On the north side of Llyn Ogwen rises the high Carneddau, much less frequented and accessible only to the stout walker. One can take in the peaks, the highest south of the Grampians – Carnedd Dafydd at 3,426 feet, Yr Elen at 3,169 feet and Carnedd Llewelyn (just over the Trust's boundary)

Tryfan, one of several rugged mountains over 3,000 feet on the Carneddau estate, is topped by Glyder Fach and Glyder Fawr. (*NT/Kevin Richardson*)

at 3,484 feet – or set one's course at a rather lower level. Perhaps the best approach is that taken in the Second World War by so many soldiers posted to Bangor to do their battle course, leaving the A55 coast road at Aber and winding up the beautiful valley of the Rhaeadr-fawr to Aber Falls, then up the Afon Goch with views over an upland landscape of drystone walls, isolated farmhouses and the occasional ancient sheepfold.

Cartmel Priory Gatehouse
Cumbria

Cavendish Street, Cartmel

Although the turret and battlements which once crowned this picturesque stone gatehouse-tower straddling Cavendish Street have been removed, it still rises imposingly above the roofs of the surrounding houses, a reminder of the need for protection against Scottish raids in the troubled border country of the Middle Ages. Apart from the church of St Mary, the gatehouse is all that remains of the Augustinian monastery founded here in 1189–90;

a strengthening of the priory's defences with the construction of the tower in 1330–40 may have been prompted by Robert the Bruce's devastating raids in the neighbourhood a few years earlier. Despite the insertion of later windows and the slate roof, the gatehouse has a substantially medieval appearance and is the only secular pre-Reformation building in Cartmel. The large room over the archway was once used for manorial courts and from 1624–1790 as a school.

Castle Coole   Co. Fermanagh

1¼ miles south-east of Enniskillen on the A4 Belfast–Enniskillen road

This austere white palace, James Wyatt's masterpiece, is one of the finest neo-classical houses in the British Isles. Built between 1789 and 1795 for Armar Lowry Corry, the future 1st Earl of Belmore, it was designed to provide a suitably grand setting for a prospective member of the peerage and also to surpass Florence Court across Lough Erne to the south, the house recently embellished by Lowry Corry's brother-in-law, Lord Enniskillen (*see* p.120).

The shady path up from the carpark by the stables suddenly emerges on the grass in front of the house to give an oblique view of the dazzling entrance façade faced in creamy Portland stone, originally shipped from Dorset to a special quay built at Ballyshannon and brought by cart and barge up Lough Erne. A pedimented portico rising the height of the house is echoed in open colonnades linking the main block to pavilions on either side, a rather old-fashioned Palladian design reminiscent of Robert Adam's Kedleston (*see* p.164), which may reflect the fact that Wyatt had to work with the foundations for a scheme of *c.*1785 by the Irish architect Richard Johnston. This constraint clearly did not dim his enthusiasm. The quality of the interior detailing is superb, ceilings by Joseph Rose and chimneypieces by Richard Westmacott matched by the craftsmanship evident in the joinery of doors and floors. The unusual survival of a complete set of building accounts and many drawings show that Wyatt even designed furniture and curtains. But he never visited Castle Coole, leaving his plans to be realised by the builder-architect Alexander Stewart.

Sadly, Lord Belmore's ambitions outstripped his purse, exhausting his funds before his new mansion was fully fitted out. Wyatt's chastely elegant in-

teriors were furnished in an opulent Regency style between 1802 and 1825 by the 2nd Earl, whose relish for the job matched that of his father. Over £26,000 spent with the fashionable Dublin upholsterer John Preston, including the price of one of the few state beds in Ireland, exceeded the cost of building the house.

Extensively restored by the Trust to reflect its early nineteenth-century appearance, Castle Coole is an intriguing blend of classical and Regency. The dignified entrance hall, with a screen of mock-marble columns and statues in niches, is painted a welcoming deep raspberry as it was by the 2nd Earl. In contrast, grey scagliola pilasters ringing the oval saloon beneath Joseph Rose's delicate ceiling echo the original colour scheme, while ceramic stoves set in niches and the curved doors following the line of the walls are again strongly reminiscent of designs for Kedleston.

The saloon is the centrepiece of the north front, dividing rooms of very different character. The dining-room on one side, still lit only by candles, is pure Wyatt, with fan-like plaster tracery arching over the curtainless windows, family portraits set in plaster panels on the slate-green walls and a delicate classical frieze. Gleaming gold plate adorns Wyatt's sideboard, produced in eleven weeks by two joiners in 1797. The drawing-room at the other end of the house is furnished with gilt couches and chairs upholstered in salmon pink and with a richly patterned nineteenth-century Aubusson carpet. The library across the hall is more comfortable, with

On sunny days, the creamy Portland stone with which Castle Coole's austere entrance front has been refaced appears dazzlingly white. (*NT*)

plump tassels and a deep fringed pelmet adorning the crimson curtains, and a plentiful supply of cushions and bolsters lying casually on the red velvet of the masculine Grecian sofas. The heavy folds of the drapes are immortalised in white marble on Westmacott's extraordinary chimneypiece, executed while Wyatt was employed on the house but not to the architect's surviving design.

Castle Coole looks out over a wooded park, landscaped in the naturalistic style in the late eighteenth century, which slopes gently down to Lough Coole, home to a famous colony of greylag geese and the site of a previous house. The double oak avenue along which Castle Coole has been approached since about 1730 is now being replanted and will reach maturity once again some time in the mid-twenty-second century.

Castle Drogo Devon

4 miles south of the A30 Exeter–Okehampton road via Crockernwell; or turn off the A382 Moretonhampstead–Whiddon Down road at Sandy Park

When Julius Drewe, the self-made millionaire, retired from his retailing business in 1889 aged only thirty-three, he was determined to set himself up as a country gentleman. Fired with the belief that he was

descended from a Norman baron, he resolved to build a castle on the acres that once belonged to his remote ancestor, apparently lord of the Dartmoor village of Drewsteignton. Although his initial grandiose plans were scaled down, Castle Drogo admirably fulfilled this ambition.

No medieval baron could have faulted the chosen site, a splendidly defensible moorland spur overlooking the gorge of the River Teign. A road runs along the top of the bluff but the castle is far more impressive if approached by the steep path leading up from the river hundreds of feet below. A jumble of granite walls and towers topped by battlements and pierced by mullioned windows suddenly rears up above the bracken-covered hillside ahead, gauntly forbidding even on the friendliest of summer days. A massive gateway tower with twin octagonal turrets on the west front sports a genuine portcullis and the heraldic Drewe lion is proudly displayed over the entrance arch.

This imposing fortress was commissioned in 1910 from Sir Edwin Lutyens, then at the height of his powers and with the transformation of Lindisfarne Castle already behind him (*see* p.180). The great architect's interiors initially seem as forbidding as the outside of the castle, with bare stone walls and unpainted woodwork suggesting cold discomfort. But Castle Drogo is a great country

The bathroom in Castle Drogo's north wing has an elaborate shower arrangement. (*NT*)

house masquerading as a fortress. In the airy, panelled drawing-room, lit by windows on three sides, soft green walls and chintz-covered sofas create a restful, luxuriant atmosphere and the agreeable bathrooms, one with an elaborate shower arrangement, were designed with pleasure in mind. Exotic Spanish furniture in several of the rooms was acquired as a result of the spectacular bankruptcy of the banker Adrian de Murrieta, friend of the Prince of Wales (the future Edward VII) and extravagant social butterfly, whose vast red-brick mansion in Sussex Drewe purchased in 1899.

Lutyens was also involved in the unexpectedly large formal garden to the north of the house, although the layout and planting probably owe more to the garden designer George Dillistone, who had worked for Julius Drewe at Culverden in Kent and was employed at Castle Drogo from 1922. Massive clipped yew hedges in geometric shapes and granite steps leading up a flight of terraces have much of the castle about them. A sunken lawn with rectangular rose beds at the lowest level is framed by Lutyens's intriguing raised walks, their sinuous curves based on patterns in Indian tilework followed by the herbaceous borders on either side. At the top of the garden more yew rings a huge circular lawn, just under 1,000 feet above sea level. To the west, where the ground falls away into the valley, magnolias, camellias, maples and cherries are planted with species and hybrid rhododendrons in an informal shrub garden created in the 1950s.

Sadly, Julius Drewe died only a year after the castle was completed in 1930, but he must have been pleased with his progress in life. Whereas his similarly wealthy retailing rivals Lipton and Sainsbury were ignored by Burke's *Landed Gentry*, the acres he acquired with the fortune amassed from his Home and Colonial Stores gained his inclusion.

Castlerigg Stone Circle Cumbria

2 miles east of Keswick, just south of the old Penrith road

This impressive late Neolithic stone circle, also known as The Carles and Druids' Circle, is dwarfed by its magnificent surroundings. Although it is set on a 700-foot plateau, the fells rise all around, forming a vast natural amphitheatre. To the north, Skiddaw and Blencathra tower over the fertile valley followed by the Keswick to Penrith road, while Helvellyn dominates the view south.

The slightly flattened circle has a maximum diameter of about a hundred feet and is formed of forty ice-smoothed volcanic boulders, the largest of them over five feet tall. A subsidiary rectangular arrangement of stones jutting into the circle on the eastern side may be a much more recent addition to the monument.

Castle Ward Co. Down

7 miles north-east of Downpatrick, 1½ miles west of Strangford village on the A25, on south shore of Strangford Lough, entrance by Ballyculter Lodge

Castle Ward, crowning a gentle slope above Strangford Lough, is a very Irish house. Although built at one period, from 1762–70, it is classical on the east side, with a central pediment supported by four columns, and Gothick on the west, with battlements, pinnacles and ogival windows. This architectural curiosity is a result of the opposing tastes of Bernard Ward, later 1st Viscount Bangor, and his wife Lady Anne. Each favouring a particular style, they agreed to differ. The interior also reflects the Wards' eccentric approach, with the rooms on his side of the house – the hall, dining-room and library – decorated in a Palladian idiom, while those on the west – the saloon, morning-room and boudoir – are in an ornate and opulent Gothick, with pointed doors and plaster vaulting. The versatile architect is unknown, although tradition has it that, like the stone of which the house is built, he may have come from Bath (the stone was brought from England in Lord Bangor's own ship and unloaded in Castle Bay below the house).

The stylistic division of Castle Ward was followed by the separation of Bernard and Anne, and by her departure for Bath. During the insanity of the 2nd Lord Bangor, his younger brother removed most of the contents of the house, but the elaborate decorative schemes have survived almost unaltered. Three-dimensional plaster motifs stand out white against the green walls of the hall; here a festoon of musical instruments, including drums and tambourines, across the room a cluster of agricultural implements, a harrow, axe and billhook. A pedimented door leads into the Gothick saloon, where ogival mirrors between the ecclesiastical traceried windows reflect a cluttered Victorian interior, with photographs on many surfaces, stuffed birds under a glass case, a gossip seat and feathery dried flowers.

(*Above*) Castlerigg stone circle, set in a vast natural amphitheatre with the Lake District fells rising on all sides. (*NT/Mike Williams*)

(*Left*) The voluptuous Gothick ceiling in Lady Bangor's sitting-room at Castle Ward was based on the fan vaulting in Henry VII's chapel at Westminster Abbey. (*NT/John Bethell*)

Next door is Lady Bangor's sitting-room, transformed by the voluptuous curves of the Gothick ceiling into a large pink tent. There could hardly be a greater contrast with the restrained treatment of the elegant cantilevered staircase, with a Venetian window on the half-landing and a frieze of acanthus-leaf scrolls on the walls.

Steps lead down past an impressive array of bells to the kitchens, housekeeper's room and wine cellar in the basement, connected by a long whitewashed tunnel to the Victorian laundry, stables and servants' quarters set round a courtyard apart from the house, as was the fashion in eighteenth-century Ireland. A former billiard-room in the basement is devoted to the exceptional Mary Ward (d.1869), scientist, painter and wife of the 5th Viscount Bangor. Delicate watercolours of wildlife vie for attention with atmospheric views of the house and estate and with cases of butterflies and insects. Most remarkable are the fruits of her pioneering work with the microscope – magnified images of the eye of a dragonfly, like a blue honeycomb, and of the silvery scales of the jewel beetle.

Castle Ward has one of the most beautiful settings of any house in Ulster, with an eighteenth-century landscape park, in the English style, sloping down to the lough and views over the water framed by mature oaks and beeches. Wildfowl glide over the water, now protected by the reserve established on the lough. Birds also enjoy the Temple Water north of the house, a serene artificial lake created in the early eighteenth century, fringed by palms and smoothly mown grass at its western end and overlooked by a little classical temple. The formal Victorian garden near the house is different in character, with grassy terraces planted with palms and roses rising from a sunken, brightly flowering parterre to a line of Irish yews and a pinetum beyond.

Corn- and sawmills, a drying kiln and slaughterhouse round a yard near the Temple Water were once the centre of a thriving agricultural estate. Here, too, is the early seventeenth-century tower-house which the Wards built soon after they came to Ireland from England. Nearby is a row of slate-roofed late Victorian cottages constructed for workers on the estate. Only a few decades before, in 1852, the village of Audleystown had been destroyed and its inhabitants transported to America to improve the view from the house. As the accounts in the estate office reveal, some left still owing rent.

The Cerne giant cut into the chalk downs of Dorset is 180 feet high and brandishes a club over 100 feet long. (*NT*)

The Cerne Giant Dorset

On Giant Hill, north of Cerne Abbas, 8 miles north of Dorchester, just east of the A352

Britain's chalk downs provide a wonderful opportunity for large-scale art, with gleaming white lines created relatively easily by scouring through the thin topsoil. Many of the surviving hill figures date from the late eighteenth and early nineteenth centuries, but the Trust's two examples (*see also* p.363) are of much greater antiquity. This huge crudely drawn naked man cut boldly into the Dorset hills is thought to date from the second century AD. As befits a giant, he stands 180 feet high and the knobbly club he brandishes in his right hand is over a hundred feet long. A cloak may once have hung over his outstretched left arm. Traditionally a fertility god, he may be a depiction of Hercules, whose cult was at its height in the late second century.

On the downs above the giant's left arm is a rectangular earthwork known as the Trendle (not owned by the Trust), which may well have had a religious or social function connected with the huge virile figure.

This unspoilt downland is part of a wide belt of chalk country stretching across Dorset which is dotted with prehistoric remains, among them a number of Iron Age hillforts in the care of the Trust (*see* p.102).

Charlecote Park Warwickshire

1 mile west of Wellesbourne, 5 miles east of Stratford-upon-Avon, 6 miles south of Warwick on north side of the B4086

Charlecote has been the home of the Lucy family for some 700 years. The present house, begun by Sir Thomas Lucy in the mid-sixteenth century, lies at the centre of an extensive wooded deer park grazed by fallow and red deer and by a herd of rare Jacob sheep introduced by George Lucy in the eighteenth century. Standing on the banks of the River Avon within easy reach of Stratford, it is here that Shakespeare is said to have been caught poaching and to have been brought before Sir Thomas Lucy, the resident magistrate, in Charlecote's great hall. (The young playwright may well have vaulted over the rough oak paling which still surrounds most of the park and which has been perpetuated since Elizabethan times.) Shakespeare took his revenge

some years later when he made fun of the knight in his portrayal of Justice Shallow in *The Merry Wives of Windsor*, with pointed reference to the Lucys' venerable coat of arms on which three silver pike rise for air.

The house itself is built of red brick to a pleasingly irregular E shape. With great chimneys marching across the roofline and octagonal corner turrets crowned with gilded weathervanes, Charlecote seems to sum up the very essence of Elizabethan England, especially when the brick-work is mellowed and burnished by the sun. Queen Elizabeth I spent two nights here in 1572, celebrated in the proud display of her arms over the two-storeyed porch. With the exception of the porch, however, most of the present building is the result of 'Elizabethan' restoration by George Hammond Lucy in the early nineteenth century. Apart from the family paintings, which hang in every room, he was also responsible for most of the furnishings, many

The early nineteenth-century scullery at Charlecote.
(*NT/Andreas von Einsiedel*)

of which came from the 1823 sale of the contents of William Beckford's Fonthill in Wiltshire. Most eyecatching is a sixteenth-century Italian marble table from the Borghese Palace, inlaid with brightly coloured birds and with a slab of onyx like a section through a fossilised tree in the centre. The general effect is rich and lush, reflecting advice from the designer and antiquarian Thomas Willement.

Two generations earlier, George Lucy, a cultivated and much travelled bachelor, had employed 'Capability' Brown to redesign the park, sweeping away the seventeenth-century water gardens (shown in the painting above Shakespeare's bust in the great hall) and altering the course of the River Hele (now the Dene) so that it cascaded into the Avon within sight of the house. The balustraded formal garden between house and river, with urns planted with geraniums and lobelia flowering pink and blue either side of the steps into the Avon, is a nineteenth-century addition. More steps lead up from the forecourt on to the Cedar Lawn, with a Victorian orangery and a rustic thatched aviary set across the grass. Beyond is the wild garden on a raised tongue of land extending north into the park, with wide views over the Avon to Hampton Lucy church. In deference to Shakespeare, a border close to the orangery has been planted with species mentioned in his plays, dog violets, columbine and cuckoo flower among them.

Some of the earliest parts of the house are in the extensive outbuildings, where the stable block includes a brew-house which was in operation until the 1890s, a wash house, and a coach house displaying a collection of vehicles used at Charlecote in the nineteenth century. But only the rose-pink gatehouse with its fretwork stone balustrade survives unaltered from Sir Thomas Lucy's original Tudor house – a tantalising taste of what must have been lost.

Chartwell Kent

2 miles south of Westerham

Six doors lead into the garden from Chartwell. From the windows of every room there are changing vistas down the little combe in which the house is built, up the wooded slope behind or over the soft Kentish countryside to the Weald. This serene setting, still breathtakingly beautiful, was to provide Winston Churchill with inspiration and

strength for over forty years, from 1922 until he left Chartwell for the last time in 1964.

The appeal of this unpretentious red-brick house, with its comfortable airy rooms created by Philip Tilden out of a gloomy Victorian mansion, lies in its powerful reflection of a great and complicated man, whose spirit still seems to linger on here. His bold, bright paintings hang throughout the house, some, such as the simple study of a magnolia on an upper landing, tranquil still lifes, others recording landscapes he loved, in France, Italy and Morocco as well as around Chartwell. A half-finished canvas stands on the easel in his surprisingly large garden studio, paints laid ready nearby. Finished pictures hang five deep on the walls round about. In the airy, flower-filled drawing-room, a card table is set for the bezique he so much enjoyed, and a painting over the fireplace records one of the finest colts from his racing stable. Velvet siren suits, his characteristic wide-brimmed hats and cigar boxes also suggest a man who relished life's pleasures.

But there are other mementoes too. In the lofty study, with its high roof open to the rafters, is the wide mahogany stand-up desk where Churchill wrote the sonorous prose of his *A History of the English-Speaking Peoples* and *The Second World War*. Here he reflected on the growing power of Germany during the 1930s, a threat which he felt was perceived by him alone. This room is still essentially as he left it, crowded with family photographs, a despatch box open on the table. A portrait of his father hangs by the fire and a drawing of his mother radiates her exceptional beauty. Medals, uniforms and other reminders of a life devoted to his country include Churchill's terse directive to Field Marshal Alexander, instructing him to expel the enemy from North Africa, and the Field Marshal's equally short reply, informing the Prime Minister that he had done so.

Chartwell is also very much a family house, with the warmth of a place which has nurtured children. The signatures of Lloyd George, Balfour and Field Marshal Montgomery in the visitors' book are interspersed with the more tentative efforts of less mature hands, friends and cousins of the four young Churchills. And it was the children who decided to mark Winston and Clemmie's fiftieth wedding anniversary by planting the glorious borders filled with thirty-two varieties of golden roses which run in a long corridor down the old kitchen garden, just yards from the wall which Churchill built when he was in the political wilderness before the Second World War.

The Churchills' spacious garden falling away to the lakes in the depths of the combe is divided by a loose framework of hedges and walls, with steps from one level to another. Stretches of trees and grass, such as the long terraced lawn in front of the house with wide-ranging views across the valley, are complemented by planting schemes reflecting Lady Churchill's love of cool colours and simple and direct effects. Her walled rose garden to the east of the house is full of pink and white blossom at the right time of year and buddleias bordering the path at the end of the terrace lawn are some of the species specially chosen to attract brimstones, tortoiseshells and other butterflies. Most evocative is the secluded goldfish pond, where an ample garden chair marks the spot where Churchill came daily to feed his golden orfe and ponder life.

Chastleton House Oxfordshire

At Chastleton off A44 4 miles south-east of Moreton-in-Marsh

On the fringes of the Cotswolds, westwards into Oxfordshire, is an unspoilt landscape of well-wooded farmland and limestone villages. Less than a mile off the main road from Oxford to Evesham, a leafy narrow lane runs steeply up through a straggle of cottages. At the top of the village, set back across a grassy court beside a stump-towered church, is a square, many-gabled Jacobean house. Of mellow local stone, with tall, three-storey ranges set round a tight internal court and mullioned windows, Chastleton is a charming and unaltered example of the kind of manor house which must have adorned a thousand English villages, lived in by families untouched by high office and national events. There are sophisticated touches, such as the arresting

The beauty of the little combe in which Chartwell lies originally attracted Winston Churchill to the place from which he was to draw strength for over forty years; sadly the beech woods rising to Crockham Hill on the other side of the valley were decimated by the Great Storm in the autumn of 1987. (*Magnum/Philippe Halsmann*)

A staircase tower dominates the east front of Chastleton House. In the foreground are the surreal forms of the topiary garden, now being coaxed back into shape. (*NT/Rupert Truman*)

south front, with its show of glass and advancing bays, and some fine plaster ceilings, but much else, such as the rough and mossy dry-stone walls lining the entrance court, is rustic and *ad hoc*.

Until it came to the Trust in 1991, Chastleton had been in the hands of the same family for almost four hundred years. Built *c.*1610–12 for Walter Jones, a successful wool merchant, who bought the estate from Robert Catesby, the future Gunpowder Plotter, it has been owned by Jones's descendants ever since, with tapestries and furniture identifiable on the inventory taken after his death in 1633. Early prosperity did not last. Although the family was staunchly royalist in the Civil War – when Arthur Jones is said to have evaded a Roundhead search party after the Battle of Worcester by hiding in a secret chamber – there were few rewards at the Restoration, and growing financial difficulties culminated in Henry Jones's imprisonment for bankruptcy in 1755. Chastleton's character comes from the slow accumulation of contents in a house that, like an old coat, was sometimes cut to fit but never drastically altered or updated. Preserving the house's atmosphere and sense of unity has been the cornerstone of the Trust's six-year restoration.

Above a substantial basement, where the smoke-blackened kitchen ceiling, said to ensure the family's luck, remains unwhitewashed, is a sequence of parlours and chambers, some tapestry hung and the grander with carved chimneypieces of stone or wood and decorative plasterwork. Panelling, now dark with age and dirt, is used like wallpaper, and there are pegged plank doors, undulating floors and unfinished corners. The plan is conservative, centred on a traditional great hall, with an oriel window lighting the high-table end and a carved strapwork screen, and with staircases in crenellated towers to either side of the house. The most ornate interior is the great chamber, where the overmantel, carved with the arms of Jones and his wife, still has traces of its rich red, blue and gold colour schemes and the ceiling is an extravaganza of trailing vines and hanging pendants; the most glorious is the bare and airy long gallery on the third floor, with its silvery panelling and plasterwork barrel ceiling. A glimpse of a more recent lifestyle is given by a spartan, unceilinged maid's bedroom open to the rafters of the roof. The long refectory table in the hall, leather chests in the gallery, and the blue and red flamestitch hangings lining a little closet are among the furnishings given on the 1633 inventory; a brief burst of refurbishment after 1697, when Walter Jones married the forceful Anne Whitmore, accounts for the James II walnut chairs and exquisite Queen Anne crewelwork; and the family's poverty ensured the survival of some seventeenth century woollen hangings that were once commonplace and are now very rare. There is also an unbroken run of family portraits, including works by Kneller and Hudson.

It was Anne Whitmore who probably laid out the topiary garden to the east of the house, with a yew circle embracing twenty-four box figures. Including such unlikely arboreal sculptures as a galleon in full sail, these are slowly being coaxed back into shape by the Trust. To the north is a sequence of grassed terraces, the one laid out as a croquet lawn recalling the nineteenth-century Walter Jones Whitmore, who first codified the rules of the game. In a field beyond the garden, on a sightline from the house, is a mature oak, said to be grown from an acorn off the Boscobel tree, and a delicious eighteenth-century dovecote stands in the parkland rising to the 860-foot summit of Chastleton Hill.

Cheddar Cliffs Somerset

8 miles north-west of Wells

On the north and west sides of the famous gorge are the Cheddar Cliffs, 375 acres of spectacular limestone cliffs and crags, acquired initially to prevent the spread of commercialisation which had begun at the gorge's lower end. Access is not for the faint-hearted. The Trust has recently devoted much effort to clearing scrub, opening up habitat for specialist limestone-loving plants such as the Cheddar pink, found nowhere else in Britain.

Chedworth Villa Gloucestershire

3 miles north-west of Fossebridge on the A429 Cirencester–Northleach road

Chedworth reveals a life of ease and luxury in Roman Britain. Consisting of low one-storey ranges fronted by verandahs set round a courtyard, with the north side extended in a long wing to the east, the villa strongly suggests the Roman equivalent of a Texan ranch. Although the walls now rise only a foot or two above the ground, exquisite mosaics

and other details were preserved by a covering of silt until the remains were discovered in 1864. The impressive dining-room, warmed by underfloor heating, is decorated with a fine pavement in red, white and blue, with drunken satyrs cavorting in Bacchic scenes and corner panels depicting the four seasons, Winter warmly clad in a hooded cloak, Spring running with a basket of flowers.

Colourful mosaics also mark the two elaborate bath complexes fed from a nearby spring, one the equivalent of a modern sauna, the other providing the steamy heat of a Turkish bath.

This lovely site in a wooded valley in the depths of the Cotswolds was first occupied in the early second century. The villa, one of many in this area, was gradually improved and enlarged over the next 250 years, probably on the profits of a thriving agricultural estate serving the important Roman towns at Gloucester and Cirencester nearby, and perhaps also benefiting from proximity to the Fosse Way linking Exeter to the River Humber.

Early in the fifth century Roman government in Britain collapsed and at some date after this Chedworth was abandoned.

Cherhill Down and Oldbury Castle Wiltshire

On the A4, between Calne and Beckhampton

The Trust owns over 500 acres of this ancient downland overlooking the Vale of Pewsey. While the vale is given over to large-scale arable farming, this is a prehistoric landscape, marked by tumuli, earthworks, long and bowl barrows, strip-field systems and ancient tracks, with the Iron Age hill fort of Oldbury Castle at the summit of the down. The Trust's acres are unimproved downland, untouched by plough or chemical spray. There are butterfly-attracting chalkland flowers on the steeper slopes, and a series of deep-cut sheltered combes, including possibly the finest example of a chalkland dry valley system in England, supports herb-rich grassland and clumps of beech.

Walkers clambering up from the A4 are rewarded with the recently restored Lansdowne Monument, built on the crest of the hill in 1845 by the 3rd Marquess of Lansdowne in memory of the economist Sir William Petty; by a fine white horse carved into the shoulder of the down (not owned by the Trust)

The warmly clad figure of Winter in a mosaic floor at Chedworth, a faggot clasped in his left hand and a hare in his right. (*NT/John Parry*)

and by exhilarating views from the 850-foot ridge. The air is like wine and from up here the cars on the A4 are reduced to toys. This is country to restore the soul.

Cherryburn Northumberland

Off A695 at Mickley, 11 miles west of Newcastle

A roughly built sandstone cottage set high above the deep green valley of the Tyne was the birthplace of the engraver and naturalist Thomas Bewick (1753–1828), known for his closely observed drawings, carved in box, of the creatures of the Northumbrian countryside. The cottage – now tiled but originally heather-thatched – looks over a sloping cobbled yard to the substantial farmhouse built in

the late 1820s by Thomas's brother William, who took over the family smallholding. Drawings of the interior of the cottage have enabled the Trust to reconstruct two rooms, and there is an exhibition on Bewick's work in the farmhouse.

Chiddingstone Kent

4 miles east of Edenbridge, 1½ miles north-west of Penshurst

This leafy single-street village is one of the most attractive of the Kentish Weald, built at a time when the Wealden iron industry was at its height and now all that remains of a much larger settlement destroyed when Chiddingstone Castle park was created. Opposite the largely seventeenth-century church of St Mary stands a perfect group of sixteenth- and seventeenth-century buildings, some half-timbered with black and white façades and overhanging upper storeys, some timber-framed with brick infilling, and all with lichen-stained red-tiled roofs.

What is now the village shop and post office is mentioned in a deed of 1453, and most of the houses probably incorporate earlier material. The sandstone block known as the Chiding Stone, by which local men are supposed to have berated their nagging wives and from which the village is said to take its name, lies in the park, below the hill crowned with the Gothick castle (not owned by the Trust).

The Chilterns

Extending from Dunstable, in the north-east, to the River Thames, in the south-west

North-west of London runs the great chalk arc of the Chilterns, its ancient beech woods, heaths and downland offering splendid walking for Londoners with a day to spare. A number of Trust holdings are scattered along the ridge: some, like the 1,100 acres of farmland and woodland based on the manor and village of Bradenham, are substantial estates; others, like the 112 acres of Watlington Hill, or the 65 acres of Pulpit Wood, protect prominent features of the landscape or important habitat. Altogether, including land attached to Hughenden (*see* p.157) and West Wycombe Park and village (*see* p.361), the Trust owns some 7,000 acres here.

From Coombe Hill, at 852 feet the highest viewpoint in the Chilterns, there are lovely views across the Vale of Aylesbury to the Berkshire Downs and the Cotswolds (*see* p.88). The handsome obelisk on the hilltop is a memorial to the men of Buckinghamshire who fell in the Boer War. On the chalk grow privet, juniper and whitebeam, with thyme, harebell, wild strawberry, bird's-foot trefoil, mullein and dog violet, but scrub would soon take over were it not for the grazing of sheep reintroduced by the Trust in recent years. At Low Scrubs, on the high ground to the east, there are woodland plants – yellow archangel, broad buckler-fern and enchanter's nightshade.

At the north-eastern end of the Chiltern arc is Ashridge. Formerly a monastic property, it was surrendered to the Crown in 1539, and then bequeathed by Henry VIII to his daughter Eliza-

beth, who spent much of her unhappy childhood here. In 1604 Sir Thomas Egerton bought the estate which remained in the Egerton family (successively Earls and Dukes of Bridgewater, and latterly Earls Brownlow, *see* p.25) until 1921.

The Egertons became enormously rich when the 3rd Duke (1737–1803) developed his coal mines in Lancashire. This 'Canal Duke', whose splendid memorial column stands on the edge of Aldbury Common, took down the old monastic buildings; James Wyatt and his nephew, Sir Jeffry Wyatville, designed the new house in Gothic style – now Ashridge College – for the 3rd Duke's successor.

The estate, enlarged to some 15,000 acres, remained well managed, private and secure until the 3rd Earl Brownlow died in 1921, whereupon Ashridge – like so many other landed estates at that time – was put on to the market to be sold piecemeal for development. Stanley Baldwin, then Prime Minister, appealed to the Brownlow trustees, local people – including the children of the six village schools – worked valiantly to raise money, and help from generous outside donors was enlisted. It was a classic National Trust campaign of its day and 1,700 acres were triumphantly bought.

The enthusiasm then generated was fully justified and has continued. The Trust's estate now covers over 4,000 acres of wonderfully varied landscape running along the hills from Berkhamsted to Ivinghoe Beacon. There are 1,200 acres of farmland; the rest is common, down and woodland.

To the north the chalk ridge of the Ivinghoe Hills compares with the best of the North Downs (*see* p.224), and has the same problems. When grazing by sheep became unprofitable in the 1930s, and even more after myxomatosis decimated the rabbit population in the 1950s, scrub encroached rapidly. Continual efforts to drive it back are gradually re-establishing the flora.

Crawley Wood, a mile to the south, rises to 800 feet, and from there, west of the B4506 from Berkhamsted to Dunstable, is wonderful wooded country, with plenty of paths. Beech, oak, larch and pine predominate but the commons have self-sown silver birch, and Sallow Copse has mature sweet chestnut. Aldbury, Berkhamsted and Northchurch Commons continue the estate across the B4506 south to Frithsden Beeches, resplendent with ancient pollarded beech. View them on a winter's evening, their gnarled encircling branches like a drawing by Arthur Rackham.

(*Opposite page*) Chiddingstone, one of the most attractive villages of the Kentish Weald, seen from the graveyard of St Mary's church. (*NT*)

The flora of Watlington Hill includes a natural yew forest and rare chalk-loving plants on the open downland. (*NT/ Nick Meers*)

Ashridge is the reward of a long campaign, and the extent of this is witnessed by the story of Dunstable Downs. Lying four miles to the north of Ashridge, this chalk ridge adjoining Whipsnade had lost its character due to encroachment by scrub. Since its acquisition in 1929–48, the whole plateau has been converted to arable land. The relict of chalk grassland has been cleared and fenced and is now grazed by sheep. Several interesting downland plants survive.

Chipping Campden Market Hall

Gloucestershire

Opposite the police station, Chipping Campden

This little gabled and pinnacled Jacobean building stands prominently in the centre of Chipping Campden, on one side of the wide high street. Like the medieval houses of wool merchants with which

it is surrounded, the market hall is built of golden Cotswold stone and roofed with stone slabs. Open arcades on all four sides give access to the cobbled floor where farmers and traders gathered to sell and buy cheese, butter and poultry.

As the coat of arms in a gable at one end signifies, the market hall was built by Sir Baptist Hicks in 1627, only two years before his death. A financier who helped support the extravagances of the court of James I, Baptist Hicks was raised to the peerage at the end of his life and is commemorated by a restrained classical monument in the south chapel of the wool church down the street.

Chirk Castle Clwyd

½ *mile west of Chirk village off the A5*

Castell y Waun – Meadow Castle – is an apt name for a building in such a beautiful situation, with magnificent views over the wooded agricultural landscape of the Welsh borders. Approached through the Davies brothers' exuberantly baroque wrought-iron gates, the first view of the castle itself comes as something of a surprise. Externally Chirk is still a fortress, its massive fourteenth-century walls fifteen feet thick and projecting drum towers rising menacingly from the hill on which it sits.

A pointed archway marked with the grooves of a portcullis leads into the internal courtyard. Here the west range still has the character of the castle Roger Mortimer started in *c*.1295 as part of Edward I's campaign to subdue the Welsh. Deep underground, reached by a spiral staircase in the thickness of the walls, is a dungeon hollowed out of the rock, only two narrow beams of light reaching those who were incarcerated here. In the courtyard outside a great shaft falls ninety-three feet to the castle well.

These reminders of the turbulent Middle Ages contrast with the domestic interiors produced by the Myddelton family who have lived at Chirk since 1595. The forbidding north range houses an elegant staircase and a suite of late eighteenth-century state apartments designed in the fashionable neo-classical style by Joseph Turner of Chester, now stripped of the neo-Gothic decoration imposed by A. W. Pugin in the 1840s. A brilliant-blue Adam-style coffered ceiling, inset with Greek mythological scenes by the Irish painter George Mullins, graces the sumptuous saloon, with gilded doors and dados, a red and white marble fireplace and Mortlake tapestries on the walls. Among the fine contemporary furniture, including a pair of stylish serpentine settees,

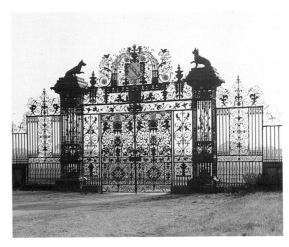

The entrance gates to Chirk Castle: exquisite baroque ironwork of 1712–19 by the Davies brothers of Bersham, who even incorporated graceful wrought-iron plants in the cage-like gate piers supporting a couple of lead wolves. (*NT*/*Jeremy Whitaker*)

is a rare signed harpsichord by Burckhardt Shudi, with eagles with outstretched wings depicted in the inlaid interior. These rooms are hung with seventeenth- and eighteenth-century family portraits, including two by the Flemish landscape painter Peter Tillemanns, and works by J. M. Wright, Michael Dahl and Allan Ramsay.

A door from the drawing-room leads into the imposing hundred-foot long gallery begun in 1670 when Sir Thomas Myddelton repaired extensive damage sustained in the Civil War. Filling the east range, and more than twice the size of the saloon, this room was conceived on the grand scale, perhaps by the gentleman-architect William Winde. Massive broken pediments crown the doors and a bold cornice of carved acanthus leaves runs above the portraits hanging on the richly panelled walls. Among the few pieces of seventeenth-century furniture is a delicate ebony Dutch cabinet inlaid with tortoiseshell and ivory and with a silver-encrusted interior decorated with scenes from the life of Christ, one showing Our Lord blessing children against the backdrop of the gabled façades of a Flemish town. Declining a peerage from Charles II, Sir Thomas accepted this cabinet instead.

Chirk lies in a mature oak-studded park, landscaped by William Emes in the late eighteenth century, in which the oldest trees date from replanting during the Restoration. On the east side of the castle the grim medieval walls are softened by roses, honeysuckle and other shrubs and plants bordering an expanse of grass and topiary yew, with a massive yew hedge cut to resemble a battlemented wall. A tiny sunken rose garden is focused on a sundial that was probably made for Chirk in the seventeenth century, and a long colourful mixed border nearby was established by Colonel and Lady Margaret Myddelton, who are largely responsible for the restoration of the garden since the Second World War. Two bronze nymphs stand guard over the steps leading down to the vine-entangled thatched hawk house on a lower lawn, picturesquely set against a rock bank planted with trees and shrubs. Other eyecatchers include the early eighteenth-century statue of Hercules, prominently placed at the top of the seventeenth-century lime avenue above the hawk house, and William Emes's delightful classical pavilion at one end of the long terrace fringing the lower lawn. This is the place to sit on a warm afternoon, gazing over the lush countryside of the Welsh borders.

Church House Devon

Widecombe-in-the-Moor, in the centre of Dartmoor, north of Ashburton, west of Bovey Tracey

The medieval church in this sadly commercialised Dartmoor village boasts a magnificent early sixteenth-century pinnacled tower, paid for by prosperous tin miners. The two-storey granite building known as the Church House in the tiny square by the lych gate is of much the same period, dating from 1537. One of the finest such houses in Devon, it is substantial and well proportioned, with round-headed two-light granite windows and a verandah supported on octagonal granite pillars running the length of the entrance front. Each pillar rests on a roughly hewn boulder. Originally a brew-house, it later became a school and is now partly leased as the village hall and partly used as a Trust information centre and shop.

Cilgerran Castle Dyfed

On rock above left bank of the Teifi, 3 miles south of Cardigan, 1½ miles east of the A478

Like the great fortress at Durham, Cilgerran is so superbly sited that it seems a natural part of the landscape. Today the ruins of this stronghold appear not so much formidable as romantic and picturesque, the inspiration of a number of artists including Turner, Richard Wilson and Pieter de Wint. Round towers linked by massive walls four feet wide in places stand on a rocky bluff above wooded slopes plunging precipitously to the gorge of the Teifi river and its tributary the Plysgog. Only a few miles from the sea, Cilgerran could be supplied by water, and also controlled the crossing point at the tidal limit of the Teifi.

Built by William Marshall, Earl of Pembroke, in about 1225 on the site of an earlier stronghold captured from the Welsh in the Norman conquest of Wales, Cilgerran was constructed only a few years after Skenfrith (*see* p.295), but already castle design had moved on. In place of a central keep, the stronghold's defensive strength is concentrated in the towers projecting from the curtain wall enclosing the tip of the promontory. The remains of a third, rectangular tower probably date from the late fourteenth century, when Edward III ordered the reinforcement of a number of Welsh castles against the threat of a French invasion. In the event, it was the south coast of England that suffered, with raids from Rye to Plymouth. A forty-foot-wide ditch separates this inner ward from the outer court, once crossed by a drawbridge to the gatehouse where the grooves for two portcullises still mark the walls. A second great ditch added further protection beyond the outer ward, where little of the original defences survives. Possibly ruined at the time of Owen Glendower's revolt in 1405, when the castle was briefly held by the Welsh, Cilgerran seems never to have been subsequently repaired.

Cissbury Ring West Sussex

1½ miles east of Findon, 3 miles north of Worthing

Often so conspicuously sited as to form local landmarks, prehistoric hill forts would rarely receive planning permission today. Cissbury is no exception. Set 600 feet up on the South Downs behind Worthing, the views from this prominent site range east to Beachy Head and west to the Isle of Wight. The hill fort itself is huge, one of the largest Iron Age examples in Britain, with a substantial ditch and earth rampart enclosing an area of about sixty-five acres. Built in 250 BC but abandoned before the Romans arrived in AD 43, the fort was apparently refortified in late Roman times, perhaps against coastal raids, and also shows traces of late Iron Age field systems.

Cissbury is notable too as one of the most important sites of neolithic flint production. Used to make implements for land clearance and as the basis of formidable fighting and hunting weapons, flint was eagerly sought by prehistoric man, who sank forty-foot shafts into the chalk here, with galleries radiating into the rock following high-quality seams. Now marked by bumps and hollows on the west side of the hill, this early industrial site was worked from c.2500 BC to 1600 BC, when new sources of flint were discovered in Norfolk.

(*Opposite page*) The romantic ruins of Cilgerran Castle, magnificently situated on a rocky promontory high above the River Teifi, have inspired a number of artists, including Turner and Richard Wilson. (*NT*)

The City Mill Hampshire

At the foot of High Street in Winchester, beside Soke Bridge

This attractive brick corn mill with tile-hung gables and a delightful island garden was built over the River Itchen by Soke Bridge in 1743 on a site that has been occupied by a succession of mills since Saxon times. The fast-flowing river which emerges in a spectacular mill race once powered several medieval mills in the city, a reflection of Winchester's early importance as capital of England and as a market for grain and wool. Already in decline by the late fourteenth century as a result of the ravages of the Black Death and the removal of the English wool staple to Calais, the city never recovered its former prosperity.

One of a number of Winchester mills recorded as being connected to the Church in Domesday Book, the Soke Bridge mill was then a property of the Benedictine nunnery of Wherwell a few miles north of the city, passing to the Crown when the monastery was dissolved in 1538–9. Some years later, in 1554, it was given to the city by Mary I in partial recompense for the expense of her marriage to Philip of Spain in Winchester Cathedral. The current mill is not in working order, but it is hoped to operate one of the undershot waterwheels and some of the mill machinery in the near future.

Clandon Park Surrey

At West Clandon on the A247, 3 miles east of Guildford on the A424

Clandon looks as if it would be more at home on the corner of a piazza in Venice or Florence than set down in the Surrey countryside. It is a massive four-square block of a house, three storeys high and eleven windows wide on the long garden façade, built in the reddest of brick with stone dressings. On the entrance front, a central pedimented section of stone stands out starkly against the red on either side, as if somebody had forgotten to colour it in. No roof rises above the crowning balustrade to relieve the austere outlines of the building.

This individual Georgian country house, built in about 1731, owes its appearance to the Italian Giacomo Leoni and is one of only five surviving buildings by this Venetian architect in England (*see also* Lyme Park, p.190). The interior is as grand as the exterior, its most impressive feature being the richly decorated formal marble hall rising through two storeys with classical statues set in niches at first-floor level. Life-like slaves supporting the central relief of Artari and Bagutti's fine plaster-work ceiling have one leg over the edge of the cornice, as if they could leap down at any moment. The white walls and ceiling, the marble floor and intricately carved marble chimneypieces over the two fireplaces all contribute to the impression of light and space, refreshingly cool on a hot August afternoon. Leoni even extended the marble floor into the grand saloon next door, clearly forgetting the absence of a Mediterranean sun in an English summer.

Clandon was built for Thomas, 2nd Baron Onslow, to replace the Elizabethan house his great-grandfather had acquired in 1641, and it has remained in the family ever since. The Onslows have traditionally followed political careers; the three who served as Speakers of the House of Commons are commemorated in portraits in the Speaker's Parlour. Here too is the 'vinegar' bible which Arthur Onslow, Speaker from 1728–61 and the most famous of the three, presented to St Margaret's, Westminster, its name deriving from

These Ch'ien Lung cranes with gilded feathers are just two of the exotically plumaged seventeenth- and eighteenth-century Chinese birds from the Gubbay Collection at Clandon Park. (*NT*)

the misprint in the parable of the vineyard. The Maori meeting house in the grounds, its steeply pitched thatched roof reaching almost to the ground, is a memorial to another eminent Onslow, the 4th Earl, who was governor of New Zealand from 1888–92 and also rescued Clandon from half a century of neglect by his great-uncle.

Most of the original contents have been sold or removed over the years, but Clandon is now filled with magnificent furniture, porcelain, textiles and carpets acquired by the connoisseur Mrs David Gubbay in the 1920s and 1930s and brought here from Little Trent Park in Hertfordshire. Apart from the English eighteenth-century furniture, which includes fine satinwood and marquetry pieces, the jewels of the collection are the fifty or so seventeenth- and eighteenth-century Chinese birds. These exquisitely moulded, vividly plumaged creatures perch on baroque brackets and adorn tables and mantelpieces, the many species represented including a pair of elegant fragile cranes in the Green Drawing Room and brilliantly blue parrots, red and green pheasants and plump ducks in the Hunting Room. A spectacular phoenix presides over the state bedroom, where the four-poster and accompanying chairs were probably made for Sir Richard Onslow, father of the builder of the house. Clandon now also houses the Queen's Royal Surrey Regimental Museum in the basement.

Claremont Landscape Garden

Surrey

On south edge of Esher, on east side of the A 307

Claremont is the product of some of the greatest names in garden history – Charles Bridgeman, 'Capability' Brown and William Kent – and one of the first and finest gardens to be designed in the natural manner, predating Stourhead (*see* p. 317) by some twenty years. Laid out round a lake on an undulating fifty-acre site falling away from the house (not owned by the Trust), Claremont is primarily a study in foliage, grass and water, where the overall effect is created by contrasts of light and shade, by the alternation of open glades with densely wooded serpentine paths and by little buildings and other features set as eyecatchers at strategic points.

Although visitors now come into the garden at the bottom of the hill, Claremont was designed to be seen from the top, looking down the broad grass path leading from Vanbrugh's dramatic castellated Belvedere (not owned by the Trust) to the yew-fringed bowling green, or out over the beeches, oaks, chestnuts and cedars to the ornamental lake with its little island crowned with a pavilion. Bordering the lake is an extraordinary turf amphitheatre, one of only two on such a large scale in Europe. Five steep, giant-size terraces form a semicircle round an oval 'stage', three more spreading out in a descending fan below. Grass ramps on either side lead up to the top. More a piece of open-air sculpture than a setting for dramatic performances, the amphitheatre's curves are framed by a backdrop of trees and ornamented with strategically placed long white benches with high backs, copies of eighteenth-century garden furniture. Across the water, heaped-up boulders and a tangle of vegetation surround a naturalistic sandstone grotto.

The gardens at Claremont were established by the Duke of Newcastle between 1715 and 1750, initially with the advice of Vanbrugh, who enlarged the house, but from 1716 with the additional assistance of Charles Bridgeman. This talented landscape designer, who created the network of avenues and paths, the grass amphitheatre and a circular pond, was one of the first to break away from the formal layouts epitomised by Le Nôtre's work at Versailles. Bridgeman's naturalistic approach was taken further by William Kent in the 1730s, who enlarged the pond into a lake, planted trees to soften the lines of paths and avenues and built a ha-ha, a section of which still exists, to allow uninterrupted views from the garden into the fields beyond. 'Capability' Brown, working for Lord Clive on his acquisition of the estate in 1768, seems to have been restrained from making his usual sweeping changes. Apart from planting the amphitheatre with trees, now removed, and building a new house (now used as a school), his main contribution was to alter the line of the old Portsmouth road to bring the prominent wooded viewpoint known as The Mound within the bounds of the garden.

During the nineteenth century, when Claremont was the home of Princess Charlotte, daughter of George IV, and then acquired by Queen Victoria for her youngest son, many exotic trees were planted throughout the estate. A camellia house was established on the terrace below the house, its site now marked by beds of tree-like specimens enclosed by railings adorned with coronets and florid Ls (for Leopold of Saxe-Coburg, Charlotte's husband). Twenty years of neglect in the twentieth century almost obscured what Bridgeman and Kent designed but, although areas which were once open glades are now thickly covered with laurel and rhododendrons, restoration has renewed the vistas which gave Claremont its eighteenth-century reputation as the most famous garden in Europe.

Claydon House Buckinghamshire

In Middle Claydon, 13 miles north-west of Aylesbury, $3\frac{1}{2}$ miles south-west of Winslow

A combination of ambition and gullibility led Ralph, 2nd Lord Verney, to create one of the most extraordinary houses in England. Inheriting the family estate in 1752, Verney initially contented himself with reconstructing and extending his father's old-fashioned Jacobean manor house, but some ten years later he embarked on a far more grandiose scheme for a great west front, partly, it seems, to produce a house to rival that of his much richer neighbour, Earl Temple of Stowe (*see* p.320). The restrained classical exterior of the surviving west wing conceals extraordinary decoration by Luke Lightfoot, an eccentric and difficult genius variously described as cabinet-maker, master builder and surveyor, but emerging at Claydon as a carver of unique talent.

Lightfoot's work in the north hall and Chinese Room is in a class of its own. Ceilings, overmantels, doors and alcoves are encrusted with lacy white woodwork. Herons, swan-like birds and fantastic wyverns with barbed tails perch on the tracery. Necks are coiled and snaky, wings outstretched, claws extended. Tiny bells hang from the roof of the built-in pagoda-like feature in the Chinese Room, decorated when the fashion for chinoiserie in eighteenth-century England was at its height. Carvings resembling oriental summerhouses surround the doors, with trelliswork connecting the supporting columns. Bamboo furniture made in Canton in about 1800 completes the effect.

Lightfoot's extravagance and the failure of a speculative housing project in which he had persuaded Lord Verney to invest led to his dismissal before the house was completed. Exquisite plasterwork adorning the saloon and staircase is by Joseph Rose, who was employed at Claydon after 1768.

A detail of Luke Lightfoot's fantastic wood-carving at Claydon House. The north hall, where this door surround can be seen, is alive with writhing foliage, swan-necked ho-ho birds and winged wyverns. (*NT*)

Working in plaster where Lightfoot worked in wood, Rose used conventional classical motifs but executed them with skill and ingenuity to create two of the finest Georgian interiors in England. The stairs themselves are one of the marvels of Claydon, with delicate ears of corn quivering in the ironwork scrolls making up the balustrade and a jigsaw of box, mahogany, ebony and ivory forming the parquetry treads.

Growing financial difficulties, unrelieved by lawyers employed to help manage mounting debts, led to the sale of the contents of the house in 1783, and Verney's grandiose ballroom and huge rotunda by the architect-squire Sir Thomas Robinson were demolished by his niece when she succeeded to the estate. The Javanese musical instruments filling the Red Room, an assortment of gongs and wood and bamboo xylophones collectively known as a Gamelan, were a present to Sir Harry Verney, 2nd Baronet, who inherited the property in 1827. Florence Nightingale would have seen this exotic gift from Sir Stamford Raffles, lieutenant governor of Java, when she came to visit her elder sister Frances Parthenope, Sir Harry's wife. Mementoes of the Lady of the Lamp are displayed in a room adjoining that where she always slept, including letters she wrote as a young girl as well as reminders of the privations she endured in the Crimea, two photographs showing how thin and frail she looked on her return. Unfortunately there is no record of what this most Victorian of ladies thought of the extravagant rococo decoration of her sister's home.

Clent Hills   Hereford & Worcester

3 miles south of Stourbridge, south-east of Hagley, north and east of Clent

The Clent Hills, with the Walton Hill commons to the east, have long been the place where people from Stourbridge, Smethwick, Halesowen, Selly Oak and Bromsgrove have come to breathe clean air and to see a fairer countryside. The grassy hills, wooded in parts, are steep but easy to walk, and the views are superb. To the north-west lies the privately owned Hagley Park, with its great eighteenth-century house and church lying snugly under the hill; beyond are Kinver Edge (*see* p.170), Wenlock Edge and the Shropshire Hills (*see* p.288). To the south, the rich farming landscape of Worcestershire stretches to the Cotswold ridge (*see* p.88), and west of that the unmistakable whaleback of the Malvern Hills (*see* p.197) rises starkly from the plain.

The view eastward is very different. Birmingham has generated much of the country's wealth, and continues to do so, but beauty is not its *raison d'être*. Far-sighted local authorities gave 360 acres of the hills to the Trust in 1959, thereby securing their future. High Harcourt farm was added in 1986.

Clevedon Court   Avon

1½ miles east of Clevedon, on Bristol road

During the nineteenth century the little seaside village of Clevedon was transformed into a fashionable resort, with Italianate villas, a pier and a Royal Hotel, but the Eltons of Clevedon Court who had done so much to improve the town lived on in the remarkable medieval manor which Abraham Elton I, a wealthy Bristol merchant, had acquired in 1709.

Despite some later additions, Sir John de Clevedon's early fourteenth-century house has survived virtually unchanged, its buttressed walls and the portcullis groove on the projecting two-storey porch suggesting that he needed to build with defence in mind. Perhaps that is why he grafted his manor on to the even earlier massive four-storey tower which rises protectively from the north-east corner. Seen from the south, the low ranges and the steeply pitched roofs studded with tall chimneys are attractively set against the thick woods of Court Hill. Terraced gardens carved out of the hillside rise sharply behind the house, planted with tender shrubs and adorned with two eighteenth-century summerhouses.

Finely crafted fourteenth-century arches on the right of the traditional screens passage bisecting the house were openings to the medieval buttery, kitchen and pantry. To the left is the great hall, now embellished with an eighteenth-century coved ceiling and thickly hung with mostly indifferent portraits of the Eltons and their relations. Sir Abraham, the 1st Baronet, dressed in his scarlet robes as Mayor of Bristol, proudly surveys the descendants who were to enrich Clevedon with literary and artistic associations. A cartoon of William Makepeace Thackeray at the top of the stairs, a shock of white hair standing out from his head and pince-nez on his nose, recalls the novelist's friendship with Sir Charles, the 6th Baronet, a gifted poet whose elegy for his two drowned sons moved his contemporaries to tears. Sir Charles's youngest daughter Jane, with whom Thackeray fell hopelessly in love, was immortalised as Lady Castlewood in *Henry Esmond*, much of which was written in the house. The poet-baronet's circle also included Lamb and Coleridge, and his nephew Arthur Hallam was Tennyson's closest friend, for whom he composed 'In Memoriam'.

The family's artistic streak appeared again in Sir Edmund Elton, whose Eltonware pots and vases made of clay from the estate, mostly in rich, dark colours but including striking sea-blue pieces with metallic glazes, are displayed in the old kitchen and whose vivid portrait by Emmeline Deane hangs in the hall. This remarkable self-taught man began his career as a potter in about 1880, building up an international reputation for his work. Fragile glass walking sticks, some shot through with spirals and twists of colour, glass rolling pins and improbable pipes tinged rose-pink, crimson and blue are part of the collection of local Nailsea glass also shown in the house.

Another side of Victorian Britain emerges on the stairs, where boldly patterned wallpaper by G.F.Bodley shows off a number of prints and engravings illustrating triumphs of engineering in the late eighteenth and nineteenth centuries, from

A net of tracery marks the window of the tiny first-floor chapel at Clevedon Court. (*NT/Jeremy Whitaker*)

Abraham Darby's iron bridge at Coalbrookdale, constructed in the 1770s, to the Menai Strait, Severn and Clifton suspension bridges and a host of viaducts and aqueducts, their delicate arches carrying the railways and canals that were vital to the achievements of the age.

A tall red and green Eltonware candlestick, designed with Sir Edmund's characteristic flair and originality, stands in the tiny first-floor chapel of St Peter, originally consecrated in 1321. A net of stone tracery filling the south wall, with brilliantly coloured stained glass by Clayton and Bell, not only recalls the patron saint of fishermen to whom the chapel is dedicated but also the Bristol Channel only a mile or so to the west, where the little islands of Flat Holm and Steep Holm stand out black against the sea in the light of a setting sun.

Cleveland Hills   North Yorkshire

8 miles south-east of Middlesbrough

High above the Tees valley at Great Ayton stands Roseberry Topping, a 1,057-foot landmark and viewpoint with the same pyramidal outline as Blakey Topping (*see* Bridestones Moor, p.43) and giving wide views over Cleveland to the North Sea. The Trust owns over 300 acres here, including a brackeny expanse of common and the approach through an important pocket of natural oak woodland (Newton Wood and Cliff Ridge Wood) flanking the south-west slope of the hill, home to spotted woodpecker, pied flycatcher and tawny owl, and rich in woodland plants.

Ten miles to the south-west, above Osmotherley, Scarthwood Moor looks north-east, up the rim of the Cleveland range, and west to the Pennines. Half hidden in the heather are burial mounds from the Bronze Age and Mesolithic remains.

Cley Hill Wiltshire

3 miles west of Warminster, on the Somerset border, on north side of the A362

As one drives west from Warminster on the A362, there are signs of a great estate on every hand. The country is well farmed, the woods well managed, the farms and cottages sturdy and well maintained. The estate is Longleat, to the south of the road, and its spreading woods were once part of the ancient Forest of Selwood.

To the north of the road a green hump appears, rising 300 feet out of the surrounding cornfields and dominating the placid Corsley valley which lies between Warminster and Frome. While not exactly dramatic, it is certainly surprising and utterly fitting in this sylvan landscape. The history of the hill is written on its slopes for the enquiring eye to read. Its shape has been altered many times since the two bowl barrows were built in the Bronze Age. The men of the Iron Age followed by building one of their ubiquitous hill forts on its summit. In the Middle Ages the hill formed the hub of the common arable field of the manor of Corsley, the village to the north. This Great Field of Cley covered 420 acres when it was enclosed in 1783. In 1588 the hill was used as one of the chain of warning beacons lit to herald the arrival of the Spanish Armada. Finally, in 1807, substantial quarrying started, to provide lime for agricultural use, and this altered the northwest and south-west spurs of the hill.

From the top the views are east beyond Warminster to further hill forts at Battlesbury and Scratchbury above the Wylye valley, west across Frome into Somerset and south over Longleat.

Cliveden Buckinghamshire

3 miles upstream from Maidenhead, 2 miles north of Taplow on the B476 from the A4

This three-storey Italianate palace floating on a chalk terrace high above the River Thames is the masterpiece of Sir Charles Barry, built in 1850–1 for the Duke and Duchess of Sutherland. An inscription in letters eighteen inches high running below the urn-studded roofline parapet records the earlier building here which was destroyed by fire – a Restoration house by William Winde for the 2nd Duke of Buckingham, much of whose character Barry preserved – as well as the construction of the present mansion. Curved corridors link the main block to two eighteenth-century wings by Thomas Archer flanking a great sweep of gravel on the entrance front, from where the drive runs straight to a monumental marble fountain, its lines echoed in a mature avenue of limes. On the west side of the forecourt a rocket-like clock-tower rears up from the ornate stable court added in 1869.

From the south Cliveden is even more impressive. Here Barry's main block rises grandly over Winde's long arcaded terrace, twenty-eight arches wide, which extends far beyond it on either side. In the centre a double staircase descends in elegant elbows of stone to the celebrated Borghese balustrade, brought here from the Villa Borghese in Rome in 1896, with elaborate pedestals framing the central opening. Beyond is a closely mown grass terrace on which beds of cotton lavender and *Senecio* fringed with box hedges and punctuated by clipped yews form a geometrical parterre.

This parterre, with its sweeping views over the beech woods framing the Thames, is a foretaste of one of the Trust's largest and most varied gardens. Some traces still remain of Charles Bridgeman's early eighteenth-century layout for Lord George Hamilton, 1st Earl of Orkney, who bought Cliveden in 1696, such as the yew walks winding above the Thames to the west of the house, and the grass amphitheatre similar to the much larger example Bridgeman designed at Claremont (*see* p.73). Lord Orkney was also responsible for the two garden buildings by the Venetian Giacomo Leoni: a little temple with a green copper dome and the charming classical eyecatcher with an elaborate pedimented arched opening known as the Blenheim Pavilion.

The garden as it is today owes much to the 1st Viscount Astor, who bought the house in 1893. He introduced the Borghese balustrade, the Roman sarcophagi and the Italian sculpture which are such a feature of the grounds. He laid out the Italianate long garden, with statuary set along grassy walks bordered with box hedges and topiary, and the informal water garden, with stepping stones leading to a brightly painted pagoda on an island and banks crowded with colourful, moisture-loving plants – golden king cups in spring, primulas, irises and day lilies – and with Japanese azaleas and rhododendrons. Lord Astor also commissioned J. L. Pearson to remodel the interior of the house, but of the three rooms shown (the house is now a hotel), the most seductive is the breakfast room, lined with

Cliveden: tradition has it that the statesman George Canning used to sit for hours at this spot gazing at the River Thames framed by beech woods far below. (*NT/Angelo Hornak*)

The view north-west from the summit of the Cloud, a gritstone outlier on the western edge of the Pennines. (*NT/Kevin Richardson*)

mirrored, green and gold rococo panelling, brought from France.

The 2nd Viscount Astor and his wife Nancy, whose vivacious portrait by Sargent is a focal point of Pearson's low-ceilinged, oak-panelled hall, made Cliveden famous as a centre of literary and political society, entertaining Henry James, Rudyard Kipling, Curzon and Churchill here. Perhaps these distinguished guests liked to sit high above the Thames under the ancient tree known as Canning's Oak, drinking in the view of the river and its hanging woods which the statesman is said to have so much enjoyed.

The Cloud   Cheshire

3 miles east of Congleton

The view from the terrace at Tatton (*see* p.329), looks south-east over gently sloping parkland and woodland to a peak rising in the distance. This miniature mountain might have been placed there by 'Capability' Brown to give point to the view, and indeed it came to the Trust with Tatton. The Cloud rises sharply to 1,124 feet from the plain, its dark heather and screes of huge gritstone boulders making a sombre contrast with the fields and

hedgerows below. The views – South Lancashire to the north, the rich farmland round Nantwich to the west, the Potteries to the south and the Pennine range to the east – are outstanding.

Clouds Hill   Dorset

9 miles east of Dorchester, $\frac{1}{2}$ mile east of Waddock crossroads on the B3390, 1 mile north of Bovington Camp

T. E. Lawrence – better known as Lawrence of Arabia, the legend of the First World War – bought this little brick and tile cottage on the slopes of Clouds Hill as a retreat from nearby Bovington Camp when he rejoined the RAF in 1925. Its tiny rooms with their simple, even austere furnishings are as Lawrence left them, a direct reflection of his monastic way of life and complex personality. His books have gone from the shelves lining the downstairs room, but the wind-up gramophone with a huge horn on which he used to play Mozart and Beethoven still dominates the music room in the roof and his cell-like bedroom, lit by a porthole window, is as it was.

Here Lawrence would come to read or write by the fire whenever he could get away from the camp, finding the peace and quiet he needed to work on his

Lawrence of Arabia died at the early age of forty-six, killed in a crash on his motor-cycle while returning to his beloved Clouds Hill. (*NT*)

revision of *Seven Pillars of Wisdom*. Friends were served picnic meals washed down with water or Lawrence's own blend of China tea, but never with alcohol.

For Lawrence the cottage was an earthly paradise. Here he returned to live out his days on his discharge from the airforce in 1935 at the age of forty-six. Five days later he was dead, killed in a fatal crash when returning to the cottage from Bovington Camp on his motor-cycle.

Clumber Park Nottinghamshire

4½ miles south-east of Worksop, 6½ miles south-west of Retford, 1 mile from the A1 and the A57, 1 mile from the M1, junction 30

In the last 250 years Nottinghamshire has changed dramatically, much of its rural landscape scarred or obliterated by industrialisation and urban growth. This 4,000-acre park which once surrounded the country seat of the Dukes of Newcastle is an acute reminder of what has been lost, a mosaic of grassland, heath, farmland and wood, rich in butterflies and visited by some 130 species of birds.

At the heart of the park is an L-shaped serpentine ornamental lake, with wooded islands dotted down its length, part of Stephen Wright's landscaping scheme for the 4th Duke in the mid-eighteenth century. The classical eyecatchers – a balustraded bridge crossing the lake and a little Doric temple on the south shore – are also his, and so too are the decorative lodges and gate piers at the park's many entrances. An extensive grassy terrace running along the north shore of the lake lies at one end of William Sawrey Gilpin's Victorian pleasure grounds, with paths winding through glades of specimen trees underplanted with shrubs.

With the exception of the Duke's study, the grandiose Italianate mansion begun in 1767 to designs by Wright was largely demolished in 1938, its extent now outlined by paving stones in the grass. The attractive stable block to the north, with a cupola crowning the clock-tower, probably predates the house. Some 400 yards away, reached along a cedar avenue, superb late nineteenth-century glasshouses overlook the former walled kitchen garden, the central palm house projecting in a fan of glass. The fig house and vineries occupying one of the long glassy wings have now been replanted, and an orchard and fruit border have been established in the upper part of the garden. Belts and clumps of broadleaved woodland, including the great lime avenue running to Apleyhead Lodge, were also nineteenth-century plantings.

Like Studley Royal to the north (*see* p. 322), Clumber is crowned by a High Victorian Gothic chapel, built in 1886–9 by G. F. Bodley for the 7th Duke of Newcastle, who, like the 1st Marquess of Ripon at Studley, was a passionate Anglo-Catholic.

Heavily buttressed walls, tall Gothic windows and a soaring 180-foot spire give the chapel the look of a parish church. Inside, it seems like a miniature cathedral, the vaulted roof in shadow high above the nave. Six brass candlesticks stand conspicuously along the elaborately carved rood screen, and ornate Flemish-style chandeliers light the Rev. Ernest Geldart's walnut and oak choir stalls, with limewood musical angels looking down from crocketed canopies on either side. Stained glass by C. E. Kempe, rich tapestries and velvets and silk altar frontals, including an early work by J. N. Comper, complete a masterpiece of Gothic revival architecture.

Coggeshall Grange Barn Essex

South of Coggeshall, on B1024 to Kelvedon

This majestic building, with a sweeping tiled roof above weatherboarded walls, is the oldest timber-framed barn in Britain. Constructed for the Savigniac monks of Coggeshall Abbey, it was built very soon after the founding of the community in 1142, probably predating the abbey church. Although the barn was extensively rebuilt in the late fourteenth century, original posts still support the roof. Not far away is a thirteenth-century chapel which stood outside the abbey gate, and some other monastic buildings are now part of a nearby farm.

Coldrum Long Barrow Kent

Between the Pilgrims' Way and the A20 Folkestone road, 1 mile east of Trottiscliffe

This impressive prehistoric burial mound is crowned by a U of standing stones and surrounded by a ditch. Like many similar features in the west of England, it is prominently placed, lying near the prehistoric track following the crest of the North Downs, later the pilgrim route from Winchester to Canterbury. A mile to the east is Trottiscliffe church, where a cabinet displays some of the human bones found when Coldrum was excavated in 1910 and 1922.

Coleridge Cottage Somerset

At west end of Nether Stowey, on south side of the A39, 8 miles west of Bridgwater

The Ancient Mariner pub at the end of Lime Street flags the rather unprepossessing cottage across the road where the young Samuel Taylor Coleridge lived for three years from 1797 with his wife Sara and infant son Hartley. Once a pretty, low, thatched building, it was substantially altered at the end of the nineteenth century and only the four front rooms are relatively unchanged. Coleridge wrote some of his best poems here, including 'Fears in Solitude', 'This Lime Tree Bower My Prison', 'The Nightingale', 'Frost at Midnight', the first part of 'Christabel' and 'The Rime of the Ancient Mariner', with its many references to places in the neighbourhood. Here, too, he eagerly started to set down the opium-inspired 'Kubla Khan', the visionary epic which came to him in his sleep and which he was unfortunately prevented from completing while it was still fresh in his mind by the interruption of 'a person . . . from Porlock'.

Mementoes of the poet now displayed here include his massive boulle inkstand, locks of his hair and letters in his distinctive hand. There are pictures of the Devonshire village where he was born, the church where he was married, the room at No. 3 The Grove, Highgate, where he died, and also of friends and acquaintances, such as Dorothy and William Wordsworth. In the little garden at the back of the house the lime-tree bower of the poem has disappeared, but the bay tree still stands as it did when Coleridge dug this plot.

Coleton Fishacre Garden Devon

2 miles from Kingswear; take Lower Ferry road, turn off at tollhouse

One of the most delightful stretches of the South Devon coastal path follows the headlands fringing the Dart estuary, looking down over wooded slopes plunging precipitously into the sea. Just beyond Kingswear, near the mouth of the estuary, the path skirts this individual eighteen-acre garden lying in

a deep combe running down to the water. The ground slopes steeply, zig-zag paths and steps linking the different levels and formal terraced gardens descending into the valley near the house. The lower combe, best seen from the gazebo perched like a look-out post on the north side of the garden, is a vast natural amphitheatre, filled with colour in spring from a display of rhododendrons, azaleas, magnolias, dogwoods, camellias and Chilean fire trees. Beyond lies the sea, with views to the glistening humps of the Blackstone rocks and the Mewstone just offshore. Craggy natural rock outcrops within the garden and the steep faces of the quarry from which stone was taken for the house add to Coleton Fishacre's distinctive character.

A wide variety of rare and exotic trees and shrubs have all been planted since 1925 when the site was acquired by Rupert and Lady Dorothy d'Oyly Carte, beneficiaries of the opera company which was for years synonymous with performances of Gilbert and Sullivan's comic creations. They also established the shelter belts of Monterey pine and holm oak which now provide essential protection and commissioned the long, low house to designs by Oswald Milne, its mullioned windows, tall chimneys and steeply pitched roofs an echo of the work of Milne's mentor, Sir Edwin Lutyens. Softened by climbers and wall shrubs, such as wintersweet, the chocolate vine and Chilean jasmine, the grey façades provide an attractive, unobtrusive backdrop to the tender, sun-loving plants round the house, including California tree poppies, the banana-scented *Michelia*, the fragrant *Camellia sasanqua* and lemon verbena.

A few yards away a wall fountain in the enclosed Rill Garden feeds the gushing stream which cascades down the valley. Each of the terraces is also enhanced by water, arum lilies setting off the rounded contours of the Lutyens-inspired concave pool on the upper level. Two more pools interrupt the course of the little stream, the lower of them flanked by a grove of large, scented rhododendrons.

Throughout the garden there are mature specimen trees, such as the massive tulip tree and the dawn redwood and swamp cypress flanking the terrace path, or the tree of heaven, handkerchief trees and snowdrop tree below the gazebo. Above the dramatic rock outcrop known as Newfoundland in the lower valley is a graceful Kashmir cypress, too tender for most British gardens, a sweet gum and the golden rain tree, notable for its long yellow spires in late summer. Autumn is spectacular here, with scarlet Japanese maples along the stream leading a memorable display of coloured foliage and purple and red berries.

Combe Martin and the Hangman Hills Devon

On the north coast, between Combe Martin and Heddon's Mouth

Exmoor National Park, nearly 20 miles across at its widest point, narrows westward, with a boundary which runs into the sea just before the resort of Combe Martin. This western extremity has some of the most dramatic coast in Devon. The windswept, humpbacked ridge which follows all this coast here approaches closest to the sea, with long, steepening slopes above some of the highest cliffs in England.

The Trust owns some 400 acres east of Combe Martin, dominated by the brooding mass of the Great Hangman, 1,044 feet above the sea. Stand on its summit on a rough day and the sea, far below, looks scarcely ruffled. The old miners' track leading towards Blackstone Point below is not for anyone who suffers from vertigo. Silver, copper, lead and manganese have been dug here since the Middle Ages. The remains of former works are all around Combe Martin, and silver mining may account for the medieval grandeur of the Trust's West Challacombe farmhouse.

The walk to the top is strenuous, and for the less adventurous the pull up to the Little Hangman, to the west and closer to Combe Martin, will suffice. The views from both are very fine, not so much seaward – for the coast runs due east and west here – as inland into the heart of the moor. These sandstone hills are covered in heather, with patches of low-growing western gorse and bracken, and grassy areas grazed by sheep. Skylarks, wheatears and stonechats abound; ravens, crows and jackdaws tease each other endlessly as they wheel about.

Across Combe Martin Bay, and therefore just outside the boundary of the Exmoor National Park, is the beautiful Golden Cove, no longer accessible since the path down to it fell away a few years ago. A viewpoint above enables one to look down to what is now a wholly sequestered beach. (*See also* the Heddon Valley, Trentishoe and Woody Bay; Lynmouth; Holnicote Estate.)

Compton Castle Devon

At Compton, 4 miles west of Torquay, 1 mile north of Marldon

A delight of towers, battlements and buttresses, this fairy-tale castle hidden in a deep lush south Devon valley two miles from the sea seems to have strayed from the set of a remake of *Camelot*. A heavy wooden door in the north front leads into a stone-flagged rectangular courtyard, where the long south side is filled by a reconstructed medieval great hall rising two storeys to the roof. A spiral staircase gives access to a minstrels' gallery at one end. A little chapel running north and south closes the courtyard on the west. Five towers, all provided with garderobes, rear up from the house itself, and a sixth, the watch-tower, is set into the south-east corner of the twenty-foot-high curtain wall which extends the defences of the entrance front.

This magical fortified house, one of very few to survive so unaltered, was built between the fourteenth and sixteenth centuries. The fortifications date from the reign of Henry VIII, when the Gilbert family who had lived here from the mid-fourteenth century probably felt threatened by the French raids on Teignmouth a few miles north along the coast and on Plymouth to the west. Although the new defences did not make the manor impregnable, they would have deterred attack from a roving shore party.

The three Gilbert boys born in the mid-sixteenth century, half-brothers to Walter Raleigh, were among the small group of Westcountrymen who earned a place in the history of Elizabethan England. John, the eldest, who became Vice Admiral of the Western Coast, played a major part in the defences against the Armada, providing for a possible landing in Torbay. And it was he who reported to Sir Francis Walsingham the capture of the Spanish galleon *Rosario*, brought into harbour here by Walter Raleigh.

His younger brother Humphrey was one of the brave men who crossed the Atlantic in fragile ships in a wave of colonisation and expansion. Armed with the first Letters Patent granted by the Crown for the 'planting' of an English colony, he claimed Newfoundland for his queen on 5 August 1583, sadly drowning when his tiny ship *Squirrel* foundered on the return voyage (*see also* Trengwainton, p.338). His torch was picked up by his younger brother Adrian, who formed a group of adventurers which included Philip Sidney, Francis Drake, John Hawkyns and Martin Frobisher as well as his half-brother. Although the colony established by Sir Walter Raleigh in Virginia in 1585 foundered, it marked the birth of English-speaking America, thirty-five years before the Pilgrim Fathers set sail.

The confidence of the age, which elsewhere led to the building of prodigy houses such as Hardwick (*see* p.142), or Wollaton Hall in Nottinghamshire, here led men to risk their lives in a quest for new lands, preserving Compton Castle as an unaltered medieval manor. Sold by the Gilbert family in 1800, and neglected for about another century, the house was bought back in 1930 and meticulously restored by Commander and Mrs Walter Raleigh Gilbert, who refurnished it as a family home.

Coney Island Co. Armagh

In Lough Neagh close to the southern (Armagh) shore

The little wooded Coney Island, at the south end of Lough Neagh, is about a mile from Maghery, from which it can easily be reached by boat. It was once joined to the mainland by a causeway, parts of which may still be seen, and was inhabited in very early times. Recent excavations have revealed traces of Neolithic settlements. St Patrick is believed to have used it as a retreat, and the shape of an ancient round tower still stands. It was used as a stronghold by the O'Neills of Tyrone during the sixteenth century and possibly earlier. The thick belt of reeds which surrounds the island provides an ideal resting place for large numbers of waterfowl.

Coniston Valley Cumbria

In the southern lakes area, to the east of the Coniston Fells

Grassy meadows and deciduous woodland sweep gently up from the shores of Coniston Water, a serene landscape with prosperous-looking farms. The Trust owns two substantial outposts on the east shore: Park-a-Moor Fell, enclosed as a sheep run by Furness Abbey in 1339, the woods along the water's edge planted much later, and Nibthwaite Woods to the south, with the tiny Peel and Fir Islands offshore. The oak woods, so peaceful now, and supporting a wide range of mosses and lichens, were busy places until this century, playing their part in local industry. Coppiced at regular intervals, they

provided not only wood for fuel but bark for tanning leather and charcoal for smelting iron ore.

On the west bank, the Old Man of Coniston stretching away upward in the background, stands Coniston Hall, with a mile of lake shore. The Elizabethan farmhouse is but a fragment of a mansion built by the Fleming family, who moved to greater grandeur at Rydal a century later. Its attractive park-like meadows were disfigured by a large camping and caravanning site when the Trust acquired the farm in 1971. The tents and caravans are now hidden in Park Coppice Wood close by.

At the head of the lake is the glorious Monk Coniston estate. Partly bequeathed to the Trust by Beatrix Potter, it comprises 4,000 acres of farmland, woodland and fell on a more intimate scale than many of the Trust's holdings. Although the Tilberthwaite Fells run up 2,502 feet to Wetherlam, north of the Old Man, the estate includes the gentle Yewdale, the south side of Little Langdale, excellent woodland, gentle walks and the beautiful honeypot of Tarn Hows. This artificial lake, made and planted in the last century deliberately to enhance the landscape, has become the most-visited spot in the Lake District. It is a place for picnicking and taking gentle strolls. Heathery mounds, stretches of short turf and a light scattering of trees make it a perfect setting for a family outing. (*See also* Gondola, p.128; Borrowdale and Derwentwater; Buttermere, Crummock Water and Loweswater; Ennerdale; Eskdale and Duddon Valleys; Grasmere Valley, Rydal, Hawkshead and Sawrey; Great and Little Langdale; Ullswater, Hartsop, Brotherswater and Troutbeck; Wasdale; Windermere.)

Conwy Suspension Bridge Gwynedd

100 yards from Conwy town centre, adjacent to Conwy Castle

Increasing trade with Ireland in the late seventeenth and early eighteenth centuries meant that goods had to be carried to and from Holyhead along the appalling roads of North Wales, with the added hazards of ferries across the wide estuary of the Conwy as well as the Menai Strait, the only alternative being a journey fifteen miles or so upriver to the first bridge at Llanrwst. In 1811 the great engineer Thomas Telford, fifty-four years old and much in demand, was asked to survey a road to Holyhead. Now followed by the A5, this route through Snowdonia is a triumph, never exceeding the gradient of 1 in 50 over which a stagecoach could make a steady 10 miles an hour.

Six years later Telford designed a suspension bridge to carry the road across the Menai Strait, only the third to be built in the British Isles and closely following the pioneering Union Bridge over the Tweed. His scheme for Conwy came shortly afterwards, his early plan for conventional arches soon abandoned in favour of another suspension bridge. The site of the crossing is magnificent. On the wooded left bank of the river the bridge seems to spring from the rocky crag crowned with Conwy Castle, the masterpiece of Edward I's great castle-builder, Master James of St George, completed in 1288. With their battlements and machicolations, the 42-foot-high turrets supporting the road look like extensions of the castle itself. Between them stretches the 327-foot span of the bridge, suspended from the graceful curve of Telford's chains, probably the only original ones still surviving on such an early bridge.

The bridge was opened in 1826, the same year that the Menai Bridge was badly damaged in a storm, convincing the old engineer that a length of 600 feet was the limit (although the young Brunel's design for the Clifton Bridge over the Avon was to exceed this span in Telford's lifetime). The bridge

The battlements of Conwy Castle echo the castellations on the turrets of Telford's suspension bridge, its 327-foot span still supported by the original massive chains. (NT/ Alan North)

and toll-house have recently been restored to their nineteenth-century appearance, with a contemporary specification used to reconstruct the road surface.

Corfe Castle Dorset

On the A351 Wareham–Swanage road

Corfe's ruins rise like jagged teeth from the summit of a steep chalk hill, a splendid strategic site guarding the only natural route through the Purbeck Hills. Although now reduced to broken towers and walls, this monument to the power of medieval kings is still architecturally striking and still dominates the little village huddled below. Even today it is easy to understand why this most defensible of all English castles was eventually reduced not by might but by treachery.

Although there may have been a royal hunting lodge at Corfe in Saxon times and King Edward is traditionally said to have been murdered here in 978, the castle was begun by William the Conqueror, whose fortifications formed part of the network of carefully placed strongholds with which he consolidated his hold on his new kingdom. These early Norman defences were gradually strengthened, with wooden features such as the original timber palisade being slowly replaced in stone. The massive keep crowning the hilltop, still rising seventy feet in dramatic fingers of stone, was completed during the reign of Henry I, who imprisoned his elder brother Robert, Duke of Normandy here in 1106. The tower-studded curtain wall looping round the crest of the hill was a later addition, dating from the early years of the reign of King John (1199–1216), when Corfe's position so close to the south coast became of considerable importance in the renewed war with France. After the loss of Normandy in 1204, the castle was in the first line of the king's defences should Philip II try to cross the Channel.

In a time when kings would travel round their kingdoms administering justice and enforcing loyalty by their presence, Corfe was a centre for government and administration as well as a stronghold. Part of the huge sum of £1,400 spent on building operations at Corfe during John's reign went to construct the king's 'Gloriette', a tower-house arranged round a courtyard in the topmost inner ward. The quality of the surviving masonry

Corfe Castle from the north-east, showing the impressive remains of the keep crowning the hilltop and a surviving stretch of curtain wall. (*NT/Martin Trelawny*)

shows that this was a building of distinction, a compactly planned domestic residence fit for a monarch, with a great hall, chapel and parlour, and chambers for the queen overlooking a garden.

Apart from a brief period in the mid-sixteenth century, Corfe remained in royal hands until it was sold by Elizabeth I to Sir Christopher Hatton, who mounted cannon on the walls in anticipation of the Spanish invasion. Some fifty years later the castle and estate were bought by Sir John Bankes, a staunch Royalist, who also purchased the neighbouring property of Kingston Lacy (*see* p.167). Of major strategic importance to both sides in the Civil War, Corfe was twice besieged. In 1643 Lady Bankes, who must have been a woman of strong character, held the castle against a force of local Parliamentarians in her husband's absence, but in the winter of 1645–6 Corfe was again attacked and fell through the treachery of one of the defenders.

The victorious Roundhead colonel, impressed by Lady Bankes's courage, not only allowed the garrison to depart but permitted his spirited opponent to take the keys of the castle with her, now to be seen hanging in the library at Kingston Lacy. Corfe's defences were savagely destroyed, leaving only the romantic remnants immortalised in Turner's evocative watercolour.

Cornish Coast

See North Cornish Coast, p.214, and South Cornish Coast, p.299.

Cornish Engines

At Pool, 2 miles west of Redruth on either side of the A3047

The tall outlines of ruined engine houses standing high up on windswept moorland or perched on lonely clifftop sites are romantic reminders of the great days of the Cornish mining industry in the mid-nineteenth century. At the height of the boom the population of the county almost doubled as newcomers flooded in to provide the manpower needed for the extraction of rich sources of tin, copper and china clay. Now only a few mines remain open, but the technology refined here was exported all over the world, from South America to Australia.

The key to the growth of the Cornish mining industry was the expiry of the patent on the Boulton and Watt steam engine in 1800. Developed in the coal-rich areas of the north, where fuel efficiency was not a prime consideration, this engine was expensive to run in the south-west where all coal had to be brought over the sea from Wales. The moment restrictions were removed, Cornish engineers – in particular Richard Trevithick (1771–1833), the first to realise the potential of high-pressure steam – set about producing more efficient engines, leading to the establishment of a number of great engine-building firms, such as Holman's of Camborne and Harvey's of Hayle. Necessity was the mother of invention, giving Cornwall the lead in mining technology that it was to hold for half a century.

The Trust owns several survivals from this great chapter in Cornish history. At the East Pool and Agar mine, straddling the A3047, is the largest of the great beam engines left in Cornwall, commissioned from Harvey's in 1891 and put to work here in 1925. With a gleaming cylinder seven feet in diameter and a huge beam weighing some fifty-two tons, this monster could lift 450 gallons of water a minute from a depth of 1,700 feet. The 1853 engine designed by a pupil of Trevithick at South Crofty tin and arsenic mine about a mile to the south-west could operate at even greater depths, raising 340 gallons a minute from 2,000 feet.

A working example of the rotative engines normally used for lifting men and materials survives at the East Pool mine, where F. W. Michell's 1887 engine made by Holman's is now powered by electricity. Francis Michell, another member of the engineering family, designed the machinery built by Harvey's in 1840 at the Levant mine north of St Just. Once again worked by steam, it is the oldest surviving beam engine in Cornwall and is memorably sited in a cliff-edge boiler house. A number of empty engine houses in the Trust's care stand in similarly dramatic situations. Wheal Prosper domi-

Towanroath engine house, romantically sited high above the sea on the north Cornish coast, is one of a number of ruined engine houses in Devon and Cornwall recalling a once prosperous mining industry. Massive rocking beams pivoted on a strengthened wall worked drainage pumps or powered winding or crushing machinery.
(*NT/Mike Williams*)

nates the cliff above Porthcew Cove, while Towan-roath engine house at Chapel Porth is perched on a ledge several hundred feet above the sea. Equally romantic is Wheal Betsy, set on lonely Black Down on the west edge of Dartmoor, its tall chimney a conspicuous sight from the A386 to Okehampton. Richard Trevithick's whitewashed thatched cottage at Lower Penponds, Camborne, from where he departed for the silver mines of Peru in 1816, is also Trust property.

Cotehele House Cornwall

On west bank of the Tamar, 1 mile west of Calstock by footpath (6 miles by road), 8 miles south-west of Tavistock

The River Tamar which divides Devon and Cornwall has proved the most effective natural boundary in England. Until the opening of the suspension bridge between Plymouth and Saltash at the mouth of the river in 1962, there was no road link below Gunnislake, fifteen miles upstream as the crow flies but almost double that distance following the twists and turns of the river. For the villages and hamlets along its banks, the Tamar was for centuries the only effective route to the outside world. So it was for this Tudor courtyard house built by Sir Richard Edgcumbe and his son Sir Piers between 1485 and *c*.1540.

Low granite ranges set round three courtyards lie at the head of a steep valley running down to the river, woodland on either side sheltering a luxuriant garden where palms, rhododendrons, azaleas, ferns and the umbrella-like *Gunnera manicata* thrive in the exceptionally mild climate. A domed dovecote and a stewpond near the house provided meat and fish for what was a largely self-sufficient community.

Cotehele quay, an example of the many which once lined the river, lies a quarter of a mile downstream. Described in 1819 as 'a very large and commodious quay with a most desirable situation on the river', the old grey stone buildings restored by the Trust are still impressive, one of them now housing an offshoot of the National Maritime Museum. A sign advertises the Edgcumbe Arms, now a restaurant, and *Shamrock*, one of the last surviving Tamar sailing barges, is berthed here (*see* p.286). The quays saw some of their busiest years at the end of the nineteenth century, when strawberries and other soft fruit from growers in the valley were taken over the river to Bere Alston

The medieval dovecote and stewpond in Cotehele's sheltered valley garden once provided meat and fish for a largely self-sufficient community. (*NT*)

station on the new Plymouth–Tavistock line. During the previous decade there had been shipments of ore from Cotehele Consols in the steep-sided wooded Danescombe valley upstream, one of over a hundred mines which exploited rich sources of copper and arsenic along the Tamar valley, its site now marked by grassy humps and some old mine buildings. The mining industry was already declining when Cotehele Consols was at its peak of production in 1844–70, and by the early years of the twentieth century many miners were seeking work overseas, some of them setting out for America as steerage passengers on the ill-fated *Titanic*.

The spruced-up buildings of Cotehele quay bear no traces of this industrial past, but hidden in the woodland across a reedy inlet to one side are the remains of a row of huge lime kilns, the arched openings which are now romantically shrouded in greenery once a source of lethal fumes. A path from here leads through woodland up the tributary valley of the River Morden to another picturesque group of estate buildings, including a three-storey eighteenth-century mill powered by an overshot wheel.

Here, too, are a wheelwright's shop, with a lathe driven by a huge flywheel, a forge where charcoal smoulders gently in the hearth, a saddler's shop filled with harness, lengths of chain and stirrups, and a sawpit and carpenter's shop.

A steep wooded ride takes visitors back to the house, past Sir Richard's massively buttressed barn flanking the route to the battlemented gateway tower. This medieval approach, the arch of the gateway just wide enough to admit a loaded packhorse, signals the character of the house, left largely undisturbed for over 200 years from the end of the seventeenth century, when the family chose to live at Mount Edgcumbe, their grander seat overlooking Plymouth Sound. The rooms are small and mostly dark, reached by flights of worn stone steps and through massive wooden doors in granite archways. Three Tudor windows light the dais end of Sir Richard's medieval great hall, with an oak refectory table marooned in the middle of the rough stone floor and whitewashed walls rising the height of the house to a decorative timber roof. Adam and Eve are carved on one of the early seventeenth-century chairs at either end of the table, and the walls are hung with a collection of arms and armour which includes Elizabethan matchlocks, Civil War breastplates and lobster-tail helmets, and some exotic pieces, such as long Indian swords and an Arab musket.

The family chambers, warmed by large Tudor fireplaces and with richly coloured hangings used like wallpaper, are far more inviting. On the bright late seventeenth-century bacchic tapestries adorning the little Punch Room, naked figures treading huge vats of grapes as if indulging in a communal bubble bath are clearly preparing a vintage to fill the arched niches in the cupboard-like wine cellar in one corner. In the Red Room upstairs, rich crimson drapery on the huge four-poster is set off by faded seventeenth-century arras on the walls, children at play with marbles and hoops on three of the panels contrasting with the scene of nightmarish violence by the bed illustrating the death of Remus. Across the landing a steeply winding stair leads to two bedrooms at the top of the three-storey battlemented tower added in 1627.

Although the east front was rebuilt in 1862, the new work blends harmoniously with the Tudor ranges behind. Two magnolias, one newly planted, frame the view down the valley garden from three long terraces created at the same time. Above the house is the walled upper garden, with lawns and specimen trees round a lily pond. Across a field from here granite pinnacles and dummy Gothic windows mask a triangular prospect tower, perhaps built to celebrate the visit of King George III and Queen Charlotte in August 1789. The panorama from the top looks west to Kit Hill and east to Dartmoor, beyond the graceful arches of the Calstock viaduct in the valley below, part of a new railway opened in 1908 whose advent killed the river traffic.

Cotswolds Gloucestershire

Between Stratford-upon-Avon, to the north, and Wotton-under-Edge, to the south

Travelling south down the M5, or on the A46 from Stratford-upon-Avon, the Cotswold scarp closes the view eastward for fifty miles to Wotton-under-Edge. The Trust's flag flies at Hidcote (*see* p.149), Snowshill (*see* p.297) and at five other places.

Dover's Hill rises above Weston-sub-Edge on the A46. Steep pasture with a woodland fringe, it forms a natural amphitheatre, but it would be no more than an incident in the escarpment if it did not commemorate Captain Robert Dover (1575–1641). A jolly, sporting lawyer, who thought life ought to be fun, he was licensed by James I to found the 'Cotswold Olimpicks'. When they started in 1612, the Games were a great success. Events included cudgel-play, wrestling, jumping, pitching the hammer, balloon (a mixture of football and handball), hare-hunting, horse racing, virgins dancing for prizes and much feasting and drinking. Banned by the Puritans when they came to power, the Games were brought back with the Restoration of 1660, and continued until 1852. They have been revived in recent years and are now re-enacted on the Friday following the spring bank holiday. Dover's Hill is a good place to walk, if steep, with views over the Vale of Evesham.

Forming a spur north of Birdlip, below the B4070, is Crickley Hill, where the Trust has joined its sixty-seven acres with seventy-eight belonging to the County Council to make a country park. Trails illustrate archaeology (Neolithic, Iron Age and post-Roman settlements), geology (oolitic limestone with outcrops of pea grit) and ecology (beech woodland and lime-rich grassland). There are spectacular views over the Severn Vale to the Malvern and the Welsh Hills.

Haresfield Beacon stands proud above the headwaters of the Severn estuary. The steeply wooded slopes, with miles of paths, run south past Shortwood (with a topograph delineating the views) to the big Standish Wood which overlooks Randwick and Ruscombe on the outskirts of Stroud.

The Trust began work at Rodborough and Minchinhampton in 1913, when the large commons were threatened by quarrying. There was a local uproar, a committee was set up, money raised and land bought and vested in the Trust. Substantial additions totalling nearly 1,000 acres have been made since, much of it high and windswept land forming an invaluable series of open spaces close to the industrial towns of Stroud and Nailsworth.

Nine miles west of Gloucester, May Hill rises to 969 feet, though the clump of trees at its summit does not belong to the Trust. The wooded and heathy skirts of the hill are attractive, there are plenty of paths, and the view from the top stretches for miles around.

Coughton Court Warwickshire

2 miles north of Alcester on east side of the A435

Only an expanse of meadow separates Coughton Court from the main Studley to Alcester road, giving passing motorists a memorable view of the great Tudor gatehouse dominating the entrance façade. Dating from the early years of Henry VIII's reign, when even in remote countryside on the southern fringes of the Forest of Arden men could at last build to please themselves rather than to protect their property, the gatehouse is a glittering glass lantern, the gleaming panes of a two-storeyed oriel window stretching the width of the two upper floors. Though Sir George Throckmorton thought it prudent to surround his new house with a moat, this may also have been regarded as a status symbol rather than as a purely defensive device. Late Tudor ranges flank the grassy lavender-fringed courtyard reached through the gatehouse passage, their domestic gabled façades covered with roses and other climbers and their half-timbered upper storeys a direct contrast with the stone splendour of the gatehouse. Yew-framed lawns at the back of the house lead down to the little River Arrow and peaceful wooded countryside beyond.

The Throckmortons first came to Coughton in 1409 and much of the fascination of the house derives from its continued association with this prominent Roman Catholic family. Increasingly prosperous during the fifteenth and sixteenth centuries, they were to pay a high price for their faith during the reign of Elizabeth I and the years that followed. Sir Nicholas Throckmorton, previously Ambassador to France, was imprisoned by the queen for his friendship with Mary Queen of Scots and his nephew executed for plotting to replace Elizabeth with her cousin. Another nephew, Thomas, was more circumspect. Although he lent Coughton to the conspirators in the Gunpowder Plot, he took care to be absent on the night of 5 November 1605 when an anxious group waited in one of the gatehouse rooms to hear news of the venture.

Like Baddesley Clinton only a few miles to the north-east (*see* p.18), Coughton was a refuge for recusants. The mass continued to be celebrated here and priests were concealed in ingenious hiding places, such as that discovered in the north-east turret, furnished with a bed and a folding leather altar. Another reminder of these times is the painted canvas hanging in the Tower Room displaying the arms of all the Catholic gentry imprisoned for recusancy during Elizabeth's reign.

Staunchly Royalist during the Civil War, the Throckmortons' loyalty was tested when the house was besieged and occupied by Parliamentary troops in 1643, the rising ground where the Roundhead army placed their guns only too visible in the view west from the top of the gatehouse tower. Two generations later the entire east side of the courtyard

The domestic half-timbered façades flanking the courtyard of Coughton Court contrast with Sir George Throckmorton's grand stone gatehouse. (*NT/Nick Meers*)

was destroyed when Coughton was sacked by a Protestant mob running wild after the flight of James II and it was never subsequently rebuilt. A number of mementoes in the house, including the shift in which Mary Queen of Scots was beheaded as well as locks of hair from the Old and Young Pretenders, recall the Throckmortons' allegiance to the Stuart cause.

In later years the family fortunes revived, partly through prudent marriages. The stone-built Gothick wings on either side of the gatehouse were added in the 1780s and the moat was filled in shortly afterwards. A mid-Victorian Roman Catholic chapel a few yards away from the house is one of the family's last and most interesting additions. Standing cheek by jowl with the ancient parish church just to the south, these three buildings are an enduring reminder of the divisions bred by religion.

The Courts Wiltshire

In the middle of Holt village, 2½ miles east of Bradford-on-Avon, on south side of the B3107

Like many of the Trust's gardens, The Courts has been created in the twentieth century. The skeleton of the garden, a largely formal layout with hedged compartments in the style of Hidcote or Sissinghurst (*see* pp.149 and 291), was partly established by the architect Sir George Hastings in the early years of the century. He planned backdrops of clipped yew to show off the stone statues which are now such a feature of The Courts, and he was also responsible for the little stone temple and the pretty eighteenth-century conservatory.

Lady Cecilie Goff, who came here with her husband in 1920, created the present seven-acre garden around the structure left by Sir George. Her lavish and varied planting schemes with subtly blended colours and textures fill long herbaceous borders in the style of Gertrude Jekyll. Beds of floribunda roses hedged with clipped yew set off a rectangular lily pond, and more water-loving plants thrive round a small lake. There are yew- and holly-hedged vistas, fine trees, and spacious lawns, and as a backdrop the eighteenth-century stone house on which the garden is centred.

The Mexican red-ink plant seen throughout the garden, its maroon-black fruits yielding a dark and potent crimson dye, is one of several reminders of The Courts's close connections with the West Country wool trade. As its name suggests, weavers brought disputes for arbitration here until the end of the eighteenth century; although the watermill which stood by the house has been demolished, the dyeing pond and the stone pillars between which wool was once hung on chains to dry have been incorporated in the garden.

Clipped yew gives the garden at The Courts an architectural framework. (*NT/Fay Godwin*)

Richard Norman Shaw's last addition to Cragside, a monumental drawing-room, is dominated by W.R. Lethaby's huge Renaissance-style marble fireplace at one end. (*NT/Charlie Waite*)

Cragside Northumberland

13 miles south-west of Alnwick on the B6341 and 15 miles north-west of the Morpeth–Wooler road

When the inventor and industrialist William Armstrong made a nostalgic visit to Rothbury in 1863 as a break from the unrelenting pressures of his factory on the River Tyne, he determined to purchase what he could of the secluded Debdon valley where he had so often wandered as a boy. Four years earlier he had seen the army adopt the new gun he had

developed after the poor British performance in the Crimean War, initiating the transformation of his works from a prosperous engineering firm to a vast industrial concern. Once primarily concerned with hydraulic machines, by the late nineteenth century Armstrong's was an international arms manufacturer, rivalled only by Krupps of Germany.

A couple of watercolours showing tall chimneys belching smoke over factory buildings ranged along the Tyne are the only direct reminders of the works which financed the rambling house set high above a ravine on the Debdon burn, with a jumble of gables, soaring chimneys, mullioned windows and half-timbering framed against a wooded hillside. But there are other pointers to the inventive mind of the man who built it. This was the earliest house in the world to be lit by hydro-electricity and water was also used to power a sawmill, a revolutionary hydraulic lift and even a kitchen spit.

Armstrong's activities are reflected too in the gradual transformation of the modest weekend retreat he had built in 1864–6. Shortly afterwards he engaged the distinguished architect Richard Norman Shaw, who over the next fifteen years turned Cragside into a country mansion and enriched it with some of his most original work. Shaw's grandest rooms were designed for important overseas clients. The King of Siam, the Shah of Persia and the Crown Prince of Afghanistan all slept in the monumental black walnut bed with solemn owls carved on the end posts and a massive half-tester which Shaw created for the guest chambers. No doubt they appreciated the plumbed-in washstand and the sunken bath in an alcove in the dressing-room next door. A long top-lit gallery, with a wooden barrel ceiling and portraits and sculpture set against deep-red walls, leads from the Owl Suite to Shaw's *tour de force*, the drawing-room completed for a royal visit in 1884. The top-lit cavernous interior is dominated by W. R. Lethaby's monumental, Renaissance-style carved marble chimney-piece, with sinuous veining in the stone round the fireplace suggesting running water. Inglenooks with cosy red leather settees are set incongruously on either side and fragile white lamps hang in clusters from the ceiling like bunches of snowdrops.

The little rooms of the original lodge and Shaw's early additions for the family are quite different in character. His beautiful and unusual library with magnificent views of the glen is perhaps the most harmonious room in the house, the warm reds and browns of the furnishings setting off brilliant-blue tiles framing the fireplace and glowing enamelled lamps along the low bookcases.

Armstrong alone seems to have been responsible for Cragside's wildly romantic setting, blasting the hillside to expose craggy rock formations and creating over 1,700 acres of pleasure grounds by planting millions of conifers, rhododendrons and alpines on what were originally bare slopes. A pinetum was established in the valley, the mature trees here now including a western hemlock, a white Colorado fir and other conifers from western North America which are among the largest in Britain, as well as outstanding specimens of oriental and tiger-tail spruces and Caucasian, Spanish and Grecian firs. Badly overgrown when the Trust took over Cragside, the grounds have now been renovated and the three-acre rock garden on the steep slope below the house, like a giant scree above the burn, has been cleared and replanted with heathers, alpines and shrubs. Before the trees grew up, the views westward from the house took in the terraced garden laid out on a south-facing slope on the other side of the valley. Reached along a steep path up from the stream, this ordered space points up the wild romanticism of the glen. Formal and contained, it includes ferneries, a fruit house and an Italian garden, and looks out over gently undulating parkland. An intricate network of paths snakes across the estate, the higher routes along the summit of the crags above the house giving dramatic views to the Cheviots, and a scenic drive of some six miles follows the perimeter of the landscaped grounds, taking in the lakes 340 feet above the house which were used to feed the hydro-electric turbine.

Cregennan Gwynedd

1 mile east of Arthog on the A493

The Cadair Idris mountains are perhaps best known after Snowdonia, and more accessible, being between the A487 and the A493 running along the south side of the Mawddach estuary. The Trust owns two substantial holdings here: Bryn Rhug, adjoining the Tan y Gadair sheepwalk on the north side of Cadair Idris, and, below the Chair of Idris, Llyn y Gadair itself. To the west, along the mountain road which rises to 750 feet above the estuary, is Cregennan, comprising two hill farms, two lakes and lovely mountainy land. The views – up to Cadair, down to Barmouth and across Cardigan Bay to the Llŷn peninsula – are superb and this is a perfect place for those whose scrambling days are over.

Croft Ambrey Hereford & Worcester

Above Croft Castle, 6½ miles south-west of Ludlow, 2¼ miles north-east of Mortimer's Cross, 1 mile east of the A4110 and Yatton

A path from Croft Castle (*see below*) leads up through a conifer plantation to this spectacularly sited Iron Age hill fort at a height of 1,000 feet on the hill above. A triple ring of banks and ditches encloses a roughly triangular area of thirty-two acres, with some additional defences on the most vulnerable southern side. Granaries and storage pits and a quantity of ironwork and decorated bronze have been found within the ramparts, evidence of occupation from about the fourth century BC until *c.*AD 50, when the Romans finally conquered Wales. The views from the fort are stunning: south over the wooded border country and west into Wales, where the hills fade ridge behind ridge into the distance.

Croft Castle Hereford & Worcester

5 miles north-west of Leominster, 9 miles south-west of Ludlow

Croft Castle is a fortress that has been gradually transformed into a country house. For centuries after the Croft family came here from Normandy some years before the Conquest, this glorious country on the Welsh borders was torn by the endless struggles and rebellions of the Marcher

Delightful Gothick details at Croft Castle include this ecclesiastical plaster decoration and the cluster columns forming the newel posts of the stair balustrade. (*NT/Jeremy Whitaker*)

lords. The four-square castle round a central courtyard built to defend the Crofts' rights and property still forms the shell of the house. Battlemented towers guarding the corners and the weathered stone of the massive external walls evocatively recall a less civilised age. The illusion of a stronghold is fostered by the convincingly medieval archway on the approach to the house, probably built in the 1790s. Even the Georgian sash windows and the delightful Gothick bays flanking the mock-Jacobean castellated porch cannot disguise what Croft once was.

The country house takes over inside. Thomas Farnolls Pritchard, the Shrewsbury architect who designed the world's first iron bridge at Coalbrookdale, was responsible for the delightful Gothick interiors introduced in 1765, his pointed arches in white plaster on a coffee background on the stairs strongly reminiscent of a row of church windows. Even the stair balustrade looks ecclesiastical: column clusters forming the newel posts are miniature versions of those which might support the vaulting of a nave. Rare and valuable furniture in the same style includes a set of Gothick chairs in dark oak with cluster-column legs and high pointed backs in the long gallery, suitable props for a dramatisation of Mary Shelley's *Frankenstein* or Horace Walpole's *The Castle of Otranto*. T. F. Pritchard also had a hand in the similarly striking but quite different decoration of the Blue Room, where *trompe-l'oeil* gold rosettes stud blue Jacobean panelling. Family portraits hang in almost every room, including a beautiful study by Gainsborough of Elizabeth Cowper, wife of Sir Archer Croft, the colours all brown and red, and works by Lawrence and Philip de Laszlo. Crofts also dominate the little church of rough local stone only a few yards from the house, where the many family memorials are crowned by a splendid early sixteenth-century altar tomb to Sir Richard and Dame Eleanor Croft, with realistic effigies showing the couple in extreme old age.

Thickly wooded parkland surrounds the castle, as it has done for centuries, the great avenues for which Croft is famous including a line of Spanish chestnuts stretching about half a mile to the west, in which some of the trees are perhaps 350 years old, and oaks and beeches flanking the long entrance drive. The ancient lime avenue which once shadowed the chestnuts has now been replanted. While most of the park escaped the attentions of an

93

improver of the 'Capability' Brown school, the late eighteenth-century landscaping of Fish Pool Valley in the Picturesque mode was a direct reaction to his ideas. This little steep-sided glen planted with mixed deciduous and evergreen trees has a dramatic wilderness quality that Brown would have hated but which is in perfect accord with the castle's Gothick interiors. Another notable feature of the 1,500-acre estate is the Iron Age hill fort of Croft Ambrey, set on a ridge a mile north of the house (*see above*).

Crom Estate Co. Fermanagh

3 miles west of Newtownbutler on the Newtownbutler–Crom road

The 1,900-acre Crom estate is a patchwork of land and water, an intricate pattern of amoeba-like islands and peninsulas separated by fingers of upper Lough Erne. Patches of cultivated land and pasture come down to the water, but the shores are mostly wooded, the varied outlines and contrasting foliage of oak, ash, beech, alder, willow, spruce and pine mirrored in the tranquil waters. Yellow and white water lilies flower profusely in summer and the rare marsh pea can be seen in the extensive banks of reeds. Wood and water birds thrive here, including a flock of the whooper swan, while feral roe deer and the red Irish hare bound away from approaching visitors.

At the centre of the estate lies the massive limestone pile of Crom Castle (not owned by the Trust), built in 1832–8 for the 3rd Earl of Erne by Edward Blore, whose assemblage of turrets, bay windows, oriels and gables fully justifies Mark Girouard's description of his work as 'gently Picturesque and gently Elizabethan'. Crowning a slight prominence in the park, the castle looks magnificent from a distance, seeming to rise out of the trees which surround it. Just below the house are a charming gabled boathouse, also designed by Blore, with a slipway into the lough, and a small Gothic teahouse placed to look over the water.

A number of other eyecatchers were added in the 1840s, most notably the round battlemented Crichton Tower like a dark finger on the tiny patch of Gad Island. A schoolhouse nestles against the trees on the Corlatt peninsula, the children who came by boat to the landing places on the shore below perhaps being ferried in a traditional Fermanagh cott. (One of these boats now waits to transport passengers from the cobbled causeway on Inisherk Island over the lough to the mid-nineteenth-century church on the Derryvore peninsula.) Nearer Crom Castle itself, the remains of a once-formidable façade stretching skywards mark the defended tower-house built here in 1610, said to have been destroyed by fire in 1764 and developed as a Picturesque folly in the nineteenth century.

This romantic landscape with its varied woodland may reflect the influence of the painter and garden designer William Sawrey Gilpin, whose uncle the Rev. William Gilpin was one of the great pioneers of the Picturesque movement. As at Scotney (*see* p.282), where he was employed some five years after Castle Crom was begun, Gilpin may have advised on the siting of the house and the vistas leading to it, and may have suggested the mixed planting which now contributes so much to the appeal of the place. He may also have had a hand in embellishing the seventeenth-century formal gardens laid out near the tower-house, although little of these now remains apart from two ancient yews, their tangled stems and branches supporting a vast tent of foliage. Like the rest of the estate, these ruined gardens are a haven for wildlife, many of the woodland and water species found at Crom, such as the purple-hairstreak butterfly or the silver-washed fritillary, rarely seen elsewhere in the British Isles.

Crom Castle: the tower on Gad Island seen through the ruins of the tower house. (*NT*)

Mellow gas lights, coloured glass, gleaming wood and the heraldic beasts guarding the row of snugs opposite the bar all contribute to the Crown Liquor Saloon's individual atmosphere. (*NT*)

Crook's Peak, Wavering Down and Shute Shelve Hill Somerset

West of Axbridge, off the A38

The Trust owns 725 acres of steep southern slopes at the western end of the Mendips, where the hills form an extensive area of rolling downland above the Somerset Levels. A landscape of combes and spurs with some craggy outcrops, much is sheep-grazed grassland, rich with butterfly-attracting flowers and herbs. There is some ancient woodland, marked by old pollards and boundary banks and including an unusual stand of yew, and pockets of heath. Rising to 763 feet at Winscombe Hill, this is a place for a brisk walk and for extensive views over Somerset and the Bristol Channel, with the M5 plunging dramatically through the ridge at Loxton Gap below.

Crown Liquor Saloon Belfast

Great Victoria Street, Belfast

The Crown Liquor Saloon glitters and gleams. Coloured glass in bright blues, oranges and reds sparkles behind the bar, mirrors reflect tilework and polished wood, and the shiny finish on the moulded ceiling is a kaleidoscope of changing patterns set up by the lively clientele below. Originally the Railway Tavern, designed to serve thirsty travellers disgorged from the terminus of the Great Northern railway across the street, the Crown was renamed in 1885 and remodelled in 1898 to produce this High Victorian fantasy, one of the greatest late nineteenth-century public houses in the British Isles.

Classical pilasters, a parapet topped with urns and a portico crowned with finials and supported by cast-iron columns add theatrical touches to the exterior, suggesting an affinity with Frank 'Matchless' Matcham's opera house only a few yards away. Inside, the Crown offers opportunities for general conviviality and secluded intimacy. A long bar runs down one side of the room, its inward curve designed for the comfort of those perched on stools along its length. Facing the bar is a row of snugs enclosed by screens of wood and coloured glass, their upholstered benches and fitted tables an echo of the railway carriages which once ground to a halt nearby. With the door shut against the noisy crowd outside, the snugs become private drinking compartments, each one guarded by crouching heraldic beasts carrying shields with Latin mottoes. Mellow gas lights, bar staff in waistcoats and bow ties and a menu board offering Irish broth and oysters in season all contribute to the Crown's individual atmosphere, a jewel of a pub in a city which boasts places of refreshment on almost every corner.

Cwmdu Dyfed

7 miles north of Llandeilo, off B4302

Deep in Welsh-speaking Wales, in a countryside of green hills, steep narrow lanes and scattered farms and dwellings, is the small hamlet of Cwmdu. In 1991 the Trust acquired the little late Georgian terrace beside the youthful River Dulais which forms the focal point of the community. Of rough stone and slate in the Welsh vernacular tradition, and washed a warm rich yellow, the terrace consists of two tiny one-up, one-downs, originally intended for agricultural workers, a village shop and a small inn that was once a farmhouse, with a lean-to stable. A riverside garden across the street still has the original stone-built lavatory range, with two 'two-holers', and the terrace is flanked, at one end, by an eighteenth-century chapel and graveyard, at the other by the chapel vestry. Here, in this small cluster of buildings, are all the elements – non-conformist chapel, vestry, pub and shop – which have fostered the distinctive Welsh identity and sense of community.

After a break of over ten years, both shop and inn are once again going concerns with the latter being run on traditional informal lines. As was the custom in rural Wales, there is no bar: beer is tapped straight from the barrel into enamel jugs, and served to customers sitting on settles and benches in what was the farmhouse parlour.

Danbury and Lingwood Commons Essex

5 miles east of Chelmsford, astride the A414

The large villages of Danbury and Little Baddow are now virtually a suburb of Chelmsford. To the west of Little Baddow the 110 acres of Blake's Wood, a chestnut and hornbeam coppice with plenty of footpaths, provide good walking, despite the damage of the Great Storm of 1987. Close at hand is Lingwood Common, at the north end of the sandy, gravelly ridge between Chelmsford and Maldon, one of the few pieces of higher ground in this part of Essex. Grazing of the common died out in the early 1920s and oak and silver birch, with pleasant grassy glades, now cover much of it.

The larger Danbury Common, at the south end of the ridge, is more open, but even here the bracken, broom and gorse are giving way to self-seeded birch and oak. The heather areas are now being reinstated by careful management. Danbury is only five miles from the head of the Blackwater estuary (*see* p.31), twelve miles from the sea coast, and, during the Napoleonic Wars when Boney was expected to invade at any moment, the east side of the common became a military camp. The site survives as a grassy open space. History repeated itself during the Second World War when Hitler failed as Boney had done, and even today the army still sometimes uses the common for training.

Dartmouth and its approaches
Devon

On the south coast, between Brixham, to the east, and Little Dartmouth, to the south-west

While Dartmouth and the coast on either side of its estuary are of great beauty, the Trust owned nothing here for most of its existence. As a deliberate act of policy, following the initial success of Enterprise Neptune, the Regional Committee decided to seek to acquire the approaches from the sea on either side of the harbour. Between 1970 and 1987 this major project was virtually completed.

The Trust now owns not only some six miles of this coast but also substantial areas of farmland behind it, particularly east of the River Dart, thus enabling the way to the coast to be made beautiful by the removal of eyesores, the planting of trees and the replacement of hedges, which in places were ruthlessly grubbed up in the agrarian revolution of the 1960s. Five miles to the east of the estuary the ancient town of Brixham, wedged into a narrow cleft above its harbour inside Berry Head, straggles up the hill on the road to Kingswear. A mile to the south, beyond an untidy fringe of holiday camps, the coast is almost wholly unspoilt.

On the west side of Sharkham Point, which is not the Trust's property, is a short stretch of cliff and the land behind it. Sharkham is a geological muddle of sandstone, limestone, tuffs and mineralised rocks, the strata tilting sharply. These cliffs are especially good for seabirds, best seen from a boat in the breeding season between mid-March and mid-June. This stretch is followed by the broken cliffs of Southdown and Woodhuish Farms, which the Trust owns, on either side of Man Sands. Here the

In South Devon the Trust has deliberately acquired six miles of coast and substantial areas of farmland to preserve the approaches to Dartmouth harbour. (*NT/Mike Williams*)

formations are Meadfoot slates and Staddon grits, the latter rock the reason for the unstable cliffs, where the broken slopes are covered with scrubby vegetation.

The attractive group of Victorian coastguard cottages at Man Sands do not belong to the Trust, nor does part of Scabbacombe Head, but beyond this all the land to the mouth of the Dart has now been acquired, and a most lovely length of coast it is. Scabbacombe Head is a nesting site for seabirds, fulmars, guillemots, razorbills and, especially, kittiwakes, who imitate their name endlessly in April, May and early June.

A mile to the west lies the Coleton Fishacre valley above Pudcombe Cove. In this valley Rupert d'Oyly Carte, the son of Richard d'Oyly Carte who produced all the operas of Gilbert and Sullivan, built a remarkable house in 1925 and laid out a substantial tree and shrub garden sloping towards the sea (see p.81).

Off Outer Froward Point is the Mew Stone, one of several off this coast. Mew is the old name for gull. Herring gulls and black-backs, cormorants and shags breed in noisy intimacy on the more sheltered faces of the rock. Here we are on a kinder soil, over the Dartmouth slates, and at once the coast becomes gentler. At Inner Froward Point pines have been planted, Monterey, maritime and Corsican, which can withstand the salt-laden gales and flourish on an inhospitable site. Hidden among the trees, and sprawling down the cliff below, are the substantial remains of a gun battery, with its attendant searchlights, built to defend Dartmouth in the Second World War. It is served by a military road from the Coleton to Kingswear lane high above. Halfway along this road is the portentous Daymark, a stone obelisk eighty feet high and mounted on tall lancet arches, erected by the Dart Harbour Commissioners in 1864 to mark the mouth of the Dart for seamen, before the days of radar beacons.

On the Dartmouth side of the harbour Dyer's Hill, high above the south end of the town, is a pleasant little wood which hides within it the old Rope Walk of the town. Every shipbuilding harbour needed to make its own ropes, and here the long terrace which the operation required was built on the contour.

Immediately to the south, across Warfleet Cove, rises the wooded hill of Gallant's Bower, the derivation of its name uncertain. During the Civil War Royalist troops raised earthworks to fortify the hill, and its ramparts and bastions are still impressive. The wood is delightful, while from the top, which is more open, there are views south and north, with the great buildings of the Britannia Royal Naval College in the middle distance.

Below, at the water's edge, Dartmouth Castle defends the narrow harbour entrance, its counterpart of Kingswear Castle on the further side. From the Bower a path leads out to Blackstone Point which shelters the west side of the harbour, and then past Compass Cove out to Little Dartmouth. This farm stretches for a mile and a half to the southwest, lovely cliffs below well-farmed fields, beyond Coombe Point to Warren Point, one of the numerous rabbit warrens on the Devon and Cornwall coast, where rabbits were bred both for their fur and their meat until comparatively recent times.

Dinefwr Park Dyfed

On the western edge of Llandeilo, off A40 (T)

At the western end of the Black Mountains, in the broad green valley of the River Tywi, is an extensive and beautiful eighteenth-century landscape surrounding an arresting Victorian mansion. Newton House, former seat of the Rice family, Barons Dynevor, dates from the mid-seventeenth century but was remodelled between 1760 and 1780, when the angle towers and crenellated parapet were added, and again in 1852, when the 4th Baron Dynevor commissioned the local architect Richard Kyrke Penson to redesign the house and face it in limestone. Penson's main façade suggests a cross between a Venetian palazzo and a French château, with an array of Gothic windows, an Italianate *porte-cochère*, and tall pyramidal roofs crowning the angle turrets.

The ruins of a former castle (owned by the Dyfed Wildlife Trust) overlooking the valley reflect Dinefwr's and the Rice family's involvement in the early history of Wales. This stonghold, rebuilt in stone some time in the twelfth century, was the capital of Deheubarth, one of the three ancient kingdoms of Wales and seat of the great Rhys ap Gruffydd, ancestor of Henry Tudor and sponsor of the first recorded eisteddfod, held in 1176. Rhys was anglicised to Rice in 1547, following the return of family lands confiscated sixteen years earlier because of a trumped-up charge of conspiracy against Henry VIII.

Looking south over the rolling green acres of Dinefwr Park, with the sea a faint strip of blue on the horizon. (*NT*)

The naturalistic landscaping of the park was the work of George Rice (1724–79) and his wife Cecil Talbot, with some advice from 'Capability' Brown, who visited Dinefwr in 1775 and is said to be responsible for some clumps of trees and a path. The 480-acre park stretches down to the banks of the Tywi, with water-meadows and abandoned meanders along the river attracting waders and overwintering birds and panoramic views over the valley from the higher ground. Mature oak woodland includes trees up to 300 years old, descendants of the ancient wildwood that was enclosed for a medieval deer-park. There are still fallow deer beneath the trees and the Trust has reintroduced Dinefwr's distinctive white cattle, a feature of the park for at least 700 years until the herd was dispersed in 1976, at the same time as financial difficulties forced the sale of the house and the home farm. With the help of local authorities and other organisations, the Trust acquired the park in the 1980s, Newton House in 1990, and is now involved in an extensive programme of restoration.

Dolaucothi Gold Mines Dyfed

At Pumpsaint, between Lampeter and Llanwrda on the A482

One of the attractions of Britain for the Romans was as a source of minerals – lead and silver from the Mendips, tin from Cornwall, iron from the Weald and the Forest of Dean. The Roman army also secured these open-cast gold workings on a remote hillside above the valley of the River Cothi, now blanketed with birch and oak woodland. Still in a remarkable state of preservation despite mining activity in the last hundred years, the Roman workings include at least five open-cast sites and a number of adits, horizontal tunnels dug into the hillside for drainage and access. Pick-marks in the rock recall the slaves who laboured here nearly 2,000 years ago, and there are also faint traces of the leats which brought water from the River Cothi and a neighbouring valley. Stored in large tanks above the workings, the water was used to wash away debris and topsoil concealing the ore-bearing rock.

A trail through the woodland with views over the valley leads to the main features of the Roman and more recent workings, and there is also a collection of 1930s mining equipment.

Dolebury Warren Avon

12 miles south of Bristol, east of the A38 above Churchill

Dolebury Warren forms the western bastion of the Mendip range, giving views across the mouth of the Severn estuary to Newport and Cardiff, the hills above Ebbw Vale and the Rhondda rising behind. There is a fine Iron Age fort, the remains of a Celtic field system and traces of a medieval rabbit warren. Although, like the rest of the Mendips, the underlying rock is limestone, there is heather representing an unusual limestone heath as well as herb-rich grassland which is a good site for butterflies. From here one can see west over Weston-super-Mare and north over the Bristol Channel to South Wales.

Dolmelynllyn Gwynedd

5 miles by road north-west of Dolgellau, on the west side of the A470

Dolmelynllyn, on the west bank of the River Mawddach, came to the Trust in 1936. Nearly half its 1,350 acres are wooded: ancient oak predominates and, although there are some beeches and conifers, they are planted with sensitivity. High above the valley is Rhaiadr Ddu, where the little Gamlan river rushes over the black rock ledges which give the waterfall its name. Visited for its romantic beauty since the mid-eighteenth century, its damp shade encourages an abundance of mosses, as well as a wonderful growth of ferns – the filmy-fern, the hay-scented buckler-fern, the mountain male-fern and the lemon-scented fern which smells of lemons when the frond is bruised.

Above the woods lies open hill crossed by dry-stone walls and with substantial remains of the Cefn Coch gold mine, worked until 1914. Three miles to the north-east, across the Dolmelynllyn sheepwalks, rises the grassy 2,475-foot summit of Y Llethr, source of the Gamlan. This is the highest mountain of the rocky Rhinogau range and has a wonderful out-of-this-world character, with vast lonely views. To the east, the heather moor of Derlwyn completes the Trust's vital holding here.

Dorset Coast

Ballard Down forms the eastern tip of the great chalk ridge of the Purbeck Hills. The sheer cliffs drop 500 feet to the sea below, with what remains of the chalk stacks called the Old Harry Rocks gradually crumbling away offshore. As well as Bronze Age barrows, there is a great view: eastward to the Isle of Wight, north over Poole Harbour with Brownsea Island in the foreground, south-west over Purbeck with Portland Bill in the far distance.

To the north, hidden from view round the wooded Handfast Point, the coast drops sharply to Studland Bay, where the Trust owns four miles of coastal land with the farms and woods behind it, over 3,000 acres of country some of which is leased to the Nature Conservancy Council as a National Nature Reserve and has restricted access. It is a place precious for its flora and fauna, particularly on the heaths where reptiles and lizards thrive and unusual plants, such as the beautiful blue heath milkwort, can be found. These sandy southern heaths are under great pressure from development, and it is fortuitous that the Trust owns this large area since it passed to it with the bequest of the Corfe Castle and Kingston Lacy estates (*see* pp.84 and 167). Active steps have now been taken to protect these rare habitats. The same bequest included two miles of the exposed and rocky coast at Langton Matravers west of Swanage, where the Trust has since acquired Spyway Farm and the old cliff quarry known as Dancing Ledge, and cliffs and undercliffs at Blacker's Hole, noted for the Early Spider Orchid.

The Trust has 450 acres at Southdown and Seabarn Farms, including the beautiful Burning and Whitenothe Cliffs. Although the Purbeck Hills finish at Lulworth, the great chalk downs continue westward to end dramatically at Ringstead Bay, where the land falls away towards Weymouth. From Ringstead to Whitenothe makes an exhilarating walk. The chalk runs into greensand, and where these have slipped over the underlying gault clay there is an exciting undercliff – dangerous for all but experienced walkers, but providing good sites for nesting seabirds. This is the country of J. Meade Falkner's romantic smuggling novel *Moonfleet*.

From Portland Bill the great shingle beach of the Chesil Bank runs north-west for 15 miles. Towards

(*Opposite page*) The Golden Cap estate preserves miles of unspoilt Dorset coast. (*NT/Fay Godwin*)

its western end, at Cogden, a 260-acre segment of coast, including a stretch of the shingle ridge and Burton Mere reed bed, came to the Trust in 1994, and seaward of the unattractive village of Burton Bradstock is the glorious expanse of Burton Cliff, rising steeply from the River Bride to a windy open bluff 100 feet above the sea.

Golden Cap is one of the Trust's great successes. When Enterprise Neptune was being planned, it was decided to build on previous experience in Devon and Cornwall and concentrate on acquiring one substantial coastal estate in Dorset, to include the essential hinterland as well as the immediate coastal strip, rather than to dissipate the available funds in small and unconnected purchases along the country's beautiful coast. In twelve years, from 1966 to 1978, the scheme was brought to fruition, both literally and metaphorically crowned by the purchase in the latter year of Golden Cap itself, 618 feet above the sea. The orange-coloured sandstone indeed shines golden above the grey cliffs on a sunny day, and from this great landmark there are panoramic views along miles of unspoilt coast, between Portland Bill in the east and Start Point, in South Devon, in the west.

The coastal walks are lovely but equally good are those in the hinterland: gentle rolling hills and valleys with seemly farm buildings, woodland, clumps of trees planted as landmarks, and views inland as well as seaward. Below the cliffs are rocky coves and little beaches reached by scrambly paths. The whole area is rich botanically, with a considerable acreage of unimproved grassland in which rare species of plants have survived. There is an intricate system of footpaths and bridleways and a good walker will need a week to get to know this magical place.

Dorset Hills Dorset

North of the A35 between Dorchester and Charmouth, and between Shaftesbury and Blandford

The A35 from Dorchester sweeps boldly west through Bridport and Charmouth. To the south, the high ground behind the coast allows only occasional views of the sea beyond. To the north lies the pastoral Vale of Marshwood and, overlooking it, a delightful series of steep hills, each with its Iron Age hill fort, built either by the Dumnonii, who controlled Devon and Cornwall, or the Durotriges

whose capital was at Maiden Castle near Dorchester, twenty miles to the east. Each hill provides a good walk and lovely views.

Pilsdon Pen, one of Dorset's best-known landmarks, and its highest hill, is at 905 feet nearly an English mountain. There are the banks of medieval pillow mounds denoting rabbit warrens within the ramparts of the fort and the panoramas from the top are superb, particularly southwards across the vale to Golden Cap, with the sea sparkling to either side.

Lambert's Castle, 842 feet high, is larger. It appears like a stranded whale, with gorse and bracken on its flanks and scrub woodland to the north. Horse races were held here at an annual fair in June which started in 1709 and continued until 1947. Coney's Castle, only a mile away, complements it but is really the spur of a ridge rather than an isolated hill. Both castles are on greensand.

At 894 feet, Lewesdon Hill commands the north side of the vale, with sweeping views over Devon, Dorset and Somerset. The most dramatic of these hills is Eggardon Hill to the east (*see* p.112), only half of which belongs to the Trust. It is bonier, more muscular, feels incredibly ancient, and the hill fort is wonderfully preserved.

Three hills of a different character lie in the east of the county and, although each has considerable archaeological remains, they were acquired for the combination of natural history, landscape and archaeology. Fontmell Down, on the chalk between Blandford and Shaftesbury, has superb views: south-west over the rich country of Blackmore Vale, north over Cranborne Chase and south towards the coast. It was bought by public subscription in 1977 as a memorial to Thomas Hardy, whose spirit hovers over so much of Dorset, and is now part leased to the Dorset Wildlife Trust. Since 1977 the Trust has acquired further land, over 400 acres in all, including Compton Down and Melbury Beacon, a major piece of preservation of what was once commonplace and is now rare. On a summer's day the down is alive with blue butterflies: the small blue, common blue and chalk-hill blue.

At Turnworth Down, in the wooded hills west of Blandford, there is more of this very special downland, and here the woods surround a Romano-British settlement on the Ridgeway. Hod Hill stands between the two downs, with a large Iron Age hill fort, the best in Wessex, and a particularly good downland flora.

Downhill House, the ambitious mansion built on the wild Ulster coast by Frederick Augustus Hervey, Bishop of Derry, is now only a ruined shell, but the little circular temple named after his cousin Mrs Mussenden still perches on the very edge of the cliffs. (*NT/Mike Williams*)

Downhill House and Mussenden Temple Co. Londonderry

1 mile west of Castlerock and 5 miles west of Coleraine on the A2 Coleraine–Downhill coast road

The wild and beautiful Ulster coast, with broom, ling and blaeberry heath clothing cliffs of limestone and basalt falling hundreds of feet to the Atlantic, was where the remarkable Frederick Augustus Hervey, Bishop of Derry and later 4th Earl of Bristol, chose to site his house. The construction of

this mansion began in about 1775, and the bleak headland round about was transformed into a landscape park, with moorland converted into 'a green carpet sprinkled with white clover' – as the Bishop described it in an invitation to his friend, the agriculturalist and travel writer Arthur Young – and thousands of deciduous and evergreen trees planted to tame the wilderness.

The Bishop's obsession with circular buildings, which reached its full flowering at Ickworth in Suffolk (*see* p.158), was heralded at Downhill. Perched right on the edge of the cliffs to the north of the house is the little Mussenden Temple, a domed rotunda crowned with a huge urn and with twelve Corinthian columns adorning the façade. The design, which was based on the Temple of Vesta at Tivoli, had been suggested to the Earl-Bishop by James Wyatt, although the long-suffering Irish architect Michael Shanahan, who had overseen the construction of the house, again executed the plans for his difficult client. The little building was named after the Bishop's attractive cousin, Mrs Frideswide Mussenden, who died shortly before it was completed in 1785, and it was fitted out as a library. Here Frederick could study undisturbed, the silence broken only by the screaming of the gulls, by the ceaseless roar of the waves breaking on the rocks below and by the Atlantic gales, which sometimes threaten to tear the building from its roots.

Downhill itself is now only a shell, a bleak ruin in the middle of the estate, but the eighteenth-century landscape park still survives. From the grand triumphal arch forming the Bishop's Gate on the Coleraine road, a path leads north to the coast along the steep wooded valley known as Black Glen, emerging on the edge of the cliffs. The Mussenden Temple stands a few yards to the west and there are glorious views beyond over Lough Foyle to the coast of Donegal. On the edge of the woods framing the view south from the house, another triumphal arch on a pedestal is the remains of the mausoleum Frederick erected in memory of his brilliant elder brother George, Ambassador to Madrid and Turin, Lord Lieutenant of Ireland and Lord Privy Seal.

Downs Banks Staffordshire

1 mile south-east of Barlaston, 1½ miles north of Stone, between the A34 and the A520

On the edge of the Potteries, only six miles south of the parish church at the centre of Stoke-on-Trent, lies Downs Banks. Industry is close at hand, but the hilly landscape encloses an oasis: a peaty valley in 170 acres of moorland covered with bracken, gorse and broom; marshy bottoms with snipe; and water-loving plants along the stream.

Dudmaston Shropshire

At Quatt, 4 miles south-east of Bridgnorth on the A442

Dudmaston lies close to some of the most beautiful countryside Britain has to offer, looking west over the River Severn to the Clee Hills. An unpretentious four-square late seventeenth-century house attributed to Francis Smith of Warwick, with some later alterations, its small-scale intimate family rooms are the ideal setting for an unusual assemblage of paintings and sculpture. This individual collection was built up by Sir George Labouchere and his wife, Rachel Hamilton-Russell, who inherited the property in 1966, the last of an unbroken line stretching back 850 years.

Lady Labouchere's interest in botanical art, continuing a long family tradition, is shown in the collection of works by such great exponents as P.-J. Redouté (1759–1840), P. Reinagle (1749–1833), G. D. Ehret (1708–70) and W. H. Fitch (1817–92). Formal studies by these masters and glowing flower canvases by Jan Van Os in the library contrast with the fresh, fluid approach adopted by Mary Grierson (b.1912), official botanical artist at Kew for twelve years. A similar love of nature is revealed in the displays of photographs and drawings by the naturalist Frances Pitt (1888–1964), who lived in this area all her life and was a close friend of the Wolryche-Whitmore family. A notebook in her neat writing meticulously records her finds.

Two rooms devoted to twentieth-century painting and sculpture, including abstracts by Ben Nicholson, sculptures by Henry Moore and Barbara Hepworth, and some rather forbidding Spanish paintings acquired by Sir George while he was Ambassador in Madrid, set a more sombre tone. Apart from flashes of red and yellow from two Poliakoffs and A. Davie's still life in red, green and orange, colours are muted: grey and black, green and brown. Chinese porcelain and French furniture are also fruits of years in the diplomatic service, as are some of Lady Labouchere's delightful topographic watercolours, including pictures of Barcelona, Bruges, India and China – such as Edward Lear's tiny study of the gardens of Government House, Calcutta, or William Alexander's cameo of a smoking Chinaman – as well as atmospheric English landscapes and local views of Bridgnorth and Shrewsbury.

Associations of a different kind are reflected in the gallery devoted to the connection between Lady Labouchere and the Darbys of Coalbrookdale, cradle of the Industrial Revolution. By a strange coincidence, Dudmaston is also linked with the twentieth-century microchip revolution, as Charles Babbage, the father of the computer, married a daughter of the house in 1814 and spent much time here.

The magnificent oaks and cedars on the terraced lawns stretching down to the lake known as the Big

Pool on the garden side of the house are reminders of another pioneer, Geoffrey Wolryche-Whitmore, who spent the first half of this century building up a national reputation for enlightened forestry on the estate. The giant cuckoo flower or ladies' smock (*Cardamine raphanifolia*) by the stream which runs into the pool was brought back from Norway by Mary Wolryche-Whitmore in the early years of this century.

A memorable display of spring and summer colour comes from mature magnolias, rhododendrons, azaleas, Japanese cherries and other shrubs, and heaths, thymes and lavenders flourish on the sunny ledges contrived on one of the sandstone outcrops which are a feature of the grounds. The wilderness garden created in the eighteenth century in the little valley known as the Dingle, with rustic bridges, ornamental waterfalls and serpentine paths leading to artful vistas, is now being restored, a rare surviving example of this gardening style.

Dunham Massey Cheshire

3 miles south-west of Altrincham, off the A56

A beautifully made hardwood model of the solar system, showing how the six known planets moved round the Sun (Neptune, Pluto and Uranus were yet to be discovered), is the centrepiece of the early eighteenth-century library, probably dating from the time of the obscure John Norris's changes to the house for George Booth, 2nd Earl of Warrington, whose cipher can be seen on many of the faded bindings in the fitted oak bookcases. Over the fireplace is a three-dimensional panoramic carving of the Crucifixion believed to be by the young Grinling Gibbons. Based on a painting by Tintoretto, the drama of the scene is enhanced by a tranquil domestic floral border.

Apart from the later insertion of sash windows, the exterior of Dunham Massey is much as George Booth left it, an attractive long, low red-brick

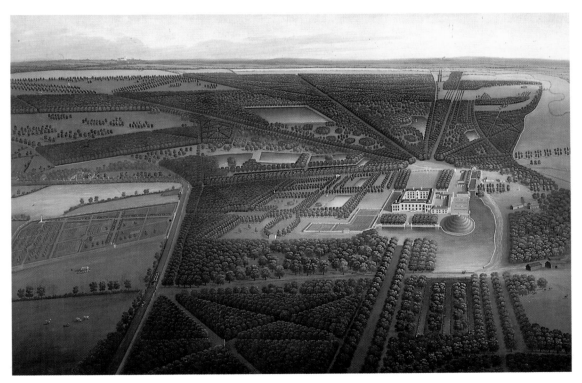

Dunham Massey from the north in *c*.1750, one of several bird's-eye views painted by John Harris the Younger which show the radiating avenues planted by the 2nd Earl of Warrington in his formal landscaping of the park. (*NT/Angelo Hornak*)

building set round two courtyards and still protected by the medieval moat that embraced the earlier Tudor house. The sombre, low-ceilinged, oak-lined chapel, made out of two rooms in 1655, and the magnificent collection of Huguenot silver are both reflections of the Booth family's ardent Protestantism. The glittering display now set out in the Queen Anne Room includes a superb wine cistern made by Philip Rollos in 1701, with the wild boars of the Booth crest formed into handles, eternally glowering at each other over the bowl.

Dunham Massey's exceptional Edwardian interiors were commissioned by William Grey, 9th Earl of Stamford, whose family acquired the estate through the marriage of George Booth's daughter to the 4th Earl. With advice from the connoisseur and furniture historian Percy Macquoid, and the outstanding firm of Morant & Co., decorators to Edward VII, the 9th Earl and his wife created rooms which rival the appeal of those from 200 years earlier. In their long saloon with a bay window arching out into the garden, Grey family portraits hang against deep-green walls suggested by Macquoid, who also advised dyeing the two mossy Donegal carpets lying on the polished boards and re-upholstering the set of early eighteenth-century walnut chairs to match the room. Yellow damask curtains hanging at the long sash windows give the final touch in a colour scheme which could well have been created for Bunthorne in Gilbert and Sullivan's *Patience*. The 9th Earl also commissioned J. Compton Hall to create an elaborate neo-Jacobean entrance front loosely based on Sudbury (*see* p.324).

A remarkable series of early views of Dunham Massey, recording its gradual transformation, hang in the great gallery, one of two rooms surviving from the Elizabethan house. Here too is Guercino's early seventeenth-century *Mars, Venus and Cupid, with Saturn as Time*, possibly purchased by George Booth but representative of the many fine pictures bought by the 5th and 6th Earls of Stamford on their Grand Tours. Perhaps the young 5th Earl commissioned two huge caricatures of his travels from Thomas Patch as light relief from the serious study of Italian art and culture.

An ancient deer park surrounds the house, enclosed by George Booth's high brick wall and still shaded by trees he established, some forming the remnants of a series of radiating avenues. Mature trees round the house, such as the two large copper beeches near the orangery (once part of the eighteenth-century walled kitchen garden) and the yews and oaks on the lawns to the east, were part of an informal Victorian and Edwardian layout which is now being re-established, with beds of rhododendrons and late-flowering azaleas, a water garden along the stream feeding the moat and a collection of skimmias. A curious mound at the north-west corner of the house, attractively smothered with acacia, laburnums and Irish ivy, may be the remains of a Norman motte, and a gabled brick mill dates from Elizabethan times (*see below*).

Dunham Massey Sawmill

Greater Manchester

In grounds of Dunham Massey (see above *)*

An attractive gabled building with mullioned windows, its warm red brick set off by the silvery trunks of beech trees, Dunham Massey mill is the only visible survivor of the Tudor hall built by Sir George Booth, 1st Baronet, most of which was reconstructed in the early eighteenth century (*see above*). Powered by a $15\frac{1}{2}$-foot-diameter overshot waterwheel fed from a continuation of the lake in front of the house, the mill was originally used for grinding corn, but in *c.*1860 was refitted as a sawmill and estate workshop. It still retains some of its Victorian machinery, including the Dunham Ripper, a big frame saw for cutting up trees, a power-fed circular saw and a crane for handling the timber, all now restored to working order.

Dunstanburgh Castle

Northumberland

9 miles north-east of Alnwick

There are no roads to Dunstanburgh. This magnificent ruin stands lonely and isolated on the Northumbrian coast, approached only by shore from Craster to the south or Embleton to the north. Built where the Great Whin Sill reaches the sea in a bold outcrop of basalt, the castle occupies a natural defensive site. To the north cliffs a hundred feet high fall sheer to the waves breaking on the rocks below; to the west the ground drops almost as precipitously to the patchwork of fields stretching away to the Cheviots; and to the south the castle

Dunstanburgh Castle from the south, showing the ruins of the massive gatehouse keep and the Lilburn Tower silhouetted against the sky beyond. (*NT/Mike Williams*)

overlooks a deep ravine-like inlet. Only on the east does the land slope gently away into the sea.

Like Cilgerran some 250 miles away looking west over the Irish Sea (*see* p.70), Dunstanburgh's might is concentrated in the massive towers which punctuate the walls enclosing the eleven-acre site. Approached from the south, where the strongest defences were needed, a substantial curtain wall with two projecting towers ends in an impressive gatehouse-keep guarding the castle's south-west corner. The two D-shaped towers bulging out round the entrance passage look formidable even today. On the north the long finger of the Lilburn Tower, its three storeys still largely intact, stands on the highest point of the bluff, often seen silhouetted against an angry sky.

Dunstanburgh was built between 1313 and 1316, the stronghold of Thomas, 2nd Earl of Lancaster, grandson of Henry III. But the Earl had little time to enjoy his castle, for he was executed only six years after it was completed, following his defeat by his cousin Edward II at the Battle of Boroughbridge. Strengthened by John of Gaunt in the late fourteenth century against the Scots, Dunstanburgh's defences were put to the test in the Wars of the Roses, when the Yorkists besieged Lancastrian forces here in 1462 and 1464. Severely damaged in these engagements, the castle was barely repaired; too remote to be useful, it was quarried for building materials and gradually decayed into an empty shell. It is now a hauntingly beautiful place, the restless murmur of the sea and the plaintive cries of seabirds wheeling overhead adding to its enchantment.

Dunster Castle Somerset

In Dunster, 3 miles south-east of Minehead on the A396, just off the A39

A few miles east of Minehead a ridge of the Brendon Hills reaches almost to the Bristol Channel, ending in a steep-sided outlier. This spectacular natural defensive site was chosen by the Norman William de Mohun as the place for his castle.

Although no trace of the original defences survives, Dunster still looks like a castle, with a tangle of towers and battlements rising romantically from the thickly wooded hill. This medieval fantasy was created by Anthony Salvin in 1868–72 for George Fownes Luttrell, whose family had lived here since 1405. It was grafted on to an earlier Jacobean house built within the confines of the original stronghold by the local stonemason William Arnold, the architect of Montacute (*see* p.202). Besieged for 160 days by Cromwell's troops in the Civil War, Dunster was considered a major threat to the Commonwealth and the regime ordered its complete destruction, miraculously issuing a reprieve when the curtain wall alone had been razed.

Struggling up the hill from the village clustered below the tor, it is easy to appreciate the defensive advantages of the castle's position. A steep slope leads up to the fifteenth-century gatehouse, and a second thirteenth-century gateway, the oldest surviving feature of the castle, gives access to what was once the lower ward. The north façade fronted by this court is dominated by Salvin's great four-storey tower on the left, bordered by an octagonal staircase turret complete with authentic medieval arrow loops. The nineteenth-century work blends so well with the Jacobean wing to the right that only details in the New Red sandstone masonry show where one ends and the other begins.

Two of the finest features of the interior were commissioned by Colonel Francis Luttrell in the late seventeenth century. He was responsible for the magnificent oak staircase with naked cherubs and dogs racing through a thick acanthus undergrowth carved on the panels of the balustrade, one of the beasts leaping over a clutch of Charles II silver shillings from the 1683–4 issue which cunningly dates the work. Of a standard comparable with the staircase at Sudbury Hall, Derbyshire (*see* p.324), this may also reflect the skill of the distinguished Edward Pearce.

Craftsmanship of similar quality is displayed in the three-dimensional plasterwork ceiling in the dining-room, thickly encrusted with flowers and foliage which almost conceal the creatures hidden in the design. Here a cherub shoots a deer with a bow and arrow; there a winged horse bursts from the centre of a blossom. A spider's web of plaster in the hall, the only original Jacobean ceiling to have escaped remodelling, looks down on the famous allegorical portrait of Sir John Luttrell, dated 1550,

This cockerel on an early eighteenth-century screen at Dunster Castle is accompanied by a hen and chicks. Much of the furniture in the castle dates from the same period, including the fine mid-eighteenth-century mahogany chairs and settee with needlework seats in the morning-room. (*NT/Charlie Waite*)

in which he is shown emerging half naked from a stormy sea while sailors abandon a foundering ship behind him. Less enigmatic but equally striking is the set of seventeenth-century painted leather hangings illustrating the story of Antony and Cleopatra which fills Salvin's gallery, the curiously expressionless faces and wooden horses redeemed by the brilliant, glittering colours produced by painting on silver foil.

A deliciously cool Victorian conservatory, like a leafy extension of the airy, pale-green drawing-room, leads out on to a sheltered south-facing terrace. Although the tor is exposed to westerly winds, the mild maritime climate allows some remarkably tender plants and shrubs to grow here, including an olive, palms and a now famous lemon, laden with fruit in midsummer. Steep paths curling round the hill below the castle are lined with fuchsias and hydrangeas, there is a grove of strawberry trees and huge conifers tower above willows, camellias and rhododendrons, the giant rhubarb-like leaves of *Gunnera manicata* and other moisture-loving plants along the River Avill in the depths of the valley.

The grassy platform which was the site of the keep and many rooms in the castle have magnificent views over the countryside around, a patchwork of small hedged fields rolling away to the hills of Exmoor which still looks very much as it is depicted in a set of early eighteenth-century scenes. To the north the tower of the village church is echoed in the folly on Conigar Hill, with the blue of the Bristol Channel beyond.

Dunwich Heath Suffolk

South off the Westleton–Dunwich road, ½ mile before reaching Dunwich

South of the now vanished Saxon capital of East Anglia, the once-prosperous town of Dunwich which was overwhelmed by the sea in the fourteenth century, lies the Trust's outpost at Dunwich Heath, between Aldeburgh and Southwold.

At first sight the heath seems unprepossessing: an oblong block of dry sandy soil covered with heather, bracken, gorse and some silver birch, the half mile of low crumbling cliffs being constantly gnawed away by the sea. Nightjars breed here in small numbers and there is a rare butterfly: the silver-studded blue. The Dunwich Rose is rare too;

it is said to have been planted in the Saxon town by medieval monks.

Dunwich Heath acts as a buffer to the RSPB's much larger Minsmere Reserve which adjoins to the south, the two holdings separated by Docwra's Ditch dug to provide both a firebreak and a reservoir, these dry heaths being much at risk from fire. The views looking down into this beautiful reserve are lovely and, half a mile to the south of the Trust's clifftop carpark, the RSPB provides hides from which the birds may be observed.

Dyrham Park Avon

8 miles north of Bath, 12 miles east of Bristol

After recording the burial of John Wynter in 1688, the local rector drew a thick line across the page. He knew it was the end of an era. Two years previously John's only surviving child, his 36-year-old daughter Mary, had married William Blathwayt, a rising civil servant, and by the end of the century this energetic, self-made man had totally transformed the Tudor manor his wife inherited, creating this great mansion set beneath a spur of the Cotswolds. Despite his loyalty to James II in the Glorious Revolution, a rare fluency in Dutch coupled with an unusual gift for administration recommended Blathwayt to William III, for whom he acted as Secretary of State from 1692–1702.

Although built over only ten years, Dyrham shows two faces to the world, reflecting Blathwayt's rising fortunes. The west front, with glorious views over the countryside towards Bristol, is an attractive building crowned with a balustrade, and with a courtyard terrace flanked by projecting one-storey wings, one of which leads to the medieval village church. An Italianate double stairway descends from the terrace to a great sweep of grass, and the façade as a whole has continental overtones, as if its architect, the shadowy Frenchman S. Hauduroy, was planning a grand Parisian town house.

By the time Blathwayt constructed the east front with its state apartments, he was important enough to command the services of William Talman, Wren's second-in-command, whose grand baroque façade is proudly surmounted by the Blathwayt eagle. The monumental orangery extending the range to the south, successfully obscuring the service quarters in the view from the hill above the house, is also Talman's.

The east front of Dyrham Park, with William Talman's orangery to the south obscuring the service quarters behind. (*NT/S. Hobhouse*)

An extensive formal Dutch water garden which once surrounded this palatial mansion has long disappeared, replaced by Charles Harcourt-Master's beautiful late eighteenth-century park, with groves and clumps of beeches, chestnuts and cedars spilling down the hillsides. But the interior still reflects the taste for Dutch fashions inspired by the new king, which Blathwayt would have had ample opportunity to see at first hand. In Talman's entrance hall bird paintings by Melchior d'Hondecoeter hang against embossed leather bought in The Hague. Door locks and hinges are engraved with tulips and daffodils in the Balcony Room and characteristic blue and white delftware is seen throughout the house, including two impressive pyramidal flower vases intended for the display of prize blooms. Sumptuous crimson and yellow velvet hangings adorning the state bed in the Queen Anne Room are typical of the rich fabrics and textiles with which Dyrham was once furnished. And then there are the paintings – cool Dutch interiors, soft land- and seascapes and serene still lifes, including works by Abraham Storck, David Tenniers the Younger and Samuel van Hoogstraeten. One of Hoogstraeten's perspective paintings shows a view through an unmistakably Dutch interior, stretching invitingly across tiled floors to a chair with a red cushion by a glowing fire in a distant room.

Eastbury House   London

In Eastbury Square, Barking, $\frac{1}{4}$ mile south of Upney station

The modern housing estate surrounding Eastbury Square could hardly be a more inappropriate setting for this red-brick H-shaped three-storey Elizabethan manor house with mullioned windows, finialled Dutch-style gables and a huge chimney-stack at the west end of the central block. With the exception of some sixteenth-century wall painting, few original interior features remain.

East Riddlesden Hall
West Yorkshire

1 mile north-east of Keighley on south side of the A650, on north bank of River Aire and close to Leeds and Liverpool Canal

Although W. S. Gilbert is said to have based the Bad Baronets in *Ruddigore* on the Murgatroyds of East Riddlesden, it seems the family does not entirely deserve its dubious reputation. Certainly the rich clothier James Murgatroyd who bought the estate in the 1630s was a respected local figure, and it is he who was largely responsible for the present house, set on a bluff above the River Aire. The impressive entrance front is dominated by a striking two-storey porch with a doorway flanked by classical columns and an ecclesiastical rose window set beneath battlements and Gothic pinnacles. To the left stretch the mullioned windows and gabled façades of the square main block of the house, while to the right a one-storey great hall forms a link to the remains of another substantial wing. Pedimented windows and other classical details on the one surviving façade of this part of the house are the work of Edmund Starkie, James Murgatroyd's great-grandson, although he may have simply refaced an older building rather than reconstructing it.

Absentee owners from the beginning of the nineteenth century ensured that this fine example of a seventeenth-century Yorkshire manor survived unaltered, although most of the 'Starkie' wing was demolished in 1905 and none of the original contents remain. Virtually empty when it was saved from dereliction by the Briggs brothers of Keighley

in the early 1930s, East Riddlesden has been refurnished by the Trust. The locally made period oak pieces which now fill the panelled family rooms include a carved and canopied early seventeenth-century cupboard in the dining-room, described by Emily Brontë in *Wuthering Heights*, and a magnificent oak settle in the drawing-room. A late sixteenth-century copper curfew for keeping in the embers of a fire overnight, a grain chest and a shepherd's chair designed with a hutch for a lamb or a dog under the seat are among a number of rare and intriguing objects in the house, and there are also displays of pewter and Dutch and oriental porcelain.

Old stone walls round a small formal garden created by the Trust at the back of the house enclose lawns bordered by pyramid apples and pears and a sunken paved rose garden defined by low box hedges. Umbrella-like Robinia trees decorate the grass on the site of the demolished Starkie wing and there is also a recently planted herb garden.

The great stone barn in front of the house, one of two shielding the hall from the sprawl of Keighley, is said to be the finest in the north of England. Tradition has it that this is a medieval barn

East Riddlesden Hall in *c*.1840 by an unknown artist; the now largely demolished Starkie wing is on the right. (*NT*)

incorporating later masonry from either nearby Kirkstall Abbey or Dalton Priory, and that the present external stone cladding was added by James Murgatroyd when he rebuilt the house, but it is more likely that the whole building was constructed in the seventeenth century. The ancient fish pond, across which visitors get their first view of the house, has more certain monastic origins. This little pool is also associated with the ghost of a woman in white, a lady of the manor who drowned here when she was thrown from her horse. Among several other apparitions said to be connected with East Riddlesden is the Grey Lady, reputed to have been shut up in her room to starve to death by her sadistic husband after she had been discovered with her lover.

Ebbor Gorge Somerset

3 miles north-west of Wells

Cheddar Gorge is only too well known, beautiful Burrington Coombe much less so, but the most lovely and least-known of these steep ravines which plunge down from the Mendip plateau to the Somerset plain is Ebbor, part leased to the Nature Conservancy Council as a National Nature Reserve. There is no road up the valley, only a path which snakes through the limestone cliffs for a mile, arched over by trees. The gorge has caves and rock shelters which were inhabited from the early Stone Age until after the Roman occupation.

Eggardon Hill Dorset

2 miles north of Askerswell, 10 miles west of Dorchester

The boundary between the parishes of Askerswell and Powerstock runs through the centre of this spectacular shield-shaped hill fort, the smooth cultivated contours of the privately owned northern half in Powerstock contrasting with the pock-marked, ridged terrain of the Trust's holding to the south, with its wealth of untouched prehistoric features. Eggardon is one of Britain's most impressive late Iron Age hill forts, superbly sited overlooking the Vale of Marshwood on the most westerly chalk scarp in England and ringed by three massive ramparts. Causeways snake through the defences on the north-west and south-east, their sinuous paths ensuring they could be properly

defended. The remains of a late Bronze Age barrow within the ramparts were respected by the Iron Age inhabitants. There are also traces of occupation here and the banks of a probably earlier enclosure.

Emmetts Garden Kent

$1\frac{1}{2}$ miles south of the A25 on Sundridge–Ide Hill road, $1\frac{1}{2}$ miles north of Ide Hill off the B2042

This little six-acre garden and arboretum stands at the highest point of Kent, on a 700-foot ridge. Once thickly screened with trees to create an inward, intimate atmosphere, the character of the garden was transformed by the freak storm in the autumn of 1987, which felled the eighty-foot beeches and oaks crowning the ridge and opened up superb vistas over the Weald as far as Crowborough Beacon to the south and north to the North Downs.

Emmetts is principally the creation of the banker

Bluebells in the garden at Emmetts. (*NT/Jerry Harpur*)

Frederick Lubbock, who bought the estate in the late nineteenth century and whose love of trees and shrubs was inspired by his friendship with William Robinson. This great gardener could well have been responsible for the layout of the arboretum planted on the shoulder of the ridge, with beautifully placed mature trees and shrubs, including a wide variety of rhododendrons and camellias as well as such exotics as the Japanese maple, the dove or handkerchief tree from China, the North American sweet-pepper bush and the Chinese ginkgo. The grassy glades are full of daffodils in spring.

A deep wooded valley, part of the Trust's 300-acre estate here, falls precipitously away from the arboretum, a contoured path leading down from the garden into the upper wood which is carpeted with bluebells in spring. Summer interest is provided by the formal rose garden beside the gaunt Victorian house, cultivars of old-fashioned varieties flowering white, pink and crimson around a central fountain. The recently restored rock garden is more intimate, with slabs of Cumbrian limestone planted with maples, dwarf pines and rhododendrons and tree heathers, and with a little waterfall cascading gently into a lily pond.

Ennerdale Cumbria

In the western lakes area

After the First World War the Forestry Commission was set up to build up the national stock of timber to replace the great acreage of mature private woodland felled between 1914–18. In 1925 it bought most of this remote valley, from Ennerdale Water up to Great Gable, and filled every inch that was plantable with Sitka spruce, a species which was dark, impenetrable and utterly alien to these hills. After an outcry led by the Council for the Protection of Rural England and the Friends of the Lake District, the Commission reluctantly agreed not to afforest the central 300 square miles of the Lake District. The Trust took a 500-year lease of plantable land at the valley head, and of the unplantable tops and screes from Great Gable to High Stile on the north, and from Great Gable to Haycock on the south. The Commission's planting was thus boxed in, but it was the warning note sounded by the amenity societies which saved the central Lake District from blanket forestry.

Later the Trust acquired the farms of How Hall, Howside and Beckfoot at the west end of the lake, Mireside on the north bank, and most of the south shore, including The Side and Angler's Crag, running up to the 7,500 wild and remote acres of Kinniside Common and Stockdale Moor. (*See also* Borrowdale and Derwentwater; Buttermere, Crummock Water and Loweswater; Coniston Valley; Eskdale and Duddon Valleys; Grasmere Valley, Rydal, Hawkshead and Sawrey; Great and Little Langdale; Ullswater, Hartsop, Brotherswater and Troutbeck; Wasdale; Windermere.)

Erddig Clwyd

2 miles south of Wrexham

Visitors to Erddig are given a special awareness of the country house as a functioning community. Instead of being welcomed at the front door, they are taken through the estate yards, an extensive and atmospheric complex of eighteenth- and nineteenth-century brick outbuildings presenting a unique picture of how these empires were nurtured day by day. Saws hang on the walls of the pit where timber was cut into manageable widths, the tools in the blacksmith's shop are the very ones that were used to repair the fine eighteenth-century ironwork screen in the formal garden, and the dry laundry sports a mangle in which clothes were pressed using the weight of a box of stones. Similarly, the tour of the house ends on the attic floor, with the spacious, airy rooms where the servants slept.

Judging by the staff portraits in the servants' hall, life was agreeable here. One of the housemaids is depicted at the age of eighty-seven and the 75-year-old estate carpenter looks spry enough to wield the axe he carries over his shoulder. In contrast to the negro coachboy who starts this unique series, they at least would have been used to the gales and driving rain which regularly sweep across Wales to batter the house.

It was weather damage which led Philip Yorke I to reface the west front of the house which his great-uncle, the successful London lawyer John Meller, had acquired in 1716. James Wyatt's rather severe neo-classical composition of the 1770s contrasts with the warm brickwork of the garden front, where a pronounced change in the colour of the materials marks the wings added in 1721–4 on either side of the late seventeenth-century central block. The length of the façades and their uniform sash windows suggest nothing so much as a row of town houses.

After the architecturally modest exterior, Meller's superb furniture and rich textiles are a surprise, his sets of silvered and walnut chairs and ornate looking-glasses all obtained from leading London cabinet-makers. Goblin-like masks smiling wickedly at each other across the head of the pier glass in the saloon are by the same hand as the carved and gilded birds on the tester of the sumptuous state bed, their exotic plumage echoed by a flock of diminutive painted companions, flashes of brilliant peacock-blue suggesting kingfishers on the wing. More birds perch in the borders of the summery Soho tapestries bought for the principal bedroom.

Philip I created the library which now displays his passionate antiquarianism as well as his great-uncle's legal tomes, and he was also responsible for the delightful Chinese wallpaper in the room next to the chapel, with handpainted cameos showing orientals at work. His concern for the past also led him to preserve the then old-fashioned garden. Although William Emes was employed to landscape

Double avenues of mature limes shade the canal in Erddig's formal garden, a rare example of an early eighteenth-century layout. (*NT/Tim Stephens*)

the park between 1767–89, contributing the original circular waterfall known as the Cup and Saucer, the hanging beech woods and picturesque walks, Philip deliberately retained the formal layout near the house, the essential features of which, such as the enclosing walls, date from 1718–32. Much decayed when Erddig came to the Trust in 1973, the garden has been reconstructed as it was in the early eighteenth century with the aid of a bird's-eye view engraved by Thomas Badeslade in 1740, and is now a rare example of a design of the period.

A long gravel path stretching away from the east front, its line emphasised by a double avenue of young pleached limes, provides a strong central focus which is continued by a canal. A decorative wrought-iron screen closes the vista at the far end and the water is shaded by magnificent mature limes on either side. To the north, apple trees planted in blocks mirror the orderly rows shown on the engraving. Plums, pears, peaches and apricots are trained on the walls, most of them varieties that were listed as growing here in 1718, and a range of flowering plants in the borders below includes old varieties of daffodils and narcissus. Immediately in front of the house, walls topped with exotically curling gables frame a Victorian parterre, its stalagmitic fountains, L-shaped beds and clipped box perfectly in tune with the formal eighteenth-century layout.

Eskdale and Duddon Valleys
Cumbria

Leading up to the Three Tarns on one side and to the Scafell range on the other

The Hardknott Pass, which links the valleys, runs through the Trust's farms of Black Hall in the Duddon valley and Butterilket in Eskdale. A great battle had to be fought in the 1930s to keep out the Forestry Commission, which had already bought land for planting (which it proposed to transform into the Hardknott Forest Park) and only reluctantly held its fire. It took thirty years before the Commission was persuaded to sell its land to the Trust which, with other gifts and purchases, now owns all the valley head from the river's source at Eskhause to the farm of Penny Hill opposite the Woolpack Inn in Eskdale. This vast area includes the 2,960-foot summit of Bow Fell, and from

Crinkle Crags to Pike o'Blisco and Three Shires Stone on Wrynose Pass, including Wrynose Bottom, Mosedale and Hardknott Pass. North of the village of Boot, the Trust's land runs up Hardrigg Gill, over the shoulder of Eskdale Fell and then up to the Scafell massif.

The valley head of the River Duddon has been secured by these manoeuvres, and by the gift in 1929 of Cockley Beck and Dale Head farms, and the valley runs away south from the central Lake District to its great estuary on which the Trust acquired the dune and marsh nature reserve of Sandscale Haws in 1984. The Duddon valley is a very special place indeed and has retained its beauty primarily because of the work of one man.

The Rev. H. H. Symonds helped to found the Friends of the Lake District in 1934 and was its Secretary until his death in 1950. Over a period he bought five farms in the valley, carefully chosen for their key positions: Browside and Thrang on the left bank above Seathwaite, and on the right, above Ulpha, Brighouse, Pike Side and Hazel Head, the last being on both sides of the beautiful road running over Birker Moor to Eskdale. By buying them himself, and because of his formidable reputation as a conservationist, he was able single-handedly to frighten off public authorities who wanted to make reservoirs and build power stations in the valley. Like Beatrix Potter seven years before, on his death he left his beloved farms to the Trust.

This area of the Lake District is rich in history as well as natural beauty. A medieval wall is a survival of the extensive monastic sheep walks which fed the wealth of Furness and Fountains abbeys, a Roman military road ran through Eskdale, from Ravenglass to Ambleside, and the Ravenglass and Eskdale railway, now a tourist attraction, was opened in 1875 to ship out iron ore.

(*See also* Borrowdale and Derwentwater; Buttermere, Crummock Water and Loweswater; Coniston Valley; Ennerdale; Grasmere Valley, Rydal, Hawkshead and Sawrey; Great and Little Langdale; Ullswater, Hartsop, Brotherswater and Troutbeck; Wasdale; Windermere.)

Exmoor   Devon and Somerset

See Combe Martin and the Hangman Hills; the Heddon Valley, Trentishoe and Woody Bay; Lynmouth; Holnicote Estate.

Falkland Memorial   Berkshire

1 mile south-west of Newbury, on the Andover road

A nineteenth-century obelisk beside the road from Newbury to Andover commemorates Lucius Gray, 2nd Viscount Falkland, and other Royalists who fell at the inconclusive 1st Battle of Newbury on 20 September 1643 during the Civil War.

Farnborough Hall   Warwickshire

6 miles north of Banbury, ½ mile west of the A423

Buried in the wooded Warwickshire countryside, this honey-coloured two-storey stone house looks out over a patchwork of fields and hedgerows to the scarp of Edgehill and the Malvern Hills beyond. It is still largely as created between 1745 and 1750 by William Holbech, who remodelled the old manor house acquired by his grandfather as a setting for the sculpture and art he had collected on a protracted Grand Tour, perhaps on the basis of designs by his close friend, the architect Sanderson Miller, who lived only a few miles away. Long façades with sash windows, pedimented doorways and a roofline balustrade reminiscent of a Palladian villa were added to the earlier classical west front commissioned by William's father.

The front door opens straight into the Italianate hall. Busts of Roman emperors and of goddesses from classical mythology look down on visitors from their niches high up in the walls, apparently ignoring the magnificent rococo decoration on the ceiling by the Yorkshireman William Perritt. The plasterwork and the copy of a view of Rome by Panini over the fireplace are a prelude to the sunny former saloon, now a family-sized dining-room, which was designed to take four large canvases of Venice by Canaletto and two of Rome by Panini. Although copies now fill the plasterwork frames set into the walls, the original scheme survives intact.

But it is the sinuous plasterwork which clamours for attention, the three-dimensional motifs white against the blue walls. A cornucopia bursts with fruit and flowers over the wall mirror between the windows, a fully-stringed violin and guns, bows and arrows reflect William's musical and sporting interests, and little dogs with upturned noses are profiled on the picture frames. Although probably also by Perritt, some of the detailing, such as the foliage curling over the mirror as if embracing it, suggests the work of Roberts of Oxford, or even the hand of an Italian craftsman. The late seventeenth-century garland of fruit and flowers ringing the domed skylight above the stairs is similarly fine, each plaster blossom, grape and pomegranate fashioned individually.

The south front surveys a stretch of grass and trees bordering a long ornamental lake below the house, one of two in the eighteenth-century land-scaped park. To the south-east William's unique grass terrace stretches three-quarters of a mile along a ridge high above the valley, its smooth sward wide enough for two carriages to pass with ease and adorned with what are probably Sanderson Miller's eyecatchers. Screened by beeches and other hard-woods to the east, the panoramic views west are seen across a bushy laurel hedge which weaves around bastion-like observation points. A little pedimented temple, its Ionic columns pleasingly weathered, is almost hidden by trees. Further along the terrace, a curving stone staircase gives access to the upper room in a two-storey domed pavilion, the rococo plasterwork picked out in white against blue echoing the craftsmanship in the house. Perhaps the Italian prisoners treated at the military hospital set up here during the Second World War, who in-scribed their names on the obelisk at the end of the terrace, appreciated the many reminders of their own country. Not so those who have promoted the route of the M40 through the Warmington valley

below the house, the advent of which has detracted from Farnborough's peace and individual charm.

Farne Islands Northumberland

2–5 miles off the coast, opposite Bamburgh, reached by motorboat from Seahouses harbour

Three names should be remembered when visiting the Farne Islands. For nearly eight centuries monks lived on the Inner Farne, and it was here that St Cuthbert, worker of miracles and revered through-out Northumbria, died in AD687. His body re-mained whole for many years and was finally transferred to Durham Cathedral in 1104 (*see* p.277). In 1838 the 22-year-old Grace Darling, daughter of the keeper of the Longstone lighthouse, rowed with her father in the teeth of a northerly gale to rescue the survivors from the wrecked steamship *Forfar-shire*. In 1848 Charles Thorp, who as Archdeacon of Durham ranked next below the Bishop in this great diocese, leased the inner islands and employed watchers to safeguard the seabird colonies during the breeding season. He bought these islands a year before his death in 1862, and his descendants continued to own them. His initiative led to the Trust acquiring all the islands as a nature reserve in 1925. The Farnes rank very highly among European reserves, and the Trust's management scheme seeks to ensure that the birds and the seals flourish while

Species nesting on the Farne Islands, one of the most important bird sanctuaries in Europe, include kittiwakes, puffins, guillemots, shags, cormorants, terns, ringed plovers and the eider duck loved by St Cuthbert, who lived as a hermit on Inner Farne in the seventh century.
(*NT/Charlie Waite*)

visitors are shown as much as is possible without endangering the habitat.

The approach is by boat from Seahouses. Although visitors may land only on the Inner Farne and on Staple Island, the teeming bird life can be seen from the boat. Sea campion covers much of the islands and fifteen species of bird nest here regularly, including four species of tern, guillemots, razorbills, puffins and the eider duck, beloved of St Cuthbert who laid down rules for its welfare.

Atlantic grey seals have been recorded in the Farnes for over 800 years. They give birth on the outer islands in late autumn, each cow producing a single pup. The sudden spread of the seal plague in 1988 has had little effect on the colony's numbers.

Felbrigg Hall Norfolk

Near Felbrigg village, 2 miles south-west of Cromer, off the A148

In 1738 William Windham II, accompanied by his multi-talented tutor Benjamin Stillingfleet, whose sartorial habits are the origin of the term 'blue stocking', set off on a protracted five-year Grand Tour. As soon as William succeeded to Felbrigg in 1749, he asked James Paine to remodel some of the rooms to provide a suitable setting for the picture collection he had acquired, the cream of which now adorns the intimate Cabinet in the west wing. Here small Dutch and Italian canvases, including twenty-six delightful gouaches by Giovanni Battista Busiri, hang three deep on crimson damask, displayed in frames which William commissioned and in a carefully balanced arrangement which he worked out.

Paine's sumptuous and beautiful eighteenth-century interiors, with some flowing rococo plasterwork by Joseph Rose the Elder, lie within a largely seventeenth-century building, the work of Thomas Windham, a descendant of the wealthy merchant who had purchased the estate in 1459, and his son William Windham I. Thomas was responsible for Felbrigg's south entrance front, a perfect unaltered Jacobean exterior, almost certainly by Robert Lyminge of Blickling (*see* p.32). Built of plaster-covered brick and flint with stone dressings, the weathered façade with its octagonal brick chimneys is now pleasingly encrusted with lichen. Two bays filled with glass and the projecting central porch are crowned with the inscription *Gloria Deo in Excelsis,*

The walled garden at Felbrigg with the octagonal dovecote, built in 1753, probably by the architect James Paine. (*NT/Marianne Majerus*)

unusually pierced through the stone parapet along the roof. Paine's Gothick library, with pinnacled cluster columns between the bookcases, was intended to complement this Jacobean façade. The exceptional collection now housed here, started by William Windham II, was greatly extended by his politician son, whose friendship with Dr Johnson is commemorated in books once owned by the learned lexicographer.

Although William Windham I was building only fifty years later than his father, a mid-century revolution in architectural styles resulted in an extraordinary contrast between their work. Walking round the house, there is an abrupt transition from the romantic Jacobean front to the ordered classicism of William Samwell's late seventeenth-century west wing, with its sash windows and hipped roof. This austere exterior hides contemporary ornate plasterwork probably by the celebrated Edward Goudge, best known for his work at Belton (*see* p.25). Peaches, pears, grapes, apricots, lemons and other fruits moulded in sharp relief on the drawing-room ceiling are accompanied by lovingly detailed depictions of pheasants, partridges, woodcock and plover. More birds dart and perch amidst lotuses and peonies on the eighteenth-century Chinese wallpaper adorning a bedroom, the relatively sombre plumage of a couple of ducks floating companionably on a pond contrasting with the brilliant-red tail feathers of a bird of paradise.

Birds also feature in the delightful walled garden to the north of the drive, where a peacock weather-vane crowns the octagonal brick dovecote at one end. The garden is partly ornamental and partly productive, with espaliered fruit trees, vines and figs on the high brick walls fronted by displays of dahlias and roses, and herbaceous borders flowering pink, blue and mauve along the Dovecote Walk. A national collection of the crocus-like Colchicums forms a spectacular fringe to the shrub borders lining the east-west central path in the latter months of the year and bees from the hives in the old apple orchard feed on the lavender planted round the pond and other scented plants.

Felbrigg's undulating park coming right up to the front of the house is studded with stands of now mature woodland. Thousands of trees – beeches, sycamores, oaks and maples – date from the time of William Windham I, who laid the foundations of the Great Wood which shelters the house from biting winds off the North Sea only two miles away. His work was continued by his son with advice from the improver Nathaniel Kent and possibly also from Humphry Repton, and was taken up again by the last squire of Felbrigg, who planted some 200,000 trees and formed the V-shaped rides commemorating VE day in Victory Wood. Memorials of a different kind, monuments to generations of Windhams, including some particularly fine brasses, fill the little flint church isolated in the park, the only remains of the village that once stood here.

Fenton House London

In Hampstead, on west side of Hampstead Grove

Hidden away in a leafy road just off busy Heath Street, this charming William and Mary house with its secluded walled garden is an oasis of peace and tranquillity in the heart of London. Standing at one of the attic windows looking out over the surrounding gardens, it is easy to imagine that Hampstead is still no more than a rural settlement on the heights

above the city. Of the many mellow brick houses built here in the late seventeenth century, when mineral springs on the slopes of the hill attracted London merchants and lesser gentry to this village in the country, Fenton House is both one of the earliest and one of the best architecturally: a square two-storey building with dormers in the steeply pitched roof and tall chimneystacks. A pediment crowning the south façade marks what was once the entrance front, from which a gravel path leads to an elaborate iron gate on Holly Hill. The house was called after the Baltic merchant who owned the property by 1793, neither the builder nor the family who commissioned it being recorded.

The home of Lady Binning from 1936 to 1952, many of the rooms in Fenton House now display the furniture, pictures and outstanding eighteenth-century porcelain which she inherited from her uncle, the connoisseur and collector George Salting, who also donated magnificent oriental porcelain to the Victoria and Albert Museum. There are two sets of seasons among the figures from the short-lived Bristol and Plymouth factories, Winter in one being

Fenton House is known for early keyboard instruments. The harpsichord, built by Shudi and Broadwood, 1770, stands in the dining-room. (*NT/Nadia Mackenzie*)

represented as an old bearded man leaning on a stick, a bundle of faggots under his arm. Two billing doves, their beaks locked together, are among the pieces from four German works, while a wall of one of the sunny first-floor rooms is filled with the blue and white Chinese porcelain which was to inspire the colouring of Delft pottery.

Much of the individuality of the house also comes from the early keyboard instruments standing in nearly every room and filling the little attics, brass hinges gleaming on the richly polished cases. Originally formed by the late Major Benton Fletcher, the collection includes harpsichords by the two most prominent makers in London in the later eighteenth century, Jacob Kirckman and Burckhardt Shudi, as well as earlier Continental and English harpsichords and spinets. A virginals dated 1664 by Robert Hatley of London could have been the instrument Pepys saw being rescued by boat from the Great Fire on 2 September 1666. Most of the instruments are kept in working order and are used by students of early music; visitors may have the enjoyable experience of wandering through the rooms to the sound of distant playing.

Terrace walks flanked by mop-head laurels in tubs and beds of lavender frame the lawn and sunken rose garden to the north of the house, a layout which may date back to the original seventeenth-century garden. Magnolias thrive on the high retaining wall, the mature trees in the orchard are laden with apples in good years and there is a well-stocked vegetable garden. Three diminutive headstones in a border near the house mark the graves of Lady Binning's beloved cats.

Figsbury Ring Wiltshire

4 miles north-east of Salisbury, ½ mile north of the A30

The defences of this sizeable early Iron Age hill fort follow the contours of a prominent, 500-foot chalk ridge. A roughly circular bank and ditch breached by two entrances enclose an area of about fifteen acres, an inner ditch forming the second 'ring' probably dug to provide material to strengthen the outer defences. A fine Bronze Age leaf-shaped sword was ploughed up here in 1704, but little evidence of permanent occupation has been found and it seems the rings may have been an occasional refuge for the local population. A rich variety of downland flowers thrives on the south-facing banks.

The Iron Age hill fort of Figsbury Ring, looking north-west over Salisbury Plain. (*NT/B.K.S. Surveys Ltd*)

Finch Foundry Devon

At Sticklepath, 4 miles east of Okehampton, off A30

Now bypassed by the busy A30, Sticklepath stands on the old route from Exeter to Okehampton, where the youthful River Taw has carved a deep valley into the northern flank of the Dartmoor massif. The nineteenth-century Finch Foundry, housed in rugged buildings of granite and cob, is the only survivor of the village's once flourishing water-powered industry. Used to produce agricultural implements and tools for the local mining and china clay industries, the foundry is still in working order, its three overshot wheels driving huge tilt hammers, a grindstone, metal-cutting shears and a polishing wheel. In business from 1814 to 1960, the foundry was always a Finch family affair, with much ad hoc patching-up of machinery and buildings.

The Fleece Inn Hereford & Worcester

In Bretforton, 4 miles east of Evesham, on the B4035

The delightfully irregular black and white half-timbered façades of this little village pub with a partly tiled, partly thatched roof date back to *c.*1400, when the inn started life as a one-storey long house, sheltering a farmer and his stock under the same

An eagle with outstretched wings forms the focal point of the rococo plasterwork in the dining-room at Florence Court. (*NT/John Bethell*)

roof. What was once the byre for the animals is now the beer cellar at the south end of the building. An inn since 1848, when Henry Byrd Taplin decided to become a publican rather than a farmer, beer was still being brewed for sale in the back kitchen well into the twentieth century.

Florence Court Co. Fermanagh

8 miles south-west of Enniskillen, via the A4 and the A32 Swanlinbar road

South of Lough Erne, the border between the Republic and Northern Ireland runs across the wild and dramatic Cuilcagh mountains. These lonely hills were the backdrop chosen by Sir John Cole for his new house, built on a site seven miles from Enniskillen where the family had been established since 1607. Sir John's early eighteenth-century building, probably little more than a hunting lodge, has long been replaced, but the name he gave it, that of his wife, lives on. And it was Florence Cole's considerable fortune that enabled their son John, 1st Lord Mount Florence, to build much more grandly than his father.

The 1st Lord's dignified house, constructed in about 1750, now forms the heart of Florence Court. Seven bays wide and three storeys high, it is built of rendered brick with stone dressings and crowned by a parapet. Delightful baroque details adorn the entrance front, giving the house an archaic touch. On the garden façade, a projecting bay window lighting the staircase stretches the height of the building, ornamented with three massive scallop shells at the top. Open colonnades with round-headed arches leading to one-storey pavilions on either side of the central block were added in 1771 by William Willoughby Cole, later 1st Earl of Enniskillen, probably to designs by Davis Ducart, the Sardinian-born architect.

The main feature of the interior is the riotous rococo plasterwork attributed to Robert West, the talented Dublin stuccadore. In the dining-room thick encrustations of acanthus foliage swirl round the central motif, where an eagle with outstretched wings is surrounded by puffing cherubs representing the four winds. Tendrils of foliage hang over the border of the design, as if new young fronds are outgrowing the frame. The acanthus theme is repeated on the staircase, where three panels filled with fluid foliage are set either side of the well. Although the contents are not original, several fine pieces of Irish furniture, such as the marquetry desk prominently decorated with scallop shells in the study, help to re-create the atmosphere of a great Irish country house.

Service rooms in the basement, including a stone-flagged kitchen with a fire-proof ceiling like a huge umbrella, look out on to cobbled courtyards on either side of the house, one a coach yard, the other housing a dairy, laundry, drying rooms and other essential facilities. A sawmill down the lane to the south is powered by an overshot Victorian water-wheel. To the north is a four-acre walled garden with an extensive clematis- and wisteria-hung pergola.

The magnificent ninety-acre park, first laid out in the eighteenth century, was improved by the celebrated Irish landscape gardener John Sutherland for the 2nd Earl, who planted many of the mature beeches, oaks and sycamores and the rhododendrons and magnolias growing in impressive clumps in the valley below the house. Here, too, there are superb examples of the graceful Florence Court weeping beech and several fine specimens of the Irish yew (*Taxus baccata* 'Fastigiata'), a freak plant discovered at Florence Court in 1767 which can only be reproduced from cuttings, but which now adorns numerous gardens and churchyards.

Formby Point Merseyside

6 miles south-west of Southport, via the A565

The proximity of the urban sprawl of Liverpool is what gives this stretch of unspoilt coast its unique value. It comprises 500 acres of sand dunes, backed by attractive pine woods, the dunes built up as the Crosby Channel silted up and the sea receded. Unusual plants grow here, due to the sweepings from grain cargoes discharged at Liverpool and

The lonely dunes and pine woods of Formby Point are only a few miles from Liverpool. (*NT/Kevin Richardson*)

washed here by the tide. The hills of Wales shape the horizon to the south-west; waders feed at the tideline. This uncommon place is highly unexpected.

Fountains Abbey North Yorkshire

2 miles west of Ripon, off the B6265 to Pateley Bridge

Fountains lies hidden away in the valley of the River Skell, with steep wooded slopes framing the long vista upstream from Studley Royal (*see* p.322). Approaching the abbey from the west, as medieval visitors would have done, is just as memorable. A narrow lane past the Elizabethan Fountains Hall, partly built with stone from the abbey ruins, suddenly opens out into the grassy court in front of the monastery. Ahead the towering west end of the nave is dwarfed by Abbot Marmaduke Huby's tower, 172 feet high, so tall that it can be seen from far away peering over the rim of the valley. To the right stretches the west range, as impressively long as Huby's tower is tall and extending over the Skell at one end. All is built of the greyish sandstone which outcrops just beside the abbey.

Fountains is not only the largest abbey in England, but has survived remarkably complete, too remote to be turned into a country house or extensively plundered for building stone after its

The monks of Fountains Abbey would not have enjoyed this uninterrupted view down the west range, as the impressive space was originally partitioned. (*NT/Charlie Waite*)

dissolution in 1539. These impressive remains illuminate the religious community which lived here for 400 years. The cloister at the heart of the abbey, the nerve centre of monastic life, still has the arched recess for the towel cupboard which the monks used when washing their hands before meals. The stone supports for the tables in the refectory itself still protrude from the grassy floor, and a flight of steps built into the thickness of the wall leads up to the pulpit where devotional works were read to the brothers while they ate.

St Mary of Fountains was established in the twelfth century as a pioneering Cistercian community, founded in 1132 by a group of idealistic monks who had rebelled against the relaxed atmosphere of their parent Benedictine house. The first Cistercians' austere and simple lifestyle is reflected in the unadorned architecture of the earliest parts of the abbey, such as the huge tree-trunk pillars supporting the cathedral-like nave. But the very success of the community was to lead to the relaxation of principles which had made it great. With the aid of lay brothers, who vastly outnumbered the monks themselves, the abbey controlled huge estates stretching west into the Lake District and north to Teesside, the source of the wealth which made it one of the richest religious houses in Britain by the mid-thirteenth century. Wool merchants who came to Yorkshire from Flanders and Italy were accommodated in self-contained suites in the guest houses still standing on Abbey Green.

This prosperity financed later building, such as the early thirteenth-century Chapel of the Nine Altars at the east end of the church, with its soaring Perpendicular window. But the greatest monument to earthly concerns, Marmaduke Huby's tower, was added in the community's final decades. A prodigy tower in the spirit of Sissinghurst or Tattershall (*see* pp.291 and 327), Huby's creation was in direct contravention of early Cistercian practice, erected to his personal glory. A magnificent example of the strength of religious faith, Fountains is also a monument to lost ideals.

4 South Quay Norfolk

In Great Yarmouth

The elegant early nineteenth-century brick frontage of this three-storey house, with a classical portico sheltering the front door and ironwork balconies decorating the sash windows on the first floor, is only a façade. Behind lies an Elizabethan building dating from 1596 in which many original features, such as oak panelling, carved chimneypieces and moulded plaster ceilings, still survive. The house is now a museum of domestic life run by Norfolk Museums Service.

Fox Talbot Museum Wiltshire

In the village of Lacock, at entrance gates to Lacock Abbey, 3 miles south of Chippenham, just east of the A350

A sixteenth-century barn at the gates of Lacock Abbey (*see* p.173) houses this museum commemorating the pioneer photographer, scientist and classicist William Henry Fox Talbot, who inherited the estate as a baby in 1800 although his family did not come to live here until 1827. A grainy, indistinct image of the latticed panes of an oriel window in the abbey is a copy of the print Fox Talbot made in August 1835 from the world's earliest negative, a scrap of paper measuring only $1\frac{3}{8}$ by $1\frac{1}{8}$ inches. Nearby is the 'mousetrap' camera commissioned from a village carpenter which was used to capture the image. Although the very first photograph was

produced by Joseph Niepce in 1826, Fox Talbot was responsible for inventing the negative-positive process which paved the way for the development of modern photography.

The ground floor of the converted barn is devoted to this exceptional man's life and work, displaying the skeletal forms of leaves and flowers captured in early experiments as well as portraits of his family and life at Lacock. Fox Talbot's achievements in other areas are also recorded, from his translation of the cuneiform inscriptions discovered in 1847 at the palaces of the Assyrian kings in what is now Iraq, to his work on microscopy, demonstrated by magnified insect wings and plant sections. Also a prominent mathematician and astronomer and a Fellow of the Royal Society, Fox Talbot's scientific

The pioneer photographer William Henry Fox Talbot in an 1866 portrait by Moffatt of Edinburgh. Fox Talbot's interest in botany and science is reflected in his studies of trees and leaves and a rare photograph of Brunel's SS *Great Britain*, taken in Bristol in 1846. (*NT*)

interests were accompanied by an appreciation of the artistic possibilities of photography, illustrated clearly by his plates in *The Pencil of Nature* (1844–6), the first book to include photographs. The museum also exhibits examples of the work of other pioneers in this field, such as Daguerre, Niepce and Wedgwood, and early photographic equipment.

Frensham Common Surrey

Astride the A287 Hindhead–Farnham road

The principal features of the 975 acres of Frensham Common are the Stony Jump – a heathery hill – and the two ponds, visited by many migrant birds. The first of many rarities recorded here was a party of black-winged stilts seen by Gilbert White of Selborne (*see* p.284). The common is large and includes places to get away from one's fellows; perfect for solitary walks.

Gawthorpe Hall Lancashire

On east outskirts of Padiham; ¾-mile drive to house on north of the A671

Set on the edge of the Pennines in the industrial area of south Lancashire, and approached from the Burnley road out of Padiham, Gawthorpe transcends its surroundings. A compact three-storey Elizabethan building with close-set tiers of mullioned windows like a huge lantern, the composition is enhanced by a prospect tower rising from the centre of the house. Very possibly the work of the talented Elizabethan architect, Robert Smythson, Gawthorpe is strongly reminiscent of his prodigy houses at Hardwick (*see* p.142) and Wollaton in Nottinghamshire.

Gawthorpe had been the home of the Shuttleworth family for some 200 years before the present house was started in 1600, financed by the fortunes of the Elizabethan barrister, Sir Richard Shuttleworth. Inside, original Jacobean ceilings and woodwork set off the nineteenth-century restoration by Sir Charles Barry, architect of the Houses of Parliament, who also made some changes to the exterior. He and his collaborators, A.W.N. Pugin and J.G. Crace, were employed in 1850–2 by Sir James Kay-Shuttleworth, the great Victorian reformer who had married the heiress to the property. Barry also laid out an Elizabethan-style formal garden, part of which still overlooks the River Calder on the north.

The interior has an atmosphere of crowded opulence. In the richly furnished drawing-room startling green curtains and velvet upholstered settees are combined with a striking carpet strongly coloured in blue and red. Photographs in ornate silver frames clutter the rare octagonal table made by Pugin and Crace. Potted ferns on pedestals, fringed table covers and a florid pink and blue Italian glass chandelier complete the effect. With the addition of a few cobwebs, it would be a perfect setting for Miss Havisham. The Jacobean frieze, with ornate three-dimensional plasterwork in which mermaids and other half-human creatures are entwined amongst writhing foliage, seems perfectly in tune with the Victorian furnishings.

The long gallery running the length of the south front on the second floor is equally evocative. Decorated with original plasterwork and hung with portraits of society figures from the early seventeenth century (some of the paintings at Gawthorpe which are on loan from the National Portrait Gallery and including a rather unflattering depiction of Charles II's mistress, the Duchess of Cleveland), this seventy-foot room still has the feel of a place where people came for exercise in inclement weather. Several rooms on the first and second floors are now given over to an exhibition of needlework, lace and costumes assembled by the Hon. Rachel Kay-Shuttleworth, the last of the family to live here. This unparalleled collection displays a wide range of needlework techniques: beautifully embroidered waistcoats, smocks, christening robes, quilts and many other pieces, largely of the eighteenth and nineteenth centuries but also including some charming modern samplers. This delightful verse, dated 1961, is embroidered with a border of seashells and mischievous fish: 'I wish I were a fish/In the Aegean Sea/Instead of which, here is my niche/In London, being me.'

The George Inn London

In Southwark, on east side of Borough High Street, near London Bridge station

Looking down into the courtyard from the wooden galleries fronting the first and second storeys of this seventeenth-century inn, it is possible to ignore the rather unattractive surroundings and to imagine the noise and excitement when the George was a major terminus for stagecoaches to all parts of England in the eighteenth and nineteenth centuries. Now the last galleried inn left in London, several similar staging-posts once stood nearby, including the Tabard where Chaucer set the beginning of his *Canterbury Tales*.

The George was built in 1677 on the site of a much older hostelry which had been destroyed by fire the year before. Originally it enclosed three sides of the yard reached through the rather un-inviting arch off Borough High Street, but two wings were pulled down in 1889. A strong period atmosphere survives inside, the coffee room lined with private drinking compartments, the bar with an open fireplace and the panelled dining-room all conjuring up the kind of establishment described by Dickens, who certainly knew the George as he mentions it in *Little Dorrit*. Even today the open galleries are the only way to reach rooms on the first and second floors.

Although it is no longer possible to stay here overnight, the George is still very much an inn. Occasional performances of Shakespeare plays foster the legend that the bard himself once acted in the courtyard.

George Stephenson's Birthplace
Northumberland

8 miles west of Newcastle, 1½ miles south of the A69, at Wylam

George Stephenson, the engineer whose revolutionary *Rocket* of 1829 paved the way for the development of the modern locomotive, was born in this little eighteenth-century stone tenement beside the River Tyne in 1781. At the time the now green valley was an industrial slum, despoiled with coal pits, ironworks and slag heaps. George's father was an impoverished colliery worker, and the Stephensons lived in just two rooms, sharing the tenement with three other families. George himself started work at the age of ten. Lying half a mile east of Wylam village, the cottage is still accessible only on foot or by bicycle. Immediately in front of the house is the track of the old Wylam colliery wagon-way, now a riverside walk, for which the Cornish engineer Richard Trevithick (1771–1833) had produced an earlier, less successful steam engine (*see also* p.85).

Gibside   Tyne & Wear

6 miles south-west of Gateshead, 20 miles west of Durham between Rowlands Gill and Burnopfield

This atmospheric property in the leafy Derwent valley is at its best at dusk, when the urns set along the roof of the chapel and the central dome are silhouetted dramatically against the dying sun. From the chapel a great avenue of ancient oaks runs over half a mile along the side of the valley, focusing on a column which rises 140 feet from the wooded hill at the far end. These features are the surviving remnants of what was once one of the greatest examples of eighteenth-century landscape design.

The Gibside estate came into the Bowes family in the early eighteenth century and it was George Bowes, who inherited in 1722, who was responsible for the transformation of the grounds around Gibside Hall. Until his death in 1760, he pursued an imaginative landscaping scheme which involved

Gibside Chapel is dominated by this rare and splendid three-tier mahogany pulpit, with its umbrella-like sound board. The chapel is shaped like a cross, with a central altar and pew filling the semicircular apses in the arms. (*NT/Nick Meers*)

radiating avenues, a series of connected buildings and wooded ravines and slopes. Although it seems he was his own landscape designer, he was probably influenced by Stephen Switzer, whose ideas form a link between the formal layouts of the eighteenth century and the 'natural' landscapes of 'Capability' Brown. Gibside is a rare survivor from this transitional period.

George Bowes commissioned the chapel to be built within six years of his death. It was begun to the design of James Paine in 1760, but the interior was not completed until 1812. In the shape of a cross with a portico reached by a double staircase, the exterior strongly resembles an Italian villa. Inside, the chapel is dominated by a three-tier mahogany pulpit which rears up behind the central altar, the umbrella-like sounding board ensuring that the preacher's message reached his flock seated below. On either side elliptical cherrywood pews for servants and visitors fill the semicircular apses in the arms of the cross. There are few other examples of such superb early nineteenth-century furnishings.

Apart from the chapel, the stables and banqueting hall by Daniel Garrett also survive, but the orangery is now a ruin and Gibside Hall itself was abandoned early this century. A circular walk takes visitors down the avenue, past the remains of house and orangery, to the column, topped by a statue to British Liberty, and then back through woodland and along the Derwent.

Glastonbury Tor Somerset

East of Glastonbury, on north side of the A361

It must be hard to visit the south-west of England without seeing the unmistakable outline of Glastonbury Tor, often from many miles away, and most visitors to Somerset take in both Wells and Glastonbury, only six miles apart, for the cathedral and the abbey. Yet how many of this multitude make the steep climb up the tor? From its summit, at 525 feet, there is a wide prospect: Brean Down and the island of Steep Holm, the Quantocks, Exmoor, much of Dorset and the distant finger of Alfred's Tower at Stourhead (*see* p.320).

The hill is conical and in certain lights appears to have been sculpted, almost terraced. This is partly due to its geological structure which is like that of Brent Knoll (*see* p.43), horizontal beds of Lower Lias clays and limestone at the base rising through the Middle Lias to a cap of hard Midford Sand, locally known as Tor Burrs. This material resists erosion better than the clays and the limestone which have gradually fretted away. A second factor which has modified the shape of the tor is its agricultural use in medieval times. When the surrounding levels were undrained it was only here, above flood level, that crops could be grown. Strip lynchets – narrow fields of unequal width – were terraced on the contours, just as one sees in a Himalayan village today, and it is the shadows cast by the supporting banks which add to the dramatic outline of the hill.

Man has occupied the tor certainly since the sixth century AD. In Anglo-Saxon and medieval times a church, possibly monastic, was founded here. At least two substantial churches were built, the latest – of which only the tower survives – probably after an earthquake had toppled its predecessor in 1275. This church was a large and sophisticated building, closely associated with the great abbey in the town at the foot of the tor, both buildings being dedicated to St Michael. After the Dissolution of the Monasteries in 1539, the church became a ruin, though the tower was restored as a historic landmark in the late eighteenth century.

Glendurgan Cornwall

4 miles south-west of Falmouth, ½ mile south-west of Mawnan Smith, on road to Helford Passage

The glorious Lizard peninsula is almost severed from the rest of Cornwall by the deep estuary of the Helford river, a tidal inlet extending more than five miles inland. Glendurgan is situated on the north side of the river, laid out in one of the secluded steep-sided valleys that are such a feature of Cornwall. Warm, wet and sheltered, this is a paradise for plants, with many tender species, such as the prickly, grey-green American aloe, flourishing in the open here.

It is no accident that Glendurgan lies only a few miles from the Fal estuary, the great deep-water harbour that was once the first port of call for shipping returning from the Americas, Africa, the Far East and the Antipodes. In the little town of Falmouth at the mouth of the river, a thriving shipping company established by the Fox family in the eighteenth century provided an ideal vehicle for importing plants from all over the world, and many

Shadows cast by medieval strip lynchets emphasise the cone-like shape of Glastonbury Tor; the fifteenth-century tower crowning the summit is all that remains of St Michael's church. (*NT/Fay Godwin*)

A spring display in the sheltered valley garden at Glendurgan. (*NT/Jerry Harpur*)

crimson, their thickly covered branches matched by the profuse blossoms of magnolias and camellias. There are delightful cameos here too, primroses, bluebells, naturalised primulas and columbines growing beneath the trees in spring, orchids and lantern lilies in quiet corners, ferns on mossy banks, and the Holy Corner planted with trees and shrubs associated with the Bible – a yew, a tree of heaven, a Judas tree, an olive and a tree of thorns. In the deep cleft of the valley, tree ferns, bamboo and the umbrella-like *Gunnera manicata* thrive in tropical luxuriance.

Serpentine paths wind through the garden, slowly descending the valley to the little fishing hamlet of Durgan, where boats are usually clustered on the shore and the air smells of seaweed. Like Trelissick only a few miles to the north (*see* p.337), this is a place where time seems to stand still, caught in the somnolence of a perpetual afternoon.

Gondola Cumbria

Coniston Pier, Coniston Water

Until the building of a rail link in 1859, the serene $5\frac{1}{2}$-mile ribbon of Coniston Water was remote and little known. A year later the railway company launched this elegant 84-foot steam yacht as an

species were to find their way to the garden Alfred Fox planted in the 1820s and 1830s. He also built the creeper-clad, lichen-stained unpretentious Victorian house at the top of the valley, looking over a sweep of grass to a foliage-framed view of the Helford. Some of the oldest trees in the garden today are probably his, such as the two magnificent tulip trees below the house. And he was responsible for the laurel maze laid out on a slope, its gently curving silvery-green hedges looking like a glistening serpent coiled up on the grass.

Alfred's son and grandson enhanced and enriched his creation, introducing some of the species which now contribute so much to the garden's character. Conifers thrive here, cedars, cypresses, pines and the weeping spruce giving a variety of colour and texture. Rhododendrons, many sweetly scented, flower pink, cream, yellow, white and deep

The gilded serpent crowning *Gondola*'s prow. (*NT/Mike Williams*)

added attraction for visitors, and it continued to ply the lake until its retirement in 1936. Fully renovated by the Trust, it now carries some eighty-six passengers on hour-long trips from Coniston Pier, its low black hull gliding effortlessly through the water and the gilded serpent on the prow glinting in the sun. When the fells darken and the distant hills are hidden in cloud, passengers can take refuge in opulent Victorian saloons fitted out with plush red seats and steam heating.

The lake scenery is memorable in all weathers and seasons, with quiet pastures, bracken-covered slopes and beech and oak woods along the shore backed by rolling moorland and mountains, the cone of the Old Man of Coniston to the west rivalled only by the peaks of the Helvellyn range to the north, usually snow-capped in winter. Halfway down the lake is the green splash of Fir Island, with its magnificent stands of Scots pine, while at the lake head the cylindrical chimneys of Coniston Hall (*see* p.83), built to a traditional Westmorland design, look across the water to John Ruskin's home at Brantwood. This is Swallows and Amazons country, with a thousand tiny creeks and bays for the little boats which powerfully evoke childhood dreams.

Goodameavy Devon

6 miles north-east of Plymouth, 2 miles south of Yelverton

The Rivers Meavy and Plym tumble off Dartmoor to meet here at Shaugh Bridge. High above stands the Dewerstone, one of a group of granite crags which provide first-class rock climbing; the longest climb of 165 feet is on the Devil's Rock towering above the trees high over the Plym.

Wigford Down above rises to 850 feet, full of the relics of prehistoric and medieval man, as is so much of Dartmoor, but as well as evidence of early man the wooded slopes of Goodameavy hide a mass of industrial remains of much later periods, all now softened by time and covered with the moss and lichen which grow so well in the damp and unpolluted Atlantic air.

Platforms made by charcoal burners for their fires are dug into the hillsides. There are abandoned granite quarries, served by a tramway the stone sleepers of which still remain, though the rails have gone. Stone was brought down a cable-operated incline, the full trucks in descent hauling up the

empty trucks from below. The quarries had their own blacksmith's cottage and smithy, now a Boy Scout basecamp. All this activity came to an end before 1914.

Gower Peninsula West Glamorgan

Immediately to the west of Swansea

Wedged between Swansea, to the east, and Llanelli, to the north, is the Gower peninsula, where the Trust has played a major part in the preservation of its beauty.

Just clear of Swansea's suburbs, the delightful Bishopston valley runs down to the sea, a mixture of old coppice woodland and limestone crags. From Pwll-du Bay, a sandy beach below a shingle ridge, the Trust's coast runs westward for five miles, round Pwll-du Head. Long-abandoned quarries make this a highly picturesque walk, but at Three Cliffs Bay there is a change. To the west of Pennard Pill is Nicholaston Burrows, with the crag of Great Tor standing proud above the dunes and where sand has been blown on to 200-foot limestone cliffs in places nearby.

The Trust owns the cliffs either side of Oxwich Point, with a short gap at Port Eynon, and then for a glorious six miles westward, to Worms Head, where there are more limestone cliffs, their strata wildly contorted and wonderfully cut about with crags and caves. The best known is the Paviland Cave, where the 'Red Lady' skeleton (later found to be male and now in the University Museum at Oxford) was ceremonially buried in prehistoric times. The cliff flora is especially good, early summer being the best time to appreciate it.

At Worms Head the coast turns north, with the 633-foot-high Rhossili Beacon rising above the great sandy sweep of Rhossili Beach. One looks south to the Devon coast, with Lundy (*see* p.189) rising sharply before it, and west to the Pembrokeshire coast (*see* p.251) fading away into the distance.

The north coast is very different, there being no more cliffs but miles of sand dunes and salt-marsh on the south shore of the Loughor estuary, four miles across at this point. Whiteford Burrows, like virtually all the Gower coast, is a very special place for bird watchers. Waders find rich feeding grounds on the tidal flats and in Landimore Marsh and Llanrhidian Marsh, which run for a further five miles east from Whiteford Point.

Three Cliffs Bay on the Gower coast, a few miles east of the long finger of Worms Head. (*NT/Mike Williams*)

(*Below*) Grange Arch on a crest of the Purbeck Hills, looking north over the unspoilt Frome valley. (*Andy Williams*)

Grange Arch   Dorset

At Creech, 3 miles west of Corfe Castle, 4 miles east of Worbarrow Bay

This simple early eighteenth-century folly, a pierced wall of lichen-stained grey Portland stone, stands on a crest of the Purbeck Hills, with magnificent views south to the sea and north over the unspoilt wooded Dorset countryside. Battlements and obelisks crown the stepped profile rising to a central round-headed arch, two smaller rectangular openings forming subsidiary features either side. Also known as Bond's Folly after its creator Denis Bond, the arch was specifically designed to be silhouetted against the skyline as seen from Creech Grange, the family house nestling in the woods below.

Grantham House   Lincolnshire

Immediately east of Grantham church

Those using the footpath through Sedgwick meadows by the River Witham can look across willow-lined banks to the garden front of Grantham House. The long two-storey stone façade attractively smothered in creeper, with its elegant sash windows, central pedimented doorway and dormers peeping over the parapet of the roof, suggests a modest country estate rather than a house set in the middle of a market town. To the left, only a stone's throw away across a road, is Grantham's cathedral-like parish church, St Wulfran's, with its soaring fourteenth-century tower and spire.

The earliest part of Grantham House, the central hall, dates from the same period, built in about 1380, but most of the building is Elizabethan or later. Sixteenth-century mullioned windows inserted by the wealthy Hall family, wool merchants of the Staple of Calais, look over the church and the entrance court on the north, while the garden façade, apart from two early windows in the central bay, was part of the eighteenth-century alterations carried out by Anne, Lady Cust, soon after 1734 when her husband bought the house. She was probably also responsible for panelling the drawing-room and for introducing the three large still lifes attributed to J. B. Ruoppolo in the hall, thought to have come from Belton House just to the north of Grantham which she subsequently inherited (*see* p.25). A walled garden leads down to the River Witham.

Grasmere Valley, Rydal, Hawkshead and Sawrey   Cumbria

Between the hills leading to Helvellyn, to the east, Easedale, to the west, and Dunmail Raise, to the north

The Trust owns a great deal in these pleasant places, much of it property acquired in the early days. There are miles of gentle walking country, with views across to the high tops, small lakes and tarns and a number of fascinating old houses. Buildings and countryside have associations with such literary names as the Wordsworths, Coleridge, de Quincey, and at Hawkshead and Sawrey with Beatrix Potter, greatest of all the Trust's benefactors in the Lakes (*see* pp.24, 151 and 372). (*See also* Borrowdale and Derwentwater; Buttermere, Crummock Water and Loweswater; Coniston Valley; Ennerdale; Eskdale and Duddon Valleys; Great and Little Langdale; Ullswater, Hartsop, Brotherswater and Troutbeck; Wasdale; Windermere.)

Gray's Monument   Buckinghamshire

At Stoke Poges, off the B473, east of the churchyard

James Wyatt's massive monument – a classical sarcophagus on a square plinth inset with inscribed panels – stands on the edge of a field just east of the churchyard which Thomas Gray immortalised in his 'Elegy' and where he chose to be laid to rest next to his mother. It was erected in 1799, twenty-eight years after the poet's death in Cambridge from 'severe internal gout', and was commissioned by John Penn, who lived nearby.

Gray's Printing Press   Co. Tyrone

49 Main Street, Strabane

The words 'GRAY, PRINTER' set above an early nineteenth-century shop front in the main street of this little border town advertise the only survivor of the printing concerns which flourished here when Strabane was an important publishing centre in the late eighteenth century. At one time there were no fewer than ten printing concerns here and Strabane had both the *Strabane Journal* and the *Strabane News-letter* before Londonderry had its own newspaper.

The works were housed on the upper floor of the long, whitewashed building over a yard at the back of the shop, now used to display nineteenth-century

Great Chalfield Manor as depicted by J.C.Buckler in 1823. Thomas Tropnell, who rebuilt the house in 1465–80, added the bellcote and spire to the little fourteenth-century church. (*John Freeman*)

printing machinery and a fine collection of wood and metal type. John Dunlap, who printed the American Declaration of Independence in 1776 and introduced the first daily newspaper in the United States, is said to have served his apprenticeship here, one of the many who learnt their trade on Strabane's two newspapers and ten presses before emigrating to America and the colonies to set up successful printing and publishing businesses.

Great Chalfield Manor Wiltshire

3 miles south-west of Melksham, via Broughton Gifford Common

When Thomas Tropnell rebuilt his house between 1465–80, England was still torn apart by the Wars of the Roses and no one could feel secure. The domestic yellow-stone building around a central courtyard was approached through a defensible gatehouse, and encircled by a curtain wall and a moat. Visitors coming to the porch could be assessed through the squint from the dining-room, and a little wicket in the front door admits only one at a time.

Seeing the house today, so peacefully set in the countryside only a few miles from Bath, it is difficult to connect it with the troubled times in which it was built. The honey-coloured stone, gabled façades and mullioned windows give it the look of a Cotswold manor, as if it has strayed from the hills to the north. Griffins holding the Tropnell arms face each other on the gables either side of the porch, while others are crowned with figures of soldiers in fifteenth-century armour, giving the house a light-hearted air.

Inside, Tropnell kept the traditional great hall rising to the rafters, lit by windows high in the walls and with a screens passage at one end. Arched openings lead to the fine first-floor rooms in the two gabled blocks flanking the hall. Both are dominated by their charming oriel windows, the beautiful semicircular example in the family's solar marked by a crown of decorative tracery on the exterior. From this window there is an excellent view of the little fourteenth-century church across the outer court-yard, which Tropnell enhanced with a bellcote and spire. From here too ladies could look down on proceedings in the hall through two of the curious stone masks with cut-away eyes which hang in the room below – one a king with ass's ears, another a bishop in his mitre, the third a laughing face. Another curiosity of the house is the mural painting in the dining-room, showing a man with five fingers on each hand. This painting may depict Thomas Tropnell himself, a 'perilous, covetous man'.

The house as it is seen today reflects Sir Harold Brakspear's restoration in 1905–12 for the Fuller family after about two centuries of neglect and disrepair, during which the east wing flanking the courtyard was demolished (the south wing, now marked only by foundations in the garden, has also disappeared). Sir Harold's sensitive and scholarly reconstruction used drawings made by Pugin's pupil Thomas Larkin Walker in 1836, when the house was already in a ruinous state. The medieval brewhouse, the former mill and the moat – created out of mill- and fish-ponds – are all reflections of an earlier self-sufficiency. Since its restoration Great Chalfield has taken on a new lease of life, now once again the hub of a rural estate including home farms, woodland, labourers' cottages and its own parish church. Few changes have marked the passing of the years on the land, with field names and bound-aries still as they are shown on a map of 1794.

Great Coxwell Barn Oxfordshire

2 miles south-west of Faringdon between the A420 and the B4019

This mid-thirteenth-century 152-foot monastic barn which once belonged to the Cistercian abbey of Beaulieu sits comfortably in a clutch of farm buildings along the narrow lane to the village church. Both the buttressed walls and the tiles covering the soaring roof which more than doubles the height of the building are of Cotswold stone, and seven-foot stone piers carry the oak posts supporting the roof timbers. Projecting porches either side of the barn, one graced with a dovecote, house the original doors, those at each end of the building being insertions of the eighteenth century designed to accommodate the larger wagons of the day.

Great Coxwell Barn, showing the original slender oak posts carrying the weight of the roof and the outline of one of the wagon doors inserted in the eighteenth century. (*NT/Nick Meers*)

Great and Little Langdale
Cumbria

7 miles and 4 miles west of Ambleside respectively

Little Langdale suffers from traffic, as it leads over Wrynose and Hardknott to the coast, but there is a reason for going there first. Built up over many years, the Trust's patchwork of ownership in Little Langdale is nearly complete, the several little farms, most with ancient houses, just right in scale for this small valley. The gift of Little Langdale Tarn in 1985 marked the fiftieth birthday of the invaluable Friends of the Lake District.

Here the road forks up to Blea Tarn on the saddle between the two valleys, and then plunges down into Great Langdale, where there is a classic view of the great semicircle of rock and fell. To the left are Pike o'Blisco, Crinkle Crags, Bow Fell and The Band; across the valley head the beetling Langdale Pikes. The farms of Stool End, Wall End, Harry Place, Middlefell Place and Robinson Place on the valley floor are larger, their fields divided by well-

Woodland above Loughrigg Tarn at the foot of Great Langdale. (*NT/Mike Williams*)

maintained drystone walls. A careful eye will notice much unobtrusive National Trust care: new farm buildings nestling by the old, a screened camping site, eroded tracks repaired. The pressure of visitors here is very great, as this is the principal approach to the most popular walks and climbs.

At the foot of Great Langdale, between Elterwater and Loughrigg Fell, is something very different. The High Close estate comprises a large house, now a youth hostel, two farms, a dozen cottages and the delightful Loughrigg Tarn below the fell. It is perfect territory for family exploration: rising to no great height, up and down country, beautifully wooded, well provided with paths. (*See also* Borrowdale and Derwentwater; Buttermere, Crummock Water and Loweswater; Coniston Valley; Ennerdale; Eskdale and Duddon Valleys; Grasmere Valley, Rydal, Hawkshead and Sawrey; Ullswater, Hartsop, Brotherswater and Troutbeck; Wasdale; Windermere.)

The Greyfriars Hereford & Worcester

Friar Street, Worcester

Thomas Grene, a wealthy Worcester brewer, built himself this fine town house on a site next to a Franciscan monastery in 1480, recording his initials on the jetties either side of the entrance. Although one of the two ranges running back from the street is Elizabethan and the present casement windows were probably inserted in the early seventeenth century, the Greyfriars is none the less a very good example of the medieval timber-framed buildings that must once have housed Worcester's wealthier citizens, the upper floor jettied out over the lower and the timbers on the long street façade set expensively close together. A double gateway large enough to take a coach gives access to a cobbled passage leading to a little courtyard.

None of the original furnishings has survived, the appearance of the house today being the work of Mr Matley Moore and his sister Elsie, who took on the derelict building from the Worcester Archaeological Society in 1943 and gradually restored it. Seventeenth-century furniture and sixteenth-century tapestries in the great hall contrast with the eighteenth-century atmosphere of the parlour, with its rare Georgian hunting wallpaper. Upstairs, a fine frieze of carved dragons is a reminder that we are now in the Welsh borders.

Greys Court Oxfordshire

3 miles west of Henley-on-Thames, east of B481

This tranquil, picturesque assemblage of trees, grass and old buildings was caught up in one of the most notorious murders of the seventeenth century. When the poet Sir Thomas Overbury died in the Tower of London in 1613 in mysterious circumstances, James I's favourite, Robert Carr, Earl of Somerset, and his beautiful wife, Frances Howard, were found guilty of poisoning him. Reprieved by the king, the two were confined at Greys Court, the home of William Knollys, whose wife was Frances's sister.

There could be few more enchanting prisons. The modest brick and flint Tudor house of the Knollyses, with some eighteenth-century improvements, is set within the courtyard of the medieval manor of the de Greys, who gave the property its name. The romantic remains of the fourteenth-century fortifications are all around, in sections of wall now festooned with climbing plants, in the lines of foundations in the grass and in the two towers across the lawn from the house, one now ruined, but the other, the Great Tower, still looking as it did when Edward III granted the 1st Lord de Grey a licence to crenellate in 1347. Its massive corner buttresses now rear up from the walled White Garden, where magnolias, Californian poppies and other white-flowering plants are set against old stone.

Other walled areas include a rose garden planted with old-fashioned species, the wistaria garden and the garden of Japanese cherries within the remains of the old tithe barn. These enclosed areas contrast with the sweep of grass to the north of the house, from where there is an uninterrupted view across the ha-ha to fields and woodland. An ancient larch on the lawn, its branches touching the ground as if to give it additional support, must be one of the oldest in the country and a Chinese bridge over the ha-ha strikes a strangely exotic note in a very English setting. A recent addition to the garden is the brick-paved turf 'Archbishop's Maze', with an armillary sphere at its centre.

Early Tudor brick outbuildings grouped around the former courtyard include a wheelhouse, where water was raised from an ancient 200-foot-deep well by a donkey wheel, the largest still surviving in Britain. In the house itself, intimate family rooms are furnished with a number of late seventeenth-

Japanese cherries
shade the fountain
garden at Greys Court.
(*NT/Nick Meers*)

and early eighteenth-century pieces. Exceptional plasterwork on the walls and ceiling of the elegant classical drawing-room, added in about 1750, may be by Roberts of Oxford.

Gunby Hall Lincolnshire

2½ miles north-west of Burgh-le-Marsh, 7 miles west of Skegness on south side of the A158

Gunby lies at the southern tip of the Lincolnshire Wolds, only ten miles from the North Sea. This is one of the most remote corners of England, a countryside of scattered villages and hamlets and of great vistas across rich arable land, criss-crossed by a network of drainage dykes in the fen country around the Wash. Gunby is out of place in these surroundings. Built of a warm rose-red brick with stone dressings, this elegant oblong with a flat roofline and a broad flight of steps rising to a pedimented front door should face an identical façade across the leafy centre of a London square. It is a town house stranded in the country.

As the keystone over the front door proclaims, Gunby was built in 1700. It was commissioned by Sir William Massingberd, whose ancient Lincolnshire family had risen from the ranks of the yeomanry in the early Middle Ages to a baronetcy by the time of Sir Henry Massingberd in the seventeenth century, helped on their way by judicious marriages. When the last baronet died only twenty years after the house was built, the property and the name descended through the female line.

The warm panelled rooms are filled with fine old paintings, furniture and china, most of which have been in the family for generations. Among the treasures is Sir Joshua Reynolds's portrait of Bennet Langton, whose son Peregrine married the heiress to the estate in 1784 and who was a lifelong friend of Dr Johnson. This association brought Gunby a very rare autographed copy of the first edition of Boswell's biography of Johnson, one of only six known to have survived and the only one in England. Bennet was also on close terms with Reynolds, who shows his friend to have been curiously effeminate, his long unpowdered hair falling in curls over his shoulders.

The gardens are another of Gunby's attractions, the present layout dating largely from the turn of the century. The old red-brick walled gardens to the north of the house are planted with traditional English vegetables, fruit and flowers, with rose-hung pergolas, espaliered apples and pears and a dovecote which predates the house. Sitting on the

The walled gardens at Gunby Hall. (*NT*)

seat against the brick wall of the dovecote and listening to the hum of insects in summer, time slips gently by. Perhaps Tennyson, born at Somersby only a few miles north, was thinking of just such moments when he wrote the autographed poem that now hangs in the front hall. Gunby, slumbering far from the nearest motorway or large town, is indeed 'a haunt of ancient peace'.

Hadrian's Wall and Housesteads Fort Northumberland

6 miles north-east of Haltwhistle, 4 miles north of Bardon Mill railway station, ½ mile north of the B6318

When the Emperor Hadrian ordered the construction of a wall from Tynemouth to the Solway Firth in AD122, eighty years after the Roman conquest of Britain, the Empire was at its height, stretching east to what is now Iraq and south to the Sahara Desert. Few other frontiers can have matched the natural grandeur of much of this northern boundary, running for mile after sinuous mile along the wave-like cliffs and ridges of the doleritic Whin Sill, its steep, craggy northern face set against the barbarians, its gentle southern slopes leading towards the civilised world. Four miles of the most dramatic section of the wall, where it rises over Hotbank Crags and Steel Rigg, are in Trust ownership, set in a landscape of vast distances, sun and shade chasing each other across huge fields bordered by drystone walls and turning the waters of a chain of little loughs from brilliant-blue to steel-grey.

Originally standing fifteen feet high and eight to ten feet broad, the wall is still impressive, although the stone watch-tower turrets which once studded it every third of a mile have entirely disappeared. Turf-capped walls forming rectangular enclosures mark the remains of three mile-castles, each once manned by some thirty Roman soldiers who moni-tored all traffic through the border at these points. The much more substantial fort at Housesteads, only one of thirteen permanent bases along the wall, conjures up an evocative picture of Roman life. Inside the standard card-shaped perimeter set right on the crest of the Whin Sill there are considerable remains of the commanding officer's house, with ranges set round an open courtyard, and of barracks for the ranks. A forest of pillars marks the site of the granary, its wooden floor raised to allow air to circulate underneath. An ingenious latrine system in the south-east corner of the compound could accommodate up to thirty men at a time on the wooden seats set over deep sewers. A hospital building and the site of the baths complex outside the fort also reflect the Roman concern with hygiene and health, although the lack of an adequate permanent water supply must have restricted the bathing facilities.

The B6318 from Greenhead to Chollerford runs half a mile south of the dolerite ridge along which the wall strides, with the Trust's farms of House-steads, Hotbank, Bradley, High Shield, East Bog, Shield on the Wall and Cawfields extending from the road up and over the ridge and down to the

valley beyond. The homesteads, modest farmhouses with clusters of low stone buildings, fit the land-scape perfectly, as do the remains of forts, mile-castles and other military works. These features survive in greater or lesser degree along the whole of the Trust's property, but the landscape is not as the Romans knew it. Then it must have been much more wooded. Centuries of enclosure have made it what it is today: a wonderful expanse of hill-farming country. The in-bye fields close to the homesteads are green and well cared for, the grassy moorland – wet in places – is grazed by sheep and cattle, small woods and shelter belts of windswept trees dot the landscape, and away to the north looms the dark bulk of Kielder Forest, the largest man-made wood-land in Britain.

An exhilarating walk west from Housesteads leads over Cuddy's Crags, Hotbank Crags and Peel Crags to the 1,230-foot crest of Winshields, the highest point on the wall. Galloway cattle and Swaledale sheep become toy animals in the wind-swept fields far below and diminutive blue and white fishing boats bob on the waters of Crag Lough. To the south, the great ditch marking off the military zone, once twenty feet deep in places, still parallels the wall for long stretches.

Hadrian's Wall faded quietly away. By the mid-fourth century troops were being withdrawn from Britain to defend Rome, and fifty years later, in AD410, the Emperor Honorius unceremoniously instructed the Britons to fend for themselves. Like Roman civilisation itself, the wall gradually de-cayed, its stone plundered for building material and gentler sections ploughed out, melting into history.

Hadrian's Wall, the most evocative symbol of the Roman conquest of Britain, snakes along the crest of Cuddy's Crags towards Housesteads. (*NT/Howard Phillips*)

Hailes Abbey Gloucestershire

2 miles north-east of Winchcombe, 1 mile east of the A46 Broadway road

Apart from seventeen cloister arches and parts of the chapter house, this great abbey with its 340-foot church is now no more than outlines in the grass. But at one time pilgrims from all over Europe flocked to this secluded spot under the wooded western edge of the Cotswolds to worship at the shrine of the Holy Blood. Authenticated by no less a person than the Patriarch of Jerusalem, this precious relic was given to the community in 1270 by Edward of Cornwall, whose father had founded

After the dissolution of Hailes Abbey in 1539, the west range of the cloister was converted into a house, as depicted in this watercolour by Thomas Robbins. These buildings were subsequently demolished and most of the once great abbey is now no more than outlines in the grass. (*NT/Rob Matheson*)

the abbey twenty years before to fulfil a vow he had made on escaping shipwreck off the Scilly Isles.

Although the abbey did not always prosper, its income fluctuating with the price of wool from its huge flocks of sheep, this gift considerably enhanced the fortunes of the struggling community, who rebuilt and extended the east end of their church to create a shrine worthy of their relic and to accommodate the throng of visitors. The foundations of five radiating chapels enclosing the ambulatory where the phial was displayed form a five-lobed leaf on the grass, the shrine itself marked by a heap of stones. Further evidence of secular concerns can be seen in the little museum, where tiles which once floored the church display the arms of the community's rich patrons, Earl Edward and his father and the principal magnate families with whom the Earls of Cornwall were associated. Intricately carved bosses housed here, including a sculpture of Jesus wrestling with a lion, also suggest how splendid the monastery once was. And the little stream which provided the monks with water still flows across the site in a deep, stone-lined channel.

One of the last Cistercian houses to be founded in England, Hailes came at the end of a great reforming wave which had started in the late eleventh century and was typified by the teaching of St Bernard of Clairvaux, who rejected all worldly values for a life of austerity and prayer. But at Hailes, as in so many other communities, the ideals faded. The early Cistercians would never have condoned the relic cult or have approved the fine fifteenth-century cloisters built partly on the profits of pilgrim donations. As at Fountains (*see* p.121), Hailes enjoyed years of prosperity at the end of its existence, but this Indian summer was terminated abruptly in 1538. In the autumn of that year Henry VIII's commissioners removed the Holy Blood to London, declaring it 'honey clarified and coloured with saffron'.

Ham House Surrey

On south bank of River Thames, west of the A307, at Petersham

Ruthless ambition created this red-brick palace beside the River Thames, with its principal rooms still furnished in the style of Charles II's court. Elizabeth, Countess of Dysart, was not content with the Jacobean house she inherited from her father, William Murray, 1st Earl of Dysart, despite the improvements he made in 1637–9. Nor was she satisfied with her husband. A close friendship with the Earl of Lauderdale, a member of Charles's Cabal Ministry, led to marriage in 1672, when the spouses of both parties had conveniently died. The haughty, rather unattractive couple confidently surveying the world from Lely's portrait in the round gallery clearly deserved each other – and together they produced one of the most lavishly appointed houses of their day.

Externally, Ham is sober enough, a three-storey U-shaped building with shallow wings flanked by colonnades projecting from the entrance front. Sixteen busts set in niches at first-floor level are companions to those in the brick wall enclosing the forecourt. Wings once also extended to the south, but these were engulfed when the Lauderdales enlarged the house.

Inside, there are few traces of the interiors created in 1610 for Sir Thomas Vavasour, Knight Marshal to James I, but several rooms still display the taste of Elizabeth's father, which reflects the period love of rich effect. Bronzing picks out martial details – a drum, armour, a cannon with a pile of shot – on the carved and pierced panels of his great staircase and on the baskets of fruit crowning the newel posts. Gilding lifts the rich panelling divided by Ionic pilasters which the Earl added to the long gallery, a suitable setting for the Restoration portraits in their sumptuous gold frames and for the copy of Van Dyck's extraordinary self-portrait, in which the artist is depicted with a huge sunflower. And William Murray was also responsible for the green closet decorated in tempera by Franz Cleyn, where

curtains on the walls once protected fifty or so small paintings.

More pompous productions by the court painter Antonio Verrio, such as his group of vacuous maidens in flowing robes representing the arts, adorn the ceilings in the apartments created for the Lauderdales on the ground floor. The richly decorated little closets where the Duke and Duchess retired for privacy or to chat with their closest friends are the most attractive rooms in these suites, the Duchess's still containing the miniature Chinese cabinet where she kept sweetmeats and tea. Richly coloured fabrics in the bedrooms – red and black, claret and egg-yellow – are re-creations of those that

This detail of a carved and gilt fireplace surround in the North Drawing Room is typical of the lavish decoration of Ham House. (*NT/John Bethell*)

The south front of Hanbury Hall, with the date 1701 above the front door. (*NT/Alastair Ogilvie*)

once hung here, evidence of luxurious tastes which also embraced silver irons for the fire, gilded looking-glasses, exquisitely crafted inlaid furniture and parquet floors. The library opening off the long gallery is also of the Lauderdales' time, with a fine built-in desk among the now-empty shelves.

The spirit of the house extends into the garden, where the formal seventeenth-century layout has been re-created. The south front looks over a broad terrace to a lawn divided into eight uniform square plats and beyond to the wilderness, where grassy walks lined by hornbeam hedges radiate from a central clearing. Little summerhouses secreted in four of the enclosures between the walks are flagged by the golden balls which crown their conical roofs, just visible over the hedges. In the secluded knot garden to the east of the house, box-edged beds punctuated by cones of box are filled with silvery Dutch and cotton lavender. Hornbeam alleys either side form restful green tunnels, cool even on the hottest summer's day. And only yards away is the

Thames, with the little ferry from Twickenham bringing visitors across the water to the house, as they have come for centuries.

Hanbury Hall   Hereford & Worcester

4½ miles east of Droitwich, 1 mile north of the B4090, 6 miles south of Bromsgrove, 1½ miles west of the B4091

James Thornhill was at the height of his career when Thomas Vernon, a successful barrister, commissioned him to decorate the staircase of his new house in 1710. Although his work for St Paul's Cathedral was still in the future, Thornhill had completed the Sabine Room at Chatsworth in Derbyshire and was halfway through his magnificent Painted Hall at Greenwich. Like this masterpiece, the Hanbury staircase is exuberantly baroque, with mythological scenes framed between classical columns on the walls and a host of deities set among clouds looking down from above. The subtle monochrome ceiling in the long hall below, probably by one of Thornhill's assistants, matches the quality of the master's work, with musical instruments and agricultural tools representing the seasons of the year separated by *trompe-l'oeil* domes and shells.

Remarkably, Thornhill's preliminary drawings were changed to include an allusion to the notorious Dr Sacheverell, who had been brought to trial earlier in the year by the Whig government for preaching a seditious pro-Tory sermon from the pulpit of St Paul's. Although he was personally unattractive, the doctor's trial made him a popular hero and the queen responded to this political blunder by gradually replacing her Whig ministers with Tories. At Hanbury, Mercury leaps away from his fellow deities above the staircase, his head still on the ceiling but his feet on the walls. A portrait of the infamous doctor in his upraised right hand is just about to be set alight. Vernon could not have stated his political sympathies more plainly.

The painted hall and staircase are the highlights of Vernon's square red-brick house, a typical example of Restoration domestic architecture in the style of Belton and Uppark (*see* pp.25 and 342), with a central cupola and dormer windows in the hipped roof. But Hanbury is individual too. Unusual French- or Dutch-style pavilions project from all four corners, and the striking pedimented entrance façade, set between Corinthian columns, has flowing carving framing the central window. Although the builder is unknown, these sophisticated details suggest the influence of William Talman, Wren's assistant, and Robert Hooke, architect of Ragley only eight miles away. Hanbury is also unusual for its detached long gallery, where some Jacobean panelling may survive from the house purchased by Vernon's grandfather in 1631. Little domed gazebos at the corners of the entrance court are Victorian.

George London's formal Dutch garden, of which only one long path remained, was reinstated in 1994, though with enclosing hedges rather than the original brick walls. A handsome orangery to one side was a mid-eighteenth-century addition to the design. Of the early eighteenth-century layout of the park, with formal avenues, only remnants survive, although a knoll on the site of the original amphitheatre still gives views to Kinver Edge, the Malvern and Clent Hills and several church steeples. Hanbury's original contents have also mostly disappeared, having been sold in 1790 after the dissipation of the family fortunes during the disastrous marriage between Emma Vernon and Henry Cecil, later Lord Exeter. Some family pieces and all

the portraits have recently returned, but the English furniture and porcelain and seventeenth-century Dutch, Flemish and English flower paintings seen in the house are largely from the collection of Mr R. S. Watney.

Hardcastle Crags West Yorkshire

5 miles north-east of Todmorden, 1 mile north of Hebden Bridge

Six miles west of Halifax, Hebden Water, which drains the great Heptonstall and Wadsworth Moors to the north-west, tumbles down to join the River Calder at Hebden Bridge, an archetypal woollen town, its long grey mills wedged beside the river and railway.

A mile up Hebden Water is New Bridge, where the Trust's property begins. To the north the Trust owns a mile of the west bank of Crimsworth Dean, with its steep woods and the little farm of Hollin Hall. To the west, Hebden Dale runs up into Wadsworth Moor, the Trust owning one or both banks for nearly three miles. Halfway up the steep wooded valley loom the Hardcastle Crags, 'stacks' of millstone grit, for generations a place for Sunday school and chapel outings. Red squirrels can be found in the oak, larch and pine woods, planted and given to the Trust by the Savile family, grandee landowners whose shooting box of Walshaw stands at the head of the dale.

The west bank was the gift of the Gibson family, whose fine late eighteenth-century cotton-spinning mill, subsequently turned over to wool, stands peacefully awaiting a new use beside the river below the Crags. High Greenwood continues the Trust land on the west bank, with three small hill farms above it. It is a most beautiful place, close to a decayed industrial area which is now being brought back to vigorous life.

Hardwick Hall Derbyshire

6½ miles west of Mansfield, 9½ miles south-east of Chesterfield

This cathedral of a house stands tall and proud on the top of a windswept hill, its distinctive many-towered outline lifting the spirits of those hurtling past on the M1. As the huge stone initials set along the roofline proclaim, this is the house of Elizabeth

Hardwick's imposing main staircase, a broad, tapestry-hung stone corridor rising across the house to the state apartments on the third floor. (*NT/Graham Challifour*)

Shrewsbury, better known as Bess of Hardwick, the formidable and ambitious squire's daughter who rose from relatively humble beginnings to become one of the richest and best-connected people in Elizabethan England.

By the time Hardwick was begun, Bess was already approaching seventy and had four marriages behind her, each of which had advanced her social position and increased her wealth. Estranged from her last husband, George Talbot, 6th Earl of Shrewsbury, the head of the oldest, grandest and richest family in England, his death in 1590 transformed her situation, providing her with the funds to finance her magnificent house. Less than a month afterwards the foundations were laid, just a few yards from the site of the manor house where Bess had been born and which she had started to remodel a few years before. But whereas Hardwick Old Hall is backward-looking and medieval, Hardwick New Hall is in a class of its own, a prodigy house by Robert Smythson, the most original of Elizabethan architects.

The strong vertical thrust of the six towers is enhanced by windows that become progressively larger up the house, giving Hardwick the appearance of a glittering glass lantern. Inside, a broad, tapestry-hung stone staircase weaves its way majestically to the state apartments lit by the huge windows on the third floor, still very much as Bess left them. Her High Great Chamber for the reception and entertainment of important guests was designed round the tapestries which still hang here, purchased new in 1587. The goddess Diana with her attendants on the three-dimensional plaster frieze above was intended as a tribute to Elizabeth I, whom Bess always hoped would visit Hardwick (she never did).

A tapestry-hung door leads into the atmospheric 166-foot long gallery crammed with over eighty pictures, many of them here in Bess's time. Portraying royalty, family, friends and patrons – evidence of her good connections – they include three of Bess's husbands and a glittering representation of the queen herself, her famous red hair piled high and her dress embroidered with sea creatures and birds and studded with pearls. Here, too, is a memorable painting of the philosopher Thomas Hobbes, tutor to Bess's grandson, the 2nd Earl of Devonshire. Hobbes is shown just a few years before he died at Hardwick, toothless in extreme old age.

Elizabethan tapestries, needlework and paintings are complemented by original furniture, such as the eglantine table in the High Great Chamber, probably made to celebrate Bess's marriage to the Earl of Shrewsbury in 1568. Its elaborate inlay is a mosaic of musical instruments, playing cards and board games, even including the setting of a four-part motet. Hardwick's unique character owes much to the 6th Duke of Devonshire, who inherited in 1811 and deliberately enhanced the antiquarian atmosphere of the house, promoting the legend that Mary Queen of Scots stayed here and filling it with additional furniture, paintings and tapestries from his other properties, particularly from Chatsworth some fifteen miles to the west.

The formal gardens to the south, laid out in the late nineteenth century, are partitioned by long walks edged with yew and hornbeam. One section has been planted as a herb garden, with a wide variety of culinary and medicinal plants known in Tudor England; another is a pear orchard, the long grass bright with bulbs in spring. Colourful herbaceous borders line some of the walls and a row of black mulberries heralds the little Elizabethan banqueting house in the south-east corner of the garden, used as a smoking-room by the 6th Duke's private orchestra who were forbidden to smoke in Hardwick itself. The surrounding 1,990-acre estate embraces two different landscapes. At the back of the house a formal stretch of grass focused on a central basin looks out across the flat, partly cultivated land on the limestone plateau east of the house. To the west is the oak-wooded, hillier terrain of the former deer park, with a series of fish ponds, an ice-house and a partly restored duck decoy. Now a country park, it is grazed by rare breeds of cattle and sheep.

Hardy Monument   Dorset

6 miles south-west of Dorchester, on the Martinstown–Portisham road

What from a distance might appear to be the chimney of a factory desecrating the South Dorset Downs is in fact a monument to Vice Admiral Sir Thomas Masterman Hardy, Flag Captain of *Victory* at Trafalgar, who was immortalised by Nelson's dying words. Designed by A. D. Troyte and erected by public subscription in 1846, it stands boldly on the crest of Black Down, from where there are glorious views over Weymouth Bay.

Hardy's Cottage   Dorset

At Higher Bockhampton, 3 miles north-east of Dorchester, ½ mile south of the A35

The main bedroom at the top of the stairs, with a window looking east towards Egdon Heath, is where the novelist and poet was born in 1840, his hold on life so tenuous that he was at first thought to be dead. Here Hardy grew up, walking six miles to school in Dorchester every day. Although he set off for London in 1862 to work as an architect, he returned five years later to practise locally, continuing to write in the little upstairs room with a window looking west to the monument on Black

Pansies, lupins, lavender, pinks, marigolds and many other old favourites crowd the sheltered, old-fashioned garden of Hardy's birthplace. The cob and thatch cottage – the front façade now faced in brick to keep the cob in place – is where Hardy began his literary career. (*NT/Eric Crichton*)

Down ten miles away (*see above*). With the success of *Far from the Madding Crowd*, published in 1874, Hardy devoted himself totally to writing and this was also the year in which he finally left the cottage for his troubled marriage to Emma Gifford, a time of deep unhappiness but also the inspiration for some of his most moving poems.

Although only a short distance from the busy main road into Dorchester, the cottage is still as quiet and secluded as it was in Hardy's day, the sheltered old-fashioned garden crowded with pansies, lupins, lavender, day lilies, pinks, marigolds and a host of other plants just as he knew it and still rich with butterflies in summer. Dating from 1800 when the family settled here, it is everybody's idea of what a cottage should look like, with casement windows peering from beneath the overhanging thatch and roses, honeysuckle and japonica smothering the walls.

Many of the settings Hardy describes so vividly are drawn from the south Dorset countryside round about. The cottage itself appears in *Under the Greenwood Tree*, in which the villagers' dance is set in the parlour to the left of the porch. And the musicians ousted by the new-fangled organ in Mellstock church echo what happened in Stinsford church, where Hardy's grandfather, father and uncle used to play the violin and cello for services and where Hardy's heart is buried. In *The Return of the Native*, wild and desolate Egdon Heath is used to symbolise the darker note which runs through so much of his writing, Hardy's concern with man's desperate struggle against the hand of an indifferent fate perhaps reflecting his own lost faith.

Hatchlands Park   Surrey

East of East Clandon, north of the A246 Guildford–Leatherhead road

Edward Boscawen, second son of the 1st Viscount Falmouth and Admiral of the Blue, financed his new house built in the late 1750s out of prize money from victories over the French in the long struggle to control trading waters which culminated in the Seven Years War. The architect of his square red-brick Georgian mansion, probably Stiff Leadbetter, ingeniously designed it with seven different floor levels. Looking at the house from the south-west, three storeys on the west front change mysteriously into two on the south. Sadly, the Admiral did not

The garden temple at Hatchlands, placed here in 1953, punctuates one of the formal vistas laid out in the early twentieth century. (*NT/A. Bartel*)

live to enjoy his new mansion, dying only a year or so after he and his wife moved in.

Hatchlands contains the earliest-recorded decoration in an English country house by Robert Adam, who was engaged in 1758, just after he had returned from his Grand Tour. Appropriately, his ceilings in the saloon and library feature a series of nautical motifs, ranging from mermaids, dolphins and sea-horses to drums, cannon and anchors. At the end of the century Joseph Bonomi made alterations to the staircase and the garden entrance and a hundred years later Sir Reginald Blomfield added the music-room in seventeenth-century style for Stuart Rendel, one-time managing partner in London of Sir William Armstrong's engineering firm (*see* p.91) and created Lord Rendel of Hatchlands.

Apart from a few pieces from the Rendel collection, such as the eighteenth-century gilt pier tables in the saloon, Adam's interiors are now complemented by pictures, furniture and keyboard instruments lent by Mr Alec Cobbe, a collector and musician who is the Trust's tenant at Hatchlands. Red silk panels in the saloon set off works by Carlo Dolci, Rubens, Frederick de Moucheron and a rare sixteenth-century altarpiece by the Florentine Alessandro Allori, and a number of portraits in the house include canvases by Gainsborough, Wright of Derby, Angelica Kauffmann and Hoppner. Among the exceptional collection of harpsichords, fortepianos and other keyboard instruments by European makers from the period *c.*1750–1840 are an Erard pianoforte reputedly made for Queen Marie Antoinette, one of the few French harpsichords to escape destruction for firewood in the years after the Revolution, and a very rare quadruple-strung piano by Conrad Graf, one of only three known such instruments by this maker. The collection is maintained for concert performance and modern visitors to Hatchlands may be lucky enough to hear the distant sound of music by Mozart, Couperin or Schubert.

Hatfield Forest   Essex

3 miles east of Bishop's Stortford, on the south side of the A120 Bishop's Stortford–Colchester road

Hatfield Forest is all that remains of the enormous Forest of Essex, a hunting preserve of the English kings since before the Conquest. The Crown relinquished its rights in 1446, and in 1729 the Hatfield part of the demesne was bought by the Houblon family, successive generations of whom drained its heavy clay, created the attractive lake, and built the delightful Shell House on its banks as a place for entertaining their friends. Just over 1,000 acres of woodland survive: great pollarded hornbeams and oaks which support a variety of rare insects associated particularly with ancient trees. The forest is divided into sections separated by permanent wood banks and is broken up with chases – wide grassy rides – and areas of woodland pasture, marsh and open water, all offering a variety of habitats for bird, animal and plant life. Thirty-six species of native trees and shrub have been found here, reflecting the forest's long continuity, as do plants such as herb Paris, oxlip and purple helleborine. Woodland flowers thrive in the glades and rides and there are nightingales, owls, woodpeckers, blackcaps and fallow deer among the trees.

Hawford Dovecote
Hereford & Worcester

3 miles north of Worcester, ½ mile east of the A449

Like Kinwarton fifteen miles or so to the east (*see* p.171), Hawford was once a monastic grange, the property of the Abbey of Evesham. The dovecote itself, a three-storey half-timbered square building standing on a sandstone plinth, with four gables pierced by mullioned windows, probably dates back to the sixteenth century. Unusually large doors on the ground floor gave access to a storage area, the birds being accommodated in the two upper storeys, where only a few of the wooden nesting boxes survive.

Hawkshead Courthouse   Cumbria

At junction of Ambleside and Coniston roads, ½ mile north of Hawkshead on the B5286

This modest two-storey gatehouse, set back from the road just outside Hawkshead, is all that remains of the medieval grange from which the monks of Furness Abbey, some twenty miles to the south, administered their extensive estates between Lake Windermere and Coniston Water. Mostly dating from the fifteenth century, it is a plain rectangular building of rough slate rubble. Carved sandstone forms the central archway, the large traceried window in the south gable and the trefoil-headed windows on the east façade. Manorial courts are traditionally said to have been held in the large upper room reached by an exterior flight of slate steps at the north end of the building.

Hawksmoor   Staffordshire

1½ miles north-east of Cheadle on the B5417

To the north-east of the little town of Cheadle, the River Churnet starts its circuitous descent to the River Trent. On its right bank the Trust owns 300 acres at Hawksmoor which has long been run as a nature reserve and bird sanctuary. It is a secretive place, providing habitats for redstarts, nightjars and warblers. Lodgepole pines and red oaks do well on the sandy soil, as, unfortunately, does *Rhododendron ponticum*.

The Heddon Valley, Trentishoe and Woody Bay   Devon

On the north coast, between Heddon's Mouth and Lynton

The most exciting approach to this superb stretch of coast forming the seaward boundary of the Exmoor National Park for nearly four miles is via the by-road from Combe Martin to Parracombe, turning north-east at Stony Corner and then over the saddle between Holdstone and Trentishoe Downs, both over 1,000 feet. The views from this road are superb: across the Bristol Channel to the hills of South Wales, along the coast to east and west, inland over much of the moor.

   In August the heather is in bloom but at any time of the year, and perhaps especially in winter, a gleam of sun can bring out wonderful colour in the varied vegetation and, if late in the day, show up the bones of the country which are invisible in summer.

The road crosses Trentishoe Down, with Bronze Age barrows to the right, and then forks. The branch to the left runs through enclosed farmland down to the little Trentishoe church, hidden at the head of its combe which falls south to the valley of the Blackmoor Brook below. The road down the combe is steep and difficult, but the alternative route from Trentishoe Down takes the branch to the right. This is a well-graded road, built as late as the 1890s, and curls down through beautiful hanging oak woods to Hunter's Inn, far below, where the Blackmoor Brook joins the River Heddon.

The Trust protects a good two miles of the Heddon Valley, with opportunities for quiet woodland walks upstream from Hunter's Inn towards Mill Farm. Below the inn, which is an information point, the walk to Heddon's Mouth provides an easy stroll along either side of the river, with a footbridge at two places. The steep slope on the west side of the valley is covered with sandstone scree. Limestone and coal were brought from Wales in small vessels which ran up on to the beach, and were then burnt in the long-disused lime kiln at Heddon's Mouth, the resulting lime being carted to farms nearby to counter the acidity in the soil.

On the east side of the beach Highveer Point soars steeply up, too steeply to scramble in comfort, and the way to it, and from there to Woody Bay, is by one of the two paths which leave the Heddon valley to strike eastwards along the contours, one from Hunter's Inn itself, the other from the upper footbridge. This is the North Devon coast at its best. By setting out at one level and returning by the other one can make a superb circular walk. Kittiwakes and fulmars swoop and call below the lower path; buzzards, ravens and jackdaws soar above the higher one, from which access can be gained to the Martinhoe Roman signal station.

Two-thirds of the way to Woody Bay both paths cross the Hollow Brook Combe, the brook dropping 800 feet in half a mile to tumble over the cliff edge. At Woody Bay the hanging oak woods, now cleared of strangling rhododendrons, curve to enclose the bay, which was once a port of call for Bristol Channel paddle steamers. The stump of the pier still stands, the walkway itself long since swept away in a storm. (*See also* Combe Martin and the Hangman Hills; Lynmouth; Holnicote Estate.)

Hembury and Holne Woods

Devon

On west bank of River Dart, west of Newton Abbot

The foothills of Dartmoor provide lovely walking country and the Trust owns two wooded properties in the middle reaches of the River Dart where the river runs off the moor.

At Hembury, on the river's west bank, where it begins to curve eastward above Buckfast Abbey, is the Iron Age hill fort of Hembury Castle, with the later motte and bailey of Dane's Castle within its substantial earthworks. The castle stands at 500 feet and surrounding it are 350 acres of oak woodland, much of it coppiced in the past, with an open heath of gorse and bracken on its west flank. Since coppicing became uneconomic two generations ago, the Trust has pursued the forestry practice of converting the coppice into an oak wood, ultimately of tall timber, by selecting the best coppice stems and removing the rest. During the work viewpoints down to the river below, and to the woods on the east bank, have been opened up and will be kept open, thus making walks along the system of rides much more interesting.

North of Hembury the river turns west, north again and then in a spectacular loop round Holne Chase, where it is joined by the Webburn river which rises on the east side of Dartmoor. It then goes south, round again to the north-west and back towards the confluence of the East and West Dart rivers at Dartmeet. It is on this higher ground, three miles below Dartmeet, that the Trust owns the Holne Woods, running for a mile on the west bank upstream of New Bridge. The trees, mainly oak, grow among the granite boulders swept off the moor during the Ice Age, and up the steep slopes to the hill farms at the edge of Holne Moor.

Hezlett House   Co. Londonderry

5½ miles west of Coleraine on the A2 Coleraine–Downhill coast road

This long, low, one-storey cottage, with Georgian sash windows half hidden by fronds of creeper and a trim thatched roof, is one of the few buildings in Ireland dating from before the eighteenth century. Probably built as a parsonage for the rector of Dunboe in 1691, it was acquired by Isaac Hezlett, a prosperous Presbyterian farmer, a century later and his descendants continued to live here for another 200 years. Apart from its age, Hezlett House is also unusual for its cruck construction, involving a frame of curved lengths of wood stretching from the floor to the ridge of the roof. Relatively common in buildings of the same date in Cumbria, this technique is rare in Northern Ireland. The tiny cottage rooms, including a womb-like kitchen painted deep red, are furnished with some eighteenth-century pieces, and one has been left open to the roof to display the carpenters' work.

Hidcote Manor Garden

Gloucestershire

At Hidcote Bartrim, 4 miles north-east of Chipping Campden, 1 mile east of the A46 off the B4081

Lawrence Johnston, the creator of Hidcote, was always very close to his mother and it was she who bought her only son this property at the northern end of the Cotswolds, with its pleasant eighteenth-century manor house, 280 acres of farmland and a lovely view west over the Vale of Evesham to Bredon Hill. There was no garden. The bones of what is now one of Europe's most famous layouts emerged over seven years of relentlessly hard work from 1905, a unique vision that was to inspire many imitations. Like Charles Wade at Snowshill, just a few miles away (*see* p.297), Lawrence Johnston was influenced by the Arts and Crafts movement, combining a formal framework with the apparent artlessness of a cottage garden. During the 1920s and 1930s, the garden benefited from the interest and advice of Mrs Norah Lindsay and from the contributions of Frank Adams, the talented head gardener.

Hedges are the skeleton and arteries of Hidcote. The varied greens of box, yew, holly, hornbeam and beech both contain and connect the outdoor rooms into which the garden is divided, and give vital protection against the winds on this 600-foot-high site. Some of the hedges are low, mere borders to planted beds, others form solid walls of green too tall to look over. Many are clipped into comfortable topiary shapes – well-fed peacocks, plump hens and contented doves – with patches of the flame flower adding brilliant red plumage here and there.

Dahlias and hemerocallis in a red border at Hidcote, with one of the brick pavilions and a glimpse of the Stilt Garden beyond. (*NT*/*Andrew Lawson*)

The garden is only ten acres in all, but the effect of the numerous compartments, as at Nymans or Sissinghurst (*see* pp.235 and 291), is to make it seem much larger. The major part lies to the south of the house, sloping down to a little stream and then rising up the other side in a long tongue of land. Here a formal long walk leading to a magnificent view framed by iron gates fringes the informal Westonbirt area, with acres of trees and shrubs planted for spring, summer and autumn colour surrounding open glades. Another long grass walk runs from east to west, rising up a flight of brick steps flanked by two charming brick gazebos topped with stone balls to the distinctive Stilt Garden, named after the tall clipped hornbeam hedges on stems which may have reminded Lawrence Johnston of features he had seen as a child in France.

Some of the garden rooms, like the Theatre Lawn, are simple arrangements of grass and hedges; others contain an abundance of plants, with species scattered as if they had sown themselves, an apparently artless but carefully contrived confusion which means that Hidcote never displays barren clumps devoid of interest. And each compartment has a character of its own. Clipped English yews form the distinctive elongated cones framing the Pillar Garden, their smooth outlines like the pieces in a giant board game emphasising the rougher textures of yuccas, herbaceous and tree peonies and decorative onions. In the White Garden, predating the more famous example at Sissinghurst, pale-blossomed species, such as the tobacco plant, phlox and the old rose '*Grüss an Aachen*', create a languorous effect, a direct contrast to the flames of orange and scarlet and the purple foliage seen in the red borders from July to October. From the Bathing-pool Garden, where the still water is closely shielded by a high hedge as if to avoid a southern sun, a path leads along a stream planted to give subtle changes of mood down the water, white magnolias threaded with blue *Brunnera macrophylla* and periwinkles giving way to orange and yellow azaleas and lilies. A hint of the Mediterranean appears again in Mrs Winthrop's Garden, named after Lawrence Johnston's mother, with its strong blue and yellow colour scheme and pots of the purple cabbage palm and the variegated agave put out on the brick paving adding to the exotic effect created by yuccas and the Chusan palm.

Everywhere there are rare and unusual plants from all over the world, some of them, such as *Mahonia siamensis* and *M. lomariifolia*, and the delectable *Jasminium polyanthum*, the fruits of Lawrence Johnston's plant-gathering expeditions to South Africa in 1927 and to China in 1931. And there are several examples of the varieties he raised and selected, such as Hidcote lavender, Hidcote hypericum and the deep-yellow rose 'Lawrence Johnston'. The latter was grown at Serre de la Madonne, Lawrence Johnston's property in the south of France where he cultivated subtropical plants too tender for the Cotswolds. Here he lived until his death in 1958 after making Hidcote over to the National Trust.

Highdown Hill   West Sussex

1 mile north of Ferring, 3 miles north-west of Worthing, 1 mile south of the A27, between the South Downs and the sea

This wooded chalky hill between the South Downs and the sea, a mile or two from the sprawl of Worthing, is crowned by the single ditch and rampart of an early Iron Age hill fort. It is a site of great archaeological importance. The Iron Age defences were built on top of the earthworks of a late Bronze Age settlement, there is evidence of Romano-British occupation in the third century AD and a rich Saxon cemetery has been excavated within the ramparts. Finds from the site are in Worthing Museum.

High Ham Mill   Somerset

2 miles north of Langport, ½ mile east of High Ham

This stately stone tower set high above Sedgemoor is the last thatched windmill in England, the reed-covered peaked cap supporting the sails perched rather incongruously on a substantial four-storey building. Dating from about 1822, the mill continued to work until the early years of this century, although its wind power was being augmented with steam by the 1890s. The miller could grind 300lbs of meal an hour in an average wind.

A pulley system was used to turn the cap, but this has not survived, and nor has most of the milling machinery. A bakehouse and the miller's cottage stand near the earth platform supporting the mill – intended to stop livestock or people wandering too close to the sails – and there is also a little privy, used until modern conveniences were installed in 1970.

High Ham Mill, a tall stone tower looking out over Sedgemoor. (*NT/Neil Campbell-Sharp*)

Hill Top Cumbria

At Near Sawrey, behind the Tower Bank Arms

The young Beatrix Potter met virtually nobody and went almost nowhere. The one bright spot in a stifling existence with her domineering parents in London was the annual family holiday, in her early years to houses in Scotland, but from 1882, when she was sixteen, to the Lake District. These brief episodes and the freedom they brought fuelled a longing for the country which emerged in meticulously observed watercolours of wild creatures and plants and in the beginnings of the animal fantasies which have delighted children and adults for over seventy years.

Beatrix's purchase of this small hill farm in 1905 was a momentous step. Presented to her parents as nothing more than a good investment (which it was), to their lonely 39-year-old daughter the little rough stone, largely seventeenth-century house with a view over Sawrey to the fells beyond represented the possibility of escape from an increasingly dreary and unchanging regime. Although she was able only to snatch weeks here in the eight years that followed, this period was to see her best work, with the production of thirteen of the stories in which rabbits, mice, squirrels, hedgehogs and other creatures become humans in miniature, all

of them illustrated with Beatrix's charming and individual paintings.

Anyone who has read these nursery classics will recognise Hill Top and its well-furnished, homely rooms, filled with accumulated clutter. The long sloping garden flanking the steep path to the house, with rows of vegetables on one side and sweet peas, phlox and hollyhocks among a medley of traditional flowers on the other, is still as it appears in *The Tale of Tom Kitten* and *Pigling Bland*. The old-fashioned kitchen range with a black kettle bubbling away strikes a reassuring note in several animal holes and burrows, the nineteenth-century dresser is featured in *The Tale of Samuel Whiskers*, and the grandfather clock with a cheerful sun on its face was the model for the one in *The Tailor of Gloucester*. Peter Rabbit's red-spotted handkerchief and the doll's house food stolen by Hunca Munca and Tom Thumb – dishes of oranges and pears and a large ham – are in one of the tiny upstairs rooms. Some grander pieces of furniture, striking an unexpected note, were acquired after Beatrix's mother died, and one of the bedrooms is hung with her brother Bertram's landscape paintings.

For the last thirty years of her life, during which she was contentedly married to William Heelis, a local solicitor, Beatrix lived as a prosperous farmer in the nearby, but much larger, Castle Cottage (not open), reserving Hill Top for those times when she wished to be alone with her memories. This period saw her love of the countryside turned outwards rather than inwards. The affection for the Lake District which is evident in her illustrations of drystone walls, stone stiles, oak woods and sweeping hillsides was now channelled into an increasing concern for the conservation of the fells and into the deliberate accumulation of land to save it from being broken up or developed. Perfectly in sympathy with the aims of the young National Trust founded by her friend Canon Rawnsley in 1895, she began to see that her own land purchases could preserve property in perpetuity if given to the new organisation. In 1930 she acquired the substantial Monk Coniston estate covering a key area of the central Lake District, half of which she immediately re-sold to the Trust, and another fourteen farms and many cottages, together totalling 4,000 acres, came to the Trust on her death in 1943. Hill Top itself was kept exactly as it was, as if Beatrix Potter could not bear to disturb the place where she found peace and fulfilment. (*See also* Beatrix Potter Gallery, p.24.)

Hindhead Commons Surrey

12 miles south-west of Guildford, on both sides of the A3

Covering 1,400 acres on either side of the Portsmouth road is a classic Trust property, built up by gifts and bequests since 1906 when the Hindhead Preservation Committee, alarmed by the rash of newly built rich men's houses, raised funds and bought over 700 acres for the Trust.

The main feature is the large natural amphitheatre of the Devil's Punch Bowl, formed by springs cutting down and back from their sources. The great curve of the bowl is dry heathland, a mix of heather, gorse, bracken and grasses, with active reclamation or areas where the heather has been invaded by birch and pine. The Smallbrook stream runs east to drain the valley, providing a wetter habitat in the bottom. As recently as 1918 squatters who had settled in the Bowl were making birch brooms for a living. The Broom Squires – or broom squarers – made brooms of birch twigs for sale on the London market.

From the carpark, on the edge of the unattractive town of Hindhead, there are glorious walks round and down the Bowl, or up to the sandstone summit of Gibbet Hill, 894 feet high, where a stone commemorates the hanging of three miscreants who murdered a sailor walking to Portsmouth (at the time the London to Portsmouth road crossed the common). From Hurt Hill, to the south-east, there are splendid views over the Weald (*see* p.356).

One and a half miles west of Hindhead lies Ludshott Common and Waggoners' Wells. Parts of the common were enclosed in the last century. Local efforts raised funds to vest over 500 acres in the Trust in 1908, now increased to 700 acres. A very severe fire burnt out 400 acres of heath and pine wood in 1980 but subsequent clearance of scrub and careful management of the regenerating heather has restored one of the best expanses of open heath in the Weald. The 'wells', man-made ponds fed by springs which form one of the sources of the River Wey, provided water-power for hammering wrought iron during the sixteenth century, and now provide a home for swans, and in high summer for dragonflies and small hot boys. Marley, south of Haslemere, is a hilltop common with steep wooded slopes split into five separate pieces. At Shottermill there are two hammerponds like those at Ludshott. It pays to explore quiet corners here with the Ordnance Survey map.

Hinton Ampner Hampshire

On the A272, 1 mile west of Bramdean village, 8 miles east of Winchester

Ralph Dutton, the 8th and last Lord Sherborne, was a man born long after his time. A true connoisseur with a wide-ranging knowledge of architecture, interior decoration and gardening, and with the income to indulge his tastes, he would have been in his element 200 years ago. Given the very different world of the twentieth century, his achievements are remarkable. The large Victorian mansion he inherited at Hinton Ampner was remodelled in 1936–9 to create a pleasing neo-Georgian house in warm red brick, a suitable setting for a distinguished collection of furniture, *objets d'art* and paintings. The framework of his individual formal garden was also established at this time, to be filled in and embellished after the Second World War, and a wooded landscape park, its features composed as carefully as if it were a work of art, gradually emerged from a former muddle of hedgerows and scattered trees to form the foreground to the unspoilt chalk countryside beyond.

The house is built near the top of a rise with the ground falling away gently to the south, a magnificent site which Ralph Dutton used to full advantage, mellow brick steps linking frequent changes of level. Much of the charm of the garden lies in the way it seems to embrace the surrounding countryside, with grassy walks leading to vistas looking north and west, and with a great sweep of Hampshire stretching away from the broad terrace on the south front. Strategically placed eyecatchers, such as the large urn centred on the north vista or the sundial lined up with an oak in the park, are all exactly right for their settings. A statue of Diana faces the sundial down the length of the 600-foot-long walk flanked with pairs of Irish yews, and a little classical temple about halfway down marks another grassy corridor aligned on the remains of an old lime avenue crossing the park. These outward-looking compositions contrast with the more inward eastern side of the garden, where steps lead down to a yew-enclosed garden room and where the deep hollow of an old chalk pit, once the village dump and now known as the Dell, is walled by sloping beds planted with hostas, paulownias, rheums and giant hogweed. High box hedges frame the curving philadelphus walk flanking the Dell, and the site of the Tudor manor beside

Sweeping views over the wooded Hampshire countryside are one of the great attractions of Hinton Ampner, as this prospect from the bay-window of the drawing-room shows. (*NT/Nick Carter*)

the house is now marked by a peaceful orchard, a mass of daffodils in spring. Throughout the garden restful colour schemes seen against a background of evergreens reflect Ralph Dutton's belief in tranquillity and harmony. There are few signs that the soil is generally very thin, with solid chalk just below the surface, but a magnificent display of magnolias and hydrangeas marks a rare patch of deep loam.

In the house, too, everything has been chosen and placed to fulfil an overall vision. The elegant drawing-room facing east and south, with a classical screen partitioning the northern end, is particularly pleasing, the opulent gold and sea-green of the walls and curtains echoed in the more subdued tones of the carpet. The furnishings are indicative of Ralph Dutton's taste, an inlaid English cabinet of about 1800 and a giltwood side table with a top of white marble and bluejohn (once in Lord Curzon's house in Carlton House Terrace) revealing his love of hardstones. A landscape by Locatelli hanging above the cabinet and canvases by Pellegrini in the hall show Lord Sherborne's appreciation of Italian seventeenth-century painting and of Venetian art in particular. Some pieces were purchased on his travels abroad, others acquired at auction, from dealers, or from houses that had been or were being demolished.

It is difficult to believe that a disastrous fire on

3 April 1960 almost completely destroyed the house and most of its contents. Lesser men would have been defeated by this tragedy, but Ralph Dutton immediately set about rebuilding and refurnishing as beautifully as before.

Holnicote Estate Somerset

Astride the A3, between Minehead and Porlock

Exmoor, the smallest of Britain's National Parks, is perhaps the most appealing of them all. Only in the most extreme weather does it appear grim, like the Peak District or Dartmoor can so easily do. Its small compass allows the visitor to absorb its character more easily, yet within it are many very different places, each quite distinct from the rest.

The Trust owns a handsome slice of the moor, a large part in Devon (*see* pp.82, 148 and 192). In Somerset the 12,000-acre Holnicote estate takes pride of place. It extends from Porlock Bay, where Trust land includes an important area of saltmarsh, eastward for four miles, with steep cliffs running up to Selworthy Beacon at over 1,000 feet, and inland over the rich farms of Porlock Vale and the beautiful villages of Allerford, Bossington, Horner,

Luccombe and Selworthy (*see* p.284). The houses, cottages and farm buildings are of cob and thatch, red sandstone and slate. Each one is seemly, fits its purpose and almost appears to have grown there rather than having been built by man. The valley farms are mixed sheep and cattle holdings while the hill farms, with steep combes running up the thin pastures next to the open moor, are much harder to work. They fit into the landscape just as the buildings do.

There are lovely walks, some of them scrambles in part, based on Selworthy. Perhaps the best is up the wooded combe above the church, where there are oak, birch, some conifers, bracken and tumbling streams. As the trees tail off one reaches open moorland, heather and bilberry, bracken and gorse, with the hill fort of Bury Castle to the west. The path leads up to the Beacon, passing the Memorial Hut, a stone shelter facing four ways to enable the walker to sit and rest in comfort whichever way the wind is blowing. The view from here is immense in every direction and, while the energetic can walk west – to Bossington Hill and Hurlstone Point above Porlock Bay – or east to North Hill and the Trust's Greenaleigh Point, above Minehead, those with less stamina can track a little west and then

The mouth of the River Aller with Bossington Hill beyond: part of the extensive Holnicote estate on Exmoor. (*NT/Alan North*)

down the wooded Holnicote Coombe and past Catherine's Well.

To the south of the vale the moor is approached through the wooded fringe as the land rises sharply. Here is the Exmoor of the travel posters. Open oak woodland, heavily exploited for coppice in the past and including an ancient wood in Horner Vale, clothes the steep slopes which run up to the open country above. It is spectacularly beautiful and so, in places near the road, such as Webber's Post, sometimes uncomfortably crowded, but one has to walk only half a mile to reach complete seclusion. Paths stretch from every direction up to the heathery slopes of Dunkery Beacon, 1,705 feet above sea level and Exmoor's highest point, marked by a summit cairn. On a clear day, there are views across the Bristol Channel and south-west to Dartmoor, and, in the foreground, across this border country's characteristic mix of farmland, wooded combe and open moorland. These diverse habitats support rare and locally specialised plants and animals, including 170 species of lichen in the Horner oak woods and the largest British colony of the rare heath fritillary butterfly on the heather moorland.

At Winsford Hill, six miles to the south, and South Hill which adjoins it, the Trust leases a further 1,300 acres of glorious moorland, an outlier of the main moor and, except beside the B3223 which crosses it to connect Simonsbath and Dulverton, rarely a soul to be seen upon it.

Horsey Norfolk

2½ miles north-east of Potter Heigham, 11 miles north of Yarmouth astride the B1159

In 1948 the Trust acquired what had been the private nature reserve of a branch of the Buxton family (ubiquitous in East Anglia), Horsey Hall with its 1,700 acres of farmland running down to the coast, and surrounding Horsey Mere with its 'marshes and marrams'. It is satisfactory that a Buxton still lives here and will arrange limited access to the mere. The area includes the farm of Heigham Holmes above the marshes of Heigham Sound which form the east end of Hickling Broad. Lovers of Arthur Ransome's *Peter Duck*, for children of all ages up to 102, will not fail to recall that Mr Duck's married daughter, Rose, lived at Potter Heigham, a mile to the south.

The Horsey windmill is not for grinding corn but is a drainage mill pumping water from the low-level system to the high, which then reaches the sea twenty-three miles away at Yarmouth. A south-east wind allows the water to escape from the mere naturally. A north-west wind, in particular during spring tides, holds up the natural flow, and pumping is necessary if flooding is to be avoided. The mill was working until 1943, when it was severely damaged by lightning. It was repaired in 1958, and may be seen by visitors.

Horton Court Avon

3 miles north-east of Chipping Sodbury, ¾ mile north of Horton, 1 mile west of the A46 Bath–Stroud road

When Robert de Beaufeu was a prebend at Salisbury Cathedral in the early twelfth century, he would have travelled from his living at Horton, snuggled in the lee of the southern Cotswolds, to Old Sarum, built within Iron Age and Norman defences high on a hill above the River Avon, and worshipped in the church which is now no more than outlines in the grass. It was this worldly ecclesiastic – who wrote a poem in praise of beer – or his successor who built the Norman hall at Horton. This remarkable one-storey building, now attached to a Cotswold manor house, stands only a dozen feet from the church for which the prebends were responsible, two carved Gothic doorways and Norman windows set high in the buttressed walls giving the hall itself the look of a simple chapel. Probably the oldest rectory in England, it looks backwards to the single-storeyed manor halls of the Anglo-Saxons.

Just as remarkable is the fifty-foot detached loggia in the garden of the manor, built some 400 years after the hall, when the prebend, William Knight, combined his ecclesiastical responsibilities with a high-flying career in the king's service. Appointed chaplain and then private secretary to Henry VIII, Knight was employed on several diplomatic missions, culminating in a visit to Pope Clement VII in 1527 in an attempt to negotiate the king's divorce from Catherine of Aragon. Knight's first-hand knowledge of Italian culture undoubtedly inspired the charming Renaissance features which he added to his manor at Horton. The open arcade of his Italian-style loggia is decorated with stucco caricatures of classical worthies, including a portrait of a bearded Hannibal, and the doorway of

the manor house is carved with helmets, weapons and foliage. Although Knight seems to have had a particular affection for Horton, one of several rich livings he enjoyed, he must have had little time to visit the magnificent thirteenth-century cathedral at Salisbury, laid out on a virgin site by the Avon as the centrepiece of the new town.

Houghton Mill Cambridgeshire

In village of Houghton, signposted off the A1123 to St Ives

One of a handful of surviving mills along the River Great Ouse, this unusually large four-storey brick and timber building rises from an artificial island two miles downstream of Huntingdon, the tarred

Houghton Mill on the River Ouse, with the fourteenth-century steeple of St Mary's church on the right. (*NT/ F. A. H. Bloemendal*)

weatherboarding of the upper storeys easily recognisable across the flat water meadows bordering the river. Once a property of Ramsey Abbey ten miles to the north (*see* p.272), there has been a cornmill on or near this site for at least 1,000 years, although the present building dates only from the seventeenth century. Three breastshot wheels – removed when the mill ceased working in the 1930s – powered the ten pairs of millstones on the first floor and the hoists in the projecting gables which raised sacks of grain for storage at the top of the building. On open days the restored machinery is operated by electricity.

Hudswell North Yorkshire

2 miles west of Richmond

Richmond, on the River Swale, is one of the most seemly towns in the north of England, emphatically a place to be walked round. In the valley below, on the south bank, lie the Hudswell Woods – Calfhall, Round House, Billybank and Hag Wood – which are all delightfully cool on a summer's day.

Hughenden Manor Buckinghamshire

1½ miles north of High Wycombe; on west side of the Great Missenden road

The six years of Tory government from 1874 saw some of the greatest successes enjoyed by any ministry of Queen Victoria's reign, including progressive social reforms and an imperialist foreign policy which gained the queen the title of Empress of India. These achievements owed much to the personal skills of the Prime Minister, Benjamin Disraeli, already seventy when the new parliament began. His radical policies had been foreshadowed some thirty years earlier in his political novels – *Coningsby* and *Sybil* – concerned with the condition of the rural and urban poor.

But this forward-looking politician still adhered to some traditional values, his strong belief that landed property was essential to support the status of a leading public figure perhaps reflecting the insecurity generated by his Italian-Jewish descent. With no great financial resources at his command, the Hughenden estate was acquired in 1847 – on the eve of his possible appointment as leader of the Conservative Party – only with the generous assistance of Lord George Bentinck and his brothers, who lent Disraeli two-thirds of the purchase price. Here he and his wife Mary Anne lived until their deaths in 1872 and 1881 respectively, entertaining many of the great political and society figures of the day and leaving an indelible mark on the house and its beautiful setting.

Hughenden stands high up surrounded by trees, with a sweeping view over lawns to the hills beyond High Wycombe. Disraeli's writings show how he loved this place, the primroses he enjoyed still sprinkling the park in spring, and the cuckoo and wood pigeons still calling in the woods. On the long terrace where he paced back and forth are the Florentine vases acquired by Mary Anne, although

his peacocks have gone, and conifers replanted by the Trust on the entrance lawn echo those Disraeli established here, as shown in an early photograph.

Inside, every room of this Gothicised three-storey Georgian house includes some reminder of the Disraelis and their friends. The staircase and hall are lined with the Gallery of Friendship, portraits of those the statesman held most dear. The library contains an autographed copy of Queen Victoria's only published work, and Disraeli's novels appear among a notable collection of 'Theology, the Classics, and History'. Upstairs, his study is largely as he left it, portraits of his parents hanging over the mantelpiece and the black-edged notepaper that he always used after his wife's death lying ready on the table.

The obelisk crowning a far hillside in the view from the windows, erected by his wife in 1862 in memory of his father, would have reminded him of the two people who influenced him most. Disraeli

Benjamin Disraeli aged thirty-six, in a portrait by A. E. Chalon painted seven years before he acquired the Hughenden estate. (*Juliet Musket*)

never let his political ambitions destroy his very evident humanity and he was the only premier other than Melbourne to be honoured with a visit from the queen. As Bismarck shrewdly observed at the Congress of Vienna in 1878, '*Der alte Jude, das ist der Mann.*'

Ickworth Suffolk

In Horringer, 3 miles south-west of Bury St Edmunds on west side of the A143

Frederick Augustus Hervey, 4th Earl of Bristol, must rank as one of the Church's more remarkable bishops. Appointed to the see of Derry, the richest in Ireland, in 1768 when only thirty-eight, his sympathy with both Roman Catholics and Presbyterians made him enormously popular, despite a sometimes light-hearted approach to his duties which once led him to organise a curates' race along the sands at Downhill (*see* p.103), rewarding the winners with vacant benefices. A large income coupled with an inherited fortune allowed the 4th Earl to embark on extensive foreign tours, now commemorated in Hotels Bristol all over the Continent, during which he amassed the works of art which he intended to display in his new house on the family's Suffolk estate.

Ickworth is as grandiose and flamboyant as its creator, a larger version of his earlier house at Ballyscullion and clearly inspired by the circular Belle Isle on an island in Windermere (as was the Bishop's little Mussenden Temple at Downhill). A huge domed rotunda decorated with classical columns and terracotta friezes is linked by curving corridors to rectangular wings, the whole building some 600 feet from end to end. But Frederick was never to see his house completed. Started in 1795 to the designs of the Italian architect Mario Asprucci the Younger, building came to a halt on the 4th Earl's death from gout in an outhouse in Italy in 1803 (from where his body was shipped back to England labelled as an antique statue). Even more tragically, the Bishop's magnificent collection had been appropriated by Napoleon's armies in 1798.

The 4th Earl's ambitious plans were realised by his son, created 1st Marquess of Bristol in 1826. The superb paintings, porcelain and furniture now displayed here largely represent the slow accumulation of several generations of Herveys, who have owned the estate since the mid-fifteenth century and most of whom have followed brilliant political careers, but much was acquired by Frederick's gifted elder brother, the 2nd Earl, Ambassador in Madrid and Turin. And it was their father, the 1st Earl, who bought the early eighteenth-century Huguenot pieces among the silver displayed in the West Corridor, the relatively restrained hand of Paul de Lamerie contrasting with more ornate rococo Italian work. One case is devoted to a shoal of silver fishes, some designed as ornamental pendants, others as scent containers, their realistic, scaly forms including a whale and a swordfish as well as more mundane species.

The 1st Marquess housed the bulk of the collection in the grand state rooms in the rotunda rather than in the wings as his father had intended. The largest room in the house is the hemispherical library across the south front, notable for its rare late seventeenth- and early eighteenth-century political periodicals and ornamented with busts of Pitt, Canning, Fox and Liverpool. Hogarth's Holland House Group on the end wall, showing the 1st Earl in the centre of a group of friends including the 3rd Duke of Marlborough, is one of a number of outstanding portraits in the house, rivalled by Velázquez's study of the Infante Balthasar Carlos, son of Philip IV, a grave little boy with two greyhounds and a huge mastiff at his feet, and by Gainsborough's full-length canvas of the colourful Augustus John Hervey, Vice Admiral of the Blue, who briefly succeeded as 3rd Earl between his two brothers. It seems this philanderer deserved his wife, Elizabeth Chudleigh, whose bigamous marriage with the Duke of Kingston in 1769 gave rise to one of the most famous scandals of the eighteenth century. Quite different in character is the charming self-portrait by Madame Vigée Lebrun, commissioned by the Earl-Bishop in Naples in 1791, the artist's severe black dress setting off her vivacious face crowned with a mop of curly hair loosely caught up in a white handkerchief. The most extraordinary exhibit is undoubtedly Flaxman's marble group, *The Fury of Athamas*, based on a scene from Ovid's *Metamorphoses*, which dominates the staircase hall. Commissioned by the 4th Earl, Athamas is here shown holding his young son over his shoulder by an ankle, about to dash him to death. A second child clings to their mother, terrified.

From the 1st Marquess's orangery, the only part of the west wing to be completed, floor-length windows lead out on to a terrace looking south over

Fine paintings in the collection at Ickworth include this charming self-portrait by Madame Vigée Lebrun, commissioned by Frederick Augustus Hervey, the Earl-Bishop, in 1791. (*NT/Angelo Hornak*)

the heavily wooded garden, where tall cypresses, yews, evergreen oak and box create the illusion of an Italian landscape. Artfully contrived vistas give enticing glimpses of the rotunda. In spring bluebells in the Silver Garden hidden in the trees form a sea lapping at hexagonal columns brought from the Giant's Causeway (*see* p.229). Subtle colours here are a direct contrast to the brassy yellow, salmon-pink and purple stripes in the Edwardian-style border fronting the nineteenth-century east wing. From the long raised terrace walk beyond the trees, created in *c.*1870 to shield the garden, there is a sweeping panorama over clumps of mature beeches and oaks in the park, many of them probably planted by 'Capability' Brown for the 2nd Earl. In the foreground, partly hidden in a dip, is Ickworth church, while an obelisk just visible above a wooded ridge on the far horizon was erected by the people of Derry in affectionate memory of their bishop.

Ightham Mote Kent

6 miles east of Sevenoaks, off the A25, and 2½ miles south of Ightham, off the A227

Descending the steep path from the carpark, Ightham Mote suddenly appears hidden in the deep, wooded valley below, its walls rising sheer from a surrounding moat. Half-timbered upper storeys project from the façade here and there, as if peering down at the little hump-backed stone bridge which crosses the water to an old wooden door. The roofline is a medley of steeply pitched gables, massive brick chimneys and moss-stained tiles. Ducks paddle about beneath the walls.

Built round three courtyards and dating originally from the fourteenth century, this beautiful manor house has retained its medieval appearance, despite many later alterations, largely because additions were always made using local oak and Kentish ragstone and were sympathetic to the ancient building. Some traces of the early house still remain. On the oak bargeboards in the cobbled courtyard, twining branches carry the Tudor rose of England, the fleur-de-lis of France and the pomegranate of Granada, the badge of Catherine of Aragon. The window of the great hall still has its original early sixteenth-century glass, in which the Tudor rose and Aragon pomegranate glow brilliantly on a sunny day. This armorial decoration is the work of Richard Clement, the great courtier

who bought Ightham in 1521 and who was anxious to display his allegiance to the house of Tudor. Less than a decade later Catherine was to be cast aside by Henry VIII, thus securely dating the period when her arms could have been added to the house.

Sir Richard Clement was also responsible for decorating the long, half-timbered room on the first floor. Now a chapel but originally intended as a gallery, its arched wagon roof is exuberantly painted to imitate a tournament tent with vividly coloured badges and emblems in red, orange, green and white representing the royal houses of England, Spain and France. The colours have faded now, but it is easy to imagine how glowing they must once have been. An elaborately decorated pulpit with Gothic tracery and choir stalls carved with grotesque faces were installed when the room was converted into a chapel, possibly in the mid-seventeenth century. There is also some fine linenfold panelling, sixteenth-century stained glass in the windows and a remarkable oak door at the west end. Dating from *c.*1640, this is older than Sir Richard Clement's alterations.

Across a landing from the chapel is the drawing-room, a startling change in atmosphere and style. One end is filled with a monumental Jacobean fireplace decorated with carved Saracen heads and painted in black and gold. The walls are covered in nineteenth-century hand-painted Chinese wallpaper and the room as a whole has a distinctly exotic flavour, although, as in the rest of the house, the furniture has been added since the 1950s when the original contents were sold.

An extensive lawn stretches up the combe north of the house, framed by woods on the steep valley sides, its regular outlines marking the site of a medieval stewpond that was once fed by the stream which now tumbles over a cascade and crosses the grass to fill the moat. A raised walk fringing the east side leads to a lake hidden in the trees beyond the lawn and to a network of woodland paths through mixed native and exotic trees underplanted with evergreens. Near the house a long border is crowded with traditional English flowers such as pinks, sweet williams, lilies and roses, but the clematis and rose pergola that once shaded the path above the west side of the lawn has disappeared.

This consciously old-fashioned garden, based on a medieval layout, reflects the late nineteenth-century's romantic view of the Middle Ages (*see also* Oxburgh, p.242) and also the influence of William

When the Tudor emblems and badges adorning the barrel ceiling of the chapel at Ightham Mote were freshly painted, the brilliant bands of colour would have echoed the decoration of pavilions and other temporary structures set up for court festivities, now only known from illustrations of the period. (*NT/Rob Matheson*)

Morris's Arts and Crafts movement (*see also* Snowshill, p.297). Although the garden was severely damaged by the Great Storm of 1987, which felled several fine cedars, Scots pine and yew, these are now being replanted and the paved Fountain Garden with pinks and rock roses in the crevices between the flags is being restored. Part of the charm of this unusual place derives from the constant sound of running water, like soothing background music.

Ilfracombe to Baggy Point Devon

On the north coast, between Ilfracombe and Morte Bay

At Morte Point the coast of North Devon, which has run due west since the Somerset border, turns south into the great sweep of Bideford Bay. It is different in character from the Exmoor coast, for here the hinterland, though it runs up to 800 feet, is all farmed. The farms extend to the cliffs and sheep graze wherever the walker can go, and in many places where he cannot.

The Trust owns nearly all of this coast, both east and west of Morte, some nine miles of very varied terrain. Ilfracombe still retains the charm of an early Victorian watering place, seemly stucco terraces ranked up the slopes above the harbour which is tucked under the steep cliff of Hillsborough on its east side. Immediately west of the town, the cliffs rise sharply to a series of rocky outcrops and this land, known as Torrs Walks, is well provided with paths cut into the slatey rock known as the Ilfracombe Beds. These lead on westward along the slopes of the Seven Hills and the Runnacleaves. Beyond Brandy Cove Point a former carriage road runs as far as Lee. The views are to the west; the air exhilarating.

The old road drops down to Lee Bay, the village in the combe behind it, and then on to the Trust's land again up Flagstaff Hill to the cliffs of Damage Barton. The Trust has made a staircase here to Sandy Cove, access to which was previously vertiginous. The cliff is particularly attractive, gorse thickets separated by humpy pasture, good for spring and summer flowers. Bennett's Water runs down to rocky reefs at Bennett's Mouth, its valley giving shelter to wintering birds.

The lighthouse on Bull Point was rebuilt in 1972 after its predecessor had become unsafe due to rockfalls. From the point the coast runs south past the sandy Rockham Beach and then curves westward to Morte. This is one of the great headlands of the West Country. Sailing ships beating up to Bristol had to weather Morte or stand offshore, for the reefs, and the Morte Stone beyond them, are perilous. In the churchyard at Mortehoe many drowned sailors are buried. The cliffs are low, still formed of slate, here called by geologists the Morte slate, but the slopes above them are grazed by sheep which keep the bracken, gorse and bramble at bay. To the west, Lundy (see p.189) looms on the horizon, and on the mainland Hartland Point at about the same distance, eleven miles south of the island.

The village of Mortehoe stands above the cliffs, followed by the hotels of Woolacombe behind Barricane Beach. Behind them the little Combesgate valley runs up to Twitchen, giving a sheltered walk on a blustery day. The Trust owns much of the farmland behind Woolacombe and this ownership has stopped the town spreading except up the hill towards the former railway station, for the line from Barnstaple to Mortehoe and Ilfracombe was a casualty of the Beeching era.

The two miles of Woolacombe Beach are all firm golden sand. Above rise the high dunes of Woolacombe Warren and, behind the dunes, the Marine Drive, a speculative venture made before 1914 in an attempt to develop this coast which thankfully never came off. It serves a most useful purpose as a carpark, not only for users of the beach but also for the elderly and disabled who can sit by their cars and absorb the atmosphere of this splendid place. Above the Drive the bold outline of Woolacombe Down forms a backdrop to the great beach.

The south end of the beach at Vention does not belong to the Trust. Its land starts at Ramson Cliff (ramson is the West Country name for the broad-leaved garlic, *Allium ursinum*), and from here the cliff path runs for a mile to Baggy Point which closes Morte Bay. Baggy is very different from Morte. Its rock is sandstone and it juts into the sea, high and bold, the house and buildings of Croyde Hoe Farm near its tip, the fields reaching out to the cliff edge. Shags and cormorants, fulmars and gulls nest on the point, with ravens, jackdaws and kestrels breeding here as well.

Isle of Wight

Although the island is small – thirteen miles from Cowes south to St Catherine's Point and seventeen miles from the Needles east to Bembridge – a great deal is packed into it, and the Trust has been active here since 1922, its estate largely built up by the efforts of a devoted Local Committee.

Much of the Trust's holding lies on the chalk hills which run right across the island. Bembridge and Culver Downs at its east end rise to 343 feet, with sheer cliffs providing safe nesting sites for seabirds (for the early eighteenth-century Bembridge windmill, *see* p.26).

At Ventnor, to the south-west, there are panoramic views from Littleton and Luccombe Downs, both seaward and north over the island to the Solent and the New Forest.

At 764 feet St Boniface Down above Ventnor is the highest point on the island. At its southernmost tip, however, the geology changes. St Catherine's Hill, with a fine view over West Wight, is chalk, while St Catherine's Down is greensand, but Knowles Farm, which runs down from there to the foreshore, is on blue lias clay, known locally as Blue Slipper. The clay is unstable and landslips are comparatively common; hence the scrubby slopes and hollows with an interesting flora. St Catherine's Point is a place where migratory birds assemble, and records have been kept by ornithologists for many years.

Westward again, beyond Brighstone, the Trust

The familiar outline of the chalk stacks known as the Needles at the westernmost tip of the Isle of Wight. The Needles Old Battery (*see* p.212) is dug into the headland above. (*NT/Nick Carter*)

protects by ownership or covenant over seven miles of coast and downland from Chilton Chine to the Needles, offering a spectacular coastal walk and at Compton Bay some of the island's best bathing beaches. Much of the land is chalk down, the thin soil covered with short downland grasses and lime-loving plants, with thickets of hawthorn and gorse and the typical downland birds: wheatears, larks and pipits. Walking is exhilarating: the chain of downs, Mottistone, Brook, Compton and Afton, the pre-historic ridgeway along the crest of the hills, the barrows from the Bronze Age and the views along the coast make this a very special place. At Motti-stone there is an additional bonus as the Trust's estate includes much of the village grouped round

the church and manor house (*see* p.206), framed by the woodland behind.

To the west, beyond Freshwater, Tennyson Down is held in memory of the poet who walked there daily when living at Farringford nearby. West High Down provides the final link which connects the westerly tip of the island to the Needles, the best known and most spectacular of all chalk cliffs.

The tallest pinnacle, known as Lot's Wife, collap-sed in 1764 and erosion still continues, but the three which remain, with the lighthouse crouched protec-tively at their outer end, live in the mind's eye of all who have seen them. Built into the cliff is the nineteenth-century Old Battery (*see* p.212), part of the defences of the Solent against the French, now restored and with an exhibition telling its history.

Newtown is something utterly different. The Newtown river, now a sequestered wooded estuary, was in the thirteenth century a flourishing harbour. What remains of the town mostly belongs to the

Robert Adam's charming fishing pavilion on the upper lake at Kedleston Hall, looking across the park to the north front of the house. There is a cold bath below the upper room, flanked by boathouses on either side. (*NT/Andrew Haslam*)

Trust and is of great interest (*see* p.213), but it is the estuary, with its seven miles of creeks and four miles of the Solent foreshore, which is especially good: oyster beds, yacht moorings, saltings and bird life, copses rich in butterflies, quietness, beauty.

Kedleston Hall Derbyshire

3 miles north of Derby, easily reached and signposted from the A38 Derby bypass

No one could describe this cold neo-classical palace as welcoming. A massive pedimented portico adorned with classical sculpture rises the full height of a three-storey central block, with curved corridors leading to rectangular pavilions on either side. Only the tower of a little medieval church peeping over the roof of the west pavilion breaks the symmetry of the façade.

Kedleston was always intended as a showpiece. Sir Nathaniel Curzon, later 1st Lord Scarsdale, began the house in 1759, only a year after he had inherited the estate. A cultivated man who was interested in the arts, he saw it as a setting for his collection of paintings and sculpture – on view to visitors from the day the house was built. The formal reception rooms and guest suite filling the central block were never intended to be used except for the entertainment of important visitors. The family lived in one pavilion, with the kitchen and domestic offices in the other.

Although work began under the direction of Matthew Brettingham and James Paine, by 1760 these two architects had been superseded by the young Robert Adam, recently returned from Rome, who transformed his predecessors' rather conventional designs. Adam's monumental marble hall, with ten alabaster columns like tree-trunks on either side and classical statues in niches along the walls, is top-lit to suggest the open courtyard of a Roman villa. The adjoining rotunda known as the saloon, its coffered dome rising to a height of sixty-two feet, was based on the Pantheon in Rome, one of the most admired buildings of classical antiquity. To either side lie formal reception rooms, Adam's hand evident in virtually every detail of their decoration. Delicate plaster ceilings in pastel shades were executed by the Yorkshireman Joseph Rose, paintings were grouped and hung according to Adam's schemes – plaster frames built into the walls in some rooms ensure his arrangements have survived – and even the furniture shows his touch, carved dolphins, merfolk and sea nymphs on the four great sofas in the drawing-room echoing the nautical theme of the Adam ceiling.

The paintings hanging double-banked in all the principal rooms, including a number of epic canvases such as Benedetto Luti's *Cain and Abel* or Samuel Koninck's *Daniel before Nebuchadnezzar*, illustrate Scarsdale's taste for seventeenth-century Italian and Dutch art. Family portraits dating back to the sixteenth century adorn the guest apartments, a charming study by Nathaniel Hone showing the 1st Lord Scarsdale walking the grounds of Kedleston with his wife. Thomas Barber's portrayal of the elderly Mrs Garrett, the housekeeper who took Boswell and Dr Johnson round Kedleston in 1777, is also memorable.

Bluejohn vases and ornaments are part of a notable collection of this prized Derbyshire stone, and Kedleston was further enriched in the early twentieth century by Marquess Curzon of Kedleston, who acquired Indian and oriental artefacts during travels in Asia and while he was Viceroy of India from 1899–1905.

The long drive from the great arched gateway of Adam's north lodge runs through his idealised landscape park, with carefully placed clumps of trees and a chain of serpentine lakes crossed by a three-arched stone bridge. Adam also designed the charming fishing pavilion on the upper lake, a Venetian window facing north over the water enabling ladies to cast a line while being shielded from the sun. Only the little cruciform medieval church remains of the village that was swept away

by Lord Scarsdale so that it would not intrude on the setting of his classical masterpiece.

To the south of the house a broad open lawn bounded by a ha-ha marks the eighteenth-century informal garden. A formal layout to the west was introduced in the early years of this century, when the hexagonal summerhouse and orangery, both designed by George Richardson in the late eighteenth century, were moved to their present positions. A pair of gates leads into the Long Walk, a winding three-mile circuit of the south side of the park with extensive views.

Keld Chapel Cumbria

1 mile south-west of Shap village, by River Lowther

The little hamlet of Keld, on the eastern edge of the Cumbrian fells, was once part of the estates of Shap Abbey, now an isolated ruin about a mile away, and this modest stone and slate building by the River Lowther was probably built by the abbey in the late fifteenth or early sixteenth century for the people of the village. Occasional services are once again held in the chapel, which was long used for other purposes.

Kent Coast: The White Cliffs

At the south-east corner of England, the rounded outlines of the North Downs meet the sea in spectacular chalk cliffs, where the advent of the Channel Tunnel has emphasised the importance of the Trust's protective role. The string of properties held here, amounting to some 560 acres and over $5\frac{1}{2}$ miles of the famous White Cliffs, lies either side of Dover: a mile of farmland and cliff at Great Farthingloe, to the west, close to the tunnel approaches; undulating, orchid-rich chalk grassland and farmland at Langdon Cliffs and Langdon Hill, behind Dover, with stunning views over the port and, on a clear day, across the Channel to France; and a number of holdings at St Margaret's Bay to the northeast, including a lighthouse (*see* p.310). Butterflies and birds abound, and there are fossils in the chalk, remains of World War II defences and exhilarating walking.

About 12 miles up the coast, the Trust protects some 550 acres of saltings, sand-dunes and mudflats at Pegwell Bay, where the River Stour winds lazily to the sea. Managed by the Kent Trust for

Nature Conservation as a nature reserve, this estuarine coast attracts migrant waders and native sea and shore birds.

Killerton Devon

On west side of the B3181, formerly the A38, Exeter–Cullompton road

Sir Thomas Dyke Acland's decision to engage the Scottish gardener John Veitch to lay out the grounds round his new house at Killerton in the 1770s was an inspired choice. Then a very young man – not yet twenty-one – who had walked from Edinburgh to seek his fortune with only ten shillings to his name, John Veitch was to become one of the greatest nurserymen and landscape designers of his day. The firm he founded was the first to send plant hunters to little-known parts of the world, from where they brought back exotic specimens that had never before been seen in England.

Killerton reflects Veitch's lifetime association with the estate. His garden – more accurately an arboretum – is laid out on the slopes of the steep volcanic outcrop known as Killerton Clump, the highest point for miles around. Paths climb ever upwards through the trees, with views down over a sea of foliage and across the flat fertile landscape of the valley of the River Clyst. Veitch's beech walk follows the contours of the hill, a cool green arch

Autumn colour on the south front of Killerton. (*NT*)

meeting overhead. Mature wellingtonias, redwoods, spruces and cedars, introduced from the Veitch nursery, tower over an almost infinite variety of rhododendrons, some of them Veitch introductions, others grown from seed brought back from the Himalayas in the 1920s, when Sir Francis Acland supported Captain Kingdon-Ward's plant-hunting expeditions, all of them flourishing in the acid soil. May and June here are magnificent, with hummocks of scarlet, crimson, yellow and white against young foliage. Earlier in the year there are daffodils between the trees and the white blossoms of magnolia, and there is autumn colour too. The more formal garden near the house – a long terrace planted with dwarf shrubs, from which Lloyd George once addressed 19,000 people in the park, and a broad herbaceous border – was created on the advice of the great Edwardian gardener William Robinson, and the rock garden by the icehouse was also added at this time.

At the edge of the arboretum, tracks continue to the Iron Age hill fort crowning the clump, first occupied in *c.*400BC, from where there are panoramas in all directions, those to south and east unfortunately marred by the busy M5 which cuts right across the view. To the north of the prehistoric earthworks trees give way to the open parkland of The Plain on the summit of the hill, with views over the Culm valley to the east and through or over the woods to the main railway line from London to Penzance far below. Deer walls on the western slopes of the hill are relics of the herd that was kept here until *c.*1920.

The house does not compete with its surroundings. A straggling buff building at the foot of the hill, later additions almost conceal the unpretentious square block built in 1778 by the Essex architect John Johnson, originally intended to be replaced by a grandiose mansion by James Wyatt on the side of the hill. Johnson's magnificent stables at the foot of the drive are a much better monument to his talent, an elegant cupola rising over the impressive pedimented archway leading into the courtyard. Another Sir Thomas – the 10th Baronet – was responsible for the Victorian chapel by C.R.Cockerell to the north of the stables, built to supersede the tiny Elizabethan building on the other side of the hill, almost all that remains of the former Acland house at Columbjohn.

Killerton's interiors, much altered over the years, recall country living between the First and Second

World Wars, when weekend parties sat down to eat off the family silver laid out in the dining-room, the most privileged female guests nearest the fire. The masculine library next door now houses the collection of the Rev. Sabine Baring-Gould (1834–1924), the larger-than-life parson of the Devonshire village of Lewtrenchard, best known for his hymn 'Onward Christian Soldiers', who is unlikely to have approved of the set of false book-backs with fanciful titles in a corner of the room. Music by Samuel Sebastian Wesley on the chamber organ dominating the music-room is dedicated to the wife of the 10th Baronet, who took lessons from Wesley when he was organist of Exeter Cathedral. More restful musical evenings are suggested by the table set up for part singing.

Many of the rooms at Killerton are now devoted to the Paulise de Bush collection of eighteenth- to twentieth-century costume, displayed on dummies in carefully composed tableaux to show the life and society of the day, flimsy floral chiffon evening gowns of the 1930s contrasting with high-necked, full-skirted Victorian gowns.

King John's Hunting Lodge

Somerset

In the Square at Axbridge, on corner of High Street

Like contemporary towns in East Anglia (*see* Paycocke's, p.245), Axbridge, Trowbridge, Bradford-on-Avon and other centres of the medieval wool trade in the West Country were once filled with prosperous merchants' houses such as this misleadingly named example of *c.*1500. A three-storey timber-framed building on the corner of Axbridge's market place, it is jettied out over the street in a double overhang. A small museum of local history and archaeology is now housed here.

The King's Head Buckinghamshire

At north-west corner of Market Square in Aylesbury

A narrow passage from Aylesbury's busy market square leads to this lovely old coaching inn with a large cobbled stable yard. Parts of the building date back to 1450, and fragments of fifteenth-century glass survive in the large mullioned and transomed window which lights the bar, once the hall of a medieval house.

Kingston Lacy Dorset

On the B3082 Wimborne–Blandford road, 1½ miles west of Wimborne

Home of the Bankes family from 1663 when Sir Ralph Bankes built a house here to replace the earlier seat at Corfe Castle (*see* p.84), ruined in the Civil War, Kingston Lacy is a monument to the eccentric and original William John Bankes (1786–1855), friend of Byron. With the aid of Sir Charles Barry, architect of the Houses of Parliament, William transformed the house into an Italianate *palazzo*, filled with pictures and other works of art he had acquired during his extensive travels in the Mediterranean. Prosecuted in 1841 for committing a homosexual act with a guardsman, he fled to Italy, where he spent the rest of his life. Although likely never to see his house again, this extraordinary man continued to concern himself with its furnishing and decoration.

Still retaining the shape of the original Restoration mansion by Sir Roger Pratt, Kingston Lacy is a symmetrical three-storey oblong with a balustrade and central cupola crowning the hipped roof. Tall chimneys give the house the look of an upturned footstool. On the grand south front a broad Italianate terrace sweeps right across the façade, with central steps flanked by urns and guarded by lions descending on to a lawn dotted with Venetian wellheads. The impressive marble staircase leading visitors up to the principal rooms on the first floor is also of Italian inspiration, provided with an airy loggia on the half-landing as if to give protection from a Mediterranean sun. One of three bronze figures set in niches here depicts brave Lady Mary Bankes, still holding the key of Corfe Castle which she twice defended for King Charles in the Civil War (the actual keys hang in the library upstairs).

No traces of Roger Pratt's house survive inside, but some rooms still remain from R.F.Brettingham's remodelling in the 1780s for Henry Bankes. The painted ceiling by Cornelius Dixon in the saloon arches over the room like elaborate wrapping paper, delicate curves and spirals of foliage

(*Overleaf*) Infra-red photography of *The Judgement of Solomon*, Sebastiano del Piombo's unfinished masterpiece at Kingston Lacy, has revealed a sword in the hand of the executioner on the right and the missing babies. (*NT/Christopher Hurst*)

echoing the rich floral borders on the opulent Savonnerie carpet. The paintings hanging two and three deep include Rubens's portraits of the Grimaldi sisters acquired by William, one encased in her gleaming wedding-dress like an exotic beetle, the other pictured with her dwarf.

The jewel of the house is the Spanish Room next door, where works William procured during his travels in Spain at the time of the Peninsular War against Napoleon are set against magnificent gilded leather hangings and seen beneath a sumptuous coffered ceiling, thought to be one of those Scamozzi added to the Palazzo Contarini on the Grand Canal in Venice. Papal power and splendour shine through Velázquez's portrait of Cardinal Massimi, clothed here in peacock blue. Another masterpiece, Sebastiano del Piombo's unfinished *The Judgement of Solomon*, dominates the dining-room.

The centre of an extensive estate (*see* p.100), Kingston Lacy is also surrounded by a naturalistic 250-acre park landscaped in the late eighteenth century, dotted with mature trees and now grazed by a herd of Red Devon cattle. The Edwardian garden being restored by the Trust includes a brightly coloured parterre to the west of the house,

where beds of forget-me-nots and crimson and yellow wallflowers in the spring are replaced by begonias and heliotrope later in the year, and a Victorian fernery to the east. A cedar walk lined with trees planted by visiting notables, including the Duke of Wellington, leads to the lime avenue and the arboretum known as the Nursery Wood beyond, where a number of young specimen trees – cedars, a swamp cypress, a wellingtonia and Brewer's weeping spruce among them – have recently been established. A pink granite obelisk, one of four in the garden, was brought here by William from a temple in the Nile which he saw on his journeys.

Kinver Edge Staffordshire

4 miles west of Stourbridge, 4 miles north of Kidderminster, west of the A449

Adjoining the large village of Kinver there rises a prominent sandstone escarpment. Once forested, it is now heathland with thickets and self-seeded birch, oak and pine.

The Trust began to acquire land at Kinver Edge

The heathland of Kinver Edge is the remnant of an ancient forest. (*NT/Will Curwen*)

in 1917 and has continued to add to its holding when the opportunity arises: its 285 acres now run with the County Council-owned Kingsford Country Park which forms the southern part of the Edge. The views to the Clent Hills (*see* p.75) and to Wenlock Edge (*see* p.289) are noteworthy, but it is the remains of the extraordinary rock dwellings tunnelled into the sandstone which have made the place famous. Some of the best are at Vales Rock, at the southern end of the Edge in Kingsford Country Park. These were well fitted up, and had beautifully laid-out gardens. The inhabitants earned a living by making besom brooms and from coppicing oak. Abandoned in the 1960s, the Edge has been occupied once again since the Trust recently rebuilt a terrace of gabled cottages set into the top of the cliff.

Kinwarton Dovecote Warwickshire

1½ miles north-east of Alcester, just south of the B4089

This substantial fourteenth-century circular dovecote sitting proudly in a field at the end of a muddy lane probably once belonged to the Abbey of Evesham some twelve miles away to the south, the only survivor of a former monastic grange. Doves are still housed in some of the 580 nesting holes built into the limestone walls, filling the air with their cooing and perching picturesquely on the red-tiled conical roof. Those who dare can climb the original potence, the ingenious manoeuvrable ladder supported on a pivoting central post which gives access to all the nesting boxes. Apart from this rare survival, Kinwarton dovecote is also notable for its fine ogee doorway.

Knightshayes Court Devon

2 miles north of Tiverton

The drunken mob who destroyed his Nottinghamshire factory on 28 June 1816 prompted the young John Heathcoat to move his revolutionary new lace-making machines to the safety of Devonshire, where he set up in one of the Tiverton mills left empty by the decline of the wool industry. The profits from what was to become the largest lace factory in the world enabled his grandson, John Heathcoat-Amory, the 1st Baronet, to purchase the Knightshayes estate and to build the idiosyncratic

This chivalric fantasy, with knights assaulting the Castle of Love, was designed by William Burges for the chimney-piece of the dining-room at Knightshayes. Like most of the other decorative fantasies he dreamed up for the house, this was never realised. (*NT/John Bethell*)

Gothic house that looks down on the little town in the valley below.

Knightshayes does not welcome visitors, the dark-red Hensley stone of the garden façade, with its pointed gables, mullioned windows and prominent gargoyles, rising forbiddingly from the terraces to the right of the drive. A rare example of the domestic architecture of William Burges, the High Victorian medievalist who is much better known for his churches, such as the masterpiece at Studley Royal (*see* p.322), this rather dour exterior was planned to conceal interiors of exceptional richness. Although Burges's designs were never executed, the schemes produced by his more conventional replacement, John Diblee Crace, were by no means subdued. Quotations from Robert Burns in gold letters several inches high run round the frieze in the dining-room, set off by dark panelling and a rich red and green wallpaper and vying for attention with the brightly painted ceiling, one of several in the house. The corbels of the principal beams are carved with creatures from the Devon countryside: a badger, a fox and an otter with a fish. The medievalism of the hall, the only room to be completed largely as Burges planned, is even more striking, with its Gothic arches, gallery, timber vault and whimsical carvings. Burges also designed the great painted bookcase with panels by Burne-Jones and Rossetti that stands here.

The Old Masters in the drawing-room, the nucleus of the collection acquired by the 3rd Baronet (1894–1972), provide a show of a different kind, including Constable's vivid red poppies like a scarlet splash on the wall by the fireplace, a misty Turner seascape, a Rembrandt self-portrait with fleshy face and thickly curling hair and Holbein's delicate *A Lady in a White Cap*, her high unmarked forehead suggesting extreme youth. Upstairs is a lower-key display of paintings by the local artist F. T. Widgery.

Although based on a nineteenth-century design by Edward Kemp, the garden owes much to the 3rd Baronet and his wife, who greatly enlarged it and made it one of the finest in the county. A formal layout near the house includes a water-lily pool in a battlemented yew enclosure and a topiary hunt on the hedges framing the lawn to the south, one of the pursuing hounds shown gathering itself to leap a leafy obstacle. To the east, grassy walks and glades cross thirty acres of rare trees and shrubs, a place of dappled shade and varied foliage. A tongue of land thickly covered with large-leaved rhododendrons contrasts with a majestic stand of Douglas fir and with the elegant, soaring trunks in the larch wood. One of the most recently planted areas is the willow garden in a little valley to the west of the house, where the grass is thick with daffodils in spring.

Knole Kent

At south end of Sevenoaks, just east of the A225

The gateway to Knole lies off the main A225 through Sevenoaks, a sudden opening between the buildings lining the road. The drive from this modest entrance emerges unexpectedly into the glorious 1,000-acre park surrounding the house, scored with deep valleys, planted with ancient oaks, beeches and chestnuts, and grazed by herds of fallow and Sika deer. As the road breasts a rise, there is a view of what looks like a compact hilltop town, with rabbit-cropped turf running almost up to the walls and a jumble of chimneys, gables, battlements and red-tiled roofs rising behind. Sprawled round courtyards like an Oxford college, Knole could house the retinue of a medieval prince. The main ranges are of rough Kentish ragstone, but hidden away in some of the minor courts are half-timbered façades, like those seen in a hundred villages round about. Inside, in contrast to the rather plain and rugged exterior, are furnishings and decoration of great richness and rarity.

The core of Knole was built by Thomas Bourchier, Archbishop of Canterbury, between 1456 and his death in 1486, when he bequeathed it to the see of Canterbury. Four more archbishops enjoyed the splendid residence Bourchier had created before Archbishop Cranmer was forced to give it to Henry VIII. The covetous king considerably enlarged his new palace, but it seems he spent little or no time here. It was later held briefly by Elizabeth I's favourite, the Earl of Leicester, but in 1566 the queen granted the house and estate to her cousin Thomas Sackville, whose descendants, the Earls and later Dukes of Dorset, and then Lords Sackville, have lived here ever since. Largely due to the cultivated 3rd Duke of Dorset, who treasured Knole's sense of age, the house was not remodelled in the classical style during the eighteenth century. It is this lack of alteration which makes Knole such a precious survival amongst the great houses of England.

Knole's collection of seventeenth-century furniture and textiles was mostly acquired by the 6th Earl some half a century after the original contents of the house had been dispersed in the Civil War. As Lord Chamberlain to William III, the Earl was entitled to take away discarded furnishings from the royal palaces and he also enriched Knole with the furniture acquired by his father-in-law, the Earl of Middlesex, who was Master of the Great Wardrobe to James I. As a result, Knole's galleries and bedchambers are filled with state beds, tapestries, chairs and stools that would once have adorned the palaces of Whitehall, Hampton Court and Kensington. For many the culmination of a visit to the house is the King's Room, where some of the rarest and finest pieces are displayed. The famous silver looking-glass, table and candlestands shine brilliantly in the simulated candlelight, drawing the eye

The west front of Knole with its battlemented gatehouse was almost certainly built by Henry VIII, but the curved gables are a later addition by Thomas Sackville, 1st Earl of Dorset, to whom Elizabeth I granted the house in 1566. (*NT/Rob Matheson*)

away from the magnificent great bed with its cloth of silver and gold and matching chairs and stools.

The furniture, the embroidered fabrics and tapestries, the ornate plaster ceilings and carved marble chimneypieces are all a reflection of the painstaking craftsmanship which created this house. Even the drainpipes have ornate leadwork heads, some in the form of a tiny castle, each one subtly individual. And each gable is crowned with a proud, beautifully carved Sackville leopard. Knole is a tribute to the genius of an unsung army of men and women as well as a memorial to wealth and power.

Lacock Abbey Wiltshire

3 miles south of Chippenham, just east of the A350

Seen across the River Avon when the sun is low, the abbey is a golden building floating in a sea of grass, its roofline punctuated by twisted chimneystacks and a prominent octagonal tower. This unusual and romantic place has a history going back over 700 years, with many echoes of the nunnery for Augustinian canonesses founded in 1232 by the redoubtable Ela, Countess of Salisbury, in memory of her husband William Longespee. At its suppression by Henry VIII's commissioners in 1539, the nunnery was granted to the duplicitous and self-seeking William Sharington, a rather unattractive man who seems to have behaved with more than the usual dishonesty in his public life but who showed both sensitivity and imagination in converting his

William Sharington's octagonal tower dominates the view of Lacock Abbey from the south-east. A doorway in the façade to the left leads to the fifteenth-century cloisters which Sharington preserved at the heart of the house he created out of the nunnery buildings. In the east front to the right, later windows have been inserted in the original medieval wall, John Ivory Talbot's gothicised openings on the first floor lighting what was the community's dormitory. (*NT/Nick Carter*)

purchase into a house, retaining much of its medieval character while also incorporating innovative Renaissance features that were rare in England at this date.

Beautiful fifteenth-century cloisters still frame a grassy court at the heart of the house, with carved bosses adorning the vaulted passages. The daughters of well-to-do families who formed the community sunned themselves on the stone seats set

into the walls or stretched out their hands to the blaze in the great fireplace preserved in the warming room on the east side. The ghost of the nunnery is also evident in the long gallery which Sharington created out of the refectory: in corbels which once supported a timber roof, in a worn section of original floor and in the 'pulpit' niche from which improving works were read at mealtimes.

The Stone Gallery on the site of the dormitory is still much as Sharington left it, furnished with a set of sixteenth-century shell-back painted chairs and with a delicately carved classical chimneypiece by John Chapman, who had also worked for the king. Renaissance features also adorn Sir William's three-storey octagonal tower. A narrow angled passage leads to the high-ceilinged chamber on the first floor where he kept valuables and important papers. This tiny cupboard of a room is almost filled by John Chapman's elaborate octagonal stone table supported on the shoulders of four satyrs and carved with the scorpions of the Sharington crest, their vicious tails and matchstick legs also recognisable in Chapman's pendants studding the vaulted ceiling. Here Sharington entertained his guests, Sir John Thynne of Longleat among them.

The newest architectural fashions were again introduced to Lacock in the middle of the eighteenth century, when John Ivory Talbot, a descendant of Sharington's niece, made extensive changes to the house and grounds. Sanderson Miller's Gothick hall, commissioned in 1753, is the first room that visitors see, entered by a prominent double flight of steps on the west front. Decorative niches with pinnacled canopies are filled with lively terracotta figures by the Austrian sculptor Victor Alexander Sederbach, a mixed company including two nuns, a bishop, a knight and a grisly skeleton dominated by Ela in heroic pose over the fireplace, a bird perching on her outstretched left arm.

In the lovely south gallery hung with family portraits, including a painting of Sir William dressed in black with a long red beard, a brown indistinct photograph placed by one of the oriel windows shows the bare outlines of the lattice panes. This blurred print was produced from a tiny negative made in 1835 by the pioneer photographer William Henry Fox Talbot, whose work is commemorated in a museum at the abbey gates (*see* p.123).

Only a low wall separates the smoothly mown lawns around the house from the rough grassland of the park, giving the illusion of an uninterrupted green sward stretching away from the abbey. Masses of *Crocus vernus* spangling the grass in early spring are followed by a spectacular display of daffodils and there are several mature specimen trees, including black walnuts, a tulip tree and a swamp cypress.

Lacock Village Wiltshire

3 miles south of Chippenham, just east of the A350

This charming village filled with unspoilt medieval buildings lying at the gates of Lacock Abbey (*see above*) seems to have been blessed with good fortune. Although there were people living here permanently in Saxon times and probably earlier, Lacock first became important in the Middle Ages following the establishment of a planned village for those working the abbey estates in the thirteenth century. Its inhabitants grew rich on the medieval wool industry and the weekly market initiated by Ela, Countess of Salisbury, the founder of the abbey. Lacock was ideally placed for both, being within a day's journey of prime grazing lands on the Cotswolds and Marlborough Downs, a staging-post on the road linking centres of the wool trade in the West Country and having access to the sea via the River Avon, which meanders past to the east. At its height in the late Middle Ages, Lacock's continued prosperity after the decline of the wool trade owed much to its position on a through route between Marlborough and Bristol, which brought wealth to the village and travellers to fill its many inns until the mid-eighteenth century. From then onwards Lacock stood still. Lack of development in the nineteenth century, when many nearby settlements expanded rapidly, was largely due to the Talbot family (*see above*), who ensured no railway lines came near the village. Lacock fossilised, resulting in one of the most pleasing and individual places in England.

The village is laid out around four main streets forming a square, the irregular terraces that line the roads being built on narrow medieval house plots running back from the frontages. Houses dating from the fourteenth to the late eighteenth century include timber-framed buildings with mullioned windows and jettied upper storeys, seventeenth-century stone cottages and elegant Georgian brick mansions, such as the two examples dated 1719 and 1779 in East Street, but recent surveys have shown that many of the apparently later buildings are older than they look and were originally timber-framed. Lichen and moss encrust stone-slated roofs and gables, and dormers add to the pleasingly varied street façades.

Of the numerous inns, the timber-framed Angel in Church Street still retains its medieval layout and the passage through which horses would be led to the yard behind, while the George in West Street has an original dog-powered spit. A magnificent fourteenth-century tithe barn would once have stored rent paid to the abbey in kind: corn, hides and fleeces. Standing slightly apart is the battlemented and pinnacled church of St Cyriac, largely rebuilt when the village was at its most prosperous in the fifteenth century and filled with stone carvings of every kind. It also contains the grandiose Renaissance tomb of Sir William Sharington, who converted the abbey into a private house. A narrow lane leads from the church to the eighteenth-century packhorse bridge over the Bide Brook and beyond to the Avon, crossed by a medieval bridge. (*See also* Fox Talbot Museum, p.123.)

Lady's Well Northumberland

At Holystone, 7 miles west of Rothbury

Lying amid farmland on the western side of the Coquet Valley, just to the north-west of Holystone village, Lady's Well is as simple as can be. A farm track leads up a slight hill to the site, a small wooded area enclosed by a low wall. The entrance is a small porched gateway from which the path runs down the embankment to the rectangular pool, rounded at one end, which lies in the base of the hollow. A stone cross stands in the shallow water, and at the western end there is a weathered statue away from the water's edge. The slopes surrounding the pool are vegetated with broadleaved trees, rhododendrons and holly, providing a secluded corner in an otherwise open farming landscape.

Lake District Cumbria

See Borrowdale and Derwentwater; Buttermere, Crummock Water and Loweswater; Coniston Valley; Ennerdale; Eskdale and Duddon Valleys; Grasmere Valley, Rydal, Hawkshead and Sawrey; Great and Little Langdale; Ullswater, Hartsop, Brotherswater and Troutbeck; Wasdale; Windermere.

Lamb House East Sussex

In West Street, Rye, facing west end of church

In 1726 a fearful storm drove the ship carrying George I from Hanover to England ashore on the sands fringing the estuary of the River Rother two miles from Rye. James Lamb, mayor of the prosperous little town, escorted the king to his house where he entertained him for three days, apparently taking in his stride the fact that his wife gave birth to a son on the first night and that the king's lack of English was fully matched by his own ignorance of German. The modest brick-fronted house which bears this exceptional man's name, one of the many

delightful buildings lining Rye's cobbled streets, had been completed just two years earlier.

Some 200 years later the house was connected with another outstanding character, in this case the American novelist and critic Henry James, who bought it for £2,000 in 1900. Already in late middle age and well established in both Europe and America, James was to reach the height of his powers here. It was at Rye that he wrote his three greatest novels, *The Ambassadors*, *The Wings of the Dove* and *The Golden Bowl*, dictating them in a sonorous voice to his secretary in a garden pavilion in the summer and in a small, sunny study in winter. Here, too, he entertained a stream of other established figures, including H. G. Wells, Ford Maddox Ford, Rudyard Kipling, Max Beerbohm and Edith Wharton.

Remarkably, after James's death in 1916, Lamb House became the home of two other novelists, the brothers A. C. and E. F. Benson. They too found the tranquil atmosphere conducive, with the neighbourhood and society of Rye clearly inspiring E. F. Benson's Lucia and Mapp novels. The books now shown in the morning-room are a more tangible memento of Henry James.

The tiny, $\frac{3}{4}$-acre walled garden, much loved by those who have lived here, contains a rich variety of plants, including a sweet gum on the central lawn, roses of many varieties and a trumpet creeper on a sunny wall.

Lanhydrock House Cornwall

2½ miles south-east of Bodmin, overlooking valley of River Fowey

Lanhydrock is lost in a long Victorian afternoon. No one is at work in the cool, tiled dairy, or in the huge stone-flagged kitchen, and buckets and brushes are lined up in the housemaids' closet ready for the next day. No sound comes from the extensive servants' quarters, where a pair of black boots stands neatly by a bed and the footman's livery lies ready to wear, while in the nursery wing all is still. Pipes lie waiting in the masculine confines of the smoking-room and the dining-room table is laid for ten, the menu already handwritten in French. The period feeling is so strong that it would be no surprise to meet a scurrying maid with a tray or to hear the Robartes family and their guests, or their nine children, coming in from the garden.

Lanhydrock's interiors vividly evoke gracious living in the 1890s. The house itself was largely rebuilt at the end of the nineteenth century after a disastrous fire in 1881, the designs by the London-trained local architect Richard Coad incorporating the latest comforts and conveniences, such as the massive radiators featured in almost every room, and also a full range of service rooms. The well-equipped kitchen area includes steam jets for scouring greasy pots in the scullery and a dairy cooled by spring water from the hill above the house, which is chanelled along runnels in the slate and marble slabs where jellies and custards were stood. At the same time Coad's exterior faithfully reflects the old-fashioned house built by Sir Richard Robartes and his son between 1630 and 1642, merging beautifully with the one wing which was not consumed in the flames. With their battlemented granite walls and mullioned windows, Lanhydrock's three ranges set round a courtyard seem typical of the conservatism of mid-seventeenth-century Cornwall. Obelisks on the projecting central porch and the ends of the wings echo those on the low wall enclosing the gardens around the house and on the enchanting detached seventeenth-century gatehouse, which seems to wear a crown.

Only the north wing, which survived the fire, gives a flavour of the original interiors. A sunny 116-foot gallery running the length of the second floor and lit by windows on either side suggests what might have been lost. The barrel ceiling arching overhead is covered with magical plaster-work dating from just before the outbreak of the Civil War. Although the twenty-four panels illustrating incidents from the Old Testament take centre stage, the delightful creatures surrounding them are far more memorable, furry porcupines, bears, armadillos and peacocks rubbing shoulders with mythical beasts, such as dragons and centaurs.

Like Coad's interiors, Lanhydrock's nineteenth-century garden is a mirror to Victorian taste. In front of the house clipped yew marks the corners of six geometric shapes planted with roses in George Gilbert Scott's formal layout of 1857 and more yew studs his intricate parterre beside the north wing, bedded out twice a year. Beyond the obelisks and castellations of the surrounding parapet, a large informal garden dating from the 1860s covers the steep slopes rising above the house. Winding paths through shrubs and trees, including displays of large Himalayan magnolias, rhododendrons and camellias, lead ever upwards, past the well used by the monks of St Petroc's Priory at Bodmin, who held Lanhydrock before the Dissolution, and the strong spring feeding the stream which chatters down the slope, its course marked by a strip of primulas, astilbes, arums, rodgersias and other water-loving plants. A long flowering season from early spring to July is extended into October in the herbaceous circle, there is spectacular autumn-colouring foliage, and Lanhydrock also boasts a national collection of crocosmias.

Vistas over the house and the wooded valley of the River Fowey culminate in magnificent views from the broad terrace walk at the top of the garden. From here the gatehouse at the head of the seventeenth-century beech and sycamore avenue leading away across the park appears set against the valley of the Fowey, with Bodmin Moor behind.

Lanyon Quoit Cornwall

4 miles north-west of Penzance, via the B3312

Lanyon Quoit stands on an open stretch of moorland in the far west of Cornwall like a giant's three-legged stool, with a trio of granite uprights supporting a fourth huge slab eighteen feet across. The remains of a neolithic chambered tomb dating from c.3500 BC, the boulders were reconstructed in 1824 after collapsing a few years earlier and their original form has been lost. The chamber was probably built as a rectangular stone box and was designed to be seen, with the huge capstone protruding from any covering mound and possibly serving as some kind of territorial marker.

Larkton and Bickerton Hills

Cheshire

4 miles north of Malpas, 12 miles south-east of Chester, east of the A41 Whitchurch road

The Peckforton Hills rise from the Cheshire plain rather like Alderley Edge (*see* p.4). At their southern tip, the 280 acres of Bickerton and Larkton Hills, with the Iron Age earthwork of Maiden Castle on one flank, are an attractive mixture of heath, woodland and little fields. This is a good place for a walk, with a network of paths and spectacular views from the long-distance Sandstone Trail following the scarp of the hills.

Lavenham Guildhall, showing the richly-carved project-ing porch and the brick and rubble plinth which supports the timber frame. The guildhall is one of a number of crooked half-timbered houses in this almost unspoilt survival of a medieval town. (*NT/John Bethell*)

Lavenham: The Guildhall of Corpus Christi Suffolk

Market Place, Lavenham

Lavenham is a medieval town, with streets of crooked half-timbered houses and a glorious late fifteenth-century church financed with profits from the wool trade. Apart from the church, one of the best buildings is the guildhall, prominently sited in the little market square. Traditional timber-framing is limewashed to a pleasing silvery-grey, the upper floor is jettied out over the lower and both are lit with oriel windows. An ornate two-storey porch projects into the square and the building as a whole rests on a brick and rubble plinth, which deepens as the ground slopes away behind.

The hall was built in about 1528–9 by the Guild of Corpus Christi, one of three in the town founded to regulate the wool trade. Used for a variety of purposes after the guild was dissolved only thirty or so years later, little of the original woodwork which must once have adorned the interior has survived, apart from the linenfold panelling lining the little room above the porch. Some carving is still visible on the exterior but it is badly weathered.

The warren of small rooms on the upper floor now houses a local museum mostly devoted to the cloth trade, displays here including, for example, the range of colours – from pale blue to black – which can be obtained from woad and a model of the tenter frames on which cloth was stretched to dry. The most unusual exhibit is a mummified cat, found in the roof where it had been placed to ward off evil spirits. Despite the guild's close association with the Church and its prominence in the great annual procession on the Feast of Corpus Christi, heavenly protection was clearly considered insufficient.

At the back of the guildhall is a walled garden with a nineteenth-century lock-up and mortuary.

Lawrence House Cornwall

9 Castle Street, Launceston

This modest Georgian brick house in the shadow of the remains of Launceston's great Norman castle was built in 1753 by the wealthy local lawyer Humphrey Lawrence and is typical of houses of the period seen in small country towns throughout England. Once the home of Caroline Pearse, a prolific Victorian author, it is now leased to the Town Council as a local museum and civic centre.

Leigh Woods Avon

On left bank of the Avon, by Clifton suspension bridge, north-east of the A369

Few people nowadays approach the city of Bristol as our ancestors did, up the River Avon from the Bristol Channel, but the motorist can enjoy the same dramatic view of the Trust's Leigh Woods, leased to English Nature as a National Nature Reserve, by leaving the M5 at junction 18 and following the A4 as it snakes along beside the river towards the old docks. The road swings round a bend to reveal one of Brunel's greatest works, the Clifton Suspension Bridge, poised 250 feet above the river. On the far bank, to the west, the woods plunge steeply down the limestone escarpment, framing the bridge. The woods formed part of the estate of Ashton Court, now the property of the city, and are the remains of a semi-natural forest of great age, with wych elm, ash, oak, small-leaved lime and two species of white-beam that grow only here. There are plenty of paths and the Nightingale valley provides a less steep approach from the riverside walk.

Leith Hill Tower and Rhododendron Wood Surrey

1 mile south-west of Coldharbour, on the A29 and B2126 roads

This battlemented Gothic folly rises from a sea of heather and bilberries clothing the highest point in south-east England. The monkey puzzles and Scots pine which until recently also crowned the sandstone ridge were decimated by the storms of 1987 and 1990, opening up magnificent views over the wooded landscape of the Weald to the South Downs and glimpses of the Channel beyond. First built by Richard Hull of Leith Hill Place in 1766, as a tablet over the door records, the tower was subsequently heightened and now rises to 1,029 feet above sea level. Over 1,000 years ago, in 851, this strategic site was secured by a Saxon army under cover of darkness, giving them the advantage in a great battle with Danish forces who had camped across the valley on Anstiebury Hill.

The slopes of the hill are wooded, with some ancient stands of oak and hazel among much replanting. On the southern slopes, just above Leith Hill Place, the childhood home of Ralph Vaughan Williams, is the rhododendron wood planted by Josiah Wedgwood, grandson of the famous potter. The collection of rhododendrons, which includes an enormous clump of *Rhododendron falconeri*, *R. arboreum*, *R. edgeworthii* and many early-flowering species and hybrids, survived the great storms but the sheltering oaks and conifers were severely depleted. Numerous azaleas and *Magnolia obovata* are among other flowering shrubs planted here.

Letocetum Staffordshire

In Wall, 2 miles south-west of Lichfield, on north side of the A5

The little Romano-British town of Letocetum grew up round a posting station on Watling Street, the main imperial route to Chester and North Wales, becoming sufficiently important to be included in a list of the twenty-eight cities of Britain produced by Nennius in the eighth century. Of the remains visible at Wall, the communal bath house is the most complete example of its kind in Britain, the extensive facilities on offer showing a full appreciation of the good life. The Roman equivalents of a Turkish bath and a sauna were part of a suite which also included cold baths, an undressing room and an exercise hall. Here the men of the community and tired imperial messengers journeying along Watling Street would spend long, indulgent afternoons (the women were allowed to bathe only in the mornings), with slaves on hand to massage scented oils into their bodies.

A courtyard building nearby, destroyed by fire in 160–170, was probably an inn. Finds from these excavations and from another Roman site, at Shenstone, a short distance to the south-east, are exhibited in a small museum.

Lindisfarne Castle Northumberland

On Holy Island, 6 miles east of the A1, across causeway

Lindisfarne's stark outline rises from the dolerite crag on which it is built as if it were part of the rock itself. The castle is accessible only by the causeway to Holy Island which is submerged for several hours at high tide; a visit here still feels like an adventure into the unknown. A cobbled approach curves steeply up the face of the crag to the entrance high above, a precipitous drop on one side, a cliff-like stone wall on the other. With spectacular views south to Bamburgh Castle and east over the water to the Farne Islands (*see* p.116), this is an entrancingly romantic place, even when lashed by the gales that come sweeping in from the North Sea.

Created in 1903 by the young Edwin Lutyens out of the shell of an originally Tudor fort, Lindisfarne's small rooms look backwards rather than forwards, with Norman-style pillars, huge fireplaces, deeply recessed mullioned windows and rounded stone arches. Varied materials and floor levels characteristic of Lutyens add to a very individual charm. Herringbone brick floors are juxtaposed with stone and timber. Some rooms are austerely whitewashed, others left bare, such as the dark drawing-room in the bowels of the building where massively thick vaults arching overhead once protected the castle's magazine. With the exception of the kitchen, where a high-backed settle and armchairs are grouped round the leaded range, none of the rooms could be described as cosy, although carved English and Flemish oak furniture, blue and white delftware and richly coloured carpets give a feel of seventeenth-century Dutch interiors.

The old fort would probably have been left to quiet decay if Edward Hudson, the founder of *Country Life*, had not happened upon it on a visit to the island and employed Lutyens to turn it into a summer retreat. He was a hospitable man who loved to entertain; a cello and music stand in the long upper gallery recall the many house parties he hosted at the castle, when the celebrated cellist Madame Suggia used to play for her fellow guests.

The castle's enchanting little walled garden, designed by Gertrude Jekyll on a south-facing slope to the north of the crag, is easily overlooked. Sheltered from the worst of the weather, it is a mass of purple, grey, pink and burnt-orange in high summer, a faithful re-creation of Miss Jekyll's original planting scheme.

Little Moreton Hall Cheshire

4 miles south-west of Congleton, on east side of the A34

The prosperous Moretons of Little Moreton Hall were gentleman farmers, profiting like many others of their kind from the sale of land following the ravages of the Black Death and the Dissolution of the Monasteries. Their timber-framed, moated house dating from c.1450 was originally only two storeys tall, the upper floor jettied out over the lower. Between about 1570 and 1580, when the size of the estate was doubled, the substantial long gallery was added to the south wing, giving the house its curiously top-heavy appearance, like a stranded Noah's Ark, and also pulling the supporting timbers out of shape, so that the building lurches drunkenly. The charming projecting gatehouse was another later addition, built towards the end of the sixteenth century.

Apart from three pieces, all the original contents have disappeared and the rooms are shown unfurnished. As a result nothing distracts from the remarkable nature of the building itself. Built in an age when wood was plentiful and half-timbered houses were two a penny in the West Midlands and Welsh Marches, Little Moreton Hall is none the less exceptional. The house seems to have been devised to display the full range of the joiner's and carpenter's art, with timbers arranged in an extraordinary variety of patterns to glorious effect. The confidence and pride of the carpenter who carried out extensive work in 1559 is proclaimed in the inscription he left on one of the prominent bay windows built for William Moreton II: 'Rycharde Dale Carpeder made thies windovs by the grac of god.' The leaded windows are similarly unusual, with the glazing patterns varying from room to room and even from window to window. Wood and glass together give Little Moreton Hall its unique and complete sixteenth-century character.

The interior is a warren, one room leading into another, some little more than cupboards, others grand chambers with fine chimneypieces and panelling, four staircases linking the different levels. A simple chapel, to which worshippers are still summoned on Sunday afternoons by a bell in the courtyard, is decorated with texts from the Coverdale and Tyndale Bible. The Moretons' religious sympathies are also evident elsewhere in the house. A frieze crowning the elaborate painted panelling in the parlour – the whole composition a rare example

Lindisfarne Castle, seen across the tiny walled garden laid out by Gertrude Jekyll on a south-facing slope nearby. (*NT*)

of sixteenth-century painted decoration – illustrates the story of Susannah and the Elders, a favourite Protestant theme. Characters are shown in contemporary Elizabethan dress, the blues and reds of their costumes still fresh and bright. In the long gallery, where the massive weight of the roof is taken by huge curved beams morticed and tenoned into the rafters, plasterwork picked out in orange and green at either end of the room depicts the virtues of hard work and the power of knowledge over superstition.

A hedge of hornbeam, thorn and honeysuckle edges the moat, enclosing a lawn planted with fruit trees and a reconstruction of an Elizabethan knot garden, with box-edged compartments filled with gravel. Two prominent mounds – one across the moat – were probably vantage points for surveying the surrounding countryside.

Llanerchaeron Dyfed

Off A482, 1½ miles east of Aberaeron

Just inland from Cardigan Bay and the sea, in the pastoral valley of the Afon Aeron, is a rare survival of the small gentry estates which were such a mainstay of the economy of rural Wales in the eighteenth and nineteenth centuries. By 1700, it had passed to the Lewis family and it was William Lewis who commissioned the young John Nash to replace an existing house. Dating from 1794, when Nash was only twenty-six, Llanerchaeron is a charming mix of the conservative and the unexpected. The plain, well-proportioned late Georgian exterior is unexceptional, but Nash included decorative oval dressing-rooms and a dramatic top-lit staircase, and his elegant service courtyard is surrounded by a verandah-shaded, slate-slabbed walkway.

The third-floor gallery at Little Moreton Hall, its timbers and windows all pulled out of shape.
(*NT/Andreas von Einsiedel*)

182

Bardsey Island, two miles off the southern tip of the Llŷn peninsula, from the headland of Mynydd Penarfynydd. (*NT/Martin Trelawny*)

The surrounding park was landscaped in the spirit of the Picturesque, with gothicised cottages and a church beside the drive used as an eye-catcher in the view from the house. Something of the family's sporting lifestyle comes through in the home farm, where the buildings round the cobbled yard, mostly contemporary with the house, include kennels for otter hounds and elegant stables, and their importance in the local economy in the little church, where forty of the sixty seats were once occupied by estate employees. But although embedded in rural life, the Lewises were not unworldly. Running through the park is the now abandoned track of the railway to Aberaeron, which the family encouraged.

Neglected for decades, both house and grounds were badly run-down when Llanerchaeron came to the Trust. Restoration has begun, but financial constraints mean the work is likely to take many years.

Llŷn Peninsula Gwynedd

In the north-west corner of Wales

Dividing Caernarfon Bay from Cardigan Bay is the Llŷn peninsula, in shape remarkably like a quarter-scale Cornwall, and with a coast equally as fine. It was the stamping ground of the three remarkable Keating sisters of Plas-yn-Rhiw (*see* p.261). Near Plas-yn-Rhiw, which stands high above the coast road, is the eighteenth-century farmstead of Penrallt Neigwl, its land running down towards the sea. A mile to the south-west, Mynydd-y-Graig rises to 800 feet, covered with bracken and heather and with a panoramic view south over Cardigan Bay. Beyond lies the headland of Mynydd Penarfynydd, and here the view opens to the west. The Gwylan Islands, a mile offshore, have a large colony of puffins and, beyond them, Aberdaron Bay is closed by the sheep-cropped turf of Pen-y-Cil, while just west of the little town a footpath leads south along the cliffs to Porth Meudwy, frequented by the rare and distinctive chough and with colonies of seals and seabirds on offshore islands. This sheltered cove was the traditional landing place for pilgrims coming back from the monastery on Bardsey Island, two miles away across the tidal race of the Sound.

Round the headland of Braich-y-Pwll the coast turns north. The views are now across to Ireland and, from the 628-foot-high Mynydd Anelog, the Wicklow Hills rise clear to the west. Below is the cove of Porth Llanllawen, where seals breed, and, beyond, the Trust's two tiny islands of Dinas Fawr and Dinas Bach and the curious Whistling Sands at

Porthor, where 73 acres are now protected by the Trust.

This is an exposed, wind-clipped coastline. Where the land turns briefly east again, low cliffs back a sheltered sandy bay and the Trust-owned village of Porthdinllaen: a huddle of cottages, the Ty Coch Inn and a Lifeboat Station looking across the bay to the triple-peaked Yr Eifl, falling almost 2,000 feet to the sea.

Lockeridge Dene and Piggledene

Wiltshire

3 miles west of Marlborough, on south and north sides of the A4 Bath road respectively

On Clatford and Fyfield Downs, west of Marlborough, and on nearby Overton Down stand thousands of the extraordinary Grey Wethers. These are sarsen stones, a hard sandstone which when on the surface is eroded by wind and rain to every sort of shape. Here they lie, as they have done since the Ice Age, although vast numbers have been taken away, both to build prehistoric circles, as at Avebury (*see* p.15), and to build churches, houses, walls and farm buildings.

The Trust owns two clusters of these peculiarly attractive stones. Lockeridge Dene, close to the village of Lockeridge south of the A4, can be seen without leaving the car. The more extensive Piggledene, to the north of the main road, needs to be walked through. Although it is entered directly from the tarmac, the dene curves westward and the bustle of traffic is soon left behind. The time for a wander here is late on a summer's evening.

(Opposite page) Vistas in the grounds of Anglesey Abbey are attractively punctuated by the white weatherboarded façades of Lode Mill. (*NT/F. A. H. Bloemendal*)

Lode Mill   Cambridgeshire

In grounds of Anglesey Abbey, 6 miles north-east of Cambridge

Lode Mill and the village which it once served are called after Bottisham Lode, an ancient man-made waterway linking with the River Cam which enabled supplies to be brought here by boat. There has probably been a mill at the junction of Bottisham Lode and Quy Water since the time of Domesday Book, but the present distinctive white weatherboarded building with a projecting lucam on the fourth floor dates from the eighteenth century. Four pairs of millstones driven by a fourteen-foot breast-shot wheel were used to grind corn until 1900, when the mill was converted to produce cement, ceasing operations altogether twenty years later. Now incorporated in the grounds of Anglesey Abbey (*see* p.5), where it provides an attractive focus for a number of leafy vistas, Lode Mill has once again been restored to working order as a corn mill.

Lodge Park   Gloucestershire

3 miles east of Northleach, across the A40 from Sherborne village

On the open Cotswold plateau west of Cheltenham is a unique survival of a finely wrought building set in a sporting landscape. Commanding sweeping views south and east towards the Thames valley is an exquisite Jacobean hunting lodge, its main façade positively crammed with architectural detail. Pedimented windows set shoulder to shoulder across the first floor carry bearded and moustachioed heads, there are exaggerated quoins, shell-headed niches and a columned portico supporting a wide balcony, and a massive classical chimneystack breaks the balustraded roofline.

This compact architectural caprice, more box than house, was built to overlook a broad grassy track edged with dry-stone walls which still runs over a mile south from the A40. From the roof and balcony of the lodge, the well-to-do would watch and bet on dogs chasing fallow deer along the course, with a finishing line marked by a ditch in front of the house. Originally consisting of just two large rooms, with a grand staircase leading to a 44-foot banqueting hall opening on to the balcony, and the roof beyond, the lodge was built in the 1630s for Sir John Dutton, a characterful hunchback known as Crump who seems to have weathered the Civil War by keeping a foot in both camps. The designer is uncertain, but may have been the local mason-architect Valentine Strong, perhaps working with the help of pattern books illustrating the kind of Italianate detail used by Inigo Jones. Crump had created a deer-park too, but in the early eighteenth century the lodge was made the focus of a 200-acre landscape by Charles Bridgeman, who planted wooded enclosures for the deer, artful clumps of trees and a double lime avenue leading away behind the house.

About the same time as Bridgeman's landscaping, the lodge was refurbished and furnished to a scheme by William Kent. In later years it was converted into estate cottages, and, in the nine-teenth century, when the gate lodges were added, turned into a house. The Trust is returning it, as far as possible, to its original configuration, with a reconstructed, Jacobean-style oak staircase leading to the banqueting hall and a copy – in plaster and wood imitating stone in the seventeenth-century manner – of the great hooded fireplace that was once here. The Kent furniture has been dispersed, although some may find its way back, but there is a show of family portraits and an atmospheric land-scape by George Lambert showing the open, well-wooded countryside of the 1740s, without the regular stone-walled fields that now dominate the view from the roof. The Bridgeman setting, too, is being clarified, with replanting of the double lime avenue.

A couple of the charming cottages in the nineteenth-century estate village at Sherborne. Built in a Cotswold vernacular style, they have stone-mullioned casements and carved drip moulds, but the village is too regimented to be the real thing. (*NT/Alastair Ogilvie*)

Long Crendon courthouse, seen through the gate leading to St Mary's church. (*NT*)

Lodge Park is part of the 4,144-acre Sherborne estate which came to the Trust in 1987. Straddling the A40 and the serene Windrush valley, this largely agricultural holding includes much former parkland and most of Sherborne village. Strung out along the valley, this is a charming collection of nineteenth-century, estate-built cottages in a Cotswold vernacular style, with gabled stone-tiled roofs and stone-mullioned windows. All are south-facing, with gardens separating them from the road. The big house, seat of the family since the sixteenth century, was sold away in 1970, and the 7th Lord Sherborne (the peerage dates from 1784 and died with the 7th Lord's cousin, Ralph Dutton of Hinton Ampner, *see* p.152) lived at the lodge. Lady Sherborne used the deer course as a runway for her aeroplane, and the short avenue of rowans now breaking the track in front of the house was planted by the 7th Lord in her memory.

Long Crendon Courthouse
Buckinghamshire

2 miles north of Thame, via the B4011, close to the church

Long Crendon courthouse lies in one of the most attractive and unspoilt villages in Buckinghamshire, its long timber-framed front façade with a jettied upper storey blending perfectly with the sixteenth- and seventeenth-century thatched cottages which line the street winding down to St Mary's church. Red handmade tiles form a warm streak of colour above the whitewashed walls. Steep wooden stairs lead directly from the street to the large room, open to the roof and floored with undulating boards, which runs most of the length of the upper storey.

Dating from the early fifteenth century or even the end of the fourteenth, the courthouse seems originally to have been built for the cloth trade, to store wool from Oxfordshire destined for the weavers of East Anglia. It was being used to hold manorial courts in the first half of the fifteenth century, and manorial business continued to be conducted here into Victorian times.

Loughwood Meeting House
Devon

4 miles west of Axminster, 1 mile south of Dalwood, 1 mile north-west of Kilmington

In the seventeenth century people walked miles to attend Baptist meetings in this little flint and sandstone building dug into the hillside, risking imprisonment, transportation or even death until the Toleration Act of 1688 legalised nonconformist forms of worship. Built as a refuge from persecution in 1653 by Baptists from the nearby village of Kilmington, Loughwood was originally buried in dense woodland and approached only along narrow footpaths. Even today it is remotely sited in rural Devonshire.

A homely thatched roof and round-headed clear-glass windows give this unassuming chapel the appearance of a cottage rather than a church, despite the surrounding burial ground and the buttressed walls. Inside, it is cheerful and airy, dominated by

The plain interior of Loughwood Meeting House, showing the unvarnished pine box pews and the musicians' gallery. (*NT/P. Lacey*)

the preacher's raised pulpit set above the baptismal pool. Unvarnished pine box pews fill the body of the chapel and the whitewashed walls and barrel roof are undecorated. Those who came from a long way away passed the time between services on Sundays in the retiring rooms underneath the musicians' gallery at the back of the building; those lucky enough to have horses quartered them in the detached stone and cob stable.

Lower Brockhampton
Hereford & Worcester

2 miles east of Bromyard on the Worcester road

When this ancient, timber-framed manor house was built, probably somewhere between 1380 and 1400, only a generation had passed since the population of England had been decimated by the Black Death. Crumbling walls on the fringes of the Malvern Hills to the east were typical of abandoned settlements on marginal land, and the economic depression of these years also saw the fragmentation of many great estates. But the middling landowners with modest holdings in well-endowed country were better placed to survive and prosper.

John Domulton, a descendant of the Brockhampton family who were here from at least the twelfth century, may have been just such a man. His delightful black and white house is small and unpretentious, but it was comfortable for its day and was built with a great chamber for the family to distance themselves from their servants and retainers. The moat with which John Domulton surrounded his property, now only surviving on three sides, may well have been necessary in the unsettled country of the Welsh Marches, but may also have been regarded as a status symbol.

The house is buried in the depths of a wooded valley, reached by a long private road off the A44 from Worcester to Bromyard which seems to descend for miles through deeply rural countryside. A little fifteenth-century timber-framed gatehouse set over the moat, its upper floor jettied out over the lower, lurches crazily towards approaching visitors, like a drunk unsteady on his feet. Set back fifteen yards or so, and facing south across a grassy court, is the manor itself, an L-shaped building in which a great hall open to the rafters filling the stub of the L is attached to a two-storey wing, where the family's

Lower Brockhampton's fifteenth-century gatehouse straddles the moat, forming a seductive aproach to the half-timbered manor beyond. (*NT/Martin Trelawny*)

Lundy Devon

11 miles north of Hartland Point

Lundy rises boldly out of the Bristol Channel eleven miles north of Hartland Point. It is the top of an undersea mountain, the water offshore deep and wonderfully clean. A little over three miles from north to south, the island, largely of granite, is only a quarter of a mile wide. The cliffs on its west coast rise to 400 feet, and although the east coast is still formidable it is gentler, with little valleys running down to rocky beaches, patches of scrubby wood and *Rhododendron ponticum*. Above the cliffs the island is flat and very exposed. The main landing-place is on an open beach at the south-east corner of the island.

The thirteenth-century Marisco Castle, on a precipice overlooking the South Light, commands the landing place. Nearby is the small village, a farm, a shop, an inn, one or two larger houses, cottages and a large Victorian church. At Mill-combe, where the road runs down to the landing place, is the seemly manor house of the island, built in 1835. At the highest point, 466 feet, stands the Old Light, a magnificent stone tower designed by Daniel Asher Alexander, architect of Dartmoor Prison. Completed in 1820, it was found to be of little use, for the fogs of the Bristol Channel obscured its beam far above the water and ships continued to drive on to Lundy's reefs. It was replaced by the North and South Lights, built at the foot of the cliffs at either end of the island and still in use, although now automated.

The island is leased to the Landmark Trust, which has done a superb job in restoring the many dilapidated buildings, removing eyesores and fostering an island community which keeps the place alive. The Landmark Trust provides a good deal of accommodation for visitors, who come here for solitude, no traffic, no noise, few people, to walk and, in particular, to watch the bird life.

The island lies on a north-south migratory route and at the right time of year there are many migrant species passing by. Kittiwakes, fulmars and Manx shearwaters nest here. There is a now very small colony of puffins, while peregrines have long nested in inaccessible eyries.

There are important heathlands and grasslands, including the rare fern *Ophioglossum*; rabbits abound and inbreeding has led to distinctive black and brown varieties. There is a type of pigmy shrew

great chamber once filled the upper floor. Red-brick chimneys rear up from the end walls.

Lower Brockhampton was constructed of massive timbers from the estate, the high quality of the woodwork particularly evident in the framework and roof of the hall. A ruined Norman chapel in the farmyard to the west of the house was probably built by the Brockhamptons in about 1180, while the mid-eighteenth-century Brockhampton Court a mile to the south (not open to the public) was commissioned by one of their descendants to replace the old-fashioned property he had inherited. The romantic manor, one of the most picturesque half-timbered buildings among the many still surviving in the Welsh Marches, was left to slumber undisturbed, appropriately set only yards away from the Paradise Brook.

Waymarked walks lead across the park and through adjoining woodland, with views of the Georgian house and across the Teme Valley.

which is found only here. The Lundy ponies, originally New Forest ponies crossed with Welsh Mountain mares, are now recognised as a distinct breed.

The Landmark Trust's handsome ship, *M.S. Oldenburg*, runs throughout the year from Bideford, and during the summer months from Ilfracombe. Arrangements for visitors are distinctly well organised. For a first visit to this very special place the inside of a week is ideal.

Lydford Gorge Devon

Halfway between Okehampton and Tavistock, 1 mile west of the A386, at west end of Lydford village

Lydford Gorge is a geological curiosity. Some 450,000 years ago the River Lyd flowed southwards along the western edge of Dartmoor, via the course of the present little River Burn, to join the River Tavy. Some disturbance of the earth's crust diverted its flow into the valley of the River West Lyd, close at hand, which then carried it away westwards from the moor, ultimately to join the Tamar east of Launceston. The phenomenon is known as river capture and its result has been the carving out of the spectacular gorge we see today, where the greatly increased volume of water from the two rivers flows over the 750-foot contour near Lydford village to drop to 300 feet at the lower end of the gorge. Its walls are now sixty feet high in places, the river bed marked with the remains of rounded basins or potholes scoured out of the Upper Devonian slates of which the gorge is formed by boulders carried down from the moor by storm water, a process which still continues.

The gorge is one and a half miles long, and near its foot a tributary stream plunges down the ninety-foot White Lady waterfall to join it. The steep sides of the gorge are thickly wooded, though a severe storm in 1977 did much damage. The trunks of the trees are covered with lichens, mosses and ferns, for the place can be like a greenhouse on a humid day. It is the potholes which the visitor remembers most vividly, the most awesome being the Devil's Cauldron below Lydford Castle.

A circular walk takes visitors down the gorge on a high-level path through the fringing oak woods, and back along the river by a much narrower, often rock-cut route, with a final precipitous descent to view the Devil's Cauldron.

Trees, mosses and ferns cling precariously to the rocky walls of Lydford Gorge, with the arch of the road bridge to Lydford high overhead and the river hidden deep in the crevasse. (*NT/A. L. Stow*)

Lyme Park Cheshire

On south side of the A6; 6½ miles south-east of Stockport, entrance on western outskirts of Disley

Used to the blinding sun and hard shadows of his homeland, the Venetian architect Giacomo Leoni must have found it hard to contend with the lowering grey skies and misty distances of the bleak Peak moors at Lyme when Peter Legh engaged him to remodel his largely Elizabethan mansion in 1725. As at Clandon (*see* p.72), Leoni responded by bringing a touch of Italy to the English countryside.

The courtyard of the Tudor house was transformed into an imitation of the *cortile* of a grand *palazzo*, ringed by shady arcades and with a double flight of steps rising to the pedimented entrance. The Mediterranean effect was later enhanced by the addition of a marble pavement and an Italian Renaissance wellhead. On the long south front built of rose-tinted stone, Leoni's great classical portico rises the full height of the house, crowned by lead figures of Venus, Neptune and Pan staring at their reflection in the lake below. Six bays separated by pilasters stretch away on either side. Something of the grand Elizabethan house still survives on the north, where a towering Tudor gateway leads into Leoni's courtyard.

Eighteenth- and nineteenth-century decorative schemes are accompanied by two surviving Elizabethan interiors: a light and airy panelled long gallery hung with seventeenth- and early eighteenth-century portraits and a richly panelled Tudor drawing-room. Leoni's saloon looking over the park through the columns of his portico has all the elegance of the eighteenth century, with a gilded rococo ceiling and oak panelling encrusted with pale three-dimensional limewood carvings. Traditionally attributed to Grinling Gibbons, one of these life-like compositions cunningly intertwines an artist's palette and brushes, a partly folded chart and navigation instruments. In another, a beautifully embroidered lace handkerchief falls in naturalistic folds.

The full-length portrait of the Black Prince in the entrance hall is a vivid reminder that the land of

One of the realistic limewood carvings at Lyme Park. The work is so fine that some of the wood is reduced to a paper-like thinness. (*NT/John Bethell*)

Lyme was won for the Legh family in 1346 on the battlefields of France. Lyme was to remain the home of the Leghs for 600 years, its contents intriguingly alluding to episodes in the family's history. A copy of Velázquez's *Las Meninas* is one of many paintings of mastiffs portraying the celebrated dogs bred here in the sixteenth century, traditionally presented as royal gifts to the courts of Europe. The ancient Greek sculptures in the library were excavated in the early nineteenth century by the intrepid Thomas Legh, whose portrait in oriental costume enlivens the staircase. His grandest find, a stele of Melisto and Epigenes of *c.*350BC, has pride of place over the fireplace, but the little tombstone of the same date in the window bay, commemorating a mother and her newborn babe, is far more memorable. A tragedy of a different kind is recalled in the Stag Parlour, where faded red covers on the Chippendale chairs were made from the cloak Charles I wore on the scaffold. Much more recently the house has been enriched by the magnificent collection of seventeenth- and eighteenth-century bracket and longcase clocks acquired by Sir Francis Legh, born at Lyme in 1919. The earliest is an instrument by Ahasuerus Fromanteel, dated 1658, one of the first pendulum mechanisms ever produced, and there are also examples of the work of masters such as Thomas Tompion and Joseph Knibbs.

The late nineteenth-century garden was laid out by William John Legh, 1st Lord Newton, who inherited the estate in 1857. Lewis Wyatt's orangery to the east of the house is fronted by a formal Victorian design, its garish colours echoed in the brightly coloured beds surrounding an ornamental pond in the sunken Dutch garden on the other side of the house. The planting along the deep ravine carved by the stream feeding the lake is quite different in character, primulas, hostas, irises and other moisture-loving plants creating an informal semi-wild area through which a path leads to a rhododendron garden on the slopes above. The similarly secluded Vicary Gibbs garden to the west of the house is called after the horticulturalist who was a friend of the family. Currently being restored, this sunken area will feature various trees and shrubs raised by Gibbs in his Hertfordshire garden, including *Sorbus hybrida* 'Gibbsii', *Berberis aldenhamensis* and *Malus aldenhamensis*.

From the terrace on the south front there are views across the lake to Lyme's medieval deer park, nine miles in circumference and already walled in

Elizabethan times. Set dramatically on a windswept ridge high above the grazing herds broods Lyme Cage, an Elizabethan hunting tower modified by Leoni, its forbidding outline crowned by domed turrets greeting approaching visitors.

Lynmouth Devon

On the north coast, east of Lynmouth, on both sides of the A39

East of Lynmouth the Trust has built up a very beautiful estate of over 1,600 acres since its first purchase in 1934. The area seems much larger, for the steep wooded valleys of the East Lyn river and the Hoar Oak Water curve deeply back into Exmoor, and their headwaters 1,000 feet above are only four miles from the sea as the crow flies.

It was this steep terrain which caused a devastating flood in August 1952. Nine inches of rain fell on the high ground in twenty-four hours. The great sponge of the peaty moorland could absorb no more and some 90 million tons of water surged down the valleys which converge on Lynmouth. Thirty-four people lost their lives in the tragedy, nearly all the bridges were swept away, as were a number of houses, the valley bottoms were scoured and much other damage was done. The sad memory of this dramatic event will abide but the scars to the landscape have virtually healed.

The Trust's property, though all contiguous, falls into two parts, the inland valleys centred on Watersmeet and the high cliffs and moorland running out to Foreland Point beyond Countisbury and east to the cliffs of Glenthorne. Although the Trust has acquired its land in many different parcels, it was originally nearly all one estate. In the first quarter of the nineteenth century a young man named Halliday, heir to a merchant's fortune, fell in love with the wild beauty of this north-western corner of Exmoor and began buying land. Halliday and his wife were philanthropists and planned to set

Foreland Point to the north of Countisbury forms the northernmost tip of Exmoor. (*NT/Roy Westlake*)

Chiselcombe Bridge over the East Lyn, rebuilt by the Trust after its predecessor was swept away in the 1952 flood. (*NT*)

up an ideal – if patriarchal – estate, peopled with tenants for whom they laid out farms and provided employment. The young couple built a romantic mansion beside the sea at Glenthorne, two miles east of Countisbury, with a drive plunging ever more steeply down from County Gate 1,000 feet above, at the border of Devon with Somerset. In 1832 they constructed Watersmeet House, in an equally romantic setting, at the confluence of the East Lyn and Hoar Oak Water, to provide a base for fishing and shooting parties. It now accommodates the National Trust's restaurant, shop and information point.

From Watersmeet paths run in every direction, many of them originally donkey tracks made by men working in the woods burning charcoal. Every twenty-five years or so the trees were coppiced; the bark was stipped for leather tanning and poles were shipped over the Bristol Channel to be used as pit-props in the Welsh coal mines. There are also signs of the mining of iron ore and a restored lime kiln. The high-level walks give the best views; those at a lower level the best peeps of rock pools and water-falls.

The woods are largely of sessile oak, with two rare whitebeams (*Sorbus devoniensis* and *S. subcuneata*), while Watersmeet is one of two places in Britain where the Irish spurge (*Euphorbia hibernica*) is found. Revelling in the damp clean air so close to the sea, lichens, ferns and mosses abound, creating a site of national importance for ancient woodland flora. The two birds most characteristic of the rivers are the grey wagtail and the dipper, always bobbing in and out of the water.

The coast is wholly different from these wooded valleys. The Foreland is all that a great headland should be, bare, sheep-grazed, facing west into the Atlantic gales. A steep path from Countisbury Hill leads down to its beach at Sillery Sands. Half a mile west of Countisbury village, with its church, pub, and a handful of cottages, is Wind Hill, with the massive earthworks of an Iron Age promontory fort. Some 2,000 years old, it was probably the site of a battle in AD878 when the Danish raider Hubba was defeated by the men of Devon.

Above the church a path leads over Butter Hill, where the roofless stone building was once a Lloyd's signal station. It now houses a television relay station which ensures that viewers at Lynmouth can receive the West Country's television services. Before it was provided they had to use the services from Wales.

The Great Red landslip on the way to the Foreland marks the point where the sandstone grits meet the slates which comprise the rest of this coast. The path then runs steeply down into Caddow Combe to the east and finishes at the Foreland lighthouse, tucked into the slope above Foreland Point. The keepers' cottages are now owned by the Trust.

At Warmersturt, a rocky knoll to the east of the combe, is a view eastwards along the Glenthorne Cliffs. This stretch of coast provides miles of walking, for more than two miles on or alongside the Trust's land, and from there for a further four and a half miles, as the crow flies, to Porlock Weir, with no road reaching the sea for its entire length. The landscape here is very different, for not only is the soil on these Lynton slates more kindly but the cliffs are sheltered from the south-west gales. Oak woodland is a prominent feature, some of it pollarded in the past, with ash, beech, rowan, sycamore and holly, and rather too much *Rhododendron ponticum*, which tends to smother the flora which would otherwise flourish here. (*See also* Combe Martin and the Hangman Hills; the Heddon Valley, Trentishoe and Woody Bay; Holnicote Estate.)

The Jekyll-style herbaceous border along the paved walk sets off a view of the east front of Lytes Cary, with the fourteenth-century chapel on the left. (*NT/L. A. Sparrow*)

Lytes Cary Manor Somerset

1 mile north of Ilchester bypass on the A303

This enchanting manor house built round a court-yard in the depths of rural Somerset bears the name of the family who lived here for 500 years, from the thirteenth to the eighteenth century. A flagged path across smoothly mown grass leads to the projecting entrance porch, crowned by the swan of the Lyte family, wings half raised as if to defend the house. Rounded topiary yews lining the path look like crinolined ladies stepping over the grass. To the left is the oldest feature of Lytes Cary, the simple little chapel built by Peter Lyte in *c*.1343, attached to the house but only accessible from the outside. Family coats of arms in red, white and yellow stand out prominently on the painted frieze added in the reign of Henry VII which decorates the whitewashed interior.

Although the north and west ranges are eight-eenth century and later, Lytes Cary has a feeling of great age, of a place that has grown out of its surroundings. The Tudor great hall between the porch and the chapel, with a little oriel off it where the family would eat in privacy away from their servants and retainers, rises the full height of the house to a magnificent timber roof, the ends of the rafters adorned with carved angels. Here, too, is a copy of Henry Lyte's *Niewe Herball*, first published

in 1578, which was translated from the work of the famous Flemish herbalist Dodoens and dedicated to Queen Elizabeth I. Subsequently known as the *Lytes Herbal*, it was still being reprinted in 1678. Henry would have enjoyed the splendid plaster ceiling in the great chamber on the floor above which his father commissioned in 1533, interlaced hexagons and diamonds studded with armorial bosses heralding Elizabethan plasterwork of a generation later. This room is also notable for a fine interior porch, covered in linenfold panelling and with a crest of trefoils.

Neglected after the departure of the Lytes in about 1748, the house was rescued in this century by Sir Walter Jenner, who refurnished it with high-quality seventeenth- and early eighteenth-century oak pieces and with fabrics in authentically medieval browns, olives and muted reds. Sir Walter was also responsible for the beautiful Elizabethan-style gar-den, with clipped yew hedges enclosing a series of outdoor rooms. A vivid herbaceous border punc-tuated with urns set between buttresses of yew leads to a long raised walk overlooking an orchard planted with the crab apples, medlars and quinces that the Elizabethans loved, graceful arches of weeping ash marking paths across the grass. Other yew compartments frame smoothly mown lawns and a pool ornamented with statues of Flora and Diana. An urn placed at the end of a hornbeam tunnel is set off by the green and white foliage of variegated weigela and a border along the south front has been stocked with species cultivated when Henry Lyte published his herbal.

Lyveden New Bield
Northamptonshire

4 miles south-west of Oundle via the A427, 3 miles east of Brigstock

Like Staunton Harold in Leicestershire to the north (*see* p.315), Lyveden New Bield is a moving testament to the strength of religious faith. This strangely compelling, roofless architectural shell, with its mullioned and transomed windows staring sightless over an empty rolling landscape of woods and cornfields, stands half a mile or so from a minor road, far from any other house. It was started in 1594 by the exceptional and talented Sir Thomas Tresham as a garden lodge to his new manor house at Lyveden, but work proceeded very slowly. Although staunchly loyal to Queen Elizabeth, who knighted him in 1575, Sir Thomas converted to the Catholic faith in 1580 and spent fifteen years of the twenty-five left to him either in prison or under house arrest for his religious beliefs, while fines for recusancy made heavy and continuing demands on

The intriguing roofless shell of Lyveden New Bield, designed in the shape of an equal-armed cross and probably still incomplete when its creator, Sir Thomas Tresham, died in 1605. (*NT/John Bethell*)

his pocket. In the circumstances it is extraordinary that he built anything at all.

Two storeys high and devised in the shape of an equal-armed cross, Lyveden New Bield's design and decoration both illustrate the Elizabethan love of symbolism and devices and unequivocally declare where Sir Thomas's religious sympathies lay. Allusions to the numbers five and seven in the design of the faces on the end of each wing are references to salvation and the Godhead. Carved emblems of the passion again refer to the mystical number seven and the eighty-one letters which made up the inscriptions running below the roof, of which only fragments remain, hinted at the nine leaves in the trefoils on the Tresham coat of arms. The fields around preserve the faint outlines of a series of canals, terraces and mounds and of an extensive diamond-patterned knot, all that remains of the grandiose formal garden with which Sir Thomas hoped to set off his new home, one of the oldest surviving garden layouts in England.

The garden lodge was probably incomplete when Sir Thomas Tresham died, just months before his son was arrested and imprisoned for complicity in the Gunpowder Plot. This intriguing ghost is a memorial to a brave but foolhardy man.

Maister House   Humberside
160 High Street, Hull

Until the building of the first commercial dock on the River Humber in 1770 heralded its gradual decline, Hull's old harbour was the focus of the town's considerable trading interests, with grand merchants' houses lining the narrow, winding thoroughfares along the river. This fine Palladian house on the High Street is one of the few surviving from this era. Rebuilt for the merchant Henry Maister after a fire in 1743, it is still substantially as finished a year later, a plain three-storey classical building fronted by railings and with a stone parapet concealing the roof. The only sign of ostentation is the fine pedimented doorcase in the centre of the façade.

This severe and dignified exterior and the sober pine-panelled counting house on the ground floor act as a foil for the superb staircase, richly decorated with plasterwork by Joseph Page, leading to what would have been the Maister family apartments. A statue of Ceres by John Cheere in a niche above the first flight surveys swags of drapery suspended from lion masks, festoons of shells and acanthus-leaf medallions and scrolls. The coved ceiling above the gallery on the second floor is similarly richly stuccoed and a fine ironwork balustrade was supplied by Robert Bakewell. The work of a highly competent architect, Maister House was probably influenced by Lord Burlington, who knew Henry Maister and whose Yorkshire home was only twenty-five miles away.

Malham Tarn   North Yorkshire

6 miles north-east of Settle

Malham Tarn, high up on the moors between Ribblesdale and Wharfedale, lies at the centre of 4,300 acres of dramatic limestone country which is farmed by the Trust's tenants with Swaledale sheep and crossbred cattle. The rock is deeply fissured, and water vanishes suddenly and reappears miles away. This is why the approach from Malham village, past the spectacular limestone cliff of Malham Cove, and up the valley to the tarn, is such an eerie landscape: humps and bumps, holes and hollows, huge boulders and outcrops of rock. Having disappeared underground, the River Aire emerges at the base of the cove. Before the Ice Age it filled the valley above and careered over the cliff in a great waterfall.

The tarn, however, sits in a saucer of Silurian slate which is impervious, dammed by glacial waste left here when the ice retreated. The mixture of limestone cliffs, known as scars, the acid 'raised bog', the alkaline fen and the nutrient-rich shallow lake make it a wonderful place for plants and an internationally important site for nature conservation and geological interests. It is worth a visit in early summer to see myriads of heart's-ease starring the sward as one approaches the tarn from the south. The mountain pansy flourishes here too, while the bird's-eye primrose (largely confined to the northern Pennines, Lake District and southern Scotland) grows in the wetter places.

Great-crested grebe, common sandpiper and coot breed on the shores of the tarn, which is stocked with brown trout. One is bound also to record that Malham Tarn inspired the social reformer Charles Kingsley to write his book *The Water Babies* (1863).

The woods, mainly broadleaved species with

Malham Tarn, a 150-acre natural lake high up on the moors between Ribblesdale and Wharfedale. (*NT/Mike Williams*)

Scots pine and larch, provide shelter and give point to the landscape. Sycamore flourishes particularly well, as it roots firmly into the fissured limestone.

The Smelt Mill, the remains of which stand south-west of the tarn, was used to roast lead and zinc ores from Pikedaw to the south. The smelted metal was then carted down to the Leeds and Liverpool canal at Gargrave.

The Pennine Way skirts the east end of the tarn, and then continues over the high ground to the north, where Great Hill, Green Hill Scar and Little Fell are all part of the Trust's estate. The Abbot Hills, in the south-east corner, remind us that this property, like Brimham (*see* p.44), was once part of the great possessions of Fountains Abbey (*see* p.121), providing it with the wool on which its fortunes were based for centuries.

Malvern Hills   Hereford & Worcester

4–8 miles south of Great Malvern, along the A449

This is the landscape captured by Elgar, whose music seems to conjure up the wooded slopes and grassy summits of the hills rising above a patchwork of fields and villages stretching away into the distance. The northern part of this fine range has long been vested in a local body of conservators, and the Trust has protective covenants over the gentler southern half. To the west, Eastnor Park drops down into Herefordshire: brackeny slopes flanking a great deer park dominated by the early nineteenth-century castle of the Hervey Bathurst/ Somers Cocks family. Above the park, Midsummer Hill (*see* p.199) is held as a memorial to a Somers Cocks relation killed in the First World War.

Manor of Cookham and Maidenhead   Berkshire

North of Maidenhead

These commons consist of more than 800 acres of land which was Crown property from before the Conquest until 1818. When the Trust acquired the land in 1934, the commons were under threat, and even now the A4 Bath road runs through the southern end at Maidenhead Thicket. From here a string of commons and greens, crossed by paths and bridleways, extends for five miles north and east to run steeply down to the Thames at Cock Marsh. Still grazed by the commoners' cattle, the marsh has a particularly good plant life.

Market House   Derbyshire

4 miles west of Matlock, on south side of the B5057, in main street of Winster

This ruggedly attractive two-storey building is one of the few clues to Winster's former importance as a market town. Built in the late seventeenth or early eighteenth century, the Market House is a pleasing mixture of brick and stone, with thick sandstone slabs covering the steeply pitched roof and mullioned and transomed windows lighting the first floor. As was traditional with such buildings, the ground floor was originally open, but its five pointed arches are now filled in. Still the dominant feature of Winster's long main street, it was bought in 1906, as the Trust's first acquisition in the Peak District. It is now a Trust information centre.

The Market House, Winster, is a reminder of the cheese and cattle fairs that were once such a prominent feature of life in the town. (*NT/Andy Williams*)

Marsden Moor West Yorkshire

7–8 miles south-west of Huddersfield, astride the A62

Marsden Moor and its outliers, Holme and Binn Moors, rise steeply on three sides of the mills and houses of Marsden, south-west of Huddersfield. This is a great sweep – some 5,700 acres – of bleak dramatic moorland, much of it over 1,000 feet above sea level and reaching 1,561 feet on Wessenden Moor. The peat blanket, habitat for mosses and moorland grasses, and for curlew, golden plover and lapwing, feeds streams tumbling down the steep-sided cloughs or valleys which dissect the upland. The Pennine Way crosses Marsden Moor, while a line of airshafts marks an older crossing far beneath, the eight-mile-long Standedge Tunnel on the railway from Ashton under Lyne to Huddersfield, one of the great monuments of nineteenth-century engineering.

Max Gate Dorset

1 mile east of Dorchester on A352

Thomas Hardy designed this tree-shrouded red-brick villa for himself and lived here from 1885 until his death, in 1928. The Hardy associations are strong, this being the place where he wrote *Tess of the d'Urbervilles*, *Jude the Obscure*, *The Mayor of Casterbridge*, and the moving poetry rooted in the disintegration of his marriage to Emma Gifford (after Emma's death, in 1912, he lived with Florence Dugdale, marrying her in 1914). Here, too, in his last years he received a stream of literary visitors, among them T. E. Lawrence, whose Clouds Hill (*see* p.79) was nearby, W. B. Yeats, Robert Louis Stevenson and Virginia Woolf. It is strange that a man so sensitive to buildings should have chosen to live in so cheerless a place, but it seems Hardy wanted convenience and privacy, and there is a fine view. Sadly, none of his contents remains (his study is re-created in Dorchester County Museum).

Melford Hall Suffolk

In Long Melford on east side of the A134, 14 miles south of Bury St Edmunds, 3 miles north of Sudbury

Set into the high brick wall bordering Long Melford's village green is a delicious octagonal Tudor pavilion, with finials rising like brick fingers at every angle and from all eight gables. This giant doll's-house faces along a grassy terrace – the former bowling-green – to one of the most satisfying Elizabethan houses in East Anglia.

As the great wall suggests, Melford faces west over the park, as if turning away from the village. Massive chimneystacks and fanciful turrets crowned

Fanciful towers crowned with onion domes and tall chimneystacks punctuate Melford Hall's warm red-brick façades.
(*NT/John Bethell*)

with eastern onion domes rise dramatically from the U-shaped red-brick mansion, with two long wings flanking the courtyard on the entrance front. The house dates from some time in the mid-sixteenth century, after the shrewd Tudor lawyer who built it, Sir William Cordell, was granted the manor that had belonged to the great Benedictine abbey of Bury St Edmunds. Despite subsequent alterations, such as the removal of the gatehouse range that once enclosed the courtyard, and the disappearance of part of the moat, the exterior is still very much as Queen Elizabeth I must have seen it when she was entertained lavishly here in 1578.

Although the house was ransacked during the Civil War and suffered a disastrous fire in 1942, there are still many associations with the Cordells and with the seafaring Parker family who bought the hall in 1786, notable for producing no fewer than three admirals. The Tudor great hall rising through two storeys is hung with both Cordell and Parker portraits and with the survey of the estate which Sir William commissioned in 1580, every field named and the long strip of the village green with the church at one end clearly shown. The panelling and Jacobean furniture in this room are a world away from the classical Regency library added by Thomas Hopper, much better known as the architect of Penrhyn Castle (see p.254), with its curved oak bookshelves, florid Greek couches and armchairs appropriately decorated with owls. Paintings of historic naval engagements fought by the 5th Baronet, Vice Admiral Sir Hyde Parker, and his second son, also an admiral, line the walls, one of the most memorable showing fireships drifting on the tide towards a British fleet on the Hudson river.

The 5th Baronet himself, who ran away from school to join the merchant navy and worked his way up through the ranks to become the most technically skilled admiral of his day, appears as a larger-than-life figure in a portrait by Romney in the little octagon off the main library. The sensitive, rather feminine boy in the miniature between the windows is his grandson Harry at the age of fourteen, lost at sea with his grandfather when the Admiral was on his way to the East Indies in 1783 to take up his last post. The ivory figures in the great hall and much of the Chinese porcelain seen throughout the house were taken from a Spanish galleon laden with presents from the Emperor of Peking to the King of Spain which the 5th Baronet captured in 1762. The house also has connections

with Beatrix Potter, whose cousin married the 10th Baronet. Mementoes of the author in the room where she always slept include the model for Jemima Puddle-duck, neatly dressed in a blue poke bonnet.

The small garden has lawns studded with domes of box and planted with specimen trees, including a Judas tree, a tree of heaven, a black mulberry and a huge copper beech. An undulating crinkle-crankle wall frames one side. The north arm of the moat is now a sunken garden by the bowling-green terrace but the west arm still runs along the village green, past some intriguing topiary figures outside the garden wall.

Middle Littleton Barn
Hereford & Worcester

3 miles north-east of Evesham, east of the B4085

Produce from the fertile Vale of Evesham once filled this coursed lias barn in market-gardening country on the banks of the River Avon. Some 316 feet long and buttressed like a church, it is both one of the largest and one of the finest in the country, although not all its wagon porches have survived.

Inside, oak framing forms an aisled bay at either end and eight base-cruck trusses divide the nine intermediate bays. The barn was built by the Benedictine monks of Evesham Abbey and may date from c.1300 or even earlier. Like Ashleworth (see p.14), the barn is part of a picturesque group of buildings which includes an Elizabethan manor.

Midsummer Hill
Hereford & Worcester

4 miles east of Ledbury, ¼ mile north of the A438 Tewkesbury road

The impressive ramparts ringing this nineteen-acre Iron Age hill fort at the southern end of the Malvern Hills enclose both the 937-foot summit of Midsummer Hill and the lower Hollybush Hill. A huge bank and ditch form the principal defences, but there are also traces of a second bank on the outer, counterscarp slope of the ditch. Scoop-shaped hollows inside the fort mark the remains of a considerable settlement which apparently included rectangular wooden houses arranged in tidy rows.

Minnowburn Beeches, Killynether and Collin Glen

Co. Down

At south end of Shaw's Bridge, Lagan river; 1 mile south-west of Newtownards; from the B38 Glen road to the foot of Collin mountain respectively

Three much valued places lie on the outskirts of Belfast. At the south end of Shaw's Bridge, over the Lagan river, the Minnowburn Beeches clothe the steep slopes as the river makes a horseshoe bend. The path up the Cregagh Glen, past Lisnabreeny, leads to a gorse-covered 400-foot hill with views over the city to Belfast Lough, east to Strangford Lough (*see* p.322) and south to the Mournes. At Newtownards, the beech woods of Killynether creep up the south side of Scrabo Hill, with a vast view over Strangford Lough to the Ards peninsula on its further shore.

West of Belfast, the stream tumbling down to wooded Collin Glen runs up the cleft between Black Mountain and Collin Mountain, a quick way out of the urban fringe to the hills above. At Glenoe, south

of Larne, in a pocket handkerchief of a glen, the Glynn river plunges over a waterfall, surrounded by beeches and ferns, past the pretty village of lime-washed cottages terraced along steep hillsides.

Mompesson House Wiltshire

In Salisbury, on north side of Choristers' Green in the Cathedral Close, near High Street Gate

Salisbury seems the perfect setting for Anthony Trollope's Barsetshire novels. It takes no effort of the imagination to see Mrs Proudie, the bishop's domineering wife in *Barchester Towers*, lifting her skirt as she crosses the smoothly mown grass of the close, or the Rev. Septimus Harding, the mild-mannered hero of *The Warden*, ending his days here quietly snoozing in the sun.

Mrs Proudie would certainly have been at home in Mompesson House, with its beautiful eighteenth-century plasterwork and marble chimneypieces and its elegant airy rooms looking over the close towards the cathedral spire soaring above the

The elegant entrance façade of Mompesson House; the grey limestone with which it is faced is set off by houses of warm red brick on either side. (*NT/John Bethell*)

rooftops. In early summer a white magnolia softens the two-storey limestone façade. A central front door is placed symmetrically between three sash windows on either side and dormers peer down from the hipped roof.

The house was built in 1701 by Charles Mompesson, MP for Old Sarum, but the sumptuous, high-quality decoration by an unknown hand was commissioned by his brother-in-law and heir Charles Longueville, son of the patron and literary executor of the poet Samuel Butler. The most spectacular plasterwork is in the staircase hall, where the bold florid designs include flowers, fruit, satyrs' masks and the head of King Midas with ass's ears. In the Green Room an eagle with outspread wings crouches in the middle of the ceiling, ready to pounce.

Later residents have also left their mark. Cool seascapes in an upstairs corridor and a scene of peaceful domesticity hanging on the stairs are two of several watercolours by Barbara Townsend, one of the three daughters of George Barnard Townsend, a local solicitor who came to Mompesson in the mid-nineteenth century. Living on here until her death at the age of ninety-six in 1939, Barbara became a legend in the close, continuing to sketch and paint right up to the end of her life, a tiny figure wrapped in layers of shawls, scarves and veils. Mompesson is also notable for the Turnbull collection of over 370 English eighteenth-century glasses, some delicately poised on slender twisted stems shot through with spirals of colour, some engraved with foliage, flowers or ears of corn.

A secluded garden at the back of the house, with a fine specimen magnolia and a wistaria- and honeysuckle-covered pergola providing welcome shade on hot summer afternoons, is bounded by the high wall of the close, partly built with material from Old Sarum. The old privy hides behind a tree in one corner.

Monk's House East Sussex

4 miles south-east of Lewes, off the former A275 (now the C7) in Rodmell village, near the church

This modest weatherboarded house at the far end of Rodmell village was the home of one of the most innovative novelists of the twentieth century. By 1919, when Virginia Woolf and her husband Leonard bought the property as a retreat from London

Monk's House, Rodmell: Vanessa Bell's watercolour sketch for a portrait of her sister Virginia Woolf, painted *c.*1933–4 in the Woolfs' London house, 52 Tavistock Square. It is inscribed 'VB to LW Christmas 1935'. The finished painting, which was exhibited in 1934, has disappeared. (*NT/Eric Crichton*)

life, Virginia's first two novels had been completed, but the experimental work which was to establish her reputation, in particular *To the Lighthouse*, *The Waves* and *Mrs Dalloway*, was still in the future. Two years earlier she and Leonard had founded the Hogarth Press at their house in Richmond, whose outstanding list, including the first published works of T. S. Eliot, was to make a major contribution to literary life. Ten miles or so across the South Downs stood Charleston, where Virginia's sister Vanessa, the gifted painter, had set up house with her art-critic husband Clive Bell and the artist Duncan Grant.

Although there are only echoes of Virginia at Monk's House, the house is full of reminders of the talented circle in which she moved. Painted furniture by her sister and Duncan Grant in a post-Impressionist style includes a table and chairs in the sitting-room: muted abstract designs in brown, blue and olive-green are relieved by a panel of peaches on the back of each chair. Books are piled on one of Duncan's tile-topped tables and a formidable portrait of Einstein in old age, his face only half-lit, is one of a number of telling photographs. China on the mantelpiece was decorated by Duncan Grant, Vanessa Bell and her son Quentin, and their work also fills the top half of the dresser in the tiny kitchen.

Every room is hung with paintings by the family circle, including Italian and Sussex landscapes and tranquil still lifes – apples or a jug of flowers – by Vanessa, as well as some of her distinctive portraits, one of them a haunting likeness of her sister. Flowering potted plants might have come from the heated greenhouses where Leonard nurtured the begonias, lilies and gloxinias with which he filled the house. A gurgling fish tank behind the sitting-room door recalls his habit of looking after ailing fish from the garden ponds, and the dogs' blue pottery water bowl is still in its place.

During the years the Woolfs lived at Monk's House, these modest simple rooms were used to entertain some of the best-known literary and artistic figures of the day, among them Vita Sackville-West, Maynard Keynes, Lytton Strachey, E. M. Forster, David Garnett and Roger Fry. A black Chinese silk shawl embroidered in pink and green, casually thrown over a chair in Virginia's sunny bedroom at the east end of the house, was a present from Lady Ottoline Morrell. Many visitors were members of the Bloomsbury Group which Virginia and Vanessa had founded with their brother Thoby and which was to give the sisters an influence far beyond their own work.

The little garden is still largely as the Woolfs left it, with a large open lawn where they played bowls and a formal walled garden with sculpture set between the flowering beds. The weather-boarded garden house, with a large window looking east towards the River Ouse and a spur of the South Downs beyond, is almost filled with the huge battered table where Virginia wrote, her distinctive blue paper spread out on top. Photographs she took at Monk's House are now displayed in the extension, accompanied by quotations from her diaries and letters.

Montacute House Somerset

In Montacute village, 4 miles west of Yeovil, on south side of the A3088, 3 miles east of the A303

Montacute invites the kind of elaborate compliment paid by one sixteenth-century visitor, who thought the fronting stone terrace superior to St Mark's Square in Venice. Probably finished by 1601, it is an H-shaped building of local honey-brown Ham stone. Like Hardwick Hall in Derbyshire (*see* p.142), Montacute is every inch an Elizabethan house, a product of a confident and enquiring age. It was designed by a local stonemason, the gifted William Arnold (*see also* Dunster Castle, p.108), for the successful lawyer Sir Edward Phelips, later Master of the Rolls and Chancellor to the Household of Prince Henry.

Montacute's long east and west façades rise three storeys to a roofline fretted with delicate chimneys, parapets and pinnacles and adorned with curved Flemish gables. Unlike a medieval house, turned inwards to a central courtyard, Montacute looks boldly out at the world through a huge display of glittering glass. Classical details on the entrance front, such as the nine curiously lumpy statues in Roman dress, betray the influence of the Renaissance, slowly filtering north from its beginnings in Italy.

The other side of the house is even more engaging. Here stonework from nearby Clifton Maybank, a splendid sixteenth-century mansion partly dismantled in 1786, ornaments the two-storey front grafted on between the existing wings in the late eighteenth century. The crowning parapet is crowded with heraldic beasts on pedestals, while shadows cast by the fluted stone pillars decorating the façade give the house a sculptural quality. Montacute's fantasy outline is continued in the spiky balustrade and the two delightful Elizabethan pavilions topped with obelisks which border the entrance court.

Although hardly any of the original contents survived the decline in the Phelipses' fortunes, leading to Montacute's sale in 1929, fine furniture and tapestries from the Sir Malcolm Stewart bequest give the rooms an authentic atmosphere. In the medieval-style great hall the early-morning sun casts richly coloured pools through the heraldic glass in the east-facing windows. Phelips portraits hang above the original panelling and an elaborate stone screen with rusticated arches set between

A meadow of spring flowers sets off a knight in armour and his gaily caparisoned horse on a late fifteenth-century Flemish tapestry at Montacute. (*NT*)

three pairs of columns runs across one end, extravagant horns curling back from the rams' heads carved on the decorative capitals. Two rare early seventeenth-century plaster panels illustrate village life, one showing a hen-pecked husband being berated by his wife as he draws beer from a barrel rather than attending to the baby he clasps in his left arm.

At the top of the house a magnificent long gallery, the largest surviving Elizabethan example in Britain, runs 172 feet down the length of the building. Used for entertaining important guests and for exercise in inclement weather, the gallery has panoramic views from the two great oriel windows framed by orange trees in pots at either end. Tudor and Jacobean paintings from the National Portrait Gallery echo the portraits of family and notables which would once have hung here, a set of stiff kings and queens like a pack of playing cards contrasting with more realistic works, such as the delightful picture showing Robert Carey, 1st Earl of Monmouth, with his family, the five adults posed as if in a photograph, or the portraits of the handsome, curly-headed Robert Sidney, 1st Earl of Leicester (1563–1626), and of little Henry, Prince of Wales (1594–1612), the child's creamy pallor emphasised by his rich crimson dress.

Although now incorporating nineteenth- and twentieth-century features and planting schemes, the extensive garden still follows the outlines of the original layout. The oriel window at the north end of the long gallery looks down on a formal rectangle of trees and grass which lies on the site of the Elizabethan garden, the raised walks framing the sunken lawn with its bracelet of clipped yew and thorn and a nineteenth-century balustraded pond in the centre probably dating from when the house was built. A border of shrub roses under the retaining wall, planted with the advice of Vita Sackville-West (*see* p.291) and Graham Stuart Thomas, includes species in cultivation in the sixteenth century, such as *Rosa gallica* 'Officinalis', the Red Rose of Lancaster, and the double white Yorkist *R. alba* 'Maxima'.

Mrs Reiss of Tintinhull (*see* p.333) was responsible for the strong colour schemes surrounding the lawn filling the entrance court, with roses, delphiniums, lupins and dahlias forming vivid splashes of red, orange, yellow and blue against dark foliage, the ideal foil for the warm yellow stone of the house.

The cedar lawn, with an arcaded garden house to which Lord Curzon, who leased Montacute in the early twentieth century, added an Elizabethan façade, lies on the site of an old orchard and the carpark fills what was the walled kitchen garden. A mature avenue of cedars, beeches and limes, fronted by clipped Irish yew, frames the west drive created in 1851–2, its lines continued in the wide grassy ride edged with limes which stretches away across the park to the east.

Moseley Old Hall Staffordshire

4 miles north of Wolverhampton; south of the M54 between the A449 and the A460

In the early hours of 8 September 1651, five days after the Royalist defeat at the Battle of Worcester, Charles II disguised as a woodcutter came through the gate at the end of the Nut Alley and moved silently up the flagged path leading to the back of the house. Waiting anxiously in the dark outside were Thomas Whitgreave, the owner of Moseley, and his chaplain, John Huddlestone. Together they escorted the king through the heavily studded back door and by the light of a flickering candle he was shown up the narrow stairs into the priest's room, now known as the King's Room.

Here he sat sipping a glass of wine while his sore feet were soothed, watching the firelight playing over the hangings of the four-poster bed where he was to spend his first night in comfort since the battle. Here, too, he was shown the hiding place barely four feet high concealed under a trapdoor in the cupboard to the right of the fireplace, the cavity where Charles was to crouch when the Parliamentarians came to the house two days later. The night after this unwelcome visit, the king mounted a horse brought to the orchard stile and rode away disguised as a serving man on the first leg of his long and hazardous journey to safety on the Continent.

Visitors to Moseley Old Hall retrace Charles's route on that fateful night 350 years ago when the Stuart cause was nearly lost. Although the façades of the Elizabethan house were faced in brick in the nineteenth century and the mullioned windows have been replaced by casements, much of the original panelling and timber framing inside the house still survives and heavy oak seventeenth-century furniture, including the bed on which Charles slept, and contemporary portraits of the king and those who helped him, all contribute to an authentic atmosphere, miraculously not destroyed by noise from the M54 only yards away. Standing at the window of Whitgreave's study over the front porch, as he and the king did, it is possible to imagine that the remnants of the defeated army will shortly appear straggling up the lane on their long walk back to Scotland. Mementoes of these perilous days include a proclamation of 10 September 1651 offering a £1,000 reward for the capture of the king and Charles II's letter of thanks to Jane Lane, who helped him to escape.

The house is now surrounded by a reconstructed seventeenth-century garden, based on a design of 1640. In the elaborate knot garden, box hedges outline a geometrical pattern like a horizontal wrought-iron screen, with each compartment filled with coloured gravels and stones. The orchard has been planted with old varieties of fruit trees, quinces, mulberries and medlars frame the path from the Nut Alley and a little herb garden now shelters beneath more box hedges. Perhaps the king saw a similar garden from the chapel windows when John Huddlestone took him to visit the oratory in the attic, now adorned with an eighteenth-century painted barrel ceiling. Charles was certainly to remember Moseley, giving Thomas Whitgreave a pension of £200 a year on his restoration in 1660 and summoning Huddlestone to administer the last rites of the Catholic Church when he lay dying in 1685.

Mottisfont Abbey Hampshire

4½ miles north-west of Romsey, ¾ mile west of the A3057

Those lucky enough to acquire monastic houses at the Dissolution were then faced with the problem of transforming them into domestic residences. Most chose to adapt the monks' living quarters, but a few ambitious men sought to incorporate the church itself into their conversions. One such was William Lord Sandys, Lord Chamberlain to Henry VIII, who was granted the priory of Mottisfont in exchange for the villages of Chelsea and Paddington and whose descendants were to move here from The Vyne (*see* p.347) after the Civil War. The silvery stone north front of his Tudor house runs the full length of what was the nave of the church and ends in the truncated tower, where the arch leading to the north transept is outlined on the façade. The medieval buttresses are now crowned with eight-

eenth-century stone balls, transforming them into ornamental pilasters. Original mullions survive on the ground floor, but sash windows were inserted above as part of extensive Georgian alterations.

The cultured world of the 1740s is far more pronounced on the south, where an elegant red-brick Georgian façade with a central pediment is framed by two shallow bayed wings stepped out from the main body of the house. Three storeys here, in contrast to two on the north, reflect the sloping site.

Few traces of the Tudor interior escaped the Georgian remodelling, but the ghost of the priory emerges in the atmospheric early thirteenth-century cellarium, with columns of Caen stone, now partly buried, supporting a vaulted roof. The main glory of the house, the Whistler Room over the cellarium, is a much later addition. This enchanting drawing-room takes its name from Rex Whistler's elaborate *trompe-l'oeil* murals imitating Gothic plasterwork, executed in 1938–9 after the completion of his mammoth work at Plas Newydd (*see* p.259). At Mottisfont Whistler had also been commissioned to design the furniture, but he never returned from the Second World War to complete his assignment.

The Abbey lies low on green lawns by the River Test, the centrepiece of beautiful wooded gardens.

The rosette-like bloom of 'Petite Lisette', one of the old-fashioned roses in the collection established by the Trust at Mottisfont Abbey. (*NT/Rob Matheson*)

Many of the mature walnuts, sycamores, Spanish chestnuts, beeches and cedars for which the property is now famous were part of the eighteenth-century grounds, but some are even older. A London plane by the river is said to be the largest in the country, its spreading branches covering some 1,500 square yards. A little Gothick summerhouse, almost surrounded by trees on the lawns to the north-west of the house, also dates from the eighteenth century and incorporates medieval floor tiles and a corbel from the priory.

The garden as it is today also owes much to Mr and Mrs Gilbert Russell, who came to Mottisfont in 1934. The north lawn bordered by a pleached lime walk and the paved octagon surrounded by clipped yew were designed by Geoffrey Jellicoe in 1936–7 and a few years later Norah Lindsay laid out the box- and lavender-edged parterre on the south front and planted wistaria, clematis and other climbers on the house. A magnolia garden and a beech circle are other notable features of the grounds, but most visitors now come to see the national collection of pre-1900 shrub roses established since 1972 in what was the walled kitchen garden. Box-edged beds round a fountain pool contain over 300 varieties, many of them cultivars developed in nineteenth-century France, such as those collected by the Empress Joséphine, but including species from all over the world. Ancient hybrids flowering white, purple, carmine and maroon mix with the tomato-red and brilliant yellow of Persian roses and the clear lemon and deep crimson of Chinese varieties. On the far side of the garden crystal-clear water still gushes from the spring which attracted the Austin canons to this sheltered spot nearly 800 years ago.

Mottistone Manor Garden

Isle of Wight

In the village of Mottistone

This young garden largely created by Lady Nicholson and her family over the last twenty years lies in a beautiful sheltered valley sloping down to the medieval and sixteenth-century manor and to the sea beyond. A flight of steps behind the house leads up to grassy terraces formally planted with roses and fruit trees. An avenue of cherries, plums and apples marks the site of the old orchard, and a broad stretch of grass sweeps up to Shern Place, an idyllic secondary valley, planted with beech and ash and carpeted with bluebells in spring, which runs up to the Long Stone on the downs above. This impressive Neolithic long barrow was probably also the site of a Saxon moot. Most of the trees in the garden are still young, but some more mature specimens, including a tulip tree, a magnolia, a liquid amber and a mulberry, date from John Seeley's restoration of the house in the late 1920s. The garden is circled by a grassy walk following the steeply sloping valley sides, with views east to St Catherine's Point and west to the spire and golden weathervane of Mottistone church.

Moulton Hall North Yorkshire

5 miles east of Richmond

This compact stone house of 1650, about a mile east of the A1, is adorned with large Dutch gables and boasts a very fine carved wood staircase.

Mount Grace Priory

North Yorkshire

6 miles north-east of Northallerton, ½ mile east of the A19 and ½ mile south of its junction with the A172

The simplicity and austerity of this little Carthusian community on the edge of the wooded Cleveland Hills is far removed from the splendours of Fountains some twenty miles to the south (*see* p.121). Whereas the remains of the Cistercian house speak of a life lived in common and of an increasing relaxation of the principles on which it was founded, Mount Grace reflects the pursuit of asceticism, untouched by the attractions of the world. The Carthusians were more hermits than monks, living apart from each other as well as in isolation from the world. Whereas other orders ate, prayed and slept together, each Carthusian lived largely in isolation in his own cell, to which meals were brought.

The main feature of Mount Grace is an extensive grass cloister, measuring 270 feet on its longest side. Ranged around it, and along one side of an outer court, are the remains of the stone-built, four-roomed cells where the little community – there is provision for only twenty-one monks – spent long hours in prayer and contemplation and in copying out devotional works. Most of the cells still show

The remains of Mount Grace Priory, showing the outlines of some of the cells where monks lived solitary lives of prayer and contemplation. (*NT/C.P. Robinson*)

the hatch through which food was served from the cloister, the right-angled bend ensuring that monk and server did not see one another. And each monk had his own walled garden, about twenty feet square, with his own garderobe at the far end. Perhaps some allowed themselves to sit here and doze in the sun on warm summer afternoons. On the north side of the cloister is the diminutive 118-foot church, a simple building that was rarely used except on Sundays and feast days, its little battlemented, pinnacled tower a telling contrast to Marmaduke Huby's soaring monument at Fountains.

But although Mount Grace turned its back on the world, sheltering behind the high precinct wall which still encloses much of the site, the community was not averse to modern conveniences. Arched recesses still visible in the cloister walls of some cells once held taps fed from a spring just outside the priory walls. Another spring was channelled to flush the drain serving the garderobes, some of which still project from the garden walls on the north side of the precinct.

Mount Grace was founded in 1398 by Thomas de Holland, Duke of Surrey and Earl of Kent, and is one of only nine charterhouses established in England, most of them part of the great Carthusian expansion between 1343 and 1414. It was surrendered quietly to Henry VIII's commissioners in December 1539, and more than a century passed before the range housing the priory's guest accommodation and kitchens was converted into the long gabled house with a projecting two-storey porch which is now such a feature of the site.

On the north side of the cloister the reconstructed cell, like a tiny two-storeyed cottage, dates from the early twentieth century, the fireplace in its living-room suggesting a degree of comfort in winter. For those who chose to live like hermits here, physical privation was probably not the major burden of the regime. The cells outlined on the grass would have been a spiritual sanctuary for the strong and resolute, but a prison for those who found they could not live with themselves or began to doubt their faith.

Mount Stewart Co. Down

15 miles east of Belfast on the A20 Newtownards–Portaferry road, 5 miles south-east of Newtownards

This long, low, grey house beautifully situated looking south over Strangford Lough is known for its association with two exceptional men, the architect James 'Athenian' Stuart and the politician Viscount Castlereagh, but it is alive with the spirit of the vivacious and brilliant Edith, Lady Londonderry, wife of the 7th Marquess, who redecorated and furnished most of the house between the First and Second World Wars.

The main block, with a huge classical portico fronting the balustraded entrance court, was built in the mid-1830s, designed by the renowned Irish architect William Vitruvius Morrison for the 3rd Marquess of Londonderry. Morrison's grandiose octagonal hall, with a black and white chequered floor and classical statues framed by Ionic pillars, fills the centre of the house, lit from above by a huge dome. A bust immortalises the linen merchant Alexander Stewart, the 3rd Marquess's grandfather, who acquired the estate in 1744, while the outstanding rust-coloured early eighteenth-century Chinese dinner service displayed here was inherited by Stewart's wife, whose brother was Governor of Bombay. Morrison's vast drawing-room divided by screens of green Ionic columns is similarly imposing, giving Lady Londonderry just the setting she needed for her lavish entertaining.

George Dance's west wing, created for the 1st Marquess in the early nineteenth century, has a lighter and more intimate touch. The delightful music-room, the least changed of his interiors, has an exquisite inlaid floor by John Ferguson, with a scalloped octagon of oak and mahogany surrounded by radiating boards of mellow bog fir enclosing a central motif like a Catherine wheel. Delicate plasterwork on the ceiling reflects the design. Double doors lead into Dance's elegant domed staircase hall, dominated by George Stubbs's intriguing painting of the racehorse Hambletonian. Shown here being rubbed down after his win at Newmarket in 1799, a race in which Stubbs felt he had been driven too hard, Hambletonian is depicted in an impossible pose, standing on his two left legs, his groom's right arm stretched like elastic over his neck.

The principal bedrooms called after European cities (Rome, Moscow, even Sebastopol), the mementoes in the Castlereagh Room and the set of Empire chairs used by delegates to the Congress of Vienna in 1815 (including those occupied by Wellington and Talleyrand) recall the proud and austere 2nd Marquess, Foreign Secretary for ten years, who died so tragically by his own hand in 1822, misunderstood by the nation to which he had devoted his life. The main architect of the act of 1801 which united Great Britain and Ireland until the creation of Eire in 1922, Castlereagh went on to play a major role in the war against Napoleon and in the Congress which concluded it, rightly regarded as the world's first summit. It is no small measure of Castlereagh's achievement that the boundaries established at this time were to endure until the start of the First World War.

The 6th and 7th Marquesses also followed prominent political careers, during which both Edward VII and the future George VI were entertained at Mount Stewart. As Secretary of State for Air, the 7th Marquess promoted the Hurricane and Spitfire fighter planes which were to prove so crucial in England's defence in the Battle of Britain in 1940 and also introduced legislation establishing air corridors. Perhaps a premonition of what was to come led him to make several private visits to Germany in the late 1930s to meet Hitler and other Nazi leaders in an effort to promote Anglo-German understanding.

The 7th Marquess's political career was mirrored in the august company which his wife entertained at Mount Stewart in the Edwardian and interwar years, the prominent figures who came here including Lord Balfour, Harold Macmillan and Ramsay MacDonald. Lady Edith's flamboyant 1920s decor, the backdrop for her glittering house parties, survives in most of the principal rooms. Salmon-pink walls in Morrison's drawing-room set off a green grand piano and comfortable chairs and sofas are spread invitingly on the pink Aubusson carpets. Subdued low-level lighting comes from lamps of every description, some made out of classical urns, others once altar candlesticks. Chinese tea caddies converted into lamp stands, chinoiserie screens and other oriental pieces were brought back from a trip to China in 1912.

Two chairs in this room and the friendly stone animals adorning a terrace on the south front – four plump dodos, a grinning dinosaur, a hedgehog and a frog among them – recall the famous Ark Club, formed at the family's house in London where Lady

Londonderry held Wednesday gatherings for political and military figures during the First World War. Members of the club were known by the names of a wide variety of creatures, including the albatross (Lord Balfour), the warlock (Winston Churchill), and the wild boar (Lord Hailsham). Appropriately, Lady Londonderry was Circe the Sorceress.

This legendary beauty, whose charm is if anything enhanced by the drab khaki uniform in the portrait showing her as head of the Women's Legion, was also largely responsible for Mount Stewart's enchanting 78-acre garden, which flourishes with sub-tropical luxuriance in the temperate climate of the Ards peninsula. Notable for a high proportion of evergreens and for species from the Southern Hemisphere, many tender trees and shrubs cultivated here are rarely seen elsewhere in the British Isles.

The formal garden around the house is laid out as a series of varied outdoor rooms reminiscent of Hidcote or Sissinghurst (*see* pp.149 and 291). A majestic flight of steps sweeps down into the Italian garden on the south front, created with the help of twenty ex-servicemen after the First World War,

where two parterres set around fountain pools either side of a palm-fringed broad grass walk are planted to give contrasting effects, one flowering strongly orange and red against violet and purple foliage, the other in softer pinks, blues, mauves and white with silver foliage. Imaginative ornamental statuary, including mischievous monkeys and winged dragons perched on columns, was all designed by Lady Londonderry. Mature trees form a continuous backdrop, casting ribbons of shade across the grass.

In the more intimate sunken garden to the west of the house, based on a design by Gertrude Jekyll, tall cypress hedges shield rose-hung pergolas and four scalloped beds round the central lawn, particularly spectacular when the vivid orange azaleas, blue delphiniums and yellow lupins are all in flower. In contrast, only blue and white flowers, such as forget-me-nots, blue and white African lilies, white roses and buddleia, are allowed in the secluded, shady Mairi Garden laid out in the shape of a Tudor rose, some of them creeping over the stone flags of the paths. Cockleshells round the central fountain pool, 'silver bells' (various campanulas) and 'pretty maids' (*Saxifraga granulata*) illustrate the well-

George Stubbs's surreal painting of *Hambletonian*. It shows the thoroughbred being rubbed down after winning a race, but the horse is balanced, unnaturally, on his left legs and the groom's arm is impossibly long. (*NT*)

known nursery rhyme, here a play on the name of Lady Mairi Stewart, the 7th Marquess's daughter, who gave Mount Stewart and many of its contents, together with an endowment, to the Trust in 1976.

Away from the house the planting is informal, with magnificent trees, shrubs and herbaceous plants along the drive, in the Lily Wood and lining the walks round the lake created by the 3rd Marquess, part of a nineteenth-century layout which Lady Londonderry embellished. There are rhododendrons of each and every variety, many sweetly scented, and species from the Mediterranean and Far East, such as the Chinese birch. Several Southern Hemisphere plants include New Zealand tree ferns, the Tasmanian cedar, eucalyptus and the rare evergreen *Gevuina avellana* from Southern Chile.

A network of interlacing paths explores the slopes of the hill beyond the lake, planted with unusual specimens such as the Kashmir cypress, the Tatarian maple, the calico bush and the fragrant South African *Buddleia auriculata*. Conical roofs glimpsed above the trees mark the Londonderrys' private burial ground, Tir Nan Og, on the summit of the hill, guarded by statues of Irish saints and with a fruiting olive, believed to have been grown from seed brought back from the Mount of Olives, spreading along the high enclosing wall. The 7th Marquess and his wife both rest here.

The octagonal Temple of the Winds, on a prominent knoll in the woods to the south of the house, is from another age, a replica, like its counterpart at Shugborough (*see* p.290), of the Tower of the Winds in ancient Athens and the only building in Ireland by the pioneering neo-classical architect James 'Athenian' Stuart. Erected by the 1st Marquess between 1782–5, it was designed as an eyecatcher and banqueting house, its sumptuously decorated upper room adorned with another star-like marquetry floor by John Ferguson, the design again echoed in plaster on the ceiling. A dew-drop chandelier hangs from the central medallion. On the floor below, long sash windows can be lowered into the basement to give an uninterrupted view over the island-studded waters of Strangford Lough to the prominent silhouette of Scrabo Tower on the opposite shore. Hitler's ambassador, Ribbentrop, could have looked back from the golf course laid out on the hill around the tower when the 7th Marquess entertained him here during a visit to Mount Stewart in the 1930s.

The Mournes Co. Down

South of Newcastle

The granite humps of the mountains of Mourne dominate the landscape of this south-east corner of Northern Ireland. Mostly smooth and rounded, with slopes of purple heather and mossy summit heaths, the hills are cleft by deep valleys and occasionally erupt into crags and cliffs. At the northern end of the range, where the mountains stand high above the coastal resort of Newcastle, the Trust has acquired 1,300 acres of prime walking and climbing country, including the 2,796-foot Slieve Donard, the highest peak, Slieve Commedagh and the whole of the upper Glen River valley, where the jagged Eagle Rock cliffs were the last northern Irish home of the sea eagle. A number of paths lead up into the mountains, including a track along the Bloody River which links with the Trust's coastal path (*see* p.224). Those who make the climb – effectively from sea level – are rewarded by spectacular views to the Isle of Man and the Lake District.

Mow Cop Cheshire

5 miles south of Congleton, 2 miles south-east of Little Moreton Hall

From a distance Mow Cop looks like a ruined medieval fortress, with a roofless round tower and what appear to be remnants of a curtain wall picturesquely silhouetted against the sky on the western edge of the Pennines. In fact this castle is a romantic sham, built as a summerhouse and eyecatcher in 1754 by Randle Wilbraham of nearby Rode Hall and placed exactly on the boundary between Cheshire and Staffordshire. It is worth braving the steep approaches for the views from the top of the 1,000-foot ridge, west over the Cheshire plain to the Welsh hills and east over the Peak District, where long tentacles reach up the valleys from the Potteries to the south. To the north, over the trees which shield Little Moreton Hall (*see* p.180), looms the futuristic dish of the radio telescope at Jodrell Bank. As an inscribed stone by the path to the summit records, in 1807 this spectacular but windswept spot was the site of a historic open-air meeting led by Hugh Bourne and William Clowes which resulted in the birth of Primitive Methodism.

The romantic silhouette of Mow Cop, perched on a rocky outcrop crowning a 1,000-foot ridge. The folly stands on the boundary between Cheshire and Staffordshire, with views west over the fertile Cheshire plain and east over the windswept expanses of the Peak. The prominent steep-sided rock known as the Old Man of Mow, a favourite haunt of climbers, stands 150 yards along the ridge to the north. (NT)

Mr Straw's House Nottinghamshire

7 Blyth Grove, Worksop

This bay-fronted, three-story Edwardian villa is like a thousand other red-brick suburban semis built for well-to-do tradesmen and professionals at the turn of the century. But the Straw brothers – William and Walter – who lived here for fifty years were anything but ordinary. Perhaps never quite recovering from the deaths of their parents, William and Florence, in the 1930s, perhaps naturally reclusive and conservative, they preserved the house as it was when their father and mother were alive, ignoring modern conveniences, such as central heating and the telephone, and the advent of radio and television.

Today, 7 Blyth Grove is partly a shrine to William and Florence, partly a uniquely well-preserved example of interwar middle-class living. Completely refurbished before the family moved in, in 1923, the house boasts dark 1920s wallpapers with decorative Sanderson borders, doors and other woodwork painted to simulate oak, and period carpets and lino. Furnishings are heavy, the rooms cluttered, with the parents' belongings still in their customary places. William senior's coats and hats still hang in the hall, Florence's piano is piled high with her music, and in their bedroom, where the brass bedstead is covered with newspaper to keep off the dust, the dressing-table still has the box for William's detachable collars and drawers of personal belongings, such as the blue sunglasses Florence wore on her annual holiday in Scarborough. The period detail even includes trade calendars advertising the grocery business which William built up, and an unheated, starkly functional 1920s bathroom. The kitchen, where bread was baked every Saturday night, is similarly uninviting, although the brothers did put in a 1950s gas stove.

The boys seem to have fitted in round their parents' space, living largely in the south-facing dining-room, one of only two rooms where a fire was regularly lit in cold weather and, in William junior's case, sleeping in a small atticky bedroom at the top of the house. An ordered routine, unchanged for forty years, included the Sunday outing to church, where the brothers always sat in the same pew, and the Sunday afternoon walk into town to inspect their grocery store and other property, while

Among the diverse objects squirrelled away in the storeroom at Mr Straw's House is an ancient vacuum cleaner, helmets from the Second World War, and bottled fruit and jam made from produce from the garden. (NT/ *Geoffrey Frosh*)

every weekday, after the shop closed, Walter would call in at his cousin's house over the road to listen to the 6 o'clock news on the radio. Both brothers liked to work in the little garden, which still has its outside privy. It seems William, who read English at university and taught for some years in London, was the dominant personality, resisting innovation and refusing to let Walter bring the car he bought in the 1960s to the house. It was William, too, who became the custodian of Blythe Grove, leaving notes around the place to record details about the family and its possessions. But he was by no means unworldly. Savings from his teacher's salary were invested in Marks & Spencer shares, worth over £150,000 at his death.

The Needles Old Battery
Isle of Wight

West of Freshwater Bay and Alum Bay

The threat of a French invasion in 1858, fuelled by Lord Palmerston's aggressively nationalistic foreign policy, threw Britain into a panic, not least because the coastal defences, little changed since Trafalgar in 1805, were clearly inadequate. This magnificently sited little fort, set 250 feet above the sea on the far western point of the Isle of Wight, was one of the new artillery works built to guard the approaches to the Solent and the major naval base at Portsmouth.

The dagger-shaped headland with precipitous chalk cliffs falling to the jagged outlines of the Needles is reached by a walk of about a mile across the downs. On the other side of a ditch cut to protect the landward approaches is the only entrance, a massive archway dated 1862. A tunnel-like passage emerges in the parade ground where five semicircular gun emplacements, two of them now mounted with guns rescued from the sea by the Trust in 1983, face west and north. Built into the rock are underground chambers for storing gunpowder, shells and cartridges, still showing the ingenious arrangements which allowed candles or oil-burning lanterns to be used without danger of igniting the powder and the system of ventilation ducts to keep the ammunition dry. From the parade ground another tunnel leads out to the look-out point positioned on the very tip of the headland where a searchlight was set up in 1899. The views are breathtaking – down on to the points of the Needles, with their wheeling colonies of cormorants and seagulls, and across the bay to the mainland, where the outline of Hurst Castle marks the western arm of the Solent. Just up the hill, on the site of the original Needles lighthouse, are the remains of the Needles New Battery, built in 1893–5 and finally closed in 1954 when the guns were scrapped.

Although the Needles batteries saw little active service, they have played an important role in military history. A massive iron ring in the parade ground of the Old Battery marks the site of the world's first anti-aircraft gun, set up here in 1913. And in 1956 the headland was the engine-testing site for the Black Knight rocket, subsequently launched at Woomera in Australia.

Nether Alderley Mill   Cheshire

1½ miles south of Alderley Edge, on east side of the A34

Nether Alderley is a most unusual watermill. On one side a long sweeping stone-tiled roof reaches almost to the ground, giving just a glimpse of warm sandstone walls. On the other the mill is wedged right up against a wooded bank, the dam of the little reservoir which provides the water to turn the wheels. The stream on which the mill was sited was too small and irregular to power the machinery effectively and this ingenious solution – with the later addition of three more reservoirs – was devised when Nether Alderley was first built, in the sixteenth century. The mill is noteworthy, too, for having a pair of waterwheels, set one below the other, a short trough leading from the first to the second. Both are twelve feet in diameter and, like all the mill machinery, date from the nineteenth century.

Four dormer windows in the sloping roof light the interior, the most remarkable feature of which is the Elizabethan oak woodwork which supports the roof. Wooden pins hold the timbers together, and some display the numbers used by the carpenters when assembling the frame. A floor of finely perforated tiles is the remains of a kiln for drying wet grain, a feature more usually seen in Scotland.

Remarkably, Nether Alderley was operating as late as 1939, over 600 years since the earliest mention of a mill here in 1290. The machinery and the culvert from the reservoir have now been restored and flour once again pours into the waiting sacks.

Newark Park Gloucestershire

1½ miles north-east of Wotton-under-Edge, 1½ miles south of junction of the A4135 and the B4058

This unusual, atmospheric house stands high on a spur of the Cotswolds looking south over steep, wooded slopes plunging to the valley of the River Severn. Buttresses, battlements and Georgian sash windows added by James Wyatt in the 1790s only partly disguise the modest four-storey Elizabethan hunting lodge built by Sir Nicholas Poyntz in *c*.1550, still surmounted by the romantic dragon weathervane with which he crowned his new property, a proud beast with a long coiled tail silhouetted against the sky. Like his father and grandfather before him, Sir Nicholas was prominent at court, becoming Groom of the Bedchamber to Henry VIII after 1539. His hunting lodge was built on monastic land granted by the king after the Dissolution of the Monasteries, formerly the property of the Abbey of Kingswood in the vale below, some materials from which were incorporated in Newark.

The Tudor building emerges most strongly on the east, where Wyatt's sympathetic hand did not destroy original features. Although Sir Nicholas's architect is unknown, this tall, symmetrical façade, with huge mullioned and transomed windows lighting the third floor, reflects the sophisticated world of the court rather than local building styles, and suggests something of the Elizabethan prodigy houses that were to follow at the end of the century (*see* pp.142 and 202). A prominent three-light oriel projects from the centre of the building and a pedimented doorway flanked by Doric columns is a remarkably pure Renaissance feature for its date. The two top floors were originally banqueting rooms, from which Sir Nicholas and his guests would have enjoyed wide views over the deer park around the house and the wooded countryside beyond.

Internally, Wyatt left the lodge more or less as it was, and Tudor fireplaces still warm some of the rooms in this part of the house, but he remodelled a second block added in the late seventeenth century, introducing neo-classical interiors. More Doric columns divide the unusual hall he inserted between the two buildings, his frieze of sheep's skulls perhaps intended to recall the wool trade which brought wealth to this area in the Middle Ages.

Formal axial gardens to the north and east were laid out by Mr Robert Parsons, the tenant from 1970 to 1994, who began to restore the property, but there are still remnants of the wild bulb garden and rock gardens created in the late nineteenth century on the slopes below the house.

New Forest Hampshire

Extends from Bournemouth, to the west, to Southampton, to the east

The Trust owns three areas of common on the edge of the New Forest. The largest, at Bramshaw to the north, covers 1,400 acres and consists of Cadnam and Stocks Cross Greens, together with the commons of Cadnam, Furzley, Half Moon and Black Hill, Penn and Plaitford. North-east of Fordingbridge lie Millersford Plantation and Hale Purlieu, over 500 acres in extent. Purlieu means land on the border of a forest, not within its boundaries but subject to forest laws controlling the hunting of game. Finally, two miles east of Ringwood, there is the small Hightown Common.

Since 1964 these commons have been included 'within the perambulation' of the New Forest and the verderers' by-laws controlling grazing apply to the Trust's land, much to its advantage. Grazing keeps the land largely as open heath, with heather and gorse interspersed with areas of woodland and with some wet places covering the gravelly peat soil. It makes good walking terrain, even better if you know your flowers, birds, butterflies and moths, for grazing stops the open places from becoming thickets.

Newtown Isle of Wight

Midway between Newport and Yarmouth, 1 mile north of the A3054

Despite its name, this shadow of a place on an arm of the Newtown estuary dates back over 700 years. Founded by the Bishop of Winchester in 1256 and laid out to a grid plan like a French *bastide*, it was at its height in the mid-fourteenth century when a community of some 300 prospered on the revenue from oyster beds, salt works and the ships using the magnificent natural harbour of the estuary, regarded as the best in the Isle of Wight. Now shrunk to a handful of scattered buildings, grassy lanes mark the lines of the town's former streets and cattle graze on what were medieval house plots, their outlines still visible in the turf. It seems Newtown never recovered from a disastrous French raid in 1377, gradually losing its trade and importance to Newport.

Surrounded by fields, oddly isolated from the rest of the village, is the little brick Town Hall of 1699, a relic of the days when Newtown elected two Members of Parliament despite its tiny population, the franchise granted in 1584 perhaps an attempt to stem the community's decline. Lit by four long round-headed windows down each side and crowned by a steeply pitched hipped roof, this simple building on an earlier stone basement was dignified by the addition of a classical portico in the late eighteenth century.

Distinguished men returned to Parliament from here until the Reform Act of 1832 include John Churchill, later 1st Duke of Marlborough (1768), and George Canning (1804), future Foreign Secretary and Prime Minister. Another of the Trust's properties initially rescued from dereliction by Ferguson's Gang (*see* p.286), the building's interior has now been refurnished and is used to display documents relating to local history and a replica of Newtown's Tudor silver mace. Not far away is Noah's Ark, a stone house of *c.*1700 that was once an inn and is now the oldest building in the village, most of the others having been rebuilt in the nineteenth century.

North Cornish Coast

Much of this coast is wild, sometimes grim. It has always been rather cut off from the rest of Cornwall and Bude is fifty miles from the main railway line at Exeter, remoter now than it was when holiday-makers could travel by train from Waterloo as far west as Padstow. That line was closed in 1966.

Except in the valleys the country is austere, windswept and treeless but grandly beautiful. There has of course been some holiday development, but it is minor, and substantial acquisitions by the Trust mean that the best of this coast is now preserved.

The spirit of Parson Hawker will always haunt Morwenstow. The Rev. Stephen Hawker (1835–74) was the subject of Baring-Gould's bestseller *The Vicar of Morwenstow* (1876) which is still in print today. A considerable poet, eccentric to a degree,

Hawker loved his people dearly. The Trust owns what was once his glebe and other land surrounding his beautiful Norman church. On the very lip of the 450-foot Vicarage Cliff is perched Hawker's Hut, made of driftwood dragged up from the rocks below. Here, clad in the fisherman's jersey he habitually wore, he wrote his ballads. This coast was a nightmare for seamen in the days of sail, for there was no harbour in which ships could take refuge in a northerly gale. Hawker attended every wreck, insisting on Christian burial for every man whose corpse was washed ashore.

In the face of the cliff is the holy well of Morwenna, virgin and saint, with a tiny well house built by Hawker, but it is dangerous to go down there. St John's Well, the ancient holy well of the parish, in the garden of the former vicarage, also belongs to the Trust. Church, farm, vicarage, holy wells, a few cottages, the wild cliff and the sea boiling on the wicked reefs far below all make this an atmospheric place.

A lane leads to Duckpool, passing the immense concrete saucer aerials of the Ministry of Defence's communications system, built in the 1970s to receive messages from orbiting satellites which keep an eye on the rest of the world. Far from being an eyesore on the high cliffs, these great constructions are beautiful as they turn gravely on their axes to perform their secret duties.

Beyond them is the Trust's 300-foot Steeple Point; below it the narrow valley leading from Coombe down to the sea. Here there are green meadows, a bustling stream and a single cottage, for the Trust has demolished the brick bungalow and large wooden shanty which formerly disfigured the beach, where a natural dam of sea-smoothed boulders holds back the pool of fresh water.

The hamlet of Coombe is a happy example of co-operation between the Landmark Trust, which owns the delightful cottages and the watermill, and the National Trust, which owns the farmland and woods for a mile inland. Above Coombe stand the handsome house and farm buildings of Stowe Barton, its fields running out to the cliffs. Stowe belonged to the great West Country family of Grenville and it was from the old Tudor house, long since demolished, that Sir Richard Grenville set out in 1591 to perform his last service for Queen Elizabeth I 'at Flores in the Azores'.

It is a stiff climb up to the cliffs from Duckpool and it can be a bracing walk for the mile and a half to

The beach at Duckpool, with part of the natural dam of sea-smoothed boulders holding back a freshwater pool. (*NT*/*John Gollop*)

Sandy Mouth. At Warren Gutter a valley drops steeply to the rocky beach where the sea has eroded away the softer bands of rock, leaving the hard bands in sharp ridges. Nearing Sandy Mouth the path crosses a sheltered valley where gatekeeper, speckled-wood and meadow-brown butterflies flourish on the kinder herbage.

At Sandy Mouth a long valley opens on to a great beach of yellow sand. When the Trust bought the place in 1978 it was a mess, with cars and caravans parked everywhere, a seedy café and overhead wires. All has been swept away, the scars made good, a carpark hidden in the landscape, a decent café built in local stone to feed families spending the day on the beach.

The cliffs here are unstable. At Houndapit Cliff, south of Sandy Mouth, the sandstone and shale rock has been buckled into a massive fold, visible on the cliff face. At its foot is a clutter of great sea-smoothed boulders which have been falling here over many thousands of years.

Dunsmouth Farm, with Menachurch Point, does not belong to the Trust but is crossed by the coastal path. The Trust's land starts again at Northcott Mouth, once a mess like Sandy Mouth, now beginning to look more seemly with cars parked back from the beach. From here for three-quarters of a mile to Bude is the much lower Maen Cliff, sheep-grazed pasture with a massive landslip at Furzey Cove making a new access to the sea.

At Crackington the rock is a particular type of shale, known to geologists as the 'Crackington formation'. Wildly contorted by movement of the earth's crust millions of years ago, it is easily fractured, landslips are common and the cliffs are layered with ledges and hollows from slips in the past.

Dizzard Point, a mile to the north, is something very rare, an extraordinary witch's wood of dwarf trees, stunted and clipped by salt spray and high winds. Mainly of sessile oak, the wood is no more than fifteen to twenty feet high, the trees straining to follow the contours of the cliff slope.

Tucked behind the beetling Penkenna Point, north of Crackington Haven, the church of St Gennys stands in a hollow behind the cliffs, some 400 feet above the sea. Grouped round a green, the church, the farm and the former school comprise the whole churchtown with not even a row of cottages. The view northward from the churchyard across the steep valley of the Coxford Water is very lovely, an Iron Age promontory fort in the foreground, the broken coast stretching away beyond. The slopes of the fort, covered with western maritime heath, are brilliant purple in high summer. The stunted thickets on sheltered parts of the cliff provide nesting cover for dunnocks, linnets, whitethroats and stonechats, the latter species rarely missing from any part of the Cornish coast.

From Crackington Haven the long proboscis of Cambeak stretches westward for a mile with a wart on the end of its nose. Here the coast turns south and the next two miles are the wildest in Cornwall. The Northern Door, a spectacular rock arch, its strata bent through ninety degrees, dominates the beach of Little Strand. Beyond it the Strangles, a beach with a fearsome reputation, is backed by screes leading up to a weird middle cliff of humps and bumps, perfect for picnicking out of the wind, and then up to High Cliff, at 731 feet the highest in the county.

The scramble path down to the beach is for the sure-footed but the walk out to the clifftop is easy and gives much of the flavour of this awesome place. Trevigue huddles in a fold behind the cliffs, its handsome Tudor farmhouse forming two sides of a picturesque enclosed court. Most of the Trust's land is farmed from here and there is a welcoming restaurant, shop and information point run by the Trust's tenant.

In the forty miles of iron-bound coast between Hartland and Padstow the picturesque Boscastle harbour is the only natural haven. It is a terrifying place to enter in anything but the calmest seas, but many sailors have sought it thankfully with this cruel coast on their lee. Penally, to the north, and Willapark, to the south, guard a gorge-like entrance which turns through two right-angles before funnelling into the mouth of the harbour. Sailing vessels could not enter unassisted. They were towed in by 'hobblers', boats with eight oars, men on either shore using guide ropes to keep them in mid-channel.

The slightest swell builds up at the narrow entrance and from early times there has been a breakwater. The present curving jetty was rebuilt by Sir Richard Grenville in 1584, deliberately made with a hollow in its centre to absorb the force of the seas, the slate stones set upright in courses allowing the water to drain out between each wave.

During the heyday of the harbour, when slate was exported in quantity, an outer breakwater was built in about 1820. More than a dozen ketches and schooners traded from here, bringing coal, iron and limestone from South Wales, timber and general mechandise from Bristol. In 1941 the outer breakwater was blown up by a drifting sea-mine. No repairs could be carried out and storms quickly began to damage the quay walls. In 1962 the Trust rebuilt the breakwater, the work taking place in winter to avoid closing the harbour to visitors, a difficult and dangerous job.

Beyond the outer breakwater is a good example of a 'blowing-hole'. At the right combination of sea and tide the thump of the swell entering the hole, the snort as the compressed air forces it back and the spurt of spume it throws across the harbour entrance is an enthralling sight.

The Palace stables at the harbour head belong to the Trust. Now converted into a youth hostel, they once housed the carthorses which worked the capstans and hauled goods from quays to warehouses. The harbour is still used by fishermen, most of whom work the rich shell-fishing grounds south of Hartland, only accessible for small boats.

The Trust owns only a handful of the buildings round the harbour but virtually all the surrounding land, including the headland of Willapark, with an Iron Age cliff castle, and, inland from it, Forrabury Common and Forrabury church which serves Boscastle. The common preserves a remarkable survival of the Celtic tenure of 'stitchmeal' and it provides a habitat for a rich and interesting flora. There are forty-two rectangular plots, thirty-four of which belong to the Trust, divided by low banks. The tenants may crop their stitches individually from Lady Day to Michaelmas (25 March to 29 September), usually with hay, corn or potatoes, but during the winter the land is grazed 'in common'. The views from Willapark are superb, both up and down the coast and inland up to the plateau which runs parallel with it.

The Valency river, which runs into the harbour, is only six miles long but drops over 600 feet. In this area of high rainfall, sixty inches and more each year, it runs brim full after a storm.

The Trust owns much of the valley as far as Newmills, steep scrubby slopes, oak woodland and a good path (there is no road) up to the delightful church of St Juliot where Thomas Hardy, as a young architect sent to restore the church, courted and married Emma Gifford, sister of the rector's wife. In February the churchyard, standing high above the river, is white with snowdrops.

The rugged peninsula of Willapark shelters the sandy beach of Bossiney Cove. John Galsworthy gave the latter name to Irene Forsyte's lover in *Man of Property* (1906). Like its namesake at Boscastle, Willapark has an Iron Age cliff castle protected by a ditch and rampart across its narrow neck. Here the local tribe would take refuge in times of strife some 2,000 years ago.

Barras Nose, to the west, was the Trust's first coastal property, bought after a local appeal in 1897, two years after the Trust was founded. There was widespread concern at the number of houses and hotels springing up to cater for the growing popularity of Tintagel, symbolised by the monumental King Arthur's Castle Hotel built by the London and South Western Railway, whose new line to Wadebridge passed only six miles away.

The massive 'island' at Tintagel, crowned by the remains of a twelfth-century castle, belongs to the Duchy of Cornwall. Beyond it the Trust's cliffs stretch for two miles to Trebarwith Strand. For centuries these cliffs were quarried for slate. At sea

A view to the Rumps, a tiny peninsula projecting from the northern corner of Pentire Head; Iron Age defences across the neck of the peninsula are still clearly visible.
(*NT/Joe Cornish*)

level the cliff face was cut back to the vertical to allow small sailing vessels to lie at its foot. The slate was lowered directly into the vessels' holds from 'whims', capstans worked by horses or donkeys. This trade survived until 1937 and a close inspection of the cliffs will pinpoint many relics of what must have been a hazardous livelihood. On these steep cliff faces are nesting sites of guillemots, fulmars, razorbills and shags, and the edible rock samphire grows near the water's edge.

Two miles to the south of Trebarwith is Tregardock, a sombre and menacing place. The approach is down a track from the farm above which curls round The Mountain, past the ruined engine house of an abandoned silver-lead mine, to enter the beach below crumbling cliffs. Together with the adjoining property of Dannonchapel, the Trust owns $1\frac{1}{2}$ miles of lonely coastline here.

To lovers of Cornwall the six miles of coast from Port Quin to Polzeath is holy ground. The cliffs, which have been wild and often grim all the way from the Devon border, suddenly become kinder. They are still high but the country begins to smile. The large parish of St Minver contains some of the best farms in the county, occupied by families who have tilled them for generations. The country has a settled look about it. The hedges, made of small stones laid dry in a herringbone pattern and filled with earth, are covered with flowers in spring and summer. May and early June are the best months. On the cliffs the vernal squill is overtaken by violets, sea-pinks, thyme, bladder campion, kidney vetch and stonecrop. In the lanes primroses are followed by a glorious mixture of bluebells, pink campion and stitchwort. Later, miles of hedges are covered by valerian in its three colours of white, pink and purple. Poppies have not been sprayed out of existence. The land has a bloom.

Port Quin can be a frightening place in a north-west gale in March, great rollers sweeping in and breaking over the road and battering the buildings at the head of the inlet. But most people see it in its summer dress, children playing in the rock pools, the little stone cottages smiling in the sun. It was a busy place in the middle of the last century. Small vessels landed coal and timber on the beach and at the two little quays, then loaded lead and antimony ores (used in ceramic glazes and in hardening other metals) from the small mines nearby. In good years large catches of pilchards were landed. The Trust has deliberately provided only a small carpark. The

approach lanes are narrow and these are Port Quin's best defence. There is no factual evidence for the legend of the lost fishing fleet, the men of the village drowned, the cottages abandoned. It seems rather that the antimony mine closed, the pilchards failed to arrive for several seasons, and the men of the hamlet were persuaded by an agent of the Canadian government to emigrate *en bloc*.

From Doyden Point there are wonderful views over Lundy Bay to the Rumps, the rocky peninsula two miles to the west over the wide sweep of Port Quin Bay, and this whole coast, much more than two miles to walk, is now the Trust's property. The three-storeyed miniature castle on Doyden Point was built by Samuel Symons, merchant of Wadebridge, soon after his purchase of the farm of Trevigo in 1827. He used it to entertain his friends, as the ample wine bins on the ground floor bear witness. The Gothic folly is built of the pockmarked stone dug on the site, a near relation of the pillow lava found at Pentire across the bay. Winter gales have scoured the soft parts of the stones into whorls and ridges. Doyden House also belongs to the Trust, now, like the castle, used for holiday flats. The square open shaft on the cliff in front of it, fenced with slate posts, connects to a sea cave below. It once formed part of the workings of the Doyden antimony mine.

The path runs over Trevan Head and steeply down into Lundy Bay, with its two coves of Lundy and Epphaven all that Cornish coves should be. The astonishing Lundy Hole in the clifftop, with an arched entrance from the sea, was once a sea cave invisible from above. The rock overhead collapsed into it centuries ago. To the west Markham's Quay lies below a vertical cliff up which sand and seaweed were hauled to counteract soil acidity and provide a fertilising mulch for the farms of the parish. They were loaded into carts and driven up the 'sanding road', which some people say was a smugglers' lane. Now wholly overgrown, it still runs up the valley to the road above.

There are dense thickets in the Lundy valley, the home of goldfinch, whitethroat and stonechat. In the clifftop fields corn bunting, skylark and meadow pipit are common. The north-facing cliffs provide perches for predators and nesting sites for seabirds. The fulmars glide effortlessly about their business just below the cliff edge, quite unworried by walkers.

Beyond Carnweather Point are the overgrown

The view west from Pentire Head to Stepper Point across the mouth of the Camel estuary, with Trevose Head beyond. (*NT/Joe Cornish*)

burrows, or waste tips, of the Pentireglaze silver-lead mine, active from Elizabethan times until a century ago. Pentireglaze Farm is the scene of Baring-Gould's thriller *In the Roar of the Sea* (1892). His picture of this countryside early in the nineteenth century still rings true.

From Pentireglaze the coast sweeps on to Pentire Farm, 360 acres bought by public appeal in 1936 when the whole farm, incredible as it may now seem, was divided up into desirable building plots. There was an immediate outcry, a committee was formed to save the farm, *The Times* published a photograph and a benefactor underwrote the appeal until the money was raised. It was this sort of event which inspired the Trust's great Enterprise Neptune Appeal nearly thirty years later.

The walk out to the Rumps, with its very well-preserved Iron Age cliff castle, is one of the classic walks of the Cornish coast. The path continues at about 300 feet outside the field hedge to Pentire Point and here the greenstone and shale give way to the pumice-like pillow lava, the product of volcanic action many millions of years ago. The views are westward across the mouth of the Camel estuary to Stepper Point with Trevose Head beyond, and up the sandy estuary to Padstow (hidden by high ground) with the dreaded Doom Bar at the entrance to the channel, covered with breakers at low water. Along the coast to the south-east is the great sandy beach of Polzeath, with some of the best surfing in Cornwall.

Bedruthan became a popular venue for carriage drives from Newquay when the town was developed as a holiday resort in the 1880s. The famous view on a fine summer's day must have appeared on more postcards than anywhere else in Cornwall: yellow sands, cottonwool clouds, a sparkling blue sea, rocks of every colour clothed in lichen, drifts of sea-pinks. Yet in a winter gale it can be an awesome sight, yellow spume scudding inland for miles.

The name Bedruthan Steps was first recorded in 1847, in the local newspaper *The West Briton*, and appears to refer to the precipitous cliff staircase which leads down to the south end of the beach, as does Pentire Steps at its north end. The name has since been applied to the several isolated stacks along the beach, the hard rock still standing after the softer rock surrounding it has been eroded away. The cliff staircase was probably originally made by miners to give access to the Carnewas iron mine dug beneath the clifftop, the remaining buildings of

which house the Trust's café and information point. After the mine closed in the 1870s the staircase was kept open. The cliffs are tortured, the strata writhing in all directions, the rock friable. The Trust has had to rebuild the staircase twice (it reopened in 1995, after being closed for some years), and techniques developed for motorway construction have been used to stabilise loose rock. As well as the staircase, the Trust owns the cliffs to north and south of the beach, but the middle section of beach and most of the stacks are privately owned.

Across the great beach Park Head stretches out to close the view to the north. Here is another Pentire Farm, one of four owned by the Trust in Cornwall (the word means headland), and the walk runs right round it. A narrow, deliberately unsignposted lane leads off the coast road. From the carpark a path runs down the valley to the sea at Porth Mear, sand and rock pools, and then round to west and south, with eight tiny coves, some accessible with great care. At the tip of the headland is a fine arch where the sea has gouged out a vein of softer rock. On a clear day the view south-west stretches for twenty-six miles down the coast to St Ives.

Shut off from the razzmatazz of Newquay by the estuary of the River Gannel, the great sandy beaches of Crantock and Holywell are both excellent for family outings and safe, providing the advice of the lifeguards is followed precisely. They attract large numbers of visitors and give enormous pleasure. But there is very much more to see, for the landscape is exceptionally diverse. As well as the beaches and sand dunes, there is a tightly grazed common, a boggy valley running down to the sea with a paradisal cove, a tidal estuary with mudflats, woodland, farmland and rocky headlands.

The River Gannel rises near the village of Mitchell, on Cornwall's spine road, the A30. Although only a small stream, it has a sizeable estuary, and until Newquay harbour was built it had a considerable trade in small sailing vessels, while wooden ships were constructed on its north bank. Most of the estuary dries out at low water and for much of the year the mudflats are alive with waders. In its lower reaches the mud becomes sand and by the time Crantock is reached it is hard and yellow. The dunes of the Rushy Green rise steeply behind the beach, always changing in shape on their seaward side but achieving stability further inland. They are held in place by the long roots of marram grass, and when too many people use the same track through the dunes the grass is killed and wind starts shifting the sand.

West Pentire closes Crantock Beach to the west, with a collapsed sea cave at its tip. The cliff turns south and opens into Polly Joke (more properly known as Porth Joke). Here the Trust fought a famous battle in the 1950s, to prevent cars driving down the valley behind the cave on to the sand; ironically, after victory had been achieved the track collapsed and is now impassable! Polly Joke is a narrow inlet of the most perfect hard sand, the bathing safe, low rock cliffs to sit on or under, rock pools, not a building or a vehicle in sight, and yet room for plenty of family parties. At low water cattle pastured on the farmland to the south come down to the beach to drink from the stream before it enters the sea, a beautiful sight.

The track, now only a footpath, leads up the valley to the Trust's carpark at Treago Mill. The stream runs through a boggy bottom and the mixture of wet habitat with the blown calcareous sand gives rise to quite different plants and insects. High above the carpark is Cubert Common. Although its underlying soil is acid, blown sand from the Holywell dunes has created a lime-rich tilth, for the sand is composed of the crushed shells of myriads of small sea creatures and is rich in calcium carbonate. So in spring the common is covered with cowslips, only found in Cornwall where there is blown sea sand. It is grazed by horses, not the best use, but while the Trust owns the freehold of the land the commoners are assured of their longstanding right to graze it.

The Kelseys, 300 acres of open headland between Polly Joke and Holywell Beach, has been farmed for centuries, the field boundaries the same now as shown on a map of 1694. Under the blown sand on its surface there is good soil which grows hay and corn for a farmer based several miles inland. Cattle are grazed after the respective harvests until ploughing begins. The walk round Kelsey Head is bracing, with sea on three sides, springy turf and offshore the rocky islet of The Chick, where seals breed. In spring and early summer the flowers are similar to those on the chalk downs of southern England, with some extras such as dwarf centaury and the deep blue vernal squill.

The modern village of Holywell has little to commend it, for what was reasonably seemly is no longer so. A cave at the north end of the beach, accessible only at low water, hides the holy well which gives the place its name. The cave is slippery and one needs to climb up towards its inner end to find the well, fed by a freshwater spring in the rock behind.

At St Agnes the landscape changes markedly for, although almost every parish in Cornwall has been worked over for its minerals in the past, here we meet the relics of mining carried out on a larger scale and until comparatively recently. The cliffs are still high, between 300 to 400 feet. From the village of St Agnes, above Trevaunance Cove, and for two and a half miles to Porthtowan the landscape is scarred by old workings for copper and tin. St Agnes was one of the great mining parishes of the eighteenth and nineteenth centuries and Seal Hole, a mine close to the village, is said to have paid vast dividends to 'Guinea-a-Minute Daniell' who, from his princely mineral income, rebuilt Trelissick House overlooking Falmouth harbour (see p.337) and planted the park and woods there. The scarred landscape, the burrows (heaps of waste rock) and the ruined engine houses with their attendant stacks have a melancholy beauty in their decay.

The Trust owns over 400 acres here, dominated by St Agnes Beacon, rising to 629 feet above St Agnes Head. Beneath the Beacon is a boss of granite, pushed up red hot from the earth's core about 225 million years ago. The great heat and pressure affected the overlying rock, while gases and liquid forced up through fissures altered its chemical composition to give veins of silver, lead, zinc, tin and copper. This mineralisation, eons ago, is the reason for the rich mining country all about the beacon. From the top there are views across the county to the south coast, on a clear day, and for twenty-six miles of this coast, from Trevose Head to the north, to Carn Naun, near St Ives, to the southwest. The beacon is covered with heather, ling and the prickly dwarf gorse which grows on all this mineralised soil, so it pays to keep to the paths. When these plants flower together in August the hill is a sheet of purple and gold.

The Trust owns Newdowns Head, north of St Agnes Beacon and near the village, but not St Agnes Head which is owned by the local authority as far as Tubby's Head where the Trust's coast starts again. The mines here were worked until the steady fall in the price of tin forced their closure in the 1920s. On a ledge below the top of the cliff is the most photogenic of all the abandoned mine buildings in Cornwall, the roofless engine house and stack of the

Towanroath Shaft of Wheal Coates, spectacularly sited high above the great sandy beach 300 feet below (*see* p.86). The miners' track from Towanroath runs down into the narrow cleft of Chapel Porth. Here a small subsidiary valley joins the path and this is the site of the chapel, possibly of the tenth century, which stood for centuries but was ruined by 1750. At high tide the sea thunders to the base of the cliff but retreats at half-tide to open up a flat sandy beach two miles long. There is good surf but it is essential to follow the lifeguard's instructions. All the way up Chapel Coombe the land is scarred by mine workings. The cliff path climbs steeply towards the vestigial ruins of Wheal Charlotte high above the sea. Beyond is the seedy holiday village of Porthtowan where developers have been active.

Between Carvannel Farm, to the east, and Godrevy Farm, to the west, the flat-topped cliffs, high and often sheer, are tidily farmed almost to their edge. All this coast was part of the great Tehidy estate of the Basset family, who prospered mightily on their mineral dues in the eighteenth and nineteenth centuries and became Lords de Dunstanville.

From Portreath the path runs steeply up Tregea Hill and along the cliff to the narrow and precipitous cleft known as Ralph's Cupboard. The sun never reaches the base of the cliffs here. Further on is Samphire Island, one of many on this coast where the edible samphire (*Crithmum maritimum*) grows profusely.

At Porthcadjack Cove, at the foot of the narrow valley below Carvannel, there is good bathing off the rocks. The next place where the beach can be reached is Basset's Cove, with a track down to the sea through former mine workings. Above it lie the remains of the earthwork of Crane Castle. From here the path follows the cliff edge, nearly sheer and at a height of 250 feet, the walk exhilarating, the view magnificent. In two miles the coast road and the cliff converge at the yawning chasm of Hell's Mouth. This is a 'horrible' place, in the eighteenth-century meaning of the word, and the walk from here round Navax and Godrevy Points is even more so. The coast provides a good habitat for flowers, for the dwarf gorse and heather provide some shelter. The royal fern (*Osmunda regalis*) grows in damp places and the sea spleenwort (*Asplenium marinum*) can also be found. Seals breed in the caverns on the east side of Navax Point and can be seen playing on the beach at Fishing Cove which is sheltered from the west. These caves can now only be entered from the sea, though one great cavern was connected to the North Cliff Mine, the workings of which honeycomb the area.

Strong currents swirl round Godrevy Point. On the day of Charles I's execution a ship containing his wardrobe and household possessions was sunk here. Its dangers are now advertised by the little white lighthouse on Godrevy Island offshore. Virginia Woolf's novel *To the Lighthouse* (1927) was entitled in affectionate memory of childhood days spent here, and lovers of that best of diaries kept by a Victorian clergyman, *Kilvert's Diary*, will remember the author's description of a fight he witnessed here between a seal and a conger eel.

Between St Ives and Land's End is granite country. The slates, shales and limestones which have run down the north coast from the Devon border have finished. Granite is everywhere, pro-

The craggy tor of Carn Galver dominates the wild moorland sweeping down to the coast road at Bosigran. (*NT/Jane Gifford*)

truding on the skyline, vast blocks tumbled about the little farms, gathered into the great hedges of the tiny fields, outcropping wherever cultivation is attempted. The houses and buildings are of granite, even the gateposts. Yet the black soil to which this intractable stone gives rise is productive, and patient clearance over many generations has made the farms of the Penwith peninsula into excellent dairy holdings, some still with the traditional herds of Channel Island cattle which look so beautiful on their rich green pastures.

Beneath the farms and the crofts, or enclosed moorland, on the higher ground lies a series of earlier landscapes going back over the centuries to the first men who lived here. Historical circumstance has preserved in this peninsula the richest large-scale prehistoric landscape in Britain. This has only become widely recognised in recent years, and is now the subject of exhaustive investigation, scheduling and, very fairly, subsidy to the farmers, who are encouraged to farm in a way which is sensitive to the needs of the archaeologist. Haunted by the ghosts of early man, grey and lonely, sparsely populated except in the mining villages near St Just, this is in many ways the most fascinating of all the differing coasts of Cornwall.

Hor Point, two miles west of St Ives, is a modest twenty-four acres of rocky cliff. It hit the local headlines in 1957 when the Borough Council proposed to tip its rubbish here. The Trust moved fast and bought the land in the afternoon before the Council met in the evening. Its members were not pleased. Hor Point remained as an isolated Trust outpost until thirty years later when it was possible to add to it the cliffs running westward to Pen Enys Point, making a mile of excellent walking.

At Zennor the Trust has built up a patchwork of ownership and protective covenants which cover virtually all the land east of the village, from Zennor Quoit, the rocky hill south of the coast road, over the lower farms and down to the cliffs. The approach is by the track through the churchtown, past Treveglos Farm (the homestead, *tre*, beside the church, *eglos*) and out to the wild grandeur of Zennor Head. Below the headland is Pendour Cove, where the celebrated Mermaid of Zennor lured the squire's son to her watery home. The legend is depicted on a bench end (now a seat) in the church. To the east are three and a half miles of cliffs running past Porthzennor Cove and Wicca Pool to Treveal Cliff, which overlooks The Carracks rocks

and Carn Naun Point beyond. The landscape is a satisfying mixture, gorse and heather on the cliffs, with many different plants in the sheltered or wetter places, and neat, granite-hedged fields inland.

The light in Penwith has special qualities which have attracted artists for more than a century. It is constantly changing and seems alive. This is the coast on which to see the phenomenon known as the 'green flash'. As the sun sinks into the sea on a summer's evening, a green light suddenly suffuses the western sky. One of the best places to see the flash is from Zennor Head.

West of Zennor the Boswednack Cliffs overlook the narrow coves of Porthglaze and Rose-an-Hales. Beyond, the bony whaleback of Gurnard's Head juts northwards, outcrops of granite at its tip. It is presumably now named after the ugly Gurnard fish, found in these waters, but its old name was Treryn Dinas, referring to the cliff castle (*dinas* means fortress), outside the ditch of which lie the remains of a medieval chapel.

At Bosigran, as at Zennor, the Trust has achieved protection of a whole landscape, this time largely by ownership, partly by protective covenants. Its 600 acres run from the summits of Watchcroft and Carn Galver, looming high over the coast road, down over farmland and out to the cliffs, taking in a remarkable early landscape, farmed for some 2,000 years, many of the field boundaries unaltered in this immense span of time.

The Trust has two farms in the valley running down to Porthmeor Cove, the third is privately owned. Their fields are mixed up in an apparently random way which makes sense when one understands how such a jigsaw happened. Each little farm needed access to water, a share of the better land as of the poorer, of the sheltered fields as well as the exposed. Overlying this ancient pattern are much later relics of small-scale tin mining, which occur almost everywhere along this coast.

The cliffs run south-west past the Great Zawn to the sheer granite precipice of Bosigran, an awesome sight but a place of pilgrimage for rock climbers who flock here from far afield. Beside the road are the ruined engine houses of the Carn Galver mine, which came to grief in 1871. Below lies Porthmoina Cove, and south of the cove the attractive Rosemergy Cliff, boulder-strewn bracken-covered land stretching for a mile between the road and the sea. The three Brandys Rocks awash in the broken water below the cliffs are so called because, seen from above, they are in the triangular shape of a *brandis*, the Cornish word for a three-legged trivet.

The unmistakable humped outline of Cape Cornwall thrusts westward below the mining town of St Just. To north and south of the Cape, from Botallack Down to Aire Point, stretch four continuous miles of Trust coastline, with high cliffs cut by parallel valleys. This is an ancient landscape, with prehistoric field systems, cliff castles and burial mounds overlain by extensive remains of some two thousand years of tin mining, including several ruined engine houses, and it is also a site of great ecological interest, with wind-sculpted coastal heath and grassland. South down the coast, the headland of Pedn-men-du, above Sennen Cove, hides Land's End from view. From here the mile of Mayon Cliff curves round Gamper, the bay north of Land's End and the Trust's furthest western outpost in Britain. (*See also* South Cornish Coast, p.299.)

North Downs Surrey

Between Farnham and Canterbury

The Pilgrims Way, the views over the Weald (*see* p.356), proximity to London and good bus and train services mean that the North Downs have long been Londoners' country and many stretches are publicly owned. The recently established North Downs Way links all these, including the Trust's considerable holdings. All are important for their wildlife, especially butterflies and orchids. Management of the downland grass requires grazing with sheep at certain times of year.

Overlooking the beautiful Tillingbourne valley, the wooded slopes of Abinger Roughs, Hackhurst Down and Netley Park rise to the escarpment. On either side of the Dorking Gap stand Denbies Hill and Box Hill while, above Reigate, Colley Hill and the woods of Gatton provide good walking. Furthest east is Oxted Downs, the most recent of many individual acquisitions, but the jewel in the Trust's North Downs crown is surely Box Hill. It takes its name from the steep chalk slopes, clothed in places with box, which John Evelyn noted in 1655. The shrub box (*Buxus sempervirens*), most commonly seen in gardens and planted as game cover in southern chalky woods, is actually native here – one of only a handful of places where it grows wild in Britain. Like the yew, also common here,

especially on the steeper slopes, and another native, it dominates small sections over thin soils, almost to the exclusion of other plants.

It is the dramatic beauty of the 400-foot escarpment of the downs, where the River Mole has cut through the hills on its way to the Thames, which has brought visitors here ever since an eye for landscape began to be cultivated in the eighteenth century. Including Mickleham Downs nearby, the Trust owns over 1,000 acres here, with wonderful walks through beech woods. The Zig-Zag road runs from the Roman Stane Street steeply up the grassy slope to the summit, giving superb views over the thickly wooded Weald, with Chanctonbury Ring, more or less intact after the Great Storm of 1987, still prominent on the South Downs twenty miles away (*see* p.309).

Stane Street ran from London to Chichester, and the Romans used the Dorking Gap as the only practicable way through the North Downs. This strategic point had been forgotten when in 1871 General Sir George Chesney alarmed the military establishment with his essay 'The Battle of Dorking', showing how an enemy force could land on the south coast and threaten London in a matter of days. Chesney's warning was acted upon and forts were built along the downs. One survives at Box Hill, another at the Trust's Colley Hill above Reigate.

The woods and gentle valleys on the north side of the hill are much less frequented, and the indigenous plant and animal life here and throughout the whole property is extremely rich. Naturalists have been coming to Box Hill for many decades, and it probably has one of the longest insect lists of any Trust property as a result. Juniper Hall is now let by the Trust to the Field Studies Council which uses the area as an outdoor laboratory.

Northern Ireland Coast

The Mourne Coastal Path is a good example of how ownership of land is much fragmented in Northern Ireland. At Bloody Bridge, just south of Newcastle, the Mountains of Mourne sweep literally down to the sea, with Slieve Donard towering above at 2,788 feet. By a series of small purchases the Trust has acquired two miles of coastal footpath along geologically interesting cliffs and boulder beaches where the yellow-horned poppy and the rare oyster plant grow. The narrow valley of the Bloody River runs up the mountains to the Saddle, and to the remarkable Mourne Wall, a high granite boundary wall which runs from summit to summit for over twenty miles. The Bloody Bridge River Path provides a point of access to the high Mournes, and from the wall the views are superb: east to Dundrum, the Murlough dunes and beyond to Strangford Lough; south to the Annalong valley below the peaks of Slieve Lamagan, Cove Mountain and Slieve Beg; north to the brooding Slieve Donard.

Dundrum Bay is of particular interest to the geographer, the archaeologist and the naturalist because much of the great range of sand dunes, which has developed across it forming the Murlough Nature Reserve, is at least 5,000 years old.

The Trust manages its 700 acres of dune as a nature reserve, but the area is big enough to allow visitors ample space and to carry on a substantial programme of research and education. The dunes support a wide range of plants, some uncommon

like the carline thistle, the Portland spurge and the pyramidal orchid, and there are valuable areas of dune heath. Sea buckthorn, planted before the First World War to stabilise blowing sand, does only too well and has had to be controlled since myxomatosis reduced the rabbit population.

There is evidence of habitation in the dunes since the earlier Neolithic period. Traces of dwellings, pottery, weapons and implements from this and later ages, as well as from early Christian and medieval times, turn up regularly as the wind removes overlying sand.

The Ards peninsula forms the east side of Strangford Lough (*see* p.322). Its sea coast is low, and here the Trust has gathered together two miles of foreshore, beach and adjoining land, from the cove with the insalubrious name of Stinking Port south round Kearney Point to Knockinelder. North of Kearney Point stands what remains of the once-flourishing village of Kearney. In 1900 seventy-five

Hexagonal basalt columns composing the cliffs of the Giant's Causeway (*see* p.229) look as if they have been sculpted out of the rock. (*NT/Mike Williams*)

White Park Bay,
a mile of golden
sand backed by low
limestone cliffs.
(*NT/Mike
Williams*)

Ireland's first nature reserve was established on the dunes at Murlough, Co. Down (*see* p.230). (*NT/Mike Williams*)

people lived here but fishing failed, farms were mechanised and many of the inhabitants emigrated. The place became virtually deserted. Thirteen cottages survive, a cluster of whitewashed buildings on the furthest point of the peninsula.

East of Bangor, at the mouth of Belfast Lough, the little village of Groomsport lies between Ballymacormick Point and Orlock Point, rocky gorsy places which have not been subjected to the municipal tidiness of the cliff walks nearer Belfast. They are places from which to watch ships entering or leaving the lough, and to see oystercatchers, stonechats, rock pipits, reed buntings, willow warblers and linnets, all of which breed here. In winter dunlin, redshank, purple sandpiper, curlew and

ringed plover feed on the shore. Ballymacormick Point is also an important botanical site.

Four miles offshore Lighthouse Island is now a misnomer, for the lighthouse has moved to nearby Mew Island. A landing permit is needed, for the island is a bird observatory where eider duck, red-breasted merganser, shelduck, fulmar and black guillemot breed, and there is an exciting colony of Manx shearwaters, which breed in rabbit burrows and emerge only at night to avoid attack by predatory gulls.

To the north and west there are three places in County Londonderry not to be missed. The estuary of the River Bann opens below Coleraine to run west to the sea at Bar Mouth. The Trust owns some 185 acres of tidal mudflats, saltings and dunes here and has established a refuge for migratory birds, where divers and auks, great-crested grebes, eiders, mergansers and kittiwakes feed offshore in autumn. Waders rest and feed here before going further south: knots, sanderlings, little stints, curlews, sandpipers, whimbrels. Later on ringed, golden and green plover, dunlin and redshank arrive, while resident duck species – mallard, teal, shelduck and goldeneye – are always about.

Across the river lie the three miles of beach and dunes of Portstewart Strand. A popular family beach, overlooked at one end by houses and hotels, with a golf course behind the dunes, it seems an unlikely candidate for preservation by the Trust, yet the Trust was the one body able to act decisively to save it.

Increased mobility had meant a growing number of visitors. The dunes were being eroded away by motor-cyclists and users of the beach, and many interesting and uncommon plants and insects were being threatened. In 1981 the Trust bought the whole and took on the unpopular job of stopping this destruction. While cars can still park on the hard sand of the beach, the dunes are slowly recovering.

West of the estuary, the ground rises and the B69 runs out to the cliff edge with a wonderful view over Magilligan Strand to the mouth of Lough Foyle. Between the road and the sea lies the extraordinary demesne of Downhill (see p.103), with the beautiful circular shell of the Mussenden Temple on the cliff edge.

The Giant's Causeway has been a mecca for tourists since the eighteenth century and, like Land's End and John o'Groats, had become sleazy with huts selling foodstuffs, drinks and souvenirs, a wishing well, a gated entrance and an admission fee. When the Trust was given the property in 1961, there was prolonged discussion as to how it should be presented, some people taking the view that the sleaziness had historic interest. Fortunately wiser counsels prevailed; the gates, huts and much else were removed, the admission fee given up. There is now an information centre, educational facilities, the Trust's own brand of souvenir shop and a restaurant. All is in good taste but another generation may question whether such a place cannot speak for itself.

In the Tertiary era, 60 million years ago, lava poured out through fissures in the earth's surface to flow over the chalk and solidify into basalt, much of it polygonal in section. Most of the columns are six-sided but columns with four, five, seven and ten sides are found. The causeway itself is fascinating,

and should be fully explored, but the coast to which it leads is truly spectacular. It was the Trust's involvement in the causeway which led to the acquisition of land, or rights of way, to make a twelve-mile walk along, above and below these wonderful cliffs, a remarkable feat of construction, some of it vertiginous and not for the faint-hearted, though this does not deter the ravens, peregrines and choughs.

There are caves, of which Portcoon Cave, west of the Causeway Hotel, can be entered from the lower path, but the most memorable features are the bays between the series of great headlands which run out to Benbane Head, with its view of Inishowen sixteen miles out to sea. Each bay forms an amphitheatre with its own particular features: manmade, like the Shepherd's Path, where 149 steps join the upper and lower paths; or natural, like the Organ, its basalt pipes forty feet high; the Harp; the Spanish Organ; Horse Back; Lover's Leap; Giant's Gate. This imposing landscape has now been designated a World Heritage Site.

East of Benbane Head, the path runs along the cliff, over Bengore Head at 374 feet, past Portfad and Port Moon, still used by salmon netsmen, to the wildly romantic and now vestigial ruin of Dunseverick Castle, the oldest and once the most strongly fortified place in Ireland. Its building was probably begun during the early Celtic period, 2,000 years ago, and Conal Cearnach, leader of the Red Branch Knights, Ulster's ancient order of chivalry, lived here. Stormed by the Vikings in 870, and again in 924, Dunseverick was held by the clan McDonnell, whose fief covered both North Antrim and Argyllshire. The last owner, Giladuff O'Cahan, was subdued by the Great O'Neill in the 1641 rebellion, and the castle, the remains of which are of the sixteenth century, was slighted by Cromwellian troops.

At Port Braddon, a tiny fishing village, the basalt finishes and white limestone begins. Here is lovely White Park Bay, acquired by the Trust in 1938 and one of the few properties gained before the Second World War. The low limestone cliffs jut out of green turf above a mile of golden sand; beyond is the little harbour of Ballintoy, and offshore are the islands of Long Gilbert, Carricknafurd, Sheep Island and Island Lean, breeding places for seabirds.

The path ends at the rock island of Carrick-a-Rede, 'the rock on the road', the road being the path of the salmon on their way to the Rivers Bann and Bush. During the fishing season, May to September,

The sixty-foot chasm between the island of Carrick-a-Rede and the Antrim coast is still spanned by a precarious rope bridge during the fishing season. (*NT*)

the sixty-foot chasm between the island and the cliff is spanned by a rope bridge. The salmon do not swim through the narrows below it but go north round the island where the fishermen have set their nets for centuries. The Trust owns a stretch of unspoilt and dramatic coatline at Larrybane, next to the rope bridge and fishery, and has blown up unattractive quarry buildings masking a former limeworks here.

The 1,000 acres comprising Fair Head, Murlough Bay and Benvan are without question the finest coastal scenery in Northern Ireland. The great headland of Fair Head is a landmark from the sea, from the air and from many miles along the adjoining coast. The dolerite cliffs rise for nearly 600 feet above the sea. The brow of the headland is heathery, wild and rocky, frequented by buzzards, ravens, peregrine falcons and quantities of choughs. A herd of wild goats lives here, moving in winter to the woods of birch, hazel and rowan on the slopes above Murlough Bay. The bay is very different:

cliffs of white chalk over red Triassic sandstone in its centre, the great basalt columns of Fair Head to the north, crumbling mica-schist to the south, a little farm perched between the woods and the sea. Among the rarer plants is Grass of Parnassus, with pure-white buttercup-like flowers in September.

Out to sea is the long low bulk of Rathlin Island, a place few people ever reach, though it looks an easy voyage. To the south, the beautiful coastal farm of Benvan is held as a memorial to the Earl of Antrim, Chairman of the Trust from 1965 until his death in 1977, whose home was at Glenarm nearby.

Cushendun lies snugly at the foot of Glendun, one of the famous Nine Glens. The River Dun rises on Orra Mountain, picks up the streams from Aggangorive Hill as the beautiful glen widens, and plunges under the fine viaduct (built by the Belfast architect Charles Lanyon in 1839) to reach the curving bay at its mouth.

The Trust owns sixty acres here, and much of the seemly village. This is partly nineteenth century, but the whitewashed terraced cottages in the square, with their mansard roofs and small-paned windows, were built in 1912 by the Welsh architect Clough Williams-Ellis.

North Norfolk Coast

The Trust has been established since 1912 on the north Norfolk coast and its initiative has brought in a number of most welcome partners, so that by far the greater part of the coast between Hunstanton and Sheringham (*see* p.288) is now managed for the preservation of its exceptional scientific interest. The Norfolk Naturalists' Trust was the National Trust's first partner; English Nature, the Norfolk Ornithologists' Association and the RSPB have also acquired reserves.

The twenty miles between the chalk cliffs at Hunstanton and Sheringham are of exceptional interest to naturalists of all disciplines, and also to geographers, for there are classic sites illustrating the phenomenon of long-shore drift, the action of waves in shifting shingle and sand along a coastline, giving a completely different shape to a system of spits and creeks in only a few years. Scientists may also observe the formation of sand dunes, the build-up of mudflats and saltings, the zonation of plants and animals on the salt-marshes according to their height above mean tide level, and the richness and variety of the bird life for which this ever-changing coast is deservedly famous. And the coast is very beautiful in a way peculiar to itself. It can be bleak, raw and very lonely but he would be a dull man whose heart strings were not touched by it.

Brancaster Staithe is the centre of the western section, and from there one may embark for Scolt Head Island, 1,620 acres of sand dune, salt-marsh, ever-changing shingle ridge and foreshore, with a ternery (in which sandwich terns are particularly abundant) at its west end, to which there is no access during the breeding season in May, June and July. The island *can* be reached over the mudflats at low water, but only by those who really know the route. The beach is little frequented and makes an exhilarating walk for the beachcomber, for as well as offering every sort of flotsam it is one of the best places for picking up complete razor shells. The island was acquired in 1923, but it was not until forty years later that the 2,220 acres of Brancaster Marshes, on the mainland opposite, were bought, adding greatly to the value of this lovely place. There is an information point at Brancaster Staithe.

One embarks at Morston or Blakeney Quay for claw-shaped Blakeney Point, 1,300 acres of shingle spit creeping ever westward and creating more creeks and mudflats as it goes. There is a large ternery and many migrant birds, including occasional rarities, which can be seen in spring and autumn. The Lifeboat House has a display which shows how Blakeney Point has been built up and describes the flora and fauna to be found here.

The 1,000 acres of salt-marsh at Stiffkey and Morston complement Blakeney Point, as the Brancaster Marshes act as a foil for Scolt Head Island. The Stiffkey marsh, with plenty of sea aster and sea lavender, provides winter feeding ground for brent geese, widgeon and teal. The Morston marsh, cut up by tidal creeks, has a population of redshank and shelduck as well as brent geese in winter. Little and common terns breed on the shingle banks. East of Blakeney, the grazing marshland of the Freshes attacts overwintering wildfowl and many other species, and the salty lagoons of Arnold's Marsh, along the coast at Salthouse, are visited by migrant waders, avocet and bearded tit. Gramborough Hill, above the marsh, also belongs to the Trust.

Northumbrian Coast

In the heavily industrialised area of Northumbria, undeveloped coast is especially precious. The Trust has three footholds, all of them on the Permian magnesian limestone which is good for both geologists and plants.

To the north of Easington lies Beacon Hill, at 279 feet the highest point on Durham's coastline, and the beach below. To the south, at Horden, there are wooded denes behind the mile of cliff where streams run down to the shore. At South Shields there is a larger foothold at The Leas, where some 300 acres of attractive grassy land lie behind three miles of limestone cliffs, with good sandy beaches. Erosion of the limestone has produced a much-indented coast, with caves, rock arches and detached 'stacks', the principal feature being the mighty arch through Marsden Rock. A large colony of kittiwakes can be found here from late winter to late summer, spending the rest of the year at sea.

North of Blyth the coast has been much less developed and, five miles south of Seahouses, the little village of Low Newton-by-the-Sea lies at the centre of the Trust's four-mile stretch which runs from Long Nanny Burn in the middle of Beadnell Bay and south round Newton Point, encompassing the whole sweep of Embleton Bay dominated by the dramatic ruin of Dunstanburgh Castle (*see* p.106).

Most of Low Newton, including the Ship Inn in the village square, belongs to the Trust. The sturdy houses nestle into this low-lying coast at the eastern tip of the Great Whin Sill. The links of wind-cropped turf, with some wet hollows, run down to the beach, and there are sand dunes in places. Oystercatchers, eider duck and rock pipits breed there and can be seen feeding among the rock pools in spring and summer, while turnstones and purple sandpipers frequent them in winter. There is a considerable kittiwake colony on the low cliff at Dunstanburgh.

The inland side of the dunes is somewhat disfigured near Low Newton by chalets, built on plots let on long leases before the Trust's acquisition, but these are forgotten at the reed-fringed sixteen acres of Newton Pool, bought as a nature reserve. Sedge warblers and reed buntings nest here, as do many common freshwater species. Ruffs, redshanks, water rail, snipe and other waders are found, and in winter tufted duck, pochard and goldeneye.

North Yorkshire Coast

On the fine stretch of coastline between Scarborough and Whitby is Hayburn Wyke, six miles north of Scarborough. High cliffs overlook a little bay with a wooded stream and waterfall, traversed – as is the whole length of the North Yorkshire coast – by the Cleveland Way footpath. After a short gap the cliffland of four farms – Rigg Hall, White Hall, Prospect House and Bent Rigg – rises up to over 500 feet, with the broken faces of Bent and Common Cliffs below.

On the south shore of Robin Hood's Bay the Trust has built up a patchwork of cliffs, farmland, disused alum and silica quarries and an abandoned brickworks, all lying behind the great peak of Ravenscar, a spectacular headland rising 600 feet above the sea. The Ravenscar Trail, starting from the Trust's centre in the village, illustrates the extraordinary geology of this unusual landscape, where pink and grey shale is capped with a thin layer of ironstone, with bands of orange-coloured sandstone called dogger and massive beds of deltaic sandstone intermixed. At the base of the cliffs are the so-called Mermaids' Tables, circular platforms of hard limestone left where the softer shale has eroded away.

Beyond the picturesque village of Robin Hood's Bay, Ness Point closes the bay to the north, with the Boggle Hole, a precipitous inlet, in the middle. As a new venture, the Trust has recently acquired the north side of the bay which surrounds the little harbour of Port Mulgrave near Staithes, north of Whitby.

Nostell Priory West Yorkshire

On the A638 out of Wakefield towards Doncaster

Sir Rowland Winn, 4th Baronet, commissioned two houses at Nostell in the mid-eighteenth century. The second, a classical building only a few feet high, stands at the foot of the south staircase of the priory. One of the most remarkable doll's houses in England, fully furnished in period style, this was built to delight an adult rather than to enchant a child. Marble chimneypieces are copied from plates in James Gibbs's *Book of Architecture* of 1728, carved mouldings and cornices in the principal rooms are picked out in gilt, and the furnishings are accurate in every detail. Little figures representing the family are looked after by servants in the Winn livery of grey and yellow and there is even a glass mouse under the kitchen table. If family tradition is correct, this minor masterpiece was the work of two young men closely associated with Rowland Winn's new mansion: James Paine, who executed and modified the plans of the gentleman-architect Colonel James Moyser, and Thomas Chippendale, both then still in their teens.

The estate had been acquired by the Winns, a family of London merchants, in 1650, ten years before the 1st Baronet was created, and the property has been held by the family ever since. The present house, built to the north of an earlier building formed out of the old priory, was created over fifty years from 1735, with a strong contrast between James Paine's rococo decoration for Sir Rowland and the severer classical designs of his successor, Robert Adam (later to oust Paine again at Kedleston, *see* p.164), for Sir Rowland's son. Fine interiors include paintings by Antonio Zucchi, among his earliest work in England, plasterwork by Joseph Rose the Younger and furniture by Chippendale.

Because only one of Adam's planned extensions to Paine's pedimented classical house was ever completed, the exterior of the priory is pleasingly asymmetrical. Adam was also responsible for the

The enchanting doll's house at Nostell Priory even includes a glass mouse under the kitchen table.
If family tradition is correct, this minor masterpiece was partly the work of the young Thomas Chippendale.
(*NT/Mark Fiennes*)

terrace fronting the entrance reached by two flights of curving steps which lifts the main façade. Inside, however, it is Paine's rooms which are the more flamboyant. Adam's beautiful hall is a serenely graceful room, with Rose's delicate plasterwork picked out against a subtly darker background. The library, with its pedimented bookcases and Zucchi's stylised classical paintings, is sombre and studious, dominated by Chippendale's superb desk in the centre of the room.

These intellectual treatments only serve to heighten the opulent over-ripeness of Paine's rooms. Zucchi's playful cherubs in the elaborate panels over the doors in the dining-room and the plaster frieze of vines and satyrs' masks suggest an appreciation of the good things in life. Paine also carried out the splendid ceiling in what is now the state bedchamber, with its trio of music-making cherubs, but the exquisite Chinese paper, with brightly coloured birds of all sizes and varieties perching on branches laden with flowers and foliage, was the choice of Chippendale, chosen to complement his rich green and gold lacquer furniture, among his most unusual work.

The 4th Baronet set his house in a park designed by Stephen Switzer, but few traces of this innovative gardener's layout survive. The main view from the house is across a sweep of grass to a natural lake and the little three-arched hump-backed bridge built in 1761 to carry the main Wakefield to Doncaster road. Adam's Gothick menagerie still stands in a clearing west of the lake.

Nunnington Hall North Yorkshire

In Ryedale, 4½ miles south-east of Helmsley on the A170 Helmsley–Pickering road; 1½ miles north of the B1257 Malton–Helmsley road

Only a brave man could have told Elizabeth I that she would never have children. The bearer of this unwelcome message was Robert Huicke, physician to Henry VIII and Edward VI as well as the queen, traces of the Elizabethan range he built while renting Nunnington from the Crown perhaps still evident in the west front. Badly damaged by Parliamentary troops garrisoned in the house during the Civil War, Nunnington was restored by Richard Graham, 1st Viscount Preston, who inherited the estate in 1685.

A convert to Rome, Lord Preston was Master of the Wardrobe to James II and one of five peers entrusted with the government of the country when James fled in 1688. Apprehended on the fishing boat which he had hoped would bear James triumphantly back to England, Preston was taken to the Tower of London and saved from execution only by the pleadings of his youngest daughter Susannah. Stripped of his offices and disgraced, he returned to Yorkshire, where he died a few years later.

Preston's south front is Nunnington's finest architectural feature, the long two-storeyed façade with projecting gables at either end appearing both welcoming and refined. Unusually, two central doors stand one above the other, with a charming wrought-iron balcony round the upper one.

Inside, the house is cosily elegant, its warmly panelled rooms filled with period furniture, tapestries and porcelain collected by the last owner. The grandest room is Preston's oak hall, with its elaborate chimneypiece supporting his coat of arms joined with those of his wife and a three-arched classical screen leading to the great oak and pine staircase climbing round three sides of a well. Preston emerges again in the two large ceiling canvases he commissioned in a small upstairs room, curiously depicting various family coats of arms against a cloudy sky, and in the little oratory adjoining a bedroom in the west wing, a reminder of his adopted faith and of the family's continued recusancy in the eighteenth century. Part of the attic above now houses the Carlisle Collection of Miniature Rooms, fully furnished in different period styles.

The delightful walled garden to the south of the house is a rare survival from the seventeenth century which still bears traces of the original formal layout. A rusticated stone gateway inserted in the south wall in the 1920s marks the site of the *clair-voyée*, a railing on a low wall which extended the view beyond the garden, shown in Samuel Buck's sketch of *c*.1720. A lawn cut to suggest the formal pattern of the parterre also shown in Buck's sketch is flanked by orchard plots. These have recently been replanted with old varieties of fruit trees, including pears and culinary and dessert apples only found in Ryedale. Clematis and roses grow against the walls. Eccentrically individual arches and gates through which the garden is approached may have helped Lord Preston recall happier times when he was Ambassador to France for Charles II.

Nymans West Sussex

On the B2114 at Handcross, 4½ miles south of Crawley, just off the M23/A23 London–Brighton road

Set 500 feet high and surrounded by the magnificent woods of the Sussex Weald, this enchanting thirty-acre garden was created over more than half a century from 1890 by Ludwig Messel and his son Leonard, and was subsequently nurtured and enriched by the Earl and Countess of Rosse. Laid out on the side of a valley, the garden is designed as a series of open-air rooms, with lichen-stained stone steps or grassy slopes connecting one levelled area with another. Trees, walls and hedges surround the rooms, sheltering the remarkable collection of rare and choice plants for which the garden is now so well known, including magnificent rhododendrons, magnolias, azaleas and camellias. Many species reflect the Messels' sponsorship of plant-collecting expeditions to the Far East, Burma, South America and Tasmania. Several plants, such as *Populus lasiocarpa, Picea likiangensis purpurea* and *Magnolia sargentiana*, were raised from seeds collected by George Forrest, F. Kingdon-Ward and others, while Chilean shrubs and trees, including *Sophora macrocarpa* and *Asteranthera ovata*, were introduced by Leonard Messel's head gardener's son, Harold Comber, who made several plant-gathering trips to this part of the world. Now much healed since the freak storm in the autumn of 1987, which completely destroyed the pinetum and felled many trees elsewhere in the garden, Nymans displays an unusually rich collection of plants and also specimens of the many that were hybridised here, including the now widespread *Eucryphia nymanensis, Magnolia* 'Leonard Messel', *M.* 'Anne Rosse' and *Camellia* 'Maud Messel'.

The heart of the garden lies in what was a walled

The rose garden at Nymans, with old-fashioned English, French and Italian shrub roses trained over arches and pillars around a fountain. (*NT/Stephen Robson*)

orchard. Entered through decorative brick arches, one crowned with pinnacles, another covered with romantically tangled roses and clematis, two peaceful walks planted for spring and summer display – a medley of red, yellow, orange, blue and scarlet – converge on an Italian fountain guarded by formally clipped yews. A prominent *Eucryphia nymanensis* is a mass of white in July and August. A hint of a Tuscan hillside is echoed in the sunken garden, where a huge grey stone Byzantine urn and a classical loggia adorned with grinning heads set off brightly planted beds flowering red, pink and mauve. Four Lawsons cypress stand sentinel on the edge of the grass.

Other features of this delightfully varied garden include beds of old-fashioned roses and the heather and rock garden created on a series of hillocks, heavy with the scent of lavender and cistus in summer and crowned by a weeping hornbeam on the highest point. The pinetum has been replanted and the magnificent wistaria pergola, knocked sideways by the storm, has been rebuilt so that visitors can again enjoy the pendant blooms in May and June. There is something of interest all year round, from carpets of daffodils in spring to the brilliant scarlet and gold of the Japanese maples in autumn. The mullions and Tudor chimneys of Ludwig Messel's pastiche fourteenth-century manor, now largely a picturesque shell after it was gutted by fire in 1947, provide a charming and romantic backdrop to the planting and to spacious lawns shaded by cedars and fringed with topiary beasts.

Much of the pleasure of the garden lies in its intimacy, and the feeling of a place secure from the world, but there are also glorious views to the heights of the Weald and to the South Downs from the balustraded terrace overlooking the park and from the perimeter walk past the little classical summerhouse and up the lime avenue. And in April cuckoos calling in the woods herald the approach of summer.

Oakhurst Cottage Surrey

In the village of Hambledon, 5 miles south of Godalming

Furnished as a labourer's cottage of the mid-nineteenth century, this little timber-framed building on the fringes of London's affluent commuter belt is a rare survival illustrating a now vanished way of life. Unlike so many other cottages of this type dating

from the prosperous fifteenth and sixteenth centuries, Oakhurst has not been modernised and gentrified in the last hundred years.

Rows of onions, cabbages and beans mingled with traditional flowers, such as hollyhocks, sweet peas and roses, crowd the little garden lining the path leading to the front door. This opens straight into the main room, a quarry-tiled kitchen dominated by a dresser set with Wedgwood willow-pattern china. A huge pot hangs over the hearth and samplers adorn the walls. A steep staircase leads directly into one of the bedrooms in the roof, lit by dormer windows. In the little back kitchen, where clothes were washed and ironed, a low bench known as a hog-form is where the hair was scraped from the family pig after it had been slaughtered, a prelude to the annual pork feast enjoyed by wealthier cottagers and so vividly described by Flora Thompson in *Lark Rise to Candleford*.

Oldbury Hill Kent

On north side of the A25, 3 miles south-west of Wrotham

The Iron Age hill fort built on this prominent sandy ridge enjoyed a magnificent defensive position, protected by exceptionally steep slopes on all sides except the north. First fortified in about 100BC, the original bank and ditch enclosing an area of 123 acres seem to have been strengthened at a later date, perhaps at the time of the Roman invasion in AD43. Natural caves in the slopes on the north-east side of the hill fort were occupied by Neanderthal huntsmen during the last Ice Age.

The Old Manor Derbyshire

At Norbury, 6 miles south-west of Ashbourne

At the north end of the seventeenth-century red-brick manor house in this leafy village on the River Dove is a low medieval building with rough buttressed stone walls dating from the thirteenth to the fifteenth centuries. The airy first-floor hall built over an undercroft and cellars has a rare king-post roof, perhaps installed here in the seventeenth century when the Tudor manor was demolished, and original Gothic two-light windows in the west wall, with stone window seats. From the little knot garden below, there is a good view of the tower of the fine fourteenth-century village church only a

Oakhurst Cottage in a watercolour of *c.*1900 by Helen Allingham. (*NT*)

The Old Post Office at Tintagel, one of the Trust's most delightful buildings. (*NT*/*Andrew Besley*)

stone's throw away, packed with monuments to the Fitzherbert family who held the manor of Norbury for over 650 years from 1125.

The Old Post Office Cornwall

In centre of village of Tintagel

The considerable increase in postal traffic resulting from the introduction of the penny post in 1844 led to a much-improved service in remote parts of the country. Tintagel, then a little-known village on the wild north Cornish coast, was blessed with its first post office, set up to receive incoming mail only in a room in this ancient cottage.

The Old Post Office is traditionally built of slate, now weathered to a uniform grey. Nothing about it is symmetrical, from the placing of the sturdy two- and three-tier chimneys to the off-centre projecting porch and the undulating roof. Dating from the fourteenth century and a rare survival of local domestic architecture, it is also now one of the few remaining picturesque buildings in Tintagel, most of the others having been ruthlessly torn down in the late nineteenth century to be replaced with a rash of boarding houses and hotels catering for Victorian romantics in search of King Arthur.

The interior suggests a very small manor house, with a diminutive hall rising to the roof in the middle of the building and a passage running through the house to the little split-level garden. The rooms are furnished with local oak pieces such as would have been found in farmhouses and cottages round about, and the post room which operated until 1892 is now fitted out as a Victorian post office.

Old Soar Manor Kent

2 miles south of Borough Green on the A25; approached via the A227 and Plaxtol

The rectangular solar block attached to a red-brick early Georgian farmhouse is all that remains of the manor house of *c.*1290 which stood here until the eighteenth century. The 28-foot solar over a barrel-vaulted undercroft was once the apartment of a medieval knight, a private retreat away from the noise and community of the great hall. Rough walls of Kentish ragstone rising to an open timber roof, a bare flagged floor and an absence of furniture underline the spartan nature of life in the Middle Ages, although the remains of a fireplace suggest some degree of comfort. Openings at the corners of the room lead to two projecting chambers, a chapel and a garderobe.

Orford Ness Suffolk

On coast between Aldeburgh and Orford

Stretching 10 miles south of Aldeburgh, with a gentle curve westwards opposite Orford, this long shingle spit is one of the most desolate and lonely places along an often wild and inhospitable coastline. Separated from the mainland by the River Ore, which it forces ever further south, the bank is still fluid and impermanent, changing shape in the winter storms which sweep in from the North Sea. Sea kale, sea pea, yellow vetch and horned-poppy

Blast-absorbing concrete pagodas dotting the lonely shingle of Orford Ness are a relic of the military research conducted here for sixty years. (*NT/Joe Cornish*)

colonise the shingle, there is a thin strip of grazing marsh, mud-flat and reed-bed on the inland side, and this rare habitat is an overwintering and breeding ground for seabirds, waders and wildfowl, including the largest colony of lesser black-backed and herring gull in East Anglia.

In 1993 the Trust acquired 5 miles, or some 1,550 acres, of the northern end of the spit. Apart from its great natural history interest, this stretch of shingle bank includes the remains of a one-time military research station, now reduced to rotting timber and concrete. First occupied in the First World War, when there was a staff of 600 and a prisoner-of-war camp here, Orford Ness was used for sixty years for testing guns, sights, explosives and aerial combat techniques. It was here, in a timber hut, that Robert Watson-Watt and his team did pioneering work on the development of radar in 1935–6, and in its last years, from 1959–71, the station was used to develop the atomic bom. Eerily futuristic concrete pagodas were built to absorb the blast should one of the tests carried out in the cavernous pits beneath them go wrong. Some structures have now been demolished, others are being allowed to gently decay, a symbol of the futility of war and man's destructiveness.

Ormesby Hall Cleveland

3 miles south-east of Middlesbrough, west of the A171

Sir James Pennyman, 6th Baronet, and his aunt Dorothy were clearly people of taste. Although 'Wicked Sir James', a spendthrift in the best eighteenth-century manner, ran through the fortune he inherited in 1770 in eight years, he spent his wealth on enlarging the Ormesby estate and enriching the house his aunt had built some thirty years earlier. Unfortunately, he was then obliged to surrender the property to the bailiffs.

Probably completed by 1743, Ormesby was designed by an unknown architect in a characteristically plain Palladian style then popular in North Yorkshire. The rather severe outlines of the high three-storey main block rising to a hipped roof are relieved only by a heavy cornice and pediments on the two main façades. Projecting porches were Victorian additions. A two-storey service wing on the east was formed out of the earlier Jacobean house, thought to have been built in about 1600, its low façades an interesting contrast to the later

Ormesby Hall's impressive late eighteenth-century stable block, probably designed by John Carr of York. (*NT/ Alan North*)

building. Although most of the original features of the service wing have been lost, one fine ornamented Jacobean doorway has survived, with the crest granted to James Pennyman in 1599 proudly displayed on the coat of arms above.

The interior of the main block is a complete contrast. Ormesby is not at all grand but the most talented of local craftsmen were employed to create the rich plaster decoration and woodwork which are now such a feature of the house. Ionic columns screening both ends of the hall and Palladian motifs here and in the library are of Dorothy's time, but Sir James introduced the delicate Adamesque ceilings attributed to Carr of York in the drawing-room and dining-room, where the silver cup he presented to Northallerton racecourse now stands proudly on the sideboard. Plain family rooms on the first floor contrast with some decorated guest rooms on the north side, one adorned with carved festoons of fruit and foliage. A notable panelled gallery runs across the house at the top of the staircase, the five pedimented doorways echoing the Palladian emphasis on symmetry and balance evident in the hall.

The house is now filled with Regency and Victorian furniture and a number of family portraits reflect the generations of Pennymans who continued to live at Ormesby despite the 6th Baronet's extravagance. Sir James's dignified stables crowned with a cupola, probably also designed by Carr of York, are now let to the mounted police.

A small rose garden and mixed flower beds and borders, some planted in cottage-garden style with delphiniums, phlox and lupins, set off the house. A holly walk shows off fancy-leaved varieties, and naturalised spring bulbs carpet the woodland towards the church, where William Lawson, author of several gardening books, was vicar in the early seventeenth century.

Osterley Park   Middlesex

Just north of Osterley station, on the western outskirts of London (Piccadilly tube line)

This grand neo-classical villa was created in the mid-eighteenth century out of a Tudor mansion built by Sir Thomas Gresham, Chancellor of the Exchequer to Elizabeth I. The ghost of the sixteenth-century courtyard house still lingers on. Delightful corner turrets crowned with cupolas, somewhat reminiscent of those at Blickling (*see* p.32), rise either side of the wide flight of steps and pedimented portico which give access to the raised courtyard. Also like Blickling, Osterley is built of warm red brick, with windows and decorative stone dressings standing out in white.

Gresham's mansion was principally transformed from 1761 by Robert Adam, who spent the next twenty years creating this superb house with its beautifully unified interiors. Statues of Greek deities standing in niches and 'antique' vases on pedestals in Adam's cool grey and white entrance hall introduce the classical theme of the house. In the airy library, paintings depicting the world

A detail from Robert Adam's decorative scheme for the Etruscan dressing-room at Osterley Park. (*NT/John Bethell*)

of ancient Greece and Rome by Antonio Zucchi crown the pilastered and pedimented bookcases. Marquetry furniture attributed to John Linnell includes a pedestal desk inlaid with trophies representing the arts, and there is a delicate Adam ceiling. Close by is an eating-room arranged in the eighteenth-century way, with the chairs against the walls and no large central table.

Adam's plasterwork also graces the three rooms which form the state apartment, and one of his most ambitious pieces of furniture, a domed eight-poster bed, can be seen in the state bedroom. The most original decorative scheme is in the Etruscan dressing-room, where ochre-coloured dancing figures and urns set beneath trellis-like arches look as if a series of Greek vases has been flattened on the walls. In contrast, and despite its Adam ceiling, the antechamber has a French flavour. All claret and gold, it is hung with richly-coloured Gobelins tapestries and lined with ornate gilded sofas and chairs by John Linnell.

Red-brick Tudor stables just north of the house survive largely intact, apart from some alterations to doors and windows, with original staircase turrets in the angles of the building. Behind are the eighteenth-century pleasure grounds, with a Doric temple and Adam's semicircular garden house among lawns, serpentine gravel paths and evergreen shrubs. The park stretches away, with majestic cedars planted in the eighteenth century shading a lake and cattle grazing beneath the trees in the Great Meadow to the west. Despite the proximity of Heathrow and the M4, Osterley still feels like a country estate.

Adam was employed by Francis Child, whose grandfather had purchased the estate in 1711 after rising from obscurity to prominence as founder of one of the first banks in England (now subsumed in The Royal Bank of Scotland). After Francis's early death at the age of twenty-eight, his brother Robert completed Osterley, but he also died prematurely, perhaps partly as a result of anxiety about his only child Sarah Anne, who eloped with the 10th Earl of Westmorland at the age of eighteen. When mildly rebuked by her mother, who pointed out she had better matches in mind, the high-spirited girl replied, 'A bird in the hand is worth two in the bush.' The father forgave his only child, but altered his will to leave Osterley and most of his fortune to Sarah Anne's second son, or eldest daughter, thus cutting out the Westmorland heir.

The luxuriant garden of Overbecks, Sharpitor, set high above the sea on the South Devon coast. Views look south-west to Bolt Head, the headland guarding the west side of the Kingsbridge estuary. (*NT/John Glover*)

Overbecks, Sharpitor Devon

1½ miles south-west of Salcombe, signposted from Malborough and Salcombe

The rolling country of south Devon lies far from any major road, crossed by a network of often steep and winding lanes. One such narrow artery leads up from the little port of Salcombe to this elegant Edwardian house set on a steep slope overlooking the sea. Like the small Victorian villa it replaced, it is known as Sharpitor after the prominent craggy line of rocks just off the coast, but the individual collections it contains bear the name of the scientist who lived here from 1928–37, Otto Overbeck.

Laid out in some half-dozen rooms, Overbecks Museum has the domestic atmosphere of a private house. Shipbuilding tools and exquisitely detailed models reflect Salcombe's heyday in the 1870s, a replica of the *Phoenix* built here in 1836 which disappeared with all hands on a voyage to Barcelona, and photographs of the stricken Swedish vessel *Herzogin Cecilie*, wrecked off this coast in 1936, poignant reminders of the hazards faced by those who put to sea. The nautical collection also includes sailors' snuffboxes and marine paintings, one of them almost certainly showing *Phoenix* in full sail in the background.

Natural history exhibits illustrate local wildlife and British shells, birds' eggs and insects, several species among the cases of butterflies now very rare. A cabinet devoted to Otto Overbeck himself contains his popular rejuvenator, patented in 1924, which was said to inject new life into the old and tired by passing electricity through the body. Perhaps clients were also urged to consume Mr Overbeck's non-alcoholic beer, another of his many inventions. A secret room under the stairs, full of dolls and toys, has been specially created for children, room settings from doll's houses which once belonged to the Overbeck family including some diminutive bamboo furniture.

The six-acre garden, which enjoys the mildest of microclimates, is the most Mediterranean in the Trust's care. Apart from the upper lawn around the house, most of it slopes steeply towards the sea in a series of sunny, sheltered terraces, where many rare and tender species thrive, among them agapanthus, mimosa, a camphor tree, olives, a Japanese banana and the ginkgo, and hundreds of fuchsias and hydrangeas. Palms, pines and cypresses flourish, the palms even seeding themselves, there are fruiting oranges in the conservatory, and pots and urns planted with agaves are placed around the garden. In March a mass of flamingo-pink blossoms visible from far beyond the garden marks the magnificent *Magnolia campbellii* for which Overbecks is famous, one of a number of fine trees planted at the turn of the century when the bones of the garden, including the terraces, were first established by Edric Hopkins. And far below there is the constant backdrop of the sea, often speckled with little boats. Cliffs across the bay run south to the dramatic headland of Prawle Point, while inland there are views to Salcombe and up the wooded reaches of the Kingsbridge estuary.

Owletts Kent

1 mile south of the A2, at west end of village of Cobham, at junction of roads from Dartford and Sole Street

This red-brick, two-storey Charles II house, with dormer windows peering over the parapet added in 1754, was built for a prosperous Kentish farmer, Bonham Hayes. His initials and those of his wife Elizabeth adorn the tall chimneys rising from the steeply pitched hipped roof and also figure prominently in the plasterwork over the staircase, the finest original feature of the interior and very unusual in such a modest house. Probably the work of Italian craftsmen, realistic, three-dimensional flowers and fruit crowd the roundels carrying the date – 1684 – and the initials of the Hayes. Bunches of grapes hanging from the ceiling suggest the figs and peaches ripening above neat rows of vegetables in the walled garden to the east of the house.

A bird-bath formed of Corinthian capitals from the old Bank of England recalls the architect Sir Herbert Baker, who was born at Owletts in 1862 and was largely responsible for the historic atmosphere of the present interiors. Known today for his imperial London buildings – India House, South Africa House and the Bank of England – and for his collaboration with Sir Edwin Lutyens in the design of New Delhi, Sir Herbert also had a successful early career in South Africa, where he built Groote Schuur for Cecil Rhodes in 1890.

Owletts reflects the architect's travels and his talents, from his carved dining-room chairs delightfully decorated with creatures symbolising the family and the house, to the Dutch grandfather clock and chest he brought back from Cape Town and his strip cartoon of the journey from Delhi to Owletts, with an early frame showing Sir Herbert and Lutyens together on an elephant. Sir Herbert also introduced the blue and gold wall-clock ingeniously devised to show the time in the countries of the Empire and a prominent feature in the airy sunny room looking over the garden, where broad lawns and a tennis court emphasise that this is a family house.

Oxburgh Hall Norfolk

At Oxburgh, 7 miles south-west of Swaffham, on south side of the Stoke Ferry road

On a fine day the octagon of Ely Cathedral can just be made out twenty miles away across the Fens from the top of Oxburgh's medieval gatehouse. This land is now cultivated, criss-crossed with drainage dykes, but, when Edward IV gave Sir Edmund Bedingfeld a licence to crenellate his manor house at Oxburgh in 1482, the site was on an island in the marsh. The Bedingfelds were to remain at Oxburgh for the next 500 years, the gradual impoverishment of the estate that resulted from their adherence to the Catholic faith also ensuring that the house survived unaltered through the sixteenth and seventeenth centuries. Still set in one of the least accessible parts of England, there is a feeling of isolation here even today.

Oxburgh is impressive from wherever you approach it, its brick ranges set around a courtyard rising from the waters of a moat on all four sides. The magnificent gatehouse with its battlemented turrets and large mullioned windows, the best-preserved part of the early Tudor house, was one of

(*Right*) Romantic Victorian embellishments to Oxburgh Hall include this heraldic fireplace, with a carved overmantel made up of genuine medieval woodwork. (*NT/ Mark Fiennes*)

the earliest to be built for display rather than defence, a forerunner of the glass lantern at Coughton Court (*see* p.89), or the prospect tower at Sissinghurst (*see* p.291). The Flemish-style stepped gables crowned with twisted terracotta chimneys, which adorn the range on either side and give the house such a distinctive outline, were added by J. C. Buckler as part of extensive restorations in the mid-nineteenth century. He was also responsible for the beautiful oriel window which fills two storeys of his authentically medieval battlemented tower in the south-east corner, looking out over the florid French-style parterre flowering in swirls of blue and yellow on the grass beyond the moat.

The interior of the house includes both Tudor survivals and atmospheric Victorian rooms. The brick-walled King's Room in the gatehouse tower with its great fireplace was where Henry VII slept when he came to Oxburgh in 1487. A priest's hole in the floor of a former garderobe off this room is an evocative reminder of the family's religious sympathies. Oxburgh's most prized possession, needlework by Mary Queen of Scots executed while she was in the custody of the Earl of Shrewsbury after her flight to England, is displayed in a darkened room nearby. These richly embroidered panels set on to green velvet, mostly delightful representations of beasts, birds and fishes ranging from the unicorn to the garden snail, are very rare specimens of the queen's work.

The nineteenth-century interiors, with designs by J. C. Buckler and J. D. Crace, are among the few examples of Catholic High Victorian taste in Britain. Crace's heraldic ceiling in the drawing-room incorporates delicately painted foliage and flowers in blue, pink and green. More heraldic devices – crimson fleurs-de-lis – are woven into the carpet of the low-ceilinged library, picking up the red in the flock wallpaper. A neo-Tudor fireplace dominates this room, the carved overmantel made up of medieval fragments from continental churches including delicate fan vaulting. The small dining-room is another rich Victorian interior, still looking exactly as it did in a watercolour of the early 1850s, the dark lustre of the panelling and of the elaborate sideboard with its crest of writhing birds relieved by vivid blue, orange and red tiles round the fireplace.

In the little chapel warmed with light cast through the great red Bedingfeld eagle in the south window, Victorian and medieval craftsmanship are again combined. The splendid altarpiece is crowned by a sixteenth-century carved triptych, purchased by the Bedingfelds in Bruges in about 1860.

Apart from the nineteenth-century Wilderness Walk to the west of the chapel and mown grass around the moat, most of the garden lies to the east of the house. A yew hedge beyond the parterre fronts a colourful herbaceous border. Behind is the fanciful, turreted wall of the Victorian kitchen garden, now planted as a formal orchard with plums, medlars, quinces and gages, and with roses, clematis and other climbers on the walls. There is also a two-mile park walk to one of Oxburgh's old shelter belts.

Packwood House Warwickshire

2 miles east of Hockley Heath on the A34, 11 miles south-east of central Birmingham

Packwood's fame rests on an evocative arrangement of trees. Across the large sunken lawn to the south of the house, a semicircular flight of brick steps leads up to a terrace walk and into the famous Yew Garden, traditionally thought to represent the Sermon on the Mount. The smoothly mown grass is dotted with clipped yews, most rising well above the heads of visitors and the tallest flanking the raised walk at the far end of the garden. Here twelve of the great yews are known as the Apostles, with the Evangelists represented by four very big specimens in the middle. From the terrace a tight spiral path edged with box ascends a hummock known as the Mount, crowned by a single yew tree. Although many of the 'multitude' were planted to replace an orchard in the mid-nineteenth century, the Master and his disciples were part of the seventeenth-century garden laid out by John Fetherston. He may also have enjoyed the sunken garden immediately in front of the house, with its delightful gazebos at each corner. One of these, dating from the time of Charles II, is ingeniously designed so that its fireplace can be used to warm fruit trees ripening on an adjacent wall. A vivid mixed herbaceous border flowering red, purple, yellow and blue near the house and crimson blooms in the box-edged rose garden act as a foil for the green of grass and trees. An intriguing sunken bath in a corner of one of the yew-hedged enclosures on the west side of the house dates from 1680. Sadly, water no longer gushes from the dog's-head spout

Packwood House: looking across the sunken garden to the raised terrace walk and the yew garden beyond.
(*NT/Derry Moore*)

in the little waterworks building adorned with the Fetherston arms.

The core of the house is a timber-framed building constructed by John Fetherston at the end of the sixteenth century. Although now rebuilt in brick and rendered over, its Elizabethan origins are still evident in the gabled roofline, massive chimneys and mullioned windows of the main block. Unlike their staunchly Catholic neighbours, the Ferrers of Baddesley Clinton (*see* p.18), the Fetherstons were politic in their allegiances. During the Civil War they seem to have offered shelter and succour as seemed expedient. Cromwell's general, Henry Ireton, slept here the night before the Battle of Edgehill in 1642 and there is a family tradition that Charles II was given food and drink at Packwood after his defeat at Worcester in 1651. Later in the century another John Fetherston added the extensive outbuildings in a rich dark-red brick, particularly fine examples of their kind.

Sold by the last of the Fetherstons in the late nineteenth century, Packwood was bought in 1905 by the wealthy industrialist Alfred Ash, also known for his fondness for the turf. Graham Baron Ash used his father's fortune to restore the house in the 1920s and 1930s, sweeping away Georgian and Victorian alterations and painstakingly acquiring features which would give Packwood a period feel, rescuing leaded casements, floors, beams and chimneypieces from other old houses. He also added the splendid long gallery and fashioned the great hall, complete with oriel window, out of an existing barn to complete his romantic vision of a Tudor house. He filled Packwood with period furnishings, including fine Jacobean panelling and an exceptional collection of tapestries, such as the seventeenth-century Brussels hanging depicting a cool terraced garden with splashing fountains and urns filled with orange trees. A long oak refectory table in the great hall and a Charles II oak cupboard inlaid with mother of pearl in the dining-room are two of the many pieces obtained from Baddesley Clinton when the finances of the Ferrers family were at a particularly low ebb.

Patterson's Spade Mill Co. Antrim

On A6, 2 miles south-east of Templepatrick

This unusual relic of Ireland's agricultural past is the last water-driven spade mill in the country. Founded in 1919 to produce a range of implements, from light tools for flower-beds to heavy-duty spades for cutting turf, Patterson's Mill was run as a family business for over seventy years. It was acquired by the Trust with all machinery and fittings intact and spades are once again being made here.

Paxton's Tower Dyfed

7 miles east of Carmarthen, 1 mile south of Llanarthney

This lonely triangular folly crowns a prominent grassy rise above the valley of the Tywi, its castellated outline, with two round turrets framing the central tower, a familiar sight to those following the A40 to Carmarthen on the other side of the river.

The tower was built between 1805 and 1808 by Sir William Paxton, a wealthy banker, as a memorial to Nelson, and originally had a banqueting room on the first floor from which the views over the valley could be enjoyed in comfort.

Paycocke's Essex

On south side of the A120 West Street, the road to Braintree, about 300 yards from centre of Coggeshall, next to the Fleece Inn, 5½ miles east of Braintree

The wealth generated by the East Anglian wool trade in the fifteenth and sixteenth centuries produced some of the most beautiful churches in the British Isles. It also enriched the homes of the merchants themselves, many of them using their fortunes to build fine half-timbered houses advertising their enhanced status. Paycocke's, a product of the early sixteenth century, is a splendid example of these buildings, its long pink and white, brick and timber street façade incorporating carpentry and carved woodwork of the highest quality.

An intricately decorated wooden beam running the width of the house beneath the five oriel windows of the projecting upper storey carries a series of delightful cameos, such as a dragon depicted upside down and a small person apparently

Paycocke's brick and timber façade on West Street, Coggeshall, showing the oak gates to the carriageway through the house and the decorative carved woodwork.
(*NT/F. A. H. Bloemendal*)

diving into a lily. Larger naturalistic figures frame the fine oak gates through which a carriageway leads to the back of the house. Closely spaced vertical timbers limewashed a silvery-grey, with brick filling the spaces that would once have been packed with wattle and daub, form the pink and white stripes that give the façade its distinctive appearance. As indicated by the four family tombs still to be seen in the parish church, the Paycockes were people of substance, the house John Paycocke built on the occasion of his son Thomas's marriage to Margaret Harrold (indicated by the initials TP and MP carved on both interior and exterior woodwork) standing out from its more modest neighbours along West Street.

Inside, it is clear that Paycocke's was a place of work and business as well as a home. Peg holes in the studs of the walls were once used to hold the warp thread of the looms, wool was stored in the roof space and the lengths of cloth were probably stretched out to dry in the garden. A display of Coggeshall lace includes a device which used water-filled flasks to magnify candlelight, thus allowing four lace-makers to work by the light of one candle.

The Peak District

Derbyshire, Staffordshire, South Yorkshire

Between Manchester, to the west, and Sheffield, to the east

Completely surrounded as the Peak District is by the great industrial cities of the North and the Midlands, it is surprising that the Trust was not involved here until 1930, when Alport Height, a hilltop near Wirksworth in the south-east corner of the area, was given anonymously. By 1940 the Trust's foothold had grown to 2,000 acres and it now owns over 36,000 acres. By far the largest holding is to the north of the A625 in the heart of the High Peak: 32,000 acres of wild landscape which is largely heather and grass moorland on the brown sandstone and black shales of the millstone grit, lying in a great horseshoe known as the Dark Peak round the much smaller area of limestone country known as the White Peak.

The Derwent estate, acquired in 1952, partly in South Yorkshire (5,000 acres) and partly in Derbyshire (1,400 acres), includes all the Howden Moors to the east of the great Howden and Derwent reservoirs which so altered the Upper Derwent valley in the years before 1914. To the west lie the 16,000 acres of Hope Woodlands which came to the Trust with Hardwick Hall (*see* p.142) in 1959. These great moors, Ronksley, Bleaklow and Ashop, mile upon mile of pale grass and dark brown peat, run in a semicircle round the valleys of the Rivers Westend, Alport and Ashop which drain the watershed into the Derwent. It was to capture the water of the two latter rivers that the vast Ladybower Reservoir was completed in 1945.

The plantations of the water companies and the Forestry Commission cover the lower slopes round the reservoirs and up into the valleys. They are less obtrusive than similar plantings in Wales or the Lake District and are not wholly coniferous; one-fifth of the 3,000 acres of publicly owned woodland is broadleaved.

In the valleys, therefore, the reservoirs and plantations serving the need for water of the great cities of Sheffield, Nottingham, Derby and Leicester have made a new landscape in this century, but above 1,000 feet – where the Trust's moors lie – the old landscape remains unchanged. The beautifully named hill sheep – White-faced Woodland, Derbyshire Gritstone and Dalesbred – are based in the valley farms, but graze for much of the year on the high moorland. The herbage – mat grass, purple moorgrass, cotton grass, bilberry and heather – suits both the sheep and the red grouse (providing there aren't too many sheep). Careful burning of the heather is necessary to give the grouse a patchwork of differently aged plants: young shoots for food, mature plants for nesting under and over-mature heather for cover. Co-operation between the National Park and landowners, of which the Trust is the largest, allows farming and grouse shooting to co-exist happily with adequate access to all these great uplands.

South of Black Ashop Moor lies the massif of Kinder Scout, rising to over 2,000 feet and including the great bowl between Kinder Edge and the Downfall where the Kinder stream spills dramatically over the cliff edge from its source in the flat peaty moors above. The moorland stretches over Swine's Back to Edale Head and Jacob's Ladder, over 3,500 acres of wild country, with the 1,600 acres of Park Hall Moor adjoining to the west. The whole acquisition, made between 1982 and 1988, with the recent addition of Hill House Farm, embracing Kinder Head, was financed by means of a public appeal, bequests, and grants from the Countryside Commission and the National Heritage

Memorial Fund. Management problems have been considerable.

The natural vegetation on the Kinder plateau has been degraded, in places eroded away altogether, due in part to atmospheric pollution, accidental fires and over-use of popular areas by walkers, but above all to overgrazing by sheep encroaching from adjoining moors. The 'hefting' of flocks, whereby ewes instinctively keep to their native moors, had broken down and the results had been disastrous. Although the Trust put in hand a vigorous programme of gathering trespassing sheep which were penned, identified and collected by their owners at regular intervals, the problem continued, so a long-term, and expensive, campaign was begun to rebuild the miles of gritstone dry walls, fence some other boundaries, and experiment with restoration of eroded areas. It is a slow business, for the soil is thin and poor, but progress is being made as techniques improve, and it is certain that eventually Kinder can be brought back to its former state.

To the south, in Edale, the Trust has built up a 2,000-acre estate of hill farms, mainly on the south side of the valley and centred on Mam Tor, 1,700 feet high. Called the 'shivering mountain' because of continual landslips over the centuries, its east face, though entirely natural, resembles a gigantic quarry. A mile to the south the narrow limestone gorge of the Winnats Pass winds steeply up from Castleton; the name is a corruption of 'wind-gates' and to be caught here in a gale confirms its aptness. The grim character of this country is not to everyone's taste, although the views north to Kinder Scout and the High Peak are superb.

The moorland of the Kinder Massif is gradually recovering from overgrazing and from damage caused by too many walkers following the popular routes. (*NT*/*Martin Dohrn*)

Landslips are responsible for the quarry-like east face of Mam Tor, the shivering mountain. An Iron Age camp on the ridge is the largest in Derbyshire. (*NT/Mike Williams*)

Longshaw, only ten miles south-west of the centre of Sheffield, contrasts with the High Peak. Mostly acquired by the Trust in two bursts, during the 1930s and the 1970s, its 1,700 acres are more varied and, although still on the millstone grit, softer in character than the great open moors.

The B6251 runs through the Padley Gorge which is cut by the Burbage Brook, sometimes just a small stream in summer but a rushing torrent in winter. Here are some of the best surviving ancient oak woodlands in the Peak District, together with the special flora and fauna which this habitat supports.

There is some valley-bottom farmland, and in the great abandoned quarries at Bolehill, the source of millstones for the local water-powered mills for centuries, numerous worked or half-worked stones still remain. From Surprise View above the quarries there is a panorama over the Derwent and Hope valleys.

To the east of the gorge, in an attractive landscape of mixed woodland, heather and coppice, stands Longshaw Lodge, built in the 1820s as a shooting box for the Duke of Rutland, now converted into flats with a Trust shop, tearoom and information room next door. Hay Wood, to the south, was once oak but clearance in the past century has allowed the invasion of self-sown birch. Tumbling Hill above the wood is the best place from which to view the whole. In the south of the

Limestone crags weathered into strange shapes tower high above the Dovedale gorge. (*NT/Mike Williams*)

National Park Derbyshire joins Staffordshire, and the landscape changes into the very different limestone valleys of the so-called White Peak. Ossoms Hill and Wetton Hill stand on either side of the narrow wooded valley of the River Manifold west of Alstonfield, where the Trust owns 900 acres of peaceful hill-farming country. Below Wetton Mill the river bed is dry during periods of low rainfall, when the river vanishes underground to reappear six miles further on below Ilam Hall. Dr Johnson refused to believe this until he had proved it to his satisfaction with marked corks!

Below Beeston Tor the Manifold is joined by the River Hamps, which also runs dry when the water level drops, flowing underground into porous limestone to re-emerge at Ilam. For two miles along the eastern bank of the Hamps the wooded slopes of Old Park Hill, Old Soles Hill and part of Little Wood belong to the Trust.

At Ilam the Manifold turns one of its many loops through Ilam Park. Ilam Hall, a Gothic extravaganza of the 1820s, was partly demolished a century later and what remains is now a youth hostel and a Trust visitor centre. The park and the hanging Hinkley Wood on the far bank of the river are pleasant places to walk, with views to Thorpe Cloud and Bunster Hill, the 'Portals of Dovedale'.

Built up since 1934, the Trust's holding in Dovedale is now over 1,400 acres, and is particularly important in terms of its beauty and popularity. The 'silver shining Dove' – with its west bank in Staffordshire, its east in Derbyshire – has been a place of pilgrimage for anglers since the middle of the seventeenth century when Charles Cotton eulogised it in his poetry and, with his friend Izaak Walton, wrote the *Compleat Angler* (1653). It is fishermen who have given the river its present character, with weirs to slow down and oxygenate the water providing a better habitat for trout and grayling.

Tourists as well as anglers began to include Dovedale in their itineraries, and the building of the railways made access to it easy. The hills are gentle and rolling, the drystone walls dividing them into jigsaw pieces, and the steep gorge of the Dove provides a vivid contrast. The river has carved its way through the soft limestone over the centuries, leaving caves, arches and pinnacles of harder rock as remnants of its former courses and tributaries. A footpath runs beside the river past the extraordinary limestone outcrops weathered into strange shapes.

Like all such rocks in beauty-spots, most of them are named: Lion Face, Lover's Leap, Dovedale Castle, Jacob's Ladder, the Twelve Apostles, Tissington Spires. With the decrease in sheep grazing, these rocks had become obscured by encroaching trees and scrub. The Trust has now cleared enough of the scrub away, revealing the rock formations. Judging the right level of clearance is a delicate matter, especially in an area so rich in nature conservation interest.

Although the dale is inaccessible by car, being crossed by a road only at Milldale, it attracts some two million visitors a year, with the three miles from Thorpe to the Milldale access point being especially popular. The hamlet of Milldale has a medieval packhorse bridge, and, next to it, a small Trust information barn. The Trust's property ends four miles beyond Milldale, past the dry Biggin Dale at the north end of Wolfscote Dale.

Peckover House Cambridgeshire

On north bank of River Nene, in Wisbech

Fluctuations in the coastline of the Wash have removed Wisbech further and further from the sea. Now some twelve miles distant, only 250 years ago the River Nene was navigable into the heart of the town and a substantial port developed on the basis of a thriving trade with the Netherlands. Although the sea traffic has long since died, imposing red-brick merchants' houses still line the river, giving this sleepy little town an elegance and importance out of all proportion to its present status. The influence of trading partners across the North Sea shows in the recurring Dutch gables and hipped roofs and also perhaps in the Friends Meeting House on the banks of the river, a testimony to the religious toleration which marked both countries and which fostered a substantial Quaker community in the town, many of whom, as elsewhere in East Anglia, played prominent roles in local affairs.

One such was Jonathan Peckover, who has given his name to the elegant three-storey Georgian town house overlooking the Nene which he bought in 1777. Five years later, in association with the Gurneys, another leading Quaker family, he established the local bank of Gurney, Birkbeck and Peckover in a wing adjoining the house, from where the business was run for almost a century until the bank merged with Barclays in 1896.

The north façade of Peckover House is more elaborate than the frontage on the River Nene, providing an imposing backdrop to the large Victorian walled garden. (*Michael Warren*)

In contrast to the rather plain exterior, the panelled rooms have fine Georgian fireplaces and a wealth of elaborate wood- and plasterwork by local craftsmen. The decoration includes both neo-classical motifs and more exuberant rococo features, such as the magnificently fluid carving surrounding the mirror above the drawing-room fireplace, with festoons of drapery suspended from an eagle with outstretched wings.

After the built-up river frontage, the spacious two-acre garden comes as something of a surprise, extending well back from the house and also running behind several other buildings along the Nene to the west. This outstanding Victorian survival is an example of the 'gardenesque' style, in which the display of individual plants is as important as the overall effect. An imposing flight of steps with a stone balustrade leads on to a spacious lawn shaded by a number of fine specimen trees, including a ginkgo, a tulip tree, redwoods, a Chusan palm and a monkey puzzle. A dark and bosky wilderness walk marking the eastern perimeter winds through laurels, hollies, box and yew, the bank of unrelieved foliage very different from the bright colour schemes backed by warm red brick in the formal walled area in the middle of the garden. Here

matching borders edged with pinks and studded with cones of roses and clematis flank the central path leading up to a little pool overlooked by a green and white summerhouse. Two topiary peacocks perch on the yew hedge dividing the garden.

Flowering pot plants fill the orangery at the other end of the path in summer and three old orange trees regularly bear fruit. Nearby is the cool green corridor of a fern house, and to the east a series of metal arches are smothered in climbing roses, the most spectacular, known as the Bandstand, carrying a white variety mingled with honeysuckle. A second lawn fills the western third of the garden. Across it, hidden in the trees, is a cats' cemetery, with a recently restored thatched reed barn beyond.

Pembrokeshire Coast Dyfed

Pembrokeshire's lovely coast has a National Park of its own, and within it the Trust is strongly represented. South of the estuary of Milford Haven lies the once-great coastal estate of Stackpole. Formerly part of the Cawdor estate, 2,000 acres of beautiful country of great variety were conveyed to the Trust in 1976. Whilst the core of the property is centred on Stackpole, with about eight miles of coastline, there is also a very fine sand-dune system at Freshwater West, one of the best dune systems in Pembrokeshire.

Stackpole Court (built in 1753 and demolished in 1962) was no great loss, as the superb landscape which surrounded it, part man-made, part natural, has survived. At the end of the eighteenth century, the valley below the house was dammed to make a freshwater lake over three miles long, and a noble eight-arched bridge was built to cross it. A generation later, the two Bosherston valleys were also dammed, the three lakes meeting above the great sandy beach at Broad Haven. One therefore approaches the sea through a man-made wooded landscape, much of it planted 200 years ago. With its miles of lakes and beautiful drives, it is comparable only to one remarkably similar estate also in the Trust's care: Penrose in the south of Cornwall (*see* p.300).

Broad Haven, surrounded by low cliffs, has dunes behind and hard yellow sand before, so there is always shelter from the wind, making it ideal for family outings. To the east is Stackpole Warren, limestone part-covered in blown sand. The close-cropped turf, with some very rare lime-loving plants and lichens, was originally enclosed as a rabbit warren providing meat in winter. The warren runs out to Stackpole Head, where the sweep of the Trust's cliffs to the north-east opens to view, stretching as far as Trewent Point above Freshwater East. Stackpole Warren and the Freshwater Lakes now fall within a designated National Nature Reserve.

Barafundle Bay, tucked in to the east of the headland, is very like Broad Haven but less frequented. Because the visitor has to walk further from the car park, it approaches near perfection, forming a delightful sandy bay. At Stackpole Quay the rock changes from limestone to red sandstone. The little stone pier was used to send away limestone when the quarries were active, and the former farm buildings are now holiday cottages. A disused quarry nearby has recently been developed as a recreational area for mixed-user groups.

St Ann's Head is the western bastion of Milford Haven. On its west side stands Kete, a mile of cliffs and farmland between Long Point and Little Castle Point. From here there are good views to the islands of Skomer and Skokholm and the property is now far more pleasant than it was when the Trust bought the land in 1967. Then it was covered with a mess of concrete: abandoned gun positions which guarded Milford Haven until 1945. Now the landscape is gradually healing after a major reclamation project undertaken by the National Park Authority.

Furthest to the west is the parish of Marloes, with a fine sandy beach linked at low tide to the rocky tongue of Gateholm Island. A mile of Trust-owned cliffs leads to the Deer Park, a heather- and grass-clad headland with an Iron Age fort embankment still evident. Seals breed in the caves beneath and a prostrate form of yellow broom grows on the windswept cliffs. At Martin's Haven, to the north, one embarks for Skomer, passing Midland Island on the way.

Virtually all the north side of St Bride's Bay is owned by the Trust or protected by means of legal covenants. The walk from Newgale to Solva, broken into mile-long sections by the rocky promontories of Dinas Fach and Dinas Fawr, can be hard-going.

The peaceful shores of Solva Creek are succeeded by three more rocky miles to Penpleidiau, with a gap south of St David's, then round the steep Porth Clais inlet (the harbour for the great monastery of St David), west to Porthllysgi Bay and out to the headland of Pen Dal-aderyn, with Ramsey Island just half a mile offshore. The views across to the precipitous coast of Ramsey are exciting, with the tide racing through Ramsey Sound around treacherous rocks disparagingly known as The Bitches. The Trust owns the whole of this Treginnis peninsula, but thereafter only small pieces of cliff until the massive St David's Head (Penmaen Dewi) which is overlooked by the rocky hummock of Carn Llidi. This is a rich site, covered with remains of the people who lived here in prehistoric times, and with a wide variety of grasses, heath and cliff plants, both common and more rare. From Carnedd Lleithir, to the east, there are good views: on a clear day north to Snowdon and west to the hills of Ireland.

Between Abereiddi, four miles to the north-east, and Porthgain is something quite different: a landscape of industrial archaeology. There are slate and stone quarries, an abandoned brickworks, the line of the railway which served them, and, at Porthgain, substantial remains of the harbour from which the products of these works were exported. It is all part of the 200-acre Ynys Barry Farm, acquired in 1985.

Two miles further east is Longhouse Farm, another splendid headland, with a promontory fort, a burial chamber with a great capstone and, tucked in on the east side (in just the same way as Porthgain is tucked under Ynys Barry), the tiny harbour of Abercastle.

Beyond a stretch of private land is the beach of Aber Mawr, with a freshwater marsh behind its pebble ridge and a submerged forest, exposed at low tide. The Trust's land here includes the wooded Aber Mawr valley, rich in birdlife, and Tregwynt home farm, with fields running out to the coast.

Sheltering Fishguard Bay from the west is rocky Strumble Head, where the prominently-placed Tre-seissylt Farm embraces the beaches of Aber Bach and Pwl Crochan. To the east lies the hundred-acre farm of Good Hope, with its craggy cliffs and small fields bounded by old turf and stone hedgebanks.

Across Fishguard Bay itself lies Dinas Island, almost circular in shape and not in fact an island but seeming so, for it is virtually separated from the mainland by a glacial overspill channel which ends as a beach on either side of the headland. Dinas Island Farm sits in the middle of its three miles of lovely coast, with Dinas Head rising 465 feet above it.

A stretch of spectacular coastline at St Elvis, Solva, on the St David's Head peninsula includes two good bathing beaches. (*NT/Martin Trelawny*)

Penrhyn Castle Gwynedd

1 mile east of Bangor, at Llandegai on the A5122

From the long upward climb off the Bangor road there is a sudden view of Penrhyn's great four-storey keep rising above the trees, with battlemented turrets at each corner. The rest of the creeper-clad building stretches away across a bluff for over 200 yards, pierced by round-headed windows and with an impressive array of towers, battlements and crenellations. The interior is even more overwhelming, with long stone-flagged corridors, high ceilings, heavy doors and panelling and a wealth of carved stone surrounding arches and doors and forming bosses, corbels, friezes and capitals. A strange population looks down from the forest of slender pillars creating blind arcades on the walls of the extraordinary staircase. Each head is different. Here is a bearded wild man, there an elf with pointed ears, somewhere else a gargoyle with interlocking teeth. Look carefully and what appears to be writhing foliage becomes a contorted face. At the foot of the staircase a semicircle of hands echoes the curve of the door into the drawing-room. Another opening leads into the galleried great hall, where Romanesque arches soar heavenwards like the transept of a cathedral. In the evening the polished limestone flags of the floor are warmed by pools of multi-coloured light from the recessed stained-glass windows.

Penrhyn is a late Georgian masterpiece, the outstanding product of a shortlived neo-Norman revival. Designed by Thomas Hopper, a fashionable architect who had been employed by the Prince Regent to build a Gothic conservatory at Carlton House, it was commissioned in 1820 by G.H. Dawkins Pennant to replace the neo-Gothic house by Samuel Wyatt he had inherited from his uncle. Whereas Richard Pennant had the benefit of a fortune made from Jamaican estates (as a result of which he strongly opposed the abolition of the slave trade), his nephew built lavishly on the profits of the Penrhyn slate quarries, exporting over 12,000 tons a year by 1792. A slate billiard table with cluster-column legs in the library and the grotesque slate bed weighing over a ton echo the basis of his prosperity.

G.H. Dawkins Pennant seems to have allowed his architect ample funds for building the castle and also for decorating and furnishing the rooms. As a result, Penrhyn is uniquely all of a piece. In the oppressive Ebony Room, original green and red curtains and upholstery and faded red damask wall hangings give some relief from the black ebony furniture and the black surrounds to the fireplace and doorways. Huge plantain leaves on the fire-screen recall the Jamaican estates. Here, too, is Dieric Bouts's (d.1475) delightful painting of St Luke sketching the Virgin and Child, the arches behind the apostle framing a sylvan landscape with a walled city. In the much lighter drawing-room next door, mirrors at either end reflect two immense metalwork candelabra.

The house was greatly enriched in the mid-nineteenth century by the Spanish, Italian and Dutch paintings collected by Colonel Douglas Pennant, 1st Baron Penrhyn, including a Canaletto of the Thames at Westminster, Rembrandt's portrait of a plain, middle-aged merchant's wife, and Palma Vecchio's *Holy Family*. His son commissioned the elaborate brass King's Bed for a visit by Edward VII when Prince of Wales in 1894. A lighter note is struck by the collection of dolls from all over the world now displayed in the stables. A museum of industrial locomotives associated with the slate industry also accommodated here includes *Charles*, a saddle tank engine that once worked the railway serving the Penrhyn family's quarries, and *Fire Queen*, built in 1848 for the Padarn Railway.

The siting of Penrhyn is superb, with views south to Snowdonia and the slate quarry like a great bite out of the hills and north over Beaumaris Bay to Anglesey. A west-facing terraced walled garden sloping steeply into a valley below the castle shelters many tender shrubs and plants, including magnolias, camellias and azaleas and the fuchsias smothering a pergola halfway down. Tasmanian ferns, palms and huge patches of gunnera grow luxuriantly in the bog garden created in the 1930s at the lowest level, and a metasequoia and a maidenhair tree are two of the fine specimen trees seen throughout the grounds, with several examples of the large evergreens popular in the nineteenth century mixed with mature beeches and oaks. A carpet of daffodils covering the slope above the drive to the entrance lodge in spring is matched by the display of snowdrops on the grass above the walled garden. From here one of the paths back to the castle passes a ruined Gothic chapel placed as an eyecatcher on a prominent knoll, a row of headstones in the dogs' cemetery at its feet commemorating Annette, Suzette, Wanda and other pets.

The neo-Norman staircase at Penrhyn Castle, smothered in decoration. (*NT/Jeremy Whitaker*)

Penshaw Monument Tyne & Wear

Halfway between Sunderland and Chester-le-Street, east of the A183

Conspicuously sited on a hilltop, and visible for miles around, this roofless classical temple surveys the grim industrial landscape of Tyneside, its honey-coloured sandstone blackened and sombre. Some hundred feet long and fifty feet wide, this impressive eyecatcher was the work of local architects John and Benjamin Green and was erected from 1844 to commemorate the radical statesman John George Lambton, 1st Earl of Durham, onetime Governor General of Canada, who had died four years earlier.

The Pepperbox Wiltshire

5 miles south-east of Salisbury, on north side of the A36

A steep rutted track off the A36 leads to the long tongue of Brickworth Down and this red-brick octagonal three-storey tower, with a weathervane crowning the pyramidal slate roof. Built by Giles

Eyre in 1606, the Pepperbox may be the earliest folly in England, or it may have been intended as a viewpoint from which ladies could follow the hunt in comfort. The windows of the room at the top of the tower have now been bricked in – and so have the open arches on the ground floor – but the views are still magnificent, the vista north-west taking in the soaring spire of Salisbury Cathedral.

Petworth House West Sussex

In centre of Petworth

A luminous landscape in the Red Room at Petworth shows the park at sunset, dark clumps of trees throwing long shadows over the lake, a stag drinking from the water in the foreground, its antlers silhouetted against the dying sun. Turner was inspired by 'Capability' Brown's masterpiece, one of the greatest man-made landscapes created in eighteenth-century Europe. Over a thousand deer graze beneath Brown's clumps of beeches, chestnuts and oaks, now seen in their splendid maturity and still impressive despite the fact that some 600 trees were brought down in the freak storm in the autumn of 1987. Trees still frame Brown's serpentine lake dominating the view from the west front and crown the ridges shading imperceptibly into Sussex downland. Far in the distance on the north-west horizon is the outline of a turreted Gothick folly, possibly designed by John Soane.

Brown's sublime landscape encloses a jewel of a house, a magnificent late seventeenth-century baroque palace filled with an exceptional collection of works of art, including fine furniture, *objets d'art* and sculpture as well as paintings. Seen from across the park, Petworth's great west front, some 300 feet long, looks as if it could have been modelled on a French château. It was the creation of the unlikeable Charles Seymour, 6th Duke of Somerset (the Proud Duke), who set about remodelling the manor house of the Earls of Northumberland on his marriage to the 11th and last Earl's daughter. The Seymour family symbol – a pair of angel's wings – is ostentatiously displayed over every window. Although only two seventeenth-century interiors survive intact, these fully reflect Charles Seymour's vanity

(*Left*) The octagonal brick eyecatcher known as the Pepperbox crowning Brickworth Down may be the earliest folly in England. (*NT/Fay Godwin*)

(*Top*) J. M. W. Turner's atmospheric *A Stag Drinking* is one of two paintings of Petworth Park commissioned by the 3rd Earl of Egremont, who also created the north gallery (*above*) to display the collection of classical and contemporary sculpture acquired by his father and himself. (*NT/John Webb, NT/Andreas von Einsiedel*)

and self-importance. The major feature of the florid baroque chapel is the family pew filling the west end. Supported by classical columns, it is surmounted by carved and painted drapery on which angels bear the Duke's arms and coronet to heaven. By contrast, the coldly formal marble hall with its black and white chequered floor must have quelled the spirits of those few visitors thought worthy to set foot in the Proud Duke's house.

As well as remodelling the house, Charles Seymour added to the art collection established by the Earls of Northumberland, which included a series of portraits by Van Dyck and works by Titian and Elsheimer. And he commissioned Grinling Gibbons to produce the limewood carvings of flowers, foliage, birds and classical vases which now cascade down the walls of the Carved Room, and Louis Laguerre to paint the Grand Staircase.

On the Proud Duke's death, the estate passed by marriage to the Wyndham family, and it was Charles Wyndham, 2nd Earl of Egremont, who employed Brown to landscape the park. A cultivated man who had profited from the Grand Tour and time in the diplomatic service, he was largely responsible for Petworth's collection of Italian, French and Dutch Old Masters. He also amassed the wealth of ancient sculpture from Greece and Rome, now of particular importance as one of only three such collections of the period to have survived intact. It includes the sensitive sculptured head fashioned in the fourth century BC known as the Leconfield Aphrodite and some good Roman portrait busts and copies of Greek originals. His son, the 3rd Earl, further enriched the house by patronising contemporary British artists. Best known as the patron of Turner, for whom he arranged a studio at Petworth, the 3rd Earl also acquired works by Gainsborough, Reynolds, Fuseli and Zoffany. And he added the fine early nineteenth-century north gallery where he augmented his father's sculpture collection with works by English contemporaries such as Sir Richard Westmacott and John Rossi, and the Irish sculptor J. E. Carew. One of the most striking pieces is the vividly fluid representation of St Michael and Satan by John Flaxman, finished in 1826, the year in which the sculptor died. Except for the spear which St Michael is about to plunge into his grovelling adversary, this powerful work, which cost the 3rd Earl £3,500, was all carved from one piece of marble.

Brown's pleasure grounds to the north-west of the house, also extensively damaged in 1987, are a striking contrast to the park. Serpentine paths wind through a thickly wooded rectangle planted with rare trees and shrubs, including tender rhododendrons, a pocket-handkerchief tree, a tulip tree and purple-leafed maples, its boundaries echoing a vanished Elizabethan layout. A little Doric temple was probably moved here when the pleasure grounds were created, but the Ionic rotunda, perhaps designed by Matthew Brettingham, was introduced by Brown. Here, too, are some of the carved seventeenth-century urns on pedestals which the 3rd Earl placed strategically in the gardens and park.

Philipps House Wiltshire

In Dinton, 9 miles west of Salisbury, on north side of the B3089

This severe neo-classical house in the Vale of Wardour was designed by Jeffry Wyatt (later Sir Jeffry Wyatville), better known for his work in the neo-Gothic style and particularly for his alterations to Windsor Castle. Philipps House, built between 1814–17, does not show this versatile architect at his most inspired. Built of local Chilmark limestone, from the same quarry that had produced the stone for Salisbury Cathedral 600 years previously, it is a plain two-storey rectangle with rows of sash windows and a parapet concealing the hipped roof, the only notable feature being a pedimented portico rising the height of the building on the south façade. A curved kitchen wing curling away from the house adds a welcome touch of asymmetry.

Wyatt's interiors are similarly austere and unadorned, the fine mahogany doors and marble chimneypieces restrained and stylised. His coolly elegant staircase, top-lit from a circular lantern, rises through the heart of the house, the grand lower flight sweeping imperiously upwards from the centre of the hall to divide at a half-landing into two parallel stairs to the first floor. Brass outlets in the flags of the hall below are remnants of the original underfloor heating system, installed in the 1820s.

The house was created for William Wyndham IV, whose family had been at Dinton since 1689 and were to live here until 1917. The undulating parkland landscaped in the eighteenth century contains some fine specimen trees, including a noble Spanish chestnut that was mature in 1700.

The early seventeenth-century Pitstone Windmill surveys a very twentieth-century skyline. (*NT/P. Lacey*)

Pitstone Windmill Buckinghamshire

½ mile south of Ivinghoe, 3 miles north-east of Tring, just west of the B488

This fascinating little building bearing the date 1627 is Britain's oldest post mill, an example of the earliest form of windmill that was developed in the Middle Ages. Unlike later mills, such as those at Bembridge or High Ham (*see* pp.26 and 150), the sails are brought into the wind by turning the building as a whole, rather than by simply revolving the cap on the top of the mill.

Pitstone's two-storey timber body, reached by a ladder, is perched some eight feet above the ground on a massive wooden post, the lower half of which is enclosed in a brick roundhouse. The building projects alarmingly on either side of its support, as if it might topple over at any moment. The tail pole sweeping down to the ground – a long beam with a wheel on the end – acted as a lever for turning the mill.

Two pairs of grinding stones, one for producing coarse meal and the other for fine white flour, are now in working order, but the mill cannot at present be turned into the wind.

Plas Newydd Anglesey

1 mile south-west of Llanfairpwll and the A5 on the A4080; 2½ miles from the Menai Bridge, 5 miles from Bangor

'I tried repeatedly in vain . . . to get some use made of my drawing.' So Rex Whistler explained his decision to join the Welsh Guards in 1940. Four years later he was dead, at the early age of thirty-nine. Fortunately for all who visit Plas Newydd, the house is full of works by this talented artist, who spent some of his happiest and most creative hours

Rex Whistler's sweeping mural at Plas Newydd is full of delightful detail, including portraits of the family dogs and Lady Anglesey's book and spectacles. (*NT/Erik Pelham*)

here. His epic mural dominating the dining-room, a dramatic view across choppy waters to an Italianate town 'bristling with spires, domes and columns' set at the foot of wild and craggy mountains, echoes Plas Newydd's own romantic position, looking over the Menai Strait to Snowdonia and north up the water to Robert Stephenson's Britannia Bridge.

Reproductions of Whistler's massive work never capture the sweep and scale of the composition or the wealth of detail it contains, with plentiful allusions to buildings the artist had seen on his continental travels and to the family of his patron, the 6th Marquess of Anglesey. Every corner is

meticulously executed. At the far end of the *trompe-l'oeil* colonnade on the left-hand side people are going about their business in a steep street running up from the water. Two women gossip; an old lady climbs slowly upward with the help of a stick; a boy steals an apple from a tub of fruit outside a shop; a girl leans out of an upstairs window to talk to a young man below. The artist himself appears in the colonnade sweeping up leaves (*see* p.vi).

The exhibition of Whistler's work in the room next door shows the range of his talent. Here are his illustrations for *Gulliver's Travels*, examples of costume and stage designs, bookplates and caricatures, and rebus letters he sent to the 6th Marquess's young son. Here, too, are drawings he did as a child, the horror of those inspired by the First World War heralding his own experiences some twenty years later. A painting of Lord Anglesey's family grouped informally in the music-room is one of many examples of Whistler's skill at portraiture, his sensitive studies of the Marquess's eldest daughter Lady Caroline, eight years Whistler's junior, suggesting a particular sympathy between artist and sitter.

Whistler's mural was part of Lord Anglesey's extensive changes to Plas Newydd in the 1930s. He and his wife converted the house into one of the most comfortable of their day, following the 6th Marquess's maxim that 'every bathroom should have a bedroom', and employed Sybil Colefax to create Lady Anglesey's feminine pink and white bedroom, furnished with a white carpet, muslin curtains and bedhangings and with a pink ribbon setting off the white bedspread. The long saloon with a view over the Menai Strait to Snowdon is also much as the 6th Marquess and his wife arranged it, with two large comfortable settees either side of the fire and four pastoral landscapes by Ommeganck dominating the pictures.

Architecturally, Plas Newydd is an intriguing and uncompromising mixture of classical and Gothick, largely the result of late eighteenth-century alterations by James Wyatt and Joseph Potter of Lichfield for the 1st Earl of Uxbridge. The classical staircase leading to a screen of Doric columns on the first floor and Wyatt's bold white friezes set against blue and red in the anteroom and octagon are a world apart from the fan vaulting in the hall, with elaborate bosses at the intersection of the ribs. This stately room rising through two storeys with a gallery at one end opens into the even more splendid Gothick music-room, probably on the site of the great hall of the original sixteenth-century manor built by the powerful Griffith family and the largest room in the house.

An early artificial limb and mud-spattered Hussar trousers recall the 1st Earl's son, created 1st Marquess of Anglesey for his heroism at the Battle of Waterloo, where he lost a leg, and also remarkable for his eighteen children and seventy-three grandchildren. Other members of the family gaze down from a wealth of portraits, including works by Hoppner, Romney and Lawrence and a Grand Tour painting of the 1st Earl, a rather plump young man in a salmon coat. Many of these came from Beaudesert, the family's Staffordshire house dismantled in 1935, which was also the source of some of the superb furniture.

Plas Newydd is first seen from above, when the path leading down from the carpark suddenly reveals the Gothick west front covered in red creeper and magnolia. The house is set off by sweeping lawns and magnificent woodland, many of the fine sycamores, beeches and oaks predating the planting undertaken with Humphry Repton's advice. Exotics thrive in the mild, wet climate and fertile soil, belts of trees to the south of the house sheltering azaleas, magnolias, Japanese maples and rhododendrons, including a number of hybrids introduced from Bodnant (*see* p.37). Formal terraced gardens are adorned with a Venetian wellhead and Italianate urns, suggesting a warmer sun than that which reddens the peaks on the far side of the water in the evening.

Plas-yn-Rhiw Gwynedd

12 miles from Pwllheli, on south coast road to Aberdaron

The long Llŷn peninsula sheltering Cardigan Bay from the full force of the Atlantic is a windswept claw of craggy moorland and tiny fields. Only in the far south-east is there shelter enough for woodland to thrive, protected by the 1,000-foot tor of Mynydd-y-Graig (*see* p.183). Below the hill, looking east over the bay, is Plas-yn-Rhiw, with a Georgian frontage hiding a much older building behind and views to Cadair Idris and south along the coast to Fishguard. On clear nights the lights of Aberystwyth beckon across the water. Even when there is a gale in the little village up the hill, it is quiet here, with a range of native and exotic plants flourishing in the mild maritime climate.

Granite walls seven to eight feet thick in the tiny parlour and the remains of a stone spiral staircase are survivals of a Tudor building on this site. As the date stone on the front of the house proclaims, it was first extended in 1634; two wings built into the hillside, Georgian sash windows and the slate-floored Victorian verandah were additions of the mid-eighteenth and early nineteenth centuries, turning the farmhouse into a gentleman's residence.

Plas-yn-Rhiw's homely interiors reflect the three forceful and indomitable Keating sisters, Eileen, Lorna and Honora, daughters of a successful Nottinghamshire architect, who bought the property in 1938 and lovingly restored it after almost twenty years of neglect. A white hat and gloves lie neatly on the patchwork quilt covering one of the simple wooden beds. A shoe rack is filled with Honora's fashionable footwear from her days in London and a successful career in the social

Looking east from Plas-yn-Rhiw, with clipped box edging thickly planted beds in the foreground and the golden sand of Porth Neigwl Bay a long streak in the distance. (*NT/Martin Trelawny*)

services. Elegant Georgian chairs, fur coats and a stole speak of comfortable gentility, and an extensive collection of popular classics suggests many evenings spent listening to the old gramophone in the parlour. Gentle watercolours hanging three and four deep on the stairs, their muted colours recording local views and landmarks, recall Honora's days at the Slade and her youthful ambition to be an artist.

The little terraced garden sloping down towards the sea, with thickly planted beds framed by box hedges, dates from the 1820s. Tender and exotic species thrive here, such as the gnarled old fig shadowing one corner of the house and the red-blossomed callistemon from Australia. Tree-like magnolias flower pale pink at the end of March and in summer the garden is crimson with a profusion of fuchsias, a source of pollen for the bees which traditionally nest under the eaves. Rough meadow grass and woodland behind the house are bright with snowdrops and bluebells in the early months of the year.

Still a legend in the neighbourhood, the sisters worked tirelessly to protect the natural beauty of the peninsula. They were often seen wrapped up warmly against the Atlantic gales, tramping the lanes to check on rubbish tips and illegal caravan sites. Fiercely outspoken in defence of their beliefs, the Keatings were personally self-effacing, little realising that the words with which they chose to honour their parents – 'there is no death while memory lives' – would serve as their own memorial.

Plym Bridge Woods Devon

3½ miles north-east of Plymouth

From Shaugh Bridge the River Plym runs south for five miles to Plym Bridge. The upper part of this section, Bickleigh Vale, is dominated by the sprawling modern barracks of the Royal Marines at Bickleigh. The lower part, for a mile and a half above Plym Bridge, is owned by the Trust, and a recent acquisition has extended this ownership for a further half mile below the bridge.

As on the high moor (*see below*), and again at Goodameavy (*see* p.129), the steeply wooded slopes of this very beautiful valley are packed with archaeological remains, most of them relics of the industries carried on here from the seventeenth century onwards.

Slates from Cann Quarry, like all long-abandoned quarries a lovely place, were used to roof Plympton Grammar School in 1664, where Sir Joshua Reynolds was later educated. Early in the nineteenth century a canal was made from here to Marsh Mills at the head of the Plym estuary. It was quickly superseded by a railway built on its towpath, and it is to trace the remains of three railways that industrial historians swarm here. The Plymouth and Dartmoor Railway was opened in 1823 to take lime, coal, timber and sand up to the moor, returning with stone and peat. The Cann Quarry Railway followed in 1834. The tracks of both these railways were removed for scrap in 1916, though many granite and slate sleepers remain. Finally the line from Plymouth to Tavistock, opened in 1859 and closed as recently as 1962, its great Cann viaduct far too solid to demolish, still strides across the narrow Plym valley.

The Trust has preserved not only these historic relics but also an invaluable lung for the people of Plymouth, for large industrial estates of high-tech factories have erupted on this north-east side of the city, with much new housing. To descend from these new landscapes into the peace of the valley and to walk, to bathe, to sleep in the sun on the shingle banks of the river is a much valued privilege.

Plym Head to Cadover Bridge

Devon

Along the River Plym, between Plym Head and Cadover Bridge

The Trust owns land in four sections of the delightful River Plym, each very different in character. The river rises at Plym Head, 1,500 feet up, below Great Gnat's Head on the high ground which dominates this southern part of Dartmoor. It runs south-west off the moor and nearly all the moorland on its left bank, 3,300 acres, belongs to the Trust for five miles down to Blacka Brook Foot, near Cadover Bridge. The rock is granite except in one place, at Shavercombe, where a shaley slate has intruded, creating a step in the stream and a waterfall.

At a casual glance this is simply peaty moorland, covered with heather and purple moorgrass, and in the wetter places with bog cotton, sphagnum moss, bog pimpernel, bog asphodel, sundew and lesser spearwort. The common birds are the birds of high open ground – meadow pipit, wheatear, skylark – and in the rougher places stonechats with ravens and crows quarrelling overhead. But all is not as it seems, for three 'warrens' into which the area is divided, Hentor Warren, Willings Walls Warren and Trowlesworthy Warren, have preserved a historic landscape of the greatest interest and rarity.

The reason for its survival is twofold. Man began to live and farm here in about 2500BC. The climate then was kinder, and he preferred to live on the uplands rather than in the dangerous undrained wooded valleys below, with wild animals and unhealthy conditions. By the time the climate became less hospitable the inhabitants possessed sufficient knowledge to move down into the valleys, clear and drain them, and cultivate their better soils. The moor was then left largely unoccupied until medieval times, perhaps from the twelfth century, when the three great rabbit warrens were constructed. This productive use of otherwise unproductive land continued well into this century,

the warrener at Trowlesworthy being the last in a very long line.

Mounds of soil and stone were thrown up, drained by a perimeter ditch, to make buries in which the rabbits lived and bred, being harvested for their flesh and fur. The warrener's chief job was to protect them from their natural enemies, weasel and stoat, and substantial traces remain of stone vermin traps, operated with a sliding shutter on the principle of the modern cage trap and surprisingly effective.

The use of land for rabbit warrens left the traces of prehistoric man largely undisturbed, as does its present use as rough grazing for sheep, cattle and ponies. The lay visitor may need help to recognise the several concentrations of ruined huts, burial chambers, cairns, small enclosures and the long stone rows whose purpose is still uncertain. Overlying these are the patterns of later land boundaries, marked by reeves, banks stretching for miles over the moor.

The best way to see this remarkable place is to organise two cars, leaving one at Cadover Bridge and driving another to White Works, an abandoned china-clay pit south-east of Princetown. From here it is two miles of rough walking to Plym Head, skirting Fox Tor Mire. The walk is down the valley, with detours into the side valleys, the Langcombe, Shavercombe and Hentor Brooks, and past the romantically named Spanish Lake.

Polesden Lacey Surrey

5 miles west of Dorking, 1½ miles south of Great Bookham, off the A246 Leatherhead–Guildford road

Polesden Lacey is alive with the spirit of Mrs Ronald Greville, captured so well in the vivacious and charming portrait which now greets visitors in the hall. Those invited to the famous weekend parties held here from 1906 until the outbreak of the Second World War included Indian maharajahs, literary figures such as Beverley Nichols, Osbert Sitwell and Harold Nicolson, and prominent politicians of the day. Edward VII was a close friend of the elegant society hostess, and the future George VI and Queen Elizabeth were lent Polesden Lacey for part of their honeymoon in 1923.

Polesden Lacey is a comfortable two-storey building sprawling round a courtyard, its large white sash windows standing out attractively against yellow stucco. The flavour of the Regency

The grounds of Polesden Lacey are laid out in a spacious Edwardian style, with sweeping expanses of grass and fine beeches, sweet chestnuts and other trees. (*NT*)

villa built in the 1820s by Joseph Bonsor to the designs of Thomas Cubitt still lingers on the south front with its classical colonnade, but the house was subsequently much enlarged and the interior transformed after 1906 by the architects of the Ritz Hotel, an essential step in the realisation of Mrs Greville's social ambitions. Here she displayed her outstanding collection of paintings, furniture and other works of art, the nucleus of which she had inherited from her wealthy father, William McEwan, founder of the Scottish brewery which still bears his name.

The range and richness of the collection, including Flemish tapestries, French and English furniture, English, continental and oriental pottery and porcelain, and European paintings from the fourteenth to the eighteenth centuries, gives Polesden Lacey its extraordinarily opulent atmosphere, vividly evoking the charmed life of the Edwardian upper classes. Some of the finest pieces were intended for very different settings. In the sumptuously decorated drawing-room glittering mirrors reflect carved and gilt panelling that once adorned an Italian palace. A richly carved oak reredos in the hall, a masterpiece by Edward Pearce, was originally intended for Sir Christopher Wren's St Matthew's just off Cheapside in London, demolished in 1881. From her father Mrs Greville inherited some Dutch seventeenth-century paintings, but she herself acquired most of the English portraits in the dining-room, such as Raeburn's charming study of George and Maria Stewart as children, the little girl holding a rabbit in the folds of her dress, and much of the cream of the collection in the corridor round the central courtyard. The pictures hanging here include an exquisite early fourteenth-century triptych of the Madonna and Child among several early Italian works, sixteenth-century portraits in the style of Corneille de Lyon and a number of atmospheric Dutch interiors and landscapes, such as Jacob van Ruisdael's skyscape of the Zuider Zee, diminutive figures on the shore dwarfed by wintry grey clouds piled overhead.

Invitation cards, scrap albums and other mementoes in the billiard-room and smoking-room conjure up the world in which Mrs Greville lived. The menu book records the salade niçoise and orange mousse on which Ramsay MacDonald dined on 17 October 1936, and the aubergines provençales given to the Queen of Spain the following day. The same names appear again and again in the visitors'

book and the same faces recur in the photographs, statesmen and royalty, such as Grand Duke Michael of Russia and Kaiser Wilhelm II, rubbing shoulders with figures from the worlds of entertainment and literature, a memorable shot showing Mrs Greville in Hollywood with Wendy Barrie and Spencer Tracy.

The atmosphere of the house extends into the garden, where spacious lawns shaded with fine beeches, cedars and limes suggest long idle summer days. Although much of the layout is a twentieth-century creation, the impressive long terraced walk, with magnificent views across the valley to the heights of Ranmore Common (*see* p.272), is a legacy from the years when Polesden Lacey was the home of the playwright Richard Brinsley Sheridan. A series of more intimate walled and hedged enclosures in what was the old kitchen garden to the west of the house include an iris garden filled with varieties popular in Edwardian times and a collection of lavenders. The rose garden centred on an Italianate marble wellhead is much larger, planted with over forty traditional and more modern varieties and with Edwardian ramblers shading the pergola walks between the beds. Mrs Greville's garden ornaments are everywhere, from the griffins on the terrace in front of the house to vases, urns and sundials placed as eyecatchers at strategic points and the statue of Diana crowning the rock garden. Mrs Greville herself lies in a yew-hedged tomb near the rose garden.

Powis Castle Powys

1 mile south of Welshpool, on the A483

Some time around 1200 the Welsh princes of Powis began building their new stronghold on this splendid defensive site, a great outcrop of limestone plunging steeply to the south with panoramic views over the River Severn to the hills of Shropshire. Although long since converted to a country house, Powis still has the trappings of a castle. Seen from across the valley, a massive Norman-style keep with three projecting towers rises to a battlemented skyline. To the left stretches the curtain wall which defended the inner bailey, now the ballroom range flanking the entrance court. In front of the castle grand baroque terraces blasted out of the rock fall to a vast expanse of lawn.

A wide flight of steps closely guarded by twin

drum towers leads up from the entrance court to a Gothic archway. The front door opens into another world, with magnificent interiors fitted out for William Herbert, 3rd Lord Powis, 1st Earl, Marquess and titular Duke, a staunch supporter of the Stuart cause who spent his last years in exile with James II. The most remarkable of his formal apartments, possibly designed by the gentleman-architect William Winde, is the state bedroom, decorated with a profusion of gilt in the 1660s and 1680s. A deep alcove is almost filled with the canopied state bed adorned with rich red hangings and gilt cresting and separated from the rest of the room by a finely carved balustrade. The only one of its kind in Britain, this barrier is a direct link with the formal etiquette of Louis XIV's Versailles, closely imitated by the English aristocracy. Velvet-covered furniture, a painted ceiling and rich tapestries contribute to the opulent effect. A huge and much more

accomplished ceiling by Antonio Verrio, based on Veronese's *Apotheosis of Venice*, with an assembly of deities seated on clouds, dominates the 1st Marquess's grand staircase.

No hint of this pomposity permeates the beautiful T-shaped long gallery, the only surviving Elizabethan interior dating from Sir Edward Herbert's acquisition of the castle in 1587. Young trees and tendrils of foliage branch across the plasterwork ceiling above the rather indifferent family portraits set against early seventeenth-century *trompe-l'oeil* panelling and the polished silver sconces forming pools of light down the room. A table carries a more than life-size marble cat, crouched aggressively over the body of a snake, ears pricked as it looks back over its shoulder, teeth bared, muscles rippling beneath its fur. This remarkable ancient Roman sculpture, perhaps modelled on a wild animal, came to Powis through the marriage of the daughter of

A lead shepherdess dances on one of the terraces at Powis, framed by Japanese wisteria and white roses.
(*NT/Ian Shaw*)

the house to the eldest son of Clive of India in 1784. The Clive Museum now adjoins the curiously elongated ballroom (originally almost twice as long), commissioned from T. F. Pritchard in 1775, in the range flanking the courtyard. Exotic cases filled with glittering gold suggest immense wealth, Indian curiosities acquired by the Great Nabob and his son, who was Governor of Madras, including jewelled slippers that once adorned the feet of Tipu Sahib, Sultan of Mysore, a gold tiger's head from his throne, a jewelled hookah encrusted with rubies, diamonds and emeralds, and sumptuously decorated padded armour. The tone is set for this exotic display by the richly coloured mid-seventeenth-century tapestry filling one wall of the ballroom, showing an embassy to Cairo or Istanbul. A potentate on a gold couch greets the ambassador against the backdrop of an eastern city peppered with onion domes, trees peeping over the walls suggesting hidden gardens.

Powis's splendid Italiante terraces, hanging over the valley below, are a fine example of late seventeenth-century taste. Who designed them and when is not known for certain, but it is likely they date from 1680s and were the inspiration of William Winde, who created similar features at Cliveden (*see* p.77), with some of the work being carried out by the French gardener Adrian Duval in the early years of the eighteenth century. Sadly, nothing remains of a contemporary water garden. Decorated with lead statues and urns and planted with clipped yews clustered closely below the castle, some lapping the terraces as if about to flow downhill, the three levels form a giant staircase descending the rock. Rare and tender plants flourish on the south-facing walls, which are hung with wistaria, magnolia and roses. These lime-tolerant species contrast with those planted in the wilderness laid out in the eighteenth century on the ridge across the valley, where the soil is acid. Here there are panoramic views of the castle from winding wooded walks through oaks, yews, rhododendrons and cedars. The formal garden by the Edwardian dower house below the castle, bordered with pyramid apple trees and crossed by a vine-covered pergola, dates from the early years of this century, when Violet Lane-Fox, wife of the 4th Earl, did much to improve the grounds. At the lowest point clipped yews like crinolined ladies look over the pond and sundial in the Fountain Garden.

The castle is surrounded by a magnificent wooded medieval deer park, its naturalistic contours and planting partly reflecting alterations by 'Capability' Brown's disciple, William Emes, who was engaged to landscape it in 1771 and diverted a public road away from the castle. Although most of the great beeches, sycamores and limes were planted between 1800 and 1850, some of the massive ancient oaks for which Powis has long been famous – and which Admiral Rodney insisted were used for the navy at the end of the eighteenth century – may be as much as 800 years old.

Priest's House   Northamptonshire

In Easton on the Hill, 2 miles south-west of Stamford, off the A43

This little two-storey stone building, with fireplaces to warm the chambers on both floors, predates the mid-sixteenth-century Reformation which turned the Church upside down. Originally intended for celibate clergy, it would have been lived in by married priests after the Reformation and was subsequently superseded by the handsome Georgian rectory standing nearby. A small museum illustrating village life in the past is housed on the upper floor.

Priest's House   Somerset

In Muchelney, 1½ miles south of Langport

The Somerset hamlet of Muchelney, once set on an island in the marshes of Sedgemoor, boasts a clutch of medieval buildings. On one side of the fine fifteenth-century church are the remains of the abbey of Muchelney, perhaps founded as early as the seventh century and the oldest in the county after Glastonbury. On the other, facing the church across a diminutive green, is this thatched stone cottage, built by the monks of the abbey in 1308 to house the vicar of the parish. Like Alfriston (*see* p.4), which it resembled in plan, this priest's house was no mean dwelling, even before it was modernised in the early sixteenth century. Although the interior has been much altered and the hall that once rose to the roof in the centre of the house is now floored over, the exterior still displays original features: a Gothic doorway, mullioned windows and the magnificent two-tiered window to the hall, with trefoil heads to the upper lights.

A Gothic doorway and mullioned windows mark the medieval priest's house at Muchelney, which faces across a tiny green to the church of St Peter and St Paul. (*NT/ Fay Godwin*)

Princes Risborough Manor House Buckinghamshire

Opposite church, off market square in Princes Risborough town centre

Sir Peter Lely, court painter to Charles II, once owned this elegant late seventeenth-century L-shaped red-brick house across a lane from St Mary's church. A little walled courtyard sets off the dignified five-bay entrance façade, with brick pilasters separating the long sash windows, a pedimented central doorway and three dormers in the roof. A Jacobean staircase with an openwork balustrade cut

from solid oak rises from the entrance hall and there is good eighteenth-century panelling in the drawing-room.

Prior Park Avon

Ralph Allen Drive, Bath

On the south-east edge of Bath, within walking distance of the city, is a secluded pastoral valley, rising with dramatic steepness to the heights of Claverton and Combe Downs. Just below the crest of the hill, strung out along the skyline, is a Palladian mansion (not National Trust) of impressive size designed by John Wood, with a porticoed central block linked by low balustrades to equally weighty pavilions on either side. When built, in 1740, this was the longest house in England. Below, a gentle curve of meadow following the contours of the combe sweeps down to a chain of stepped ponds, with a serene Palladian bridge sitting above the first of the cascades that links one level to another. Woodland on the slopes to either side, a mosaic of beech and yew, ash and larch, fences the valley in. This is a composition that works on two scales. The valley itself is small and intimate, but its dramatic setting, high above Bath, gives views out over a much wider landscape, looking across the Avon to the curving Georgian terraces which are contemporary with the house.

Developed between 1734 and 1764, Prior Park is one of the most important survivals of eighteenth-century landscape art, showing, in just thirty years, the evolution from an earlier taste for more formal layouts to the kind of highly contrived naturalism favoured by 'Capability' Brown, one of the two major figures linked with the scheme, and the artful use of a borrowed landscape. It was the creation of Ralph Allen, one of the big men of Georgian Bath. A Cornishman who made a fortune in postal distribution, Allen used his wealth to buy land around Bath, including the Combe Down quarries which

provided stone for the Georgian city. The story goes that his great house at the top of the combe, for 'all of Bath to see and to see all of Bath', was partly a statement, an advertisement for the golden lime-stone which his quarries produced.

The valley garden below the house became more extensive as the years passed. Allen's first layout, extending only about halfway down the combe, was a formal design, with a gradually narrowing, straight-sided stretch of grass framed by urns and hedges focusing on a round pond. Beyond the hedge to the east there was probably a kitchen garden; to the west, with the help of the poet Alexander Pope, who had a similar feature in his garden at Twickenham, then a fashionable Thames-side retreat outside London, Allen laid out a wooded Wilderness area, with shady serpentine paths running through thick shrubbery past a series of surprises, among them a serpentine lake curving round the hillside, a grotto (for Mrs Allen), a rustic sham bridge, and a fine cascade. In the 1750s, Allen extended the garden down the combe, damming the stream to create the three ponds and adding the

Prior Park, showing the Palladian bridge being restored and Ralph Allen's great house at the head of the valley.
(*NT/Chris King*)

Palladian bridge. Now one of only three surviving in England, the bridge was probably designed by Richard Jones, Allen's Clerk of Works, as a direct copy of the earlier one at Wilton House (the third is at Stowe, *see* p.320). Trees were planted to frame a new cascade below the pond, a Gothic temple was built on the edge of the Wilderness, and there was a general softening of the woodland outline. Only ten to fifteen years later, before the new plantings would have had time to grow up, let alone mature, the naturalisation was taken a step further. On the advice of 'Capability' Brown, who visited Prior Park in the early 1760s, the formal pond and its setting were swept away and the woods given their present, gently swelling contours. The Wilderness, though, hidden away in its wood, was left alone.

Apart from the drive driven through the Wilderness in 1834 by the then owner, Bishop Baines, who also added the double flight of urn-studded steps descending from the portico, and the filling in of the serpentine lake and its replacement with a *sotto voce* pond, later owners (the house became a Catholic seminary and then a co-educational public school, which it is today) left the valley largely untouched, although allowing structures to decay and woods and paths to become overgrown.

When Prior Park came to the Trust, in 1993, it was in an advanced state of decay. Restoration has begun with essential maintenance on the bridge and other structures, with clearance of the laurels and brambles which had overrun woods and pasture, and with re-establishment of footpaths and new planting. With the exception of the elms that would have featured strongly in the original woodland, the aim is to return the landscape to its appearance in 1764, when Allen died, including the re-creation of now lost features of the Wilderness, such as the lake and cascade.

A circular walk takes visitors round the combe along footpaths of limestone quarry waste, as Allen had them. Except where it descends at the foot of the valley, the path is mostly high level, giving shifting views down into the combe and out across Bath, with the tower of ancient Widcombe church as a focal point just beyond the lower boundary, as it was in the eighteenth century. The meadow is being grazed as it was in Allen's day, and above the woods the park runs into the fields and leafy hedgerows of the Trust's Rainbow Wood and Pope's Walk properties, thus extending the protected landscape of the Bath skyline (*see* p.23).

Quarry Bank Mill Cheshire

1½ miles north of Wilmslow off the B5166, 2 miles from the M56, exit 5, 10 miles south of Manchester

The cotton industry was marked by a watershed in 1783. The patents protecting Richard Arkwright's revolutionary new spinning machine were challenged and overthrown, opening the way for a huge expansion in factory-produced yarn. One of the first to take advantage of the new opportunities was the young Samuel Greg, the son of a prosperous Belfast merchant, who found a suitable site for a water-powered mill in the isolated Bollin valley some ten miles south of Manchester and established a new cotton-spinning business here in 1784. As the mill prospered, it was enlarged, and a little village complete with school, shop and chapel was built in the early nineteenth century to house the growing labour force.

This early industrial complex now lies at the centre of some 284 acres of well-wooded park following the River Bollin, some exotic trees and

Robert Greg built Oak Cottages for the workers at his mill. Each house consisted of a cellar, parlour and scullery with two bedrooms upstairs. Exceptionally, each had its own privy and also a sizeable garden where the families could grow their own vegetables. Oak School, now the Styal County Primary School, closes the end of the street. (*NT/Mike Williams*)

shrubs a legacy of landscaping in the late nineteenth century. The surroundings seem delightfully rural, with grass and trees setting off the red-brick four-storey mill with its cupola, tall chimney and impressive rows of windows. Samuel Greg lived in the elegant white Georgian house only a stone's throw away, and a smaller but no less comfortable residence on the upstream side was inhabited by the mill manager, responsible for controlling the flow of water which powered the factory.

Although later generations of Gregs moved to the grandiose Victorian house which looks down on the mill from high up on the side of the valley, the family never lost the humanitarian interests which are so evident in the layout of the village. Behind each red-brick cottage are the remains of a privy, a great luxury at a time when such facilities were usually shared between several families. And the long gardens, now mostly gay with flowers, were once allotments where tenants could grow their own vegetables. Some thatched, half-timbered buildings, including the impressive Oak Farm which once provided the village with fresh dairy produce, are remnants of a medieval settlement. Nearest to the mill is the Apprentice House, built in 1790 to accommodate the children who then made up about a third of the workforce. This double-gabled three-storey building was home to up to a hundred pauper apprentices brought in from work-houses, most of them on seven-year contracts to work twelve hours a day, six days a week. Neat rows of vegetables in the garden, including the red-veined leaves of cottagers' kale, illustrate the traditional produce the children grew in their spare time, although their diet largely consisted of bread, milk, porridge and potatoes. On Sundays, they went twice to church, walking across the fields to Wilms-low before the village chapel was built.

Although none of the original machinery survives, Styal has been restored as a working museum of the cotton industry. A giant waterwheel powers spinning machinery and some thirty looms packed together in the weaving sheds added by Greg's eldest son Robert in the mid-nineteenth century. The cloth produced is a coarse calico, a replica of what was manufactured here. The noise in the weaving sheds and the lack of space round the flying machinery give some idea of what conditions must have been like during the mill's heyday, when tired children could be disfigured for life if they nodded off over their work.

Quebec House Kent

At east end of the village of Westerham, on the north side of the A25, facing junction with the B2026 Edenbridge road

A high brick wall on a sharp corner on the road from Westerham to Sevenoaks conceals the un-pretentious gabled façades of Quebec House, where James Wolfe spent the first eleven years of his life. His parents rented the house, then known as Spiers, in 1726, and James was born a year later. The house was subsequently extensively altered but has now been returned to its seventeenth-century appearance. Basically square, it is built of a pleasing mixture of brick and Kentish ragstone and has three distinctive gables on each façade. This is a homely, welcoming place, its character signalled by the fact that visitors ring the bell for admittance, as if paying an afternoon call.

The low-ceilinged, panelled rooms contain many mementoes of General Wolfe and his victory at Quebec in 1759, when he defeated the French forces under the command of Montcalm by scaling the Heights of Abraham above the town. A pencil sketch of Wolfe to the left of the fireplace in the Bicentenary Room was drawn by his aide-de-camp on a page torn from a pocket book while they were in the field. The curiously pointed profile, a cartoonist's dream, is easily recognisable in a number of other paintings in the house.

Wolfe's travelling canteen in a corner of the Bicentenary Room gives a glimpse of the comforts enjoyed by an officer on campaign in the mid-eighteenth century. Clearly the finer things in life were not entirely discarded, as the canteen contains a cruet and glass decanters as well as more mundane objects, such as a griddle and a frying-pan. In the same room is the finely quilted dressing-gown in which Wolfe's body was brought back to England from Quebec. A seventeenth-century staircase leads up to a tranquil panelled drawing-room on the first floor, furnished with William and Mary and Queen Anne pieces and a 1788 Broadwood square piano, and warmed by an open fire on cold afternoons. An imaginatively staged exhibition in the old coach house across the walled garden describes the Quebec campaign and its background and gives details of Wolfe's life. Three niches in the south wall of this building are thought to be bee boles where bees were kept in old-fashioned straw skeps, or hives, possibly to aid the pollination of fruit trees on the wall.

Rainham Hall Essex

The Broadway, just south of the church, 5 miles east of Barking

This elegant Georgian house, set back from the road behind beautiful wrought-iron gates and railings, was completed in 1729 for the merchant and shipowner John Harle. In the domestic Dutch style, with red-brick façades and stone dressings and dormers in the hipped roof, the main feature of the exterior is a fine carved wood porch with Corinthian columns. Inside, the house has been little altered, original doorcases, fireplaces and softwood panelling helping to convey a strong sense of period.

Ramsey Abbey Gatehouse

Cambridgeshire

Abbey School, at south-east edge of Ramsey, at point where the Chatteris road leaves the B1096, 10 miles south-east of Peterborough

In 969 St Oswald, Archbishop of York, and Ailwyn, foster brother of the Saxon king Edgar, founded a Benedictine abbey on a remote island in the Fens. Only fragments survive, the remains of an ornate late fifteenth-century gatehouse with a richly carved oriel window above the entrance doorway suggesting how sumptuous the abbatial buildings must once have been. A small room to the right of the gateway is filled with an impressive mid-thirteenth-century marble tomb, with a time-worn effigy clutching a huge key in its right hand. An intriguing mystery surrounds the identity of the frost-damaged figure. Once taken to represent Ailwyn, it is now thought the carving may be a retrospective image of a Saxon prince.

Ranmore Common Surrey

2 miles north-west of Dorking, adjoining the south boundary of the Polesden Lacey estate

Running along the ridge of the North Downs north-west of Dorking and forming the attractive backdrop to the view southwards from Polesden Lacey (*see* p.263) are the 470 acres of Ranmore Common. On each side of the road from Dorking to East Horsley there are grassy strips much used by families out for an afternoon, but it is the old wood pasture sloping north which provides good walking and exploring territory, for very varied vegetation grows on these clay caps and chalky slopes. Below Denbies, the country house of Thomas Cubitt, the early nineteenth-century developer of Belgravia, a further 250 acres of steep hillside with varied chalk downland flora and fauna make up with the Polesden estate a fine stretch of beautiful landscape.

Rievaulx Terrace and Temples

North Yorkshire

2½ miles north-west of Helmsley on the B1257

Like Fountains Abbey thirty miles away to the south-west (*see* p.121), the Cistercian abbey of Rievaulx (not owned by the Trust) was established in a secluded valley where the monks could pursue their vocation untroubled by the world. Today their great monastery at the head of Ryedale is an evocative ruin, the walls of the mid-thirteenth-century church rising powerfully from the valley floor, the three tiers of windows in the nave still remarkably untouched by time. Above the abbey, Rievaulx Terrace winds like a serpent across the side of the hill, a gently curving walk giving changing vistas over the valley below. Sometimes there are glimpses through the trees to the three-arched bridge crossing the River Rye, sometimes branches frame a stone farmhouse or cottage on the far hillside. And then the ruins of the abbey are gradually visible, culminating in a view down the length of the great nave. In the same way, John Aislabie had devised his garden at Studley Royal a few years before to focus on the abbey ruins which lay just beyond his boundaries (*see* p.322).

Little Palladian temples punctuate either end of the terrace. To the south there is a delicate domed temple, its circular form completely enveloped in a colonnade. Inside, a richly decorated white plaster trellis, possibly the work of Giuseppe Cortese who was employed at Studley, stands out vividly against the blue of the dome. The interior of the porticoed and pedimented rectangular Ionic temple is yet more magnificent, with brilliantly coloured frescoes by Giuseppe Borgnis and carvings covered in gold leaf. It was intended as a banqueting house, and the central table is improbably set for a meal. Both temples may be the work of the gentleman-architect

One of the two Palladian temples set either end of Rievaulx Terrace. (*NT/Joe Cornish*)

Thomas Robinson, who was more spectacularly involved in Claydon House (*see* p.74).

With its two temples set on a thickly wooded hillside and its views over the ruined abbey in the valley below, Rievaulx is a romantic Italian landscape brought to life, as if a canvas by Claude or Poussin had been translated into a Yorkshire setting. This idealised creation was the vision of Thomas Duncombe III. He had inherited both Rievaulx and the adjoining Helmsley estate from his father in 1746 and must have wanted to complement, if not surpass, the more formal terrace his father had laid out in front of his house on the other side of the valley. Like William Aislabie's additions to his father's garden at Studley, Thomas Duncombe's terrace is a product of the eighteenth-century taste for the informal and the picturesque

and of a new appreciation of the drama in a natural landscape. As the agriculturalist and travel writer Arthur Young said in the late eighteenth century, 'This is a most bewitching spot.'

The River Wey and Godalming Navigations Surrey

Running between Godalming and Weybridge

Although bridged by the M25 and close to London's suburban sprawl, this tranquil waterway snaking twenty miles through Surrey from Godalming north to the River Thames is still remarkably rural, with cows grazing placidly in meadows on either side, views to church towers and wooded hills and whitewashed lock-keepers' cottages fringing the towpath. The 15½-mile stretch along the River Wey from Guildford to Weybridge was opened for navigation in 1653 on the initiative of Sir Richard

Once crowded with barges carrying agricultural produce and timber to London, the peaceful waters of the Wey and Godalming Navigation are now thronged with pleasure boats.
(*NT/Andy Williams*)

Weston, who introduced the principle of the lock, but the remaining four and a half miles upstream to Godalming were not completed until about a hundred years later. When finished, there were sixteen locks to negotiate between Godalming and the Thames.

Once crowded with barges loaded with agricultural produce and timber for London, the river lost its importance with the coming of the railways, although the waterway continued to be used commercially until about 1960. Walkers now enjoy the 20 miles of towpath running alongside and a disused railway line and there are pleasure boats for hire. With its tranquil backwaters, the canalised river is also an important wildlife corridor in a heavily populated area.

Ross Castle Northumberland

12 miles north-west of Alnwick, south-east of Chillingham

Rising out of the moors to the east of Chillingham Park is the conical hill of Ross Castle, where the Trust holds 7½ acres. There are no castle ruins, only vestigial remains of the Iron Age hill fort, but the view from this remote property is memorable: seaward to Holy Island, Bamburgh and the Farnes (*see* p. 116), south to the rich land between the hills and the sea, west to the Cheviot Hills and Scotland.

The Round House and Naval Temple Gwent

1 mile east of Monmouth between the A466 and the A4136

The prominent 800-foot hill known as The Kymin is renowned for its wide-ranging views over the Wye and Monnow valleys, said to embrace nine counties. The Trust owns nine acres of the high ground and the two structures which crown it. In the late eighteenth century members of a local dining club formed the habit of meeting here on summer evenings for a cold supper and in 1794 built the round battlemented banqueting house on the brow of the hill for use in bad weather, each of its windows placed so as to enjoy a spectacular panorama. Nelson's celebrated victory over the French in the Battle of the Nile four years later inspired the construction of the little temple in honour of the British navy which stands nearby. Its pyramidal stepped roof suggests an Egyptian summerhouse, despite the prominent statue of Britannia which crowns the structure and the medallions recording the names and principal achievements of sixteen great eighteenth-century admirals. When Nelson himself visited this spot in 1802, he thought it was one of the most beautiful places he had ever seen. History does not record the feelings of Emma Hamilton and her husband who were accompanying him on his journey down the Wye.

Rowallane Garden Co. Down

11 miles south-east of Belfast, 1 mile south of Saintfield, west of the A7 Downpatrick road

The drumlin landscape of Co. Down, with outcrops of basalt scraped bare by glaciers long ago and stony moraines left as the ice retreated, is harsh farming country, where little fields formed on the thin soil are edged by drystone walls built up from material laboriously cleared by hand. Features which would defeat most cultivators are the very essence of Rowallane. Established on the fields of a hill farm, the informal planting follows the lie of the land, banks of shrubs turning back on themselves round a hillock and natural rock gardens formed on craggy basalt outcrops. Areas known as the Paddock and the Spring Ground conjure up the flocks and herds which once grazed here, and a network of drystone walls still traces the skeleton of the farm, those marking the boundaries of the holding nicely coursed.

Although started by the Rev. John Moore in the late nineteenth century, this unique tree and shrub garden is largely the creation of his talented nephew who inherited the property in 1903. Hugh Armytage Moore's particular genius lay in his ability to choose a plant for a setting, enhancing the natural landscape rather than adapting it to his own designs. The garden is particularly known for spectacular displays of rhododendrons and azaleas, which flourish on the acid soils in the mild wet climate; a large clump of bright red rhododendrons by the little pool contrasts with a bank of trifoliate varieties flowering in twilight colours – pink, mauve and blue – or with the tiny yellow flowers of *Rhododendron lutescens*. Many rare and exotic species, some sent back by E. H. Wilson, G. Forrest, F. Kingdon-Ward and other collectors from the Far East and the southern hemisphere, include the Chilean fire bush, the handkerchief tree and magnificent southern beeches. This is a garden where the beauty and subtle variety of foliage can be fully appreciated, every hue and tone of green seeming to contribute to the woodland framing the open area of grass known as the pleasure ground, setting off the gay blue bandstand moved here in the 1860s.

A long drive lined with rhododendrons and specimen conifers and punctuated with tall stone cairns erected by John Moore leads up from the Belfast road. Rare bulbs, tender shrubs and climbing plants shelter in the walled garden beside the house, including the chaenomeles, viburnum, hypericum and primula named after Rowallane, a scented magnolia, fuchsias, hostas, colchicums, vivid blue and purple drifts of the Himalayan blue poppy, and a collection of the red- and purple-flowering penstemons. To the east is the Spring Ground, the rocky pastures on which it was created being known for producing the first new grass of the year. Rhododendrons and azaleas backed by maples, birches and other trees line a grassy glade leading gently downhill, yellow with daffodils in spring. At the bottom a massive basalt outcrop harbours a wide range of alpines and heathers. Blue gentians cling to pockets of soil, primulas flower in shady corners and the rock is bright with dwarf rhododendrons and daffodils early in the year. Up a little clearing from here is the natural whinstone outcrop shaped like a bishop's chair, known as the Bishop's Rock.

The tree and shrub garden at Rowallane, known for spectacular displays of rhododendrons and azaleas. (*NT/ John Bethell*)

Rowallane is spectacular in March, April and May, and again when there is autumn foliage and berries encrust trees and shrubs in the Paddock. And this was the land once judged by the Rev. John Moore as 'not fit to graze a goat'.

Royal Military Canal
Kent and East Sussex

3½ miles of canal bank between Appledore and Warehorne

Like the Needles Old Battery (*see* p.212), the Royal Military Canal running for twenty-eight miles between Hythe and Rye along the inner edge of Romney Marsh was built in anticipation of enemy action which never came. Dug in 1804–7 to a width of sixty feet and a depth of nine feet, it was intended as a line of defence against a landing by Napoleon's forces and the military road behind it for moving troops rapidly along the coast. It is now considered one of the most important surviving examples in Europe of a linear military defence system. Once the danger of a French invasion had passed, it was very quickly made suitable for commercial traffic, which only ceased in 1909. The Trust owns a beautiful 3½-mile stretch between Warehorne and Appledore. Walkers heading west along the sometimes tree-lined towpath see the Isle of Oxney swelling out of the landscape ahead, while to the left the marsh stretches away to the sea.

Rufford Old Hall Lancashire

7 miles north of Ormskirk, in village of Rufford on east side of the A59

Like his father, grandfather and great-grandfather before him, Sir Thomas Hesketh married an heiress. Certainly no expense was spared on the half-timbered manor house he built in *c.*1420, establishing the family seat for the next 350 years. Although only the great hall survives in its original form – the west wing being now no more than marks in the grass and the east wing having been extensively rebuilt – what remains speaks eloquently of wealth and position. The great hall, forty-six feet long and twenty-two feet wide, was built to be admired, crowned by a fanciful hammer-beam roof in which each massive timber is fretted with carved battlements. Angels – all but one now wingless – look

down from the ends of the supporting beams while carved roof bosses display the arms of the great Lancashire families with which Hesketh was allied.

A massive, intricately carved movable wooden screen with three soaring finials like a pagoda takes the place of the more usual partition in houses of this date separating the hall from the traditional screens passage. This deliberately theatrical set piece, backed by blind quatrefoils lining the upper wall of the passage and placed within a wooden arch supported by beautifully decorated octagonal pillars, must have delighted William Shakespeare if there is truth in the legend that he performed here while in Sir Thomas's service. A canopy of honour curves over the far end of the room, where the lord and his guests would have sat at high table, their special status further emphasised by the great bay window looking north. A long refectory table, richly carved oak chests, and pieces from the Hesketh collection of arms and armour add to the house's atmosphere. The exterior is similarly fine,

The great hall at Rufford Old Hall is noted for its hammer-beam roof and the richly carved movable screen which stands at one end. (*NT/Andreas von Einsiedel*)

an impressive display of studding, quatrefoils and wood-mullioned windows greeting visitors as they come up the drive.

A Carolean wing juts out at right-angles to the medieval great hall, its symmetrical gabled façade built of warm red brick contrasting strangely with the black and white timbering. A castellated tower peering over the angle between the two ranges is a later addition, a feature of the nineteenth-century building which joins the great hall to the Charles II wing. Partly formed out of the old medieval east range, this wing of the house includes a spacious drawing-room stretching the full length of the first floor, with a sixteenth-century open timber roof and a spy-hole looking down into the great hall below. As elsewhere in the house, richly carved court cupboards, spindle-backed rush-seated chairs and oak settles of the seventeenth and eighteenth centuries demonstrate the skills of local craftsmen.

Outbuildings house the Philip Ashcroft Museum of Rural Life, a unique collection of objects and implements illustrating village life in pre-industrial Lancashire. Relics of the local cheese- and butter-making industries are displayed alongside a man-trap and an unusual water-filter made from local red sandstone.

Runnymede Surrey

On the Thames, ½ mile above Runnymede bridge, on south side of the A 308

These sleepy water meadows beside the River Thames are where King John signed Magna Carta on 12 June 1215, ending nine days of negotiations with his rebellious barons. Subsequently regarded as a fundamental statement of human rights, the libertarian principles thought to be enshrined in Magna Carta formed the basis of English law and were eventually incorporated in the constitutions of many other countries, including the United States. Appropriately, therefore, this peaceful spot was also chosen to honour the American President John F. Kennedy after his assassination in 1963 and to commemorate 20,455 airmen lost without trace in the Second World War.

Monuments to Magna Carta (erected 1957) and John F. Kennedy (1965) stand one above the other on the wooded slopes rising steeply from the meadows, while the crest of the hill, from where there are magnificent views towards London, is crowned by the extensive Commonwealth Air Forces Memorial (1953). Two bungalow-like lodges with deep hipped roofs bordering the road to Windsor and two kiosks at the Egham end of the property by Sir Edwin Lutyens were erected in memory of the 1st Lord Fairhaven (*see* p.5), whose widow presented the meadows to the Trust. Lutyens also designed the pairs of memorial pillars flanking both sets of buildings with inscriptions recording Lord Fairhaven's bequest and the charter granted in 1215.

St Cuthbert's Cave Northumberland

10 miles north-east of Wooler

St Cuthbert's Cave, situated in the wooded Kyloe Hills on the mainland opposite Holy Island, is believed to have been used as a hermitage by St Cuthbert in AD 674, or, alternatively, as a temporary resting place for the saint's body during its century-long journey through the country to Durham. It is a remote, tranquil spot with exceptional views over some of the most outstanding scenery in Northumberland.

St George's Guildhall Norfolk

In King's Lynn, on west side of King Street close to the Tuesday Market Place

Medieval King's Lynn was a market town and port of considerable importance, trading in wool and agricultural produce across the North Sea and to Scandinavia. The Guild of St George was one of the largest of the sixty or so that flourished here in late medieval times, and this substantial building by Tuesday Market, the biggest surviving medieval guildhall in England, is a graphic illustration of the wealth and status of the fraternity.

Although the 107-foot great hall on the first floor has been converted into a theatre and the building as a whole is an arts centre, many original fifteenth-century features survive, such as the five massive buttresses against the north wall and the open timber roof. There are also traces of the Georgian theatre constructed here in 1766. An adjoining Tudor house and the long row of medieval warehouses running down to the River Ouse from the west end of the guildhall are also owned by the Trust.

St John's Jerusalem Garden Kent

3 miles south of Dartford at Sutton-at-Hone, on east side of the A225

After the noise and traffic of Dartford, this cool, secluded garden moated by the River Darent seems an oasis of peace and serenity. Undulating lawns planted with a broad avenue of chestnuts stretch away from the house to limes and willows edging the moat. Spring and summer flower borders are bright with bulbs and herbaceous plants and there are a number of fine specimen trees, including a descendant of one of the St Helena willows under which Napoleon was buried.

Approached down a short drive from the village of Sutton-at-Hone, the first view of St John's, a pleasant two-storey stuccoed building with dormers in the steeply pitched roof, is framed by the branches of a huge Cedar of Lebanon. This magnificent tree was probably planted by Abraham Hill in the late seventeenth century at the same time as he made alterations to the house. Sash windows and rich plasterwork inside the house were later additions by Edward Hasted, the eminent local historian, who lived here from 1755–76.

The oldest part of St John's is the former chapel, with buttressed flint walls and tall lancet windows, all that remains of the former Commandery of the Knights Hospitallers of the Order of Saint John of Jerusalem. Established here in 1199, they live on in the name of this delightful property.

St Michael's Mount Cornwall

½ mile south of the A394 at Marazion

St Michael's Mount rises from the sea off the Cornish coast as if a spiny sea monster were arching its back below the waves, its dramatic profile crowned by Arthurian battlements and towers. When the skies are grey and an Atlantic gale is sending breakers crashing on to the rocks, it is easy to imagine that the Archangel St Michael did indeed do battle with the Devil here. On still summer evenings the island is another world, floating serenely in a crystal-clear sea.

This strange hybrid is part religious retreat, part fortress, part elegant country house. Associated with Christianity since the fifth century, when St Michael is said to have appeared to some local fishermen, it became an important place of pilgrimage in the Middle Ages, when the attraction of the saint's shrine was enhanced by the charms of the jawbone of St Appolonia of Alexander, said to cure those suffering from toothache. The heart of the castle today is a little fourteenth-century granite church built on the highest point of the island, the major survival from the Benedictine priory established here in the twelfth century, daughter house of the much grander Mont St Michel set on another rocky outcrop some 150 miles across the Channel. Two beautiful fifteenth-century rose windows light the building, angels in flowing robes forming swirls of olive-green, blue, red and orange in that at the west end.

What was probably the monastic refectory is now the impressive Chevy Chase Room, called after the prominent and unusual plaster frieze on which rabbits, boars, stags, a bear and a fox are being pursued by men with spears and guns. Some of the hunters' dogs have got away from the pack and are perched mischievously on top of the frieze. Appropriately furnished with a gleaming seventeenth-century refectory table, the room is dominated by the royal coat of arms picked out in gold and red over the fireplace, set up here in celebration of Charles II's restoration to the throne. The massive granite walls are probably those built in the twelfth century but the arching timber roof dates from 300 years later.

The guardroom in the entry range, the garrison room embedded in the rock, an old sentry box overlooking the steep cobbled path up to the castle and gun batteries pointing out to sea recall the 200 years when the Mount was a manned fortress, a major link in England's defences against the Spanish Armada (a beacon lit on the church tower in 1587 heralded the approach of the fleet) and a Royalist stronghold in the Civil War until the castle's surrender in 1646. The last military governor, the Parliamentarian Colonel John St Aubyn, began the conversion of the fortress into a private house and his descendants continued to live here for the next 300 years. Sir John St Aubyn, 3rd Baronet, transformed the ruined lady chapel into the elegant blue drawing-room, early rococo Gothic plasterwork picked out in white against the blue walls, niches filled with pink Italian vases in jasper and alabaster and fine Chippendale furniture upholstered in blue conjuring up the cultivated world of Georgian England.

Far below, on the steep exposed lower slopes

St Michael's Mount at high tide, with the wall of the little harbour visible to the right of the island.
(*NT/Howard Phillips*)

of the rock, is the St Aubyn family's terraced rock garden and eighteenth-century walled garden. Despite the sea gales, rare tropical and subtropical plants flourish here.

From the castle terraces there are magnificent views over Mount's Bay along the Cornish coast and inland to rolling granite moors, while far below a thread of ant-like people crossing the causeway leading back over the sands to Marazion at low tide could be medieval pilgrims. A row of whitewashed cottages huddles above the claw-like harbour on the sheltered north side of the island, where sailing ships once loaded Cornish tin and copper for the Continent.

Salcombe Devon

On the south coast; about 9 miles of coastline on either side of the harbour

This is one of the Trust's longest stretches of coastline, running from Prawle Point, three miles east of Salcombe, to Bolt Tail, six miles to the west, nine miles in all.

Prawle is the southernmost tip of Devon. The name means the look-out hill, and it has been used for this purpose since early times, through many wars, and is manned today by HM Coastguard. Elender Cove, to the west, does not belong to the Trust, but immediately beyond it is the beautiful sandy Maceley Cove, and from here the Trust's ownership is continuous to Salcombe.

The shapely Gammon Head shelters Maceley Cove from the west, an easy scramble out to its tip, and from here there is a wonderful view: westwards over the bay to Bolt Head, inland to the neat fields of the South Hams, and seawards where ships pass frequently up and down Channel.

The path runs west past the promontory of the Pig's Nose, where a delightful valley leads up to the village of East Prawle, past Moor Sands and along Decklers Cliff, once farmed as the field hedges show but now overgrown. Rickham Sands, below the Gara Rock Hotel (converted from a row of former coastguard cottages), is a good beach. The little whitewashed and thatched building above it was the coastguard's look-out.

Overhead glide kestrels, buzzards and ravens, while seabirds and waders frequent the rocks and beaches below the cliffs. From Gara Rock there are paths at two levels along Portlemouth Down and

past Limebury Point into Salcombe harbour. Below the low cliffs are little sandy coves, sheltered, wholly delightful, until the large beach of Mill Bay where the Trust's property ends.

At the head of the harbour South Pool Creek strikes off to the north-east and, on the opposite bank, where the Kingsbridge estuary continues to the north, is Snape's Point. These 150 acres of farmland with two miles of estuary coast are important in the landscape because the Trust's ownership will stop the expansion in this direction of Salcombe, a former shipbuilding town and commercial harbour, now wholly devoted to the boating fraternity.

West of the harbour entrance the Trust's land starts again above South Sands, at Overbecks (*see* p.241). The Courtenay Walk (Courtenay being the family name of the Earl of Devon who formerly owned this land) leads steeply upwards above Stink Cove – the stink due to seaweed which collects here – to Sharp Tor 400 feet above the sea. There is a topograph showing what there is to see in the wide prospect to east and north. The path follows round Starehole Bay, all that a cliff path should be: craggy outcrops of rock, brackeny slopes, tidy fields inland, the sun glittering on the sea far below.

In 1936 the four-masted barque *Herzogin Cecilie*, one of the great fleet of grain ships trading out of Mariehamm in Finland, struck the Ham Stone, a rock offshore round Bolt Head to the west. The damage was thought to be slight and she was towed round and beached here in Starehole Bay to be unloaded. Before this could be achieved a storm blew up and broke her back. On a still, clear day the ghostly outline of her hull can be seen on the sandy bottom of the bay.

Bolt Head is marginally higher than Sharp Tor and, because the coast turns sharply west at the opening of the harbour, it is very impressive when seen from a boat immediately below. The Warren stretches for a further two and a half miles of excellent walking to Soar Mill Cove, with its good sand and rock pools at low water, perfect for family picnics. Eighteen miles to the west, beyond Plymouth, stands the Eddystone Light, just visible from the higher ground in daylight, unmistakable at night.

Cathole and West Cliffs follow, some of the fields above the cliff bounded by upright slabs of the local mica schist, a slaty stone produced by the pressure of volcanic action. Then the path leads across

Bolberry Down, high above Slippery Point and Fernyhole Point, evocative names, far below. Whether in summer or winter the air is sparkling, the walk exhilarating, the views of cliffs, sea and ships, and inland across the South Hams to Dartmoor, unsurpassed.

Finally the path goes past Ramillies Cove, named not after the battle but the ship, a ninety-gun second-rate ship of the line wrecked here in 1760, and round Bolt Tail to the picture-postcard village of Hope Cove, tucked inside the headland, a walk to remember.

Saltram Devon

2 miles west of Plympton, 3½ miles east of Plymouth city centre, between the A38 Plymouth–Exeter road and the A379 Plymouth–Kingsbridge road

Anyone who has travelled by train from Plymouth to London will know the pleasure of seeing the Saltram estate shortly after leaving the city, when the line suddenly emerges on the banks of the River Plym and the wooded slope of the park rises on the other side of the estuary. With a view over Plymouth Sound to the trees of Mount Edgcumbe, this is a perfect position for a house, and the building created here lived up to its setting. Saltram is essentially a product of the eighteenth century, the rooms with their original contents summing up all that was best about this elegant and civilised age.

The remodelling of the house was the work of John and Lady Catherine Parker, who wrapped three classical façades round a Tudor core and the three-storey seventeenth-century block which John's father had purchased in 1712. But it was their son, John Parker, 1st Lord Boringdon, who invited Robert Adam to Saltram and who amassed the outstanding collection of pictures. Already at work on Kedleston Hall (*see* p.164) and Osterley (*see* p.240), Adam was at the height of his career and his rooms at Saltram, in which he designed everything, including the door knobs, are exceptional examples of his style. In the great neo-classical saloon, delicate plasterwork attributed to Joseph Rose stands out white against the eggshell-blue and burnt-yellow of the coved ceiling. Blue damask lines the walls, setting off the four great looking-glasses and the paintings hung as Adam intended. A magnificent Axminster carpet echoes the design of the ceiling and gilded chairs and sofas line the walls.

Another aspect of the eighteenth century is reflected in the morning-room, far more intimate and relaxed than the saloon, where a quartet of cloud-based cherubs makes music in the rococo plaster ceiling. Paintings hang triple-banked in the fashion of the day, their gilded frames glowing against red velvet.

The picture collection is still virtually as Lord Boringdon left it, including ten paintings by his close friend Sir Joshua Reynolds. During their long association, Reynolds not only portrayed Lord Boringdon and his family but also advised him on his other acquisitions, among them works by Angelica Kauffmann and a number of Italian, Dutch and Flemish paintings. Other delights at Saltram are the eighteenth-century Chinese wallpaper, some of it depicting those curiously elongated figures so familiar from Japanese prints, and an essentially eighteenth-century kitchen, with a battery of gleaming copper pans.

Ten paintings by Sir Joshua Reynolds at Saltram, including this study of the 1st Lord Boringdon's wife and son, reflect the artist's close friendship with the family. Reynolds advised Lord Boringdon on his other acquisitions and it is probable that most of the continental works at Saltram were bought on his recommendation. (*NT/ Rob Matheson*)

A pleasant Victorian informal garden lies to the west of the house, a soothing mixture of lawns, wooded glades and shrubs, with grass walks bordered by magnolias, camellias, rhododendrons and a number of good specimen trees. A long lime avenue is ribboned with daffodils in spring and bright with patches of cyclamen in September. An octagonal mid-eighteenth-century Gothic belvedere at the end of this walk was probably built by Harry Stockman, the estate's talented carpenter, as was the elegant pedimented orangery of 1775 by the house, still full of citrus fruits which are set out round a fountain pool in summer. Stockman also created the chapel nearby, adding battlements, buttresses and pointed windows to what was originally a barn. The extensive deer park formed in the mid-eighteenth century was landscaped in the style of 'Capability' Brown, but the magnificent views depicted by William Tomkins's delightful landscapes in the garden room have been ruined by Plymouth's urban sprawl. Recently planted shelter belts will eventually hide this intrusive reminder of the twentieth century, but passengers on the main Plymouth to London line will still be able to enjoy a glimpse of the amphitheatre, a mid-eighteenth-century folly nestling in the woods on the other side of the Plym estuary.

Sandham Memorial Chapel

Hampshire

4 miles south of Newbury, ½ mile east of the A34

Service in Greece and in a military hospital during the First World War inspired the visionary and touching murals by Stanley Spencer which fill this chapel. These are not horrific, tortured scenes of trench warfare but cameos of everyday activities which convey a sense of human companionship rarely found in civilian life. Soldiers in Greece are shown filling their water bottles, dressing under mosquito nets, cooking breakfast in the open and picking bilberries. In the hospital they sort laundry, polish taps and make beds. Spencer's greatest work, the *Resurrection of the Soldiers*, hangs above the altar. A stream of white crosses leads towards Christ standing in the middle distance, gathering crosses from the fallen in his arms. Soldiers emerge from their graves, shake hands with their comrades, clean buttons and wind puttees. Here, as throughout this powerful cycle, everyday life is touched by the immortal.

The 1920s red-brick chapel was built to Spencer's instructions by Mr and Mrs Behrend specially to house the murals, which were painted, on large seamless canvases, between 1927 and 1932. It was subsequently dedicated to Mrs Behrend's brother H.W. Sandham, who died in the First World War.

Sand Point and Middle Hope

Avon

5 miles north of Weston-super-Mare

Weston-super-Mare is all that a Victorian resort ought to be, its genteel stone villas ranked above its rather muddy beach with a pier and all the attractions that such places provide. Immediately to the north of the town is something quite different. Weston Woods, with deciduous trees and sunny glades, overlook Sand Bay. One and a half miles across the beach is the Trust's Sand Point, a limestone cliff with attractive outcrops of rock and fine views across the Bristol Channel. On its north side, at Swallow Cliff, there is a good example of a raised beach, formed in the distant past when the sea level was different. Trust land extends a further half mile east along the low cliffs of Middle Hope, where a loop walk takes in the buildings of Woodspring Priory, recently restored by the Landmark Trust.

Scotney Castle Garden   Kent

1½ miles south of Lamberhurst on the A21

Like Sissinghurst only a few miles to the east (*see* p.291), much of Scotney's charm derives from the romantic buildings incorporated in the garden. A rich variety of flowering shrubs and trees laid out on the steep slopes of a bluff overlooking the little River Bewel provide a charming backdrop to the picturesque moated ruins in the floor of the valley. Now serene and peaceful, with roses, ivy and other climbing plants encrusting the ancient stonework, the castle was originally built during the troubled decades of the Hundred Years War when men of substance needed to protect their property. Although not as vulnerable to French raids as Bodiam on the River Rother to the south, where Richard II directed Edward Dalyngrigge to fortify his estate

Orderly rows of tents, the soldier handing round bread and the thick pieces of bacon frying for breakfast in Stanley Spencer's *The Camp at Karasuli* illustrate the sense of companionship in his murals at Sandham Memorial Chapel. (*NT*)

(*see* p.35), Scotney was strategically sited where the road from Rye and Hastings crossed the valley of the Bewel. A massive round tower rising picturesquely from the lake-like moat, with a projecting parapet at roof level, and a ruined gatehouse are the remnants of the fortified house Roger Ashburnham constructed here in *c*.1378–80. A brick Elizabethan range adjoining the tower is all that survives of the sixteenth-century additions, and jagged walls with gaping windows mark a substantial seventeenth-century wing.

The magical twenty-acre garden which now sets off these fairy-tale remains was created from 1837 by Edward Hussey III, whose grandfather purchased the estate. As well as commissioning Anthony Salvin to build a neo-Tudor house on the bluff above the valley, he engaged William Sawrey Gilpin, the artist and landscape gardener, to advise on the creation of its surroundings. In view of the dramatic nature of the site, this was an inspired choice. Gilpin was a disciple of Richard Payne Knight and Sir Uvedale Price, the leading exponents of the Picturesque style, in which the naturalistic but carefully manicured landscapes of the 'Capability' Brown school were rejected in favour of the illusion of the beauty of nature untamed, as in a painting by Salvator Rosa. Scotney offered considerable potential, with its genuine medieval ruin backed by a steeply rising slope and the added interest of a deep quarry left where the stone for the new house had been extracted.

The first view of the garden is one of the best.

Standing on the semicircular bastion below the new house, the visitor looks down from the stone parapet over the quarry and the slope of the valley, thickly planted with trees and shrubs, to the moated remains of the old castle. On the other side of the river the park rises gently to woodlands of beech and oak. Walking along the top path from here, different vistas and perspectives open up, with glimpses of the seventeenth-century tower of Goudhurst church away to the north. Come here in April, when the magnolia in the quarry is in bloom, and the Japanese maples are unfurling their leaves. Or aim to see the azaleas and rhododendrons in flower, a blaze of yellow, orange, purple and red cascading down the slope towards the moat in early summer. Later in the year pink, white and mauve roses encrust the old walls of the castle, and the air above the little formal herb garden created round an Italianate carved wellhead is heavy with the scent of aromatic plants. Luxuriant vegetation almost smothers a little red-tiled boathouse, with pinnacles and bargeboards adorning the gable ends.

Carefully preserved by later generations of the Hussey family, the only modern note in the garden is the *Reclining Figure* by Henry Moore hidden away on a little isthmus in the lake, a tribute to the memory of Christopher Hussey who greatly enhanced the beauty of Scotney and gave it to the Trust.

Segontium   Gwynedd

On the A4085 Llanbeblig road, on south-east outskirts of Caernarfon

Edward I's great castle at Caernarfon was partly built of dressed stone plundered from a much earlier stronghold, the Roman fort of Segontium on the top of a hill about half a mile east. One of over thirty forts built to control the rebellious tribes in the valleys west of the Rivers Severn and Dee, Segontium was sited in a commanding position on the Menai Strait, within easy reach of the Snowdon massif and the Llŷn peninsula and with routes inland to the much larger garrisons based at Chester and Caerleon. Founded in AD78, it was held until about 390, longer than any other Roman fort in Wales, probably a reflection of its strategic importance. The perimeter defences were strengthened over the years, a ditch and clay rampart pierced by four wooden gateways being gradually replaced in stone.

The 5½-acre site is crossed by the Caernarfon to Beddgelert road and only the ground plan of part of the northern half is excavated. The fort was of the usual playing-card shape and laid out to a standard design, with barracks for the men in tidy rows either side of the commander's house and the head-quarter's building in the middle of the compound, the latter displaying the remains of an underfloor heating system. There are no visible signs of the two large granaries which housed a year's supply of corn for the garrison (up to 1,000 strong), but a rather basic bath suite added in the late third or early fourth century shows facilities here were less lavish than at Letocetum (*see* p.179). A site museum covers Roman military life in general, as well as the history and interpretation of Segontium itself.

Selborne Hill   Hampshire

4 miles south of Alton, between Selborne and Newton Valence, west of the B3006

There seems no danger that Gilbert White, the greatest of so many parson-naturalists, will ever be forgotten. His *Natural History and Antiquities of Selborne* has never gone out of print and much of his parish remains as he knew it. The Trust's 700-foot Selborne Hill, with White's zig-zag path climbing to the top of the beech hanger, the little valleys below and his house – now the Wakes museum (not NT) – are perfect for a quiet expedition.

Selworthy   Somerset

On the Holnicote estate, astride the A39, between Minehead and Porlock

At first glance the thatched, cream-washed stone cottages climbing the hill to the fifteenth-century church of All Saints seem typical of this area. Unlike neighbouring villages, however, Selworthy was largely rebuilt in 1828 by Sir Thomas Acland of Killerton (*see* p.166), who designed a group of cottages in a local idiom set loosely round a long green. A philanthropist who wished to provide housing for the pensioners on his Holnicote estate (*see* p.154), Sir Thomas was probably inspired by his friend John Harford, who had commissioned Nash to design Blaise Hamlet for his aged retainers twenty years earlier (*see* p.32).

Both settlements are examples of the cult of the

When Sir Thomas Acland rebuilt Selworthy in 1828 for the pensioners on his estate, he used traditional materials and designs to produce a consciously old-fashioned village. Cream-washed, thatched cottages straggle up the hill to All Saints church, their gardens sheltered by the trees Sir Thomas planted in the steep valley and on the hill above. (*NT/David Noton*)

Picturesque, but they could hardly be more different. Whereas Nash's cottages are self-consciously flamboyant and exaggerated, those at Selworthy are gentle variations on the vernacular, with tall chimneys, deep thatched eaves, eyebrow dormers and projecting ovens. They are magnificently set, in a steep wooded valley on the northern fringes of Exmoor. The view from the church at the top of the village looks over a patchwork of thatched roofs and neat cottage gardens to the heather- and bracken-covered heights of Dunkery Beacon, the highest point on the moor. Whether the pensioners thought their surroundings worth the red cloaks they had to wear on Sundays is not recorded.

Shalford Mill Surrey

1½ miles south of Guildford, on east side of the A281

This large eighteenth-century watermill sits confidently astride the Tillingbourne, a tributary of the River Wey. Two timber-framed upper storeys attractively hung with warm red tiles are built on a brick ground floor, with three brick arches on the upstream side channelling the water of the river through the mill. A prominent projecting gable at third-floor level housed the hoist which once raised sacks of grain for storage in the large bins running the length of the attic.

All the principal machinery is still intact, but the mill can no longer be worked as only the top half of the fourteen-foot waterwheel remains. This is a breastshot wheel, driven by the water hitting the paddles halfway up the wheel rather than falling from above as in the more efficient overshot design (*see, for example,* Nether Alderley Mill, p.212). A vertical shaft made from a single pine trunk transmitted power from the wheel to three pairs of millstones, one of which is still complete, and to the hoist in the attic and winnowing and grading machinery on the second floor.

Shalford Mill is of particular interest because it is one of the properties that were presented to the Trust by the anonymous band of conservationists known as Ferguson's Gang, who used to meet here in the 1930s. Part of the building is now converted into a house and is privately let.

Shamrock Cornwall

Cotehele quay, on west bank of the Tamar; 1 mile west of Calstock by footpath (6 miles by road), 14 miles from Plymouth via Tamar Bridge, 2 miles east of St Dominick

Until the 1920s when competition from road and rail transport killed off the use of sail, a fleet of sturdy barges worked the coasts of Devon and Cornwall and the many river estuaries reaching into the heart of the peninsula. Everything was carried by water, from brick, limestone and coal to general provisions, loaded and landed on beaches or at one of the many old stone quays on the Rivers Fal, Dart, Tamar and Lynher.

Built in 1899 in a Plymouth yard, *Shamrock* is one of the last Tamar barges, a ketch-rigged (two-masted) 57-foot cargo boat typical of those which once crowded the river. Originally designed for inland waters and used to carry fertiliser and other bulky cargoes, she would have been a regular visitor to the little quay at Cotehele (*see* p.87) on the Tamar where she is now permanently berthed. She was later modified for work in the open sea, ending her days in the 1960s prospecting for tin in St Ives Bay and as a salvage vessel and diving tender. Reduced to a rotting hulk by 1974, she has now been fully restored.

An outstation of the National Maritime Museum housed in one of the attractive grey stone buildings on Cotehele quay tells the story of *Shamrock* and of the once-flourishing local shipping industry.

(*Right*) Bernard Shaw was active right to the end of his long life. One of the many personal relics on display at Shaw's Corner is his membership card for the Cyclists' Touring Club; it is dated 1950, the year he died aged ninety-four. (*NT*)

Shaw's Corner Hertfordshire

At south-west end of the village of Ayot St Lawrence,
2 miles north-east of Wheathampstead

This rather undistinguished Edwardian villa is
where the Irish dramatist and critic George Bernard
Shaw moved in 1906 at the age of fifty to enjoy a full
and fruitful old age. Apart from the museum room,
which shows such gems as the old-fashioned steel-
rimmed spectacles Shaw wore in his later years and
his membership card for the Cyclists' Touring Club
dated 1950, the year in which he died, the house is
still arranged very much as it was in his day and is
filled with echoes of his individuality and genius. It
is almost as if the great man has just gone out for the
afternoon, taking a hat from the collection in the
hall. In the study his typewriter sits waiting on the
desk, with his pens to one side and the pocket
dictionaries he used for immediate reference ranged
below the window on to the garden. Perhaps his
secretary Miss Patch is away, as her little desk in the
corner of the room is unnaturally tidy. One of the
drawers of the filing cabinets behind where she sits
carries a characteristic Shavian label: 'Keys and
Contraptions'.

In the drawing-room next door a bronze bust by
Rodin perfectly captures the craggy head, with its
rather prominent nose and full beard. Shaw hardly
used this room after his wife died in 1943, preferring
to sit in an armchair by the fire in the dining-room
after eating an early vegetarian dinner. Photographs
of Gandhi, Lenin and Stalin above the fireplace
reflect Shaw's socialist views and the room is
dominated by Augustus John's glowing oil portrait. From here Shaw used to step out into the
garden for his regular evening walks, or to bury
himself in the little shed where he did much of his
writing, safe from interruptions, sitting in the
wicker chair which is still pulled up to the table at
which he worked.

Sheffield Park Garden East Sussex

Midway between East Grinstead and Lewes, 5 miles north-
west of Uckfield, on east side of the A275

This peaceful hundred-acre woodland garden set on
the edge of the Sussex Weald is large enough to
accommodate a flood of visitors in the summer
months without losing its character. Focused on a
chain of lakes, the garden is criss-crossed by gravel
and grass paths which weave and loop through the
trees, sometimes bordering the water, sometimes
veering away from it. It is possible to wander for an

Autumn colour round
the top lake at
Sheffield Park, with
Wyatt's Gothic
mansion in the
distance.
(*NT/Ian Shaw*)

287

afternoon here without discovering the full range of the planting or retracing one's steps.

The garden is the creation of Arthur G. Soames, who acquired the estate on the death of the 3rd Earl of Sheffield in 1909 and devoted the next twenty-five years to transforming and extending the landscape park which 'Capability' Brown had laid out for the 1st Earl at the end of the eighteenth century. The neo-Gothic mansion (not owned by the Trust) which James Wyatt designed in 1775 to crown the 1st Earl's new property rises like a fairy-tale palace at the top of the garden, a great tracery window prominent in the end façade.

The 3rd Earl extended Brown's original two lakes to create a T-shaped chain, with picturesque cascades joining one level to another. From the top bridge over the first cascade, one can look back at Wyatt's pinnacled and battlemented fantasy mirrored in the waters of the first lake or down the impressive 25-foot drop to the length of the second, where palms flourishing on grassy islands immediately below the rocky falls add a suggestion of tropical luxuriance. Rafts of water lilies dot the surface of the upper lakes in summer, flowering white above the dividing cascade, red and pink below the falls. An impressive range of trees and shrubs lines the shores of the lakes, each species added and placed in an inspired planting scheme which has resulted in one of the finest woodland gardens in the British Isles.

Sheffield Park is said to be at its best in the autumn, when deep-blue water on crisp sunny days sets off turning leaves, a number of tupelo trees (*Nyssa sylvatica*) providing particularly spectacular displays. In spring there are wild daffodils and bluebells, and the flowers of the Japanese magnolia, like a cloud of exotic butterflies against the bare March twigs. Only a couple of months later the garden is ablaze with flowering shrubs, including an important collection of Ghent azaleas with honeysuckle-like blooms and banks of rhododendrons flowering blue, purple, yellow and wine-red, many of them sweetly scented. Spotted orchids appear in the long grass fringing the Queen's Walk circling one of the lower lakes, now a conservation area for wild flowers.

Although the freak storm in the autumn of 1987 thinned the trees framing and sheltering the garden, many exceptional mature specimens survived, including ancient chestnuts and oaks old enough to rival those at Croft Castle (*see* p.93) and already full

grown when William of Orange landed in 1688. Others are conifers planted by the 3rd Lord Sheffield at the end of the nineteenth century. Exotics from the Far East are also well represented, such as the dawn redwood from east Asia, at one time thought to be extinct, the feathery Chinese honey locust and *Pinus armandii* and the rare Nikko maple. A shady stream garden created over the last ten years is now well established, primulas, hostas, lilies and other water-loving plants flowering in a strip of pink, white and blue beneath the trees.

Sheringham Park Norfolk

2 miles south-west of Sheringham, 5 miles west of Cromer, 6 miles east of Holt

The 770 acres of Sheringham Park, mostly lying tucked behind the coast road near the holiday town of Sheringham, are what Humphry Repton called his 'most favourite work'. The parkland landscape was conceived for Abbot Upcher to whom Repton presented a Red Book of especial charm in 1812. The woodlands contain magnificent displays of rhododendrons and azaleas of many varieties and the rolling parkland itself is adorned by an ornamental temple, suggested by Repton but actually built in 1975. North of the coast road, the land slopes gently down to soft eroding cliffs of glacial clays, sands and gravels. This part of the property includes half a mile of coast, with a dramatic section of the North Norfolk coastal path, and is designated as a Site of Special Scientific Interest on account of fulmars which nest on the cliff face.

In 1994 the Trust's holding here was extended by the 100-acre Weybourne Woods, adjoining the park.

Shropshire Hills Shropshire

Northern extremity extends from the Severn gorge to Montgomery on the Welsh border, and the southern extremity from Cleobury Mortimer to Knighton

Among the glorious hills of Shropshire, including Brown Clee, Titterstone Clee and the Stiperstones, is the great Long Mynd. West of the A49 lies Church Stretton, its hotels and boarding houses starting to climb up the hill behind but petering out as if the effort were too much, and with good reason, for the mynd, from the Welsh *mynydd*, or mountain, has

The Sheringham estate includes a dramatic section of the North Norfolk coastal path. (*NT/Angelo Hornak*)

always been a real barrier, shielding the Welsh from the forays of the Marcher barons.

The great ridge, running for ten miles from south-west to north-east and three or four miles wide, is broken by steep valleys known as hollows or batches, and for centuries was a wilderness of heather and grass, grazed only by sheep and ponies. Early in the morning the valleys are sunlit; as the sun moves they fall into shadow. The light can be dramatic: in stormy weather the clouds race across the hills, shafts of sunlight suddenly striking a distant spur. Along the spine runs the Portway, a Bronze Age ridgeway which later became a route for cattle drovers from Wales to the Midlands.

All this beauty seemed at no risk until the Forestry Commission turned its acquisitive eye towards these border hills. Here was cheap land to buy and plant, easier to afforest than the true mountain land in north and central Wales. The great Mortimer and Clun Forests began to blanket the

hills and crept up from the south on to Long Mynd itself; the contrast at Minton Batch, where the Trust's open hills join the dark conifers, is an object lesson. In 1965 an appeal was launched and 4,700 acres were bought, with over 1,100 since. About half the high land, which rises to over 1,100 feet, now belongs to the Trust. It is superb for walking – up one hollow, along the ridge, back down another, or from Church Stretton up and over the top to Ratlinghope or Asterton, hamlets buried in the broken country stretching into Wales. The lie of the hills means that only from the 2,197-foot summit at Pole Bank can one see the whole panorama over Wales, the Marches and the West Midlands. On a clear day the view is from Cadair Idris to the Cotswolds, from the Brecon Beacons to Beeston Castle, near Chester.

Five miles across the A49, to the east, is a very different ridge, the narrow limestone escarpment of Wenlock Edge, running for fifteen miles on the same south-west to north-east alignment as the Long Mynd. Approached from the east it is un-dramatic: farmland rising gently to a scrubby skyline, with an occasional view down into Hope-dale below giving a sense of height. From the west it rears up as a harsh cliff, hacked about by quarry men and lime burners for centuries, menacing in certain lights.

The Wenlock limestone, formed in the Silurian period some 420 million years ago, developed as a barrier reef on the edge of a continental shelf when a deep ocean covered what is now land to the west. Built up largely from the skeletons of small marine creatures, the rock is full of fossils. The overlying thin soil has a rich flora of orchids, quaking-grass, yellow-wort, carline thistle and bushes of yew and spindle smothered in old-man's beard.

The Trust owns some five miles of Wenlock Edge, from Much Wenlock south to Easthope, including two viewpoints: Major's Leap, from where the Royalist Major Smallman jumped to elude his Parliamentarian pursuers (see p.366), and the crag of Ippikin's Rock. They lie either side of the road which slithers down the Edge to the village of Hughley, celebrated by A. E. Housman.

Contrasting with the harshness of Wenlock Edge and the magnificence of the Long Mynd is Hopesay Hill, lying north of Aston-on-Clun in the peaceful hilly country west of Craven Arms. The hill, a gentle ridge with paths leading to modest views, is used as a sheepwalk. Housman's quatrain sets the scene perfectly: *'In valleys of springs of rivers, By Ony and Teme and Clun, The country for easy livers, The quietest under the sun.'*

Shugborough Staffordshire

6 miles east of Stafford on the A513

The two Anson brothers born in the 1690s took very different paths in life. George, who went to sea at the age of twelve, rose to be 1st Lord of the Admiralty and gained both fame and fortune on an epic four-year circumnavigation of the globe in the 1740s, during which he captured a treasure-laden Spanish galleon. Much of the Admiral's wealth went to help his cultivated elder brother Thomas improve the three-storey late seventeenth-century house on the banks of the River Sow which he had inherited in 1720, financing the charming domed pavilions with semicircular bay windows by Thomas Wright of Durham which now frame the central block. The massive two-storey portico dominating the entrance front was a later addition,

part of Samuel Wyatt's alterations for the 1st Viscount Anson at the end of the century. Similarly, Wyatt was responsible for the central bow on the garden façade, and for the verandahs fronting the links to the pavilions on either side.

A leading spirit of the Society of Dilettanti which promoted the art of classical Greece, Thomas Anson's interiors reflect his interest in the ancient world. Six sombre Piranesi-like paintings of classical ruins by Nicholas Thomas Dall adorn the dining-room, large and imposing enough not to be overshadowed by Vassalli's arresting plasterwork gently curving overhead. The low-ceilinged library, with a shallow arch set on Ionic columns dividing the room, is more welcoming, the apparently classical marble busts set along the bookcases including a nineteenth-century study of one of the family with a rabbit as well as likenesses of Plato and Hercules.

Neo-classical motifs also mark Wyatt's interiors. Giant yellow scagliola columns punctuate the walls of his curiously elongated saloon, their reflections in the pier glasses on the end wall making the room seem even larger than it is. Joseph Rose the Younger's coved ceiling in Wyatt's impressive Red Drawing Room is decorated with delicate compositions reminiscent of a Wedgwood vase. This room also displays remnants of Thomas Anson's famous picture collection, mostly dispersed with the rest of the contents in the 1842 sale precipitated by the extravagance of the 2nd Viscount, created 1st Earl of Lichfield. A number of paintings connected with the estate have also survived, including two portraits of Corsican goats, noble-looking beasts with corkscrew horns, part of a herd of this rare breed established by Thomas Anson. Magnificent French furniture in the principal rooms was acquired by the 2nd Earl when he set about rescuing the house in the 1850s.

A gold repeater, a snuffbox made of wood from one of his ships, Spanish coins and his commission from George III are among several mementoes of the gallant Admiral. One of his officers designed the little Chinese house by the Sow, set off by a pagoda tree and other oriental shrubs, but the rococo plaster ceiling and superb Chinese painted mirrors which once adorned it are now in the house, complementing the oriental porcelain and other chinoiserie acquired by the brothers.

Formal terraced gardens punctuated by cones of golden yew and classical urns lead down to the river, arches and pillars trailing roses and clematis partly screening the Victorian-style rose garden round a central sundial. The long loop of the Ladies' Walk meanders through the wild garden to the south where daffodils and bluebells beneath the trees in spring are followed by the dark-purple and creamy-yellow blossoms of groups of rhododendrons and azaleas. Thomas Wright's Picturesque ruin on the banks of the Sow, a crumbling array of columns and walls topped by the statue of a druid, is outclassed by the classical monuments based on buildings in ancient Athens in the park which Thomas Anson commissioned from James 'Athenian' Stuart. A triumphal arch stalks across the grass on a rise above the drive like a creature from outer space. Two pedimented porches with fluted columns project from the octagonal Tower of the Winds in the valley below and a shady knoll is crowned with the Lantern of Demosthenes, a cluster of columns topped by three dolphins supporting a tripod and bowl. No later development dulls the impact of these re-creations, only a gentle roar and tremors in the ground betraying the presence of the Stafford to Stoke main railway line buried in a tunnel beneath the triumphal arch.

Sissinghurst Castle Garden Kent

2 miles north-east of Cranbrook, 1 mile east of Sissinghurst village on the A262

The beauty and charm of this exceptional garden set high on a ridge above the Vale of Kent owe much to the Tudor buildings around which it was created and which form a romantic backdrop to the planting. The focal point of the garden is a four-storey red-brick Elizabethan prospect tower with two octagonal turrets, a remnant of the great mansion built by Sir Richard Baker in the mid-sixteenth century, one of the first houses in England constructed in brick and so magnificent that it was chosen by Elizabeth I for a three-day visit during her Progress through the Weald in 1573. Across what was the outer courtyard, the long entrance range of an earlier house is pierced by a gabled archway, crowned with three slender Tudor chimneys. On the other side of the tower two arms of an ancient moat are still filled with water and elsewhere in the garden are remains of Tudor walls, a cottage which was once part of the south wing of the Elizabethan mansion and a sixteenth-century

priest's house. Despite over 200 years of neglect and decay, these romantic remains inspired the novelist and biographer Vita Sackville-West to purchase the property in 1930 and with the help of her husband, Sir Harold Nicolson, the diplomat and literary critic, to create one of the greatest gardens of the twentieth century.

Like Hidcote (*see* p.149), Sissinghurst was conceived as a series of intimate open-air rooms, bounded with red-brick walls or with hedges of

Four Irish yews round the central copper in the cottage garden at Sissinghurst set off the red, yellow and orange planting scheme. (*NT/Eric Crichton*)

(*Overleaf*) The west front of Shugborough in *c.*1768 by Nicholas Dall. The Chinese house half hidden in trees beside the River Sow still survives, but James 'Athenian' Stuart's orangery and the classical ruin on the near bank of the river have disappeared. A number of other works by Dall at Shugborough include panoramic views of the park and James Stuart's monuments. (*NT/Erik Pelham*)

yew, rose or hornbeam and with long linking walks stretching across the garden. The design, which has the happy effect of making the whole seem larger than it is, was Harold Nicolson's achievement, but it was his wife who devised the inspired planting schemes, using colour and texture to build the effects which make Sissinghurst so individual. As Vita Sackville-West herself observed, there is a southern feel about the place, perhaps partly conjured up by the lush Kentish countryside. Faint echoes of a Mediterranean villa are strengthened in the profuse planting of figs and vines, and in the terracotta Tuscan pots which adorn the lime walk. In the cottage garden even the dreariest English weather cannot subdue the tangle of tulips, columbines, irises, tiger-lilies and dahlias planted here, flaming yellow, orange and red against the paving stones and old bricks of the paths. A prolific white rose cascades over the cottage at one end. A different tone is set by the tranquil grassy walk leading down to the moat, flanked on one side by a border of azaleas, on the other by the old brick moat wall, dotted with wild flowers clinging to the mortar in spring. The nuttery beyond the azaleas ends in a yew-enclosed herb garden, crowded with aromatic and medicinal plants, camphor, woad, rue, lovage and apothecary's rose among them.

One of the best places to appreciate Sissinghurst is from the top of the tower, reached by a spiral staircase which leads up past the cluttered room where Vita Sackville-West wrote, its walls lined with books reflecting her special interests – gardening, literature, history and travel. From the roof there is a view down on to the rose garden, planted with old-fashioned species grouped round a little lawn. The rich colours when the bushes are in flower contrast vividly with the ghostly, surreal tones in the tangled White Garden on the other side of the tower, where all the blossoms are white and much of the foliage is grey. White lavender, clematis and the white double primrose echo the planting described in one of Vita's letters on display in the tower, where there is also a plan by Harold Nicolson detailing daffodils, narcissi and forsythia for the end of the lime walk.

Beyond the borders of the garden, the tower looks out over woods, fields and oasthouses to a distant ridge of the North Downs, with the spire of Frittenden church in the middle distance. Perhaps Elizabeth I was taken up the tower to admire the view when she was entertained here.

Sizergh Castle Cumbria

3½ miles south of Kendal, north-west of the A6/A591 interchange

Sizergh is dominated by the fourteenth-century fortress at its heart. The Stricklands who have lived here for 750 years were one of the great military families of the north, and the house they constructed in about 1350 reflects both their status and the vulnerability of these acres within reach of the Scottish border, part of the lowland corridor leading south between the Lakeland hills and the inhospitable North Yorkshire moors. The once-moated stronghold rises almost sixty feet to the battlements, its limestone rubble walls still formidable despite the later mullioned windows and the softening blanket of Virginia creeper.

Tudor and Elizabethan additions, partly hidden behind a Georgian veneer, adjoin the pele tower and long low Elizabethan service wings with soaring chimneys flank the entrance courtyard. Double doors that once opened into the great hall now give access to a carriageway running through the castle, with a grand stone and oak staircase rising from one side.

Early Elizabethan woodwork in several of the rooms gives Sizergh its special flavour. Although the superb panelling that once adorned the Inlaid Chamber was sadly sold to the Victoria and Albert Museum, only a small section remaining to show what has been lost, craftsmanship of similar quality is displayed in the five intricately carved armorial chimneypieces, four of which date from 1563–75. The rest of the panelling is also very fine, the oldest in the house being the oak linenfold work dating from the reign of Henry VIII in a passage room. Intriguingly, a lozenge design on the woodwork in the old dining-room and one of the bedrooms reappears on the backs of three Elizabethan oak chairs in the pele tower. Here, too, there are unusually richly decorated carved oak benches produced in the mid-sixteenth century.

A number of Stuart portraits and personal royal relics, such as a silk and gold bedspread which once belonged to James II, advertise the Stricklands' adherence to the Catholic faith and devotion to the Stuart cause. Refusing to desert the royal family after 1688, Sir Thomas Strickland and his wife accompanied James II into exile in France where Lady Strickland was governess to the young prince.

Terraced lawns, their retaining walls bright with

The extensive rock garden at Sizergh Castle, the largest artificial example owned by the Trust, was created by Hayes of Ambleside in 1926 on the site of an old orchard. It is planted with dwarf conifers, Japanese maples and an exceptional collection of hardy ferns. (*NT/Robert Thrift*)

shrubs and climbers, lead down from the south front to the lake. Possibly created in the seventeenth century out of what was once part of the moat, the lake was much enlarged in 1926 when the terraces were built. Orchids and Lent lilies (wild daffodils) flowering in the grass of the meadow above the lake are part of a native limestone flora which reflects the rock outcropping all over the estate in screes, cliffs and pavements, but the extensive rock garden covering an acre was constructed of Westmorland stone in 1926 by Hayes of Ambleside, who arranged the little stream tumbling across it into the lake in a series of pools and falls. The crevices between the water-worn stones support a wide variety of plants, including primulas, astilbes, impressively large dwarf conifers, Japanese maples and an exceptional collection of hardy ferns, examples of the grey and

maroon *Athyrium nipponicum* 'Pictum', *Dryopteris erythrosora* and *Adiantum venustum* among them. A good herbaceous border beside the rock garden gives colour throughout the season and there is a rose garden beyond the gates, with an avenue of Beissner's rowan setting off shrub roses, hydrangeas, eucryphias and other flowering shrubs.

Skenfrith Gwent

6 miles north-west of Monmouth, 12 miles north-east of Abergavenny, on north side of the B4521 Ross road

The remains of some eighty castles scattered across South Wales recall the long drawn-out conflict between the Welsh and the English following the Norman Conquest. The little early thirteenth-century fortress of Skenfrith, set on low ground by the River Monnow, is one of the more important survivals, part of a trio (with White Castle to the south and Grosmont to the north) protecting a natural routeway into Wales. Washed by the river on one side, the castle is protected by a wide moat –

now a dry ditch – on the other three. Above these defences rise the remains of the massive curtain wall, best preserved along the river, ruined circular towers, from which attackers could be subjected to deadly raking fire, projecting boldly from the four corners. A large round keep in the style of those being built by the French king at this period rises forty feet from the centre of the enclosed court, constructed on a mound which probably formed part of a more primitive fortress established here in the decades after the Conquest.

Skenfrith is the work of Hubert de Burgh, Earl of Kent, who was granted the 'Three Castles' by King John and may have been influenced in his design by what he had seen while imprisoned in France. Like the builder of Bodiam away to the east (*see* p.35) two centuries later, the Earl of Kent was concerned with acquiring a nobleman's residence as well as a castle, the foundations and lower walls of his hall range still to be seen against the west curtain wall. Little changed since it was built, Skenfrith is a splendid example of the castles which foreshadowed the formidable symmetry of Edward I's great fortresses.

Smallhythe Place Kent

At Smallhythe, 2 miles south of Tenterden, on east side of the Rye road

This modest half-timbered sixteenth-century farmhouse belonged to the legendary actress Dame Ellen Terry for nearly thirty years, from 1899 until her death here on 21 July 1928. Appropriately, she first saw Smallhythe in the company of Henry Irving, the manager of the Lyceum Theatre in London's Covent Garden, with whom she created a famous theatrical partnership that lasted for twenty-four years.

Her attractive house stands at one end of the straggling hamlet, with a steeply sloping red-tiled roof and sturdy brick chimneys outlined against the Kentish marshes stretching away on all sides. With the sea ten miles away as the crow flies and the once sizeable stream bordering the garden shrunk to a narrow ditch, it is difficult to believe that the farm was formerly Port House to a thriving shipyard, catering for a procession of boats unloading at the wharves along the creek. A duckweed-covered pool marks the site of the repair dock used for some 400 years until the seventeenth century.

The house is now preserved as a theatrical museum, full of mementoes of Ellen Terry's long and eventful life and of the world in which she moved. In the large beamed kitchen which she used as a dining-room, with traditional wheel-back chairs ranged round the walls, a refectory table in the middle of the warm red-brick floor and a high-backed settle by the fire, two walls are devoted to David Garrick and Sarah Siddons. Other exhibits connected with famous names from the past include an affectionate message from Sarah Bernhardt – '*Merci*, my dearling' – written with a flourish on the cover of a dressing-table, Sir Arthur Sullivan's monocle, with his autograph on the glass, a chain worn by Fanny Kemble and a visiting card from

The actress Ellen Terry, whose spirit lives on at Smallhythe Place. The daughter of Benjamin Terry, a well-known provincial actor, Ellen Terry was steeped in the theatre from birth (appropriately enough, in theatrical lodgings in Coventry) and acquired a considerable reputation for her performances when still a child. (*NT*)

Alexandre Dumas, whose *La dame aux camélias* inspired Verdi's *La Traviata*. A letter in Oscar Wilde's languorous scrawl in an adjoining room begs Ellen Terry to accept 'the first copy of my first play', adding 'perhaps some day I shall be fortunate to write something worthy of your playing'. Here, too, is her make-up box; a sponge, a mirror and a large swatch of grey hair are prominent among the notably sparse contents, which seem barely adequate for someone of Terry's stature.

Upstairs there are displays of the lavish silk and velvet costumes which Irving created for Terry, much criticised for their extravagance, including the famous moss-green beetle-wing dress she wore as Lady Macbeth in 1888 and the vivid scarlet robes in which she portrayed a memorably touching Portia in *The Merchant of Venice*. The more private face of the great actress is revealed in her simple, low-ceilinged bedroom, still very much as she left it, with brightly patterned rugs on the bare boards of the floor, rotund pottery pigs on the mantelpiece and a view out over the marshes from the casement windows. Kate Hastings's pastel portraits of her mother and of her two children, Edith and Edward Gordon Craig, offspring of Terry's liaison with the architect and theatrical designer Edward Godwin, hang above the bed with its theatrical curved Empire ends. The wooden crucifix Gordon Craig made for his mother stands on the bedside table, next to a worn copy of the Globe Shakespeare annotated in her distinctively generous hand. Something of the great actress's integrity and resolution also emerges in a much-read edition of Robert Louis Stevenson's 'Christmas Sermon', one of the many underlined passages exhorting 'If your morals make you dreary, depend upon it they are wrong.'

Snowshill Manor Gloucestershire

3 miles south-west of Broadway, 4 miles west of junction of the A44 and the A424

The old lady who showed her grandson the family treasures hidden away in her Cantonese cabinet on Sunday afternoons could not have known that this was to be the inspiration for one of the most extraordinary collections ever assembled by one person. Charles Wade, born in 1883, was clearly an unusual little boy and he grew up to be a most exceptional man. A talented artist, craftsman and professional architect, once he had inherited the family sugar estates in the West Indies he devoted his life to restoring the Cotswold manor house he bought in 1919 and to amassing the wide-ranging exhibits now displayed here.

Snowshill is an L-shaped building of warm Cotswold stone, with a warren of rooms on different levels leading off one another. The Tudor hall house of *c.*1500 at its heart, still evident in the huge fireplace on the ground floor and in two ceilings upstairs, was substantially rebuilt in about 1600 and altered again in the early eighteenth century, when the curiously attractive south front was added. Here Georgian sash windows on the left side of the pedimented main entrance contrast with mullioned and transomed casements to the right, giving the house a slightly rakish air.

Every inch from ground floor to attics is devoted to Charles Wade's acquisitions, most of the rooms christened with bizarre names such as Dragon, Meridian, Top Gallant and Seraphim. Mr Wade did not set out to accumulate things because they were rare or valuable, but saw his pieces primarily as records of vanished handicrafts. As a result, the Snowshill collection is unique, displaying an unclassifiable range of everyday objects, from tools used in spinning, weaving and lacemaking to baby minders (one for use on board ship), prams, early bicycles, exquisite bone carvings made by French prisoners of war, eighteenth-century medicine chests cunningly contrived to carry a mass of little bottles and gaily painted model farm wagons. One room is devoted to pieces connected with the sea, such as compasses, telescopes and ship models, another to musical instruments, arranged as a playerless orchestra, and yet another (his Seventh Heaven) to many of the toys Mr Wade had as a child. Perhaps the most remarkable spectacle is in the Green Room, where suits of Japanese Samurai armour topped with ferocious masks threaten visitors in a theatrically staged display. A sense of order everywhere shows that this is no random, magpie collection but a reflection of a serious purpose.

The charming steeply sloping terraced garden was largely designed by Wade's friend, M. H. Baillie Scott, a fellow architect with whom he had worked when employed by Raymond Unwin in London before the First World War, but Wade altered and adapted the original structure. It is laid out as a series of interconnecting but separate garden rooms, with arches and steps leading from one to another

Early bicycles at Snowshill, just one facet of Charles Wade's wide-ranging collection in this Cotswold manor house. (*NT/Erik Pelham*)

and with roses and other climbing plants trailing over the dividing walls. Flagged paths, carefully contrived vistas down and across the slope, many features and centres of interest and Wade's old-fashioned planting schemes reflect the influence of the Arts and Crafts movement, with its preference for cottage-garden styles. A long path bordered with pillars of clipped Irish yew leads past the grassy Armillary Court, dominated by a tall sundial, to the medieval dovecote, where birds roosting on the steeply pitched roof stand out brilliantly white against the stone flags. A Venetian wellhead at one end of a lower terrace balances the small water-lily

pool at the other, with colour from a bracelet of crowded borders.

This garden is ideally suited to the Cotswold house it sets off, the blue, mauve and purple of delphiniums, larkspur and lavender blending beautifully with the honey-coloured stone. Garden seats, tubs and other woodwork are also blue, painted the dark shade with a hint of turquoise which Charles Wade used as a foil to grass and foliage. And always there is the backdrop of a far wooded hillside across the valley.

Only yards from the manor house is the little cottage where Charles Wade lived without electricity and with a fireplace with two bread ovens as the only means of heating and cooking, the walls and even the ceiling of his kitchen/living-room covered with a multitude of useful objects, from bowls and tankards to farm tools. Seeing these spartan conditions and the workshop where he spent so many happy hours, it is easy to believe, as Queen Mary said after visiting Snowshill in 1937, that the most notable part of the collection was Mr Wade himself.

Souter Lighthouse Tyne and Wear

2½ miles south of South Shields, on A183

Just south of the Tyne estuary, overlooking a stretch of unspoilt limestone coastline owned by the Trust (*see* The Leas, p.231), is a prominent clifftop lighthouse, its 76-foot tower painted in bold red and white stripes. Built in 1870, it was the first lighthouse to be powered by an alternating electric current and could be seen from some 19 miles out to sea. A focal point on a stretch of open grassy clifftop, the lighthouse dominates a row of nineteenth-century coastguard cottages and other ancillary buildings. A nearby array of limekilns is a reminder of former quarrying along these cliffs, and there was once a colliery village here too.

South Cornish Coast

A few miles south of Land's End, St Levan church, vicarage and farm lie back from the coast in a sheltered valley. Seawards, the headland of Pedn-mên-an-mere commands the view across the bay to the superb headland of Treryn Dinas, owned by the Trust since 1933. As the sun goes down in the west, or as the water sparkles in the moonlight, the view is unforgettable. A steep path descends to Porthcurno, one of Cornwall's finest beaches, and also a place of significance in the history of communications. Given to the Trust by Cable & Wireless plc in 1994, it was the landing point for cables linking Britain to the world telegraph network. More than two miles of Trust coastline runs on from here past Pedn-vounder Beach (pronounced Pedneyfunder) beneath Treen Cliff to the east, where a steep path gives access to a curving strand of the finest sand. The bathing is good if the sea is calm, but care should be taken of the sand bar which builds up offshore in some seasons and can cause currents.

The rocket-like tower of Souter Lighthouse, set on limestone cliffs just south of the Tyne estuary, and visible, when it was working, from far out in the North Sea. (*NT/Matthew Antrobus*)

The granite here is in blocks, cube piled on cube, for all the world like a child's bricks. Arrows painted on the rocks lead the way to the Logan Rock (the Cornish verb *log* means 'to heave', 'to move'; the name of the rock is pronounced 'loggan'). There were formerly many such in Cornwall, formed by weathering over an immensely long period, and this celebrated specimen has been visited by tourists since the eighteenth century. It is said to weigh sixty-two tons and to have rocked easily before 1824 when Lieutenant Goldsmith, nephew of the poet, landed with a party of sailors and with a good deal of effort and ingenuity succeeded in dislodging it. A fine old row ensued. Petitions were dispatched to the Admiralty and the Lords Commissioners sent a peremptory order to Goldsmith to replace the rock. This needed much greater effort, and spars, cables and sheaves were sent from Devonport Dockyard at Goldsmith's expense. At last all was made ready and with a long heave and a strong heave the rock was reset. Half the county attended the occasion and Goldsmith became a hero.

Beyond Treryn the path leads across Cribba Head and steeply down to Penberth, the most perfect of Cornish fishing coves. The Trust owns most of the valley behind the cove and its policy is to let the little granite cottages to those who earn their living here, fishing and growing violets and narcissi for the early markets, though this latter trade has largely ceased due to competition from flowers grown under glass. The fishermen have formed a co-operative society and fishing flourishes. Crab and lobster pots are no longer made from withies grown in the valley, for they last for only two seasons whereas the modern steel and plastic pots last for eight or ten. The boats are small, up to sixteen feet, because of the limited space available for pulling up clear of high water. This is an inshore fishery, boats going five or six miles out to sea, from St Michael's Mount to the Wolf Rock twelve miles to the southwest, or sometimes round Land's End to the Brisons, a group of rocks off Cape Cornwall. Fish are caught by hand-lining, three-quarters of the catch being mackerel, with some pollack and colefish. The shell fishery is for lobster and crab and high prices are given by buyers from France.

St Michael's Mount (*see* p.278), even more beautiful than its French namesake, presides grandly over Mount's Bay. To the west the view from the island looks over the expanse of Penzance, but to the east it is closed by Cudden Point, a miniature version of Gurnard's Head in shape (*see* p.223), with the low, open fields of Trenow in the foreground. Five miles to the east there is Trust land on either side of the privately owned Rinsey Head. Lesceave Cliff, west of the headland, seals off the scattered development of Praa Sands, a wilderness of caravans, chalets and bungalows where the Trust preserves a patch of scrub above the beach. To the east Rinsey Cliff surrounds a delightful cove and sets off the roofless engine house and stack of Wheal Prosper (*see* p.86), a copper-mining venture which closed in about 1860. Beyond Rinsey lies the bold Trewavas Head, only part of which the Trust owns, and the coast is also privately owned from there to Porthleven, once busy with shipbuilding and fishing, dying since the 1950s but now reactivated by a purchaser of the harbour and shipyard who has injected fresh capital and new ideas.

The 1,600-acre Penrose estate, the largest gift ever made to the Trust in Cornwall, stretches for six miles south-east to Gunwalloe. The freshwater lake of the Loe (from *logh*, the Cornish word for a pool) runs inland for over a mile, cut off from the sea by the great shingle beach of Loe Bar. Carminowe Creek forms a branch of the lake to the east. The wooded banks are utterly peaceful and the Trust owns the whole of the surrounding landscape. It was a far-sighted condition of this princely gift that cars should be kept well away and the lake should remain free of boats and waterskiers. So the Trust has made a number of small carparks set back from the water, linked by a network of footpaths which provide delightful walks. Cliffs, shingle beach, sea and freshwater, with woodland, reed marsh and farmland, make up an unforgettable whole.

The Loe was not originally a lake but the estuary of the River Cober, with the port of Helston at its head, but by the thirteenth century the shingle bar had formed, cutting the town off from the sea. The shingle is nearly all of flint and where it comes from is an unsolved mystery, possibly a sea-bed deposit offshore. Extensive tin and copper mines on the high ground above Helston drained into the Cober valley, bringing down vast quantities of silt which have gradually filled the upper end of the lake to form Loe Marsh, a large area of willow and alder,

(*Opposite page*) Pedn-vounder Beach, with the giant boulder known as the Logan Rock perched precariously on the jagged granite headland across the sand. (*NT/Rob Matheson*)

with reeds lower down, reminiscent of a tropical mangrove swamp. After heavy rain the water level rises rapidly, often flooding the lower parts of Helston in the past. The mayor of the town then paid three halfpence to the lord of the manor of Penrose, who allowed a channel to be cut through the bar, which none the less soon closed again. The latest channel had to be cut in 1984 and it remains to be seen whether the improvements will avoid future flooding.

The Loe is probably the most important place in Cornwall for wintering wildfowl. Widgeon, teal, mallard, shoveller, pochard, tufted duck and coot appear each year, while a few mallard, coot, moorhen and mute swans nest here. Herons and cormorants can always be seen and rarer birds, particularly migrants in season, stay for a few days. In high summer the lake suffers from the phenomenon known as eutrophication. An algal bloom turns the surface of the water green and de-oxygenates it, which is harmful to the fish and other creatures living in the lake. The bloom has become worse with the use of modern fertilisers on the land draining into the pool, not to speak of sewage effluent draining into the lake from Helston and the large naval aerodrome at Culdrose.

The woods are largely mixed hardwoods, with Monterey cypress and Monterey pine near the sea. Beside the drive at Bar Lodge, at the north end of the bar, is a colony of an exotic plant from Chile, a member of the pineapple family, *Fascicularia pitcairniifolia*, with long spiky leaves, red at the base, and blue flowers. On the cliff below the lodge flourishes the Hottentot fig, *Carpobrotus edulis*, with brightly coloured flowers from May to August.

South of Loe Bar the beach, and most of the cliff, belongs to the Trust as far as Gunwalloe Fishing Cove. The rusting winches above the cove came from ships wrecked on this coast and were used by local fishermen to haul their boats clear of the surf. From the cove a lane leads the weary walker to refreshment at the Halzephron Inn nearby. After a short gap the Trust's land starts at Halsferran Cove and runs over the high Halzephron Cliff to Dollar Cove, then past the church to Gunwalloe Church Cove.

Church Cove was the scene of a famous Trust battle. The Trust had long owned Gunwalloe Towans east of the stream but could not control what happened to the west. The gift of the Penrose estate in 1974 brought the cove into one ownership

and it became possible to make a carpark behind Winnianton Farm, and to stop parking on the beach and dunes which had become degraded by overuse. Some people protested at losing what they looked upon as a right to park; others applauded the Trust's initiative. There were some lively scenes. The benefit has been incontestable; visitors can now sit in comfort round the cove clear of cars.

The church of St Winwaloe, tucked under the cliff beside the beach, is sited on the very edge of its parish because — from about the sixth century — there was an important settlement here which later became a royal manor. The Cornish section of Domesday Book begins 'the King holds Winneton'. The Towans were bought by the Trust in 1956 to avert the very real threat of development as a major caravan site. The golf club, started in 1890, had gone bankrupt and the course was to be sold. The Trust was able to raise the wind, buy the land, let it for grazing for some years, and then lease it to a reconstituted golf club for this very suitable use.

Beyond the Towans Poldhu Cove, with fine hard sand and safe bathing, is dominated by the massive bulk of the former Poldhu Hotel, built in 1899 and now made into flats. When the railway arrived at Helston a series of large hotels was built round the Lizard coast, served by the Great Western Railway's motor-bus service, a trailblazer in its day. South of the hotel the monument at the cliff edge commemorates Guglielmo Marconi, who in 1901 received here the first transatlantic wireless message, sent to him from Newfoundland. In 1923 he successfully tested his short-wave beam system which revolutionised long-distance communication. Marconi came here because the geology of the Lizard peninsula provides a stable base for wireless reception. It is no coincidence that at Goonhilly Downs, three miles to the south-east, there now stand the great saucers of the Satellite Earth Station, beaming messages round the world day and night.

Mullion Cove is a picture-postcard place, and deserves its fame, but the once beautiful approach leading down to it has been much spoilt in recent years by bungalows and caravans. The harbour walls, built in 1893–5 by Lord Robartes of Lanhydrock (*see* p.176) to provide shelter for the fishermen's boats in the open cove, are made of local greenstone, a basalt-like rock of great hardness which strikes fire with flint. The picturesque Winch House at the head of the slipway is older, built for the capstan used to haul boats clear of the sea before the harbour was constructed, and now housing a modern motor winch. This coast faces directly into the Atlantic gales and the Trust has to spend substantial sums in keeping the quays in repair. At low water a tunnel dries out to lead through the cliff to a secluded sandy beach to the south.

Predannack Cliff runs with the three small farms of Predannack Wollas, two of which belong to the Trust. The Cornish suffix *wollas* means lower and is always found, as here, in conjunction with the suffix *wartha*, meaning higher. This is a typical medieval farming settlement, the three farms huddled together with their own enclosed fields nearby, each grazing the unenclosed moorland and cliff 'in common'. However, no farmer can today afford a boy to look after grazing animals and the common grazing had become neglected, overgrown with scrub which smothered the cliff flowers. The Trust has therefore erected unobtrusive fencing to enable grazing to start again. The rarer flora is rapidly recovering: hairy bird's-foot trefoil, prostrate dyer's

greenweed and fringed rupturewort, with sheets of blue-flowered squill in spring.

To the east the Trust unusually owns half of Predannack airfield, the other half being owned by the Ministry of Defence. From 1939–45 Spitfires and Hurricanes were based here and the airfield is now used for training pilots from the naval air station at Culdrose. The reason for the Trust's acquisition is that some of the best areas of the unique Lizard heath grow within the perimeter fence.

Two miles to the south lies Kynance Cove, which has long been a place of pilgrimage. The hard yellow sand, the crystal-clear water, the rocky islets offshore and the mottled brown, red and green serpentine rock made Kynance a Victorian water-colourist's dream. Until 1987 the surroundings were marred by a large car-park with commercial buildings on the skyline; these have since been acquired by the Trust, eyesores removed and the landscape restored. Even more popular as a tourist attraction is Lizard Point, the two-pronged prow of the

The tiny harbour at Mullion Cove, built in 1893–5 by Lord Robartes of Lanhydrock (*see* p.176). (*NT/Mike Williams*)

peninsula, where the Trust now owns the furthest tip, the most southerly point of mainland Britain. There has been remedial work here too, with half a mile of dry-stone wall, known in Cornwall as a hedge, built along the access route. The coastal footpath which links all these holdings runs on past the former Lloyds Signal Station, on Bass Point, and north up the Lizard's eastern flank. Here is Landewednack Church Cove, with an abandoned and beautiful cliff-edge quarry to the north and, half a mile beyond, Inglewidden, with the spectacular collapsed cave known as the Devil's Frying Pan.

The steep slope leading down to Cadgwith Cove is covered with a dwarf wood of wind-clipped elms, apparently unique in Britain for this species. Lime-washed cottages cluster round the beach, some of them still thatched, and a small community of fishermen work from the cove, mainly in the shellfish fishery. On the headland to the north is a little stone building, formerly the coastguard's watch-house, and from here there is a lovely cliff walk, all on the Trust's land, past Kildown Cove and Enys Head down to Carleon Cove. The shingle on the beach is of many colours, much of it sea-washed pebbles of serpentine, and the curved capstan house and three-storey warehouse which now stand so picturesquely above the beach are all that remains of the substantial works of the Lizard Serpentine Company (1853–93), where machinery driven by water-power cut and polished objects made of this colourful rock: fonts and pulpits, tombstones, chimneypieces, urns and ornaments, even complete shop fronts. A few miles beyond, round Black Head, the Trust owns a stretch of coastal farmland and cliff running south from the rocky promontory of Chynalls Point.

The estuary of the Helford river has suffered from development above Helford Passage and particularly at Port Navas, both on the north bank, but the greater part of it is beautiful to a degree, the upper reaches wooded, remote, peaceful, a place to drift in a boat with only the occasional dip of one's oars. The Trust owns only three stretches of the south bank. Upstream of Helford village is the sheltered Penarvon Cove, cradled by low wooded cliffs, almost like a scene from *Treasure Island*. Here the Trust owns forty acres and the cottages in the valley and on the bluff opposite Helford Passage. A mile further west is the entrance to Frenchman's Creek, the wooded inlet leading south from the estuary ever narrowing until the tree branches meet

overhead at the head of the little creek. Merthen Wood, on the north shore, a great bank of wind-trimmed oak coppice, is privately owned, but opposite lie the fifty acres of the Trust's Tremayne Wood, surrounding the boathouse and quay which served Trelowarren, a romantic Tudor house hidden away in a wooded valley two miles to the south. The wood is of beech, ash, oak and sweet chestnut, with a good ground flora in the leaf mould below, in early spring carpeted with wood anemones, the flowers varying from purest white to a clear Cambridge blue.

On the north bank of the estuary is the hamlet of Durgan, where the Trust owns half the cottages and the garden of Glendurgan (*see* p.126) in the valley rising above it. Early traders from the Mediterranean called here for tin which was exported from Cornwall long before the arrival of the Romans. There is still some fishing, but Durgan's chief function today is as a sheltered base for the fleet of small boats which ride at their multi-coloured buoys, the wooded cliffs rising above them. The best approach is by water, for the non-resident visitor has to park his car half a mile before reaching the hamlet.

Bosloe lies to the east, the substantial and seemly house built as a rich man's holiday retreat in 1880, and now divided into three holiday houses by the Trust. With it runs farmland sloping down to the water's edge and joining Durgan with the Carwinion valley, then a short privately owned gap before the bold headland of Mawnan Shear at the mouth of the estuary. This formed part of the glebe of the vicar of Mawnan whose church tower peers out of the trees at the top of the cliff, with Parson's Beach beneath. From the headland the views over the estuary to Nare Point, and three miles up it to Merthen Wood, remain in the memory. Rosemullion Head juts eastward as Falmouth Bay sweeps in towards the Helford river. The Trust owns the coast on both sides of the headland for more than a mile, with little coves and nearby rocks which are good for bathing.

The grandest harbour in the English Channel, Falmouth has a long history. The newer town, behind the big beach of Gyllyngvase, has a proper sea front. Pendennis Castle, on the headland above it, built by Henry VIII, guards the entrance to the old town inside the estuary. Pendennis was the last fortress, but for Raglan, to hold out for King Charles in the Civil War, and the parish church is

Kynance Cove on the south coast of Cornwall, much painted by Victorian tourists. (*NT*)

dedicated to King Charles the Martyr. As well as the old quays and warehouses there is a modern ship-repair yard with an immense dry dock, big enough to take supertankers. The three parts of the town – the seaside resort, the old port, the ship-repair yard – hang together and make a walk through the streets and alleys in the higher part of old Falmouth an exciting experience, with views of all these activities over the chimneypots, and the broad sweep of the great estuary running up to the deep water of the Carrick Roads at its head. Overlooking the Roads, where the River Fal opens into its estuary, is the dignified façade of Trelissick House, standing high above the water and looking down over its park the full length of the harbour and out to sea. A lovely circular walk leads from the garden (*see* p.337) through the waterside woods to King Harry Ferry, the quiet Lamouth Creek beyond it, and then back through further woodland and park.

On the opposite bank of the Fal lies Turnaware Point, a pleasant place for picnics and blackberry-ing, with a safe beach. Past the headland flows the busy traffic of the river: small cargo boats bound for

Truro, river trips to and from Falmouth, fishermen and dinghy sailors and, from October to March, the stoutly built oyster boats which here continue the only fishery where no boats with engines are allowed. Truro Corporation, as owner of the oyster beds, decrees that to give equal opportunity to each fisherman no motor boats should be used. Whenever the weather is favourable in the winter months the 'working boats' can be seen beating up and down the estuary trawling the oysters from the bottom. On this east shore of the harbour the Trust owns virtually all the farmland from St Just to St Mawes, rising steeply from the water's edge to the escarpment, a splendid backdrop to the great sheet of water, with a waterside walk between the two villages.

St Anthony Head protects Falmouth from the east, the lighthouse at its foot shining its white beam to mark the entrance to the harbour, the light flashing through a red sector to warn of the dangerous Manacle Rocks across the bay. The headland was fortified at least from the year of Trafalgar in 1805 and further strengthened in 1853 and 1885. It continued to be manned by a coastal artillery unit until 1957. By that time not only had it been cut off by a high iron fence but it was covered in Nissen huts and with gun and searchlight positions erected during the Second World War. With generous help from local people, the Trust was able to buy the land, remove the concrete and the hutments (though the underground magazine remains) and encourage the natural vegetation to recover, a major piece of landscape restoration. From here there are magnificent views over Falmouth Bay and much of this part of Cornwall, with a topograph to name the places one can see.

From Porth, at the peninsula's north end, where there are hidden carparks, a circular walk runs for three and a half miles round the north end of the parish, and this can be doubled in length by making an extra circuit on the public path round the privately owned farm of Place Barton. The paths run partly on the clifftop, partly along the creek sides, partly through woodland, a wonderfully varied walk with water and boats always in sight, and seabirds and estuary birds to be seen. Porthbeor and Towan beaches on the sea coast provide good bathing with sand, sun and shelter. It is hard to imagine now how the latter beach, a curving strand with fields sloping gently down to the sand, was disfigured by up to 150 summer caravans before the

Trust acquired the land and brought this use to an end.

To the north of St Anthony much of the coast of this large bay, three miles across but six miles as the shore runs, belongs to the Trust. The sandy beach of Porthcurnick is sheltered by the low green headland of Pednvadan. It was bought because the land behind the beach had become over-commercialised and was a mess. Caravans, huts and cars were scattered higgledy-piggledy and could be seen for miles. Removal of this clutter, realignment of fences and planting of trees showed that the landscape was quite easily restored, given initiative and local support.

Treluggan Cliff continues the walk northwards, covered with blackthorn, bracken, furze and willow, good cover for small birds, with little sandy coves on the rocky foreshore below and the Trust's farmland above running back to the coast road. The beach at Pendower, with a pleasant long low hotel behind it and a handful of houses above, is popular with people from Truro, Cornwall's county town. Sand dunes behind the beach screen the carpark and the few buildings, and on a hot day the Trust's path up the wooded Pendower valley behind the beach gives a shady walk.

The Trust owns the farmland behind the coast for the next few miles and has thus been able to remove many eyesores which had accrued there. Once the ugly buildings and overhead wires had gone it is hard to imagine how they got there in the first place, for to allow such things now would cause an outcry. The Trust's long campaign to preserve the coast has caused a radical change in public opinion on these matters over the last forty years.

Nare Head is one of Cornwall's great headlands and can be reached either by the coast path, from east or west, or by car as far as the carpark hidden in an old quarry on the spine of the headland. The road there leads past the spreading new buildings of Penare Farm, which sit in a hollow in what is now a substantial holding made up from five small (and now uneconomic) farms. The homestead provides an example of how large-scale farming can be made to fit into a beautiful landscape without harming it.

The contrast between this south coast of Cornwall and the more exposed north coast is apparent. The views from the coast inland show the country to be prosperous and smiling, very different from the barer, bleaker land a comparatively few miles away. The panoramas over Gerrans Bay to the west, and the even larger Veryan Bay to the east, take in a series of small headlands, cliffs and beaches, the slopes all covered with the typical shrub cover of this coast, hawthorn, blackthorn, bramble, willow, bracken, ivy and good cliff flowers where there are more open patches. Half a mile off Nare Head the Gull Rock rises steeply out of the sea, the rocky island a nesting place for hundreds of seabirds, given by a former member of the Trust's staff to complete its ownership here.

The Trust's land runs most of the way to Portloe, still an active fishing hamlet, its harbour a narrow inlet in the cliffs, but the coast is privately owned for three miles thereafter, most of it by the Caerhays estate, presided over by a picturesque castle, designed by the architect John Nash in 1808, its towers and turrets backed by a steep wooded slope where there is a famous shrub garden.

The east side of Veryan Bay is closed by the unmistakable profile of the Dodman, its mighty Roman nose standing out bold and proud. The visitor can drive to the carpark in the hamlet of Penare, which lies in a hollow on the Dodman's spine, but the better approach is along the coast. From Porthluney Cove, below Caerhays Castle, the path runs past the Trust's remote Lambsowden Cove and the privately owned Greeb Point to Hemmick Beach. Here are pebbles of many different colours, worn smooth by the action of the waves. The rock is 'mineralised' with veins of white, pink, green and brown, and these veins give each pebble its own character. A rock arch leads west to the smaller Percunning Cove. To the east a path made by the Trust climbs steeply up to the Dodman, the Point itself a promontory fort cut off by the deep ditch known as the Balk. The high granite cross on the summit was erected in 1896 by a rector of Caerhays to act as a mark for fishermen and as a reminder of the all-seeing eye of Providence. When the work was finished the rector consecrated it and spent the night at its foot. Some way back from the cross is a tiny watch-house for the coastguard, apparently the only survivor of this early nineteenth-century pattern built in the great days of sail, when every yard of the coast was patrolled twice daily, originally in an attempt to stop smuggling and later as a safety measure, for there is scarcely a mile of these coasts that has not had its wreck. There have been many wrecks on the Dodman itself; the currents are notorious and vessels which over-ran Falmouth at night in dirty weather have ended their days here. In 1897 the destroyers *Thresher* and *Lynx* went ashore in thick fog, and in 1957 the pleasure boat *Darlwin*, returning from Fowey to Falmouth with a full load of holiday visitors, sank with all on board.

East of the Dodman the gently curving sweep of Vault Beach leads out to Lamledra where the Trust owns most of the farm and the headland of Maenease Point. The path down to the beach is easy and the fine gravel of which it is composed is as pleasant as sand. Round Maenease the cliffs run down to Gorran Haven. The harbour, beach, church and old village, with Mr Cakebread's excellent baker's shop, are delightful but sadly large numbers of bungalows built in recent years disfigure the slopes above.

St Austell Bay, four miles across, is the seaward face of Cornwall's only large industry, the production of china clay, based on the granite ridge rising to over 1,000 feet at Hensbarrow behind the town of St Austell. From here clay is dug, by computer-controlled water cannon, settled out, purified, dried and exported all over the world, a very large industry but nowadays almost wholly automated and employing far fewer people than in the past. The clay is exported in deepwater ships, up to 15,000 tons in size, from the port of Fowey, in shallow draught coasters from Par, the industry's own port in the north-eastern corner of the bay, and in small quantities from the early nineteenth-century port at Charlestown, in the north-western corner of the bay. Between the two harbours there is a golf course, much holiday development and houses for china-clay executives.

On either side of this developed coast, however, two great headlands run southward to contain the bay to east and west; on the west side Black Head, on the east The Gribbin, both backed by substantial agricultural estates. In the 1960s the three hereditary owners, with great foresight, agreed to a scheme proposed by the Trust to keep these long arms of St Austell Bay inviolate. As a result the Trust now owns the headlands on each side of the bay, and holds protective covenants over six miles of adjoining farmland and cliff. These protect the coast from Gamas Point, near Pentewan, round Black Head to include the west side of St Austell Bay, and, on the east side, from Polkerris round The Gribbin to Polridmouth on its east flank. Thanks to three people, St Austell Bay can continue in its invaluable commercial use while still retaining its beauty.

In misty weather The Gribbin's 260-foot snout can be confused with the Dodman, nine miles to the south-west. For this reason it carries a 'day mark', a slender eighty-foot stone tower erected by Trinity House in 1832. The three seaward faces of the tower are painted in broad red and white stripes, the effect more handsome than bizarre. On either side crouch wind-pruned plantations of sycamore, ilex, beech and *Rhododendron ponticum*. They survive tenaciously in the teeth of winter gales. On the western cliff is probably the one station in Cornwall of the sea buckthorn, *Hippophaë rhamnoides*, a grey-leaved prickly shrub with bright orange berries in autumn. Below the cliff on the eastern side there are small sandy coves, the preserve of those who scramble there across the rocks beneath.

More easily accessible is Polridmouth (called Pridmouth), a beautiful beach surrounded by the woods of Menabilly, the seat of the Rashleigh family since the sixteenth century. Pridmouth is reached by paths from Coombe to the east, or from Menabilly Barton to the west. Menabilly appears as Manderley in Daphne du Maurier's *Rebecca* (1938) which begins 'Last night I dreamt I went to Manderley again', and in which the woods, the beach and the coast are faithfully recorded. The path from the beach leads up through a little wood, along the clifftop fields and down again after a mile to Coombe Haven, on Trust land all the way. The farm at the valley head takes its name from the place and was once a dower house of the Rashleighs. Beyond Coombe Haven is a former golf course, now grazed by sheep, and the Trust's woodland behind St Catherine's Point at the entrance to Fowey. There are exciting views up the harbour, always busy with small boats, and several times a day the deep blast of a siren can be heard heralding a large ship arriving with a pilot to creep up the harbour to the jetties upstream and load china clay destined for ports all over the world.

The curious object surrounded by iron railings on top of St Catherine's Point is the mausoleum erected in 1867 by William Rashleigh of Menabilly in honour of himself and his family. Above the harbour mouth is St Catherine's Castle, one of the many coastal forts built by Henry VIII to protect the growing shipping trade at the dawning of the first Elizabethan age. Fowey has a long and stirring history as a sea port, and in the French wars of the fourteenth and fifteenth centuries its ships were in the van of the English fleet.

Fowey is closely associated with 'Q' (Sir Arthur Quiller-Couch), who died in 1944 and is commemorated by a great monolith of granite on Penleath Point where the beautiful creek of Pont Pill branches off east of the main estuary. Almost all this side of the harbour is owned by the Trust. Hall Walk, below the ancient vehicular ferry at Bodinnick, is celebrated for an incident in the Civil War when Charles I narrowly missed decapitation by a Parliamentary cannon ball lobbed across the water from Fowey. The Walk was the promenade of the ancient house of Hall behind the cliffs, seat of the Mohun family who owned the parish of Lanteglos, and is held by the Trust in memory of the men of this parish and of Fowey who gave their lives in the Second World War. The path leads from Hall Walk along the north bank of the wholly unspoiled creek of Pont Pill and descends through a wood to the delightful hamlet of Pont, where the Trust has rebuilt the quays and restored the footbridge connecting them. The path continues along wooded slopes on the south bank, with lovely views over the harbour, to reach the passenger ferry at Polruan which takes pedestrians across the estuary back to Fowey.

From Polruan eastwards lie eight miles of quiet and peaceful coast, not rugged or wild, though the cliffs are high and the spray flies in winter gales, but a smiling land of good farms, many of them occupied by members of the Talling family who have long farmed here, and centred on the two beautiful churches of Lanteglos and Lansallos. Except for the farms of Raphael and Lizzen west of Polperro, all now belongs to the Trust.

A path from Pont leads up a bosky valley to Lanteglos church, mainly of the late fourteenth century and dedicated to St Wyllow. It lies in a hollow behind Pencarrow Head, two steep miles away from its village of Polruan inside the mouth of Fowey harbour. As with so many Cornish churches, the 'churchtown' is in the middle of the parish whereas the population lives elsewhere. The Trust owns Churchtown Farm beside the church, which has been well restored and is flooded with light from windows of clear glass. At the east end of the south aisle there is a beautiful brass of Thomas de Mohun from the first decade of the fifteenth century. From the church Saffron Lane leads up to the coast where a footpath runs out to Lantic Bay, the sheltered cove west of Pencarrow Head. A precipitous path descends to the big curving beach, with small coves beyond giving excellent bathing. At the back of the beach grow several plants at home in the shingle: sea holly (*Eryngium maritimum*), sea kale (*Crambe maritima*) and the beautiful pink sea bindweed (*Calystegia soldanella*), an exotic cousin of the common bindweed found in gardens.

Pencarrow Head is on two levels. From its crown at 447 feet the views are enormous. To the east Rame Head marks the end of Cornwall; far beyond it Bolt Tail in south Devon reaches out into the Channel. Westward the noble Roman profile of the Dodman on the far side of St Austell Bay is backed by the Lizard peninsula, curving away to the south, a panorama of some seventy miles. Beneath this high point the headland steps down in a series of giant strides to 150 feet above the water, with the wholly unspoilt Lantic and Lantivet Bays on either side. While Lantic has its one big beach, Lantivet is quite different, with a series of little beaches, each guarded by reefs largely covered at high water, below cliffs of no more than a hundred feet. Many of Lantivet's beaches can be reached from the cliff path, though the more inaccessible may call for a bit of rock climbing. Lansallos Beach, at the foot of West Coombe below Lansallos church, is a perfect semicircle, guarded by rocks and approached through a track cut in the cliff face just wide enough for a horse and cart. The place is the epitome of a smugglers' cove and it is not so long ago that contraband was landed here. The track runs steeply up to the fifteenth-century church of St Ildierna, one of those shadowy female saints with whom Cornwall is richly endowed. The church has a fine wagon roof, many of its original pews, simple slate floors, and an atmosphere of peace. Its tower alone is visible from the cliffs and seems to ride in the sky as it appears and disappears from view.

From West Coombe the path is cut halfway up the cliff, with rocky crags jutting out above. Ravens, kestrels and peregrines wheel and float above these cliffs which run unbroken to Polperro with not a single house in sight. At all times of year there are interesting flowers, for in the kind Cornish climate autumn runs into spring with no perceptible break. Centaury, both in its common form and the rarer *Centaurium pulchellum*, can be recognised by its bright pink flower from June to September. Great mats of thyme abound in the cliff turf. Mallow grows near the base of the cliffs and, hugging the ground closely, the inconspicuous but beautifully named orchid, lady's tresses (*Spiranthus spiralis*),

flowers in August and September. Walk here on Christmas Day and a dozen plants will be in bloom.

As the path approaches Polperro little hedged enclosures begin to appear, now overgrown. So closely are the cottages of the village packed into the narrow coombe in which it lies that there is no room for gardens. In the past some fifty little plots were dug in the cliffs, closely hedged with veronica and escallonia, to enable cottagers to grow flowers and vegetables. The Net Loft, wedged into a cleft behind the Peak Rock at the harbour entrance, has been restored by the Trust. Built of local stone and slate, it appears to grow out of the rock. Polperro harbour and the huddled cottages of the old village are undeniably picturesque but the village has been prostituted by the tourist trade and is best avoided in the height of the visitor season. Beyond lies the Warren, a mile of cliff bequeathed to the Trust by Angela Brazil, writer of stories for schoolgirls, and a pleasant breezy place it is. The Trust's land stops at Talland Bay, with another fine church standing high over the sea, but then starts again to round Hore Point and the sweep of coast eastwards to the hotels of Looe, giving another mile and a half of good walking. (*See also* North Cornish Coast, p.214.)

South Downs Sussex

Between Winchester, to the west, and Eastbourne, to the east

Gilbert White (*see* p.284), visiting Sussex in 1773, described the South Downs as 'that chain of majestic mountains'. Although only rarely above 800 feet, these rolling chalk hills running 150 miles from Beachy Head to the Hampshire border are one of England's most evocative features. Rising from the south to steep, north-facing scarp slopes, cut by characteristic dry valleys, traditionally grazed to a botanically rich, close-cropped turf and rich in remains of early man, this is a treasured and vulnerable landscape in the most densely populated part of the country, where new bypasses and other developments are continually eroding what countryside remains. Partly due to the relaunching of the South Downs appeal in 1991, the Trust's holdings of fragile downland landscapes are now substantial, amounting to well over 7,500 acres and including some of the region's most prominent viewpoints and landmarks. The emphasis has been on acquiring ancient escarpment landscape, where the Trust is encouraging a continuance of sheep grazing and where areas ploughed in recent years are being returned to grass.

Most of the Trust's land lies in West Sussex. The 3,520-acre Slindon estate, 6 miles north of Bognor Regis, offers a large expanse of sweeping downland, with hanging beech and ash woods on steep scarp slopes, a flint and brick village with seventeenth-century cottages, and a substantial section of Stane Street, the Roman road from London to Chichester, with traces of its ditch-flanked, rammed chalk and flint surface running for 3¾ miles across the downs. To the north of Slindon park the ruined arch against the skyline is Nore folly. Above it lie Coldharbour Hill and Glatting Beacon, with breathtaking views south across the Channel and north over the Weald. Some 11 miles north-west, on the crest of the Downs near Uppark (see p.342), is the expanse of Harting Down, where, as elsewhere, the small hummocky mounds of the yellow wood ant show that the grassland has not been ploughed for a long time, and also close to the border with Hampshire is the 1,100-acre Woolbeding estate, near Midhurst, which includes a hanging wood above the River Rother.

Further east, Trust properties ring the sprawl of Brighton and Hove. Overlooking Shoreham at the western end are Southwick Hill and Shoreham Gap on the dip slope of the Downs, with the Brighton bypass carried in a tunnel under the hill. Further

north, Fulking escarpment, Edburton Hill and Newtimber Hill offer over 600 acres of open downland and magnificent north-facing scarp. The spectacular Devil's Dyke cutting into the scarp is the largest chalkland dry valley in England, the grassland flora includes orchids and the rare red star thistle, and from the top of Newtimber Hill, which can be reached by a shady walk through a hanging ash wood on the north side, there are views seaward and across the Weald, and also into the curving valleys of the large downland estate of Brighton Corporation which adjoins the property.

Two further viewpoints along this stretch of the Downs are also in Trust hands. Less than a mile away, north across the busy A23, is the recently acquired, 677-foot Wolstonbury Hill, site of an extensive Iron Age hill fort, while over the border into East Sussex, 6 miles north of Brighton, is the prominent 813-foot summit of Ditchling Beacon, with traces of another hill fort and views over the mouth of the River Ouse. Also recently acquired are the Black Cap estate west of Lewes, straddling the South Downs Way, and the 348 acres of Frog Firle Farm, between Alfriston and Seaford, which includes some water-meadow along the River Cuckmere and a fine white horse cut into the downland turf.

Most of these properties lie within the Sussex Downs Area of Outstanding Natural Beauty, and many are skirted or crossed by the South Downs Way. This is life-enhancing country, with a sense of space and distance, sheep dotted on springy turf, skylarks singing overhead, and perhaps a glimpse of a chalkhill blue or marbled white butterfly (see also Cissbury Ring, p.70; Highdown Hill, p.150).

South Foreland Lighthouse Kent

3 miles east of Dover, between St Margaret's Bay and Langdon Cliffs

The Trust's string of properties along the white cliffs of Dover (see p.165) includes this lighthouse set on downland on South Foreland Point. Sited to guide mariners past the shifting shoals and banks of the notorious Goodwin Sands, the lighthouse dates from 1843, when the light was an oil lamp. Marconi used the 69-foot tower for his first successful trials in radio navigation, making contact with the East Goodwin lightship, ten miles away, on Christmas Eve 1898. There are views over Dover docks and

The sweeping downland of the Slindon estate is crossed by Stane Street, the Roman road from London to Chichester. Now a bridle path, this 3½-mile stretch made of rammed chalk with ditches on either side is the best-preserved section of the road. (NT)

Speke Hall, built over a century from 1490, has some of the finest black and white timberwork in England. (*NT/ W. R. Davis*)

the Channel from the balcony round the light, and walkers along the cliffs between here and Dover can take a zig-zag path down to the shore and the wreck of the sailing ship *Preussan*, which ran aground here in 1910.

Speke Hall   Merseyside

On north bank of the Mersey, 8 miles south-east of the centre of Liverpool, 1 mile south of the A561, on west side of Liverpool airport

A carved overmantel in the great parlour depicts the three generations of the wealthy gentry family largely responsible for this magical half-timbered moated manor house. Henry Norris to the left, accompanied by his wife and five children, carried on the building started by his father on inheriting the estate in about 1490. In the centre sits Sir William, whose considerable additions in the mid-sixteenth century may be explained by the nineteen children grouped at his feet (the son killed in battle is accompanied by a skull and bones). To the right is Edward, who recorded his completion of the house with an inscription dated 1598 over the entrance and is shown with his wife and two of their children.

These men built conservatively, each addition merging perfectly with what had gone before and with no hint of the Renaissance influences that were becoming evident further south. Four long, low ranges enclose a cobbled courtyard, jettied gables topped with finials projecting unevenly and apparently haphazardly from the façades, and the rough sandstone slabs covering the roof contributing to a charmingly crooked effect. Leaded panes appear dark in the riot of black and white timberwork, among the finest in England. An Elizabethan stone bridge crosses the now grassy moat to the powerfully studded wooden doors which give access to the interior. Walking through is a surprise: two huge yews known as Adam and Eve shadow the courtyard, their branches rising above the house.

Surviving Tudor interiors live up to the promise of the exterior. In the light and airy T-shaped great hall rising to the roof, a series of plaster heads looks down from the crude Gothic chimneypiece stretching to the ceiling. The naive decoration here contrasts with the sophisticated carving on the panelling at the other end of the room, with busts of Roman emperors set between elegant, fluted columns represented in high relief. In the great parlour next door, panels in the superb early Jacobean plaster ceiling are alive with pomegranates, roses, lilies, vines and hazelnuts; bunches of ripe grapes and other fruits dangle enticingly and rosebuds are about to burst into flower. A spy-hole in one of the bedrooms and hiding places throughout the house reflect the Norrises' Catholic sympathies which brought them to the edge of ruin in the seventeenth century, culminating in the loss of the family estates after the Civil War.

After years of neglect following the death of the last of the family in 1766, the house was rescued in the late eighteenth century by Richard Watt, whose descendants introduced the heavy oak furniture in period style which contributes to Speke's unique atmosphere. The more intimate panelled Victorian rooms in the north and west wings were created by the shipping magnate F. R. Leyland, who leased the house and carried on Watt's restoration after his early death. A noted patron of the arts, Leyland was responsible for hanging the early William Morris wallpapers which are now a feature of Speke and he also entertained the painter James McNeill Whistler here.

The house lies buried in bracken woodland only a stone's throw from Liverpool airport, a green oasis in the heart of industrial Merseyside. A wide ride leads to the great embankment which shelters the property to the south. Those who struggle up the steep grassy slope are rewarded by a panoramic view of the River Mersey stretching away in a shining sheet of water to the smoking stacks of Ellesmere Port on the other side of the estuary.

Springhill Co. Londonderry

1 mile from Moneymore on Moneymore–Coagh road

Four flintlocks used to defend Londonderry when it was besieged by James II's forces in 1688–9 are among many mementoes of the Protestant military family who built this modest manor house and lived here for 300 years. Although the Conynghams acquired the estate in 1658, the house dates from the end of the seventeenth century, when 'Good' Will

Conyngham's marriage articles required him to build for his bride (a copy of the contract now hangs in the hall).

First seen at the end of a long straight avenue, Springhill could well be a French *manoir* transported miraculously to Ulster. Long sash windows march across the simple whitewashed façade under the steeply pitched slate roof, those either side of the central front door only two panes wide. Hexagonal one-storey bays added in the eighteenth century extend the house on either side, as if they have snuggled up to it for warmth, and long, low buildings once used as servants' quarters flank the entrance courtyard. Old yews shade the house, the remnants of an ancient forest which once stretched for miles along the shores of Lough Neagh, clothing the ridge on which the estate stands.

Springhill's eighteenth- and nineteenth-century interiors are redolent of the Conyngham family and their connections. In the library to the right of the hall, Kneller's portraits of William and Mary were presented by the king to Sir Albert Conyngham, who commanded the Inniskilling Dragoons, for his services to the Protestant cause. The medicine chest full of bottles and drawers in this room also has military associations, used by the 3rd Viscount Molesworth, connected to the Conynghams by marriage, during the War of Spanish Succession (1701–14), when he was the Duke of Marlborough's aide-de-camp. The exceptional collection of books, mostly acquired in the eighteenth century, includes a very early edition of Gerard's *Herbal* and first editions of Hobbes's *Leviathan* (1651) and Raleigh's *History of the World* (1614). Walnut William and Mary fiddleback chairs surround an Irish table in the dining-room on the other side of the house, from where there are views over the park to the tower at the end of the beech walk.

A gateway from the entrance court leads into the laundry yard, with its original seventeenth-century slaughterhouse and turf shed. A changing exhibition of costume over the last 200 years is on show in the old laundry building: the Trust's collection includes important eighteenth-century garments, a wide range of nineteenth-century costume and flimsy evening dresses of the 1920s and 1930s. The little walled garden beyond the outbuildings, where herbs surround a tiny camomile lawn, is overlooked by a defensible two-storeyed seventeenth-century barn, its interior spanned by roughly hewn oak beams.

Long low buildings flanking Springhill's entrance court-yard were once servants' quarters. (*John Bethell*)

Sprivers Garden Kent

2 miles north of Lamberhurst on the B2162

An unpretentious mid-eighteenth-century house attractively hung with red tiles, the brick façades embracing an older building behind, stands at the centre of a small formal garden with walled and hedged compartments very similar to those depicted on an eighteenth-century print. Although mostly devoted to grass, with clipped yew and box seen against a backdrop of fine trees, there is also an extensive herbaceous border, spring and summer bedding and a walled rose garden. A little classical temple on the edge of the main lawn, the focus of a short avenue of pear trees, marks the site of an eighteenth-century eyecatcher, but numerous other garden ornaments and pieces of statuary are part of the displays of Chilstone Garden Ornaments, who use Sprivers as a showground.

Standen West Sussex

2 miles south of East Grinstead

Standen is a most unusual house, built in 1892–4 and yet not at all Victorian, designed all of a piece and yet seeming to have grown out of the group of old farm buildings to which it is attached. This peaceful place on the edge of the Weald was designed by Philip Webb for the successful London solicitor James Beale, who wanted a roomy house for his large family for weekends and holidays. It was one of Webb's last commissions and is also one of the few unaltered examples of the work of this talented architect, so much less well known than his flamboyant contemporary Richard Norman Shaw. A lifelong friend and professional associate of William Morris, Webb shared Morris's views on the value of high-quality materials and craftsmanship. His aim was to design good, plain buildings, with comfortable interiors that could be lived in, an ambition which Standen fulfils in every respect.

As shown in Arthur Melville's delightful water-colour, painted when he visited the Beales for a weekend in 1896, Standen sits on a terrace facing south over the River Medway to Ashdown Forest. It is part-built of stone from the hill behind, with upper storeys weatherboarded and tile-hung in the Wealden fashion to produce red and white façades. An attractive arcaded conservatory stretches away from the five-gabled garden front, with its tall chimneys reminiscent of Norman Shaw rising almost to the height of the tower holding the water tanks.

The rooms are light and airy, furnished with Morris's wallpapers and textiles, with richly coloured William de Morgan pottery, such as the ochre-red ware in a cabinet in the drawing-room, and with a pleasing mixture of antiques and beautifully made pieces from Morris's company. The house was lit by electricity from the beginning, and many of the original fittings still exist. Webb's delicate wall lights in the drawing-room hang like overblown snowdrops, casting soft pools of light on the blue and red hand-knotted carpet and the comfortable chairs covered in faded green velvet supplied from Morris's workshops. Engraved sunflowers on the burnished-copper plates supporting the light brackets echo the design of the wallpaper and complement the swirls of foliage and tulips on the brass cheeks of the fireplace. A view through to the conservatory from this room shows cane furniture set enticingly amidst a profusion of plants. All the rooms reflect Webb's meticulous concern with every detail. The dining-room at the end of the south front, its distinctive grey-green panelling setting off blue and white Chinese porcelain, has an east-facing breakfast alcove, where the little round table flanked by oak dressers lined with china is flooded with sunshine in the early morning. Curiously, the first floor reveals that the Beales were expected still to rely heavily on washstands and hip baths, with only one bathroom provided for twelve bedrooms.

The south-facing, steeply sloping garden which falls away from the house reflects changes over several decades by a number of different hands. A fussy gardenesque layout by the London landscape gardener G. B. Simpson, who was employed before Webb and planned his design to focus on a differently sited house, was then modified by his successor, who favoured a simpler approach con-

(*Right*) A tapestry panel by Burne-Jones on the stairs at Standen. (*NT*)

centrating on grass and trees. The planting, on the other hand, was undertaken by James Beale's wife Margaret, who established a wide collection of colourful and unusual plants at variance with the quiet restful vistas Webb hoped to achieve.

The end result, although based on no coherent overall plan, is both individual and charming, with many changes of level linked by flights of steps and magnificent views across the valley. Webb's terraces, with his summerhouse set on the topmost level, descend the hill in giant leaps, their outlines followed by stepped yew hedges. Hydrangeas, azaleas, kalmias and rhododendrons surround several areas of grass, such as the upper lawns with their spangling of ladies'-tresses orchid in September, and fine trees include the Monterey pine, a tulip tree, a weeping holly and a handkerchief tree. The little quarry which supplied the stone for the house is now attractively leafy and overgrown, supporting a colony of royal fern, primulas, anemones and the pale-yellow hoop-petticoat daffodil.

Staunton Harold Church

Leicestershire

5 miles north-east of Ashby-de-la-Zouch, west of the B587

Sir Robert Shirley, 4th Baronet, must have been a very brave if rather foolhardy young man. The splendid church he built in 1653, one of very few erected between the outbreak of the Civil War and the Restoration, was an open act of defiance to Cromwell's Puritan regime, showing Sir Robert's identification with the High Church Anglicanism of the martyred king and advertising his wealth. The incensed Cromwell retaliated by demanding money for a regiment of soldiers, throwing Sir Robert into the Tower of London when he refused to comply. There he died, aged only twenty-seven.

Staunton Harold is this ardent Royalist's memorial. Built in the revived Gothic style which symbolised continuity with the old Church, its prominent pinnacles, embattled parapets and imposing tower suggest a medieval building. Fine carved woodwork by a joiner named William Smith survives unaltered inside. Double rows of oak box pews fill the nave, lit by single-armed candlesticks attached to the divisions. Oak panelling lines the walls and faces the columns of the nave and a magnificent Jacobean screen supports the organ loft

at the west end. The organ itself, which predates the church, is one of the oldest English-built instruments still in its original condition. Swirls of blue, black and white representing the elements in chaos draw the eye high overhead to a wonderfully abstract version of the Creation dated 1655. The Puritans would have regarded both this display and the fixed altar in the chancel as idolatrous.

The only two later features in the church are Robert Bakewell of Derby's early eighteenth-century ornate wrought-iron screen in the chancel arch and the marble tomb to Robert Shirley's great-grandson, who died of smallpox in 1714. The young man lies propped on his right elbow, as if eagerly surveying the world he has left.

Stockbridge Hampshire

At the junction of the A30, the A272 and the A3057

The Trust is lord of the manor of Stockbridge and administers the common marsh, where ancient rights of grazing are still exercised, and the manorial waste, which includes the wide verges of the A30 which runs through the neat Georgian main street. A mile to the east is Stockbridge Down, where the Trust's 150 acres are grazed by its own flocks of sheep to maintain the rich, butterfly-attracting downland flora. Both marsh and down are designated Sites of Special Scientific Interest.

Stoneacre Kent

At north end of Otham village, 3 miles south-east of Maidstone, 1 mile south of the A20

Prosperous yeomen farmers and other men of moderate means in the late Middle Ages built to a standard pattern that endured for generations. The core of these houses was a central hall open to the rafters, with two floors of smaller chambers on either side, a layout which reconciled increasing pressures for individual privacy with the traditional communal life.

This attractive half-timbered Wealden house, dating from about 1480, was typical of its time, following the plan already established in the little Alfriston Clergy House built over a century earlier (*see* p.4). But Stoneacre's individual character, created by Aymer Valance in the early twentieth century, sets it apart. Impressive timberwork spans the great hall, with a rare and beautiful king-post, devised as a cluster of columns, supporting the ridge of the roof from the gigantic tie beam which stretches the length of the room. A massive brick chimney built in the 1920s rises the height of the hall from the fifteenth-century fireplace introduced by Mr Valance on the south side, a collection of warm-toned Hispanic plates along the chimney breast enhancing the soft pinks of the brickwork. Morning and evening sun pours through the leaded panes in the two twelve-light windows facing east and west.

This fifteenth-century core with its solar block to the south is now the centrepiece of a much larger building. Half-timbered wings in complete harmony with the medieval work were created by Mr Valance using timber, windows and furnishings from dilapidated Tudor houses, some of which were acquired as complete buildings. Badly neglected before he began his restoration of the property, Stoneacre is a fascinating exercise in the fruits of inspired scholarship.

Stonehenge Down Wiltshire

1–3 miles west of Amesbury, at junction of the A303 and the A360

Few visitors to the world-famous monument (not owned by the Trust) on Salisbury Plain realise that the surrounding windswept downland contains numerous other prehistoric remains, many of which are on Trust land. To the north of Stonehenge, parallel banks and shallow ditches about a hundred yards apart define the enigmatic late Neolithic feature known as the Cursus, a great sweep of grass which has been variously interpreted as a racecourse and as a processional way. Running for one and three-quarter miles from west to east across a shallow valley, it is now largely ploughed out in its eastern half but rises impressively to a barrow silhouetted on the horizon in the other direction. Far more indistinct – indeed, practically invisible on the ground for most of its length – is the processional way known as the Avenue. Dating from *c*.2000BC, it extends one and a half miles from Stonehenge to the River Avon. The western half, running north into the shallow valley crossed by the Cursus and then turning east to climb uphill to the skyline, is Trust property. Shallow banks and ditches are just discernible on the bend and two young beeches planted on the ridge, now only a

couple of feet high, will usefully flag the outer edges of this feature in future years.

Far more impressive are the Beaker and Bronze Age barrow cemeteries dating from *c*.2500–2000BC which crown the low ridges ringing Stonehenge at distances of half a mile to a mile. One of the most prominent, flanking the southern edge of the Cursus, lies in open grazing land, the grassy mounds swelling on the skyline looking like a row of hats or upturned bowls. The New and Old King barrows extending for over half a mile along the ridge crossed by the Avenue were in open country when recorded by the antiquary William Stukeley in the early eighteenth century, but now appear as dark shapes in beech woods on the crest of the hill (trees growing actually on the barrows, obscuring their outlines, have recently been cleared). The impressive mounds here – over a hundred feet across and eight to twelve feet high – are almost all bowl barrows, the earliest and simplest form of these features, but the Cursus group contains fine examples of bell barrows, in which a flat platform, or berm, separates the central mound from the encircling ditch. Both these types and the rarer pond, saucer and dish barrows can be seen in the Winterbourne Stoke cemetery in the angle between the A303 and the A360 to the west. Just off the roundabout where the two roads intersect is a fine Neolithic long barrow dating from *c*.3000BC, its irregular profile, partly concealed by scrub, probably mistaken for a dump of waste material by many passing motorists.

Several of the cemeteries are illustrated in William Stukeley's *Stonehenge*, published in 1740, and most of the barrows were excavated by Sir Richard Colt Hoare of Stourhead (*see below*), who set out to record the prehistoric remains of Wiltshire in 1803–10. His considerable finds, many of which are now displayed in Devizes Museum, included both skeletons and cremated remains interned in coffins and urns and a variety of grave goods – amber beads, bronze daggers, pins and tweezers, various jars and cups and work in gold.

Many more barrows stud the rolling countryside round about, some hidden in woods, others isolated prominently in fields or on the crests of ridges. An even greater number have probably been ploughed out, together with the remains of field systems and settlements. Although we see the barrows grassed over, it is likely they were originally bare chalk mounds, appearing startlingly white in a green and brown landscape. Each marked the grave of a Wessex chieftain or of a member of his family, the upper echelons of a sophisticated society which profited from trade in tin, copper and gold with the Continent and which had mastered skilled metal-working techniques.

Stourhead Wiltshire

At Stourton, off the B3092, 3 miles north-west of Mere

The fine house on a ridge of the Wiltshire Downs is overshadowed by the magical garden created in a steep-sided combe which falls away to the west. Sheltered and enclosed by windbreaks planted along the rim of the valley, the perfect eighteenth-century landscape preserved here looks inward, with views over wooded slopes to the serene artificial lake in the depths of the combe. A number of little classical temples along the shore are seen framed against the trees in a sequence of contrived vistas which shift and change according to the viewpoint on the path round the lake. Stourhead is as much a work of art as the idealised landscapes it imitates, designed as a series of experiences and never the same however often it is visited. In spring, a carpet of tiny wild daffodils is mirrored in the water and the magnolias are in bloom. In summer, silvery-white willows along the shore appear iridescent against the darker foliage behind and patches of deep-crimson and purple rhododendrons mark the upper slopes. In autumn, Japanese maples bring flashes of fire to the russet-brown and fir-green of the woods. The trees are a magnificent mix of beeches, oaks and other native species and exotics, among them the Norwegian maple, tulip trees, cedars, the dawn redwood and the Japanese *Pinus parviflora*.

Stourhead is primarily the creation of Henry Hoare II, son of the London banker who built the Palladian house (*see below*), although later members of the family, in particular Sir Richard Colt Hoare, (*see below*), enriched the garden by widening the range of species, introducing flowering shrubs and exotic trees, and also made some more fundamental changes. Perhaps turned in on himself by the tragic loss of both his wives, the garden was to be Henry's absorbing interest for forty years from 1741, its design a direct expression of the eighteenth-century taste for the world of ancient Greece and Rome and of the reaction against the formal landscapes of the

preceding century typified by Versailles. Henry's model could well have been one of Claude Lorraine's romantic and atmospheric paintings of the countryside around Rome, with little temples set in a leafy arcadian paradise.

The only professional engaged in the creation of the garden was the architect Henry Flitcroft, who designed the classical eyecatchers. His dignified Pantheon, with a broad flight of steps leading up to a pedimented portico, crowns a rounded slope above the lake, the curve of the dome continuing the contours of the grass. His tall, circular Temple of Apollo enclosed in a continuous colonnade sits high up on a knoll, looking imperiously out over the island-studded water. Across the valley, steps lead down through a leafy tunnel to the dripping grotto on the edge of the lake, its sombre rock-shadowed pools adorned with sculpture. John Cheere's hoary long-haired river god sits half in and half out of the water, one arm raised as if to welcome visitors, his flesh unhealthily white in the gloom of the cavern. His companion, a nymph of the grot, circles her head protectively with her left arm as she sleeps, oblivious of the cascade streaming down from her bed. Close by on the path above is a fantasy from another century, the Gothic cottage added by Sir Richard Colt Hoare in 1806, its prominent traceried windows and rough slab tiles almost buried in vegetation.

Although Henry Hoare originally hid the estate village on the edge of the valley behind a screen of trees so that it would not intrude on his design, the row of tiled cottages with mullioned windows stretching down to the Palladian bridge over an arm of the lake adds to the charm of his creation. Opposite is the medieval parish church, picturesquely crowned with fretwork parapets and filled with monuments to the Hoares and their predecessors, the Stourtons. Just beyond the churchyard, dominating the view over the lake to the Pantheon, rises the slender column of the medieval cross which Henry acquired from the City of Bristol in the 1760s, its tapering length suggesting the spire of a buried church.

The garden was intended to be seen from above, approached by the shady walk from the house which suddenly emerges on the edge of the combe to give a view of shining water through the trees. Visitors taking this upper route rather than following the road through the village catch a glimpse of the entrance front of Henry Hoare I's austere neo-classical house facing east over the park to distant wooded hills. The son of Sir Richard Hoare, the founder of the family bank, Henry had purchased the estate in 1717, three years after it had passed out of the hands of the Stourton family who had lived here for 700 years. He immediately demolished the existing house and employed Colen Campbell, a leader of the fashionable neo-classical revival, to build this replacement, one of the first Palladian houses in England. Campbell, who published his designs for Stourhead in 1725 in the third volume of *Vitruvius Britannia*, derived his ideas from a house that Palladio built in the 1560s: a five-bay, two-storeyed building in the villa style with a pedimented portico rising the height of the façade. This square main block is now flanked by pavilions added in the 1790s to house a picture gallery and library. The rather severe lines of the façade are softened only by two flights of steps rising to the entrance, their end pillars supporting stone basins surmounted by the Hoare eagle, and by the three lead statues set above the portico.

Sadly, the original decoration was destroyed by the fire which gutted this central block in 1902. More or less faithful Edwardian reconstructions of Campbell's intentions by the local architect Doran Webb and the more prestigious Sir Aston Webb who replaced him are now sandwiched between the Regency rooms in the pavilions, both of which survived virtually unscathed. The contents, a rich collection of family heirlooms with finely crafted furniture by Thomas Chippendale the Younger, reflect the interests of several generations of the Hoares and the addition of pieces from Wavendon, the family's house in Buckinghamshire, in the nineteenth century.

The nucleus of paintings, sculpture and *objets d'art* acquired by Henry Hoare II to embellish his father's new house was greatly extended by his grandson Sir Richard Colt Hoare, who inherited in 1785. This eminent antiquary, scholar and county historian was an omnivorous collector, amassing a magnificent library in one of his purpose-built extensions and displaying the pick of his grandfather's collection together with his own acquisitions of works by Italian and British contemporaries in the other. Although some of the finest were sold in the late nineteenth century, the paintings still hang triple-banked against pea-green walls, simple gilt frames contrasting with florid rococo creations on the end wall. Cigoli's *Adoration of the Magi*

dominates the room, an expression of great tenderness lighting the face of the grizzled king in an ermine-fringed cloak who kneels at the Virgin's feet.

Similarly, although many of his books have now been dispersed, Colt Hoare's evocative green and white library is one of the most beautiful surviving Regency rooms in England, the arch of the high barrel-vaulted ceiling echoed in the curved alcoves lined with books. Thomas Chippendale's rich mahogany furniture (including massive staircase-like library steps), gilded calf bindings and the deep-green and ochre carpet all contribute to a feeling of luxurious opulence, while the muted tones are lifted by flashes of colour from the painted glass high up in the lunettes at either end of the room. Of the other treasures in the house, perhaps the most memorable is the seventeenth-century 'Pope's cabinet' designed like the façade of a Renaissance church, a framework of ebony and bronze setting off a multi-coloured inlay of marble, porphyry, jasper and other ornamental stones.

Stourhead Estate Wiltshire

At Stourton, off the B3092, 3 miles north-west of Mere on the A303

To most people Stourhead means the finest landscape garden in the south of England and a great house with a fine collection (*see above*), but its estate of 2,019 acres has much to show the walker.

The wooded escarpment between Warminster and Wincanton forms the western edge of the chalk country centred on Salisbury Plain. It is divided between three estates: Longleat to the north, Maiden Bradley in the middle reach, and Stourhead to the south. Each of these overlooks the pastoral country to the west with its market town of Shepton Mallet. Stourhead's share of this lovely country provides three very different walks.

First a woodland walk. South of the chain of lakes in the landscape garden, the River Stour winds its way through a steep wooded valley towards Gill-

(*Opposite page*) The Temple of Apollo on a knoll above the lake at Stourhead is one of several eyecatchers punctuating vistas across the valley. (*NT/Charlie Waite*)

ingham, passing the hamlet of Gasper. A circular walk from Stourton leads via Bonham to the footbridge over the river below Gasper Mill, now a private house. In the woods above there are several thousand minuscule quarries, named Pen Pits. Archaeologists have shown that they were dug from about 1800 BC to extract lumps of greensand which were then made into grindstones and whetstones. The path runs up through the woods, past the Pen Pits, to Pear Ash and then turns north to return to Stourton past the former hound kennels between New Lake and Turner's Paddock Lake.

The second walk is through a more contrived landscape, north of the garden. It starts past the east entrance front of Stourhead House and continues west into Long Lane, a disused road which formerly carried traffic running west from Salisbury. The lane becomes a tarred road and one is conscious of fine planting, an avenue of beeches on the ridge. Then, on the left, Six Wells Bottom plunges south-west to the lake far below. The woods on either side of this grassy combe give it great beauty. Near the top St Peter's Pump collects the springs at the head-waters of the river to serve the chain of lakes. A mile and a half to the west is one of the Trust's finest follies, the great red-brick mass of the three-sided Alfred's Tower, 160 feet high, perched on the edge of the escarpment. Alfred is said to have rallied his troops here against Danish invaders in AD 879. The tower was started in 1762 and stood unharmed until 1942 when it was hit by an aircraft, knocking off the spire which was eventually replaced in 1985. The views from the top of the tower, across the whole of Somerset, are superb, and it is usually open in the summer when the weather is fine. From Hilcombe Farm, some way below the tower, the walk returns to Stourton through the woods to the west of the garden.

The third walk is very different. East of Stourton one leaves the wooded country for the open, not to say very exposed, upland and takes lanes and field paths north of Search Farm up to White Sheet Down, and from there up White Sheet Hill, 802 feet high. There are Neolithic and Iron Age earthworks, almost obligatory on these West Country hills, but the visitor has much else to appreciate for this is the best sort of chalk grassland, springy underfoot, skylarks trilling overhead, and the views are superb: west back to Stourhead and Alfred's Tower, south-west over the Blackmore Vale, north-east towards the Deverills.

Stowe Landscape Gardens
Buckinghamshire

3 miles north-west of Buckingham, off A422

Laid out over some 560 acres of undulating Buckinghamshire countryside is a vast eighteenth-century landscape, with sweeping tree-framed vistas to distant arches, temples and other eye-catchers, a chain of lakes crossed by a Palladian bridge, the model for that at Prior Park (*see* p. 268), and a central focus on an impressive classical house (not National Trust). Conceived on a heroic scale, its various buildings the size of houses rather than ornaments, this is more a private world than a garden, with a bucolic naturalism that has architectural jewels rising out of rough grassland and emerging from belts of woodland. A grand note is struck right from the start, with an approach down a straight $2\frac{1}{2}$-mile avenue from Buckingham and glimpses of a 60-foot-high Corinthian arch on the skyline ahead. The arch overlooks a valley and Stowe's stunning north–south main vista, running gently down to the lakes and up a broad sweep of grass to the house crowning the opposite slope. Always impressive, this romantic Claudian view is magical in the low sun of a summer's evening or a winter's afternoon, when shadows etch the sculptural façade of the house and fall long over the grass.

Stowe has an important place in the history of landscape design. Leading landscapers, architects and sculptors, among them Charles Bridgeman, Sir John Vanbrugh, William Kent and James Gibbs, were employed here and the layout, gradually developed over some eighty years, pioneered the eighteenth-century swing away from formality to the kind of artful naturalism practised by 'Capability' Brown. Still in his twenties, Brown was head gardener here for a decade from 1741 and was married in 1744 in the medieval church enveloped in the garden, all that remains of the former village.

Stowe is the work of three generations of the upwardly mobile, politically ambitious Temple-Grenville family, who enshrined their Whiggish prejudices in the garden architecture. The transformation of what had been a formal terraced garden was started by Richard Temple (1675–1749), later Viscount Cobham, who, funded by marriage to a rich brewery heiress, devoted periods in the political wilderness to extending his house and garden. Of his earlier formal design, only the innovatory

The delicious Oxford bridge at Stowe, with one of the Boycott pavilions beyond. The eighteenth-century landscape, laid out over 560 acres, is devised as a series of vistas to distant arches, temples and other eyecatchers. (*NT/Rupert Truman*)

encircling ha-ha devised by Charles Bridgeman, with military-style bastions at the southern corners, survives unaltered, but the garden still boasts Vanbrugh's domed rotonda and his lakeside pavilions, which now frame the vista to the Corinthian arch.

An increasingly naturalistic approach from the 1740s, with the addition of temples and other monuments by Kent and Gibbs, most of them classical but one a turreted, triangular Gothic fantasy faced in orangey ironstone which now graces a sheep-grazed meadow, was continued by Cobham's nephew, Earl Temple (1711–79). As arrogant and self-important as his uncle, Temple was also a man of taste, who used continental artists such as Giovanni Battista Borra and Vincenzo Valdrè to alter and embellish existing buildings, gave the house its magical south front and created the glorious main vista to the Corinthian arch. Both arch and house were the work of his architect cousin Thomas Pitt, Earl Camelford, who designed the former to be lived in, tucking windows into the sides, and based the latter on designs commissioned from the more exalted Robert Adam. The final touches were added to Stowe by Earl Temple's nephew, George Grenville (1753–1813), created Marquess of Buckingham in 1784 as a reward for services in Ireland, but, to his chagrin, never Duke (an honour achieved by his son).

Growing financial difficulties in the nineteenth century, when the 2nd Duke ran up huge debts, resulted in the sale of most of the estate and the family collections in 1848. In 1921, the house became a public school, which it is today. Despite valiant efforts, the designed landscape and its monuments continued to decay and in 1989, thanks to an anonymous benefactor and the National Heritage Memorial Fund, the gardens were handed over to the National Trust, which has now begun a massive, long-term restoration programme.

The extensive visitor tour is partly a feast of changing vistas, like a series of landscape paintings, partly a window on to the classical, literary and political world in which Stowe is embedded. A little valley below the house is named for the Elysian fields of classical mythology, with a dammed stream to imitate the serpentine River Styx and a curved screen by Kent, like a wayside shrine, carrying portrait busts of Whig-approved heroes, from King Alfred and Shakespeare to the now-forgotten MP Sir John Barnard, who supported Lord Cobham in voting against Walpole's excise bill; an island carries a monument to the dramatist William Congreve, Cobham's friend and drinking companion; and there are direct historical references too, such as the 100-foot column erected in 1759 to commemorate General Wolfe's death on the Heights of Abraham. Despite the golf course laid out below the house, surrounding Vanbrugh's rotunda with a patchwork of greens and fairways, and the glimpses of school tennis courts, this is one of the most memorable of planned landscapes.

Strangford Lough   Co. Down

Stretches from Strangford inland to Newtownards

This great tidal inlet, twenty-three miles from Angus Rock at its mouth to its headwaters at Newtownards, is not only very beautiful, dotted with 120 little islands, but immensely rich in wildlife. On each tide millions of gallons of water flow through the Narrows, creating a turbulent current which ensures an even mix of nutrients and food and forms a series of differing habitats throughout the lough. Soft corals, sponges and anemones, mussels, sea squirts and brittle-stars live on the bottom, feeding on the food suspended in the water. Crab and starfish eat these filter-feeding animals, while octopus and fish take crabs, shrimps and worms, themselves being preyed on by seals and porpoises. On the shore and on the islands there is a rich resident bird life, made richer by the several migrations. Wildfowl and waders pass through on their way north in early spring, while terns arrive from Africa in order to breed. As the terns leave to go south, the waders return at the end of summer: black-tailed godwit, curlew, golden plover. In autumn more waders arrive – knot, turnstone, lapwing, Brent geese from Arctic Canada – to feed on the mudflats and in some cases to rest before going further. In really cold weather they are joined by great-northern divers, bar-tailed godwit and other birds driven by storm. Big flocks of wintering wildfowl include widgeon from Russia, whooper swans from Iceland, teal and pochard.

This great natural reserve was at risk from uncontrolled shooting, from disturbance by a population made mobile by cars and by lack of management techniques. The Trust already owned Castle Ward (*see* p.57), overlooking the Narrows, but the rest of the shore and the islands belonged to numerous individuals and there was no chance of acquiring the whole. In 1966, however, the Trust took the lead by making an agreement with the several wildfowling clubs, working out management plans with many of the owners, and, later on, acquiring a number of islands and stretches of foreshore. Following the purchase, with funds donated by *Daily Mail* readers, of 12 miles of shoreline along the Narrows and the southern end of the Ards Peninsula in 1990, most of the foreshore is now in Trust hands. The plan has largely been achieved. Strangford Lough is now managed in the interest of its wildlife, and those who use the lough for their enjoyment can still do so.

Studley Royal   North Yorkshire

2 miles west of Ripon, off the B6265 to Pateley Bridge

The Studley Royal estate hides an enchanting formal water garden, with mirror-like moon pools – one round and two crescent-shaped – set in smoothly mown grass reflecting classical statues and the Tuscan columns of a pedimented temple. Laid out in the steep-sided valley of the River Skell, the water garden is framed and contained by the foliage of beeches, yews and Scots pine on the slopes above. More sculpture, a grotto and a rustic bridge provide points of interest on the walk circling the garden, while a pinnacled Gothic tower and a domed rotunda perched high up on the side of the valley were designed as eyecatchers to highlight a series of views across the glassy ponds. This is a serene and peaceful place, a restful combination of still water with green grass and trees. At one end of the garden the canalised Skell cascades into a lake, while upstream the river has been dammed to form a sweep of water curving round the mound known as Tent Hill towards Fountains Abbey (*see* p.121).

This rare survival was the inspiration of John Aislabie, who inherited the Studley Royal estate in 1699. An able and ambitious politician who rose to be Chancellor of the Exchequer, his meteoric career was brought to a sudden end in 1720 by his involvement in the South Sea Bubble, which led to his expulsion from Parliament. Returning to Yorkshire in the same year, he devoted himself to the garden he had started in 1716, perhaps regarding it as a refuge from the world. A beautiful naturalistic park surrounding his creation, with deer grazing beneath mature oaks, beeches, chestnuts and limes, reflects landscaping in the late eighteenth and early nineteenth centuries, but it also bears traces of the seven great intersecting avenues which John Aislabie designed to focus on features of the estate, on the tower of Fountains Abbey, or on a distant view of Ripon Minster. The house which he built to replace the medieval manor in the park, probably with advice from Colen Campbell whose enchanting banqueting house crowns the Coffin Lawn, has disappeared. Like the earlier building, this was

extensively damaged by fire and only the impressive stable block (not owned by the Trust) remains.

Below the lake the Skell plunges into a natural gorge, rustic bridges carrying the path following the stream back and forth over the river. Beech woods tower over the valley, accentuating the drama of the steep cliffs outcropping on either side. Although only one of the eyecatchers built on prominent crags survives, this intentionally wild landscape is still largely as conceived by Aislabie's son William, one of the first examples of the Picturesque style in England and a direct contrast with the formality of his father's water garden. William was also responsible for purchasing the Fountains Abbey estate in 1768, and for the great sweep of grass framed by woods on the valley sides which now leads up to the ruins. And he engineered what is probably Studley's most memorable feature,

Balthazar Nebot's view of Studley Royal in c.1760 shows the cascade into the lake from the water garden, with the Gothic octagon tower high up on the left and the domed Temple of Fame, which was later to be moved to the other side of the valley, on the right. White swans as shown in the painting have been re-introduced by the Trust. (*NT/Tony Whittaker*)

the surprise view of the abbey from high up on the east side of the valley, the culmination of the vista path which winds past the octagon tower and domed temple.

The only major subsequent addition to the estate was the High Victorian Gothic church built in the park in 1871–8 for the 1st Marquess and Marchioness of Ripon. The masterpiece of William Burges, its highly ornate interior includes a painted multitude of richly coloured angelic musicians on a gold background thronging the sanctuary and stained-glass windows representing the Book of Revelation. This magnificent building is seen impressively silhouetted on the horizon at the far end of the majestic lime avenue which climbs slowly to the skyline through the gate into the park from the estate village of Studley Roger.

Studley Royal is not only a remarkable survival but a unique illustration of the development of landscape gardening during the course of the eighteenth century, the formality of the early years of the period being gradually rejected in favour of the kind of naturalistic landscapes seen in the park, below the lake and in the setting of the abbey.

Sudbury Hall Derbyshire

6 miles east of Uttoxeter at the crossing point of the A50 Derby–Stoke and the A515 Lichfield–Ashbourne roads

Sudbury is the most idiosyncratic of the many great houses created during Charles II's reign, built to a consciously outdated plan incorporating a great hall and long gallery and yet fashionably decorated. The message of the exterior is similarly contradictory. Diapered brickwork and an array of mullioned and transomed windows suggest a Jacobean house, but the hipped roof and gleaming central cupola, visible for miles around, are characteristic of the age. George Vernon, who started his new house the year after he inherited the Sudbury estate in 1659, seems to have acted as his own architect and to have adapted his original ideas over some forty years as knowledge of London fashions gradually filtered through to remote Derbyshire.

Competent but uninspired early work by local men contrasts with the skills displayed by the London craftsmen Vernon employed as time went by, such as Edward Pearce, Grinling Gibbons and the plasterers Bradbury and Pettifer. The balustrade of Pearce's carved pine staircase, one of the finest of

its date, is a mass of writhing foliage, with baskets of fruit set on the newel posts. Pettifer's plasterwork overhead is similarly rich, garlands of fruit and flowers and acanthus scrolls forming three-dimensional encrustations. And yet twenty years after this work was finished Vernon employed Louis Laguerre to paint mythological scenes in the plasterwork panels, a taste of the exuberant baroque style popular at court.

Another painting by Laguerre fills a plaster wreath on the ceiling of the saloon. One of the richest of Sudbury's interiors, Pearce's pedimented and gilded woodwork panels displaying a series of full-length family portraits are strongly reminiscent of his contributions to Wren's city churches. But even his work is outclassed by the Grinling Gibbons carving over the fireplace in the drawing-room next door, fruit, flowers, dead game and fish all depicted with life-like realism.

After so much unrelieved grandeur, the decoration of the sunny 138-foot long gallery running the

Naturalistic baskets of fruit crown the newel posts of Edward Pearce's superb carved pine staircase at Sudbury Hall, for which he was paid £112 15s 6d. The baskets of fruit could be removed and replaced with lanterns or candelabra at night. (*NT/John Bethell*)

length of the south front is unexpected. At first glance Bradbury and Pettifer's intricate plasterwork appears to repeat established motifs. But all is not what it seems. The classical busts portrayed along the frieze are humorous caricatures, while a lion, a horse, a boar and other animals leap gaily out of the swirls of foliage on the ceiling and grasshoppers dance playfully round the sunflower rosette adorning the central window bay.

The small family rooms at the east end of the house contrast with the magnificence elsewhere. Lady Vernon's cosy sitting-room, with its leaf-green walls and tranquil view over the lake below the south front, has a communicating door to her husband's study. It is easy to imagine them talking through it, and walking together across the passage to eat in the small dining-room.

Although Sudbury has lost most of its original contents, there are family portraits in almost every room, including works by Lawrence, Hoppner and S. M. Wright, and a few outstanding furnishings remain. In the room where Queen Adelaide slept when she rented the house in the 1840s, a seventeenth-century Flemish ebony cabinet is enchantingly decorated with scenes of the Creation by Frans Francken the Younger. The first panel shows a purple- and red-robed god hovering above an endless expanse of ocean, brooding on what he is about to unleash.

Sugar Loaf and Skirrid Fawr

Gwent

3 miles north-west and 3 miles north-east of Abergavenny

North of Abergavenny, between the rivers Usk and Honddu and on either side of the A465, are two prominent outliers of the sandstone mass of the Brecon Beacons (*see* p.41). West of the road is the cone-shaped 1,950 Sugar Loaf, given to the Trust in 1936. Its Welsh name is Pen-y-fâl, but its English name, a reference to the way sugar was once sold, has survived in this English-speaking part of Wales. To the east is the 1,596-foot Skirrid Fawr, where the Trust has held 205 acres of the summit since 1939.

The hills are areas of open heather and bilberry moor, coarse tussocky grassland, bracken and ancient oak woodland, with some crags and scree. The easiest way up both is from the south, with views from the summits of the Usk Valley, the Black Mountains and across the Bristol Channel.

Skirrid Fawr, a 1,596-foot outlier of the Brecon Beacons north-east of Abergavenny. (*NT/C. M. Radcliffe*)

Sussex Coast

Like the North Downs (*see* p.224), the South Downs meet the sea in a spectacular cliffline, with a long, undeveloped stretch running out to the knob of Beachy Head between Eastbourne and Seaford. The Trust owns over 700 acres here, including three and a half of the turf-thatched humps known as the Seven Sisters. This is a switchback landscape of chalk hills and dry valleys, much cultivated during the Second World War and so with a rich flora only along the cliffline and in untouched pockets. There are prehistoric remains too, and the buildings at Birling Gap, being refurbished by the Trust, include a row of nineteenth-century coastguard cottages set end on to the shore, and gradually disappearing as the sea eats into the soft and friable cliffs. The Trust's two other holdings along this coast are quite different in character. The coast east of Hastings, where the Trust owns Fairlight Cliff and adjoining farmland, is known for its geologically interesting, fragile mudstone cliffs; while westwards, guarding the mouth of Chichester harbour, is the claw-like spit of East Head, a tongue of dunes, saltings and sand and shingle beach which is one of the most important sites in western Europe for overwintering waders and wildfowl.

The Seven Sisters, perhaps the most famous stretch of coast in southern England. (*NT/Michael Dohrn*)

Sutton House London

At the corner of Isabella Road and Homerton High Street, Hackney

An inner-city borough in East London is the setting for one of the few surviving examples of a Tudor red-brick house. At the west end of Homerton High Street, where it starts to swing north, is a three-storey H-shaped house set back from the road across a paved yard, with diamond diapering marking the west wing. Dating from 1534–5, Sutton House was built for the high-flying courtier and statesman Sir Ralph Sadleir (1507–87) in what

was then desirable countryside on the edge of Hackney village, with open fields between here and London. Right-hand man to Thomas Cromwell, Sadleir survived his patron's fall in 1540, and was one of those who tried the ill-fated Mary Queen of Scots in 1586. His house has had a more chequered career. Remodelled in *c.*1700, when the Tudor gables and mullioned windows were replaced with the present elegant sashes and roofline parapet, divided into two in *c.*1750, partly faced in heavy stucco in the mid-nineteenth century, reunited in 1904, Sutton House has served as school, working men's institute and offices as well as one or more private dwellings. After a recent period of uncertainty and decline, it has now been restored by the Trust and is both a show place and a cultural centre.

The restoration has exposed original features

hidden behind later alterations and, apart from the great hall that once filled the bar of the H, the basic Tudor plan also survives, with staircases in the wings and a few cupboard-like garderobes. The parlour in the west wing is one of the finest Tudor interiors in London, with oak linenfold panelling running from floor to ceiling and a fireplace of carved Reigate stone, and on the first floor, above what was the great hall, is the airy, high-ceilinged great chamber, lit by windows to both north and south. As in the parlour, the panelling here has been rearranged, and some of it is Jacobean rather than Tudor, but this is a striking room, its effect enhanced by Sadleir family portraits, an oak refectory table and a Charles II dresser. Other features reflect later history. There is painted Jacobean strapwork imitating what richer folk would have had executed in stone or wood, a panelled Georgian parlour in a delicate mint green and Georgian barley-twist balusters on the east staircase, and a Victorian study. There is also one surviving leaded and mullioned Tudor window, looking out on to the secluded, flagged court at the centre of the house. None of the sparse contents is original but all is in keeping, including a couple of reproduction seventeenth-century harpsichords.

Sutton House is a centre for the local community as well as a place of historic interest. These children are in the Tudor parlour, lined with linenfold panelling. (*NT/Chris King*)

'Finds' on display – thimbles, bobbins, scissors, pins and the odd shoe – date from the school years, and a squatter has left a sinister red and black eye on the wall of an attic room. The Wenlock Barn closing the court, a balconied hall with an open timber roof built by Lionel Crane, son of the Arts and Crafts designer Walter Crane, is now a function room and the house is also a showcase for Hackney's sizeable community of artists, said to be the largest in Europe, whose work is shown in a first-floor gallery.

Tattershall Castle Lincolnshire

On south side of the A153, 15 miles north-east of Sleaford, 10 miles south-west of Horncastle

Ralph, 1st Lord Cromwell, was an ambitious man, reaching the climax of his career as Treasurer to Henry VI in 1433–43. His sturdy brick tower, rising over a hundred feet from the Lincolnshire Fens and visible for miles around, is one of the most striking monuments of the later Middle Ages, all that survives of the great castle he created here.

Tattershall looks both forwards and backwards. By 1430, when Cromwell started on the extensions to the existing buildings at Tattershall, keeps had gone out of fashion in England, but were to be built for another century or so in France. The magnificent products of Franco-Burgundian culture, so exquisitely illustrated in the *Trés Riches Heures* of the Duc de Berry, may well have inspired the young nobleman, who would have had ample opportunity to see them while serving with the English army in the Hundred Years War. Like its French counterparts, Tattershall has an air of unreality, as if it too had stepped from a contemporary manuscript. In the years that followed, many other men of substance were to reach skywards in buildings which were essentially status symbols.

Although outwardly defensive, with machicolated fighting galleries underneath the battlements and girdled by two moats, this is in fact a domestic country mansion masquerading as a fortress, with large and plentiful windows and several entrances. One great chamber fills each of the four floors above the vaulted basement, with the Treasurer's personal bedchamber at the top of his tower-house. Carved stone chimneypieces displaying the purse of his office and elaborate window tracery point to luxuriously fitted interiors.

Large windows lighting the upper floors reveal that Tattershall Castle is a domestic country mansion masquerading as a fortress. (*NT/Brian Lawrence*)

Tattershall is as significant for its material as its design. Although bricks were used in the eastern counties in the thirteenth and fourteenth centuries, they were usually concealed under plaster. Tattershall is one of the earliest examples of the deliberate choice of this material (*see also* Sissinghurst, p.291), with its decorative possibilities exploited in the rows of corbels at the top of the façades. Inside, the skill of the craftsmen Cromwell employed shows particularly in the spiral staircase that fills one of the corner turrets, with its finely moulded stone handrail fashioned in the wall, and in the brickwork of the decorative vaults.

Cromwell was a man of the world, acquiring large estates across the East Midlands and building manor houses elsewhere as well as constructing his lavishly-appointed tower-house at Tattershall. He was also a creature of his age, concerned for his fate in the next world as much as his comfort in this one. Like other great men of his time, he anticipated the Last Trump by endowing a memorial college, set only a few yards from his castle. Apart from a ruined, two-storey brick building, possibly offices and lodgings, only the beautiful collegiate church, with its armorial stained glass and mutilated brass commemorating Cromwell and his wife, still survives, the attractive row of almshouses having been rebuilt in the seventeenth century (neither is owned by the Trust).

In the late Middle Ages this considerable complex of buildings, rising like an island of the civilised world from the sea of the Fens, tellingly revealed the self-importance and aspirations of the man who created them.

Tatton Park Cheshire

3½ miles north of Knutsford, 4 miles south of Altrincham, 3½ miles from the M6 at Manchester interchange

A hundred pairs of eyes watch visitors to Tatton's Tenant's Hall, where the walls are hung with the sporting trophies acquired by the 4th Lord Egerton in Africa and India. This restless man, who once lived with a tribe in the Gobi Desert, also experimented with short-wave radio and had his own aeroplane. His 1900 Benz proudly displaying the number plate M1 was the first car to be registered in Cheshire.

The 4th Lord's inquiring mind seems to have been an inherited trait. In all the Wyatt family's plans for the remodelling of the house, for which they were employed at Tatton between 1774 and about 1825, the library is most prominent. A comfortable room filling the centre of the garden front, it was designed to be used, not admired. Books lie companionably on the reading chairs and stands, leather-padded armchairs are drawn up by the fire and a library ladder invites inspection of the topmost shelves. There is something for everyone here, including Jane Austen first editions, volumes of music, and illustrated works on the arts and classical antiquities, mostly finely bound. The nucleus of the collection is the sixteenth-century library acquired by Thomas Egerton, founder of the family fortunes, who rose from unpromising beginnings to become Lord Chancellor of England.

Lewis Wyatt's formal drawing-room hung with cherry-coloured silk is much grander, with a relentless coffered ceiling and with gilt-framed chairs and sofas carved in a sinuous rococo style by Gillows of Lancaster that would not seem out of place in a Venetian *palazzo*. Van Dyck's *Martyrdom of St Stephen* seems curiously appropriate in these unrelaxed surroundings, cherubs hovering overhead to receive the saint's soul. Two moody Venetian views by Canaletto are full of delightful detail, the scene on the quay in front of the Doge's Palace including a little white dog with a jaunty tail trotting purposefully along among the figures going about their business.

Lewis Wyatt was also responsible for the inspired treatment of the staircase in the centre of the house, giving a vista through a colonnade-like series of arches on the first floor. The Regency lifestyle for which Tatton was designed emerges strongly here, every bedroom except one sporting a dressing-room. Each suite was originally distinguished by the colour of its textiles and the wood of the furniture, the pieces in the principal apartment being of mahogany inlaid with ebony.

The Wyatts' exterior is a pure neo-classical design, with a giant pedimented portico dominating the south front, a low-pitched roof and almost no decoration except for chaste swags in panels over the sash windows. Only the dining-room remains from the eighteenth-century house that William Tatton Egerton so ruthlessly swept away, green walls setting off superb rococo plasterwork.

The atmosphere of opulent grandeur extends into the gardens, where herbaceous borders face across sweeping lawns. Flower-filled urns look down on Sir Joseph Paxton's grassy terraces on the south front, with shallow flights of steps descending to a fountain surrounded by an Italianate parterre. The classical conservatory, now furnished with nineteenth-century plants, is Lewis Wyatt's; Paxton designed the fernery, but the roof has been raised to allow for the huge New Zealand tree ferns which now reach to the glass. More informal planting – azaleas, rhododendrons, a collection of conifers and many other shrubs – surrounds the artificial lake known as the Golden Brook, almost concealing the Japanese garden laid out here in 1910, a mosaic of water and islands authentically planted with Japanese maples, dwarf conifers, Kurume azaleas and evergreens, and dotted with stone lanterns. A mound crowned with white stones simulates snow-capped Mount Fuji. Another surprise is the small beech maze hidden behind a bank of rhododendrons beside the long avenue known as the Broad Walk, one of only three such features in the Trust's care (*see* Glendurgan and Greys Court, pp. 126 and 135).

The Home Farm at Tatton Dale was once the heart of the extensive Egerton estates, with pig sties, stockyards and stables surrounding the office from which nearly 1,000 tenant properties were administered, and workshops where everything needed on the estate would be produced, from coffins to horseshoes. Humphry Repton produced a Red Book for the extensive park, but most of the landscaping probably dates from William Emes's work in the mid-eighteenth century, with some early nineteenth-century modifications by John Webb. Flocks of Soay and Hebridean sheep mingle with the red and fallow deer beneath the trees, and the remains of the medieval manor house are used to introduce visitors to the realities of pre-modern life.

The Doge's Palace and Riva degli Schiavoni, one of two views of Venice by Canaletto at Tatton Park. (*NT*/*John Bethell*)

The Teign Gorge Devon

3 miles north-east of Moretonhampstead, on both sides of the B3212

The River Teign rises at Teign Head below White-horse Hill in the north of Dartmoor and runs north and east past Gidleigh and Chagford, gathering side streams as it goes until in the parish of Drewsteignton, where its bed is at about 500 feet, it has to pierce the range of hills, 400 feet higher, which run parallel to the north-east side of the moor and which are outliers of it. From this point, far below Lutyens's masterpiece of Castle Drogo (*see* p.56), the Teign follows a wooded gorge for some seven miles east, to Steps Bridge at Dunsford.

The Trust owns two substantial lengths of the gorge. At the upper end its property extends from Dogmarsh Bridge below Chagford down to Fingle Bridge, with paths on both sides of the river. On the north bank there are paths at two levels. The Hunter's Path runs along the side of the gorge above Sharp Tor and Hunter's Tor and here, below Castle Drogo, a weir across the river dams water to serve the turbine which makes electricity for the castle. The Fisherman's Path, beside the river, is also easy walking, though the granite gives way to the crumbling rock of the culm shales below Hunter's Tor.

The south bank is very different. Opposite Castle Drogo Whiddon Park rises sharply from the river up to 750 feet. Here is an unaltered Tudor deer park, made by Sir John Whiddon in about 1570. While there is no herd of fallow deer here nowadays, the colossal deer hedge made of immense blocks of granite to contain the herd still stands eight to nine feet high. The park is wonderfully picturesque, with granite outcrops, groves of ancient oak, ash and rowan, broom and gorse, bracken and bilberry, and a lichen and invertebrate community associated with ancient trees that has survived from pre-Neolithic woodland. The Trust owns Whiddon Wood, to the west of the park, and also the conifer plantations between here and Fingle Bridge.

From this latter bridge down to Clifford Bridge the gorge is privately owned, but on the north bank the beautiful hanging oaks of Dunsford Wood belong to the Trust, and then continuously to Steps Bridge. On the opposite bank the woods on either side of the Doccombe stream belong, including St Thomas Cleave and running up to the B3212, as does Bridford Wood to the south of this road. Miles of paths traverse these steep woods, with peeps far down to the river below, and because oak woods let in much more light than, say, beech or conifers, there is an interesting flora beneath the trees.

Templetown Mausoleum

Co. Antrim

In Castle Upton graveyard, Templepatrick

The quiet graveyard at Castle Upton outside Templepatrick is dominated by this perfect neo-classical temple, erected by Sarah Upton in 1789 in memory of the Hon. Arthur Upton who had died twenty years earlier. The mausoleum is now partly smothered in creeper with red and green tendrils exploring the dignified entrance façade. Urns in niches flank a rusticated arch and three more crown the parapet above the simple inscription. Coade stone plaques commemorate other members of the Upton family. One of the finest monuments ever designed by Robert Adam, the mausoleum is also one of the few examples of the architect's work in Ireland. Adam was commissioned to give a new look to Castle Upton (not owned by the Trust), but the house was subsequently remodelled and only his castellated stables near the graveyard have survived.

Theatre Royal Suffolk

In Westgate Street, Bury St Edmunds, on south side of the A134 from Sudbury

This delightfully intimate theatre, seating an audience of just under 300, is one of only three surviving Georgian playhouses. Built in 1819, it dates from an era when Bury was a provincial capital and farmers and gentry from miles around crowded into the town for the short autumn season. Comfortable red plush seats have replaced the benches in the pit, but original boxes still fill the dress circle and the stalls are authentically raked steeply towards the stage. This little jewel is the creation of William Wilkins (1778–1839), an experienced theatre designer and one of the leading neo-classical architects of his day, who was later to produce the National Gallery and the screen at King's College, Cambridge. Winged sphinxes and griffins decorate the dress circle and another classical frieze adorns the proscenium arch.

Original boxes still line the dress circle of Bury St Edmunds's tiny Theatre Royal, built in 1819, but the benches in the pit have been replaced by comfortable plush seats. (*NT*)

The pink, white and grey façade on Westgate Street, with a projecting glazed portico, is dwarfed by the huge buildings of the Greene King brewery, an ever-present reminder of the years the theatre lay forgotten. The coming of the railways in the 1840s, which transported those in search of good entertainment speedily to Norwich or London, hastened a decline which had set in a decade or so earlier and which could not be halted even by the staging of the world première of *Charley's Aunt* here in 1892. Greene King & Sons, who used the theatre as a barrel store, also played a prominent part in its revival in 1965.

Tintinhull Somerset

5 miles north-west of Yeovil, ½ mile south of the A303, on east outskirts of Tintinhull

Formal pools, varied borders and secluded lawns in this tiny, entirely satisfying walled garden are divided by clipped hedges and seen against the backdrop of an unpretentious seventeenth- and early eighteenth-century house built of warm Ham stone. The west façade added in *c*.1722, where mullioned and transomed windows glow like liquid gold in the evening sun, overlooks one of Tintinhull's most charming features, a grassy, walled

forecourt guarded by stone eagles set high on gate piers. Domes of box like vast green hedgehogs line the central path, and roses and clematis climb the walls. A flight of steps leads into the court from the central porch flanked by Tuscan columns, its curved pediment echoed in the shallow triangle breaking the roofline above.

A yew- and box-fringed path punctuated by shallow flights of steps runs gently downhill from here, past an apse-shaped lawn dominated by a huge *Quercus ilex* and through a thicket of azaleas to the fountain pool which closes the vista. An opening in the hedge to the right gives a view of smoothly mown grass framing a tranquil sheet of water, with the classical columns of a little stone loggia overlooking the far end. A feeling of the Mediterranean is enhanced by terracotta pots marking the corners of the pool, but the springy turf and the thickly planted borders on either side are quintessentially English.

The garden is still largely as created by Mrs F. E. Reiss, who moved here with her husband in 1933. This inspired plantswoman used flower and foliage, colour and texture to make pictorial compositions, setting them within an architectural framework defined by yew and box hedges and linked by axial paths, a series of outdoor rooms in the style of Hidcote (*see* p.149). She knew the value of

Tintinhull: the vista up the garden to the west end of the house from the fountain pool. (*NT/Neil Campbell-Sharp*)

alternating sunlight and shade in creating the spirit of a garden and how blue can be used to light dark corners. Most of the borders are mixed, mingling small trees, flowering and foliage plants, grasses and bulbs. Schemes and patterns are never repeated. Whereas one of the long beds flanking the rectangular water-lily pool is planted in deep bright colours, mostly yellow, orange and red, the other is a subtle blend of softer shades – pink, violet, and blue – with silver and grey foliage. There are many individual species here to delight the keen plantsman, but Tintinhull is above all a garden where the overall effect amounts to far more than the sum of its parts.

Townend Cumbria

3 miles south-east of Ambleside at south end of Troutbeck

Townend is a rare and remarkably intact survival of the house of a family of yeoman farmers. Largely dating from the seventeenth century, with lime-washed walls, mullioned windows and a slate roof topped with six round chimneys, it is one of the finest examples of domestic Lake District architecture. Just across the lane, dating from the same period as the house built on a much grander scale, is the homestead's stone-and-slate galleried barn, with a ramp up to the granary floor and the date 1666 carved on one of the lintels.

The Browne family who lived here for over four centuries were sheep farmers, who seem to have gradually risen in society through careful manage-

The long seventeenth-century oak table under the window in the firehouse at Townend was assembled *in situ*. (*NT/John Bethell*)

ment of their affairs and judicious marriages. Much of Townend's attraction derives from the fact that its contents reflect slow accretion by several generations of the Brownes. In the little library, Milton rubs shoulders with Clarke's sermons, Walton's *Compleat Angler*, a history of England and volumes of farming periodicals. None of the books is very rare or valuable, but the collection as a whole gives a unique insight into the interests and preoccupations of a rural middle-class family.

The preservation of the house and its contents owes much to the last George Browne (1834–1914), who was both a noted antiquary and a gifted joiner and woodcarver. The rooms are filled with ornate examples of his work, from the richly carved chairs in the firehouse, the oldest part of the building, to the little spindle-fronted cupboard in one of the bedrooms, in which no two spindles are alike. Such minor masterpieces speak of long winter evenings by candlelight round the fire.

The wealth of heavy oak furniture displayed at Townend also includes the long seventeenth-century dining-table in the firehouse, undoubtedly assembled *in situ*, where the Brownes would have taken meals with their farmhands and servants. From the kitchen next door, an early seventeenth-century spiral staircase winds steeply upwards to the austere quarters for the housekeeper and maids, with a pair of clogs set out ready for the morning by one of the beds.

Among many other treasures is a series of charming naive paintings of the family's sheep by the local nineteenth-century artist William Taylor Longmire. Perhaps he took his models from the ancestors of the beasts which still graze the fells rising behind the house.

George Browne's notebooks have enabled the Trust to re-create the small garden as it was in the Edwardian era. Roses and a traditional mixture of cottage-garden flowers, such as delphiniums and sweet peas, fuchsias and potentillas, crowd the beds, rhododendrons and damsons are planted on the banks and there is fruit from apples, gages and plums.

Town Walls Tower Shropshire

Overlooking the River Severn on the south side of Shrewsbury

Despite Edward I's conquest of Wales in the late thirteenth century, towns in the Welsh Marches still needed to be defended against the possibility of insurrection in the west. Of Shrewsbury's walls studded with twelve watch-towers only fragments now remain, including this four-storey fourteenth-century tower overlooking a great loop of the River Severn on the south side of town.

Toys Hill Kent

2½ miles south of Brasted, 1 mile west of Ide Hill

A mile and a half east of Sir Winston Churchill's beloved Chartwell (*see* p.61) lies Toys Hill, which was once part of the commons of Brasted Chart. Its 363 acres, rising to over 800 feet and including the highest point in Kent, have been built up from a tiny beginning in 1898. Local people no longer graze pigs and cattle, quarry stone, or cut peat or firewood, but the old pollarded beeches provide fascinating relics of a former land use. Sadly, only a few of these survived the Great Storm of 1987, but the Trust is now actively managing regenerating woodland and seeking to conserve aspects of the historic landscape, such as pockets of heath and wood pasture.

Treasurer's House North Yorkshire

In Minster Yard, York, on the north side of the minster

Treasurer's House borders a narrow medieval cobbled street in the shadow of York Minster, only a stone's throw from the east end. Once attached to one of the wealthiest and most sought-after benefices in England, successive treasurers of the cathedral lived here from 1100 until the office was abolished under Henry VIII. Little remains of the medieval building or of the earlier structures suggested by the Roman column in the cellars.

The present elegant and roomy town house has had many and varied owners, including John Aislabie of Studley Royal (*see* p.322) and Dr Jacques Sterne, whose novelist-nephew Laurence Sterne, despite becoming a prebendary of the minster in 1741, satirised the inward-looking society of the

cathedral set in his *A Political Romance* (1759). Sterne's savage attack on local ecclesiastical courts provoked the banning of the book.

The attractive garden front, with its classical central entrance bay, dates from about 1630. The charming curved Dutch gables adorning the projecting wings on either side are also seventeenth century, but the Venetian windows in the façades below were added about a hundred years later. Although the entrance from the garden leads into a galleried hall with a medieval flavour, most of the interior dates either from the seventeenth century or early in the eighteenth. The thin, beautifully carved balusters on the stairs, possibly the work of the highly skilled local carpenter-architect, William Thornton, whose magnificent woodcarvings are the chief glory of Beningbrough Hall (*see* p.26), date from the later period, as does the airy, panelled drawing-room looking over the garden.

Subsequently divided into three separate dwellings, the house was rescued by the wealthy industrialist and aesthete Frank Green, who acquired it in 1897. Removing all nineteenth-century alterations and additions, Green carefully restored the house to what he thought was its original appearance, creating a huge hall out of the two-storey central block, with a half-timbered gallery supported on classical columns. Appropriate antiques were used to form a sequence of period rooms. Furniture reflecting the craftsmanship of two centuries includes a fine oak refectory table of *c*.1600, a marquetry grandfather clock of 1680 and three early eighteenth-century tester beds in the rooms where Edward VII, then Prince of Wales, his wife Alexandra and their daughter Victoria slept when visiting the house in 1900. Three pairs of ornate early eighteenth-century giltwood mirrors make the drawing-room seem even larger than it is and an exquisite walnut secretaire-bookcase of the same period stands in the staircase hall. The house is further enriched by collections of china, pottery and glass and by a number of English and Flemish portraits from the sixteenth to eighteenth centuries.

The formal walled garden fronting the principal façade was established between 1897 and 1900 by Frank Green and is largely as he left it. A central sunken lawn is bordered on one side by a pollarded plane-tree avenue and there are raised terrace walks running along the south-west and south-east walls. Nothing in the garden can compete with the view of the minster towering above it.

The view of Carrick Roads from Trelissick, with boats at anchor off Mylor harbour across the water and Pendennis Castle crowning the promontory on the horizon. (*NT/ Andrew Besley*)

Treasurer's House Somerset

Opposite church in middle of village of Martock; 1 mile north-west of the A303 between Ilminster and Ilchester

Of the clutch of late medieval priests' houses owned by the Trust (*see, for example,* p.267), this comfortable building of mellow Ham stone, marked by a traceried two-light window and set back from the street through an archway, is perhaps the grandest. At the heart of the house is a sizeable two-storey hall completed by 1293, an original collar-braced timber roof arching above it. The solar block at right-angles to the hall is even earlier, but the kitchen on the other side was added in the fifteenth century. Martock was begun by the Treasurer of Wells Cathedral, who had acquired the twelfth-century village church from the French monastery of Mont St Michel in 1227–8. The above-average quality of the accommodation he enjoyed at this occasional country residence was no more than appropriate for a high official of the Church.

Trelissick Cornwall

4 miles south of Truro, on both sides of the B3289 above King Harry Ferry

Trelissick is set in the kind of country which evokes Daphne du Maurier. The estate stands at the head of the estuary of the River Fal, a ribbon of deep water running far inland with smaller creeks and inlets branching off on either side. Woods of oak with areas of beech and pine clothe the slopes leading down to the water, hanging over the tidal mudflats in the creeks. It is easy to imagine smugglers coming into these lonely inlets under cover of darkness. Below the house the romantically named King Harry Ferry is the only connection across the water to the Roseland peninsula on the other side. The estuary itself is still a major deep-water harbour, where huge oil tankers and cargo ships ride at anchor only yards offshore.

Although there was an ornamental woodland area on the slopes leading down to the Fal from the house remodelled by Peter Frederick Robinson in 1825 (not open to the public), the present garden was largely created by Mr and Mrs Ronald Copeland after she inherited the property in 1937. Mr and Mrs Copeland planted many of the species that flourish in the mild Cornish air, including the

337

rhododendrons and azaleas which are now such a feature of the garden, hydrangeas, camellias and flowering cherries, and exotics such as the ginkgo and various species of palm. They also ensured that the blossoms they nurtured had a wider, if unknowing audience. Mr Ronald Copeland was chairman and later managing director of his family's business, the Spode china factory, and flowers grown at Trelissick were used as models for those painted on ware produced at the works. The Copelands' family crest, a horse's head, now decorates the weathervane on the turret of the stable block, a pair to the Gilbert squirrel on the splendid Victorian Gothic water tower, an echo of the family who lived here in the second half of the nineteenth century (their ancestor, Sir Humphrey Gilbert, was lost at sea in his tiny ship *Squirrel* after discovering Newfoundland; *see* Compton Castle, p.82).

The feeling of the garden is intimate and small scale, with beeches, conifers and other trees sheltering and enclosing the valley and many changes of level and perspective. Paths bordered by high hedges suddenly open out into an area of grass, such as the spacious main lawn shaded by a large Japanese cedar. Although there are glimpses of the estuary through the trees, views are generally inward, across the valley and down to the dell at the heart of the garden, thickly planted with species hydrangeas, large-leaved rhododendrons and other exotic plants, including a banana, the Chilean fern and the Australian tree fern, and dotted with yellow and pink patches when the primulas are in flower. A narrow path leads to the rustic bridge over the Ferry Road, a green canyon through the heart of the garden. Beyond lies the wide slope of Carcadden, planted informally with conifers and a collection of choice shrubs, including hydrangeas, camellias, flowering cherries, rhododendrons and magnolias and with orange azaleas grouped round some purple-leaved nuts and maples. Trelissick also boasts the Trust's only fig garden, in a small enclosure near the entrance.

Only by the house does the view open out, where Robinson's imposing columned portico rising the height of the south front looks out across a great sweep of grass to Carrick Roads. On a clear day Pendennis Castle can be seen silhouetted on one of the promontories that guard the entrance to the estuary, while across the water little boats like outsize gulls ride at anchor off Mylor harbour. Much of the woodland hugging the shores of the estuary was planted by Thomas Daniell, Robinson's patron, whose father had bought the estate in 1800 with an inherited fortune from tin-mining interests. The carriage drives Thomas laid out in the park are now leafy woodland walks, an attractive adjunct to the tree-shaded lawns and paths in the garden itself.

Trencrom Hill Cornwall

3 miles south of St Ives, 4½ miles north-east of Penzance, 2 miles west of junction of the A30 and the A3074

A single wall following the contours of the hill and incorporating natural outcrops of granite traces the irregular outline of this small Iron Age hill fort dating from the second century BC, superbly sited on a gorse-covered tor in the far west of Cornwall. The remains of over seventeen hut circles have been found in the one-acre enclosure. To the north the fort looks over a typically Cornish patchwork of tiny stone-walled fields towards the blue expanses of St Ives Bay and the Atlantic beyond.

Trengwainton Cornwall

2 miles north-west of Penzance, ½ mile west of Heamoor on the B3312 Penzance–Morvah road

This long strip of a garden climbs gently uphill for about a third of a mile following a little stream. Still not yet mature, it was largely created after 1925 by Lieutenant Colonel Sir Edward Bolitho, who inherited the rambling Victorian mansion (not open to the public) looking down the valley. Like the secluded gardens of Glendurgan and Trelissick a few miles east (*see* pp.126 and 337), Trengwainton is particularly favoured climatically, well watered and rarely experiencing severe frosts. A remarkable collection of tender and half-hardy trees, shrubs and other plants has been established here, many of which could only be grown under glass elsewhere in the country.

But the skeleton of Trengwainton is much older. The tall beeches and oaks along the stream and sheltering the house, without which the little valley would be open to the full force of the westerly gales, were planted in the early nineteenth century by Rose Price, the son of a rich West Indian sugar planter. A considerable income from the Jamaican plantations was also responsible for the unusual walled garden at the foot of the drive, expensively constructed with brick, a warmer material than the native granite. Designed as a series of compartments, the garden's dividing walls have a steeply sloped bed of banked-up soil on their western side, a rare survival of a practice that was common in the late eighteenth and early nineteenth centuries. Like vineyards on south- and west-facing slopes, these beds reap the full benefit of the sun, producing early crops of vegetables and succouring tender plants.

Five varied compartments on the south side of the walled area suggest the back of a row of town houses, with handkerchief-sized lawns dominated by a magnolia or some other large species and with borders filled with a variety of plants – camellias, eucalyptus, the Chatham Island forget-me-not, the snowy-yellow *Azara dentata* from Chile, the passion flower, a climbing hydrangea from Japan or *Cassia corymbosa* from tropical America, with golden-yellow flowers which last through the autumn months. In late spring the air is filled with the fragrance of sweet-scented tender rhododendrons, many of them, such as *Rhododendron macabeanum*, *R. elliottii*, *R. taggianum* and *R. concatenans*, raised from seed brought back from the foothills of the eastern Himalayas in 1927–8 on an expedition partly financed by Colonel Bolitho.

Massed banks of rhododendrons flower scarlet, white and purple in the woods leading up to the house. Australian tree ferns and graceful feathery bamboos shadow the stream and the primulas, lilies and other water-loving plants which hug its banks. Hundreds of hydrangeas give the woodland a pale-blue wash in late summer. To the left of the house a sheltered enclave contains a fifty-foot *Magnolia sargentiana robusta*, its large pink flowers the highspot of any spring visit to Trengwainton.

Most of the garden is inward-looking, with walls and thick vegetation giving a sense of enclosure. But on the lawns in front of the house the vista suddenly opens out, an arch of beech framing a memorable view of St Michael's Mount (*see* p.278) rising like a fairy castle in the bay far below.

Trerice Cornwall

3 miles south-east of Newquay, via the A392 and the A3058

Trerice is not grand. A small but quite sophisticated Elizabethan house built of local buff-coloured limestone, it escaped later alteration in the prosperous eighteenth and nineteenth centuries, the heyday of the Cornish mining industries, perhaps

The sloping beds in the walled garden at Trengwainton produce early crops of vegetables; in the foreground, a young variegated yucca is sandwiched between clumps of the canna lily and *Libertia grandiflora*, an iris-like plant from New Zealand. (*NT/Tymn Lintell*)

339

The entrance front of Trerice, showing the decorative scrolled gables which are such a feature of the house and two projecting bays of the Elizabethan E-plan. The local limestone of which it is built has weathered over the years to a silvery grey. (*NT/Stephen Robson*)

because its owners chose to live elsewhere. Belonging to the Arundells, one of the great families of Cornwall, for over 400 years, in 1802 it passed to the Aclands, whose principal estates were in Devon and Somerset (*see* Killerton, p.166).

The nature of the house is heralded in an approach down a narrow winding lane, with hedges high on either side. An unpretentious gateway leads into a small grassy walled garden in front of the house, where two granite Arundell lions guard the path to the front door. Trerice faces east, its traditional E-shaped façade with a central porch surmounted by decorative scrolled gables in the Dutch style; unusual in Cornwall, their presence here perhaps reflects Sir John Arundell's service in the Low Countries for Elizabeth I. The bay to the left of the porch is entirely filled by the two-storey

window lighting the great hall, original sixteenth-century glass still composing many of the 576 panes supported by a lattice of mullions and transoms.

The glory of Trerice is the sunny, south-facing great chamber on the first floor, which Sir John Arundell probably created out of a medieval solar. The room is richly decorated with bold Elizabethan plasterwork over the fireplace and on the splendid barrel ceiling, one of the best of the period in the West Country. Although, apart from the twenty-foot table in the hall, made for the house in the early eighteenth century, none of the furniture is original, there are some good oak and walnut pieces, including a longcase clock by Thomas Tompion, a Queen Anne escritoire and an eighteenth-century travelling case fitted out with bottles for wines and spirits, and also some fine Chinese and English eighteenth-century porcelain. Paintings by John Opie, who was born at Trevallas, only fifteen miles away, add an appropriately Cornish flavour, among them portraits of his two wives, Mary and Amelia. There are also many reminders of the Arundells' devotion to the royal cause in the seventeenth century. The hall is filled with Stuart portraits and a haunting picture of Charles I by Henry Stone hangs in the court chamber upstairs. The face is careworn, the eyes withdrawn and watchful. Also in the house is an enchanting Jacobean embroidery panel, believed to depict Charles with his queen, Henrietta, giving him a bunch of flowers while a large snail crawls between them and a long-eared rabbit looks on.

Across the cobbled, walled courtyard behind the house lies a magnificent great barn of a size and age – it probably dates from the fifteenth century – rarely seen in Cornwall. A ramp from the flat lawn above, where the Home Guard drilled in the Second World War, leads to the lawn-mower collection in the hayloft of the former stable. Some very early machines here were produced after Mr Budding's initial invention of 1831.

Few traces remain of the small, old-fashioned enclosed gardens known to have surrounded Trerice until 1915. Steps from the grassy court in front of the house lead up on to what was the bowling-green and another flight from there to an upper lawn, from where there is a roof-level view of the gables on the east front. The garden to the south has vanished completely and the grass here is now planted with fruit trees set out in the quincunx pattern used in the seventeenth century, where every tree is in line with its neighbour from wherever it is viewed. An early fifteenth-century chapel has also disappeared, although its site lives on in the field name Chapel Close.

Treryn Dinas Cornwall

4 miles south-east of Land's End, 7 miles south-west of Penzance

The jagged granite headland of Treryn Dinas juts into the sea at the southern end of the Penwith peninsula, an inhospitable jumbled mass of rock exposed to the full force of westerly gales and battered by Atlantic breakers. Several Iron Age forts were built on promontories such as this round the coasts of Wales and Cornwall, the need to defend only one approach presumably compensating for the bleak sites. At Treryn Dinas the headland is cut off by four parallel banks and ditches, the outermost, probably dating from the first century BC, an earthwork of immense size. The famous 66-ton rocking boulder known as the Logan Rock is contained within the defences (*see also* p.300).

Tudor Merchant's House Dyfed

Quay Hill, Tenby

Like Aberconwy House (*see* p.1), this narrow late fifteenth-century three-storey building looking down Bridge Street only yards from the harbour is typical of the prosperous medieval dwellings that would have crowded the lanes of this little town when it was a thriving port in the fourteenth and fifteenth centuries. Sturdily built of lime and sand-stone rubble, the house still retains a garderobe turret rising the height of the building, its original jointed roof trusses and a circular chimneystack characteristic of this part of Wales. Although the interior has been much altered, a late medieval trailing flower pattern painted in red, black and yellow on wet plaster emerged from beneath no fewer than twenty-three coats of whitewash on the only surviving original partition.

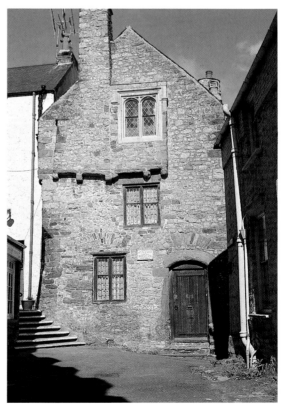

Tudor Merchant's House. (*NT/Vernon D. Shaw*)

Tŷ Mawr Gwynedd

At the head of the little Wybrnant valley, 3½ miles south-west of Betws-y-Coed, 2 miles west of Penmachno

This little sixteenth-century farmhouse hidden away on the eastern edge of the Snowdon massif, with its rough stone walls, slate roof, massive chimneys and deep-set windows, is typical of Wales's scattered upland dwellings. This isolated spot was the birth-place of Bishop William Morgan (*c.*1541–1604), whose translation of the Bible into Welsh is still in use today. Realising that the Welsh had no alter-native to the Latin service after the Reformation, in 1563 Elizabeth I ordered the four Welsh bishops and the Bishop of Hereford to produce a translation of the Prayer Book and the Bible within three years. The New Testament published in 1567 was a stilted, pedantic text, bearing no comparison to William Morgan's triumphantly fluid masterpiece produced in Armada year (1588) with a dedication to his queen. Alas, although the bishop was born and grew up in this remote valley, the farmhouse almost certainly postdates him.

Ullswater, Hartsop, Brotherswater and Troutbeck

Cumbria

North of Patterdale; near the Kirkstone Pass; and 3 miles south-east of Ambleside respectively

These places are the eastern protectorates of the Trust's Lake District empire. In 1911, because of the threat of building development, its first acquisi-tion was Gowbarrow Park on the west bank of Ullswater, a medieval deer park with the waterfall of Aira Force which had long attracted visitors. Glencoyne Wood, fine oak woodland to the south, was added in 1928, and twenty years later the magnificent gift of Glencoyne Park joined the two together so that the Trust now owns the whole of the south-western quarter of the shores of Ulls-water. Glencoyne is one of the Trust's largest sheep farms, running up its own valley to Hartside at 2,481 feet on the north, and on the south along the Glenridding Screes to Raise at 2,889 feet. This high ground is part of the Helvellyn ridge between Thirlmere and Ullswater, the Glencoyne Beck being the boundary between Cumberland and West-morland. In 1984 Matterdale and Watermillock

Commons were added, making over 7,000 acres of particular beauty, the thickly wooded slopes above the lake thinning out as the fells rise above. There is a link with Wordsworth, who wrote 'I wandered lonely as a cloud' after a walk beside Ullswater.

To the south, the A592 makes its way up to the Kirkstone Pass, bypassing the village of Hartsop and the 1,708 acres of Grove Farm running up into the Hayswater and Pasture Beck valleys. The farms of Hartsop Hall and Caudale Beck, which includes the delightful small lake of Brotherswater, lie on both sides of the road, the 2,072-foot summit of Hart Crag to the east complemented by that of Middle Dodd on the west. East of Hart Crag is one of the most famous farms in the Lake District, the 2,000-acre Troutbeck Park, left to the Trust by Beatrix Potter in 1943. The Troutbeck valley stands mercifully clear of the hurly-burly of Ambleside, Windermere and Bowness, and the Trust owns other fine farms here: The Howe, Long Green Head, Stonethwaite and Townend (*see* p.334).

Uppark West Sussex

5 miles south-east of Petersfield on the B2146, 1½ miles south of South Harting

The serene two-storey house built in about 1690 for Lord Grey, Earl of Tankerville, owes its existence to his grandfather's invention of an effective method of pumping water to great heights, without which the commanding site on a crest of the South Downs would have been impractical.

The amoral and duplicitous Lord Grey is one of many colourful characters connected with the estate, emerging remarkably unscathed from his involvement in the Duke of Monmouth's rebellion against James II, perhaps because he turned king's evidence. His new house, thought to be by William Talman, was in the latest Dutch style. Standing four-square like a giant doll's house, it is built of red brick with weathered, lichen-tinted stone dressings and dormer windows in a hipped roof. A pediment crowns the south front and detached mid-eight-eenth-century stable and kitchen blocks neatly balance the composition on either side.

The rich interior is mostly the work of Sir Matthew Fetherstonhaugh, who bought Uppark in 1747. This cultivated man, heir to the vast fortune of a distant relative, redecorated most of the principal rooms and enriched the house with a

Troutbeck Park Farm with the Tongue rising behind it; bought by Beatrix Potter in 1923, this major estate was left to the Trust on her death twenty years later. (*NT/Robert Thrift*)

The A592 climbs steeply to the Kirkstone Pass from the southern end of Ullswater. (*NT/Robert Thrift*)

The cool dairy at Uppark with a frieze of clematis bordering the white tiles is where Sir Harry Fetherstonhaugh courted his future bride, the young Mary Ann Bullock. (*NT/Tim Stephens*)

magnificent collection of carpets, furniture and works of art, much of it, such as portraits by Batoni and four harbour and coastal scenes by Joseph Vernet, purchased on a Grand Tour with his wife Sarah in 1749–51. The couple were responsible for the hauntingly beautiful white and gold saloon, with its delicate plaster ceiling, ivory silk brocade curtains framing the long south-facing windows and with paintings set into fixed plasterwork frames in the Adam style. Fireplaces inlaid with Sienese marble warm both ends of the room, one of them carved with the Sienese wolf suckling Romulus and Remus. Sarah also introduced the highly-crafted Queen Anne doll's house made for her as a child, with diminutive landscape paintings on the walls, hallmarked silver and gleaming glass on the dining-room table and silver and brass fire irons. Meticulously dressed dolls people the mansion, those representing the family identifiable by their wax faces, the lower orders depicted in wood.

Matthew's only son Harry inherited his parents' good taste and enriched their collection. But in other respects he was a prodigal young man, with a love of hunting and the turf which is echoed in his sporting pictures and silver-gilt cups. His close

friend the Prince Regent was a frequent guest at the lavish house parties staged at Uppark, with superb meals produced by Harry's French chef Moget. It was on one of these occasions that the fifteen-year-old Emma Hart, the future Lady Hamilton, is said to have danced on the dining-room table, only a few months before Harry heartlessly discarded her. Perhaps he remembered Emma when, in his seventieth year, he married young Mary Ann Bullock, his head dairymaid, in 1825. Largely because of this girl and her sister Frances, who joined the household, Uppark was to survive the nineteenth century little changed.

A cream and green Victorian kitchen, with a long scrubbed table and gleaming pots and pans, the butler's pantry next door and other service rooms are full of echoes of life below stairs. Easy chairs are drawn up by the fire and tea is laid on a tray in the sunny room where H. G. Wells's mother presided as housekeeper from 1880–93, not far from the long whitewashed tunnels leading to the old stable and eighteenth-century kitchen blocks down which her son chased the maids.

Much of Uppark's charm derives from its setting, with a great stretch of grass planted with mature trees sweeping away from the house and leading the eye across a rolling landscape to the sea. Humphry Repton, who added the pillared portico to the north front, was probably also responsible for Mary Ann's elegant dairy, its white tiles decorated with a blue and green frieze of clematis, and for the little Gothic summerhouse.

One of the more traumatic events in the Trust's recent history was the fire at Uppark in 1989, from which most of the furniture and paintings were rescued but which largely destroyed their eighteenth-century setting. The recently completed, 5½-year restoration has restored the air of faded elegance which makes the house so attractive. Plasterwork has been re-created, intricate mouldings and architraves re-carved, new curtains woven and wallpaper printed. New has been carefully matched to old, even to the extent of imitating picture-protected patches of wallpaper and time-darkened white paint, but almost every room has also been left with scorched floorboards and chimneypieces and other reminders of the fire, or with unfinished, newly created detail, such as an ungilded ornamental cherub. Wherever possible, fire-mangled and shattered fittings have been put back together, with painstaking reconstruction of

lanterns and chandeliers, reduced to twisted metal shapes and fragments of glass, and the piecing together of a scagliola table-top. The whole exercise has been a valuable learning exercise in applying traditional skills.

All this, and much else, is conveyed in an extensive highly visual exhibition on the fire (fought with water piped from the main at the foot of the Downs) and the whole restoration process. At the house itself, all drama has gone. As before, the most enduring memory is of mellow pink brick and lichened stone against a life-enhancing view. And martins have returned to nest under the eaves.

Upper Wharfedale North Yorkshire

North-west of Kettlewell, on B6160

This 5,590-acre Pennine estate in the well-wooded pastoral valley of the upper Wharfe includes some of the finest countryside in the Yorkshire Dales National Park. This is an ice-smoothed, limestone landscape, with a broad, glacier-moulded valley floor walled by steeply rising slopes soaring a thousand feet to the high fells. Farms and bridges are built of the local stone, and dry-stone walls edge

The green and grey, ice-smoothed landscape of Upper Wharfedale, criss-crossed by dry-stone walls.
(*NT/Mike Caldwell*)

the fields, carving the valley floor into a geometric patchwork and running up the hillsides to the acid moorland on the tops. In places the limestone shows through, outcropping in white scars on steeper slopes and in the bed of the river.

The Trust's estate includes eight upland farms, a former deer-park and substantial stands of ancient oak woodland on the valley sides. Most of the farms are being run in the traditional way and there are over a hundred of the sturdy roughwalled field barns, as big as houses, which are such a distinctive feature of this landscape. Each set in its own meadow, they were used to house cattle and their fodder over the winter. The Yockenthwaite stone circle, the remains of a Bronze Age burial mound, is a reminder of how long this country has been settled. Norse pastoralists, moving their stock from valley to fells in the summer months, gave the landscape its evocative names, such as gill, scar, tarn and beck, and in the Middle Ages Wharfedale was part of the great monastic sheepwalks which fed the riches of Fountains (see p.121) and Bolton abbeys. The walls criss-crossing the farmland are relatively recent additions, most of them dating from the Enclosure Acts of the late eighteenth and early nineteenth centuries, when the field barns were also built.

Now this is walking country, traversed by the long-distance Dales Way which follows the valley and with a network of other footpaths. There are dunlin and golden plover on the heights, waterfalls on the gills tumbling into the Wharfe, and long views over a soft green and grey landscape.

Upton House Warwickshire

1 mile south of Edge Hill, 7 miles north-west of Banbury, on west side of the Stratford-upon-Avon road

People reveal themselves in how they choose to live. Walter Samuel, 2nd Viscount Bearsted, had the great good fortune to inherit the wealth acquired by his father, who built up the Shell organisation from very small beginnings in the late nineteenth century to an international corporation. Innumerable bequests to charities, hospitals and schools are eloquent testimony to the 2nd Viscount's humanitarianism, but those who did not know of his activities would gain a sense of his benevolence towards his fellow men by visiting Upton.

Many of the outstanding works of art which fill every room are concerned in one way or another with human beings. Among a number of works by fifteenth- and sixteenth-century masters is El Greco's *El Espolio* (the Flagellation of Christ), the spears of the soldiers grouped behind Our Lord suggesting a crown of thorns. In another strongly atmospheric work, Brueghel's *Dormition of the Virgin*, Our Lady is shown receiving a lighted taper from St Peter in a dimly lit room. The use of grey and black alone gives the picture a ghostly quality as if both the radiant figure in the bed and the shadowy, hooded women crowding round are not of this world. Serene Dutch interiors and landscapes with diminutive figures set against immense skies include Saenredam's cool study of St Catherine's church, Utrecht, beetle-like clerics and two men inscribing a stone set into the floor dwarfed by the soaring arches of the nave. A little dog is silhouetted against the magnificent tiered screen enclosing the east end, the central pulpit proclaiming this is a Protestant church.

Dogs feature more prominently in the sporting pictures in the dining-room. Here, too, hang Stubbs's *Haymakers*, *Reapers* and *Labourers*, the weariness evident in the horses about to take away a laden cart as real as the chill of Hogarth's early winter morning in front of St Paul's, Covent Garden, one of the paintings for his engraved series, *The Four Times of Day*.

Lord Bearsted's collection of china and porcelain is similarly wide-ranging. Here, again, figures feature prominently, among the most memorable being two Chelsea pieces in the long gallery depicting a wet nurse suckling a swaddled baby and a shepherd teaching his shepherdess how to play the flute, holding the instrument for her as she blows. People even adorn the eighteenth-century furniture in this room, embroidered with scenes of weaving, grape-treading and other occupations.

Architecturally, Upton is a mongrel. A baroque broken pediment on the long entrance façade advertises the modest Restoration house now overwhelmed by eighteenth-century and later additions. Percy Morley Horder's comprehensive reworking for Lord Bearsted transformed the interior into one of the most luxurious houses of the 1920s, though it has the impersonality of a hotel or liner of the period. In contrast, the gardens are full of character, descending steeply from the cedar-framed lawn and broad double terrace fronting the south façade to a chain of ponds in the valley below. A collection of asters flourishes on the warm dry terrace banks and cascades of wistaria and sprays of roses overhang the Italianate balustraded stairway added in the 1930s, its lichen-stained steps leading into the depths of the combe. The mellow brick wall of the old kitchen garden on the slope of the valley still carries espaliered fruit trees as it did in the seventeenth century, and sets off borders of lavender, hollyhocks and lupins among the rows of vegetables.

Orderly planting here, and in the little yew-enclosed rose garden, contrasts with the wilder bog garden in a natural amphitheatre to the west of the house where another combe joins the first. Sheep graze on the other side of the valley and over a mile away, just visible from the terrace, a lake reflects the columns of a little eighteenth-century Tuscan temple.

Vale of Ffestiniog Gwynedd

Running from Blaenau Ffestiniog to Porthmadog

Above Penrhyndeudraeth, the Dwyryd river curls placidly up the Vale of Ffestiniog's water meadows for five miles. On the north bank are the hanging oak woods which make the valley so lovely. When they were threatened with conversion to conifer woodland in the 1960s, Coeddyd Maentwrog, in the upper part of the vale, was acquired intact, while Coed Cae Fali, lower down, had already been partially replanted. Now some 470 acres are in the Trust's hands and the oak woods are being revitalised. Plenty of paths and the Ffestiniog railway above the tree line make access easy.

The Vyne Hampshire

4 miles north of Basingstoke, between Bramley and Sherborne St John

This long U-shaped red-brick house with purple diaperwork lacing the façades is set low in a hollow. There is a pedimented portico on the garden front and the original mullions have been replaced with mid seventeenth-century sash windows, but the E-plan is that of a Tudor house. Dating from some time between 1500 and 1520. The Vyne was built for William, 1st Lord Sandys, whose long career in the service of Henry VIII culminated in his appointment to the office of Lord Chamberlain in 1526.

Seen from the other side of the lake bordering the spacious, shady lawns on the north side of the house, Sandys's battlemented chapel juts out conspicuously on the far left. One of the most perfect private oratories in England, this lofty room rising the height of two storeys is still largely as it was built in 1518–27. Intricately carved canopied stalls facing across the chapel are fringed by richly coloured blue, yellow, orange and green early sixteenth-century Italian tiles that were found in the grounds. Morning sunlight streams in through the three magnificent stained-glass windows above the altar apse, rivalled only by those of similar date in King's College, Cambridge. The depictions of Henry VIII and Catherine of Aragon, the queen accompanied by a little dog, would have been hidden from view when the king came here with Anne Boleyn in 1535.

The oak gallery stretching the length of the west wing on the first floor is another survival from the Tudor house, one of the finest examples of its date in Britain. The delicate pale linenfold panelling which lines the walls from floor to ceiling carries a wealth of carved badges and devices, including the Tudor rose and Catherine of Aragon's pomegranate and the curious portcullis-like hemp bray used in the separation of flax fibres, crest of Sir Reginald Bray, uncle of Lord Sandys's wife. The white marble of a seventeenth-century classical fireplace in the middle of the east wall is echoed in a series of portrait busts set down the room, a mixed company in which portrayals of Shakespeare, Milton and Mary Queen of Scots rub shoulders with a typically arrogant Nero and a world-weary Seneca.

Lord Sandys's service to Henry VIII was rewarded at the Dissolution of the Monasteries with the gift of Mottisfont Abbey (*see* p.205) and it was here that the family retired when impoverishment in the Civil War forced the sale of The Vyne in 1653. The new owner was another successful and astute politician, Chaloner Chute, shortly to be Speaker in Richard Cromwell's parliament, who reduced the size of the house and added the classical portico on the north front, thought to be the earliest on a domestic building. His grandson Edward acquired the Queen Anne furniture and Soho tapestries now displayed in the house, such as the hangings

(*Overleaf*) The outstanding art collection at Upton House includes Pieter Brueghel the Elder's *Dormition of the Virgin*, in which most of the light in the picture comes from Our Lady herself. (*NT*)

347

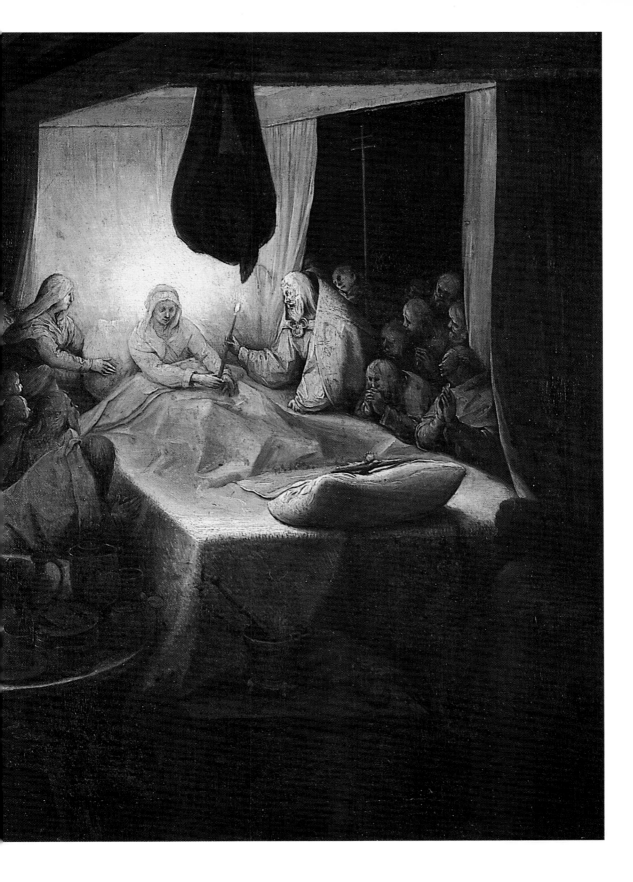

John Chute's additions to The Vyne in about 1750 included the tomb chamber off the Tudor chapel, where a grandiose monument commemorates his distinguished ancestor, Speaker Chaloner Chute. (*NT/James Pipkin*)

depicting oriental scenes in the room next to the gallery, full of gay spotted butterflies and darting birds and with a monkey sitting in a palm tree. Chute's great-grandson John, friend of Walpole, made notable alterations in about 1750, creating the theatrical classical staircase, with its moulded ceiling in pale blue and white, a first-floor gallery fringed with ornate fluted columns and busts of Roman emperors on the newel posts.

John Chute was also responsible for the tomb chamber off the chapel, built in honour of his distinguished ancestor. Here the Speaker lies immortalised in Carrara marble on the top of a box-like monument loosely disguised as a Greek temple. His life-like effigy rests on an unyielding plaited straw mattress, his head supported on his right arm, one finger extended along the curve of his brow.

Waddesdon Manor Buckinghamshire

6 miles north-west of Aylesbury, on the A41, 11 miles south-east of Bicester

The great châteaux of the Loire valley made such an impression on the young Ferdinand de Rothschild, grandson of the founder of the Austrian branch of this famous banking family (*see* p.11), that he determined to model any house he might build on what he had seen in France. This magnificent palace designed by Gabriel Hippolyte Destailleur fulfilled the young Baron's dreams, its pinnacles, mansard roofs, dormer windows, massive chimneys and staircase towers reproducing the characteristic features of Maintenon, Blois and other French Renaissance châteaux. The 45-year-old Ferdinand purchased the hill on which Waddesdon is set from the Duke of Marlborough in 1874, carving out a platform for his mansion and importing half-grown trees to clothe the slopes. Building materials were brought up by cable, while the timber was hauled laboriously up the hill by teams of horses.

This pastiche château has similarly extravagant, French-inspired interiors, with a procession of high-ceilinged reception rooms re-creating the elegant splendour of the pre-Revolutionary regime. Profiting from Baron Haussmann's remodelling of Paris for Napoleon III, Ferdinand was able to obtain panelling from the buildings destroyed to form the city's great boulevards, and this elaborately decorated carved woodwork can be seen in almost every room. Royal fleurs-de-lis feature prominently on the Savonnerie carpets, a representation of the Sun King himself appearing on one from a set Louis XIV commissioned for the long gallery of the Louvre. Eight pieces of furniture were made for the French royal family by the great Jean-Henri Riesener, the leading cabinet-maker of his day, including a marquetry writing-table created for Marie Antoinette and a drop-front secretaire ordered for Louis XVI by his wife. Elegant little tables with delicate gazelle-like legs contrast with the Baron's massive cylinder-top desk that once belonged to the dramatist Beaumarchais and a monumental black and gold secretaire surmounted by a clock and crowned by a huge gilt eagle. Teardrop chandeliers are reflected in mirrors with elaborately carved gilt frames and every surface is crammed with clocks, Sèvres and Meissen porcelain and *objets d'art*, such as a gold snuffbox that once belonged to Louis XV's mistress, Madame de

Pompadour, with her pet poodle and spaniel shown cavorting on the lid. Paintings by Watteau, Lancret, Boucher and Greuze help to create a sense of pre-Revolutionary France.

These sumptuous French pieces are harmoniously combined with a superb collection of English eighteenth-century portraits, including works by Gainsborough, Reynolds and Romney, and with a number of seventeenth-century Dutch paintings, such as Jan van der Heyden's tranquil view of an Amsterdam canal, characteristic red-brick stepped gables reflected in the still waters, a garden scene by de Hoogh, and Rubens's dreamy *The Garden of Love*. One of the two galleries leading from the main entrance is dominated by two huge canvases of Venice by Francesco Guardi, one a view to Santa Maria della Salute and San Giorgio Maggiore, two gilded and canopied gondolas gliding across the water between them, the other looking towards the Doge's Palace from across the lagoon.

The recent completion of an extensive programme of restoration and conservation undertaken by the Rothschild family has returned Waddesdon's Bath stone to its original striking yellow and opened new rooms to view. Oenophilists are now tantalised by a 'library' of Rothschild vintages on view in the wine cellars and there has been a wholesale rearrangement of the first floor of the house. Part is now given over to a display of Sèvres porcelain, and a suite of rooms has been fitted out with decorative eighteenth-century French panelling which was removed from Baron Ferdinand's London house at his death in 1898 and has been in store ever since. Also newly on show are paintings commissioned by the late James de Rothschild from the artist and stage designer Léon Bakst, who incorporated portraits of the family and their friends in panels illustrating the story of Sleeping Beauty.

A broad flight of steps leads down to the Italian fountain on the balustraded terrace behind the house, adorned with some of the garden sculpture acquired by Baron Ferdinand and surrounded with clipped yew. Beyond stretches the wooded park, part of the extensive grounds designed by the French landscape gardener Lainé. Hidden away to the west of the house is an enchanting eighteenth-century-style aviary, its presence heralded by whoops, twittering and chirruping from the exotic inhabitants, including peach-faced lovebirds, the toucan and other brightly coloured creatures, many of them bred at Waddesdon.

Wakehurst Place West Sussex

1½ miles north-west of Ardingly, on the B2028

Only a few miles from the sprawl of Crawley and the noise of Gatwick airport, a deep secluded valley of the Sussex Weald has been transformed into one of the most magical of woodland gardens. The valley doubles back on itself in a great two-mile horseshoe, with steep wooded slopes walling it in on either side. Miles of footpaths thread its length, and a stream has been dammed and channelled to create cascades, ponds and a lake.

This private world, conceived on the grand scale, is primarily the creation of Gerald Loder, later Lord Wakehurst, who bought the estate in 1903 and devoted the next thirty-three years to improving it, but previous owners also contributed by planting the now mature wellingtonias and other exotics. Now home to some 7,500 kinds of plants, Wakehurst is leased to the Royal Botanic Gardens, Kew, forming a valuable, virtually pollution-free addition to their London acres.

The most formal part of the garden lies around a weatherbeaten Elizabethan mansion (no displayed interiors), its mellow sandstone walls, mullions and finialled gables forming an attractive backdrop to views across smooth lawns. To one side are two walled gardens. Clipped yew surrounds an ornamental fountain and round beds planted for spring and summer colour in The Pleasaunce, with a yew arch framing a vista through the more extensive cottage garden created in memory of Sir Henry Price, who continued Gerald Loder's work. Here clumps of sweet peas, clematis, phlox, roses, hydrangeas and other soft-coloured plants flower purple, white, blue and pink.

Elsewhere, Wakehurst is less restrained and more exotic. Near the house, descendants of many of the original Australasian and South American species introduced by Gerald Loder still flourish, such as the Tasmanian waratah, with its distinctive red claw-like flowers, and hoherias from New Zealand, a mass of white in summer, and paths lead on to a lushly planted water garden, with giant Himalayan lilies. Deeper into the valley, the garden becomes wilder. Sandstone outcrops along the southern rim, with great blocks heaped up into craggy tors giving views across wooded slopes fading into the distance.

Tragically, the storms of 1987 and 1990 wreaked havoc at Wakehurst, bringing down over 15,000

Nowhere in the woodland garden of Wakehurst Place is far from water. (*NT/Michael Brown*)

trees and devastating the rock walk leading from one outcrop to another along the top of the valley, where stricken trees dislodged boulders as they fell. The hard work of clearance and restoration is now complete: the rhododendron walk near the house, which was torn apart by the storms, has been replaced by an Asian heath garden, to display shrubs found naturally above the tree line, and the re-planted tree collections have been arranged geographically, so as to imitate natural forest. Trees to be seen here include the North American redwood, Monterey pine and hickory, species from the Mediterranean and Near East, and a collection of southern beech, as well as groves of oak, beech and birch and other native species. There are still fine rhododendrons deep in the valley, and Wakehurst is also known for bluebells and Lent Lilies carpeting the woodland floor in spring and for autumn colour.

Wallington Northumberland

12 miles west of Morpeth on the B6343, 6 miles north-west of Belsay on the A696

Many country houses are hidden behind walls or screens of trees, but there is nothing secluded about Wallington. The pedimented south front of this square stone building crowns a long slope of rough grass, in full view of the public road through the park. Nor is there a lodge or an imposing gateway. The pinnacled triumphal arch built for the house was found to be too narrow for coaches and now languishes in a field.

Wallington is largely the creation of Sir Walter Calverley Blackett, who in *c.*1738 commissioned the Northumbrian architect Daniel Garrett to remodel his grandfather's uncomfortable house. Garrett's cool, Palladian exteriors are no preparation for Pietro Lafrancini's magnificent rococo plasterwork in the saloon, where delicate, feminine compositions in blue and white, with winged sphinxes perched on curling foliage, garlands of flowers and cornucopias overflowing with fruit, suggest an elaborate wedding cake.

Oriental porcelain in the alcoves on either side of the fireplace is part of a large and varied collection, much of it the dowry of Maria Wilson, who married into the family in 1791 just a few years after the house had passed to Sir Walter's nephew, Sir John Trevelyan. A bizarre Meissen tea-set in the parlour

features paintings of life-size insects nestling in the bottom of each cup. Even more extraordinary is Wallington's Cabinet of Curiosities, which Maria also introduced, its strange exhibits ranging from a piece of Edward IV's coffin to stuffed birds set against painted habitats and a spiky red porcupine fish like an animated pin cushion.

The hall rising through two storeys in the middle of the house reflects another era. Created in 1853–4 out of what was an internal courtyard, this individual room was the inspiration of the talented Pauline Trevelyan, whose vivid personality attracted a stream of artists and writers, including Ruskin, Swinburne and Rossetti. Under her influence Rossetti's friend William Bell Scott was commissioned to produce the eight epic scenes from Northumbrian history, with panels illustrating the death of the Venerable Bede and Grace Darling in her open boat rescuing the men of the *Forfarshire*. In the canvas showing the landing of the Vikings, savage heads on the prows of the silent fleet emerge out of the gloom over the sea like an invasion of prehistoric monsters. Ruskin and Pauline herself, among others, painted the delicate wild flowers – purple foxgloves, brilliant-red poppies, yellow columbine – on the pillars between the panels. The family's later connection with the Macaulays brought associations with scientists and politicians as well as artists and writers, and Lord Macaulay wrote his monumental history of England here, working at the desk in the study.

Sir Walter Calverley Blackett's spirit lives on in the 13,000-acre estate which he transformed, laying out roads, enclosing fields, building cottages, planting woods and devising follies. His formal pleasure grounds, with straight-edged ponds and woods and radiating avenues, were later converted into a naturalistic landscape park, possibly with the advice of the young 'Capability' Brown, who was born nearby and went to school on the estate and who, in about 1765, was employed to design the setting for the ornamental lake at Rothley. But Sir Walter himself was responsible for damming the River Wansbeck and for James Paine's imposing three-arched bridge below the house.

Sir Walter also laid out the walled garden half a mile east of the house in the sheltered dell running down to the river; what was a vegetable garden with fruit and flower borders is now an unexpected delight of lawns and mixed herbaceous beds following the lines of the valley. The shady path to the gate

Grace Darling rescuing the men of the *Forfarshire*: one of William Bell Scott's epic mural panels at Wallington illustrating episodes from Northumbrian history. (*NT/A.C. Cooper*)

leads past two wooded ponds, the slope above the second still crowned with a long brick wall that sheltered an earlier kitchen garden and with the porticoed, pedimented façade of what was the gardener's house. Flights of steps sweeping down from the terrace at the head of the present garden embrace Lady Mary Trevelyan's pond in a stone niche created in 1938, the source of the little stream chattering down the valley, its course marked by dwarf shrubs, herbaceous plants and alpines.

To one side a raised terrace walk high above the valley carries a little brick pavilion, formerly the head gardener's lodging, surmounted with the owl of the Calverley crest, and Sir George Otto Trevelyan's 1908 conservatory, where his giant fuchsias, one nearly eighty years old, still flourish round a marble fountain. A hedged nuttery on the slopes below marks the site of the former vegetable patch, while across the valley a broad sloping mixed border includes phlox, lilies, hostas and fuchsias among a selection of bulbs, shrubs and herbaceous plants chosen for colour effect. Although this is the Trust's coldest garden, roses, honeysuckles, clematis and sun-loving plants thrive against the south-facing walls. There is also a national collection of elders here, their scarlet and purple-black berries conspicuous in late summer and autumn.

Most of the estate is now enclosed farmland, but there are lovely walks through the woods near the house and along the Wansbeck. Recently, too, the Trust has opened a seven-mile walk making use of two disused railway lines, the Rothbury line (closed in 1963) and the Wannie line (closed in 1966), with waymarked paths across the fields linking the sections of grassy track.

Wasdale Cumbria

South-east of Middle Fell, Seatoller and Yewbarrow

A 'horrid' place in the eighteenth-century meaning of the word, the Wasdale valley, only four miles in length, is dramatic and can be awesome. At its head is Scafell Pike, the highest point in England at 3,206 feet, and at its foot Wastwater, the deepest lake in the country. It is the great screes on the south bank of the lake, plunging down to the water's edge, which give a grim note to its spectacular beauty.

The Trust acquired the farms of Wasdale Head Hall, Middle Row, Row Head and later Burnthwaite under Kirk Fell at a time when forestry

syndicates, formed to take advantage of tax concessions, were actively seeking land for planting. It was of the utmost importance to keep the farms and their great sheepwalks – High Fell, Eskdale Fell, the head of Mosedale, the south side of Pillar to the Black Sail Pass and Yewbarrow running down to the head of the lake – clear of blanket forestry.

By 1979 the Trust had acquired virtually the whole of Upper Wasdale, and none too soon, for a new threat was at hand. British Nuclear Fuels Ltd, needing more water for their works at Sellafield, sought to take it from Wastwater by building a massive weir which would facilitate the raising or lowering of the level of the lake at will. At the same time similar proposals were made for Ennerdale Water by the North West Water Authority. A great battle ensued and the trump card turned out to be the Trust's statement that, even if planning consent *were* granted, it would rely on its legal right to ask Parliament to protect its inalienable land as a matter of national importance. The battle was won and the beauty of Wasdale was preserved. (*See also* Borrowdale and Derwentwater; Buttermere, Crummock Water and Loweswater; Coniston Valley; Ennerdale; Eskdale and Duddon Valleys; Grasmere Valley, Rydal, Hawkshead and Sawrey; Great and Little Langdale; Ullswater, Hartsop, Brotherswater and Troutbeck; Windermere.)

Washington Old Hall Tyne & Wear

5 miles west of Sunderland, 2 miles east of the A1, south of Tyne tunnel

Two nineteenth-century watercolours in the parlour show Washington Old Hall as it once was – a modest manor house on the edge of Washington village, just below the church on its wooded hill and with cornfields stretching away behind it. Although the village has now been swallowed up by Washington New Town, the house looks over a little green valley to the red-brick mansion which was the home of the Bell family, connected by marriage to the Trevelyans of Wallington (*see* p.353), and it is still possible to shut out the twentieth century here.

Washington Old Hall is not a grand house. Rebuilt on twelfth-century foundations in the early seventeenth century, its rough unornamented sandstone walls suggest a family of moderate means. The interior was conventionally designed on an H-plan, with a great hall occupying the centre of the building. Two arches from the original house lead from the hall into the kitchen.

This unpretentious building was the ancestral home of George Washington, elected first President of the USA in 1789; his direct ancestors lived here for five generations and the property remained in the family until 1613. Mementoes of the American connection and the struggle for independence can be seen throughout the house. A portrait of George Washington executed on drum parchment while he was on campaign as leader of the rebel forces hangs alongside a letter from Percy, 2nd Duke of Northumberland, who served with the British troops. A lottery ticket signed by Washington is displayed upstairs, by a uniform of the Washington Greys in a glass case.

Although none of the furniture is original, it is all in tune with the house and includes some interesting pieces, such as the seventeenth-century baby-walker in the bedroom and the beautifully embroidered stumpwork cabinet in the parlour.

A print of Mount Vernon, given by President Jimmy Carter when he visited the house in 1977, symbolises the importance of a more recent American connection. Washington Old Hall was divided into Georgian tenements and during the nineteenth century became increasingly dilapidated. Its condition was so bad by the 1930s that demolition was seriously considered and only a concerted effort saved the building. Generous gifts from across the Atlantic made restoration possible and the people of the USA continue to offer much-needed help, many of them visiting the Old Hall every year.

The Weald Surrey

Between the North and South Downs

The Trust's properties in the Weald lie on the chalk hills of the North and South Downs and the sandstone ridges between them. They provide easy walking and picnicking in lovely surroundings and, above all, views over a wooded prosperous countryside which, despite the continual pressure of development, is still very beautiful indeed.

On Leith Hill, at 967 feet the highest ground in south-east England, Richard Hill of Leith Hill Place built the comparatively modest 64-foot tower (*see* p.179) so as to get the full benefit of the view from this sandstone ridge. The Trust owns nearly 900 acres, partly to the north but mainly to the south of the ridge, and much of it is woodland, running eastwards to Coldharbour Common, with its modest village. Although the estate is fragmented, it ties in with the commons of Wotton and Abinger nearby and provides a wonderful 'lung' only forty miles from central London.

The Weir Hereford & Worcester

5 miles west of Hereford on the A438

Steep south-facing banks fringing one of the great bends on the River Wye as it meanders slowly eastward are the site of the Parr family's unusual garden created in the 1920s, informally planted with trees and shrubs and improbably held in place by masses of reinforced concrete which prevent it tumbling into the water. A walk through beech woodland high above the Wye leads to the much-altered eighteenth-century villa (not open to the public) at the top of the garden, from where paths criss-cross the slopes at all levels, sometimes punctuated by flights of steps. Yew, privet and laurel grow well on the grassy banks, with willow along the river itself, and there are also a number of exotic trees and shrubs, such as the Japanese maple. Spectacular displays of daffodils and bluebells in spring are followed by a carpet of the brilliant-yellow rose of Sharon in summer, when butter-coloured flowers completely smother the slopes at one end of the garden. A small rockery of Cheddar limestone hides a shaded lily pond fed by a trickling stream.

The views over the River Wye are spectacular, across a wooded pastoral patchwork grazed by sleepy cows to the slopes of the Black Mountains, with the tips of the Brecon Beacons beyond.

Wellbrook Beetling Mill

Co. Tyrone

4 miles west of Cookstown, ½ mile off the A505 Cookstown–Omagh road

Like the wool industry in medieval England, linen manufacture was of major importance in eighteenth-century Ireland, particularly in the north, where new landowners from England and Scotland were anxious to maximise the return on their estates. Official encouragement included the set-

For some 200 years linen was given a gleaming sheen at Wellbrook Beetling Mill by being pounded with heavy hammers such as these. (*NT/Alan North*)

ting-up of a Linen Board in 1711, the removal of duty on Irish linen imported into England, and a body to fund development. Although some spinning and weaving continued to be done in the home, the industry was increasingly mechanised, with many mills established on the rivers around Belfast. Beetling was the last stage in the process, in which the cloth was pounded with heavy hammers for up to two weeks to give it a gleaming sheen.

This functional isolated building in a remote valley west of Cookstown is the only surviving part of the once-extensive Wellbrook linen works. Built in 1765 and modified in the nineteenth century, it continued operating until 1965, although the main bleaching mill closed about a hundred years earlier. Seven beetling engines, their hammers resembling rows of organ pipes, were powered by a sixteen-foot-diameter breastshot waterwheel set against the eastern gable of the long two-storey mill. Water for the wheel was brought from a weir on the Ballinderry river a few hundred yards away, an impressive wooden aqueduct on brick piers transporting it the last fifty feet or so. After beetling, the cloth was hung to dry on the upper floor where the airing racks and louvred windows still survive, and was then folded on a special table for dispatch.

Now restored to working order, the mill once again reverberates to the heavy pounding of the beetling hammers. There is also a display illustrating the Irish linen industry.

Wellington Monument   Somerset

2 miles south of Wellington on the A38, just west of the Wellington–Hemyock road

Anyone travelling south-west along the M5 or by train from Taunton to Exeter will recognise this stark stone obelisk, rearing 175 feet from the Blackdown Hills on the Devon–Somerset border. Designed in 1817 by Thomas Lee, the architect of Arlington Court (*see* p.10), it was commissioned by a group of local gentry to commemorate the achievements of the Duke of Wellington, whose victory at the Battle of Waterloo was no doubt still fresh in their minds. The Iron Duke would probably have appreciated the military advantages of such a splendid position, with breathtaking views in all directions, but this is not a place to be visited in cold weather, when the wind whistles ferociously round the tiny room reached by a spiral staircase at the top of the monument.

Wembury and the Yealm Estuary
Devon

On the south coast, 5–6 miles east of Plymouth

To the south of Plymouth the coast is somewhat unattractive, what with the grim heights of Staddon overlooking the great breakwater at the mouth of the Sound and HMS Cambridge, the naval gunnery school near Heybrook Bay, although the latter is fenced off. But as the coast turns east into Wembury Bay there is a change.

The church of St Werburgh stands above the beach, a narrow valley curving inland behind it, the now much enlarged village mercifully hidden from view by the contours. The rocky island offshore, owned by the Ministry of Defence as it lies within the danger area of the gunnery school, is the Great Mew Stone, once occupied as the ruined cottage by its shore attests.

The Trust has owned the valley pastures and the south-facing cliffs running east to Warren Point since 1939, a most timely gift as it prevented development of a prime coastal site at a time when planning control was minimal. In 1975 it became apparent that the beauty of the Yealm estuary was seriously at risk. The villages of Newton Ferrers and Noss Mayo were already bursting with retired people and the rebuilding to a near motorway standard of the A38 from Exeter to Plymouth would increase the existing pressure for moorings and accommodation from people with boats. The planning authority would have found it hard to contain this pressure by itself and welcomed the Trust's initiative in launching a Yealm Estuary Appeal for funds to buy as much as possible of the unspoilt estuary and the sea coast. The appeal was a resounding success, partly because it transpired that many people then in their sixties and seventies had spent their honeymoon on the estuary, had fond memories of it, and sent handsome cheques.

The Trust was able to buy nearly three miles of magnificent coast from Noss Mayo, well up the estuary, round Gara Point at its mouth, and then eastwards to Saddle Cove beyond Blackstone Point, and – equally important – the farmland behind and above it, some 440 acres in all.

The waterside woods in the estuary are peaceful and sheltered, with glimpses of water and brightly coloured boats below. In Passage Wood, and again in Brakehill Plantation, the path is at two levels and emerges from the latter wood on to the open cliff above Mouthstone Point. From here there is a breezy coastal walk with wonderful views: east across Bigbury Bay to Bolt Tail, west to Rame Head and for many miles along the Cornish coast to the great headland of the Dodman (*see* p.307). The walk is along the Revelstoke Drive, well graded because it was built for horsedrawn carriages towards the end of the last century by Lord Revelstoke of Membland Hall. His large estate here enabled him to build this drive for nine miles round his property and very proud of it he must have felt. Sadly, as a member of the Baring family, he was involved in the 1890 crash of the family's bank and had to sell up to meet the bank's creditors. It is nice to be able to record that Baring Brothers made a generous contribution to the Trust's appeal to buy this land.

The attractive Warren Cottage above Blackstone Point was originally occupied by the warrener for, like so many places in similar situations on the coast, there was a large rabbit warren here well into the nineteenth century. The cottage was later enlarged for the Baring family, who used it as a base on a summer's day. It is now privately occupied.

In 1987 the Trust was able to buy a further two miles of the very similar cliffs running eastwards from Saddle Cove, round Hilsea Point to Stoke Point, a further 360 acres, making a superb stretch of wholly unspoilt coast.

Wensleydale North Yorkshire

1 mile south-east of Bainbridge on the A684

The Trust owns two properties in Wensleydale. East Scar Top Farm, south-east of Bainbridge, runs from a valley to the top of Addleborough which, at 1,564 feet, gives a wonderful view down the dale on a clear day. South of Layburn, Braithwaite Hall, a hill farm of 750 acres, has a handsome late seventeenth-century farmhouse (*see* p.40).

Westbury Court Garden
Gloucestershire

Westbury-on-Severn, 9 miles south-west of Gloucester on the A48

Only a man with a passionate interest in gardens would devote all his money to creating a new one rather than modernising an antiquated house, as Maynard Colchester I, co-founder of the Society for the Propagation of Christian Knowledge, chose to do at Westbury between 1696 and his death in 1715. Even more remarkably, his formal layout in the newly fashionable Dutch style inspired by the accession of William and Mary is still largely as planned, the only water garden of its kind in England not to be swept away under the influence of 'Capability' Brown and Humphry Repton and the vogue for 'natural landscaping'.

Westbury lies in water meadows by the River Severn, laid out on the kind of level, well-watered site that abounds in the Netherlands. Water, grass and clipped evergreens are key elements in the garden, with beautifully cut hedges fringing tranquil canals, and balls and pyramids of box and yew punctuating shady lawns and formally planted beds. Delicious red-brick pavilions peer over walls and hedges, and sheltering trees cast long ribbons of shade across the grass. The garden is ordered and serene, with the neatness and pleasing symmetry of a sampler. It is also small-scale and intimate, quite different in character from formal gardens of French inspiration with their distant vistas and grand avenues.

The route from the carpark brings visitors through the high brick wall bordering the garden on the west to the edge of the long canal, a watery corridor stretching 450 feet to a wrought-iron screen giving tantalising glimpses of the country-

Kip's engraving of Westbury Court Garden in *c.*1707, showing the tall Dutch pavilion looking down the long canal, a simple parterre, and orderly rows of what could well be vegetables among the fruit trees, emphasising the garden was productive as well as ornamental. (*NT*)

side beyond. Old varieties of apples, pears and plums are espaliered against the warm brick, and the grass under the wall is thick with daffodils, crocuses and tulips in spring. A tall, dignified two-storey pavilion faces down the canal, long sash windows in the Dutch style lighting the upper room and an open loggia at ground level suggesting the building is on stilts. On fine days the sun draws flashes of fire from the gilded ball crowning a little cupola.

Another delightful brick building, its pyramidal roof concealed by a parapet ornamented with stone balls, overlooks a second T-shaped canal paralleling the first, with a statue of Neptune riding a dolphin adorning the arm of the T. On the other side of this gazebo is a small walled garden, with shady arbours rounding the corners and box-edged beds planted with old roses and a rich variety of other plants known in England before 1700, including humble cottage-garden flowers such as the primrose, violet and lily of the valley. Quinces, medlars and other old varieties of fruit trees arranged in a quincunx pattern in roughly mown grass close by partly surround the geometrical beds of a simple parterre, its smooth lines and curves echoing the design shown in Kip's engraving of Westbury executed in *c.*1707.

Although the garden was the inspiration of Maynard Colchester I, the T-shaped canal and some other features, such as the gazebo, were probably added by his nephew, Maynard Colchester II. Unlike his uncle, the younger Maynard turned his attention also to the house, although no traces now remain of the Palladian mansion with which he replaced the Elizabethan manor or of the nineteenth-century building which succeeded it. The garden itself was neglected for some 150 years and almost disappeared in recent times. It has been re-created by the Trust, which has planted it with species listed in Maynard Colchester I's original documents or which are known to have been in cultivation at the time. Although few of the original trees survive, an evergreen oak at the end of the T-canal is thought to be the oldest in the country, planted in the early 1600s.

West Green House   Hampshire

1 mile west of Hartley Wintney, 10 miles north-east of Basingstoke, 1 mile north of the A30

This peaceful, homely, eighteenth-century house set in wooded parkland was remodelled in about 1750 by General Henry Hawley, whose brutality to the Scots after the Battle of Culloden five years earlier had earned him the nickname 'Hangman Hawley'. It is strange that this hardened and apparently vicious soldier should have left such a serene and charming memorial. The house is roughly square, built of mellow red brick, with sash windows, pedimented dormers in the hipped roof and stone vases crowning the corners of the roofline. Almost a quarter of the building is taken up by the two-storey panelled saloon, more appropriate to a much larger house, running the length of the garden front, five busts in niches replacing windows at first-floor level on the exterior.

A door from the saloon leads out on to grassy terraces rising towards the park, a row of clipped hornbeams standing to attention along the highest level. A large walled kitchen garden on the slope to the left of the terraces is a pleasing mixture of vegetables, flowers and fruit, with old apple trees outlined against the warm red brick and acting as supports for roses and clematis. Food plants are integrated in an ornamental design, with rows of vegetables set between box-edged paths radiating outwards from the decorative fruit cages at the top of the garden. A narrow herbaceous border runs the length of the north side, the ornamental species planted here chosen for their pale-coloured flowers and interesting foliage.

A gate and steps in the west wall lead to the herringbone brick path across the wild garden, where the long grass hides fritillaries, naturalised martagon lilies and the native Hampshire elecampane. Beyond, at the highest point of the garden, is Quinlan Terry's exotic *trompe-l'oeil* Nymphaeum, surely a stray from the pleasure grounds at West Wycombe Park (*see below*). Other garden buildings include a small orangery and the charming monkey house, a late eighteenth-century stone building commemorating General Hawley's favourite spaniel. A field to the south is being developed as an eighteenth-century-style pleasure ground, with serpentine walks and exotic garden buildings set round a small lake. Newly planted avenues of chestnut and lime link the garden to the park beyond, where rare breeds of sheep and cattle graze beneath the trees.

Westward Ho! to Hartland Point
Devon

On the north coast, 4 miles east of Hartland on the B3237

Beyond the caravans and chalets of Westward Ho! rises the gorse-covered hill given to the Trust in memory of Rudyard Kipling. From its slopes there is an unspoilt view west to Hartland Point.

Ornamental fruit cages in the walled garden at West Green House form the focuses of radiating paths. (*NT/Neil Campbell-Sharp*)

In 1988 the Trust acquired from the Pine-Coffin family a major section of this coastline, the seaward part of the Portledge estate which runs for five miles from Green Cliff to Bucks Mills and includes the wooded Peppercombe valley.

Clovelly is justly celebrated, and its long ownership by one estate has kept this most picturesque of all coastal villages largely unspoilt. The village and the park of Clovelly Court are surrounded by woods, and the Trust's property starts where these woods end, a mile and a half to the west. From here a glorious three miles of coast runs almost to Hartland Point.

Windbury Head, at the east end, has an Iron Age hill fort on its 486-foot-high summit. Below it is the wooded Beckland Combe, down which Beckland Water rushes to plunge over the cliff in a waterfall which is a dramatic sight after heavy rain.

The Trust owns much of the farmland behind the cliffs and cars can be parked at Brownsham, East Titchberry and Exmansworthy. The cliffs are high, running from 350 feet up to over 500 feet at Fatacott, and bleak except in the few places where trees can grow. The rocks are shales, slates and carboniferous sandstones, exposed in a spectacular rockfold at Shipload Bay at the west end, where there is the only access to the beach.

The fragile nature of the rock here means that the undercliff tends to slip away, and on this slipped area are thickets of stunted oak, ash and sycamore, with thorn, gorse and sally willow giving good cover for small birds. Buzzards, kestrels and fulmars all nest in the vicinity. The bay is reached by 273 steps, rebuilt by the Trust in 1981 to replace an earlier staircase carried away by a landslip.

Westwood Manor Wiltshire

1½ miles south-west of Bradford-on-Avon, in Westwood village

The sixteenth century was a golden age for the west of England, when men amassed considerable fortunes in the profitable cloth trade with Antwerp and built the many fine but unpretentious houses which are such a feature of towns and villages in this part of the country. One of these men was Thomas Horton, who acquired a little fifteenth-century manor built by a prosperous Wiltshire farmer and transformed it into a house more fitting for someone of his status and position. Further embellish-

ment in the early seventeenth century resulted in the fine plasterwork and panelling now found in many of the rooms.

Westwood is both dignified and welcoming. A modest L-shaped building of warm local stone, its low ranges frame a grassy court crossed by flagged paths, with a great medieval barn just a stone's throw away. One of the most satisfying rooms is the parlour over the hall, with its unusual interior porches, an elaborate plaster ceiling and a show of early keyboard instruments. The long, low window giving on to the courtyard from this room has a beautiful view of the little village church and over the valley of the River Frome beyond.

West Wycombe Park
Buckinghamshire

At west end of West Wycombe, south of the Oxford road

Everything about West Wycombe bears the stamp of the man who created it, the mercurial dilettante Sir Francis Dashwood. Armed with the fortune his father had made in trade with Africa, India and the East, Sir Francis interleaved several visits to Italy with tours as far afield as Russia and Turkey. Months of foreign travel not only gave him opportunities to indulge in his fondness for practical jokes but also an appreciation of art and a depth of learning that were to lead him to be a founder member of the Dilettanti Society in 1732, an important influence on English taste. Now remembered chiefly for his connection with the notorious Hellfire Club, which met in caves (not owned by the Trust) burrowed into the hill rising steeply to the north, the more serious side of his character is demonstrated in a successful political career. Although disastrous as Chancellor of the Exchequer in 1762, he proved himself a more than able joint Paymaster General in the years that followed.

Sir Francis was largely his own architect, aided by Giovanni Servandoni, Nicholas Revett and the draughtsman John Donowell. Between 1735 and 1781 the square Queen Anne building he inherited was transformed into a classical mansion and filled with paintings and furniture acquired on his Grand Tours. In his remodelling, Sir Francis was no more than a man of his time; it is the detail and mix of decorative styles which give West Wycombe its highly individual character. An unusual double colonnade rising to roof height stretches almost the

The east front of West Wycombe Park from across the lake. The huge portico is one of the highly individual features designed by Sir Francis Dashwood. (*NT/Vera Collingwood*)

full width of the long south front, rivalling the huge porticoes decorated with frescoes which dominate the short sides of the house. The interior is a mixture of the old-fashioned and the innovative, the voluptuous and the restrained, with artfully placed gilt mirrors reflecting glittering vistas through the house. Sensual baroque painted ceilings by the Italian Giuseppe Mattias Borgnis, brought specially to England for this commission, adorn some of the principal rooms, his *Triumph of Bacchus and Ariadne* in the Blue Drawing Room a riot of overweight cherubs, heavily muscled bodies and flowing drapery. Elsewhere Sir Francis opted for delicate rococo plasterwork or classical compositions by William Hannan. Innovative ceilings in the hall and dining-room by Giuseppe's son Giovanni herald the neo-classicism of the late eighteenth century.

Hardly altered since Sir Francis's death, the house still displays his fine eighteenth-century furniture and his catholic collection of lesser Italian masters. Superb chimneypieces in many of the rooms include work by Sir Henry Cheere, such as the elaborate pink and white marble fireplace carved with birds in high relief in the music-room, billing and cooing doves on one side balanced by an owl devouring a

small bird on the other. Sir Henry was probably also responsible for the deceptively simple plaque in the study, showing cherubs warming themselves by a fire, two naked figures stretching out their hands to the blaze while their companions fetch wood. The mahogany staircase inlaid with satinwood and ebony is similarly fine, one of very few examples of work of this kind (*see also* Claydon House, p.74).

The naturalistic pleasure ground is also Sir Francis's creation, a remodelling of his own earlier, more formal layout, with a series of classical temples and follies forming eyecatchers in contrived vistas. From the north front of the house the ground falls away into the wooded valley which hides the village (*see below*), rising again to the church Sir Francis rebuilt inside a prehistoric earthwork on the top of the hill opposite, its massive golden ball glinting in the sun on fine days. A sweep of grass stretches to the shores of a lake, where the colonnade of a classical temple on one of the islands shows white against the surrounding foliage. Garden buildings by Nicholas Revett include a cottage disguised as a church and a colonnaded circular dovecote with a pyramidal roof known as the Round Temple. John Donowell was responsible for the Temple of Apollo next to the house, a gigantic grey arch of flint and stone with the motto of the Hellfire Club engraved on an inset panel. The domed classical temple on a grassy mound in the woods to the west of the lake, with an open colonnade enclosing a statue of Venus, is one of three eyecatchers commissioned from Quinlan Terry in recent years.

West Wycombe Village

Buckinghamshire

2 miles west of High Wycombe, on the A40

For centuries the principal route from London to Oxford, the Midlands and Wales passed through West Wycombe, nurturing the creation of this exceptional village, its long main street lined by timber-framed, flint and brick cottages, many of which date from the sixteenth century or earlier. One of the oldest buildings, the fifteenth-century Church Loft, was originally a rest house for pilgrims. Later travellers were catered for by several coaching inns, three of which survive, and there are also some more gracious façades among the traditional cottage frontages, such as the Queen Anne Steps House.

The village was acquired by the Dashwood family, as part of the West Wycombe estate, in 1698, and lies just outside the gates of Sir Francis Dashwood's great house (*see above*).

White Mill   Dorset

Off B3082 north of Sturminster Marshall

This substantial brick and tile corn mill, in a peaceful setting on the banks of the sluggish River Stour, is one of the most important vernacular buildings on the 8,795-acre agricultural estate attached to Kingston Lacy (*see* p.167). Largely rebuilt in 1776, but probably marking a mill site recorded in Domesday Book, the mill still has its original highly crafted elm and applewood machinery, now very rare.

White Horse Hill   Oxfordshire

6 miles west of Wantage, 2 miles south of Uffington, on south side of the B4507

Whoever outlined the famous white horse set 800 feet up on the scarp of the Berkshire Downs had an eye for his work. With only a few well-placed lines

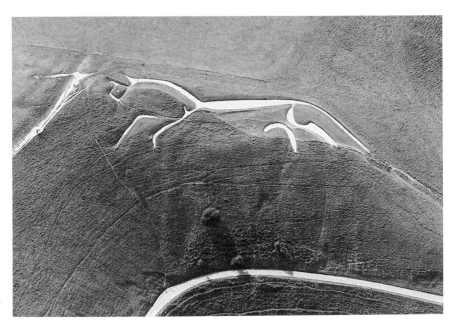

Flowing lines outline the White Horse on the crest of the downs above Uffington. (*NT*)

he created the impression of a proud and powerful animal, eternally prancing above the vale which bears its name. Closely resembling the tiny stylised animals depicted on coins of the first century BC, the White Horse may well have marked the territory of a local Iron Age tribe, either the Dobunni, who were centred on Cirencester, or the Atrebates, who had their capital at Silchester.

Just above the horse is the Iron Age hill fort of Uffington Castle, its powerful earth ramparts a familiar landmark to those walking the prehistoric track known as the Ridgeway along the crest of the downs. The prominent natural knob of Dragon Hill just below the chalk figure is where St George is supposed to have slain the dragon.

Wichenford Dovecote

Hereford & Worcester

5½ miles north-west of Worcester, north of the B4204

Perhaps built at the same time as the adjoining farmhouse was given its elegant late seventeenth-century façades, this tall timber-framed black and white dovecote strikes a similarly domestic note, mown grass surrounding the sandstone plinth on which it stands. A lantern crowning the steeply pitched roof admitted birds to some 550 nesting boxes stacked on short brick piers.

Wicken Fen Cambridgeshire

Access south of the A1123 at the village of Wicken, 3 miles west of Soham, on the A142; 17 miles north-east of Cambridge, via Stretham on the A10

Scientifically one of the most important wetland nature reserves in Western Europe, Wicken Fen is virtually all that remains of the once-vast area of undrained fen which covered 2,500 square miles from Lincolnshire to Suffolk, now called the Fens of the Great Level. The small population which lived here were a law unto themselves, and bitterly resented the progressive draining of the Fens by rich entrepreneurs, foremost among them the 1st Duke of Bedford, whose forebears had grown immensely rich with plunder from dissolved monasteries. The Duke employed the Dutch engineer Cornelius Vermuyden to drive what is now called the Old Bedford River through the area, to join the

River Great Ouse at Downham Market and from there drain to The Wash.

What the Duke began continued apace, and the reclamation took place of what became some of the richest farmland in the country, now well below sea level and kept dry by immense pumping stations, for once drained the peat contracts and the level of the soil falls.

Because the Sedge Fen at Wicken has never been drained, it now stands as an island several feet above the surrounding land, and water has to be pumped up into it to maintain its character. The Trust has restored an old drainage windpump to help in this most necessary task and the boundary banks have been sealed to prevent water escaping down on to surrounding arable land. If left to itself the fen would dry out, the aquatic plants would die and clog the open water which would subsequently be invaded first by reeds, then by willows, alder and buckthorn, changing finally into oak and ash

As well as a long list of resident and visiting birds, Wicken Fen is particularly rich in insects and flowering plants. The character of this important wetland reserve now has to be artificially maintained as, left to itself, it would gradually dry out and would eventually be colonised by forest trees. (*NT/Ray Hallett*)

woodland. So very careful management is needed to keep a balance between reed and sedge beds, 'carr' – as the scrub is known – and open water.

Wicken Fen is wonderfully rich in plant and bird life, and particularly in insects, with over 5,000 species, including 700 moths and butterflies, 200 spiders, of which some are unique to Wicken, over 300 species of flowering plants and a long list of birds, including marsh and Montagu harriers, bittern, great-crested grebe, bearded tit, black tern, duck, owls, and many waders and small marshland species.

Wightwick Manor West Midlands

3 miles west of Wolverhampton, up Wightwick Bank, beside the Mermaid Inn, just north of the A454 Bridgnorth road

In 1848 seven young men barely out of their teens – including Holman Hunt, J. E. Millais and Dante Gabriel Rossetti – founded the Pre-Raphaelite Brotherhood, a revolt against the artistic establishment and what they perceived as the emptiness and

Burne-Jones's *Love Among the Ruins* at Wightwick Manor, the tendrils of briar rose an echo of the thorny forest he created at Buscot Park. The sitter for the male figure was Gaetano Meo, a favourite Pre-Raphaelite model, who became a designer of mosaics. (*NT*)

artificiality of contemporary art. The group was short-lived, but its ideals were enormously influential, feeding into the reaction against mass production and return to pre-industrial techniques which became identified with William Morris and the Arts and Crafts Movement. Rossetti, Madox Brown and Burne-Jones were among the founders of Morris's design and furnishing company, which started life as an artist's co-operative in 1861.

Wightwick Manor is one of only a few surviving examples of a house built and furnished under the influence of the Arts and Crafts Movement. Morris wallpapers, textiles and carpets and William de Morgan tiles and Benson metalwork supplied by his company set off paintings and drawings by Ford Madox Brown, Holman Hunt, Millais, Burne-Jones and Ruskin, and books from Morris's Kelmscott Press. The Jacobean furniture, oriental porcelain and Persian rugs with which the house is also furnished complement rather than compete with the nineteenth-century work, echoing Morris's appreciation of good craftsmanship from any period.

Built in two stages in 1887 and 1893, the half-timbered, pseudo-medieval house was commissioned by the industrialist Theodore Mander, a paint and varnish manufacturer, from the Liverpool architect Edward Ould. The later, eastern half is more richly decorated and is clearly inspired by the Tudor buildings of the Welsh Marches. Decorative black and white timbering, in stripes, swirls and quatrefoils, rises from a plinth of local stone, with banks of spiral Tudor chimneys crowning the gabled roofline.

In keeping with the exterior, the heart of the house is a great parlour in the form of a feudal hall, with an open timber roof painted by the talented Charles Kempe. A minstrels' gallery across one end, a deeply recessed fireplace alcove and extensive use of panelling add to the medieval atmosphere. Kempe was also responsible for the glowing colours in the painted windows and the deep plaster frieze telling the story of Orpheus and Eurydice that may well have been inspired by that in the High Great Chamber at Hardwick (see p.142). Orpheus sits with his harp in a forest, enticing a whole menagerie of beasts with his music, from a trumpeting elephant to a kangaroo and a peacock with a golden tail. Morris's last woven fabric design – white and pink blossom on a deep-blue ground, like a meadow full of spring flowers – hangs below the frieze and Benson chandeliers light the displays of Chinese porcelain and the long refectory table down the centre of the room. The gallery end of the hall is dominated by Burne-Jones's romantic *Love Among the Ruins*, his tendrils of briar rose entangling the ardent couple recalling those in his masterpiece at Buscot Park (see p.47). This eclectic mix of antique and Victorian appears throughout the house, as in the drawing-room, where a superb Italian Renaissance chimneypiece is inset with rich green tiles by William de Morgan featuring a bestiary of mischievous creatures. Photographs of the Pre-Raphaelites and their associates on an upstairs landing include one showing William Morris and Burne-Jones with their families, in which only Mrs Morris looks straight at the camera.

The attractive garden, first laid out on the advice of the painter Alfred Parsons, was considerably extended by the Edwardian landscape architect Thomas Mawson. Formal walks framed by clipped yew and golden holly lead to a rose garden overlooked by topiary peacocks or down to a more informally planted area round two ponds linked by a little stream. More topiary yew forms a narrow path across the lawn fringing the broad stone terrace with an oak balustrade which Thomas Mawson added to the south front in about 1910. Pieces of stonework from the Houses of Parliament adorned the nuttery, and a wooden bridge over the road up to the house is similar to one across the River Cam at Queens' College, Cambridge. A beech planted by Queen Mary when Duchess of York in 1900, one of several trees associated with royalty and political figures, is now old and gnarled.

Wilderhope Manor Shropshire

7 miles south-west of Much Wenlock, 7 miles east of Church Stretton, ½ mile south of the B4371

This gabled, unspoilt Elizabethan manor stands on the south slope of Wenlock Edge (see p.289), deep in the remote wooded Shropshire landscape evoked so vividly in the work of the local novelist Mary Webb, who used Wilderhope Manor as her model for Undern Hall in *Gone to Earth* (1917). Built of local grey limestone with tall brick chimneys and a stone-tiled roof, this is a delightfully asymmetrical house, with a curious detached pediment marking the off-centre entrance in the south-east front. Mullioned windows in the varied three-storeyed gables on this side of the house look out over the River Corve deep in the valley below.

Apart from the notable circular wooden staircase capped by a conical roof which ascends right through the house, the main feature of the interior is its unexpected plasterwork ceilings, executed with such skill that they were once thought to be the work of Italian craftsmen rather than by a provincial team. The initials of Francis and Ellen Smallman, who built Wilderhope in about 1586, recur frequently in the moulds punctuating the plaster ribs, alternating with standard motifs such as the Tudor rose, the fleur-de-lis and the portcullis.

The spot known as the 'Major's Leap' on Wenlock Edge nearby commemorates Francis and Ellen's descendant, Thomas Smallman, a supporter of the Royalist cause in the Civil War, who was imprisoned at Wilderhope. Escaping into the garden, probably by means of an old garderobe flue, he evaded his pursuers by riding his horse over Wenlock Edge. Although his unfortunate mount was killed, the major's fall is said to have been broken by a crab-apple tree.

Willington Dovecote and Stables

Bedfordshire

4 miles east of Bedford, just north of the Sandy road

The serrated roofline of this imposing sixteenth-century dovecote built by Sir John Goshawk, Cardinal Wolsey's Master of the Horse, can be seen for miles across the flat Bedfordshire countryside. Built on a scale commensurate with the large mansion to which it was once attached, the dovecote's kidney-shaped nesting boxes set into the thickness of the stone walls could accommodate some 1,500 birds. Stepped Dutch-style gables are supported on thirteenth-century corbels, probably filched from local priories at the Dissolution of the Monasteries. Across the road is a contemporary barn-like building with late Gothic windows where the young John Bunyan, born at Elstow only five miles to the west, once stayed, leaving his signature and the date, 1650, etched on a stone fireplace.

Cardinal Wolsey's Master of the Horse built this imposing dovecote rising high above the flat Bedfordshire countryside at Willington. (*NT*)

2 Willow Road London

Near junction of Willow Road and Downshire Hill, Hampstead

Next to some assertive Victorian villas on the western edge of Hampstead Heath is an unobtrusive three-storey, brick and concrete rectangle with a flat roof and an uninterrupted expanse of glass lighting the first floor. Compact and all of a piece, what appears to be one house is in fact a terrace of three, with a hidden basement giving on to gardens behind.

This piece of pre-war modernism was the work of the anglophile Austro-Hungarian architect Ernö Goldfinger (1902–87), who designed the central house for his artist wife Ursula Blackwell and their children and lived here from 1939 until his death. The first example of modern architecture to be acquired by the National Trust, 2 Willow Road still has its original fixtures and fittings, including some of Ernö's prototype furniture, and the Goldfingers' important collection of contemporary art, reflecting their close links with the avant-garde. The couple met in Paris, where he had trained with Auguste Perret, known for his innovative use of reinforced concrete, and she was a student of the painter Amédée Ozenfant, who reacted to cubism by advocating a return to a minimalist representational art, in which forms are reduced to 'pure' outline. The Goldfingers came to London in 1934, but in these pre-war years Ernö's designs, apart from some work for the toy firm Abbatt, were largely unexecuted. After the war, he was responsible for some of London's now deprecated developments, notably the large office complex at Elephant and Castle and high-rise housing in Kensington.

Willow Road, built partly to impress Ursula's parents, heirs to the Crosse & Blackwell fortune, probably sees Ernö at his best. No. 2 is by no means large, but there is a sense of both space and light, with the glass walls of the main rooms drawing the eye out over the heath in front and on to the south-facing balcony and gardens behind. Ernö's hand is in every detail. A spiral staircase is the backbone and main artery of the house, carrying the concrete frame. Wrapped round it on the first floor is a versatile space, with movable partitions and a change in floor level indicating dining-room, studio and living-room. Above is the nursery and bedroom floor, with compact internal bathrooms lit through the flat roof. Built-in wardrobes are flush with the

The sunny living-room at 2 Willow Road, with a picture window onto the garden and a built-in frame to display works from the Goldfingers' art collection. (*NT/Angelo Hornak*)

wall, study bookshelves are recessed into a room partition, and the studio has a tall cupboard for Ursula's canvases. The furniture too is functional, with upturned anglepoises either side of the low double bed in the master bedroom, a lino-topped dining-table on a lathe base, and dining-chairs made out of tubular metal and plywood.

But this is not an austere house. On the walls are some of Ursula's surreal anatomical studies, abstract and figurative works by Ozenfant, Delaunay, Max Ernst and Bridget Riley and a strong portrait of Ursula by the Goldfingers' close friend Man Ray, the living-room area has a parquet floor and oak-veneer panelling, and there are gay scarlet doors and areas of deep crimson paint. Clearly, too, Gold-

finger was a man with pretensions. The basement was designed with accommodation for two servants, and his house is the only one in the terrace to be provided with two garages, one of which has an inspection pit.

Wimpole Hall   Cambridgeshire

8 miles south-west of Cambridge, 6 miles north of Royston

When Rudyard Kipling visited his daughter Elsie here, a few months after she and her husband Captain George Bambridge took up residence in 1936, he was moved to remark that he hoped she had not bitten off more than she could chew. Two years later the Bambridges embarked on the restoration and refurnishing of the largest house in Cambridgeshire, whose red-brick and stone façades, three and four storeys high in the central block, stretch nearly 300 feet from end to end. From the double staircase leading up to the entrance set beneath a pediment on the south front, a 270-foot-wide avenue lined with young limes runs over two miles into the distance. Immediately in front of the house urns and busts on pedestals flank the courtyard like guards standing rigidly to attention.

The largely eighteenth-century façades added to the original mid-seventeenth-century core date from Wimpole's golden age. From 1713–40 the house was the property of Edward Harley, 2nd Earl of Oxford, who entertained Swift and Pope among a brilliant circle of writers, scholars and artists, and whose household included a Master of the Horse, a Groom of the Chamber and a Master of Music. Perhaps it was for the latter and his orchestra that Lord Harley commissioned James Gibbs's overwhelming baroque chapel, Bavarian in its opulence, which is a principal feature of the house. In Sir James Thornhill's *trompe-l'oeil* decoration, statues of Saints Gregory, Ambrose, Augustine and Jerome stand in niches between pairs of classical columns, their shadows etched sharply on the stone behind. Gregory leans eagerly forward with a book in his hand, as if about to escape his perch, while half-naked St Jerome displays a splendidly muscled physique. The east wall is filled with Thornhill's *Adoration of the Magi*, in which the Three Kings are accompanied by a sizeable retinue of armed men and Mary herself sits amid a romantic classical ruin, her ruddy-faced, bearded husband watching quietly in the background.

Gibbs also designed the long library to house Harley's collection of books and manuscripts, the largest and most important ever assembled by a private individual in England, later to form the nucleus of the British Library. An oak and walnut pulpit on castors gives access to the upper shelves and a brown, pink and beige carpet picks up the subdued tones of the plaster ceiling. This noble room is reached through a stately 52-foot gallery, created by Henry Flitcroft for Wimpole's next owner, Philip Yorke, 1st Earl of Hardwicke, as a setting for his finest paintings. Now used to display pictures particularly associated with the house, such as *The Stag Hunt* by John Wootton, who frequently visited Wimpole in Lord Harley's time, the room's long sash windows framed by red curtains and the grey-green walls help to create an atmosphere which is both restful and warm.

Wimpole's crowning glory, John Soane's Yellow Drawing Room, was added fifty years later for Philip Yorke's great-nephew, the 3rd Earl. Running from the north front into the centre of the house, Soane's domed oval at the inner end is lit from a lantern in the roof above. With semicircular apses set either side of a central fireplace on the far wall and a large painting of playing cherubs above the chimneypiece, the effect is to suggest a chapel transformed into a room of exceptional elegance and grace, with the yellow silk on the walls setting off blue silk upholstery on the gilt chairs and long settees curved round the apses. Soane's indulgent bath house, with its grand double staircase sweeping down to a tiled pool holding over 2,000 gallons, is a delightful reminder of another side of eighteenth-century life.

Wimpole's setting, an extensive 350-acre wooded park, fully matches the grandeur of the house and reflects the influence of some of the most famous names in the history of landscape gardening. The great lime avenue running two and a quarter miles

The eighteenth-century belief that dips in cold water could cure a number of maladies, including headaches and the vapours, probably prompted the 3rd Earl of Hardwicke to install a plunge bath at Wimpole Hall. (*NT*)

to the south, its unyielding lines striking through a patchwork of fields like a grassy motorway, was created by Charles Bridgeman, employed by Lord Harley in the 1720s to extend an elaborate formal layout which already included the much smaller east and west avenues to either side of the house. Originally elm, all three have been replanted, the south avenue using limes grafted and budded from mature trees Bridgeman established elsewhere in the park.

Remarkably, these remains of what was once an extensive scheme of axial avenues, canalised ponds, ha-has and bastions survived the attentions of 'Capability' Brown and his disciple William Emes later in the century, both of whom set about 'naturalising' the park. The view from the north front, artfully framed by the clumps of trees with which Brown replaced a felled avenue, looks over his serpentine ornamental lake to the three-towered Gothick ruin by Sanderson Miller which he erected as an eyecatcher on a hillock. Brown's belts of trees defining and sheltering the park were thickened and extended by Humphry Repton, who produced a Red Book for the 3rd Earl in 1801, but Repton also re-introduced a touch of formality, creating the small flower garden enclosed by iron railings on the north side of the house. A recently reinstated parterre here is planted with *Anemone blanda* in spring and hardy fuchsias and violas later on in the year.

Sir John Soane's home farm to the north of the house, built in a pleasing mixture of brick, wood, tile and thatch, was also commissioned by the 3rd Earl, who was passionately interested in farming and agricultural improvement. Gaily painted wagons and carts now fill the imposing thatched barn, but the surrounding paddocks and pens make up Wimpole's rare breeds farm. Unusual farmyard livestock here include the bright chestnut Suffolk Punch, once used as a work-horse on nearly every farm in East Anglia. The parish church only a few yards from the house, substantially rebuilt to Flitcroft's design in 1749, is all that remains of the village swept away to create the park. In the north chapel, the only part of the medieval building not demolished in the mid-eighteenth century, the recumbent effigy of the 3rd Earl with his coronet at his feet dominates a number of grandiose monuments to successive owners of the palatial house, sleeping peacefully in the midst of all they once enjoyed. Banks and ditches in the grass to the south

mark the house plots of medieval villagers who tilled the land centuries ago, the ridge and furrow they created still visible on a slope of old pasture.

Windermere Cumbria

Runs for 10 miles, with Waterhead and Ambleside to the north, Bowness-on-Windermere to the east, and Newby Bridge to the south

The largest of the English lakes became accessible by rail in 1847 when the line from Oxenholme, near Kendal, reached Birthwaite and the town of Windermere sprang up there. Wordsworth was horrified when substantial villas suddenly appeared on the east shore, summer homes of Manchester businessmen: 'Persons of pure taste throughout the island, by their oft-repeated visits to the lakes, testify they deem the district as a sort of national property, in which every man has a right and interest who has an eye to perceive and a heart to enjoy.' It took another fifty years before his views began to be heeded, and the Trust's early efforts were not at Windermere but at wholly unspoilt Derwentwater (*see* p.38) and Ullswater (*see* p.342).

The Trust's first purchase in the valley, in 1913, was on the east shore at Queen Adelaide's Hill, west of the town of Windermere, and even today it owns little of the east side of the lake, where development still proceeds. Nevertheless, acquisitions have been made over the years, and some of the viewpoints, such as Jenkin Crag, Post Knott, Cockshott Point and its country park at Fell Foot, provide magnificent panoramas across the lake to the Langdale Pikes and the Coniston Fells.

On the west side the entire shore has been acquired, from Bee Holme and Wray Castle near the head of the lake, with the extensive Claife Woods running down to the ferry to Bowness. The Trust has been able to give access to this shore, to hide away caravan sites, and to build, at Low Wray, its first basecamp, where volunteers can live in modest comfort while working for the Trust, paying for their keep, and giving much in the way of sweat, toil and goodwill. (*See also* Borrowdale and Derwentwater; Buttermere, Crummock Water and Loweswater; Coniston Valley; Ennerdale; Eskdale and Duddon Valleys; Grasmere Valley, Rydal, Hawkshead and Sawrey; Great and Little Langdale; Ullswater, Hartsop, Brotherswater and Troutbeck; Wasdale.)

Win Green Hill Wiltshire

5 miles south-east of Shaftesbury, ½ mile north-east of the
B3081

South-east of Shaftesbury and north-east of Bland-ford lies the high ground of Cranborne Chase. At 911 feet, Win Green Hill is the highest point of the chase, with a circular clump of trees at its summit. The views stretch from the Quantock Hills, to the west, to the Isle of Wight far away to the south, but it is the country nearer at hand which is so well worth exploring once one has surveyed it from this little-visited Trust outpost.

Winkworth Arboretum Surrey

Near Hascombe, 2 miles south-east of Godalming on east
side of the B2130

Although only a few miles south of Guildford, Winkworth feels as if it is in the depths of the country. The sweeping views across the valley from the steep hillside on which it is planted are to green fields with sheep grazing on the skyline against the blue of distant ridges. Waterfowl trek with deter-mination across the still waters of two lakes; sometimes there is a boat apparently becalmed on the water, a rod and line over the side.

Winkworth is largely the creation of one man, Dr Wilfrid Fox, who started work on clearing and planting the neglected woodland thickly blanketing the slopes soon after he acquired the land in 1937. Ancient oaks, clumps of hazel and belts of old pines are remnants of the original vegetation, now form-ing useful cover and windbreaks for young plants and more tender species. Unlike the more cultivated and continued landscapes of Sheffield Park (*see* p.287), Winkworth is naturalistic and unmanicured, with long grass and bracken under the leaf canopy. Some 1,300 different shrubs and trees are now established here, including important collections of maples, hollies, birches, cherries, whitebeam, mountain ash, rhododendrons and azaleas.

Sandy paths lead along the contours of the hill or plunge precipitously downwards. An impressive narrow corridor of over a hundred steps leads up from the boathouse at the end of the lower lake known as Rowe's Flash, the azaleas planted thickly either side providing an unforgettable display in the spring. Floral attractions also include pink and white blossoms in the magnolia wood (where there

are species in flower from March to the end of September) and the rich colours of the rhododen-drons massed near the carpark. A stretch of wood-land along the lower lake, left more or less in its natural state as a reserve for wildlife, is a carpet of bluebells in spring, and several specimens of *Eucry-phia nymanensis* are smothered in drifts of white in high summer, two of them standing watch over Sir Hugh Casson's memorial to Dr Fox.

But Winkworth is at its most spectacular in autumn, with the rich scarlet, orange and yellow foliage of the maples, tupelo trees and Japanese cherries showing in brilliant patches against more sober greens and browns and the blue of conifers. Berries – red, yellow, pink and purple – adorn the stands of whitebeam and ash, and the azalea steps are again showy with colour.

The lakes and varied habitats are a magnet for birds, the company of resident coots, moorhens, tufted ducks and Canada geese often swelled by herons and kingfishers. Tree-creepers scurry up and down the oaks in the wood fringing the upper lake, also a haunt of woodpeckers and nuthatches. Hearing the birds in full song on a warm summer's evening brings home the extent to which bird life has been impoverished elsewhere.

The Wirral Merseyside

9–18 miles north-west of Chester

The Wirral peninsula divides the mudflats of the Mersey from the sands of Dee, two great rivers conditioned by their very different hinterlands. At low water Caldy Hill provides views over five miles of islands, bars and spits to Point of Air lighthouse across the mouth of the Dee. From the gorsy Thurstaston Common, and from Harrock Wood behind it, there are similar views across the estuary to the Clwydian Hills.

Witley and Milford Commons
Surrey

7 miles south-west of Guildford, 1 mile south-west of
Milford between the A3 London–Portsmouth and the A286
Milford–Haslemere roads

The 400 acres of Witley and Milford Commons have changed their spots during the Trust's ownership. Before 1914 they were much as they had always been: open heath grazed by cattle and horses, with bracken cut for bedding of stock, areas of birch and some pine.

During the First World War the commons were requisitioned as army camps (Aldershot and Bordon are each within ten miles) and much cut up, but after the Trust acquired them in the 1920s this damage largely healed over, although grazing was never fully resumed.

In 1940 the army came again. Roads and sites for buildings were gouged out with bulldozers, and alien materials were brought in, damaging the natural drainage and destroying the vegetation. When the army left, roads and foundations were removed and soil was brought from elsewhere to make good. Since then invasion by bracken and scrub has been the biggest management problem and the Trust has carried out much work to ensure that dry heath and boggy areas remain open, while retaining some woodland areas and scrub. There is an interpretation centre, with nature trails and exhibitions which take advantage of the unusual recent history of this open-air schoolroom.

Woolsthorpe Manor Lincolnshire

At Woolsthorpe, 7 miles south of Grantham, ½ mile north-west of Colsterworth, 1 mile west of the A1

The premature and sickly boy born in this modest limestone house on Christmas Day 1642 came into a world which believed that the Earth was the centre of the Universe. He grew up to be the leading scientist of his day, whose work was to lay the foundations of modern scientific thought and to show that our planet is merely a satellite of the Sun. The boy was Sir Isaac Newton, the offspring of a prosperous Lincolnshire farmer who died two months before his son's birth. While his mother raised a second family nearby, Isaac spent an isolated and introverted childhood at Woolsthorpe, cared for by his grandmother. Although he left to pursue his studies in Cambridge in 1661, he returned to Woolsthorpe again in 1665 when the university was closed by the plague. That year was to see some of Newton's most fruitful work, including the discovery of the principle of differential calculus.

With its mullioned windows and simple T-shaped plan, Woolsthorpe is a typical early seventeenth-century manor house, and was bought by Isaac's grandfather, Robert Newton, in 1623. Its

plain rooms have been sparsely furnished to reflect the lifestyle of a moderately wealthy yeoman family. Upstairs is the room which Isaac used when he came back from Cambridge to see his mother, now hung with a portrait of the great man by Thornhill and prints of other famous scientists of the day, many of whom fell out with their brilliant but difficult contemporary. Also here is a copy of the third edition of Newton's major work, the *Principia Mathematica*.

Although there is little in the house to evoke the man himself (a roughly drawn church scribbled on the kitchen wall is, alas, unlikely to be his handiwork), a gnarled old apple tree in the garden may be a graft from the famous specimen which helped Newton with his work on gravity.

Wordsworth House Cumbria

Main Street, Cockermouth

Three men born in the early 1770s and known as the Lake Poets did much to change contemporary views of landscape, their appreciation of the wild beauty of nature suggesting new ideals for people seeking an escape from the realities of the Industrial Revolution. Of the three, William Wordsworth was the most innovative. Although he followed Robert Southey as poet laureate, Wordsworth's best work permanently enlarged the range and subject matter of English poetry, outclassing Southey's more pedestrian creations and the products of Samuel Taylor Coleridge's wayward genius. Wordsworth's love of the Lakes shows above all in the fact that he chose to live here all his life.

Although the adult Wordsworth is mainly connected with the southern Lakes, his formative years were spent in the north, in the little market town on the River Derwent where his father was agent to Sir James Lowther. The Georgian house where he was born on 7 April 1770, almost two years before his sister Dorothy, stands at the west end of the main street, its garden stretching down to the river and only a stone's throw from the ruined castle from which William derived so much inspiration.

Seven of the modest family rooms are furnished in eighteenth-century style, as the Wordsworths might have had them, and include some pieces which belonged to the poet in later life – his painted bookshelves, his sofa, his early nineteenth-century longcase clock and his white and gold porcelain inkstand. Southey's fine Georgian walnut chairs grace the drawing-room, which is hung with early prints of the Lake District. And the terrace above the Derwent at the end of the garden is where Wordsworth spent so many happy childhood hours with his beloved sister Dorothy. Sadly, the death of their father when Wordsworth was only thirteen resulted in the break-up of the family home.

Ysbyty Estate Gwynedd

South of Betws-y-Coed, astride the B4406 and the B4407 and on the south side of the A5 and the A470

Another great block of land besides the Carneddau (*see* p.53) which came to the Trust with Penrhyn Castle (*see* p.254) is the 21,000-acre Ysbyty estate. This is very different in character from the Carneddau, for, although the latter is farmed, Ysbyty has many more holdings and it has always been the Trust's policy to help its tenants maintain their traditional way of life, hard though this can often be. Many of the farms are remote and in some the same families have farmed for generations. Visitors must remember to stick to the tracks, to shut every gate and keep dogs very strictly under control.

The southern part of the estate is largely open moorland, with the beautiful Llyn Conwy set in its midst. The northern section is mostly farmland interspersed with woodlands on the middle slopes, with the hills above. Just outside the village of Penmachno, visitors can see Ty'n-y-Coed, a nineteenth-century farmhouse and smallholding illustrating the traditional Welsh way of life; four miles north-west, in the Wybrnant valley, is the equally emotive Tŷ Mawr (*see* p.342).

Properties not described in the Text

England

Avon

Barton Rocks, Winscombe 79½ acres of farmland.

Bristol *Frenchay Moor*: 8 acres, 2 miles south of Winterbourne on the B4427. *Shirehampton Park*: 99 acres, part used as a golf course, overlooking the River Avon. *Westbury College*: College Road, Westbury-on-Trym. Fifteenth-century gatehouse of the College of Priests, founded in the thirteenth century, of which John Wycliffe was a prebend.

Failand 4 miles west of central Bristol, on south side of the A369. 363 acres, including several farms and woodland.

Monk's Steps, Kewstoke On north edge of Weston-super-Mare. 2½ acres, including the Monk's (or St Kew's) Steps.

Redcliffe Bay Coastal belt of 2 acres crossed by the mariners' path from Clevedon to Portishead.

Bedfordshire

Sharpenhoe: The Clappers and Roberts Farm On the Chilterns, 1½ miles south-west of Barton-in-the-Clay. 136 acres, crowned by Clappers Wood.

Berkshire

Ambarrow Hill ½ mile south of Crowthorne station. 11 acres of pine-clad hilltop.

The Holies, Streatley 118 acres of chalk downland and woodland at the Goring Gap.

Bucklebury 8 miles east of Newbury. 102 acres of agricultural land adjacent to Bucklebury Common.

Finchampstead Ridges and Simons Wood ¾ mile west of Crowthorne station, on the south side of the B3348. 60 acres of woodland and a heather ridge. *Heath Pool*: A pond and 12 acres of woodland. *Simons Wood*: 63 acres of woodland, with access from Heath Pool.

Hunts Green: Badgers 1 mile south of Boxford. Thatched cottage in the village (not open to the public).

Lardon Chase Just north of Streatley, on the west side of the A417. 38 acres of down. *Lough Down*: 28½ acres adjoining Lardon Chase.

Pangbourne Meadow Just below Pangbourne bridge, east of the B471. 7 acres on the south bank of the Thames.

Windsor: The Goswells Between Thames Street and the Thames. 3 acres.

Buckinghamshire

Aylesbury: The Cottage A small three-storey dwelling adjacent to the King's Head hotel.

Coombe Hill (q.v.) *Low Scrubs*: 12 acres of woodland adjacent to existing Trust land.

Dorneywood South-west of Burnham Beeches, 1 mile east of Cliveden. The house, contents and 215 acres given as an official residence for a Secretary of State or a Minister of the Crown. Not open to the public.

Greenlands estate North-east of Henley. Four viewpoints covering 2½ acres north and south of the A4155.

Hogback Wood 1 mile west of Beaconsfield station. 22½ acres of woodland.

Hughenden Manor (q.v.) *Hanging and Flagmore Woods*: 33¼ acres of mixed woodland adjoining manor woodland. *Naphill Farm*: 138 acres of agricultural land and woodland.

Medmenham: Lodge Farm 3 miles south-west of Marlow, on north side of the A4155. 75 acres. A seventeenth-century farmhouse and three modern cottages (not open).

Pulpit Wood 1½ miles north-east of Princes Risborough, 2½ miles south-west of Wendover. 65 acres of Chiltern beech woodland with prehistoric hill fort.

Stowe: Castle Farm 57½ acres of farmland adjoining Stowe Landscape Gardens (q.v.).

Whiteleaf Fields ¾ mile north-east of Princes Risborough. 3 acres opposite the Nag's Head Inn at Monks Risborough and 2 acres extending for about ¼ mile on either side of the Icknield Way.

Cambridgeshire

Wicken Fen (q.v.) 128 acres of pasture adjoining fen.

Wisbech: 14 and 19 North Brink Early eighteenth-century houses, one much altered, flanking Peckover House (q.v.) on the north bank of the Nene (open by appointment).

Cheshire

Eddisbury Park Field 1 mile east of Macclesfield on the Buxton road. 16 acres of park-like meadow, 700 feet above sea level.

Hare Hill 1 mile west of Prestbury, 4½ miles north-west of Macclesfield. 284½ acres of park and farmland with woods and a small garden forming part of the Alderley Edge escarpment; fine views to the north-east; connecting path to Alderley Edge estate (q.v.).

Helsby Hill ½ mile east of Helsby, just east of the A56. 40 acres of the summit, on which is part of an Iron Age promontory fort, and wooded lower slopes.

Lyme Park (q.v.): **Drinkwater Meadow** 56 acres of pasture and coniferous shelter belt.

Maggoty's Wood ½ mile north-west of Gawsworth, 3 miles south-west of Macclesfield. 2½ acres of wood including the grave of Maggoty Johnson, an eccentric eighteenth-century dramatist and dancing master.

Mobberley 3 miles north-east of Knutsford. 20 acres of meadow protecting the church.

Mow Cop *Old Man of Mow*: 150 yards north of Mow Cop (q.v.). 2 acres of land round prominent rock on Cheshire/Staffordshire border.

Cleveland

Brotton: Hunt Cliff and Warsett Hill 153 acres, including ⅔ mile of coast with 330-foot cliffs and undercliff.

Hummersea, Skiningrove 57 acres of coastal cliff-top, 14 miles north-west of Whitby.

Loftus: Park Street Houses Farm 140 acres of scenic undercliff and clifftop.

Cornwall

The Birdcage, Port Isaac A tiny, five-sided, three-storey slate-hung cottage perched high above the harbour, now a holiday cottage.

Bodigga Cliff 1 mile east of Looe. 43 acres of rough cliffland and foreshore.

Bodrugan's Leap 1½ miles south of Mevagissey, just south of Chapel Point. 5 acres of the headland from which Sir Henry Trenowth of Bodrugan, pursued by Sir Richard Edgcumbe of Cotehele (q.v.), is said to have jumped into the sea and escaped to France.

Booby's Bay 2¾ acres of cliffland, including Constantine Island.

Boscathnoe Farm 3⅓ acres of pasture and woodland opposite entrance to Trengwainton Garden (q.v.).

Boscregan Farm 2 miles south-west of St Just. 69 acres of farmland behind Hendra Cliff (q.v.).

Bosigran and Carn Galver: Porthmeor (q.v.) 3 miles north-east of Morvah, 2 miles south-west of St Ives, on either side of the B3306. Lower Porthmeor, a farmhouse, cottage and outbuildings with 6 acres of meadow and moor.

Cadsonbury Near New Bridge, 2 miles south-west of Callington. 84 acres, including important hill fort crowning a steep isolated hill in the Lynher valley.

Camel Estuary: Fishing Cove Field, Trebetherick 6¼ acres.

Chapel Carn Brea 3 miles north-east of Land's End between the A30 and the B3306. 53 acres, including several Bronze Age barrows. The 'first and last' hill in England.

Erth Barton and Erth Island 1½ miles south-east of St Germans, 4 miles west of Saltash. 198 acres of saltings and foreshore.

Fal Estuary *Ardevora*: 32 acres of foreshore on the east bank. *Trelonk*: 22 acres of foreshore on the east bank.

Fowey (q.v.) *Penpoll Creek*: 14 acres at entrance to creek. *Readymoney Copse*: ¼ acre. *St Saviour's Point*: 6 acres at Polruan (q.v.). *Station Wood*: 31 acres of woodland and meadow on right bank of estuary.

Godrevy Point 56 acres of beach south of the point.

Helford River (q.v.) *Carne Vean*: 2½ acres on south side of Gillan Creek with two typically Cornish stone and cob cottages (not open). *Nansidwell*: 53 acres forming a valley running down to the sea. *Gillan Creek*: 3-acre wood forming north bank. *Pengwedhen*: 34 acres of farm and woodland to west of Helford village.

Trewarnevas and Coneysburrow Cove: 5½ acres 2 miles east of Manaccan.

Lerryn Creek On east bank of Fowey estuary. Wood and parkland, circular walks.

Lizard Peninsula (q.v.) *Beagles Point*: 74 acres. *Bosun's Whistle*: A small bungalow on the narrow lane leading to Lizard Point. *Lowland Point*: 57 acres of farmland and wild cliffs overlooking the Manacles Rocks, the scene of many shipwrecks. *Parn Voose Cove and The Balk*: 27 acres. *Polurrian Cove*: 5 acres of open cliffland on south side of cove. *Sea Breeze*: A 1920s stuccoed bungalow. *Tregullas and Tregominnion Farms*: 123½ acres, including Pen Olver headland. *Wartha Manor*: A substantial late Victorian house on Lizard Point (not open).

Mount's Bay 29 acres of coastal farmland at Boat Cove, overlooking St Michael's Mount.

Park Head, St Eval 6 miles south-west of Padstow. A wild 222-acre headland dominating this part of the coast and including Diggory's Island and six round barrows. Beach Head NT, the Trust's coastal base-camp, is at the centre of the property.

Polperro (q.v.) *Chapel Cliff*: 91½ acres of cliff and farmland on west side of harbour. *Raphael Cliff*: 16 acres of coastal scrubland within a Site of Special Scientific Interest. *Talland Hill*: 3 acres of woodland and scrub standing prominently about Polperro harbour.

Port Gaverne ¼ mile east of Port Isaac. 16 acres, including beach, foreshore and fish cellars and five cottages (not open).

Porthcothan 5 miles south-west of Padstow. 28⅓ acres forming north side of inlet and ¼ mile of coast.

Porthminster Point On south edge of St Ives. 12 acres of cliffs and small fields, including several rocky coves.

Rosemergy, Morvah 2 acres of land adjacent to the Trust's existing land at Rosemergy (q.v.).

Rough Tor 3 miles south-east of Camelford. 174 acres of moorland, rising to 1,296 feet, the second highest point in Cornwall. Includes Bronze Age settlement and Second World War memorial.

St Agnes (q.v.) *Wayside Cottages*: Three Cornish stone cottages (not open), with 1-acre garden.

St Anthony-in-Roseland *The Court, Bohortha*: Three thatched cottages (not open), with ½ acre of land.

St Mawes (q.v.): **Newton Farm** 93 acres of land lying behind the Trust's property at Newton Cliff.

Tintagel (q.v.) 4½ acres of pasture and scrub overlooking Tintagel Island. *Glebe Cliff*: 71 acres between Tintagel church and the sea. *Higher Penhallic Point*: 3½ acres just south of Glebe Cliff. *Lower Penhallic Point*: 13 acres on south side of Glebe Cliff.

Tregassick and Trewince On the east bank of the St Mawes estuary. 143 acres of farmland embracing the hamlet of Porthcuel and including 1½ miles of estuary shore.

Treligga Near Delabole. 2¼ acres.

Trelissick (q.v.): **Lamouth Creek** 14 acres. 11 acres of woodland and pasture, with 3 acres of foreshore along the north bank of Lamouth Creek, connecting the main part of Trelissick with Round Wood. *Pill Creek*: 4½ acres of pasture overlooking creek. *Pill Farm*: 182 acres, including a farmhouse, woods and foreshore.

Watchcroft 166 acres of heathland straddling B3306 1 mile north-east of Morvah, and including western part of Trevean cliffs.

West Penwith 16 acres of the Cot Valley, St Just.

Whitesand Bay 5 miles west of Torpoint, 3 miles north-west of Rame Head. *Sharrow Point and Higher Tregantle Cliffs*: 69 acres of cliffs overlooking White-sand Bay, with the eighteenth-century Sharrow Grot hewn out of the cliff-face. *Trethill Cliffs*: 69 acres of farm and cliffland on coast road to Portwrinkle.

Cumbria

Ambleside *Birdhouse*: Two fields of 6 acres by Amble-side Roman Fort; no public access. *Borrans Field*: 21 acres on the left bank of the River Brathay where it flows into Windermere; also the remains of Ambleside Roman Fort. *Fishgarths Wood*: 23¾ acres of mixed deciduous woodland. *Force How and Bridge How Coppice*: 17½ acres of mixed woodland on the south side of the River Brathay, above Skelwith Bridge, and running down to the southern side of Skelwith Force. *Fox How Farm and Deer Hows Wood*: 67½ acres of farmland, pasture and woodland. *Great Bog*: A field of 1½ acres beside Lake Road, Ambleside. *Kelsick Scar and High Skelgill Farm*: 215 acres of wood, fell and farm ½ mile south-east of Ambleside. *Martins Wood*: 10 acres of agricultural land 2 miles south-east of Ambleside. *The Rashfield or Dora's Field, Rydal*: 1½ acres 1½ miles north-west of Ambleside bought by poet Wordsworth in 1826. *Scandale Fell*: 320 acres with some enclosed pasture and extensive views of Lake Windermere. *Skelwith Bridge*: 25 acres of traditional oak woodland within Brunt How Wood. *Wansfell*: 190 acres of wood and grassland on east side of Windermere with fine views over lake; also Stagshaw Garden, a woodland garden with azaleas and rhododendrons created by C. H. D. Acland.

Arnside *The Knott*: 1 mile south of Arnside. 212½ acres overlooking Morecambe Bay. *Heathwaite*: 60 acres of limestone grassland and woodland adjacent to Arnside Knott.

Borrowdale (q.v.) *Banks Intake*: 186 acres of lonely fellside on east side of Langstrath Beck. *Bull Crag*: 86 acres at foot of Langstrath. *Castle Head*: 20 acres of woodland rising to 529 feet with famous view of Derwentwater from top. *Johnny's Wood and High Doat*: 80 acres of woodland and fell. *Langstrath Intake*: 80 acres of open hillside. *The Lordship of the Manor of Borrowdale*: Surface rights over 7,200 acres of fell. *Nook Farm*: 150½ acres of fields and farmland south-west of Rosthwaite. *Red Brow*: 3 acres. *Seathwaite Farm*: 636 acres at the head of the valley. *Seatoller Farm*: 963½ acres reaching to the top of Honister Pass. *Stonethwaite and Rosthwaite*: 534 acres, including nine cottages, Stonethwaite Farm, Croft Farm and The How, a hill in the middle of Rosthwaite village. *Yew Tree and Longthwaite Farms*: 582 acres of farmland and fell.

Buttermere Valley (q.v.) *Folder's Wood*: 2½ acres of woodland near Cockermouth. *Hobcarton Crag*: 27½ acres of the face of the crag, 4 miles west of Derwentwater. *Woodhouse*: A small guesthouse and 23½ acres on the shores of Crummock Water.

Cautley: Cross Keys Inn 5 miles north-east of Sedbergh on the A683. Built c.1600 and altered in the early eighteenth and late nineteenth centuries. Once an unlicensed inn.

Coniston Water (q.v.) *High Arnside Farm*: 305 acres rising to 750 feet 2½ miles north-east of the lake. *Hoathwaite Farm*: 112 acres on west shore.

Dalton Castle A fourteenth-century tower in the main street of Dalton.

Derwentwater (q.v.) *The Bield, Grange in Borrowdale*: 4½ acres and a detached house. *Castle Crag, Hollows Farm (and other properties)*: 302 acres between Rosthwaite and Grange including many famous viewpoints. *Castlerigg Fell*: 947 acres of fell on east shore of lake. *Cockshott Wood, Friar's Crag, Stable Hills and Calf Close Bay*: 139 acres of farm and woodland in continuous stretch on east side of lake. Ruskin memorial on Friar's Crag. *Coombe allotment and Troutdale*: 184 acres of craggy wooded land on east flank of Borrowdale. *Crosthwaite, Skiddaw Cottage*: ½ mile north-west of Keswick; not open. *Crow Park*: 40½ acres on north shore of lake. *Derwent Island*: 7 acres. *Grange Fell*: 311 acres, including King's How and the Bowder Stone. *Great Wood, Keswick*: 237 acres of woodland. *Hawse End*: 22½ acres on west shore of lake. *High Rigg Fields*:

49 acres ¼ mile west of Grange. *Isthmus*: 9 acres of woodland with cottage (not open) and bathing place. *Long Corner Cottage, Grange-in-Borrowdale*: not open. *Lord's and St Herbert's Island and Rampsholme*: Wooded islands totalling 11½ acres in Derwentwater. *Manesty Park*: 139 acres of park, woodland and rough land at south end of lake.

Duddon Valley (q.v.) *Baskell Farm*: 216-acre farm. *Fenwick Farm, Thwaites*: 65 acres of stock farm with views out to sea. *Low Hollin House*: 1 mile north-east of Seathwaite; not open. *Sandscale Haws*: 651 acres of sand dunes and marsh at the mouth of the Duddon estuary. *Tongue House and Long House Farm*: 245-acre hill farm 1 mile north-east of Seathwaite. *Troutal Farm*: 145 acres on left bank of River Duddon. *Wallowbarrow Crag*: 465 acres of rough fell, woodland and farmland on right bank of River Duddon.

Dunthwaite 2 miles west of north end of Bassenthwaite. 427 acres of farm and woodland bordering the Derwent, including Dunthwaite House (not open), dating from 1785, and Kirkhouse Farm.

Ennerdale (q.v.) *Crag Fell*: 294 acres of fell on south shore of lake. *Valley Head Fell*: 3,624 acres of fell on both sides of the River Liza.

Eskdale (q.v.) 57 acres of valley-bottom meadow, rough grazing land and enclosed fell around the Woolpack Inn, and grazing rights for 600 sheep on Eskdale Common. *Boot*: 5 acres near the church and 15 acres of agricultural land nearby. *Burnmoor Tarn*: 57½ acres beside path from Eskdale to Wasdale. *Field Head Farm*: 119 acres at the foot of Eskdale under Birker Fell. *Gill Bank Farm*: 87 acres of in-bye land east of the Whillan Beck with rights on Eskdale Common. *High and Low Intack*: 13 acres of rough grazing with an oak wood. *Kirkhouse*: 13½ acres of rough grazing. *Taw House Farm*: 223 acres near the head of the valley, including Bird How Cottage (not open). *Wha House Farm*: 189 acres adjoining Taw House Farm.

Grasmere (q.v.) *Alcock Tarn, Brackenfell and Chapel Green*: 97 acres including fell behind Dove Cottage stretching up to and including Alcock Tarn. *Allan Bank*: 94 acres, including house and garden in Grasmere village where Wordsworth lived between 1808–11 (not open). *Broadgate Field*: 3½ acres in Grasmere village. *Butterlip How*: 6 acres rising behind the village. *Church Stile*: Sixteenth-century cottage, one of the oldest in Grasmere village; information centre. *Dunnabeck Paddock*: 1½ acres. *Easedale*: 217¼ acres, including Easedale House (not open), and Brimmer Head Farm. *Grandy Close*: six modern cottages with 3 acres. *Lakeside Land*: 20 acres on south-west shore of Grasmere. *Low Fold*: 4¾ acres with a house. *Moss Parrock*: ½ acre in Grasmere village. *Nicholas Wood*: 10½ acres of woodland beside path from Grasmere to High Close. *St Oswalds*: House (not open) and 3 acres ½ mile west of village. *Stubdale Cottage*: 2½ acres and a cottage at foot of Easedale; not open. *Town Head Farm*: 224 acres at head of Grasmere valley with landlord's flock of 350 sheep. *Underhelm Farm*: 80 acres with landlord's flock of 220 sheep and a 1-acre paddock. *White Moss Intake*: 6½ acres of rough pasture 1 mile east of village. *The Wray*: 15 acres of meadow and rough pasture adjoining Allan Bank Park.

Hawkshead (q.v.) *Blelham Tarn*: 26 acres 2 miles north-east of Hawkshead. *Cam Stones, Outgate*: 13 acres of farmland, pasture and meadow. *Dan Becks*: 154½ acres 1½ miles north-east of Hawkshead. *Green End*: 177 acres north-east of Hawkshead, including a house near Colthouse, Syke Side Farm and Latterbarrow. *High Wray and Tock How Farms*: 263 acres near village of High Wray. *Honeysuckle Cottage*: A seventeenth-century cottage in the centre of the village. *Loanthwaite*: 163 acres 1 mile north of Hawkshead, including Crag Wood, two farms and eighteenth-century house (not open). *Low Wray Farm*: 385 acres 2½ miles north-east of Hawkshead; includes Blelham Bog. *North Fen*: 17 acres on north-east edge of Esthwaite Water. *Outgate*: 18 acres of mixed woodland and a paddock. *Round Parrock Wood*: 1 acre 1 mile north-west of Hawkshead.

The Langdale Valleys (q.v.) *Brunt How*: 1½ acres beside Langdale road. *Brunt How Wood*: 19½ acres of oak woodland on northern slope of lower River Brathay. *Elterwater*: 8 acres and a house. *St Anne's Studio, Chapel Stile*: two cottages and a garden (not open).

Leconfield Commons 715 acres of Wastwater and 31,215 acres of common land of the Manors of Derwent Fells, Braithwaite and Coledale, Kinniside, Netherwasdale and Eskdale, Mitredale and Wasdalehead.

Lonsdale Commons 16,842 acres. All the high land from Seat Sandal and Stone Arthur on the slopes of Helvellyn to the head of Great Langdale. At the lower level, the bed of Grasmere Lake and parts of Rydal Water, White Moss and Elterwater Commons are included.

Newlands Valley: High Snab Farm 4 miles south-west of Keswick. 93 acres.

Overwater Lake 68 acres of lake and foreshore.

Plumpton Marsh 7 acres of coastal saltmarsh on Leven estuary, 1 mile east of Ulverston.

Sawrey (q.v.) *Tower Bank Arms*: Adjacent to Hill Top (q.v.). Let as an inn.

Sizergh Castle (q.v.) *Cowgarth Wood*: 7 acres of mixed woodland on a steep hillside.

Solway Commons On the south shore of the Firth. 170 acres of common land and 1½ miles of coastline.

Stockdale Moor 4 miles south of Ennerdale. 2,507½ acres, including a long barrow and other prehistoric remains.

Ullswater Valley (q.v.) *Beckstones Farm*: 138-acre hill farm with landlord's flock of 250 sheep. *Great Mell Fell*: 2 miles south of Troutbeck; 379 acres including rounded hill crowned with tumulus rising to 1,760 feet. *Howe Green Farm*: 509 acres at Low Hartsop in Patterdale; mostly fell grazing with landlord's flock of 220 sheep. *Matterdale: Home Farm. Millses Farm*: 92 acres adjoining Gowbarrow Park. *Patterdale, Goldrill House*: used as a youth hostel. *Riddings Plantation*: 146 acres of open fell adjoining Gowbarrow Park. *Side Farm*: 107 acres on east shore of Ullswater.

Wasdale (q.v.) *Bowderdale*: 5 acres on north shore of lake. *Gill, Broadgap and Buckbarrow Farms*: 255 acres of in-bye farmland on the Gosforth to Wastwater road with landlord's flock of 5,097 sheep. *Harrowhead Farm*: 86 acres of in-bye land south of Gosforth to Wastwater road with landlord's flock of 200 sheep and grazing rights on Nether Wasdale Common. *Guards*: Adjacent to Cathow Bridge, Nether Wasdale. 2½-acre field adjoining existing Trust land. *Nether Wasdale*: 1,530½ acres of farm and woodland. *Wasdale Hall*: 53½ acres of farm and woodland at foot of Wastwater.

Wetheral Woods 21½ acres on left bank of River Eden, 5 miles east of Carlisle.

Whitehaven: St Bees Two cottages adjoining lighthouse and a small building previously used as a foghorn station. Not open.

Windermere (q.v.) *Allen Knott and Latter Heath*: 75 acres, 2 miles north of station. *Ash Landing, Far Sawrey*: Two fields of 6½ acres. *Bordriggs Brow*: ¾-acre viewpoint, ½ mile south of Bowness. *Cockshott Point*: 21 acres on the outskirts of Bowness, including Rectory Farm. *Common Farm*: 169 acres on outskirts of Windermere. *Crosthwaite estate*: 1,960 acres on east side of lake consisting of six farms. *Fell Foot Park*: 18 acres of parkland with exotic shrubs and trees on east shore of lake. *Ladyholme*: ½-acre island. *Moorhow*: 43 acres overlooking lake, 2 miles north of Fell Foot Park. *Post Knott*: 7 acres of rough land above Bowness. *Rampholme Island*: 1-acre wooded island. *St Catherine's estate*: 53 acres of old parkland and woodland surrounding a now demolished mansion on east side of lake. *Storrs Temple*: Early nineteenth-century folly (no access).

Derbyshire and the Peak District

Alsop Moor Plantation 8 miles north of Ashbourne. 16½ acres.

Castleton 5½ acres at Odin Mine.

Curbar Gap ½ mile east of Curbar village, 2½ miles south of Padley. 8½ acres with fine views of Derwent valley.

Derwent Estate: Ashes Farm 100 acres of hill farm with traditional farmhouse.

Dovedale (q.v.) *Biggin Dale*: 51 acres on western slopes of Wolfscote Hill. *Thorpe Pastures*: 194 acres of limestone grazing bordering River Dove. *Wolfscote Hill*: 34 acres of summit, 1½ miles south of Hartington; views.

Duffield Castle ½ mile north of Duffield station, 2½ miles south of Belper, on west side of the A6. 2½ acres with foundations of Norman keep razed in 1266.

Eccles Pike 1½ miles west of Chapel-en-le-Frith. 35 acres on summit.

Edale (q.v.) *Dale Head Farm*: 174-acre hill farm at head of valley. *Dore Clough Farm*: 90 acres adjoining Dale Head Farm. *Dunscar Farm, Castleton*: 72½ acres of pasture and woodland surrounding traditional farmstead. *Edale End Farm*: 91 acres of hill grazing with some coppice and a farmhouse, 2 miles south of Hope. *Greenlands Farm*: 58½ acres on lower slopes of Mam Tor. *Harrop, Fullwood Holmes and Upper Fullwood Farms*: 246 acres, 1 mile north of Hope, including Roman road and ¾ mile of River Noe. *Lee and Orchard Farms*: Hill farms totalling 346 acres at head of Edale. *Lord's Seat and Ashton Bank*: 47 acres including prehistoric barrow; views. *Lose Hill Pike or Ward's Piece*: 55 acres of bare hilltop, 2 miles east of Edale village. *Upper Booth Farm*: 124-acre hill farm astride Crowden Brook.

Eyam: Riley Graves ½ mile east of the village. A steep hillside with the graves of seven members of the Hancock family who died of the plague in one week in August 1665.

Hayfield estate 248 acres of land adjoining Kinder Reservoir.

High Wheeldon 5½ miles south-east of Buxton, 1 mile north-east of Longnor, 4 miles north-west of Hartington. 33 acres forming a shoulder of part of the range bounding the east bank of the Dove.

Hope Woodlands (q.v.) *Crookhill Farm*: A 324-acre upland hill farm with views over Ladybower Reservoir. *Two Thorn Fields Farm*: 367 acres of farmland and buildings surrounded by the Trust's High Peak estate.

Lantern Pike 1½ miles north-west of Hayfield. 32 acres of moorland hilltop with views.

Longshaw estate (q.v.) *Curbar Gap*: 1½ acres of gritstone walled upland grassland, with views of Derwent valley. *Froggatt Wood*: 76 acres of woodland and pasture, 3 miles south of Hathersage. *The Grouse Fields*: 29 acres of upland moorland and grassland bounded by gritstone walls. *Hathersage: Little Moor*: 25½ acres at foot of the Millstone Edge. *Outseats*: 116 acres of traditional farmland, 1½ miles north of Hathersage. *White Edge Moor*: 124 acres of moorland.

Manifold and Hamps Valleys (q.v.) *Apes Tor*: Rock-face forming northern spur of Ecton Hill. *Throwley estate*: 222 acres on the banks of the Hamps and Manifold.

Miller's Dale and Ravenstor 2 miles south of Tideswell, astride the Wye. 64 acres.

Shining Cliff Wood Alderwasley, 4 miles north of Belper. 200 acres of woodland on west bank of Derwent.

South Head Hill 7 acres. Part of Kinder holding.

South Ridge Farm 4 miles north of Chapel-en-le-Frith. 28 acres rising over 1,000 feet.

Stanton Moor Edge 2 miles north of Winster, 4 miles south-east of Bakewell. 32 acres, extending over ¾ mile and rising over 900 feet.

Taddington Wood 1½ miles east of Taddington. 49 acres of wooded slopes.

Winster: 3 and 4 Woolley's Yard Two small Derbyshire stone terraced houses. Not open.

Devon

Bigbury-on-Sea: Clematon Hill On south side of the B3392. 7 acres, with views over the River Avon to Bolt Tail.

Branscombe and Salcombe Regis (q.v.) *Southcombe Farm*: 111½ acres of farmland and adjoining cliffs and foreshore.

Buckland Abbey (q.v.) 220 acres of Place Barton Farm and 414 acres of woodland on banks of River Tavy.

Burrough Farm, Northam 44½ acres running down the left bank of the Torridge estuary.

Clovelly (q.v.) *Abbotsham*: 16 acres of farmland with spectacular views of Bideford Bay. *Gawlish*: 28½ acres of cliffland. *Mount Pleasant*: 1 acre, with a view over Bideford Bay.

Combe Wood, Combe Raleigh 1 mile north of Honiton. 18 acres.

Dart Estuary: Crownley Wood 6 acres of woodland, including foreshore adjoining Bow Creek on River Dart.

Dart Estuary: Dartmouth (q.v.) *Compass Plantation*: 2¼ acres of woodland overlooking Dart estuary. *Hoodown Wood*: 33½ acres of woodland overlooking Dart estuary. *Long Wood*: 101 acres of oak woodland and foreshore on east bank of Dart estuary.

Dart Estuary: Kingswear (q.v.) *Higher Brownstone Farm*: 298 acres. *Hoodown*: ½ acre. *Inverdart*: 2 acres. *Nethway Wood*: 17 acres of mixed woodland and furze.

Dumpdon Hill, Luppitt 2 miles north of Honiton. 62 acres of common, including Iron Age hill fort.

Dunsland 4½ miles east of Holsworthy, 9 miles west of Hatherleigh, to north of the A3072. 92 acres, including site of Dunsland House, of Tudor origin with seventeenth-century alterations, burnt down in 1967.

East Titchberry Farm 1 mile east of Hartland Point, north-west of the A39. 120 acres, including 1 mile of cliff with an ancient farmhouse (not open).

Exmouth: Lower Halsdon Farm 110 acres of pasture along ¼ mile of the Exe estuary.

Hartland: Exmansworthy Cliff 40 acres of coastal land.

Heddon Valley (q.v.) *Mill Wood*: 60 acres of mainly deciduous woodland with some rough pasture.

Hembury (q.v.) *Burchetts Wood and Beechwood Copse*: 25 acres of woodland. *Butterfly Meadow*: 3½ acres of unimproved wet meadow.

Killerton (q.v.) 6,088 acres of farmland and woodland, the villages of Broadclyst and Budlake and hamlets of Westwood and Beare.

Lee to Croyde (q.v.) *Combegate Beach*: 6 acres. *Morte Fields*: 30 acres. *Potters Hill*: 30 acres overlooking Morte Bay. *Sandleigh*: A house and farm buildings adjoining Baggy Point car park. *Town Farm*: 114 acres. *Woolacombe Barton*: 545 acres of steeply sloping land.

Little Haldon 3 miles north-west of Teignmouth, on east side of the B3192. 43 acres of heath, with views over Exe estuary and Dartmoor.

Lympstone 7 miles south-east of Exeter. 6½ acres on east side of the Exe.

Moretonhampstead Almshouses On east edge of town, on north side of the B3212. Thatched, granite building of 1637 with open colonnade facing street (not open).

Old Blundell's School, Tiverton In Station Road. Famous grammar school built in 1604 and mentioned in *Lorna Doone*. Now dwelling houses.

Orcombe and Prattshayes 2½ miles east of Exmouth. 126 acres, including a mile of high red sandstone cliff, the foreshore east from Exmouth promenade and the ancient house of Prattshayes (not open).

Parke, Bovey Tracey Just outside Bovey Tracey, on north side of the B3344. 200 acres of parkland in the wooded valley of the River Bovey, 40 acres of woodland and 3 acres of Rolls Meadow. House leased to Devon County Council as headquarters of Dartmoor National Park Authority.

Plym Bridge Woods (q.v.) *Boringdon Gate Piers*: Late seventeenth-century granite piers, once entrance to Boringdon House, seat of the Parker family before they moved to Saltram (q.v.), ½ mile south-east of Plym Bridge. *Mainstone Wood and Plym Bridge Meadow*: 66 acres of woodland and meadow.

Portledge estate 770 acres of agricultural land, cliffs, beaches and foreshore.

Portlemouth Down: High House Farm 50 acres of farmland and rough grazing.

Ringmore: Higher and Lower Manor Farms 245 acres of farmland, including a mile of coast, west of Bigbury-on-Sea.

Rockbeare Hill (Prickly Pear Blossoms Park) 3 miles west of Ottery St Mary, on west side of the B3180. 22 acres of heath and woodland at top of the hill.

Shute Barton 3 miles south-west of Axminster, 2 miles north of Colyton on the B3161. 16½ acres, including remains of manor house built over three centuries from c.1380. Detached sixteenth-century gatehouse altered c.1830.

Sidmouth *Combe Wood Farm*: 61 acres, including 8 acres of cliff. *Pond Meadow*: Steep 6-acre pasture. *Rock Cottage*: Regency-style house on Sidmouth sea-front. *Sid Meadows*: 14 acres of meadow adjoining River Sid.

South Milton 2 miles west of Kingsbridge. 75½ acres, including South Milton Sands and Southdown Farm.

Teign Valley (q.v.) *Bridford Wood*: A further 44 acres of sessile oak woodland.

Welcombe and Marsland Mouths On border of Devon and Cornwall. 1 acre.

Westward Ho!: Kipling Tors 18 acres of gorse-covered hill at the west end of the town, the scene of much of Kipling's *Stalky and Co.*

Withleigh 3 miles west of Tiverton in valley of the Little Dart. *Buzzards*: 82 acres of coppice and water meadows. *Huntland Wood*: 27 acres of hanging woodland on east bank of river. *Nethercleave*: 30 acres of steep pasture on east bank of river.

Dorset

Belle Vue Farm, Isle of Purbeck 2 miles south-west of Swanage. 51 acres of rough grazing above the cliffs.

Bottle Knapp Cottage, Long Bredy, Dorchester A seventeenth-century cottage and 3 acres of pasture.

Burton Bradstock *Bindbarrow*: $18\frac{1}{2}$ acres of unimproved grassland.

Corfe Castle (q.v.) *Boar Mill*: $\frac{1}{2}$ acre, with mill, mill cottage and bakery (not open). *The Box of Delights*: Small shop in village square.

Crook Hill, Beaminster 6 acres. A fine viewpoint near Winyard's Gap.

Golden Cap Estate (q.v.) *Black Venn*: 49 acres of cliff and undercliff. *Cain's Folly*: 31 acres of undercliff and rough pasture, including a stretch of coastal path. *Chardown Hill and Upcot Farm*: 405 acres with views of coast and inland to Lambert's Castle and Pilsdon Pen (q.v.). *Doghouse Hill*: 130 acres, including spectacular 300-foot-high cliffs. *Downhouse Farm*: 194 acres of farmland and undercliff with grazing rights over Eype Down and two barrows on Thorncombe Beacon. *Filcombe and Norchard Farms*: 252 acres of farmland and woods. *Hardown Hill*: 25 acres with views north over Marshwood Vale and south to the sea. *Ridge Cliff and West Cliff, Seatown*: 195 acres of cliff, undercliff and farmland. *The Saddle*: 8 acres. *St Gabriel's*: 192 acres of undercliff and clifftop, including a group of thatched cottages and a ruined thirteenth-century chapel. *Shedbush Farm*: A 61-acre grassland farm. *Ship Farm*: A 39-acre grassland farm. *The Spittles*: 126 acres leased as a nature reserve. *Stonebarrow Hill and Westhay Farm*: 335 acres, including part of the coastal footpath.

Kingston Lacy Estate $1\frac{1}{2}$ miles north-west of Wimborne Minster, on west side of the B3082. 8,795 acres, including house by Pratt and Barry (q.v.), fourteen farms, parts of villages of Shapwick and Pamphill, including the Vine Inn at Pamphill, National Nature Reserve of Holt Heath and Iron Age fort of Badbury Rings (q.v.).

Melbury Down 243 acres, mostly agricultural unimproved chalk downland, adjoining Melbury Beacon (q.v.).

Pamphill $6\frac{1}{2}$ acres of largely agricultural land adjoining the Kingston Lacy estate.

Tolpuddle: Martyrs' Memorial 7 miles north-east of Dorchester, on south side of the A35. A seat commemorating the labourers condemned to transportation in 1834.

Ware Cliffs, Lyme Regis $29\frac{1}{2}$ acres, immediately west of Lyme Regis, forming a sheltered valley of unimproved grassland above the Cobb and undercliffs.

West Bexington *Labour-in-Vain Farm, Puncknowle*: 225 acres, farmhouse and small cottage. *Lime Kiln Hill*: 37 acres of rough grazing and farmland with former stone workings.

Winyard's Gap Above Chedington, 4 miles southeast of Crewkerne, on south side of the A356. 16 acres of woodland.

Durham

Blackhills Gill 110 acres of clifftop and arable hinterland 7 miles north of Hartlepool.

Ebchester 10 acres of woodland on the right bank of the Derwent, 12 miles south-west of Newcastle.

Hawthorn Dene and Chourdon Point 165 acres of wooded dene, beach, clifftop and arable, 6 miles south of Sunderland.

Horden (q.v.) 88 acres, including Warren House Gill and part of Fox Holes Dene together with clifftop and beach; the 500th mile of coastline bought through the Enterprise Neptune Appeal.

Moor House Woods 70 acres of woodland beside the River Wear, 3 miles north-east of Durham.

Essex

Dedham *Bridges Farm*: 79 acres, just west of the village. *Dalethorpe Park*: $16\frac{1}{2}$ acres of pasture by River Stour. *Dedham Hall Farm and Lower Barn Farm*: 228 acres of grazing meadow. *Lower Barn Farm*: 277 acres of grazing meadow to east of Dedham. *Sherman's Hall*: An early Georgian house in the main street (not open).

Rayleigh Mount 6 miles north-west of Southend. 4 acres with the motte of a Norman castle abandoned in the thirteenth century.

Saffron Walden: Sun Inn At the junction of Church Street and Market Hill. A many-gabled building incorporating a fifteenth-century hall house and with seventeenth-century pargeting. Now an antique shop.

Gloucestershire

Bibury *Arlington Row*: A row of early seventeenth-century stone cottages (not open), formed from earlier industrial building. *Rack Isle*: 4-acre field opposite the Row, bounded by water on three sides, where wool was hung on racks to dry.

Chipping Campden (q.v.) *The Coneygree*: $13\frac{1}{2}$ acres of old park preserving the surroundings of the church.

Ebworth *Blackstable Wood*: $65\frac{1}{2}$ acres with fine beech trees, near Painswick, north of the B4070. *Ebworth Lodge*: $1\frac{1}{4}$ acres with a cottage and garden. *Lord's and Lady's Woods*: 21 acres of beech wood overlooking Sheepscombe village. *Overton Farm, Sheepscombe*: 608 acres of Cotswold farmland. *Workmans Wood, Sheepscombe*: 288 acres of woodland.

Eden's Hill $2\frac{1}{2}$ miles east of Newent. $1\frac{1}{2}$ acres.

Frocester Hill and Coaley Peak Near Nympsfield between Stroud and Dursley. 13 acres of particular botanical interest on the Cotswold escarpment.

Newark Park (q.v.) 750 acres of woodland and agricultural land, on a spur of the Cotswolds.

Painswick: Little Fleece A small Cotswold town house, probably seventeenth-century. Let as a bookshop.

Snowshill: Piper's Grove $43\frac{1}{2}$ acres of sloping pasture and woodland with a farmhouse.

Stroud Properties *Besbury Common*: 8 acres above Golden Valley. *The Great Park, Minchinhampton*: $31\frac{1}{2}$ acres of pasture parkland adjoining Minchinhampton Common (q.v.). *Highlands Cottage Field*: 3 acres of permanent pasture at Pinfarthings. *Hyde Commons*: 11 acres in village. *Littleworth Common and St Chloe's Green*: 11 acres adjoining Minchinhampton Common (q.v.). *Stockend and Maitland Woods*: 61 acres on Scottsquar Hill. *Watledge Hill*: $4\frac{1}{2}$ acres of common.

Woodchester Park 504 acres of a deep, secluded valley north-west of Nailsworth, formerly an eighteenth-century park.

Wotton-under-Edge $12\frac{1}{2}$ acres of steeply sloping pasture at junction of Coombe Road and Adey's Lane on northern outskirts. *Westridge Woods*: 43 acres on escarpment above the B4060.

Greater Manchester

Medlock Vale $1\frac{1}{2}$ miles north-east of Ashton-under-Lyne. 16 acres on banks of Medlock, with Hen Cote Cottage (not open) at Daisy Nook.

Hampshire

Hamble River At Curdridge, 1 mile below Botley. 74 acres of wood and agricultural land. A nature reserve.

Ludshott (q.v.) *Bramshott Chase*: 38 acres, $\frac{1}{2}$ mile south-east of Waggoners' Wells (q.v.). *Passfield Common and Conford Moor*: 231 acres of common, with some woodland, astride the B3004 2 miles north-west of Liphook.

Newtown Common: Barn Plot $\frac{1}{4}$ acre, 3 miles south of Newbury.

Odiham: King John's Hunting Lodge 2 miles north-east of Odiham. Small eighteenth-century eye-catcher in Jacobean style in a formal garden (not open). $\frac{1}{2}$-acre lake.

Selborne: Selborne Hill (q.v.) 4 miles south of Alton, between Selborne and Newton Valence. $249\frac{1}{2}$ acres of common and woodland where Gilbert White made many observations recorded in *The Natural History of Selborne*. *The Long and Short Lythes*: 21 acres, principally hanging beech woods overlooking Selborne stream.

Sparsholt: Vaine Cottages 3 miles west of Winchester. Two thatched cottages (not open).

Speltham Down, Hambledon 17 acres, mainly unimproved downland.

Woolton Hill: The Chase 3 miles south-west of Newbury. $139\frac{3}{4}$ acres of woodland threaded by a chalk stream, with a small farm. A nature reserve.

Hereford & Worcester

Birmingham Properties *Chadwich Manor Estate*: 432 acres, mainly agricultural and woodland, on south-west edge of Birmingham; includes early eighteenth-century manor house (not open). *Cofton Hackett*: 44 acres of farmland, 2 miles east of Chadwich estate. *Frankley Beeches*: $23\frac{1}{2}$ acres of hilltop crowned with conspicuous clump of beeches. *Groveley Dingle*: 180 acres of wooded and agricultural land on southern edge of Birmingham; mainly a bird sanctuary. *Sling Pool*: 4 acres, including a pool, in a small valley running down from the Clent Hills (q.v.).

Breinton Springs On left bank of Wye. 14 acres of farm and woodland.

Brilley: Cwmmau, Fernhall and Little Penlan Farms 428 acres of farmland and woods on the borders of Herefordshire and Powys, including interesting timber-framed farmhouses with stone-tiled roofs (not open) and a small motte.

Clump Farm, Broadway To south of the A44, $\frac{1}{2}$ mile south-east of Broadway. 85 acres of farmland on the Cotswold escarpment. Wide views.

Court Farm, Broadway 50 acres of pasture and orchard on Cotswold scarp.

Knowles Mill $1\frac{1}{2}$ miles north-west of Bewdley, on south side of Dowles Brook. Set in 4 acres of orchard.

Ledge Bank Wood 16 acres of woodland on high ground on northern edge of the Cotswold scarp, 15 miles north-east of Cheltenham.

Malvern Hills (q.v.) *Foxhall*: 5 acres on east slope. *Pink Cottage*: Near Foxhall; not open. *Tack Coppice*: $\frac{3}{4}$ acre.

Mayhill Common 74 acres of heathland common with fine views towards the Welsh and Malvern Hills.

Pengethly Park 4 miles west of Ross, on north side of the A49. 118 acres of farm and woodland.

Poor's Acre $1\frac{1}{2}$ miles west of Woolhope, 6 miles south-east of Hereford. $17\frac{1}{2}$ acres bordering road in middle of Haugh Wood.

Walford 3 miles south of Ross-on-Wye, off the B4234. 35 acres overlooking the Wye valley with views to the Welsh hills.

Hertfordshire

Ashridge (q.v.) *Duncombe Farm*: 3 miles north of Berkhamsted. Valley-head farm comprising 60 acres of agricultural land, with nineteenth-century farm buildings and eighteenth-century farmhouse. *Hudnall Common*: 116 acres. *Land in the Golden Valley*: Near Berkhamsted. 120 acres of parkland at the southern end of the Golden Valley, adjoining Trust woodland on two sides and the gardens of Ashridge House on the third. *Little Heath*: 20 acres. *Waterend Moor*: $4\frac{1}{2}$ acres of wetland by the River Gade.

Barkway: Berg Cottage A small thatched cottage, bearing the date 1687, at south end of village. Also one modern cottage. Not open.

Morven Park $\frac{1}{2}$ mile north of Potters Bar, on east side of the A1000. A Victorian house (not open) and 36 acres.

Isle of Wight

Borthwood Copse 2 miles west of Sandown, $\frac{1}{2}$ mile north of the A3056. $57\frac{1}{2}$ acres of wood, almost all that remains of a once extensive medieval hunting forest.

Brighstone A terrace of thatched, chalk-block eighteenth-century cottages in North Street.

Cowes: Rosetta Cottage Small Victorian house and garden in Queens Road. Let as a holiday cottage.

Gatcombe Estate: Chillerton Down $64\frac{1}{2}$ acres of downland to the east of Chillerton village in the middle of the island.

Newport 35A St James Street.

Newtown (q.v.) Midway between Newport and Yarmouth. *Hamstead*: 78 acres adjoining river. *Harts Farm*: 35 acres of pasture, including large part of ancient borough. *Hollis Cottage and The Clammeries*: Stone cottage and wooden bungalow opposite Noah's Ark (q.v.); not open. *Old Vicarage Copse*: 7 acres. *The Quay Fields*: 12 acres of pastureland running down to Ducks Cove. *Town Copse*: 12 acres just east of Newtown. *Walter's Copse*: 48 acres of woodland, mostly oak, running down to Clamerkin Creek.

St Catherine's (q.v.) *Sudmoor Point*: 44 acres of farmland and cliff.

St Helen's *Priory Bay, Horestone Point*: $1\frac{1}{4}$ acres of wooded coastline. *Priory Woods*: 55 acres of coastal woodland at Priory Bay. *St Helen's Common*: $9\frac{1}{2}$ acres and a cottage, 1 mile north-west of Bembridge. *St Helen's Duver*: A 30-acre spit of sand and shingle stretching almost across the mouth of Bembridge harbour.

Ventnor: *Chert and Little Chert*: Two 1970s properties built on the undercliff. *Luccombe Farm*: 244 acres of downland, meadow and cliff.

West Wight *Brook Chine*: 73 acres of grazing land and shore astride the Military Road at Brook. *Hanover Point and Shippards Chine*: $26\frac{1}{2}$ acres of coast with $\frac{1}{4}$ mile of sandstone cliffs. *Headon Warren and West High Down*: 459 acres of downland, heath and agricultural land. *Tapnell Down*: 35 acres.

Kent

Appledore: Hallhouse Farm 8½ miles north-west of New Romney. Late fifteenth-century yeoman farmer's house with 6½ acres of pasture.

Crockham Hill *Close Farm*: Stone and tile-hung farmhouse, ½ mile east of Crockham Hill. *Grange Farm*: 2 miles south of Westerham, on north-east side of the B2069. 296 acres.

Dover (q.v.) *Foxhill Down*: 52 acres of cliffland immediately east of Dover. Chalk downland interspersed with scrub; Site of Special Scientific Interest.

Elham: Kingpost A terraced town house dating from the sixteenth century in the centre of Elham.

Gover Hill 1 mile west of West Peckham, 3 miles south-east of Ightham. A 1½-acre hilltop.

Harbledown: Golden Hill 1 mile west of Canterbury, just south of the A2. 2½ acres.

Ide Hill 2½ miles south of Brasted, 1 mile east of Toys Hill (q.v.), on west side of the B2042. 33½ acres comprised of wooded hillside overlooking the Weald and a mill field.

Loose: Wool House 3 miles south-east of Maidstone, ¼ mile west of Cranbrook road. A fifteenth-century half-timbered house, formerly used for cleaning wool.

Mariner's Hill 1½ miles south of Westerham, on east side of the B2026. 26½ acres with views across the Weald.

One Tree Hill 2 miles south-east of Sevenoaks, on east side of Knole Park (q.v.). 34 acres said to contain Roman burials.

St Margaret's Bay (q.v.) *Bockell Hill*: 11½ acres of grazing land. *Kingsdown Leas*: 11 acres of clifftop. *Kingsdown Wood*: 8 acres of woodland on Wood Hill, prominent in coastal landscape. *The Leas*: 10 acres along top of chalk cliffs on east side of bay. *Lighthouse Down*: 10 acres, mostly cliff.

Sole Street: Tudor Yeoman's House 1 mile south-west of Cobham, on west side of the B2009. Sixteenth-century house of timber construction restored by Sir Herbert Baker.

Stone-in-Oxney 5 miles south-east of Tenterden. 5 acres of glebe and 26 acres of pasture round church, including the old school.

Toys Hill (q.v.) *Octavia Hill Woodlands*: 103 acres adjoining Toys Hill. *Outridge Farm*: 93½ acres of woodland on north-east slope of Toys Hill, including listed farm and oast buildings (not open). *Parson's Marsh*: 18½ acres of woodland 1½ miles south of Brasted. *Scord's Wood*: 61 acres, west of Ide Hill.

Wrotham Water ½ mile east of Wrotham, on south side of Pilgrims' Way. 260 acres, mainly farmland, at foot of the North Downs. *Great and Little Spratts*: 11½ acres adjoining Wrotham Water on north. *Hognore Farm*: 64 acres on lower slopes of North Downs. *Pilgrims' Way*: 16½ acres of wood and arable land. *Trottiscliffe*: 30 acres on the scarp slope of the North Downs, including some agricultural land and woodland. *Wrotham Water Farm*: 77 acres at foot of North Downs.

Lancashire

Gawthorpe Hall (q.v.): **Habergham Plantation** 2 acres of wood and scrub.

Holcombe Manor, Clitheroe 916 acres of moorland.

Silverdale 1 mile north-west of Carnforth. *Bank House Farm*: 66 acres, including about ⅓ mile of limestone coastal fringe, overlooking the salt-marshes of the Kent estuary. *Castlebarrow*: 21 acres overlooking Morecambe Bay. *Eaves and Waterslack Woods*: 106 acres of wooded hill, including 1-acre quarry. *Lambert's Meadow and Burton Well Wood*: 14 acres. *Low Town Field and High Town Field*: Two fields next to Bank House Farm. *Jack Scout*: 16 acres of coastal limestone pasture and scrub overlooking Kent estuary.

Stubbins West of Stubbins, 5 miles north of Bury, 1 mile north of Ramsbottom. 436 acres, including two farms and six cottages, rising to 800 feet.

Leicestershire

Charnwood Forest: Ulverscroft 6 miles south-west of Loughborough, between the B5350, the B591 and the B587. 84-acre nature reserve on one of highest points of Charnwood Forest. *Rocky Field and Rocky Plantation*: 20 acres.

Lincolnshire

Belton House (q.v.) 9½ acres in Belton village, including post office, smithy, two cottages, Bede Houses and Old School.

Gunby Hall (q.v.) 1,400-acre estate, including fifteen farms.

The Old Rectory, Bratoft Part of Gunby Hall property (q.v.); not open.

Tattershall Castle (q.v.) 15 acres of agricultural land at Castle Farm.

Woolsthorpe Manor, Grantham A traditional farmstead next to the manor with a range of brick and stone buildings.

London

97–100 Cheyne Walk, Chelsea Most of Lindsey House, one of the finest seventeenth-century exteriors in London, built in 1674 on the site of Sir Thomas More's garden. Not open.

Chislehurst (Kent) *Camden Court Land*: A roadside strip with a row of limes. Together with *Oak Bank Estate*, a strip at the top of Station Hill, part of a scheme to preserve Chislehurst Common.

East Sheen Common Adjoining Richmond Park on the north. 53 acres.

Hawkwood (Kent) Between Chislehurst and Orpington. 245 acres of farm and woodland adjoining Petts Wood property.

33 Kensington Square House on west side built in 1695, home of Mrs Patrick Campbell. Not open.

Petts Wood (Kent) Between Chislehurst and Orpington, on west side of the A208. 88 acres of wood and heath.

40, 42 and 44 Queen Anne's Gate, Westminster Part of a street of Queen Anne houses, headquarters of the Trust until 1983. Not open.

'Roman' Bath, 5 Strand Lane Remains of a bath, restored in the seventeenth century. Its origins are disputed.

Selsdon Wood (Surrey) 3 miles east of Croydon, ½ mile south-east of Selsdon. 198½ acres.

Squire's Mount, Hampstead On south-west side of Hampstead Heath. A group of late eighteenth-century buildings and 1½ acres of garden. Not open.

Wandle Properties *Happy Valley*: 2 acres on west bank of River Wandle. *Merton Abbey Wall*: On west bank of River Wandle, running south from Colliers Wood High Street. *Morden Hall Park*: 124 acres, including Morden Hall, the cottage and seventeen other houses (not open). The park is intersected by the Wandle. *Wandle Park*: 2 acres known as Millpond Gardens, behind the Royal Six Bells Inn near the Abbey Wall. *Watermeads*: 13-acre nature reserve on River Wandle.

Merseyside

Liverpool: 20 Forthlin Road, Garston A 1950s brick-and-tile council house, former home of the McCartney family, where the Beatles were formed.

The Wirral (q.v.) *Burton Wood (Cheshire)*: 8 miles north-west of Chester above village of Burton. 20½ acres of woodland, mainly conifers. *Heswall*: 39½ acres of meadow and arable land on the Dee estuary with fine views across to North Wales.

Norfolk

Bale Oaks In the village, 8 miles north-east of Fakenham. A group of ilexes close to Bale church.

Blakeney Point (q.v.) *Freshes*: 196 acres of grazing marshland east of Blakeney. *Friary Farm*: 80 acres, including a listed farmhouse, a windmill and saltmarsh.

Branodunum Roman Fort 23 acres including the site of a former Roman shore fort. Access along the North Norfolk coast footpath.

Bullfer Grove 4½ miles south-west of Holt. 8½ acres of woodland.

Burnham Overy 1 mile north of Burnham Market, on the south-east side of the A149. *Burnham Overy Watermill*: Three-storey mill and maltings dating from late eighteenth century, mill house and two cottages, with 39 acres. Converted to residential accommodation, including two holiday flats. *Duchess's Pightle*: a 1½-acre field on edge of River Burn valley. *The Tower Windmill*: Built in 1816 on brow of hill a few hundred yards east of watermill. Not open.

Darrow Wood 15 acres near Denton village. Contains remains of eleventh-century motte and bailey.

Cawston The duelling stone and the plot on which it stands, close to the old Woodrow Inn on the B1149 Norwich to Holt road.

Holme-next-the-Sea 5½ acres of grass-covered dune, part of Holme Bird Observatory.

Salthouse Broad (q.v.) *Great Eye*: On north coast, ½ mile north of Salthouse, off the A149. About 2 acres of sand and shingle, which is being gradually eroded by the sea.

West Runton ¾ mile south of West Runton station, between Sheringham and Cromer. 71½ acres, including the highest point in Norfolk. Site of iron-working in Saxo-medieval times. *Beeston Regis Heath*: 37 acres with fine views of coast. *Incleborough Hill and Town Hill*:

28 acres of open hill and woodland with magnificent sea views. *Row Heath and the Canadas*: 70½-acre conifer plantation.

Northamptonshire

Brackley Park 3 acres of open space on east side of High Street, Brackley.

Canons Ashby (q.v.): **Hillview** A three-bedroomed cottage and meadow.

Northumberland

Beadnell Dunes ¼ mile north of Beadnell, east of the B1340. 9 acres of sand dunes stretching from the northern edge of Beadnell village to Link House.

Beadnell Lime Kilns ½ mile south-east of Beadnell, 2½ miles south of Seahouses. A group of eighteenth-century lime kilns by the sea.

Buston Links 18¼ acres of sand dunes, to the south of Alnmouth village.

Druridge Bay 2 miles north of Cresswell village, 1½ miles east of the A1068. 99 acres of sand dunes and grass hinterland stretching along a mile of coastline.

Dunstanburgh Castle, Embleton Links and Low Newton-by-the-Sea (q.v.) *Craster*: 273 acres of coastal farmland between village and castle. *Newton Links*: 55 acres of sand dunes and rough grazing, south of the Long Nanny in Beadnell Bay. *Newton Point*: 117 acres of coastal rough grazing and pasture.

Hadrian's Wall Estate (q.v.) *Causeway Farm, Bardon Mill*: 28½ acres. *Crag Lough*: 26½ acres. *Peel Cottage*: Adjacent to the Pennine Way, to be converted into a bothy for climbers and walkers. *Well House*: 23 acres, including 440-yard stretch of the wall.

St Aidan's and Shoreston Dunes 2 miles south-east of Bamburgh, east of the B1340. 60 acres of sand dunes with views of the Farne Islands.

Wallington, Cambo (q.v.) *Codger Fort*: On east edge of estate. Built in 1769 by Thomas Wright of Durham. *The Riding*: A terraced house in Cambo village.

Nottinghamshire

Colston Bassett: Market Cross 10 miles south-east of Nottingham, 5 miles south of Bingham. Eighteenth-century square head surmounted by a ball, with Doric shaft on moulded medieval base.

Oxfordshire

Ashdown (q.v.): **Alfred's Castle** An Iron Age fortified enclosure.

Aston Wood 1½ miles north-west of Stokenchurch, astride the Oxford road. 104 acres of beech wood on an escarpment of the Chilterns.

Burford: Beech Grove Farm A 49-acre Cotswold farm with a stone farmhouse, traditional barns and pasture.

Buscot: The Old Parsonage Adjacent to Buscot village. House built in 1703 of Cotswold stone.

Chastleton: Blue Row A row of four eighteenth-century quasi-almshouses.

Coleshill South of Buscot, astride the B4019. 3,620 acres of farm and woodlands, including Iron Age hill fort on Badbury Hill and Coleshill village with farmhouses and cottages of Cotswold stone.

Coombe End Farm On west side of the B471, 2½ miles north of Pangbourne. 213 acres high up on the Chilterns and a partly seventeenth-century house (not open).

Kencot Manor Farm 5 miles south of Burford, 1½ miles east of the A361. A small early seventeenth-century house with 2½ acres and stone barn. Not open.

Rotherfield Greys: The Lordship of the Manor 3 miles north-west of Henley-on-Thames, off the B481, 1½ miles from Peppard, near Bolt's Cross. 25 acres of common land, including Greys Green and Shepherds Green.

Ruskin Reserve, Cothill 3 miles north-west of Abingdon. 4½ acres of marshy woodland.

South Leigh: Little Bartletts 2½ miles east of Witney. 1 acre with two seventeenth-century cottages (not open to the public).

Steventon: Priory Cottages 4 miles south of Abingdon, ¼ mile west of the A34. Part of former monastic buildings converted into two houses, one of which contains the great hall of the Priory. South Cottage only open.

Watlington: Watlington Park 1 mile south of Watlington Hill (q.v.). 150 acres of beech woods.

Shropshire

Hillcrest: Lee Brockhurst 10 miles north-east of Shrewsbury. 40 acres of pasture and woodland forming part of Lee Hill.

Long Mynd (q.v.) *The Batch Land*: 25 acres of farmland. *Carding Mill Valley*: 250 acres including Burway and Bodbury Hills. *The Wern*: 9½ acres of woodland.

Lydbury North 20 acres of woodland at Walcot.

Morville Hall 3¼ miles west of Bridgnorth on the A458, 5½ miles south-east of Much Wenlock. 134 acres, including an Elizabethan house altered and enlarged in the eighteenth century. *Morville Glebe*: 3½ acres of grazing pasture and stream.

Wenlock Edge (q.v.) *Blakeway Coppice*: 213 acres of mixed woodland and pasture forming 2 miles of the escarpment slope, with a small nineteenth-century cottage. *Harley Bank*: 72 acres of wooded western slope above village of Harley. *Longville Woodland* 154 acres running for about 2 miles along Edge.

Wilderhope Manor (q.v.) 300 acres of farmland and woodland and Wilderhope Manor Farm.

Somerset

Barrington Court (q.v.) Six thatched cottages and a range of model farm buildings constructed by Colonel Arthur Lyle in the 1920s.

Dunster Castle (q.v.) *Grabbist Hill*: 1 mile west of Dunster village. 55 acres of open space with steep wooded hillside giving views over Dunster Castle to Quantocks and Exmoor, 10¾ acres of plantation and 4½ acres of heath.

The Quantocks *Beacon Hill and Bicknoller Hill*: 2½ miles east of Williton, 6 miles west of Holford, off the A39. 626½ acres of moorland, including Iron Age fort of Trendle Ring. Magnificent views. *Broomfield Hill*: 110 acres, 6 miles north of Taunton. *Fyne Court*: 6 miles north of Taunton at Broomfield, 9 miles south-west of Bridgwater. 67 acres, the former pleasure grounds of the now demolished home of the pioneer electrician Andrew Crosse. Headquarters of the Somerset Trust for Nature Conservation and Visitor Centre for the Quantocks. *Great and Marrow Hills, Triscombe*: 226 acres of moor, grass and woodland with fine views to Brendon Hills and Exmoor. *Holford Fields*: 3 miles west of Nether Stowey, on west side of the A39. 27½ acres of pasture and orchard. *Longstone Hill*: 61 acres of open moorland adjoining Willoughby Cleeve. Fine views. *Shervage Wood*: 2 miles west of Nether Stowey, on south side of the A39. 136 acres of oak woodland, oak coppice and moorland with views over the Bristol Channel. *Willoughby Cleeve*: ½ mile west of Holford. 77½ acres of woodland, agricultural land and moorland.

Sedgemoor and Athelney *Cock Hill*: ¾ acre on the crest of the Polden Hills, with views over the Somerset levels. *Ivythorn and Walton Hills*: 89 acres of open land and wood. *Red Hill*: 2½ acres of hilltop on southern edge of Sedgemoor with views to Glastonbury Tor (q.v.), the Quantocks and the Mendips. *Turn Hill*: 1¼ acres looking across the battlefield of Sedgemoor.

Stoke-sub-Hamdon Priory In North Street, just north of the A3088, 2 miles west of Montacute. 2 acres. Fourteenth- and fifteenth-century farm buildings of Ham stone which include the great hall and screens passage of the former residence of the priests of the chantry of St Nicholas established by the Beauchamp family. Great hall only visitable.

Wells: Tor Hill Just east of the city, on the north side of the Shepton Mallet road. 19½ acres, with views of the cathedral.

West Pennard Court Barn 3 miles east of Glastonbury, 7 miles south of Wells, 1½ miles south of West Pennard. Fifteenth-century barn of five bays, with a roof of interesting construction.

Staffordshire

Churnet Valley (q.v.) *Toothill Wood*: West of Alton, north of the B5032 Cheadle to Ashbourne road. 10-acre wood opposite Alton Towers, including viewpoint of Toothill Rock.

Shugborough (q.v.) *Great Haywood Bank*: 63 acres of wood and parkland.

Suffolk

Flatford *Flatford Mill and Willy Lott's House*: On north bank of the Stour, 1 mile south of East Bergholt. 16 acres, including the mill and the mill house dating from the fifteenth century which belonged to John Constable's father and were the subject of some of the artist's most famous paintings. Willy Lott's House dates from the early seventeenth century. Not open. *Bridge Cottage*: 1 mile south of East Bergholt. Sixteenth-century thatched cottage, tearoom, shop and boating facilities with a ¾-acre garden, next to the River Stour and Flatford Mill. *Judas Gap Marsh*: 5½ acres. *Miller's Field*: 19 acres of grazing land. *River Field and Gibbonsgate Pond*: 18½ acres of grazing land and pond adjoining Willy Lott's House. *The Valley Farm*: 17 acres, including a half-timbered fifteenth-century house.

Kyson Hill ¾ mile south of Woodbridge, 1 mile east of junction of the A12 and the B1438. 4 acres of parkland overlooking River Deben.

Lavenham: Lock-up and Mortuary A small brick building in the grounds of the Guildhall (q.v.).

Outney Common, Bungay Six 'goings' or rights of pasturage on the 495-acre common in the loop of the River Waveney.

Pin Mill: Cliff Plantation $\frac{1}{2}$ mile north of Chelmondiston village, 5 miles south-east of Ipswich, on south bank of the River Orwell. 17 acres of natural woodland.

Thorington Hall 2 miles south-east of Stoke-by-Nayland, on north side of the B1068. An oak-framed, plastered, gabled house dating from *c*.1600, extended *c*.1700 and repaired in 1937.

Surrey

Abinger Hammer: Piney Copse $4\frac{1}{2}$-acre wood.

Blackheath $\frac{1}{2}$ mile south of Chilworth and Albury station, on the ridge south of the Guildford to Dorking road. $19\frac{1}{2}$ acres of heather- and pine-clad land.

Bletchingley: Sandhills Estate 3 miles east of Redhill, south of the village of Bletchingley. 419 acres of agricultural land and woods.

Box Hill (q.v.) *West Humble Chapel*: $\frac{1}{2}$ mile from Box Hill station, along the lane to Bookham. The remains of a late twelfth-century chapel, built for those unable to cross the river to Mickleham church.

Brockham: The Big Field An open field of 48 acres.

Cobham: Cedar House Overlooking the River Mole on north side of the A245. A fifteenth-century H-shaped building, altered and enlarged in the seventeenth and eighteenth centuries, with a great hall with an open-timbered roof.

Eashing Bridges and Cottages $1\frac{1}{2}$ miles west of Godalming, just east of the Guildford bypass. A medieval double bridge over the River Wey and a carrier stream, with 5 acres and two cottages (not open to the public).

Eastlands, Weybridge Nineteenth-century house (not open to the public) and 7 acres.

Effingham 56 acres of agricultural land close to National Trust property at Polesden Lacey (q.v.).

Ewell: Hatch Furlong 6 acres.

Frensham Common (q.v.) *Frensham Little Pond*: $66\frac{1}{2}$ acres, including a nature reserve, cottage and boathouse.

Godalming: 116–122 Ockford Road Modernised cottage (not open to the public).

Godalming Navigation (q.v.) *Peasmarsh*: 3 acres of disused railway line surrounded by Trust land.

Grayswood Common 1 mile north of Haslemere, east of the London road. $16\frac{1}{2}$ acres.

Guildford *Shalford Common*: $9\frac{1}{2}$ acres of agricultural land. *Weir House*: Probably mid-eighteenth-century building with nineteenth-century additions, overlooking weir on the River Wey at Millmead, with 5 acres of meadows. Not open.

Hambledon $2\frac{1}{2}$ acres near the church. *Glebe House*: With seven cottages and 24 acres. Not open.

Harewoods At Outwood, 3 miles south-east of Redhill, 2 miles east of Salfords, 2 miles south-east of Bletchingley. 2,034 acres of farms, woods and cottages, including Outwood Common.

Hindhead (q.v.) *Beacon Hill*: $33\frac{3}{4}$ acres of pine-covered heathland on south side of Frensham road. *Nutcombe Down, Tyndall Wood and Craig's Wood*: 107 acres of heath and wooded valley between the Haslemere and Portsmouth roads, south of Hindhead. *Polecat Copse*: 36 acres, mostly woodland, south of Nutcombe Down. *Pollock's Path*: A lane and a small piece of land, 1 mile south-west of Hindhead. *Stoatley Green*: 5 acres, 1 mile north of Haslemere station. *Windy Gap*: 15 acres of heath. *Woodcock Bottom and Whitmore Vale*: $155\frac{1}{2}$ acres of wood and heath, including Golden Valley, on south side of Frensham road.

Hydon's Ball and Hydon Heath 3 miles south of Godalming, $1\frac{1}{2}$ miles west of the B2130. 126 acres of heath and woodland.

Leith Hill (q.v.) North-west of the A29, west of the A24 and south of the A25. *Coldharbour Common*: 104 acres of woodland and open space, including Coldharbour village green, war memorial and cricket pitch. *Duke's Warren*: 4 miles south-west of Dorking, between Wotton and Coldharbour Commons. 193 acres of heath and wood. *Mosses Wood, Cockshot Wood and Tanners Wood*: 79 acres, much of it bluebell wood, between Coldharbour and top of Leith Hill. *Pond Cottage, Broadmoor*: $\frac{1}{2}$ acre. *Severell's Copse*: At Friday Street, 1 mile east of Abinger. 59 acres of mixed woodland on east side of valley.

Little King's Wood On south escarpment of North Downs, above Gomshall. 60 acres of mixed woodland.

Oxted Downs (q.v.) *South Hawke*: $4\frac{1}{2}$ acres of down and woodland. *Hanging Wood*: $4\frac{1}{2}$ acres on south slope of North Downs with fine views.

Park Downs 1 mile south-east of Banstead, overlooking the Chipstead valley. 74-acre open space.

Sandhills Common ½ mile west of Witley station, west of the A283. 11½ acres.

Six Brothers' Field ½ mile south of Chaldon, midway between Caterham and Merstham. 7 acres.

Swan Barn Farm On east edge of Haslemere, north of the B2131. 73 acres of farmland, woodland and chestnut coppice, and pasture.

Thursley: John Freeman Memorial 2 miles north of Hindhead, ½ mile west of the A3. 8 acres protecting the church, a memorial to the poet John Freeman, who is buried in the churchyard.

Sussex: East

Battle: Lake Meadow Opposite the Chequers Hotel. 4½ acres preserving the view to the north.

Exceat Saltings South of Exceat Bridge, on west bank of the Cuckmere river. 4½ acres overlooking the saltings and a small piece of the saltings themselves.

Nap Wood 4 miles south of Tunbridge Wells, on the A267. 107 acres, predominantly oak wood.

Telscombe 3 miles north-west of Newhaven, 1½ miles north of Peacehaven. Much-altered manor house with garden in the village. Not open.

Winchelsea *Crutches Farm*: 281 acres of sheep and arable farm ½ mile west of Winchelsea. *Wickham Manor Farm*: 1 mile south-west of Winchelsea, on road to Pett. 394 acres of farmland, including much of the ancient town of Winchelsea, a much-altered mid-fifteenth-century farmhouse (not open) and 1½ miles of the Royal Military Canal (q.v.).

Wych Cross: The Warren 2½ miles south of Forest Row, just east of the A22. 15 acres of woodland.

Sussex: West

Bosham: Quay Meadow 4 miles west of Chichester, 1 mile south of the A27. 1 acre, between the church and the creek, with associations with King Canute and where Earl Harold set sail for Normandy in 1064.

Donnington: The Old Manor House A Queen Anne manor house (not open) and 11 acres of pasture.

Drovers Estate Astride the Midhurst to Chichester road, north of the Goodwood estate. 1,097 acres of farms, woods and typical Sussex agricultural country.

Durford Heath 2½ miles north-east of Petersfield, on south side of the A3. 62 acres, mostly old oak coppice.

Lavington Common 2 miles south-west of Petworth. 77 acres of heather- and pine-covered heathland with three round barrows.

Marley (West Sussex and Surrey) *Kingsley Green Common*: 2 miles south of Haslemere, on the Chichester road. 7 acres. *Marley Common and Wood*: 132 acres of high common and steep woodland, on west side of the A286. *Marley Combe*: 19 acres. *Marley Heights*: 1½ acres of a viewpoint known as the Terraces.

Pangdean Farm, Pyecombe 80 acres of chalk downland and arable (to be converted back to downland).

Selsfield Common 4 miles south-west of East Grinstead, on east side of the B2028. 7 acres.

Sullington Warren ½ mile east of Storrington, 8 miles north of Worthing, just north of the A283. 63 acres, with views of the North and South Downs, straddled between two lines of bowl barrows.

Terwick: Church Field ¾ mile east of Rogate, on south side of the A272. 9 acres adjoining church.

Warren Hill 8 miles north of Worthing, on west side of the A24, astride the A283. 243 acres, including Washington Common, woods, a farm, a house and eight cottages. Views of Chanctonbury Ring and the South Downs.

Woolbeding 2 miles north-west of Midhurst. 1,102-acre agricultural estate with farms, woods and commons and a house.

Tyne & Wear

Washington Old Hall (q.v.) *Jacobean Garden*: ¾-acre garden overlooked by the Old Hall.

Warwickshire

Earlswood Moat House On south edge of Birmingham, 1 mile east of Earlswood Lakes station. A small, timber-framed house, mainly of the late fifteenth century but much restored, with 65 acres of pasture and woodland. Not open.

Farnborough Hall (q.v.) 588-acre estate with farmland and mixed woodland.

Stratford-upon-Avon: 45/45a Wood Street and 65/66 Henley Street Partly sixteenth-century half-timbered buildings containing three shops.

West Midlands

Knowle: Children's Field Between Kixley Lane and Knowle church, 9 miles south-east of central Birmingham. 3 acres.

Wiltshire

The Combes, Hinton Parva 39 acres of chalk downland with an unimproved hay meadow and medieval lynchets.

Dinton 9 miles west of Salisbury, on north side of the B3089. *Dinton Park*: 205½ acres, including a farm, three cottages, part of an Iron Age hill fort, and Philipps House (q.v.). *Hyde's House*: Wren-style, early eighteenth-century house (not open to the public) incorporating Tudor portions.

Great Chalfield Manor (q.v.) 42½ acres of agricultural land.

Little Clarendon and Lawes Cottage ¼ mile east of Dinton church. 29 acres with a stone late fifteenth-century house (Little Clarendon) and the seventeenth-century stone Lawes Cottage (not open), once the home of the composer William Lawes (1602–45).

Salisbury *Joiner's Hall*: In St Ann Street. Timbered façade of former hall of a livery company, dating from *c*.1550.

Warminster: Boreham Field 6 acres.

White Barrow ¾ mile south of Tilshead, 7 miles north-west of Stonehenge, ¼ mile west of the A360. 3 acres, including a Neolithic long barrow.

Yorkshire: North

Bransdale 6 miles north of Helmsley, on North Yorkshire Moors. 1,925 acres of farmland in a valley surrounded by high moors.

Cayton Bay and Knipe Point, Scarborough 88 acres of cliff and undercliff and 6 acres of agricultural land.

Farndale Woodlands 32¼ acres of mixed woodland in Upper Farndale, 8 miles north of Kirbymoorside, known for wild daffodils.

Fountains Abbey (q.v.) *How Hall Farm*: 27½ acres with a house, and a tower chapel of medieval origin prominently set on a hill near the abbey. *Swanley Grange and land at Mackershaw*: 85 acres of agricultural land and buildings beside the abbey.

Malham Tarn 72 acres of pasture with ancient limestone walls and lynchets below Malham Cove. *Darnbrook Farm*: A 2,868-acre hill farm in a dramatic upland landscape including limestone outcrops, waterfalls, hay meadows and heather moor. *Town Head Barn*: Traditional Dales barn on the edge of Malham village.

Newbiggin East Farm 1 mile north of Filey Brigg. 500 yards of steep dramatic cliff and 25 acres of clifftop.

Ripon: Sanctuary Cross At Sharow, ¾ mile north-east of Ripon. The stump of the only surviving cross marking the limits of sanctuary attached to St Wilfrid's Abbey.

Robin Hood's Bay (q.v.) *Bay Ness Farm*: 176½ acres, including superb cliffs forming northern headland. *Bottom House Farm*: 198 acres with ⅔ mile of spectacular coast, north of Robin Hood's Bay. *Ravenscar*: 260 acres, including 1 mile of coastline and spectacular cliff scenery. *Ravenscar: Bent Rigg Farm*: 96 acres of clifftop, including part of Cleveland Way. *Ravenscar Brickyards*: 16 acres, including a disused quarry and site of former brickworks. *Ravenscar: Church Farm*: 30 acres of pasture. *Ravenscar: Stoupe Brow Farm*: 72 acres of farm and coastal land. *Rocket Post Field*: 12 acres of coastal land and cliff adjoining village. *Smails Moor*: 15-acre cliff field.

Runswick Bay, Whitby 26 acres of heritage coast, including 11 acres of slumped cliff.

Saltwick Nab 1 mile east of Whitby, off the A171 and the A169. 7½ acres of cliffland, including low, rocky nab jutting into sea.

Stainforth Bridge 2½ miles north of Settle, just west of the B6479. A seventeenth-century single-span bridge over the River Ribble.

Staintondale: Rigg Hall Farm Between Hayburn Wyke and Ravenscar. 91½ acres of farmland with over ½ mile of superb cliff.

Yorkshire: West

Hardcastle Crags (q.v.) *Crimsworth Wood*: 9 acres of mixed broadleaved woodland and steep rough grazing. *Gibson Wood*: 44 acres on west bank of Hebden Water. *High Greenwood Wood and Black Dean*: 112 acres, including three small farms and fine woods, west and south of Hebden Water. *Ingham Wood*: 9 acres of mainly beech woodland.

Wales

Clwyd

Glyn Ceiriog 8 miles north-west of Oswestry. 5 acres of meadow and a mile of the Glyn Valley Tramway.

Graig Fawr: Dyserth 2 miles south of Prestatyn. $61\frac{1}{2}$ acres, including a limestone hill, a smallholding and a Site of Special Scientific Interest.

Llangollen: Coed Hyrddyn (Velvet Hill) 76 acres above road from Llangollen to the Horseshoe Pass. Fine views.

Dyfed

Ceibrw Bay, Moylegrove $6\frac{1}{2}$ acres.

Cippin Fach and Gernos, St Dogmaels 106 acres comprising 1 mile of coastline. Views to Llŷn peninsula.

The Colby Estate 973 acres of farm and tranquil woodland, including $\frac{3}{4}$ mile of coastline, 12 farms and smallholdings and 7 cottages. Panoramic views.

Colby Lodge Early nineteenth-century house (not open to the public) designed by a pupil of John Nash, with 28 acres of walled garden and grounds, in a beautiful, secluded wooded valley.

Dolaucothi Estate At Pumpsaint, on the A482, between Llanwrda and Lampeter. 2,522 acres of farm and woodland extending along Cothi valley from Pumpsaint village, including Dolaucothi Arms Hotel and Dolaucothi Gold Mine (q.v.) and several cottages in Pumpsaint.

Lawrenny 71-acre hanging wood on east side of Castle Reach of River Cleddau.

Little Milford On the Western Cleddau, 3 miles south of Haverfordwest. 72-acre woodland estate with three houses.

Llanerchaeron (q.v.), **Pontbrenmydyr** Mid-eighteenth-century, limewashed cob-walled cottage.

Llanrhian: Barry Island Farm 200 acres of coastal farmland.

Llanunwas Just west of Solva, linking Trust-owned Morfa Common and land in Solva on Pembrokeshire coast. 141 acres of farmland, comprising 2 miles of rugged coastline, traversed by the coastal footpath. Iron Age promontory fort at Porth-y-Rhaw.

Lochtyn, Llangranog 213 acres of farmland just north-east of village, including $1\frac{1}{2}$ miles of cliff, an island and two beaches. Splendid views.

Long House Farm Near Abercastle. 151 acres of farmland comprising $2\frac{1}{2}$ miles of scenic and rugged coastline with two small islands: Ynys-y-Castell and Ynys Daullyn. Iron Age promontory fort.

Lydstep Headland 4 miles south-west of Tenby, $1\frac{1}{2}$ miles east of Manorbier. 54 acres of headland.

Manorbier Bay: Manorbier Cliff 48 acres, including red sandstone cliffs with views west to St Govan's Head.

Mwnt On the coast about 4 miles north of Cardigan. 98 acres of coastland.

Mynachdy'r Graig 153 acres of coastal farm with dramatic cliffs and views of Cardigan Bay.

Newquay to Cwm Tydu *Caerllan Farm*: 73 acres with 880 yards of coastline. *Coybal*: 37 acres of coastal land, 1 mile south-west of Newquay. *Craig-yr-Adar*: 1 mile of cliffland adjoining Coybal property. *Cwm Soden*: 53 acres of partly wooded coastal valley. *Cwm Tydu*: Lime kilns and 2 acres at mouth of valley. *Llwynwermod*: 17 acres of woodland and meadow at head of Cwm Soden valley. *Penparc Farm*: 120 acres including 1 mile of coastline and $\frac{3}{4}$ mile of westerly bluff of valley. *Pen-y-Graig Farm*: A 76-acre coastal farm near Newquay, with a small beach, an island and an Iron Age hill fort. *Pottre*: 20 acres of partly wooded valley slope, adjoining Llwynwermod Wood and running down to the Ferwig river.

Penbryn *Llanborth Farm*: 95 acres, with $\frac{1}{2}$ mile of coastline immediately north-west of hamlet. *Pencwm*: 29 acres of woodland and pasture west of Llanborth Farm leading to $\frac{1}{4}$ mile of coast.

Ponterwyd: Bryn Bras 12 miles east of Aberystwyth, just south of the A44. 234-acre sheep farm above magnificent gorge of Rheidol.

St Bride's Bay (q.v.) *Carn Nwchwn to Nine Wells*: 111 acres between St David's and Solva. *Lower Treginnis Farm*: 250 acres; the most westerly mainland farm in Wales, with views to Ramsey Island and across the bay. *Marloes: West Hook, Trehill and Runwayskiln Farms*: 524 acres on south arm of bay. *Pointz Castle*: $\frac{1}{3}$ acre with Norman motte. *Pwll Caerog Farm*: a 244-acre coastal farm with farmhouse, two Iron Age promontory forts and $\frac{1}{2}$ mile of coastline. *St David's*: 234 acres, 2 miles north-west of St David's. *St Elvis, Solva*: 276 acres, immediately east of Solva harbour. *Upper Solva to Cwm Bach, Newgale*: 203 acres. *Upper Treginnis*: 116 acres of farmland with a range of nineteenth-century buildings (not open) on the St David's Head peninsula (q.v.). *Whitesands Bay to Porth-clais*: 81 acres of cliffs.

St David's Commons 860 acres of common between St David's and Fishguard and around both cities.

Tregoning Hill On east headland of Towy estuary, 1 mile south of Ferryside. 20 acres of cliffland with views of Carmarthen Bay.

Wharley Point, Llanstephan 386 acres of farm and cliffland at the confluence of the Taf and Towy estuaries.

Williamston Park The promontory between the Creswell and Carew rivers, south-east of Lawrenny. 52 acres of one of Carew Castle's two medieval deer parks, extensively quarried in the eighteenth and nineteenth centuries and now a nature reserve.

Gwent

Betws Newydd 4 miles north of Usk, 4 miles west of Raglan. *Coed-y-Bwynydd (Coed Arthur)*: 25-acre hilltop with views of Usk valley.

Clytha Park Estate 3 miles west of Raglan. 371½-acre estate, including house set in parkland, two farms and a late eighteenth-century Gothic castle.

Pant Skirrid Wood and Caer Wood 3 miles north-east of Abergavenny. 35 acres of mixed hardwood and conifers astride approach to Skirrid Fawr (q.v.).

Park Lodge Farm, Llwyndu 489 acres near Abergavenny.

Gwynedd

Aberglaslyn Pass (q.v.) *Coed Aberglaslyn*: 68 acres of mixed woodland rising steeply above Pont Aberglaslyn to the head of the pass. *Bryn-y-Bont, Nantmor*: 45 acres of mainly pasture with outcrops of woodland. *Bryn-y-Felin, Beddgelert*: 45 acres, including wooded bank, open grassland with old copper workings and pasture running down to the River Glaslyn, with monument known as Gelert's Grave. *Parc Bach*: 5 acres of oak woodland.

Anelog: Tan-y-Fron A 14½-acre smallholding with a farmhouse and grazing rights on Anelog Common.

Beddgelert *Coed Cae Morys*: 28 acres of broadleaf woodland on western side of Glaslyn valley. *Craflwyn Hall Estate*: 230 acres of mountain, a period residence, farm buildings and cottages. *Hafod y Porth*: 937 acres of farmland, including farm buildings. *Llywelyn Cottage*: A largely seventeenth-century, traditional stone and

slate Welsh cottage used as an information centre and shop.

Cadair Ifan Goch On east side of the Conwy valley, 3 miles north of Llanrwst, ½ mile east of the A470. 1½-acre rocky promontory.

Cae Glan-y-Mor On the Menai Strait in Anglesey between road and railway bridges. 11 acres preserving view over strait and Snowdon range. *Ynys Welltog*: ½-acre rocky island in the Menai Strait.

Carreg Farm, Aberdaron 143 acres of headland adjoining coastal slopes of Dinas Fawr and Dinas Bach, an Area of Outstanding Natural Beauty.

Cemaes On east side of Cemaes Bay, Anglesey. 51 acres of cliff and agricultural land. *Tyn Lan, Llanbadrig*: Two small coastal fields of two acres.

Cemlyn (q.v.) *Felin Gafnan and Trwyn Pencarreg, Anglesey*: 36 acres of coastal smallholding and rocky headland. *Pancarreg*: 25 acres of pasture and ¼ mile of unspoilt coast.

Cregennan (q.v.) *Ffynnon Arthog*: 115 acres on north-east slope of Braich Ddu.

Derlwyn 2 miles north-west of Ganllwyd village, 6 miles north-west of Dolgellau. 114½ acres of rough heather moorland and half a small lake.

Dinas Gynfor 2 miles north-east of Cemaes, Anglesey, 5 miles west of Amlwch. 4½ acres of cliffland, the northernmost point of Wales, including part of Iron Age promontory fort.

Dinas Oleu Above south end of Barmouth. 4½ acres of cliffland overlooking Cardigan Bay, the first property acquired by the Trust (in 1895), and ½ acre of steep grass-covered bank. *Cae Fadog*: 12 acres of cliffland above Barmouth.

Dolobran and Braich-melyn 1 mile north-west of Dinas Mawddwy, 9 miles east of Dolgellau. Two Welsh mountain farms totalling 120 acres and rights of pasturage over a further 121 acres.

Gamallt 3 miles north-east of Ffestiniog. 300 acres of moorland with half of two lakes.

Glan Faenol 3 miles south-west of Bangor, 7 miles north of Caernarfon, off the A487. 314 acres of farmland and woodland bordering the Menai Strait.

Hafod Lwyfog 5 miles north-east of Beddgelert, ½ mile east of the A498. 314 acres overlooking Llyn Gwynant.

Harlech *Allt-y-Mor*: 1 mile south of Harlech, on the Barmouth road. 1¼ acres with footpath to sea. *Coed*

Llechwedd: Just north of Harlech, below the B4573. 11¼ acres with views over bay.

Llandanwg: Y Maes Immediately south of Llandanwg and adjoining the Artro estuary. 24 acres surrounding the medieval church of St Tanwg.

Llanddona: Bryn Offa and Ffynnon Oer, Anglesey 1½ acres of common and adjoining clifftop field overlooking Red Wharf Bay.

Llangoed: Fedw Fawr, Anglesey 45½ acres of common.

Llanrwst: Tu Hwnt I'r Bont At west end of old bridge over the Conwy, on the B5106. A fifteenth-century stone building once used as a courthouse.

Lledr Valley: Rhiw Goch On the A470, about 2 miles north-east of Dolwyddelan. 163 acres with views over valley.

Morfa Bychan 1¼ miles south-west of Porthmadog. 85 acres of golf course and sand dunes with about ½ mile of seashore.

Mynachdy, Llanfairynghorny, Anglesey 412 acres of farmland including 3¼ miles of coastline.

Mynydd Bychestyn, near Aberdaron 46 acres of common between Mynydd Gwyddel and Pen-y-Cil.

Penarfynydd, Rhiw 245 acres of agricultural land and rough clifftop grazing with magnificent views of Llŷn peninsula and Meirionnydd coast.

Pen-y-Graig, Rhydwyn, Llanrhuddlad, Anglesey 8 acres of former agricultural land with fine views over Holyhead Bay.

Pistyll Farm, Nefyn 240 acres of farmland, including a mile of coastline.

Plas-yn-Rhiw Estate, Llŷn (q.v.) *Foel Felin Wynt*: 6-acre hill north-west of Mynytho, with extensive views seaward and of Snowdon range. *Mynydd Cilan*: 70 acres of cliff with extensive views. *Mynydd Rhiw*: 146 acres of common on summit. *Porth Orion*: 9 acres of cliffland adjoining Mynydd Anelog and 1 acre adjoining Dinas Fawr and Dinas Bach (q.v.). *Porth Ysgo*: 22 acres on south coast of Llŷn; beautiful sandy bay surrounded by cliffs with waterfall and stream. *Rhiw Wood*: 150 acres of conifer, wood and heath. *Tan-yr-Ardd with Penmynydd*: 19½ acres of moorland on slopes of Mynydd Rhiw, with small traditional cottage.

Porth Gwylan 1 mile east of Tudweiliog on the Llŷn peninsula. 54 acres, including the harbour of Porth Gwylan.

Rhyd 3 miles north-west of Maentwrog. 114 acres of enclosed mountain bordering Rhyd, with fine views over Tremadog Bay.

Swtan, Church Bay, Anglesey 13½ acres of coastal land.

Tal-y-Braich Uchaf 2½ miles west of Capel Curig. A sheepwalk of 1,075½ acres in the Ogwen valley next to the Trust's Carneddau property (q.v.), and including the summit of Pen yr Helgi Du.

Ty Gwyn and Ty'n y Maes Farms, Nant Ffrancon, Bethesda Two farms of 494 acres and two cottages adjoining Trust's Penrhyn estate (q.v.).

Tywyn-y-Fach (Sandburrows), Abersoch At north-east end of Abersoch, 6 miles south-west of Pwllheli. 19 acres of sandhills covered with thorn scrub and bracken.

Uwchmynydd Fields 16 acres on the Llŷn peninsula between Mynydd Mawr and Mynydd Bychestyn, forming part of an unspoilt ancient field pattern.

Y Llethr 4½ miles north of the A496 at Borthwnog, Dolgellau. 250 acres, including summit of Y Llethr, the highest peak of the Rhinogau; adjoins sheepwalks of Dolmelynllyn estate (q.v.).

Ynysgain 1 mile west of Criccieth. 198 acres comprising about 1 mile of coastland and foreshore, including the mouth of the Afon Dwyfor.

Ynys Tywyn On south-east side of Porthmadog, near the harbour entrance. A 2-acre rocky knoll with fine views.

Powys

Brecon Beacons (q.v.) *Berthllwyd Farm*: 163 acres of sheep farm including a Site of Special Scientific Interest. *Carno Wood*: 37 acres. *Cwmoergwm*: 93 acres of farmland at head of a mountain valley 3 miles south of Llanfrynach.

Henrhyd Falls and Graigllech Woods 11 miles north of Neath, midway between the A4067 and the A4109. 188 acres, including 37½ acres of deep wooded ravine and the famous waterfalls.

West Glamorgan

Gower Peninsula (q.v.) *The Bulwark*: A hill fort and 87 acres of common. *Notthill*: 5 acres of rocky and bracken-covered hill with wide sea views, 9 miles south-west of Swansea, ½ mile east of Penmaen. *Penmaen Common*: 36 acres. *Pennard Cliff*: 248 acres with views of Somerset coast from Pwll-du Head, 7 miles south-west of Swansea. *Pilton Green and Pitton Cross*: Two small commons totalling 23 acres, 2 miles and 3 miles east of Rhossili. *Pitton Cliff*: 38 acres. *Raised Terrace*: 55 acres of narrow coastal plateau between Rhossili Down and Rhossili Bay, including a nineteenth-century house and stone outbuildings. *Rhossili Down* (q.v.): Nos. 2 and 3 Coastguard Cottages, now an information centre. *Rhossili: The Vile*: 65 acres within the medieval field system. *Ryers Down*: 35 acres. *Thurba Head*: 53 acres, with an early earthwork. *Welsh Moor*: 146-acre common.

Northern Ireland

Co. Antrim

Carrick-a-Rede (q.v.) *Larrybane*: 58 acres of coastline, including disused basalt quarry and limeworks.

Cushleake Mountain 2,963 acres of blanket peat bog, important for breeding birds, rare plants and butterflies.

Fair Head and Murlough Bay (q.v.) *Murlough Cottage, Bothy and Land*: 17 acres of coastline in Murlough Bay.

Giant's Causeway (q.v.) *Innisfree Farm* 62 acres immediately south of Giant's Causeway. *Land at Aird*: 94 acres of coastal heathland and farmland of high landscape and nature conservation value.

Island Magee, Larne *Ballykeel*: 36 acres of semi-improved grassland, cliff face and undercliff. *Skernaghan Point*: 113 acres of coastal land.

Layde 2 miles north of Cushendall. Coastal path leading to small beach.

Torr Head to Coolranny Path 7½ acres acquired for a coastal path.

White Park Bay: 'Rossneath' A three-bay cottage with garden at Portbraddan.

Co. Armagh

Ballymoyer 4 miles north-east of Newtownhamilton, 8 miles west of Newry. 49 acres of wooded glen.

Derrymore House 1½ miles north-west of Newry. A thatched eighteenth-century manor house, the home of Isaac Corry, Speaker of the Irish House of Commons, and 48-acre park.

Co. Down

Ballymacormick Point (q.v.) *Cockle Island*: ½ acre.

Blockhouse Island and Green Island Two islands totalling 2 acres at the mouth of Carlingford Lough. Important nesting sites for common, Arctic and roseate terns.

Castle Ward (q.v.) *Strangford Bay Path*: From Castle Ward to Strangford village, along the east shore of Strangford Bay.

Clough Castle 24 miles south-east of Belfast, 5 miles north-east of Dundrum. Norman motte and bailey with 1 acre.

Lisnabreeny, Cregagh Glen 1⅓ acres of wooded glen completing ownership on both sides of the river.

Mount Stewart (q.v.) *Clay Gate Lodge*: 200 Portaferry Road, Newtownards. Single-storey gate lodge with stone walls and slate roof and ⅛ acre.

Orlock Point Near Groomsport, 3 miles north-east of Bangor on the A2. 29 acres.

Strangford Lough (q.v.) *Anne's Point*: 12 acres of freshwater marsh and conifer woodland. *Ballyhenry Island*: 5-acre rocky island overlooked by Castle Ward (q.v.). *Barr Hall and Green Island*: 17 acres in a narrow strip above high-water mark but including some foreshore and salt-marsh. *Darragh Island*: 21-acre island north of Ringhaddy Sound. *Gibb's Island*: 13 acres of island and mainland linked by a causeway. *Glastry Ponds*: 40 acres of disused clay pits and adjoining land. *Greyabbey Bay*: 3,608 acres of land, foreshore and sea bed. *Horse Island*: 46 acres of mainland and island south of Kircubbin. *Janes's Shore, Downpatrick*: 5¾ acres of woodland on banks of River Quoile. *Salt Island and Green Island*: 68 acres. *Taggart Island*: 94 acres. *Walter Meadow and Woods*: 26 acres north of Portaferry.

Co. Fermanagh

Tonregee Island Almost 5 acres forming part of the Belle Isle estate.

Co. Londonderry

Rough Fort 1 mile west of Limavady, on the Londonderry Road. An unexcavated rath or ring fort of 1 acre, surrounded by Scots firs, oaks and beeches.

Useful Addresses

Headquarters
36 Queen Anne's Gate, London SW1H 9AS
0171-222 9251

London Information Centre for personal callers
Blewcoat School, 23 Caxton Street, London SW1H 0PY
0171-222 2877

Membership
PO Box 39, Bromley, Kent BR1 3XL
0181-315 1111

Finance; Internal Audit; Trading; Volunteer Unit
Heywood House, Westbury, Wiltshire BA13 4NA
(01373) 858787

Cornwall
Lanhydrock, Bodmin PL30 4DE (01208) 74281

Devon
Killerton House, Broadclyst, Exeter EX5 3LE
(01392) 881691

Wessex (Avon, Dorset, Somerset, Wiltshire)
Eastleigh Court, Bishopstrow, Warminster,
Wiltshire BA12 9HW (01985) 843600

Southern (includes Hampshire, the Isle of Wight,
South-Western Greater London, Surrey and West
Sussex)
Polesden Lacey, Dorking, Surrey RH5 6BD
(01372) 453401

Kent & East Sussex (includes South-Eastern
Greater London)
The Estate Office, Scotney Castle, Lamberhurst,
Tunbridge Wells, Kent TN3 8JN (01892) 890651

East Anglia (Cambridgeshire, Essex, Norfolk,
Suffolk)
Blickling, Norwich NR11 6NF (01263) 733471

Thames & Chilterns (Buckinghamshire,
Bedfordshire, Berkshire, Hertfordshire, London
north of the Thames, and Oxfordshire)
Hughenden Manor, High Wycombe,
Bucks HP14 4LA (01494) 528051

Severn (Gloucestershire, Hereford & Worcester,
Warwickshire)
Mythe End House, Tewkesbury, Glos GL20 6EB
(01684) 850051

South Wales (Dyfed, Gwent, West Glamorgan,
southern part of Powys)
The King's Head, Bridge Street, Llandeilo,
Dyfed SA19 6BB (01558) 822800

North Wales (Clwyd, Gwynedd, northern part
of Powys)
Trinity Square, Llandudno, Gwynedd LL30 2DE
(01492) 860123

Mercia (Cheshire, Merseyside, Shropshire,
Greater Manchester, most of Staffordshire, part of
West Midlands)
Attingham Park, Shrewsbury, Shropshire SY4 4TP
(01743) 709343

East Midlands (Derbyshire, Leicestershire,
Lincolnshire, Northamptonshire, Nottinghamshire,
South Humberside, parts of Cheshire, Greater
Manchester, Staffordshire, South Yorkshire and
West Yorkshire)
Clumber Park Stableyard, Worksop, Notts S80 3BE
(01909) 486411

Yorkshire (includes North, South and West
Yorkshire, Cleveland and North Humberside)
Goddards, 27 Tadcaster Road, Dringhouses,
York YO2 2QG (01904) 702021

North-West (Cumbria and Lancashire)
The Hollens, Grasmere, Ambleside,
Cumbria LA22 9QZ (015394) 35599

Northumbria (Durham, Northumberland and
Tyne & Wear)
Scots' Gap, Morpeth, Northumberland NE61 4EG
(01670) 774691

Northern Ireland
Rowallane House, Saintfield, Ballynahinch,
Co. Down BT24 7LH (01238) 510721

Royal Oak Foundation, Inc.
285 West Broadway, Suite 400, N.Y., N.Y. 10013–
2299, USA (001-212 966 6565)

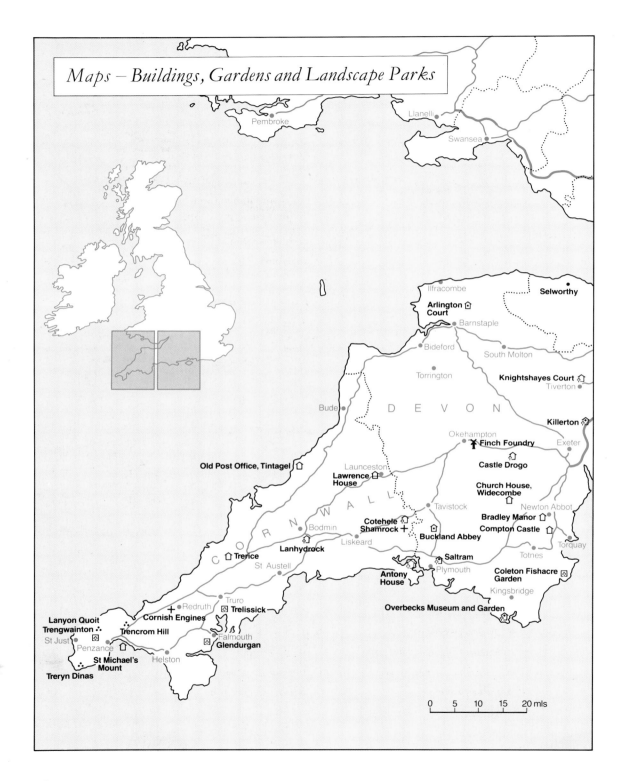

Maps – Buildings, Gardens and Landscape Parks

Pembroke

Llanelli

Swansea

Ilfracombe

Selworthy

Arlington Court

Barnstaple

Bideford

South Molton

Torrington

Knightshayes Court

Tiverton

D E V O N

Bude

Killerton

Okehampton

Exeter

Finch Foundry

Old Post Office, Tintagel

Castle Drogo

Launceston

Lawrence House

Church House, Widecombe

Newton Abbot

C O R N W A L L

Tavistock

Bradley Manor

Bodmin

Cotehele Shamrock

Compton Castle

Torquay

Lanhydrock

Liskeard

Buckland Abbey

Trerice

Totnes

St Austell

Saltram

Plymouth

Coleton Fishacre Garden

Antony House

Kingsbridge

Truro

Redruth

Cornish Engines

Trelissick

Overbecks Museum and Garden

Lanyon Quoit

Trengwainton

Trencrom Hill

St Just

Penzance

Falmouth

Glendurgan

St Michael's Mount

Helston

Treryn Dinas

0   5   10   15   20 mls

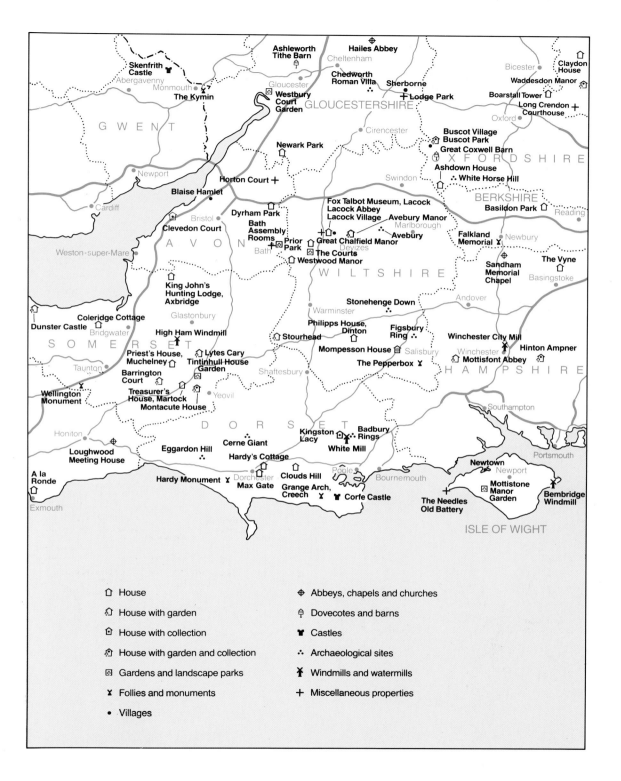

Skenfrith Castle
Abergavenny
Monmouth
The Kymin

G W E N T

Newport

Cardiff

Ashleworth Tithe Barn
Cheltenham
Hailes Abbey
Bicester
Claydon House
Chedworth Roman Villa
Sherborne
Waddesdon Manor
Gloucester
Westbury Court Garden
Lodge Park
Boarstall Tower
Long Crendon Courthouse
GLOUCESTERSHIRE
Oxford
Buscot Village
Cirencester
Buscot Park
Great Coxwell Barn
Newark Park
OXFORDSHIRE
Ashdown House
Swindon
White Horse Hill
Horton Court
BERKSHIRE
Blaise Hamlet
Fox Talbot Museum, Lacock
Lacock Abbey
Basildon Park
Reading
Dyrham Park
Lacock Village
Avebury Manor
Marlborough
Bristol
Bath Assembly Rooms
Avebury
Clevedon Court
Great Chalfield Manor
Falkland Memorial
Newbury
A V O N
Prior Park
Devizes
The Vyne
Bath
The Courts
Sandham Memorial Chapel
Weston-super-Mare
Westwood Manor
W I L T S H I R E
Basingstoke
King John's Hunting Lodge, Axbridge
Stonehenge Down
Andover
Coleridge Cottage
Glastonbury
Warminster
Dunster Castle
Bridgwater
Philipps House, Dinton
Figsbury Ring
Winchester City Mill
High Ham Windmill
Stourhead
Hinton Ampner
S O M E R S E T
Mompesson House
Salisbury
Winchester
Mottisfont Abbey
Taunton
Priest's House, Muchelney
Lytes Cary
Tintinhull House Garden
The Pepperbox
H A M P S H I R E
Barrington Court
Shaftesbury
Wellington Monument
Treasurer's House, Martock
Montacute House
Yeovil
Southampton
Cerne Giant
Kingston Lacy
Badbury Rings
Newtown
Honiton
Loughwood Meeting House
Eggardon Hill
Hardy's Cottage
White Mill
Newport
Portsmouth
A la Ronde
D O R S E T
Hardy Monument
Dorchester
Clouds Hill
Poole
Mottistone Manor Garden
Exmouth
Max Gate
Grange Arch, Creech
Bournemouth
Bembridge Windmill
Corfe Castle
The Needles Old Battery
ISLE OF WIGHT

🏠 House

🏠 House with garden

🏠 House with collection

🏠 House with garden and collection

▣ Gardens and landscape parks

✗ Follies and monuments

• Villages

⊕ Abbeys, chapels and churches

🕊 Dovecotes and barns

♜ Castles

∴ Archaeological sites

🗼 Windmills and watermills

+ Miscellaneous properties

397

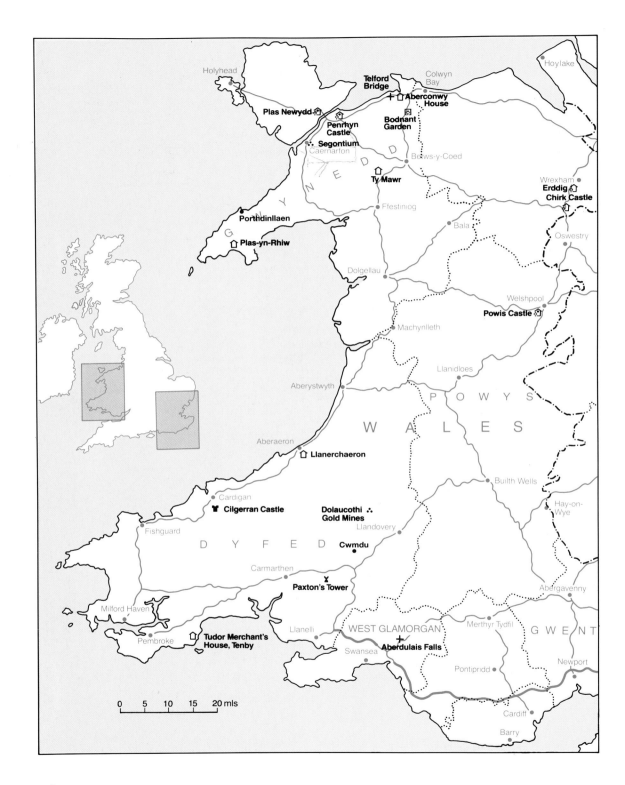

Holyhead

Colwyn
Bay

Hoylake

**Telford
Bridge**

Plas Newydd 🏠 **Aberconwy
House**

**Penrhyn
Castle** **Bodnant
Garden**

Segontium
Caernarfon

Betws-y-Coed

G W Y N E D D

Ty Mawr

Ffestiniog

Wrexham

Erddig
Chirk Castle

Bala

Oswestry

Porthdinllaen

Plas-yn-Rhiw

Dolgellau

Welshpool

Powis Castle 🏠

Machynlleth

Llanidloes

P O W Y S

Aberystwyth

W A L E S

Aberaeron

Llanerchaeron

Builth Wells

Cardigan

Hay-on-
Wye

Cilgerran Castle

**Dolaucothi
Gold Mines**

Llandovery

Fishguard

D Y F E D

Cwmdu

Carmarthen

Abergavenny

Paxton's Tower

Milford Haven

Llanelli

WEST GLAMORGAN

Merthyr Tydfil

G W E N T

Pembroke

**Tudor Merchant's
House, Tenby**

Swansea

Aberdulais Falls

Newport

Pontipridd

Cardiff

Barry

0   5   10   15   20 mls

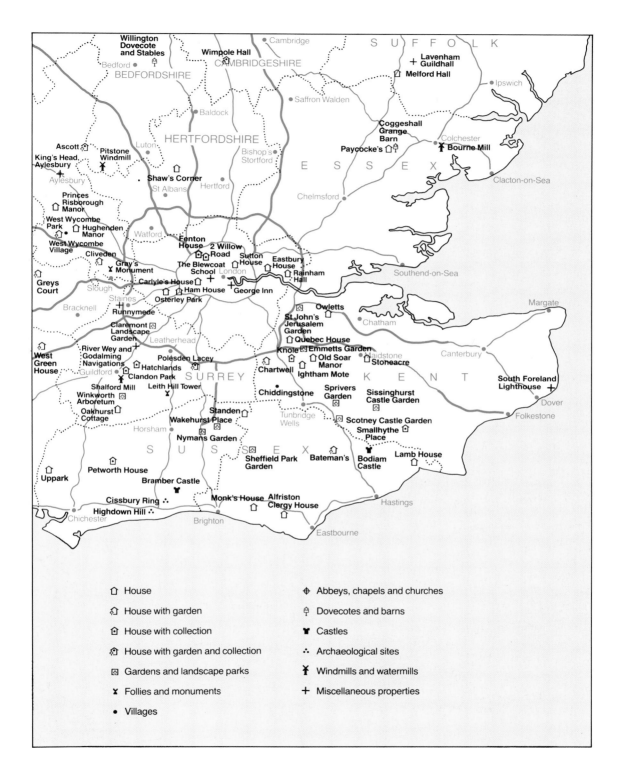

Willington Dovecote and Stables
Wimpole Hall
CAMBRIDGESHIRE
Cambridge
SUFFOLK
Lavenham Guildhall
Melford Hall
Ipswich
Bedford
BEDFORDSHIRE
Saffron Walden
Baldock
HERTFORDSHIRE
Luton
Bishop's Stortford
Coggeshall Grange Barn
Colchester
Paycocke's
Bourne Mill
Ascott
Pitstone Windmill
King's Head Aylesbury
Aylesbury
Shaw's Corner
St Albans
Hertford
ESSEX
Clacton-on-Sea
Chelmsford
Princes Risborough Manor
West Wycombe Park
Hughenden Manor
West Wycombe Village
Cliveden
Watford
St Albans
Fenton House
2 Willow Road
Sutton House
Eastbury House
Southend-on-Sea
Gray's Monument
Carlyle's House
The Blewcoat School
London
Rainham Hall
Margate
Greys Court
Slough
Staines
Ham House
George Inn
Osterley Park
Bracknell
Runnymede
Owletts
Chatham
Claremont Landscape Garden
Leatherhead
St John's Jerusalem Garden
Quebec House
Canterbury
West Green House
River Wey and Godalming Navigations
Polesden Lacey
Hatchlands
Knole
Emmetts Garden
Old Soar Manor
Stoneacre
Maidstone
KENT
South Foreland Lighthouse
Guildford
Clandon Park
SURREY
Chartwell
Ightham Mote
Dover
Shalford Mill
Leith Hill Tower
Chiddingstone
Sprivers Garden
Sissinghurst Castle Garden
Folkestone
Winkworth Arboretum
Oakhurst Cottage
Standen
Wakehurst Place
Tunbridge Wells
Scotney Castle Garden
Smallhythe Place
Horsham
Nymans Garden
SUSSEX
Sheffield Park Garden
Bateman's
Bodiam Castle
Lamb House
Uppark
Petworth House
Bramber Castle
Cissbury Ring
Highdown Hill
Chichester
Monk's House
Alfriston Clergy House
Brighton
Hastings
Eastbourne

House
House with garden
House with collection
House with garden and collection
Gardens and landscape parks
Follies and monuments
Villages

Abbeys, chapels and churches
Dovecotes and barns
Castles
Archaeological sites
Windmills and watermills
Miscellaneous properties

399

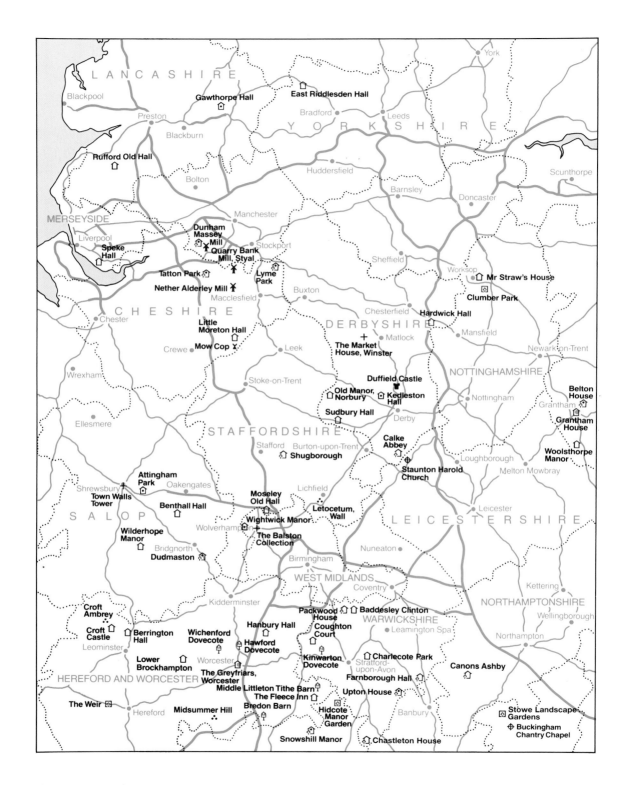

LANCASHIRE

Blackpool

Gawthorpe Hall

East Riddlesden Hall

Preston

YORKSHIRE

Blackburn

Bradford

Leeds

York

Rufford Old Hall

Bolton

Huddersfield

Barnsley

Doncaster

Scunthorpe

MERSEYSIDE

Manchester

Liverpool

Dunham Massey

Stockport

Sheffield

Worksop

Speke Hall

Mill

Quarry Bank Mill, Styal

Mr Straw's House

Tatton Park

Lyme Park

Clumber Park

Nether Alderley Mill

Buxton

Chesterfield

Macclesfield

Hardwick Hall

Chester

CHESHIRE

DERBYSHIRE

Matlock

Mansfield

Newark-on-Trent

Little Moreton Hall

Crewe

Mow Cop

Leek

The Market House, Winster

NOTTINGHAMSHIRE

Wrexham

Stoke-on-Trent

Duffield Castle

Nottingham

Belton House

Ellesmere

Old Manor, Norbury

Kedleston Hall

Grantham

STAFFORDSHIRE

Sudbury Hall

Derby

Grantham House

Stafford

Burton-upon-Trent

Calke Abbey

Loughborough

Woolsthorpe Manor

Shugborough

Staunton Harold Church

Melton Mowbray

Attingham Park

Oakengates

Lichfield

Leicester

Shrewsbury

Town Walls Tower

Moseley Old Hall

Letocetum, Wall

LEICESTERSHIRE

SALOP

Benthall Hall

Wolverhampton

Wightwick Manor

Nuneaton

Wilderhope Manor

Bridgnorth

The Balston Collection

Dudmaston

Birmingham

WEST MIDLANDS

Coventry

Kettering

NORTHAMPTONSHIRE

Kidderminster

Croft Ambrey

Packwood House

Baddesley Clinton

WARWICKSHIRE

Wellingborough

Croft Castle

Berrington Hall

Wichenford Dovecote

Hanbury Hall

Coughton Court

Leamington Spa

Northampton

Leominster

Hawford Dovecote

Worcester

Lower Brockhampton

Kinwarton Dovecote

Charlecote Park

Canons Ashby

Farnborough Hall

Stratford-upon-Avon

The Greyfriars, Worcester

HEREFORD AND WORCESTER

Middle Littleton Tithe Barn

Upton House

The Fleece Inn

Bredon Barn

The Weir

Hereford

Midsummer Hill

Hidcote Manor Garden

Banbury

Stowe Landscape Gardens

Snowshill Manor

Chastleton House

Buckingham Chantry Chapel

400

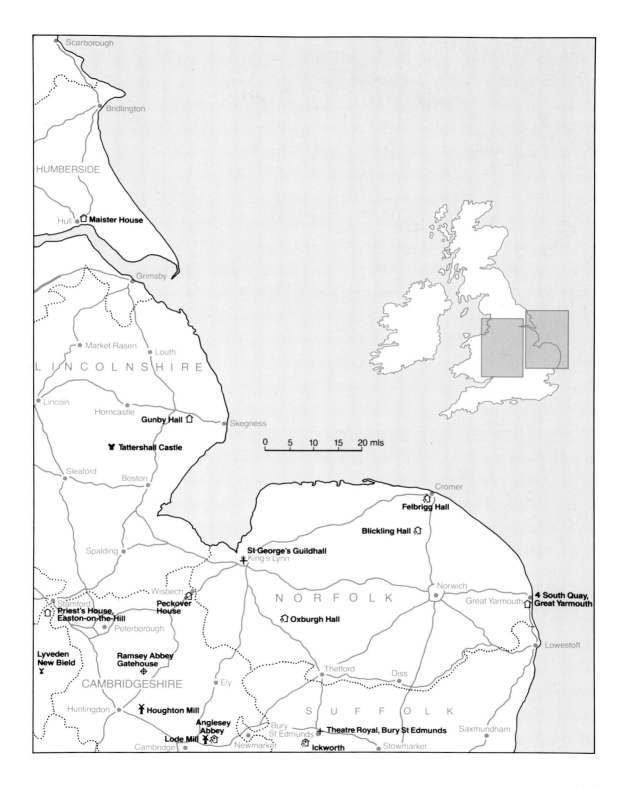

Scarborough

Bridlington

HUMBERSIDE

Hull □ **Maister House**

Grimsby

LINCOLNSHIRE

Market Rasen ● ● Louth

Lincoln ●

Horncastle ●

Gunby Hall □ ● Skegness

♈ **Tattershall Castle**

Sleaford ●

Boston ●

Cromer

♙ **Felbrigg Hall**

Blickling Hall ♙

Spalding ●

St George's Guildhall
King's Lynn ✙

Wisbech ●

Peckover House ♙

Stamford ●

Priest's House, Easton-on-the-Hill ⌂

NORFOLK

Norwich ●

Great Yarmouth ● ⌂ **4 South Quay, Great Yarmouth**

♙ **Oxburgh Hall**

Peterborough ●

Lowestoft ●

Lyveden New Bield ⸸

Ramsey Abbey Gatehouse ⊕

CAMBRIDGESHIRE

Ely ●

Thetford ● Diss ●

SUFFOLK

Huntingdon ●

⸸ **Houghton Mill**

Anglesey Abbey

Lode Mill ✹⌂

Cambridge ● Newmarket ●

Bury St Edmunds ✙ **Theatre Royal, Bury St Edmunds** Saxmundham ●

♙ **Ickworth** Stowmarket ●

0   5   10   15   20 mls

401

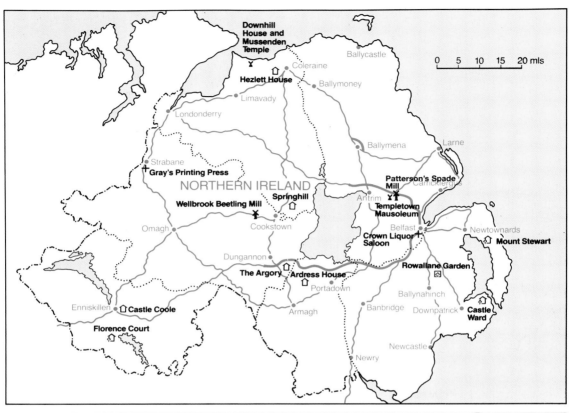

Downhill House and Mussenden Temple
Ballycastle
0 5 10 15 20 mls
Coleraine
Hezlett House
Ballymoney
Limavady
Londonderry
Ballymena
Larne
Strabane
Gray's Printing Press
NORTHERN IRELAND
Patterson's Spade Mill
Carrickfergus
Springhill
Antrim
Wellbrook Beetling Mill
Templetown Mausoleum
Cookstown
Omagh
Belfast
Newtownards
Dungannon
Crown Liquor Saloon
Mount Stewart
The Argory
Ardress House
Rowallane Garden
Portadown
Ballynahinch
Enniskillen
Castle Coole
Armagh
Banbridge
Downpatrick
Castle Ward
Florence Court
Newcastle
Newry

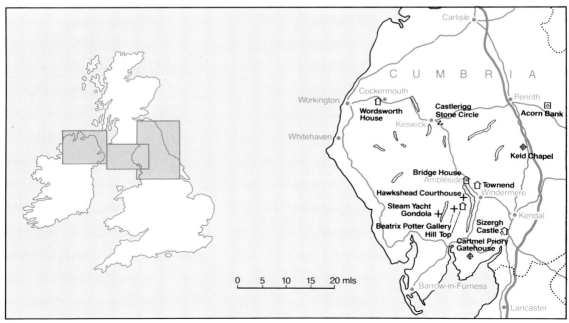

Carlisle
C U M B R I A
Cockermouth
Penrith
Workington
Castlerigg Stone Circle
Wordsworth House
Acorn Bank
Keswick
Whitehaven
Keld Chapel
Bridge House
Ambleside
Townend
Hawkshead Courthouse
Windermere
Steam Yacht Gondola
Kendal
Beatrix Potter Gallery
Sizergh Castle
Hill Top
Cartmel Priory Gatehouse
0 5 10 15 20 mls
Barrow-in-Furness
Lancaster

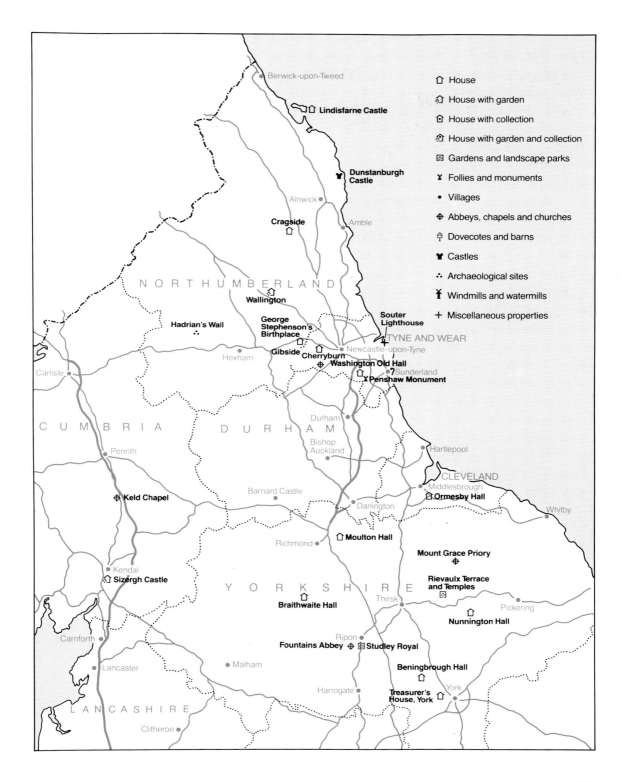

House

House with garden

House with collection

House with garden and collection

Gardens and landscape parks

Follies and monuments

Villages

Abbeys, chapels and churches

Dovecotes and barns

Castles

Archaeological sites

Windmills and watermills

Miscellaneous properties

Berwick-upon-Tweed

Lindisfarne Castle

Dunstanburgh Castle

Alnwick

Amble

Cragside

N O R T H U M B E R L A N D

Wallington

Hadrian's Wall

George Stephenson's Birthplace

Souter Lighthouse

TYNE AND WEAR

Hexham

Newcastle-upon-Tyne

Gibside

Cherryburn

Washington Old Hall

Sunderland

Penshaw Monument

Carlisle

C U M B R I A

D U R H A M

Durham

Bishop Auckland

Penrith

Barnard Castle

Keld Chapel

Darlington

CLEVELAND

Middlesbrough

Ormesby Hall

Hartlepool

Whitby

Richmond

Moulton Hall

Mount Grace Priory

Kendal

Sizergh Castle

Y O R K S H I R E

Rievaulx Terrace and Temples

Thirsk

Pickering

Braithwaite Hall

Nunnington Hall

Carnforth

Ripon

Fountains Abbey

Studley Royal

Lancaster

Malham

Beningbrough Hall

Harrogate

Treasurer's House, York

York

L A N C A S H I R E

Clitheroe

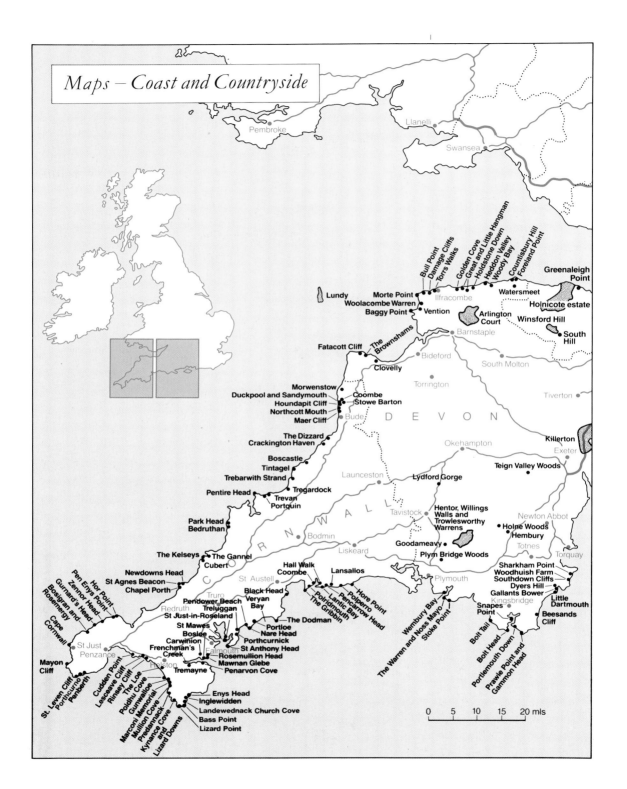

Maps – Coast and Countryside

Pembroke

Llanelli

Swansea

Lundy

Bull Point
Damage Cliffs
Torrs Walks
Golden Cove
Great and Little Hangman
Holdstone Down
Heddon Valley
Woody Bay
Countisbury Hill
Foreland Point

Greenaleigh Point

Watersmeet

Morte Point
Woolacombe Warren
Baggy Point

Ilfracombe

Vention

Holnicote estate

Winsford Hill

South Hill

Arlington Court

Fatacott Cliff
The Brownshams

Barnstaple

Bideford

South Molton

Clovelly

Tiverton

Morwenstow
Duckpool and Sandymouth
Houndapit Cliff
Northcott Mouth
Maer Cliff

Coombe
Stowe Barton

Torrington

D E V O N

Bude

Killerton

The Dizzard
Crackington Haven

Okehampton

Exeter

Boscastle
Tintagel
Trebarwith Strand

Lydford Gorge

Teign Valley Woods

Pentire Head

Tregardock
Trevan
Portquin

Launceston

Park Head
Bedruthan

C O R N W A L L

Tavistock

Hentor, Willings Walls and Trowlesworthy Warrens

Holne Woods
Hembury

Newton Abbot

The Kelseys
Cubert

The Gannel

Bodmin

Goodameavy

Plym Bridge Woods

Totnes

Torquay

Newdowns Head
St Agnes Beacon
Chapel Porth

St Austell

Hall Walk
Coombe

Lansallos

Liskeard

Plymouth

Sharkham Point
Woodhuish Farm
Southdown Cliffs
Dyers Hill
Gallants Bower

Hor Point
Pen Enys Point
Zennor Head
Gurnard's Head
Bosigran and Rosemergy

Truro

Black Head
Veryan Bay

Hore Point
Polperro
Pencarrow Head
Lantic Bay
Polridmouth
The Gribbin

Little Dartmouth

Beesands Cliff

Cape Cornwall

Redruth

Pendower Beach
Treluggan
St Just-in-Roseland

Nare Head

The Dodman

The Warren and Noss Mayo
Wembury Bay
Stoke Point

Snapes Point

Kingsbridge

St Mawes
Bosloe
Carwinion
Frenchman's Creek

Portloe
Portholland
Porthcurnick
St Anthony Head

Bolt Tail

Bolt Head

Portlemouth Down
Prawle Point and Gammon Head

Mayon Cliff

St Just
Penzance

Helston

Tremayne

Rosemullion Head
Mawnan Glebe
Penarvon Cove

Falmouth

St Leven Cliff
Porthcurno
Penberth

Cudden Point
Lesceave Cliff
Rinsey Cliff
Poldhu Cove
Gunwalloe
Mullion Cove
Predannack
Kynance Cove
and Lizard Downs

The Loe
The Cove
Marconi Memorial

Enys Head
Inglewidden
Landewednack Church Cove
Bass Point
Lizard Point

0   5   10   15   20 mls

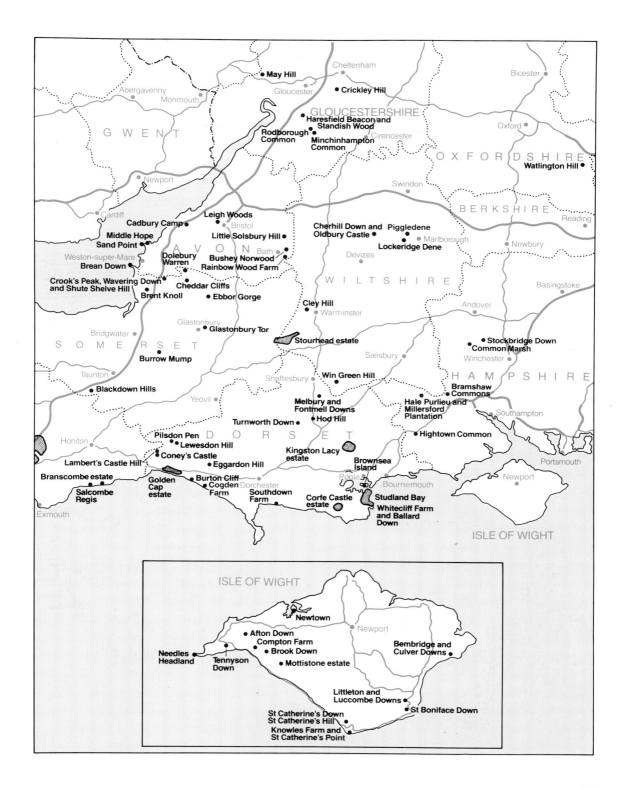

May Hill

Crickley Hill

GLOUCESTERSHIRE

Haresfield Beacon and
Standish Wood

Rodborough
Common

Minchinhampton
Common

Cirencester

OXFORDSHIRE

Watlington Hill

GWENT

Abergavenny

Monmouth

Gloucester

Cheltenham

Bicester

Oxford

Swindon

BERKSHIRE

Newport

Cardiff

Newbury

Reading

Leigh Woods

Cadbury Camp

Bristol

A V O N

Middle Hope
Sand Point

Little Solsbury Hill

Cherhill Down and
Oldbury Castle

Piggledene

Weston-super-Mare

Dolebury
Warren

Bath

Lockeridge Dene

Marlborough

Brean Down

Bushey Norwood
Rainbow Wood Farm

Devizes

Basingstoke

Crook's Peak, Wavering Down
and Shute Shelve Hill

Cheddar Cliffs

W I L T S H I R E

Brent Knoll

Ebbor Gorge

Cley Hill

Andover

Glastonbury

Glastonbury Tor

Warminster

S O M E R S E T

Bridgwater

Stourhead estate

Salisbury

Stockbridge Down
Common Marsh

Burrow Mump

Winchester

Taunton

Shaftesbury

Win Green Hill

H A M P S H I R E

Yeovil

Bramshaw
Commons

Blackdown Hills

Melbury and
Fontmell Downs

Hod Hill

Hale Purlieu and
Millersford
Plantation

Southampton

Turnworth Down

Honiton

Pilsdon Pen

D O R S E T

Lewesdon Hill

Coney's Castle

Kingston Lacy
estate

Hightown Common

Lambert's Castle Hill

Eggardon Hill

Brownsea
Island

Portsmouth

Branscombe estate

Golden
Cap
estate

Burton Cliff

Cogden
Farm

Poole

Bournemouth

Newport

Salcombe
Regis

Southdown
Farm

Dorchester

Corfe Castle
estate

Studland Bay

Exmouth

Whitecliff Farm
and Ballard
Down

ISLE OF WIGHT

ISLE OF WIGHT

Newtown

Afton Down

Compton Farm

Brook Down

Bembridge and
Culver Downs

Needles
Headland

Tennyson
Down

Mottistone estate

Littleton and
Luccombe Downs

St Catherine's Down
St Catherine's Hill

St Boniface Down

Knowles Farm and
St Catherine's Point

405

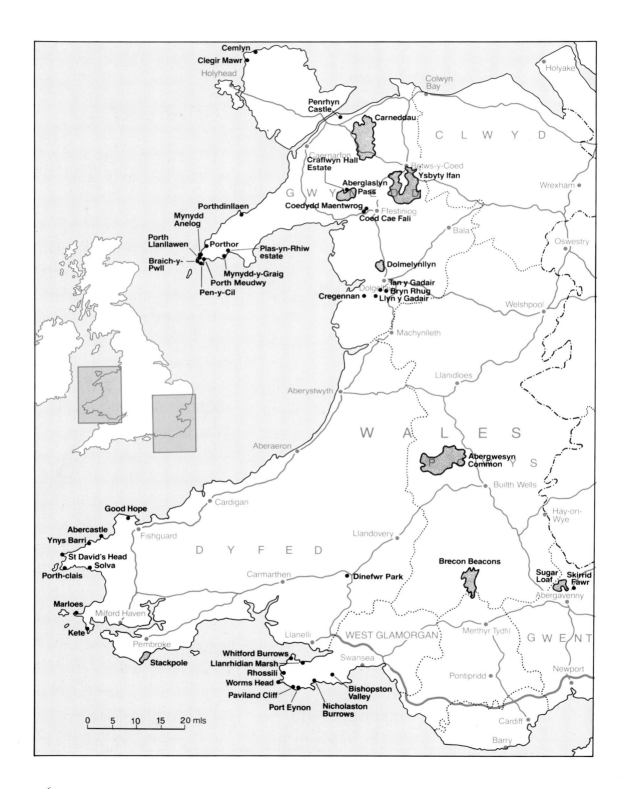

Cemlyn
Clegir Mawr
Holyhead
Colwyn Bay
Holyake

Penrhyn Castle
Carneddau
C L W Y D

Caernarfon
Craflwyn Hall Estate
Betws-y-Coed
Wrexham

G W Y
Aberglaslyn Pass
Ysbyty Ifan
Porthdinllaen
Coedydd Maentwrog
Ffestiniog
Oswestry
Mynydd Anelog
Coed Cae Fali

Porth Llanllawen
Porthor
Plas-yn-Rhiw estate
Bala

Braich-y-Pwll
Mynydd-y-Graig
Dolmelynllyn

Porth Meudwy
Pen-y-Cil
Tan y Gadair
Welshpool
Bryn Rhug
Dolgellau
Cregennan
Llyn y Gadair

Machynlleth

Llanidloes

Aberystwyth

W A L E S

Aberaeron

Abergwesyn Common
Builth Wells

Cardigan
Hay-on-Wye

Good Hope
Fishguard
Llandovery

Abercastle
Ynys Barri
St David's Head
Solva
Carmarthen
Dinefwr Park
Brecon Beacons
Sugar Loaf
Skirrid Fawr

Porth-clais
Abergavenny

Marloes
Milford Haven
Llanelli
WEST GLAMORGAN
G W E N T
Kete
Pembroke
Merthyr Tydfil

Stackpole
Swansea
Pontipridd
Newport

Whitford Burrows
Llanrhidian Marsh
Rhossili
Worms Head
Bishopston Valley
Paviland Cliff
Port Eynon
Nicholaston Burrows

Cardiff
Barry

0   5   10   15   20 mls

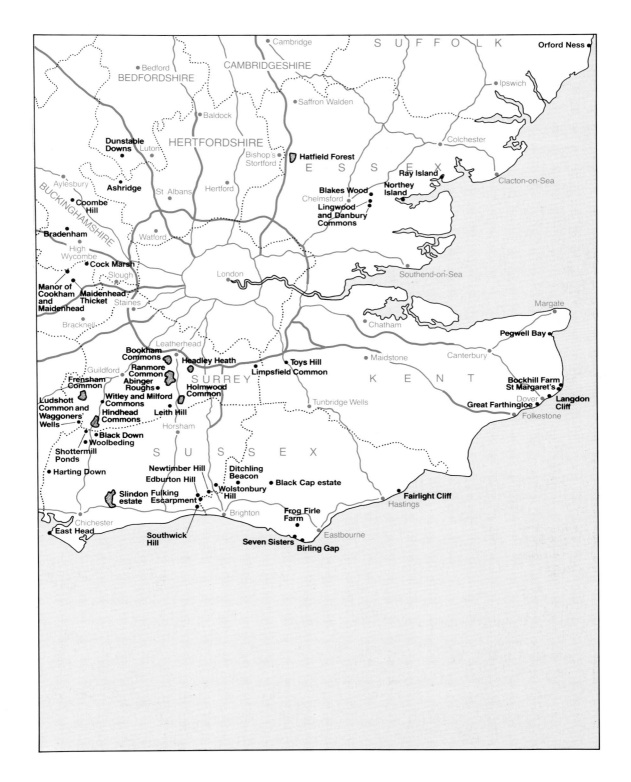

407

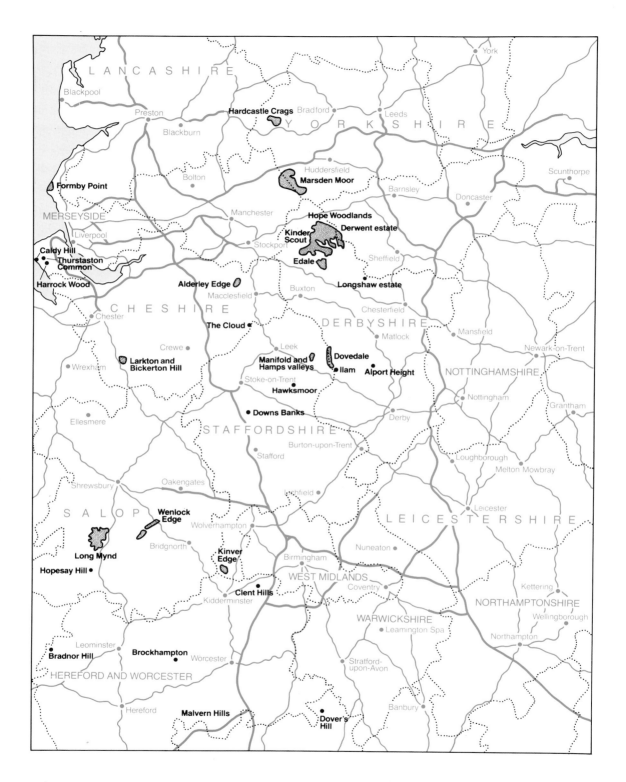

408

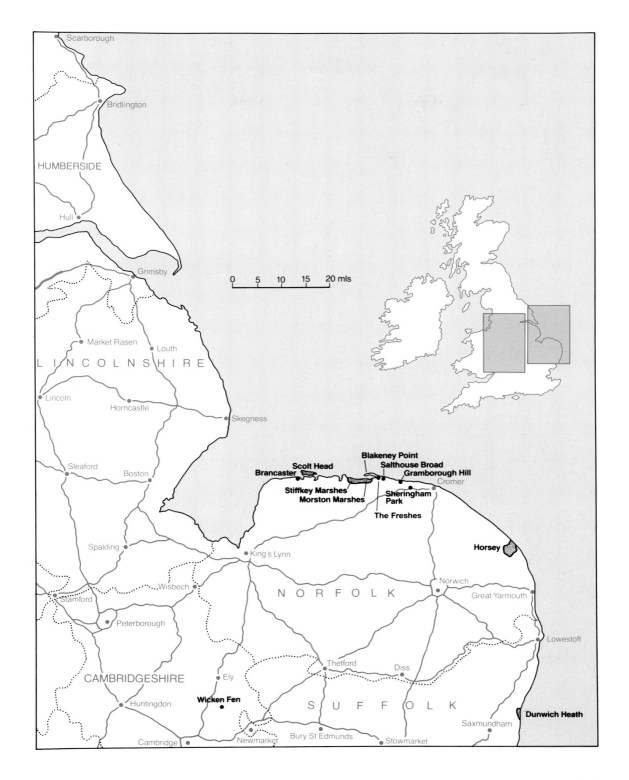

Scarborough

Bridlington

HUMBERSIDE

Hull

Grimsby

0   5   10   15   20 mls

L I N C O L N S H I R E

Market Rasen   Louth

Lincoln

Horncastle   Skegness

Sleaford

Boston

Spalding

Scolt Head   Blakeney Point
Brancaster   Salthouse Broad
                              Gramborough Hill
                                              Cromer
Stiffkey Marshes
Morston Marshes   Sheringham
                                      Park
                        The Freshes

King's Lynn   Horsey

Wisbech   N O R F O L K   Norwich

Stamford   Great Yarmouth
Peterborough

                                                          Lowestoft

CAMBRIDGESHIRE   Thetford   Diss

Ely   S U F F O L K

Wicken Fen

Huntingdon   Saxmundham
                                              Dunwich Heath

Cambridge   Newmarket   Bury St Edmunds   Stowmarket

409

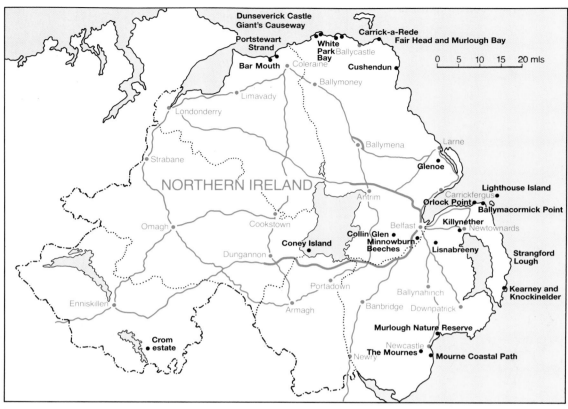

Dunseverick Castle
Giant's Causeway
Carrick-a-Rede
Fair Head and Murlough Bay
Portstewart
Strand
White
Park
Bay
Ballycastle
Bar Mouth
Coleraine
Cushendun

0 5 10 15 20 mls

Limavady
Ballymoney

Londonderry
Ballymena
Larne

Strabane
Glenoe

NORTHERN IRELAND
Lighthouse Island
Carrickfergus
Orlock Point
Antrim
Ballymacormick Point
Killynether
Omagh
Cookstown
Belfast
Newtownards
Collin Glen
Minnowburn
Beeches
Coney Island
Lisnabreeny
Strangford
Lough
Dungannon
Portadown
Ballynahinch
Kearney and
Knockinelder
Enniskillen
Banbridge
Downpatrick
Armagh

Crom
estate
Murlough Nature Reserve
Newcastle
The Mournes
Mourne Coastal Path
Newry

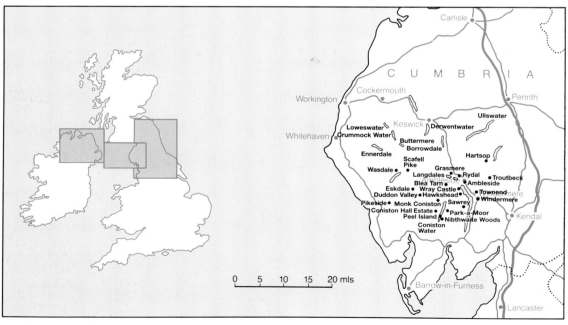

Carlisle

C U M B R I A
Cockermouth
Penrith
Workington
Ullswater
Keswick
Derwentwater
Loweswater
Crummock Water
Whitehaven
Buttermere
Borrowdale
Hartsop
Ennerdale
Scafell
Pike
Wasdale
Grasmere
Langdales
Rydal
Troutbeck
Blea Tarn
Ambleside
Eskdale
Wray Castle
Townend
Duddon Valley
Hawkshead
Windermere
Pikeside
Monk Coniston
Sawrey
Coniston Hall Estate
Park-a-Moor
Peel Island
Nibthwaite Woods
Kendal
Coniston
Water

0 5 10 15 20 mls

Barrow-in-Furness
Lancaster

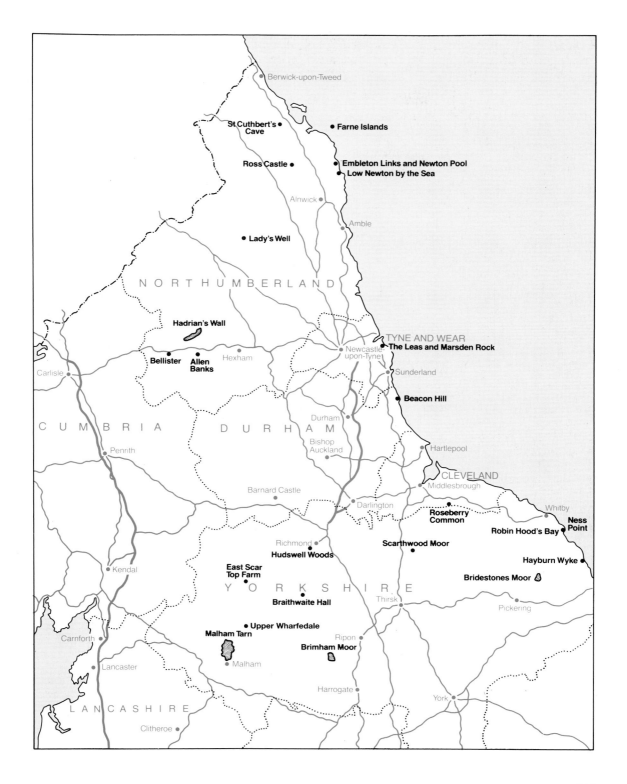

Berwick-upon-Tweed

St Cuthbert's Cave •
● Farne Islands

Ross Castle ●
● Embleton Links and Newton Pool
● Low Newton by the Sea

Alnwick

Amble

● Lady's Well

N O R T H U M B E R L A N D

Hadrian's Wall

Hexham
TYNE AND WEAR
Newcastle-upon-Tyne
● The Leas and Marsden Rock

Bellister
Allen Banks

Carlisle
Sunderland

● Beacon Hill

C U M B R I A   D U R H A M

Durham
Penrith
Bishop Auckland

Hartlepool

CLEVELAND
Barnard Castle
Middlesbrough
Darlington

Whitby
● Roseberry Common
● Ness Point
Robin Hood's Bay ●

Richmond
● Scarthwood Moor
Hudswell Woods

Hayburn Wyke ●

East Scar Top Farm
Bridestones Moor

Kendal
Y O R K S H I R E
Thirsk

Braithwaite Hall
Pickering

● Upper Wharfedale
Malham Tarn
Ripon
Brimham Moor

Carnforth
Malham

Lancaster
Harrogate

L A N C A S H I R E
York

Clitheroe

Index

Page numbers in *italics* refer to illustrations